P9-APC-106

GALLIPOLI

ALSO BY PETER HART
1918: A Very British Victory
Aces Falling: War Above the Trenches, 1918
The Somme
Bloody April: Slaughter in the Skies Over Arras, 1917
Somme Success: The RFC and the Battle of the Somme

WITH NIGEL STEEL
Tumult in the Clouds
Defeat at Gallipoli
Passchendaele
Jutland 1916

GALLIPOLI

PETER HART

OXFORD
UNIVERSITY PRESS

OXFORD
UNIVERSITY PRESS

Oxford University Press, Inc., publishes works that further
Oxford University's objective of excellence
in research, scholarship, and education.

Oxford   New York
Auckland   Cape Town   Dar es Salaam   Hong Kong   Karachi
Kuala Lumpur   Madrid   Melbourne   Mexico City   Nairobi
New Delhi   Shanghai   Taipei   Toronto

With offices in
Argentina   Austria   Brazil   Chile   Czech Republic   France   Greece
Guatemala   Hungary   Italy   Japan Poland   Portugal   Singapore
South Korea   Switzerland   Thailand   Turkey   Ukraine   Vietnam

First published in Great Britain in 2011 by Profile Books Ltd

First published in the United States in 2011 by Oxford University Press, Inc.
198 Madison Avenue, New York, New York 10016

www.oup.com

Oxford is a registered trademark of Oxford University Press

Library of Congress Cataloging-in-Publication Data
Hart, Peter, 1955–
Gallipoli / Peter Hart.
p.   cm.
"First published in Great Britain in 2011 by Profile Books"—T.p. verso.
Includes bibliographical references and index.
ISBN 978-0-19-983686-4 (hardcover : alk. paper)
1. World War, 1914–1918—Campaigns—Turkey—Gallipoli Peninsula.   2. Great
Britain. Army. Australian and New Zealand Army Corps.   3. World War,
1914–1918—Participation, Australian.   4. World War, 1914–1918—Participation,
New Zealand.   5. World War, 1914–1918—Participation, British.   I. Title.
D568.3.H37   2011
940.4'26—dc22   2011015975

1 3 5 7 9 8 6 4 2

Printed in the United States of America
on acid-free paper

CONTENTS

PREFACE

GALLIPOLI. IT WAS A LUNACY that never could have succeeded, an idiocy generated by muddled thinking. The Great War stalled when the huge continental armies of Germany and France fought themselves to a standstill on the Western Front in 1914. For the Allies, the grim business of killing Germans, wearing them down to the point that their armies collapsed, would take four more painful years. The British were very much the junior partner to the French, yet in 1915, long before they had the military capability, they engaged in a series of military adventures that sought an easier route to victory. Of these the most doomed, the most pointless, was the attack on the Gallipoli Peninsula, the aim of which was to gain control of the Dardanelles Straits that separated Asia from Europe and take Turkey out of the war. Apologists for the campaign have pointed to its imagined benefits, thereby not only removing one member of the alliance that was propping up Germany but also influencing the wavering Balkan states into joining the Allies. This would result in the pressure being taken off Russia, while the opening of the sea route to the south Russian ports in the Black Sea would allow the export of desperately needed munitions to feed the Russian guns on the Eastern Front. Much of this view is sheer nonsense.

Moreover, from the British perspective few military operations can have begun with such a cavalier disregard for the elementary principles of war: Gallipoli was a campaign driven by wish-fulfilment rather than a professional assessment of the strategy and tactics required. Right from the beginning it was a distraction from what should have been the main business of the war: concentrating scarce military resources on defeating the Germans on the Western Front. Although surprise is usually crucial to any successful campaign, in this case at a strategic level it was meekly surrendered by allowing small-scale naval attacks months before the main assault. Any brief tactical possibilities the British may have contemplated were dissipated by plans that failed to focus sufficient force to secure any significant objectives, while carrying out the first ever contested landings against a modern weapons system. Logistical incoherence was guaranteed by the decision to try and wage a major campaign thousands of miles away from Britain with neither the necessary resources nor infrastructure to ensure success. The British units sent out to fight were for the most part only half-trained, inexperienced in modern combat and poorly led, in sharp contrast to the better trained, battle-hardened, well-led Turks. This truly was a disaster in the making.

Gallipoli proved to be a key moment for two of the most significant individuals of the twentieth century: Winston Churchill, the First Lord of the Admiralty, and Mustafa Kemal, then an officer in the Turkish Army. Churchill pushed his luck once too often and ended up justly vilified for the dreadful consequences of his strategic incompetence. The setback would have ended the career of a lesser man; even he had to spend ten years in the political wilderness. For Kemal, Gallipoli was an opportunity. Before the Great War he had been a frustrated politician-soldier, but at Anzac he demonstrated the keen military skills and a messianic style of leadership that were to give him the post-war platform to seize the reins of power in Turkey and become the head of his people as Kemal Atatürk.

Gallipoli was a truly international campaign involving troops from a multinational Allied task force made up of British, French, Australian, New Zealand and Indian troops. As ever, the British and Anzac forces are right at the centre of our tale. But this book seeks to tell the story from all sides and Turkish sources have been incorporated into the narrative of battle wherever possible to give a more rounded picture of events than has hitherto been presented. They were, after all, the victors in 1915; the story they tell is one of equal heroism and superior military competence. The role, too, of the French has long been unfairly downplayed; it could be argued that they were the most effective fighting unit at Gallipoli. Well trained and supported by a sufficiency of artillery batteries armed with the highly regarded 75mm guns, they proved a formidable fighting force. But they were cruelly hamstrung in their efforts on the right flank at Helles by the threat of flanking fire from the Asiatic coast just across the Dardanelles, combined to lethal effect with the terrible ground configuration that thwarted their efforts in the Kereves Dere sector. This book attempts to put the French contribution more appropriately at the heart of events.

The true picture of war is a jigsaw puzzle made up of thousands of individual stories from men unfortunate enough to have experienced it. In battle few knew what was going on just fifty yards away, so the overall picture created depends very much on the individual stories chosen. I have tried to use sources that reflect elements of both the commonality and the uniqueness of the Gallipoli experience, using the now-stilled voices of the soldiers who were there to bring their terrible experiences back to life. The original quotations have, where necessary, been lightly edited for overall readability. Thus punctuation and spellings have been largely standardised, material has occasionally been re-ordered and irrelevant material has been omitted, usually without any indication in the text. Nevertheless, changes in the actual words used in the original sources have been avoided wherever possible.

Overall the book aims to expose the futility of the campaign while showing what it was like to fight at Gallipoli almost a hundred years ago. It does not cover every battle, but pursues a course through the most tactically illuminating and some of the previously less well-documented episodes, which I hope are covered in more detail here than in most other books.

Gallipoli is an epic tragedy with an incredible heroic resilience displayed by the soldiers at the centre of our narrative. But historians must beware of being caught up in the romance of the campaign and sucked into thinking that it was either a justifiable operation of war or that it had a realistic chance of success. The Western Front was where the war would be decided and the German Army defeated. Although there were important lessons to be learnt from the Gallipoli campaign it was a futile and costly sideshow for all the combatants. This is their story.

1

DODGING THE ISSUE

The only place that a demonstration might have some effect in
stopping reinforcements going East would be the Dardanelles –
particularly if, as the Grand Duke says, reports could be spread at the
same time that Constantinople is threatened. We shall not be ready for
anything big for some months.[1]

Secretary of State for War Lord Kitchener

THE GREAT WAR was a continental war that would be decided on the
Western Front. Right at the start of the war the Germans unveiled their
latest version of the Schlieffen Plan, which entailed holding the Russians
back on the Eastern Front while seeking to knock out France. This set the
tone for the whole war. It was a battle between heavyweight continental
armies relying on conscription to mobilise millions of trained men. In this
battle of the giants Britain was a mere pygmy with her small regular volunteer army of just 250,000. She had agreed to deploy the British Expeditionary Force (BEF) alongside the French on the Western Front, as to leave
France to fight by herself was to guarantee German victory. Although the
fighting would spread across the globe, the result of the war would be
decided – no less than with the Seven Years War, the Napoleonic Wars and
the Franco-Prussian War – by the course of the fighting in Europe.

What was it that toppled Turkey into this Great War of the European
Powers? What was it that caused a country evenly balanced between

her ambitions and her well-justified fears of looming disaster to plunge into the war in November 1914 – a war for which she was by no means ready? Was there ever any real advantage to be gained by poor benighted Turkey, whichever side won? Both the Allies and the Central Powers had their greedy eyes fixed on various portions of the Turkish domain. Where they did not actually plan to seize territory, they sought either increased political influence or long-term economic gains and looked forward to future depredations. Whatever protestations they might make, the Great Powers all had an unspoken agenda that boded ill for the Turks once the war was over. Why then did the Turks expose themselves to a lottery where the winner would take all, but that winner could never be Turkey? A refusal to be dragged into such a dangerous morass alongside a diligent armed neutrality would have served Turkey far better. Most of all the Turks required time to modernise their country; time to husband their strength for the battles to come against the predators that surrounded them.

Turkey was not a nation state in the contemporary sense but the remains of the once-great Ottoman Empire.[2] Of its approximately 40 million population at the end of the nineteenth century about half were ethnic Turks. The rest were a collation of Greeks, Arabs, Slavs and many other races scattered more or less wherever the tides of history had washed them. Religious differences added a further spice to this complex ethnic mix. As the various layers of European Turkey were peeled off with the onset of independence for Greece, Rumania, Serbia, Montenegro and Bulgaria, one effect of the removal of these largely Christian countries from the Ottoman Empire was a consequent rebalancing towards a generally Muslim character. This growing source of national identity was counterbalanced by the effective economic penetration of Turkey by the Great Powers which, coupled with a crippling national debt, made economic regeneration exceedingly difficult. The country was therefore still largely agricultural, with little heavy industry or exploitation of natural resources. Infrastructure improvements were financed from abroad and often reflected a foreign agenda that was not in Turkey's long-term interest. Even her army and navy were dominated by foreign military missions.

The floundering government of Sultan Abdul Hamid was first challenged in 1908 by a partial coup led by the 'Young Turks' of the prosaically named Committee of Union and Progress. This was a fractured group of dissidents but the key groupings lay among young army officers and civil servants. Their common desire was to modernise the Ottoman Empire and thereby reverse its long term decline. The parliament was restored, but the Young Turks at this stage did not actually seize power and the Sultan continued to rule in a somewhat amorphous situation. The real revolution came in 1909 when a half-hearted counter-revolution gave the Young Turks the opportunity to mobilise and take full control. A brief period of martial law followed and the Sultan was deposed before parliament was re-established. Yet it was still difficult to see how modernisation could be achieved without ceding even more control to foreign powers. And those powers seemed to be circling ever closer: indeed, Italy launched a direct attack on Turkey in 1911, seizing both Tripolitania and the Dodecanese Islands; France's lust for Syria was evident; and greedy European eyes lingered on almost every portion of the former empire. The economy remained moribund and nothing seemed to have changed. A serious political crisis emerged in 1912 as more liberal elements tried to manipulate the political system to remove the increasingly dictatorial Young Turks.

The Turkish weakness demonstrated in the war with Italy encouraged the Balkan states and the First Balkan War broke out as the Balkan League of Serbia, Greece, Bulgaria and Montenegro attacked Turkey in October 1912. The Turks failed to concentrate their forces and in just a couple of months were soundly defeated, with severe losses. An armistice was called in December 1912 and negotiations at a peace conference convened in London seemed liable to strip Turkey of all her European Balkan possessions. Yet these defeats gave the Young Turks a chance to restore their position. A volatile 31-year-old army officer named Enver Bey, enraged by the suggestions of surrendering Adrianople and Thrace to Bulgaria to gain peace, led an armed raid on the Sublime Porte which forced the Grand Vizier to resign. Further complex manoeuvrings enabled the Young Turks to regain political control and brought together the three men who would dominate the political scene in Turkey in 1914: Djemal Pasha, Mehmed Talaat and Enver Bey. They then withdrew from the peace negotiations and the war accordingly resumed in February 1913. Further military disasters followed, forcing them to accept defeat and the loss of both Adrianople to the Bulgarians and Yannina to the Greeks at the Treaty of London in June 1913. Yet just when it seemed all hope was lost, the Balkan League spontaneously imploded. A bitter dispute over the spoils of war caused Bulgaria to launch a pre-emptive strike on Greece and Serbia over their unresolved conflicting territorial claims, thereby triggering the Second Balkan War in June 1913. When Rumania and Montenegro joined in, Bulgaria found itself badly isolated and was forced to withdraw from Thrace. Turkey took immediate advantage and succeeded in regaining Adrianople without becoming entangled in serious fighting before the war ended in August 1913, with Bulgaria having lost most of its earlier spoils of war.

The recapture of Adrianople seemed to cement the authority of the Young Turks across the country and in particular with the army – their real power base. They had been through the fire and their aims were now far more clearly defined by what they had abandoned: Islamism had been strongly associated with the Sultan's regime; liberal support was not compatible with the methods they used to attain and retain power. What was left was the drive to modernisation and an increased nationalistic concentration on their Anatolian heartlands – the area that would become the beating heart of modern Turkey.

The British claimed a theoretical long-standing friendship with Turkey, but this was an amity that could easily be confused with enmity. Britain had taken control of Egypt and Cyprus in the late nineteenth century. In 1914 the British had a new interest in the oilfields of the Persian Gulf and it did not take great insight to guess their ambitions in the Mesopotamian area. The regular outbursts of popular indignation in Britain at various real or imagined Turkish atrocities were not only hypocritical, given the not infrequent incidents of similar deplorable behaviour by the British Empire throughout her history, but also largely synthetic, whipped up by politicians looking for a convenient external enemy. There was no genuine friendship for Turkey emanating from Britain. Her Naval Mission in Constantinople under Rear Admiral Arthur Limpus was there to strengthen the Turkish Navy, but only so it could act as a barrier to Britain's potential rivals in the Middle East. There was no altruism in the gesture: Britain and her businessmen were doing very well out of Turkey and the status quo was quite satisfactory. The whole situation was further complicated by Britain's 1904 entente with France and Russia in response to the new threat from Germany across the North Sea. This change in strategic priorities rendered Britain not only far more ambivalent about the long-term future of Turkey, but also no longer quite so concerned over the control of the eastern Mediterranean.

Germany was another false friend to Turkey. Her apparent camaraderie was largely a thing of smoke and mirrors deployed in the service of long-term ambitions to secure new commercial spheres of influence stretching from the Rhineland to the Persian Gulf. Symbolic of this was the Germans' heavy commercial involvement in the construction of the so-called 'Baghdad to Berlin' railway. They also supplied a Military Mission to strengthen the Turkish Army in counterpoint to the British Naval Mission. In November 1912 Germany despatched the modern battlecruiser *Goeben*, accompanied by the light cruiser *Breslau*, to Constantinople. The effect was to demonstrate to the Turks that, not only was the German Empire the dominant military force in Europe, but it had serious pretensions to challenge the Royal Navy for control of the seas. For the next two years the *Goeben* and the *Breslau* remained in the Mediterranean area acting as symbols of nascent German naval power. Regular visits of the *Goeben* to anchor off the German Embassy at Constantinople soon became a focal point of admiring comment among Turkish society. When volunteers from the *Goeben* crew helped quench a serious barrack fire during a visit to the city in May 1914, this only added popular acclaim to the growing prestige of the German Navy.

> The struggle had lasted for hours – hours of toil, fire-fighting and rescue. There was no danger that was not faced. All had attacked the raging flames like heroes. Suddenly, with a terrific roar, a wall had collapsed and buried four good fellows. We dragged them out from the smoking ruins of the masonry. Four German seamen had given their lives at the burning of a Turkish barracks. All Constantinople sincerely mourned these four brave *Goeben* men. The funeral was a thing never to be forgotten.[3]
>
> Seaman Georg Kopp, SS *Goeben*

On 28 June 1914 the assassination in Sarajevo of Archduke Franz Ferdinand, the heir to the throne of the Austro-Hungarian Empire, by a Serbian nationalist triggered an unfortunate sequence of events. Posturing diplomacy, precautionary mobilisations, alliance commitments and long-standing military plans added lethally to the mix. At first the Turks watched from the sidelines with a degree of hope that the situation would turn out to their advantage, as had been the case in the Second Balkan War. One young Foreign Office official at the British Embassy watched the fluctuating Turkish moods with a professional eye:

> We gazed on distant war-clouds through the light glow of Japanese lanterns. The change came with the publication of the Austrian note. The feeling that predominated at Constantinople at the outset was more or less a reflection of that which, as far as we could see, obtained in London; sympathy with Austria was considerable amongst diplomats. Austrians are generally liked as personalities, and from Constantinople the Serb can be observed rather too closely to pass for a *'chevalier sans reproche'*. The Turks, I fancy, in so far as they understood it all, were in the first phase not sorry that Serbia was to get a trouncing. Later, they rejoiced in the thought that thieves would fall out and honest men come by their own, and they calculated on a Turkish re-conquest of Salonika, for Greece was at that time their bête noire.[4]
>
> Charles Lister, British Embassy, Constantinople

When it became apparent that the situation was escalating out of control, it became equally evident that isolation could be very dangerous in a world at war. Turkey needed strong friends; the question was how to choose them? There were attractions to an alliance with Germany, whose military and naval resources would be a sure source of strength. Germany also posed a less immediate threat to Turkey than the Entente Powers of Britain, France and Russia, as she had far less obvious territorial ambitions.

> It is difficult for us to make out the Turks' attitude towards Germany. I don't think the Turk has any liking for the German; he looks on him as useful, and has boundless confidence in his efficiency. It was this conviction, that Germany was sure to win, which had to be met. There is, after all, something to be said for those who were throughout convinced that it was in Turkey's interest to go to war on Germany's side, such as Enver and others of the soldiers. Turkey could alone hope from the Central European Powers for any reversal of the Balkan settlement arrived at in 1913; France was herself at war and therefore unable to lend Turkey money. This fact precluded any possibility of peaceful regeneration and raised the spectre of internal disruption and the fall of the Enver regime. Add to this the dazzling nature of the German promises.[5]
>
> Charles Lister, British Embassy, Constantinople

On the other hand, the other Central Powers – Austria-Hungary and Italy – were recent enemies and enduring grievances remained. It was a complex situation, with no clear-cut course of action evident to most Turkish politicians. Some favoured an alliance with the Entente; others an armed neutrality. Although there was a fair degree of confidence that Germany was capable of defeating the French and Russians, there was an equal hesitation to trust their entire future on such a gamble. Many Turks also feared that their army was not yet ready for war so soon after its traumatic experiences in the Balkan Wars. Crucially the key Young Turks, Enver, Djemal and Talaat, were in favour of an alliance with Germany. Ignoring doubts even in their own cabinet, they negotiated a secret Turko-German alliance. Under the treaty conditions Germany promised to help recover the Turkish territories lost in recent wars and to guarantee her current borders – if Turkey joined the war in the event of a Russian attack on Germany. The whole treaty was immediately overtaken by events when, the day before it was to be formally signed on 2 August, the Germans declared war on Russia. This did not prevent the Germans exerting pressure on Turkey to join the war, but a lack of consensus among Turkish politicians severely restricted the actions of the pro-Germany faction, especially when Italy and Rumania both failed to honour their treaty obligations to join the war. Although the Turks began their long mobilisation process they could hardly leave their Balkan and Russian borders unguarded as Europe plunged into war.

Amid this state of febrile diplomatic tension the Turks were rashly provoked. It was almost as if the British government had set about creating a situation designed to deliver a pre-packaged Turkey into the ranks of the Central Powers. First, there was a staggering degree of *laissez faire* at the Foreign Office. When the crisis reached its heights, where was Sir Louis Mallet, British ambassador to Turkey? It might have been expected that he was straining every sinew to counter the machinations of his German opposite number Baron Hans Freiherr von Wangenheim. Incredibly, he was on holiday from 14 July to 16 August. He should of course have returned to his post in Constantinople in order to monitor the local situation, analyse the possibilities and judge what diplomatic responses could be made. In circumstances where a simple gesture of friendship to Turkey might well have resolved the situation and maintained her neutrality – which was, after all, her default position – the British exuded nothing but casual indifference.

Yet it went far further than that. The gradual loss of her offshore islands in the Aegean had drawn Turkey's attention to her fundamental naval weakness. The British Naval Mission had been advising expenditure on destroyers or torpedo boats to defend home waters, but the Turks looked forward to a possible resumption of war with Greece and so had contracted to purchase two dreadnought battleships constructed in British naval yards. The exorbitant cost of these ships was met by public subscription – the *Sultan Osman* and the *Reshadieh* were therefore close to the hearts of the Turkish people. They were fast approaching completion in the summer of 1914. With war imminent it was tempting for the British to take over the two ships and at a stroke augment the Grand Fleet for the naval battles with the German High Seas Fleet. The man who had to make the decision was the First Lord of the Admiralty, Winston Churchill. He sought legal advice and was informed by a senior legal officer in the Foreign Office that there was no precedent for seizing foreign warships in time of peace; if at war it was a matter of right and the question was simply whether or not to exercise that right. At that time Britain and Turkey were not at war; indeed, Britain was not at war with anyone. The political risks were high but Churchill was by nature an adventurer and he decided that the shipbuilders should use every means possible to delay, indeed actively thwart the departure of the two ships. Then, if war came, they were to be seized immediately. In taking this course of action Churchill had clearly decided that the acquisition of two dreadnoughts was well worth the risk of a dangerous rupture with Turkey. The ships were finally taken over on 1 August.

But was it worth risking Turkish neutrality at this crucial time in 1914? To turn Churchill's later arguments against him: was it worth risking the geographical isolation of Russia, the closure of the Dardanelles, a new menace to the hard-pressed Russian Army in the Caucasus and a possible threat to the Suez Canal linking Britain with India and the East? Was it worth risking all this for a couple of battleships? The dreadnoughts *were* desperately needed. The German High Seas Fleet could pick its own moment to secure maximum advantage when the Grand Fleet, given the usual problems of ships refitting and the vagaries of war, might have only a bare superiority, or even mere parity. Yet when the consequences of war with Turkey are factored in, the effect of adding the renamed *Agincourt* and *Erin* to the Grand Fleet was ultimately to drain away far more capital ships and the precious destroyer escorts to the far reaches of the eastern Mediterranean when the situation in the North Sea was still by no means resolved.

Despite this grievous provocation, when the British declared war on Germany on 4 August the Turks still backed off. For the moment at least they would examine their options and remain neutral.

> The Turks had viewed our entrance into the field with mixed feelings; they had hoped we should look on and, in company with themselves, play the part of the fox that sucked the bone for which the lions were fighting. They were rather impressed by our intervention; but I doubt if they thought we could really do much to benefit our allies, who in their view were certain to be beaten crushingly. The Turk has very little idea of sea power as a factor in war. He imagined that England could not come to very much harm, but he could not conceive sea power as an aggressive force in world warfare.[6]
>
> Charles Lister, British Embassy, Constantinople

Germany did not give up hope and, to their ill-concealed chagrin, the officers at the German Military Mission in Turkey were ordered to remain at their station pending the outcome of events. This was a wise decision for the slow-burning fuse of Turkish resentment at the confiscation of the *Sultan Osman* and the *Reshadieh* would continue to gnaw at the entrails of Turko-British relations. Despite this, with splendid duplicity, the Turks even pondered the unlikely possibility of an alliance with Russia. It seemed for a while that the most that Germany could hope for from Turkey was a benevolent neutrality. But then again, in a short war, that was all that Germany required.

Meanwhile, a pair of grey shadows was flitting across the Mediterranean. Early on 4 August, the *Goeben* and the *Breslau*, under the command of Rear Admiral Wilhelm Souchon, failed in an attempt to disrupt the embarkation at the French North African ports of Bone and Phillipeville of the French XIX Corps bound for Marseilles and deployment on the Western Front. The French Mediterranean Fleet seemed paralysed by the onset of war with Germany on 3 August; in particular, its commander, Vice Admiral Augustin Boué de Lapeyrère, was fixated with the necessity of covering the safe passage of the troop convoys rather than any thought of seeking out and destroying the *Goeben*. His overall tardiness and obsession with convoys rendered his entire fleet redundant in the operations that followed. He could, and should, have intercepted the Germans, but his obtuseness allowed them to steam off unscathed.

Souchon then suffered a heart-stopping moment at 09.46 on 4 August when he encountered the British battlecruisers *Indomitable* and *Indefatigable* under the overall command of Captain Francis Kennedy. It was unfortunate for the Royal Navy that the British ultimatum to Germany had expressly stated that war would start at midnight on 4 August, some fourteen hours later – in other words, they were technically not yet at war. Kennedy, proving himself neither as disobedient, reckless, nor as resourceful as his illustrious predecessor Lord Horatio Nelson, sailed past the *Goeben* on the opposite course, before turning hard about to pursue his prey in accordance with the tedious strictures of international law. Now it was a race and, as the *Goeben* was theoretically capable of higher speeds, the question was whether she could reach her top performance hampered as she was by her increasingly fragile boilers. It was a matter of life or death and every available man was sent deep into the bowels of the ship to assist the stokers.

> The overheated air affected lungs and heart. Shut off from the outer air by the armoured deck, we worked in the compressed atmosphere forced down through the ventilators. There was an infernal din going on in the interior of the ship. The artificial draught roared and hissed from above into the stokeholds, drove into the open furnace doors, fanning the glowing coal and swept roaring up the smoke stacks. In that hell below, with a temperature of 50° Centigrade, coal was wearyingly trimmed and flung into the furnaces.[7]
>
> Seaman Georg Kopp, SS *Goeben*

Despite their engine problems, the German ship managed to outstrip the pursuing British battlecruisers and disappeared into the night long before the midnight deadline was reached. Souchon hastily refuelled at Messina, Sicily, thus taking advantage of the continuing Italian neutrality, but well aware that he would be obliged to leave within twenty-four hours. By this time Admiral Sir Archibald Berkeley Milne, Commander of the British Mediterranean Fleet, had disposed his battlecruisers west of Sicily with the intention of blocking off Souchon should he attempt to resume his attacks on the French convoys or break through to the Atlantic. Only one light cruiser, the *Gloucester*, watched the southern exit of the Messina Straits. At the same time the *Defence, Warrior, Duke of Edinburgh* and *Black Prince* of the 1st Cruiser Squadron, under Rear Admiral Ernest Troubridge, were stationed to guard the approaches to the Adriatic where it was feared that the *Goeben* might be heading in order to augment the Austro-Hungarian Navy (despite the fact that Austria's enemy status was not yet formally confirmed). When the *Goeben* and the *Breslau* emerged on 6 August the *Gloucester* tracked their progress and signalled to Troubridge in good time for him to make an interception. Weighed down by the uncertainties of engaging a modern German battlecruiser with his obsolescent armoured cruisers, Troubridge knew that he would be outclassed.

> It was plain I could never bring her to action in the open sea. Her speed – 27 knots – her effective gun range of 14,000 yards against our speed – a doubtful 19 – and effective gun range of 8,000 yards ensures her escape at any time she so desires, or alternatively, a position of great advantage at a range which we could not hope to hit her, while making four good targets for her long range fire.[8]
>
> Rear Admiral Ernest Troubridge, HMS *Defence*, 1st Cruiser Squadron

Troubridge, all too aware of his vulnerability, rightly or wrongly, chose to avoid action. Even as he took the decision to turn away early on 7 August, he was in tears.[9] Afterwards he would prove the perfect scapegoat, not wholly blameless and therefore ideal to conceal the incompetence of others. Once again Souchon was able to disappear into the night.

Unknown to the British and French naval commanders, Souchon had been given new orders to try to reach Constantinople following the signing of the Turko-German treaty on 2 August. The Germans were well aware of the potential damage to the British if they could inveigle Turkey into the war; the *Goeben* and *Breslau* offered them a real opportunity. The British were still far more preoccupied with their hopes and fears for a decisive clash with the High Seas Fleet in the North Sea; the question of the exact whereabouts and activities of a single German battlecruiser was of far less importance to the Admiralty, although they still managed to send a stream of confusing signals which further muddied the situation in the Mediterranean. A similar distraction engaged the French Navy, which by then had more than half an eye on the possibility of a major fleet action with the Austro-Hungarian Navy. And so it was that at 17.00 on

10 August Souchon appeared, as if by magic, off the entrance to the Dardanelles, whereupon the *Goeben* and *Breslau* were allowed safe passage by the Turks, their arrival cloaked by the transparent ruse that Germany had 'sold' them to Turkey to replace the ships 'stolen' by perfidious Albion. Not only did this present the Germans in a very flattering light but also the near-miraculous escape of the German ships was taken to show that the Royal Navy did not, after all, rule the waves. At a stroke the attractions to Turkey of the putative alliance signed with Germany became all the more tempting.

Yet, despite it all, the Turks were still prevaricating, still avoiding a formal declaration of war. Meanwhile, the British ineffectually protested that as Turkey was neutral the German warships should have been turned back, the *Goeben* and the *Breslau* interned and their German crews expelled. The Turks were more than willing to promise that the crews would be sent back, but were reticent as to when that might happen. Britain had been comprehensively hoist by her own petard. Within days the British Naval Mission in Constantinople was first sidelined and then rendered redundant as the redoubtable Souchon was appointed to command the Turkish Navy.

> The initial error had been in our impartial recognition of the transfer of the German ships to Turkey. Once that had been conceded; once we had failed to demand internment in a certain time, and, failing such internment, sent our ships up the Narrows – then but little mined – we could only work for the postponement of the final rupture between Turkey and the Triple Entente Powers.[10]
>
> Charles Lister, British Embassy, Constantinople

As the situation deteriorated Lister began to hanker for a more active role in the war. He was an unusual young man as, although the son of a lord, he had conceived a passion for socialism and joined the Labour Party while still at Eton. Now he was ready to join an even greater struggle. His request to the Foreign Office for a year's leave of absence from his post was granted and he returned to England in October 1914.

The end game in Turkey was nigh. Enver, who had taken increasing political control of the situation, unilaterally instructed Souchon to take the *Goeben* and *Breslau*, accompanied by various Turkish cruisers and destroyers, on an aggressive sortie into the Black Sea on 26 October. On 29 October Souchon's ships, divided into four squadrons, launched attacks on the Russian ports of Sevastopol, Feodosia, Yalta, Odessa and Novorossiysk, which, as intended, provoked Russia into a declaration of war on Turkey on 2 November 1914. The British reaction was swift. Churchill ordered the navy to strike at the Turkish forts at the entrance to the Dardanelles even before his government had completed the formalities of declaring war on Turkey. On 3 November the *Indomitable* and *Indefatigable* bombarded the European forts, while the French ships, the *Suffren* and *Vérité*, opened fire on the Asiatic forts at the entrance to the Dardanelles. The magazine at Sedd el Bahr, on the northern side, was detonated, killing eighty-six members of the Turkish garrison in an action still remembered as a war crime in Turkey. Ironically this British success coloured their perceptions of the feasibility of setting ships against forts and at the same time intensified Turkish efforts to improve their Dardanelles defences. The ill-conceived naval operations that were to follow would cost hundreds of Allied lives. After this false dawn, the situation militated against any further immediate action against Turkey in the Dardanelles as the gravity of the situation on the Western Front sucked in both attention and any spare resources.

Churchill was horrified by reports of the bloodbath of trench warfare, which reinforced his desire to use the potential of the Royal Navy to achieve victory. The question was how? Even before the stalemate on the Western Front, Churchill was keen to move the war along, by deploying naval power to harass and confound his enemies with a variety of ingenious schemes. One recurring fantasy was to establish a destroyer base on the German islands of Borkum or Sylt in the North Sea, thereby provoking a huge naval battle and a presumed British victory. Churchill foresaw a dramatic landing of Russian troops on the German Baltic coast, leading inexorably to German defeat. Then there was the incredible plan to use the British Expeditionary Force (BEF) in a series of landings on the Belgian and Dutch coasts in defiance of all common sense and minor inconveniences such as Dutch neutrality. Another scheme, directed against the Turks, was to use the Greek Army to seize the Gallipoli Peninsula and thereby allow a British fleet to enter the Sea of Marmara. This Anglo-Greek Scheme was originally drawn up by Rear Admiral Mark Kerr, the Chief of the British Naval Mission in Greece, and in its most ambitious format envisaged diversionary attacks using in total 50,000 men, while 2,000 would capture the Kum Kale forts, 30,000 would take the Bulair Lines and 60,000 would land along the coast south of Gaba Tepe to take the Kilid

Bahr forts from the rear. This scheme had been rendered stillborn, at least in the first instance when the Greeks, hampered by internal political divisions, remained resolutely neutral.

Churchill was not alone in harbouring doubts as to the efficacy of committing the nation's strength to the Western Front. The Chancellor of the Exchequer, David Lloyd George, pointed to imagined opportunities from attacking Austria or by threatening the Turks with a landing at Alexandretta in Syria, while a speculative memoranda from Maurice Hankey, the Secretary of the War Council, recommended Balkan alliances to threaten Turkey. Gradually the concept of operations against Turkey seemed to be drifting to centre stage.

Then, on 1 January 1915, against this backdrop of increasing debate, the Russians asked for a naval or military demonstration against the Turks to ease the pressure caused by the Turkish offensive driving through the Caucasus mountains. The Russians had attacked the Turks almost immediately war broke out via the Caucasus and had caught the Turks, who were not yet fully mobilised, by surprise. A counter-attack had restored the situation, but then Enver, determined to regain territory lost to the Russians during the Russo-Turkish War of 1877–8, personally led the Third Army into an encircling offensive centred on Sarikamis, deep in the Caucasus mountains, on 22 December. This apparently rash move was initially successful, cutting off a substantial Russian force and threatening a repeat of the Tannenberg fiasco meted out to the Russians by the Germans on the Eastern Front back in August 1914. It was at this point that the Russians appealed for help.

The logical British response should have been regretful refusal. The BEF was already fully committed and needed every reinforcement it could get. At the same time the Grand Fleet, commanded by Admiral Sir John Jellicoe, had been stripped of its notional superiority by a series of unfortunate incidents. The sinking of the *Audacious* on 27 October 1914, the damaging collision between the *Conqueror* and the *Monarch* on 27 December, miscellaneous engine problems and the usual refits had left it for a brief period with potentially just seventeen dreadnoughts, to the fifteen of the High Seas Fleet. The departure of three of Jellicoe's battlecruisers in operations to avenge the humiliating defeat suffered by the British South Atlantic Squadron at the hands of the German East Asiatic Squadron at the Battle of Coronel on 1 November 1914 had left his margin of superiority wafer thin. Then there was the worrying question of the superior construction and resilience of German dreadnoughts, intended mainly for operations in the North Sea, in contrast to the British ships which had to have the capability of serving across the oceans.

Despite these pressing considerations, Lord Herbert Kitchener, the Secretary of State for War, went only halfway to a sensible position of refusing to send any aid. In his interim reply he pointed out that there were no troops available, but added the rider that if there was any demonstration in favour of the Russians it would have to be naval and at the Dardanelles. By introducing this qualification he left the gate not just ajar, but hanging off its hinges. At the Admiralty, the First Sea Lord Admiral Sir John Fisher was ambivalent about such a demonstration. Dubious as he was about the validity of further naval bombardments following the experiment of November 1914, he nevertheless saw possibilities if the navy was supported by a large army generated by the Bulgarians, Greeks, Serbs and Russians – not the most likely collection of bedfellows. In contrast, Churchill saw this as the chance to push forward one of his favoured schemes and, on 3 January 1915, he convened a meeting of the Admiralty War Group, which sent a message to Vice Admiral Sackville Carden, Commander of the East Mediterranean Fleet, asking him whether it was practical to force the Dardanelles by ships alone using only the older pre-dreadnoughts and some measures to reduce the risk of Turkish mines. This reasonable enough question was fatally loaded by a final statement which indicated clearly the answer Churchill required: 'The importance of the results would justify severe loss.'[11] The answer was unsurprising as Carden responded that, although the Dardanelles could not be rushed, they 'might be forced by extended operations with a large numbers of ships'.[12]

This was very different from Fisher's view that the operation would require large numbers of troops in support, but by this time Churchill had attained a position of ascendancy at the Admiralty. Ten years before Fisher had been a pre-eminent figure in the Royal Navy forcing through innovations such as the genesis of the *Dreadnought*. But, having been recalled from retirement in October 1914, he was finding that, at nearly 74 years old, his naturally combative eccentricity had met its match in Churchill. Fisher's views wavered wildly depending on whom he was dealing with. To Jellicoe he appeared firm in maintaining the strength of the Grand Fleet, but in his dealings with Churchill he veered from manic support of the wildest schemes to an equally hysterical opposition. His recall from retirement had been a terrible mistake. This chronic instability at the heart of the Admiralty left Churchill pulling the strings and able to sideline or simply ignore professional naval advice at will.

The consequences would be apparent at the meetings in January 1915 of the War Council. The future strategic direction of the British war effort was largely entrusted to this committee, which combined elements of the Cabinet and the Committee for Imperial Defence. Made up of leading politicians and their service advisers, its aim was to focus discussion rather more closely than had proved possible in Cabinet, yet its own constitutional position remained somewhat vague. The first two meetings, on 7 and 8 January, had given a firm commitment to fight side by side with the French on the Western Front, but it had also been decided to discuss at a further sub-committee possible alternative fronts for deployment of the New Armies that were being raised by Kitchener in his capacity as Secretary of State for War. The intention was to have serious plans ready for alternative deployments should the French no longer need support, or no further advance be possible on the Western Front. At the meeting on 13 January, Churchill was armed with Carden's freshly minted outline plan to force the Dardanelles using ships alone, which had reached the Admiralty on 11 January. Although Churchill put his case persuasively to the assembled War Council, the proceedings degenerated into near farce. Every wild scheme for alternative theatres of war was given a renewed airing and every hobbyhorse dusted off in the rambling debate that followed. In the end nothing of consequence resulted apart from the poorly expressed instruction that the Admiralty should prepare a naval expedition 'to invade and take the Gallipoli Peninsula, with Constantinople as its objective' commencing February 1915.[13] Churchill had got his way and Fisher had failed to express adequately his opposition to a solely naval scheme.

However, this decision taken by the War Council on 13 January 1915 cannot just be attributed to the actions of Churchill. Every minister and service adviser present was directly culpable for allowing Britain's strategic priorities to drift in an effort to find an easy solution to the pressing problems that weighed down on them in the first years of the Great War. First of all they placed at risk the naval war against Germany, which at that stage should have been firmly centred on the prospective battle for control of the North Sea. Geography and the distant blockade of the Grand Fleet had given *de facto* control of the seas across the globe to the Royal Navy once the last of the German commerce raiders and the East Asiatic Squadron had been destroyed. Although the blockade of Germany was not dramatic in its results in the short term, that did not remove its primacy at the centre of British global strategic policy. A naval defeat and loss of control of the seas would surely doom Britain. As Churchill himself put it, 'Jellicoe was the only man on either side who could lose the war in an afternoon.'[14]

One thing was certain: Germany would never be beaten by an ill-conceived adventure launched against Turkey. There was no back door to Germany; no easy route to victory; no allies propping her up, the removal of which would trigger a sudden collapse. Germany operated on interior lines of communications and, even in the event of a Turkish defeat, would merely have rushed reinforcements to the Austrians to make the Balkan mountain ranges all but impregnable. If Germany was to be defeated, then better by far on the Western Front where the British and French could fight side by side and with a minimum of logistical problems. Britain had to fight the war as it was, not how visionaries dreamt it might be. Germany was encamped in France, occupying a good part of the industrial heartland, with armies poised ready to strike at Paris and to seize the Channel ports. Britain could not just abandon her ally while pursuing quixotic adventures in the Middle East. The defeat of France would recast the map of Europe for a generation or more. To any British statesman worth his salt it was axiomatic that no one country could be allowed to secure hegemony over Europe. And it was equally crucial to prevent Germany from gaining control of the Channel ports which would raise the spectre of an invasion of Britain.

Above all the guilty men of the War Council forgot the sound principle of war: concentrate on the main enemy on the main front. They were generally motivated by the best of intentions, yet their names should be recalled with at the very least a raised eyebrow: Prime Minister Herbert Asquith, Chancellor of the Exchequer David Lloyd George, Foreign Secretary Sir Edward Grey, Secretary of State for War Lord Kitchener, First Lord of the Admiralty Winston Churchill, the former Conservative Party leader Arthur Balfour, the Lord Chancellor Lord Haldane and Liberal politicians Lewis Harcourt, Reginald McKenna and the Marquess of Crewe. They and their advisers, Cabinet Secretary Maurice Hankey, First Sea Lord Sir John Fisher and Chief of Imperial General Staff Lieutenant General Sir Archibald Wolfe Murray, were the men that bore the collective responsibility for everything that was to follow. Their excuse was that they believed they were only using a fleet of obsolescent ships that could abandon operations if they ran into trouble. This is fatuous. A serious operation of war should not be undertaken in such a casual fashion; hundreds of men's lives cast away on a whim, as if in a mere game of sport that could be abandoned at half time. Many of those responsible managed to evade the consequences of their culpability during their lifetimes, but history has a long memory.

Turkey was a distinctly unthreatening opponent if left to her own devices. The Turks could try to promote a Jihad, or holy war, among the Muslim populations of the British Empire, the threat of which remained a constant fear for many British statesmen for whom memories of the Indian Mutiny of 1857 still had a considerable resonance. In theory the Turks could also cut British oil supplies in Mesopotamia, but this had already been secured by a small expeditionary force in December 1914, which could have held back any Turkish retaliatory forces till doomsday. It was only British hubris that promoted a series of wasteful expeditions up the Tigris and Euphrates rivers in 1915. The Turks could launch an attack from Palestine across the Sinai Desert on the Suez Canal to cut the British route to India; they did indeed try, but, as we shall see, they failed. And of course Turkey could invade the Russian southern flanks through the Caucasus mountains – the very action that had triggered the Russian request for help. Yet even before the British response had been decided on, the Russians, assisted by atrocious winter conditions, had achieved the destruction of the Turkish threat.

The Russians encircled in Sarikamis had not given up, as predicted by Enver, but had fought on, buying time during which the weather drastically worsened. The temperatures plummeted far below zero and the ill-equipped Turks were soon freezing to death in their thousands. The Turks were also slightly outnumbered by the Russians, who had reorganised their forces and launched a counter-attack on 2 January 1915, which in turn threatened to encircle the Turkish Third Army. The result was a disaster for the Turks as the whole of their IX Corps was cut off and destroyed within a week. All that was left for the Third Army was a defensive posture; it posed no further threat to the Russian borders in the Caucasus. There was clearly no longer any need for British diversionary operations, but by then events had gained a momentum of their own.

Once the Admiralty had been given its instructions, the planning – such as it was – began in earnest. Carden had already provided a draft outline detailing the seven stages of attack on the various layers of defences that defended the Dardanelles: the outer and intermediate forts, before facing the challenge of the batteries in the forts overlooking the Narrows where the Straits measured just under a mile across. In essence the British plan was to out-range the Turkish guns and grind down the forts' resistance before closing in with minesweepers to destroy them at close range. It was originally intended that the fleet would be made up of obsolescent pre-dreadnoughts, but it was inevitable that this principle would not be observed. First, at the instigation of Fisher, the super-dreadnought *Queen Elizabeth* was added, ostensibly to calibrate her massive 15-inch guns against the Turkish forts; then a battlecruiser, the *Inflexible*. And of course the *ad hoc* fleet still called on far too many of the workhorse destroyers that were needed back in the North Sea to screen and defend the Grand Fleet. Every one of these ships could be seen as a tooth drawn painfully from Jellicoe's jaw. As the fleet was augmented Fisher's irrationality increased as the stresses of his two-faced position towards Jellicoe and Churchill, reflecting in turn the inherent dichotomy between his inner caution and wilder schemes, drove him to distraction. Fisher's wild threats to resign multiplied as he came to deny all responsibility for the earlier War Cabinet decision of 13 January and the planning process that he had been directly involved in just days before. This mini psychodrama came to a head at the War Cabinet meeting on the Dardanelles on 28 January. Fisher screwed up his nerve to defy Churchill, and indeed created an embarrassing scene by petulantly storming away from the Cabinet table with the intention of resigning. Kitchener managed to placate him and the meeting reconvened with Fisher's protest generally discounted as another emotional outburst that signified little from a man many regarded as a loose cannon. It was soon forgotten amid the general enthusiasm for the scheme and all it could achieve – if successful. Not only would Turkey be out of the war, but the sea route to Russia would be open. After Kitchener reiterated that the naval attack could be broken off at any time, the decision to proceed was confirmed. But there were still no troops available for military operations.

Some of the Cabinet seems to have envisioned a Turkish defeat triggering a rash of declarations of war on the Central Powers from the Balkans. Yet the individual Balkan states held contradictory war aims, sought alliances that were not feasible and demanded conditions that no one could meet. In truth, they were all waiting for the winner of the global conflict to become apparent, at which point they would join pellmell in the race to the finish and the despoliation of the losers – whoever they might be. Complicating the issue was the general confusion relating to the situation in the Balkans: a messy Gordian knot. There was just so much seething hatred, some nurtured across generations, but a substantial portion emanating from the recent Balkan Wars. To become the ally of one country entailed the unthinking enmity of another. The Balkan states were riven with racial, regional, religious, cultural and political chasms that could not be bridged by negotiation.

One existing ally was more than willing to become involved. The French were concerned at British ambitions in the Near East, with particular reference to Syria, which they saw as being within their own sphere of influence. As a result they wanted to march closely in step with the British in any Middle Eastern expedition for long-term imperial considerations. Thus, although the French Naval Minister, Victor Augagneur, was sceptical of the chances of a solely naval operation succeeding in forcing the Dardanelles, his underlying attitude was clear:

> Not to take part in the operation would have been, in case it succeeded, to witness the appearance of the English fleet alone before Constantinople. For us French, who are deeply involved in the Orient, it would have been a very painful renunciation of our national pride and perilous for our interests.[15]
>
> Naval Minister Victor Augagneur

He was even willing to allow the proposed joint British and French fleet to be commanded by the British, despite the August 1914 agreement that the French would command any naval operations launched in the Mediterranean.

The Russians, keen to promote their own interests, also wanted to get involved. As soon as they heard of the joint Anglo-French fleet they feared that if Constantinople fell then they would be prevented from seizing the Turkish capital – a long-term aim of Russian foreign policy. Their concern was reflected in an offer to support British and French ambitions, not only in the break-up of the Ottoman Empire, but also elsewhere in the globe. But, and it was a big but, *only* if the Russians were allowed to occupy Constantinople. The Allies may have all been on the same side, but they each had their own rather than any common agenda. The horse trading commenced and by mid-April the deal was done. On the map, at least, the Ottoman Empire had been dismembered and shared out between the British, the French and the Russians. The predators had gathered. Now all that was required was the defeat of the Turks.

2

NAVY IN ACTION

Nearly all the papers talk the most abject rot about this campaign and I find it rather annoying when I read that the people who have been holding us up for the last month only have two old guns and a catapult in each fort, can only fire at ranges of 100 yards and not straight at that![1]

Midshipman Herbert Williams, HMS *Agamemnon*

ONE SHADOW SHOULD HAVE BEEN CAST over the operations even before they started. Presumptions of easy success were based on the perception that the Turks were deficient in military skills, grit and determination. Yet just a few days after the War Council made its decision the Turks launched a daring attack on the Suez Canal. The importance of the Suez Canal to the British Empire as the main route to India and the East made it an obvious target for the Turks, but first they would have to cross the Sinai Desert. A total of 25,000 Turkish troops and Arab irregulars, accompanied by artillery, advanced across the desert in three columns. With them they took galvanised steel boats and pontoons dragged by teams of oxen. The logistical difficulties of crossing the arid landscape were considerable, as the animals required to carry the water and food supplies themselves needed water and fodder, which had to be carried by yet more pack animals. The British were not unprepared: Major General Sir John Maxwell, commander of the army in Egypt, had some 30,000 polyglot troops under his command, including two Indian Army divisions, the territorial 42nd Division and the Australian and New Zealand Army Corps (ANZAC Corps). His main defences were on the western bank of the canal, but strong outposts were established on the eastern bank. The British, enjoying the benefits of aerial reconnaissance, were well aware of the approach of the Turkish forces as they painfully trudged across the desert in late January 1915. However, a night march concealed the final stages of the Turks' approach to Ismailia on the canal just north of the Bitter Lakes.

The attack across the canal was launched by the main column and two flanking forces in the early morning of 3 February 1915. They were soon sighted and a vigorous fire totally disrupted the crossing. Although many of the Turks panicked, caught in boats holding about thirty men each, two companies managed to cross the canal and establish a small bridgehead which was then supported by the Turkish artillery firing over the canal. But the British brought their ships up the canal to fire directly into the Turkish positions. Repeated counter-attacks by an Indian brigade wiped out most of the isolated force on the western bank and the Turks ordered a reluctant retreat back across the desert. The Turks had been far too optimistic in their plans. Yet they had performed reasonably well, dragging themselves across the hostile desert environment and then fighting with considerable courage. Perversely, the Allies seemed to have taken this plucky failure as another sign that the Turks were militarily negligible.

It was not so much the Turks' military competence that worried the Royal Navy senior admirals but rather the sanity of what they were being asked to achieve in taking and holding the Gallipoli Peninsula. How could ships take and hold an area of ground? Already two battalions of Royal Marine Light Infantry had been despatched by the Admiralty to take possession of the island of Lemnos, which had been captured by the Greeks from the Turks in 1912 but which they had now conveniently abandoned so that the British could make use of its natural harbour of Mudros without compromising Greek neutrality. These marines would then be available to be used as demolition parties to complete the destruction of the Turkish batteries in the Dardanelles. Kitchener also promised to make troops available for the later stages of the operations if needed. This opened a Pandora's box. If troops could be sent later, why not immediately so as to be ready at the point of need rather than when it might be too late? Admiral Sir Henry Jackson summed up the Admiralty view on the

Carden plan: 'The naval bombardment is not recommended as a sound operation unless a strong military force is ready to assist it, or, at least, to follow it up immediately the forts are silenced.'[2] Proposals multiplied for additions to this force, with the Royal Naval Division (RND) being sent out in February, the ANZAC Corps already in Egypt and the French having promised a division for any land operations. This fatal drift, reflecting the faulty thinking that had triggered the initial decisions, soon spread into the War Council itself when, on 16 February, it decided that the regular 29th Division should be sent out to act as further support for the naval operations. But Kitchener, wary as ever of major troop commitments away from the Western Front, had changed his mind by the 19 February meeting of the War Council. He subsequently acidly enquired at the next meeting, on 24 February, what all these forces were required for when Churchill had already promised the Dardanelles could be forced without troops. Nevertheless Kitchener showed his own inner weakness and inability to maintain a coherent thought pattern by stating at the same meeting that if the fleet did not succeed by itself, the army ought to see the business through and there was no going back. As ever, Kitchener feared that embarrassment in the Dardanelles might inspire a revolt in India or promote trouble in Egypt and thereby threaten the Suez Canal.

The despatch of the 29th Division to the eastern Mediterranean became the weathervane of Kitchener's confidence, or rather lack of it, in the navy's progress. Promised, then withheld, it was finally despatched on 10 March. The gathering amorphous force took another step forward when Kitchener appointed General Sir Ian Hamilton to take command of what had almost by default become the Mediterranean Expeditionary Force (MEF) on 12 March 1915. There were even hopes of cooperation with a Russian fleet and army corps should the Allies break through and threaten Constantinople itself. Therefore, as a single service endeavour, the naval campaign was already compromised before it had started.

After a long interval following the experimental bombardment back on 3 November 1914, the Allied fleet commenced the first stages of Carden's methodical plan with the shelling of the Sedd el Bahr (Fort No. 3), Kum Kale (Fort No. 6) and Orkanie (Fort No. 4) at the entrance of the Dardanelles at 09.51 on 19 February 1915. The Royal Navy had never practised firing at shore targets. Now it was shooting at long range, each ship only using a single gun at a time in order to save ammunition and wear to

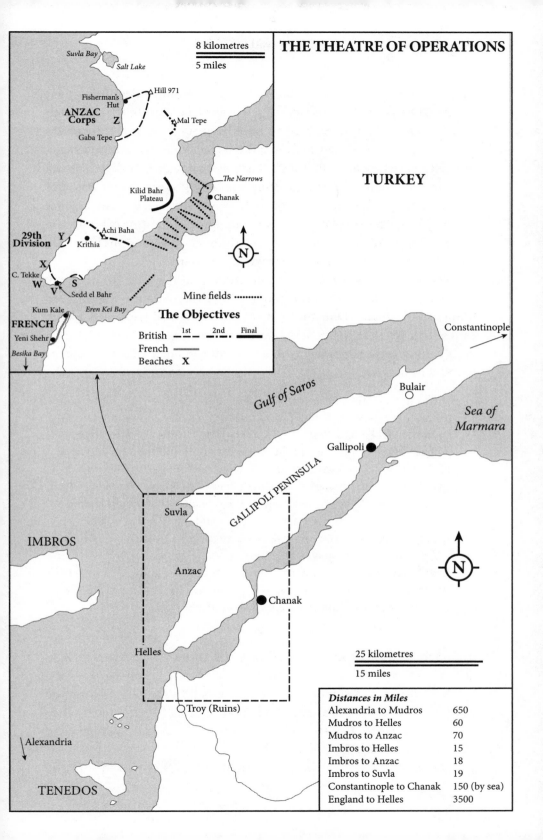

THE THEATRE OF OPERATIONS

8 kilometres
5 miles

Suvla Bay
Salt Lake
Fisherman's Hut
Hill 971
ANZAC Corps
Z
Mal Tepe
Gaba Tepe

TURKEY

The Narrows
Kilid Bahr Plateau
Chanak

N

29th Division
Y
Achi Baba
Krithia
X
C. Tekke
W
V
S
Sedd el Bahr
Eren Kei Bay
Kum Kale
FRENCH
Yeni Shehr
Besika Bay

Mine fields ··········

The Objectives

	1st	2nd	Final
British	---	---	—
French	—		
Beaches	**X**		

Constantinople

Gulf of Saros

Bulair

Sea of Marmara

Gallipoli

GALLIPOLI PENINSULA

Suvla

IMBROS

Anzac

N

Chanak

Helles

25 kilometres
15 miles

Troy (Ruins)

Alexandria

TENEDOS

Distances in Miles

Alexandria to Mudros	650
Mudros to Helles	60
Mudros to Anzac	70
Imbros to Helles	15
Imbros to Anzac	18
Imbros to Suvla	19
Constantinople to Chanak	150 (by sea)
England to Helles	3500

the gun barrels. The gunners soon found they had difficulties hitting their targets. The minimal results were to prove all too typical of the campaign that followed. The forts seemed to have been subdued, but then would miraculously resume their fire once the naval shells had stopped dropping all around them. Unless a shell actually hit a gun, or detonated an ammunition dump, the damage done was largely superficial; it was later estimated that just 2–3 per cent of shells would hit such a small target at 12,000 yards. The Turkish crews were safe underground or behind solid earthworks, shaken undoubtedly by the thunderous explosions but ready enough to emerge to man the guns when necessary.

Bad weather soon hampered operations and the next major attack on the entrance forts was carried out on 25 February. As the ships moved into position the forts burst into life as if nothing had happened a week earlier. Fort No. 1 at Helles made excellent practice with its two 9.4-inch guns pelting the *Agamemnon* with shells. Midshipman Herbert Williams found it unnerving.

> It was not exactly a bean feast this time and we had a very unpleasant 10 minutes and at the time I would have given anything in the world to have been back at Portland. I was stationed in the conning tower and so had quite a good view. I found that watching the enemy's guns fire and waiting 15 seconds or so for the screech of the projectile coming over was a distinctly nerve-wracking experience. I kept on wondering whether it would be the next one or the one after that would lay me out. I had to go for a stretcher party once and if any outsider had seen me streaking across the upper deck he might have mistaken me for a really good runner. I have come to the conclusion that only those who have been in action during the course of their lives know what real funk is. A little blood makes such an awful mess and I thanked heaven I was not a doctor, as a small fragment of shell makes a ghastly wound.[3]
>
> Midshipman Herbert Williams, HMS *Agamemnon*

In just ten minutes the *Agamemnon* was hit seven times, but not badly damaged. Attacked from three sides, the forts began to show signs of wear and tear with guns dismounted. Their fire ground to a halt, allowing the warships to close to a near point blank range of 2,000 yards where they could open up with their secondary armaments. All in all it was one of the more successful days for Carden's fleet.

The next day, 26 February, the pre-dreadnoughts moved into the

Straits, firing into the reverse side of the entrance forts and then moving to engage the intermediate forts, including Forts Dardanos (Fort No. 8) and Messudieh (Fort No. 7) up to Kephez Point. While this was going on it was decided that impromptu naval landing parties would complete the destruction of the forts and abandoned gun batteries at Kum Kale and Sedd el Bahr. A demolition party of fifty sailors under Lieutenant Commander Eric Robinson raised from the *Vengeance* and accompanied by fifty marines, landed unopposed at Kum Kale pier at 14.30. They shook out and began to move south through the cemetery outside Kum Kale to Fort No. 4 at Orkanie Mound. A vigorous opposition soon built up, pressing in from across the River Mendere on their left and centred on the Yeni Shehr windmills behind the battery. Despite heavy fire Robinson managed to blow up two Turkish guns on Achilles Mound and then pushed on to destroy the last remaining 9.4-inch gun of the Orkanie battery. His one big advantage was the support of the *Vengeance*, *Dublin* and *Basilisk* lurking close offshore. This was to some extent neutralised when it became apparent that the naval gunlayers would have great problems picking out their targets, which were often either screened by features in the foreground, or merged seamlessly into the background haze.

> We were laying off the Asiatic side covering our party, and had been watching Eric Robinson strolling round by himself under heavy rifle fire from the neighbouring rise, like a sparrow enjoying a bath from a garden hose, until the *Dublin* turned the hose off with some nicely placed salvos. He and his party and escort were returning to the boats, when a fresh turmoil started all round them. They had now passed out of sight in the trees of Kum Kale cemetery, and none of us could see what was happening. At length they got a signal through to say they were held up with the main body of the enemy in a large domed tomb. The control could see the tomb and I could just distinguish its top when they put me on. It was invisible at the guns, but I was able to note its whereabouts in the treetops, and went down to let off a 6" lyddite. The range was short and the rangefinder had it exactly, so the first round sent the tomb and fragments of its inmates, both ancient and modern, flying heavenwards. Using the burst as a starting point there was no further difficulty in taking the guns on to any other target to get our people clear.[4]
>
> Captain Bertram Smith, HMS *Vengeance*

Lieutenant Commander Robinson, who had taken extreme personal risks trying to reduce casualties to a minimum, was subsequently awarded the VC. A similar landing at Sedd el Bahr by a party from the *Irresistible* succeeded in demolishing the main battery of the old fort but was unable to advance up to Fort No. 1 when resistance strengthened. These landings were repeated in the days that followed, in order to check results and ensure the complete destruction of all the guns, thereby silencing the entrance forts.

These British raids were in effect taking the Turks through a step-by-step guide to the weaknesses of the Turkish defences at the entrance to the Straits. The final stage of this tactical primer occurred on 4 March when a larger scale enterprise met with a far more vigorous Turkish response. Two companies of the Plymouth Battalion, Royal Marine Light Infantry (RMLI) were assigned to the landings at Kum Kale and Sedd el Bahr. At 10.30 the marines landed at the small Camber harbour that nestled below Sedd el Bahr village and alongside the fort. Among them was Lieutenant Charles Lamplough.

> When we got just off Sedd el Bahr the fleet started bombarding like blazes. It looked very nice and as if we should have no opposition. Well, we got into our cutters and finally got ashore and everything looked in our favour. The patrols got out and went up the cliff. One went to the top through the fort and the others straight up. When they got to the top they got it thick – poor old Baldwin was very soon caught. He got one through the head and died a little time after. Then we had a good deal of firing. I finally found we could not get up there as they were in the ruined houses sniping us, so we found where they were. I came down to the beach and signalled which houses we wanted shelling and they let them have it. Then I took my patrol up and we did not have much opposition. Dickinson got hit in the leg and had to be taken off but he is alright – but Jones of 14 Platoon was killed and also Dyter of 13 Platoon. We had quite a nice little scrap and then they sent a lot of shrapnel over, but they did not get us.[5]
>
> Lieutenant Charles Lamplough, Plymouth Battalion, RMLI

Lance Corporal Harold Benfell was one of the first ashore, his patrol cautiously feeling their way into the Sedd el Bahr fort. At first everything seemed quiet enough.

I signalled back to the officer commanding that all was quite clear, the place seeming to be forsaken and quite dead; but we found it very much alive. Within 10 minutes I received two bullets – one through the top left pocket and another under my right arm. For a second I stood gazing around to see where the man was that fired but he was concealed. More bullets came across and I made my way inside the fort for cover, though very little was to be found. I was followed there by two other men out of my section and we considered ourselves cut off from all communication. An hour passed away before we could get out of this place and the three of us lay there on the ruined wall which had been blown down by our ship's gun. The bullets were whizzing around us and I can assure you we had a very warm time.[6]

Lance Corporal Harold Benfell, Plymouth Battalion, RMLI

Given this hot reception, a request was made for reinforcements but it was decided to withdraw the landing party instead at around 15.00 under covering fire from the ships. They had managed little more than the reported destruction of two Nordenfelt guns. Their comrades fared no better at Kum Kale. Indeed, having landed a little after 10.00 at Kum Kale pier, they soon encountered a far greater number of purposeful Turks. They too achieved little and were only rescued by dint of a helpful series of interventions by the supporting ships.

We had little opposition and a few casualties before landing, but after it got hotter as there were about half a dozen windmills which were full of snipers so it held up our job, until they signalled back to the Navy who concentrated their fire on them and up they went like skittles, the best bit of firing I saw during the whole war.[7]

Private Ben Sinfield, Plymouth Battalion, RMLI

The withdrawal was chaotic, with the destroyers having to move in close to provide covering fire while smaller boats rescued the isolated stragglers before it was completed at 19.45. The Turks were becoming far more accomplished at working round the threat posed by naval gunfire.

Meanwhile the main naval operations proceeding in tandem against the intermediate forts were not progressing well. Carden was cautious in deploying no more than three of his pre-dreadnoughts at a time, thereby at a stroke reducing the potential for a truly crushing bombardment of the targeted forts. This, combined with the limitations on firing salvos, meant that little was achieved. Some imagination was shown on 5 March when the 15-inch guns of the *Queen Elizabeth* were fired right across the peninsula at the Kilid Bahr group of forts: Rumili Medjidieh (Fort No. 13), Fort Hamidieh II (No. 16) and Fort Namazgah (No. 17). But there were problems in achieving coordination by wireless with spotting ships in the Straits; it was hoped that the seaplanes from the *Ark Royal* would be able to correct the fire. So it was that at 11.00 Flight Lieutenant W. H. S. Garnett and his observer, Lieutenant Commander H. A. Williamson, took off in their Sopwith seaplane with hope in their hearts.

> It was a perfect day, with just the right amount of wind for taking off from the water, and we were soon in the air. It was an exhilarating moment. There below was the *Queen Elizabeth* with her eight 15-inch guns ready to fire and trained on the coast. The conditions were ideal; stationary ships and stationary target, only eight miles apart, and perfect visibility. I was filled with confident expectation. We soon reached 3,000 feet and were ready to cross the peninsula to the target. Then it happened. In a moment the machine was out of control and we were hurtling towards the sea.[8]
>
> Lieutenant Commander H. A. Williamson, HMS *Ark Royal*

The seaplane's propeller had broken up in midair and it was a miracle that both Williamson and Garnett survived. The next seaplane to take off could not gain sufficient altitude and the pilot was wounded by a rifle bullet in the leg, forcing him to return. So far nothing had been achieved and a third seaplane seems to have only sent one successful range correction. Similar forays from the *Queen Elizabeth* over the next two days were no more successful. It was evident that the frightening limitations of the seaplanes made them all but useless for effective observation. To compound the insult, the *Queen Elizabeth* was also chivvied mercilessly by howitzer batteries, causing some superficial damage to her superstructure. In the end the idea was abandoned.

As the operations progressed it was becoming increasingly evident that the forts and minefields were not the only threats the fleet would have to overcome.

> We were being fired on by concealed howitzers. They are beastly things to deal with as they fire from behind a hill and all you know about

them is that shells are falling all around. You can't even tell what
direction they come from and so it is impossible to hit back. When
these batteries are located by aeroplanes they move. Luckily they
are not big guns, but this high-angle fire is very objectionable as the
projectiles come pretty nearly straight down on to a ship's deck and side
armour is no good.[9]

Midshipman Herbert Williams, HMS *Agamemnon*

The howitzers could cause superficial damage to the pre-dreadnoughts, but
the main threat posed by their shells was to the converted fishing trawlers being used as minesweepers. With a maximum speed while sweeping
of only six knots they made easy targets as they tried to make progress
against the three to four knot current pouring through the Dardanelles
out into the Aegean. This vulnerability made their formerly civilian crews,
who had been signed up for 'Hostilities Only', very nervous. Even when
they were belatedly augmented, and finally replaced by, regular naval volunteers, the combination of heavy shell fire directed by searchlights at
night, currents and prevailing winds severely hampered their activities.
On the night of 14 March Lieutenant Commander John Waterlow took
command of the trawler minesweeper flotilla, from the boat commanded
by Lieutenant Pitts. By this stage each trawler had aboard an officer, a
petty officer and a signaller, all naval volunteers. They made a determined
effort and managed to reach the Kephez minefield.

Searchlight after searchlight began to open on both sides, and the fire
became denser and was delivered from both banks. For the first time I
heard shells whistling over my head. Like everybody does I ducked but
got over the desire to do that in a very few minutes. I asked the skipper
how he liked it, and he said he'd rather be fishing! By the time we got
into the minefield the fire was terrific. Both banks blazed incessantly,
and with the glare of the searchlights, which never left us for an
instant, it was bright as day. A veritable hail of shell fell all around us. It
was now that the Royal Naval Reserve Petty Officer proved himself. He
had been standing quietly in the wheelhouse, arms folded majestically
across his breast above the cork lifebelt, when the two trawlermen
at the wheel lost their heads and began to cringe. Lieutenant Pitts
sent them below, and the old Petty Officer took over the wheel and
steered absolutely unperturbed. A 6-inch shell hit the funnel so close

to my head that scraps of paint and smuts covered me. The noise was deafening and made one's head ache.[10]

Lieutenant Commander John Waterlow, HMS *Blenheim*

In these stressful circumstances, the minesweeping process became a hit-or-miss affair, as they worked in pairs about 300–500 yards apart, each dragging a heavy paravane 'kite' underwater between which ran a sweep wire designed to cut the mooring cables of the mines. When the mines floated to the surface they were sunk by rifle fire.

It was becoming apparent that over the long winter months since the first naval shots of the campaign in November 1914, the Turks had managed to create a formidable, integrated defence system to guard the Straits. The big guns in the forts attracted most attention, serving to keep the pre-dreadnoughts at long range, but it was the minefield batteries and mobile howitzers that nullified the minesweepers' efforts. At the heart of the defences were the minefields that threatened carnage if not properly swept and ruled out any attempt to rush the slow-firing forts. Torpedo tubes aiming across the Narrows threatened a further layer of disaster, although the potential threat was far greater than the reality. Finally, the *Goeben* herself lay in wait, tucked behind the Nagara Point, and ready to pick off any Allied ship that turned the 90-degree corner dictated by the narrow navigational channel. As a battlecruiser she was probably the equal of any of the Allied fleet, save only the *Queen Elizabeth* – banned by Fisher from entering the Straits – and the *Indefatigable*, an equally well-armed, but weakly armoured, early British battlecruiser.

With frustration beginning to show at the slow progress, it was decided to launch an attempt to force the Narrows on 18 March 1915. This decision was complicated by the failure of Carden's health under the manifold stresses of command. He was forced to return home, to be replaced by his second-in-command acting Vice Admiral John de Robeck. The plan was to accelerate the grinding-down of the Turkish defences in controlled stages by telescoping the process into a couple of days, although there was still no intention of attempting a suicidal rush of the Straits. Simple in concept, the idea was to divide the Allied fleet into three lines of ships. The most modern ships were to go first in Line 'A': the *Queen Elizabeth*, *Agamemnon*, *Lord Nelson* and *Inflexible*, with the *Prince George* and the *Triumph* guarding their flanks. They were to sail up the Straits and open fire at the forts on either side of the Narrows. Next would come Line 'B' made up of the French ships *Suffren*, *Bouvet*, *Gaulois* and the *Charlemagne*, which would pass through the Straits and press forwards, reducing the range to as close as 8,000 yards. Line 'C', made up of the *Ocean*, *Irresistible*, *Albion*, *Vengeance*, *Swiftsure* and *Majestic*, would act as reliefs, replacing damaged ships and allowing the attack to be pressed home without diminution of fire. Minesweeping would commence after a couple of hours, once the Turkish fire had been mastered, and would allow the fleet to close the range still further. The fleet would then withdraw overnight before completing the destruction of the Narrows forts on 19 March prior to finally forcing the Straits. However, this sober-looking plan had not allowed for a splendid piece of initiative by the Turks. The minelayer the *Nusrat* had stolen out unobserved on 8 March and managed to lay a line of mines, not across the Straits as might have been expected, but parallel to them in the Eren Keui Bay, where Turkish observers had seen the Allied battleships manoeuvring during the previous bombardments.

It must have been an amazing sight as the Allied fleet passed into the Straits at 10.30 on the beautiful sunny morning that was Thursday, 18 March 1915. The sea was full of ships and to the Turkish observers it may have seemed that nothing could withstand such an awesome display of naval might; but the more thoughtful of the British naval officers realised that it would not be easy. Captain Bertram Smith of the *Vengeance* had tried his best to prepare his gunnery officers for the spotting difficulties he knew they would experience.

> The conditions were a contrast to those at sea. There, to some extent at least, the ship is a ship, the sky is sky, and the sea is sea; in fact you either see your target or you do not. Here, when firing at long ranges, as in the Narrows attack, you might be looking at your target yet never distinguish it; it was part of the landscape's background and in certain lights merged into it. As soon as we knew what our position would be for the attack on the Narrows I roped in the midshipmen and had the landscape of the Narrows projected horizontally from bearings from the chart, and vertically from contours on the map of the peninsula. Suggestions of details were then sketched in their proper places to suit the nature of building, such as a thin inverted 'V' as minaret of a mosque, a thin horizontal rectangle for barracks, or, in the case of batteries, a hint of their shape, with details, where known, carefully

eliminated, so as to leave a hazy outline in keeping with what we should see. Batteries and prominent features were marked with their numbers or description.[11]

Captain Bertram Smith, HMS *Vengeance*

The pre-dreadnoughts might be nearing obsolescence, but they had been the pride of the Royal Navy just ten or so years before and with their menacing turrets they were still formidable-looking weapons of war. The *Lord Nelson* and *Agamemnon*, the last of the pre-dreadnoughts built for the Royal Navy, were armed with a potent arsenal of four 12-inch, ten 9.2-inch and twenty-four 12-pounder guns. Midshipman Alfred Langley was on duty in one of the twin 9.2-inch turrets of the *Lord Nelson*.

The turret that is visible above the deck may be compared with the head of a giant mushroom. Suspended from the floor of the turret a long circular trunk – the mushroom stalk – reaches down to the bottom of the ship into the shell rooms and magazines. Lifts travelling up and down the trunk supply ammunition to the guns. The whole of the turret-trunk structure, weighing hundreds of tons, rests and rotates on a ring of enormous steel rollers carried by the ship. We crawled into the turret through a small hatch in the thick armour plating forming the roof. A confined space dominated by the huge breeches of the two guns met the eye. All around a tangle of machinery and instruments seemed to leave little room for the gun's crew, but somehow when they had all squeezed into their separate niches the turret did not feel overfull. 'Free the turret!' ordered the Lieutenant in charge and, on a great locking bolt being withdrawn, we were free to train in the direction of the enemy.[12]

Midshipman Alfred Langley, HMS *Lord Nelson*

As the pre-dreadnoughts glided into the Straits the turret gun crews leapt to their tasks surrounded by the awesome machines that encapsulated many of the most modern technologies of their age. Men and machines operated in synchronised harmony as at about 11.30 the huge ships opened fire on the forts.

An immense clatter now reverberated throughout the metallic enclosure as the gun's crew tested the machinery. Empty ammunition cages rattled and banged up and down the trunk; the guns rose and fell as the elevating ram slid out and in; breeches swung open and closed with a clang; telephones rang; interlocking gears clicked; telescopic rammers shot out to incredible lengths and collapsed as quickly into an inoffensive silence. Nearly all the machinery was worked hydraulically at a pressure of a thousand pounds to the square inch. In every pipe liquid hissed and surged and occasionally, from a leaky joint, spouted with bullet like velocity into the well below the guns. In a few minutes the deafening din ceased as abruptly as it began. The gear had been tested, found correct, and was reported so to the central control station. 'Load with lyddite shell!' In a moment the whole gun's crew were again alert and active, whilst the deafening clatter recommenced only to die away again within half a minute when the guns were loaded. It was still impossible to fire because the switch completing the electrical firing circuit was not yet made. Another peaceful pause before, 'All guns to the ready!' With a snap the switch was made and a low buzzing sound indicated that the circuits were alive. Now everyone was tense and silent. It was not difficult to imagine, lying ready to leap into cataclysmic activity, the huge charge of cordite concealed in the chamber of the gun. Unconsciously one noted that the breech was properly closed, that all men were clear in the rear where the gun would leap in recoil. One wondered if everything was sound. A merely microscopic fault in the great steel barrel might have caused a calamity. The seconds dragged on. Still the soughing from the hydraulic valves and the electrical buzzing were the only sounds inside the turret. The waves breaking against the side of the ship could be plainly heard. Suddenly two rings on the fire gong, 'Stand by!' One ring, 'Fire!' and with a 'CR-RR-UMPH!' the gun would leap back into the turret and start slowly to run out. The air in the gunhouse, suddenly compressed then released by the great mass of the gun, was rent at the same time by the noise of the explosion. Before the reverberations had died away the gun's crew, with febrile activity, were reloading.[13]

Midshipman Alfred Langley, HMS *Lord Nelson*

As the British Line 'A' advanced into the Straits it came under a considerable amount of harassing fire from howitzers lurking unseen in the surrounding hills. Regimental Sergeant Major David Hepburn, lent to the navy and in charge of two 6-inch howitzers placed aboard the *Prince George*, was busy observing the performance of the Turkish batteries.

These howitzers are evidently laid on squares and fired when the ships enter their area – a chart of the water area is marked off in squares, each square having a certain range and direction from the guns. An observer with a similar chart would order the guns to be fired when the target entered the square. These howitzers would undoubtedly do great havoc if more accurately served. The howitzers seem pretty accurate in themselves as three and four shells invariably fall together in quite a small area. The shells have a deafening detonation on bursting; high explosive and well-detonated. The fuses are too sensitive though to my idea, which would greatly help a ship struck by them, as the shell would burst on the upper deck before it could reach the vitals of the ship. All the same I should consider them the Turks' best weapons. I got hit by a small splinter of high explosive shell which stuck in my temple – went in like a needle. Luckily it was a very small piece or I should not be writing this.[14]

Regimental Sergeant Major David Hepburn, Royal Garrison Artillery (attached to HMS *Prince George*)

The rate of fire of the forts would slacken markedly from time to time, promoting hopes that some serious damage had been caused, before resuming seemingly unharmed. At 12.06, de Robeck considered that it was time to order the French Line 'B', under Rear Admiral Émile Guépratte, to pass through and close the range. The *Gaulois* and *Charlemagne* had moved up on the European flank of Line 'A' while the *Suffren* and *Bouvet* passed by on the Asiatic side. From high up in the sky Lieutenant L. H. Straw had a wonderful view.

I was nailed to the sky in a bright seaplane over the fleet and forts. The *Bouvet* and *Gaulois* far up on the Asiatic side hammering away at close quarters; the *Vengeance* and two others of ours doing the same on the Gallipoli side. The *Queen Elizabeth*, *Inflexible*, *Suffren* and *Agamemnon* behind firing over them at the forts up at Chanak and Kilid Bahr and all these forts replying so that the whole water was churned up. Not a single soul to be seen on the decks, just the flash of guns to show that they were alive. Shells falling in the water look like concentric circles of white on the outside merging into deep brown in the centre when seen from straight above. When at an angle you only see the column of water.[15]

Lieutenant L. H. Straw, HMS *Ark Royal*

The French ships came under tremendous pressure as the forts burst back into life as they closed to within 9,000 yards. Soon afterwards, when the *Suffren* was hit by a heavy shell that penetrated through to a magazine, some quick thinking by a young officer proved vital.

> In a few minutes the flagship was hit by a large number of heavy shells, one of which caused major damage: a casemate and a turret were knocked out of action and all of their crew killed and incinerated. There was an escape of flame and burning gases into the port magazine and the boiler-room, with fires between decks and the destruction of the port fire control station. The port magazine was flooded to save the ship from the threat of explosion. A sharp turn to port and the forward funnel was blown away. Desiring to salute our brave men, I went straight down. The scene was tragically macabre: the image of desolation, the flames spared nothing. As for our young men, a few minutes ago, so alert, so self-confident, all now lying dead on the bare deck, blackened burnt skeletons, twisted in all directions, no trace of any clothing, the fire having devoured all.[16]
>
> Rear Admiral Émile Guépratte, *Suffren*

In the press of battle the gunners had been caught breaking safety rules and, as the flash spread, a cataclysmic explosion threatened.

> In these circumstances time was running out for our ship. It was going without doubt to explode with all hands, if a young gunnery officer named François Lannuzel, acting with initiative beyond praise, hadn't saved the ship by hurriedly ordering the flooding of the magazines. He ran through the smoke to Commander Petit-Thouars saying, 'I hope I haven't over reached myself, but seeing that the *Suffren* was in grave danger of explosion I've just flooded the magazine without orders.'[17]
>
> Rear Admiral Émile Guépratte, *Suffren*

Of course Lannuzel was the hero of the hour, for he had undoubtedly saved the French flagship and most of her crew from an explosive finale. The British watched the hard pounding with unstinting admiration.

> I say, 'Hats off!' to the Frenchmen, two of their cruisers now passed up the lines and took up a position ahead of our ships over on the Asiatic side in a direct line with Dardanos Fort close to Chanak. If anyone went over into hell these two French cruisers did. At times it was impossible

to see them for the spray that was thrown up by the shells falling all
around them – the fort was firing like hell.[18]

Able Seaman Daniel Cemm, HMS *Prince George*

This tremendous duel lasted until just before 14.00 when the *Bouvet* in
rapid succession was hit by a heavy shell and then almost immediately ran
on to a mine just as the British ships in Line 'C' were moving up to relieve
the French. Captain Ashir Arkayan watched the results with considerable
satisfaction from his Turkish gun battery.

> The *Bouvet* started to withdraw, but at that moment a cloud of red and
> black smoke arose from under the ship, which may have struck a mine.
> Immediately after this there was a much more violent explosion. We
> believed that a shell from Mejidiye had blown up the magazine. The
> ship heeled over at once and her crew poured into the sea.[19]

Captain Ashir Arkayan, Artillery, Fifth Army

From the *Prince George* they had a close-up view of a naval catastrophe.
When things go wrong at sea they usually go wrong with a terrifying
suddenness.

> We saw an immense cloud of black smoke ascending from the
> Frenchman's starboard quarter. Almost immediately she began to heel
> over towards us and gradually, steadily and gracefully, she continued
> to heel till her masts lay on the water. A second or two in that
> position, then, just as steadily she continued to heel over till she lay
> keel uppermost – she was perhaps half a minute in that position then
> quickly slid under the water. From the time we saw the smoke till she
> disappeared was barely 3½ minutes. No noise; nothing horrifying in the
> sight – our imaginations supplied the horror.[20]

Regimental Sergeant Major David Hepburn, Royal Garrison Artillery attached to
HMS *Prince George*

It was a dreadful sight, immortalised in a few smudgy photographs that,
as Hepburn implies, can never convey the horror of what happened in the
bowels of the *Bouvet* as water flooded her with breakneck speed. Seaman
Sauveur Payro had been sent to fetch more ammunition when the explosions happened.

The boat immediately listed to starboard. I was completely covered in the coal dust which came from the bunkers. I went to the signal ladder and with the second mate we climbed up. From the bridge I got myself on to the funnel which was entering the water. Then I climbed on to the hull. I believe that the second mate was trapped and he fell into a hatch way. From the keel I threw myself into the water.[21]

Seaman Sauveur Payro, *Bouvet*

Luckily he was a good swimmer, but it was still touch and go whether he would survive.

I couldn't rise to the surface because of the tug of the water. I was in the water for some time, then, when the bottom of the ship touched the bottom of the sea, I came straight up, either because the ship touched bottom or the boilers exploded. I couldn't breathe; blood was coming out of my mouth, my ears. When I was on the surface again, if I hadn't found this piece of wood I would have been finished. I managed to grab one of the hammocks and held it between my knees. I saw another chap crying out to me to save him and I told him to come closer to me so that he could be on one end of the plank and me on the other. But when the English came to fish us out of the water I saw that both his legs had been cut off. He died three days later.[22]

Seaman Sauveur Payro, *Bouvet*

The *Bouvet*'s crew had scant chance of escape. As she disappeared she took with her Captain Rageot de la Touche and 638 of his crew. The few that did survive were picked up by the British.

As she disappeared, a few men could be seen getting out of the tops, also one man who ran along a gun muzzle and who went into the sea off that. Our picket boat went in and picked up seven survivors and also sank a mine fairly close. The Turks ceased fire as she went and, for a while, the boats were not molested in their errand of saving life. But before many minutes were up the Turks started bursting shrapnel over the place.[23]

Commander George More, HMS *Lord Nelson*

The *Prince George* picket boat picked up nearly forty swimmers in the pandemonium. It seems that in total sixty-six survived.

Our picket boat was there. All at once these few survivors that were rescued sent up a cheer and sang their national anthem. The water all around where the ship had foundered was a mass of wreckage of all descriptions, there was a huge upheaval of water caused by air escaping from the sunken ship. These Frenchmen did not seem a bit downhearted over their ducking, they were all more or less joking and laughing, but I expect that they thought themselves lucky to escape with their lives.[24]

Able Seaman Daniel Cemm, HMS *Prince George*

Still the duel carried on as the Allies' shells crashed down on the forts, which reserved their fire for targets that were properly within range. Then they could really strike back. Deep down inside the 12-inch magazine on the *Ocean* in Line 'C' was Petty Officer George Morgan.

We soon began to 'pay our respects' to the forts ashore, giving and taking as fast as we could send up ammunition. No thoughts of anything now but charges and shells. 'What the Dickens was that?' said one to me, as a monster shell must have struck the armoured belting. 'Oh! Someone's false teeth have fallen in the shell room,' said another. It was like being in a huge tank, with a party outside, with different size hammers belting away. Every now and then the ship would heel over, trembling, the thump of the propellers going now hard, now soft. The news came down that we were doing good work.[25]

Petty Officer George Morgan, HMS *Ocean*

When the shells hit home the results could be petrifying, as Midshipman Langley discovered when the *Lord Nelson* was hit.

In the middle of the afternoon my own turret was directly struck by an enemy shell. Two sightsetters were wounded and one of the 9.2" guns damaged. This did indeed give us a very exciting moment. To the din and fumes inside the turret were added the deafening crash of the shell bursting outside, the cries of the injured men, the pungent smell of the smoke drifting in through the gun ports. A minute later, when we cautiously opened the armoured hatch in the turret roof to evacuate the sightsetters, a volume of salt water poured into the turret. A cry of, 'She's sinking!' was quickly suppressed, but it was indeed an excusable cry from the wounded men who had been cooped up in a dim armoured dungeon full to the brim with fumes and smoke, reverberating intolerably with the clang of machinery, the roaring of the guns, the bursting of shells, and shuddering bodily like some huge wounded animal when struck by the enemy's fire. The deluge of water puzzled us considerably, but it was soon traced to a water pipe, running along the superstructure behind the turret, which had been severed by a fragment of the same shell that directly struck us.[26]

Midshipman Alfred Langley, HMS *Lord Nelson*

The trawlers had been ordered forward to sweep ahead of the fleet but the *Nusrat* line of mines remained undetected. At 16.11 the *Inflexible*, which had already been hit by several shells, ran on to a mine on the starboard bow causing severe damage which forced her to retreat, taking in considerable water as she limped away out of the Straits. She would ultimately only survive by dint of beaching herself on Tenedos Island. Just three minutes later, at 16.14, the *Irresistible* detonated a mine and began to slowly settle while the Turks redoubled their efforts to finish her off as she began to drift further into Eren Keui Bay.

A great shock was felt which lifted the whole ship up. She at once listed to starboard, having been struck in the starboard engine room, which filled up very quickly – a warrant officer and three men being drowned. The bulkhead between the two engine rooms gave way and she righted a bit. The order was given for everyone to come on deck. Everybody came up from below and started throwing everything that would float overboard, as we thought that we should have to swim as there were not any destroyers or anything near. We were subjected to heavy fire from the forts. We were hit twice by shells, one lyddite on the after conning tower and another which entered the Commander's upper deck cabin after passing through the officers' WCs.[27]

Midshipman Owen Ommanney, HMS *Irresistible*

Fortunately, most of her crew were evacuated by the destroyer *Wear*. As soon as they were safe, de Robeck commanded the leading ships to fall back before ordering a 'General Recall' at 17.50. Too many ships had been lost to accept with any equanimity. Unaware of the existence of the rogue line of Turkish mines, de Robeck and many other senior officers leapt to the natural conclusion that the Turks were deploying a deadly form of floating mine, drifting down on the prevailing current to create havoc. As the retreat began, the *Ocean*, which had been attempting without success to take the *Irresistible* in tow, was circling round and it was no surprise to observers when she too hit a mine at 18.05. Petty Officer George Morgan was still far below the waterline in the magazines; he knew he had little time to escape.

> I was about to hand out a half-charge on the loading tray, when 'Bang!!' The force of the blow picked me off the floor with the 85lb half-charge in my arms. We didn't need ask what that was. The order came, 'Close magazines and shell rooms!' The men all went up the trunk from the magazine. Before I could leave it was my duty to see all ventilators and bunker plates fastened and water tight, doors shut and voice pipes shut off in case they wanted to flood the magazine to avoid explosion. It only took a few minutes, but it seemed such a time to me – at last it was finished. There was only one way for me to escape and that was through the shell-room escape hatch. I only had a few minutes – I had to retrace my steps and undo and refasten all I had done. I hurried – any moment they may flood the magazine. As I opened the shell room door I heard a faint hissing and a rumbling noise. It was dark now, the electric lights were smashed. It was the swishing water and lumps of coal rolling about in the bottom of the ship. Then the danger I was in dawned upon me. I had to think and act quickly. I crossed to the shell-rack and scrambled up on the shells. Up I went and groped for the hatch. To my joy it was opened. I was soon through and closed it behind me. My troubles were not over. Supposing the other hatch was closed? Anyone seeing it open in passing would close it. I lost no time but rushed towards it. Just as I reached the ladder I heard someone raising the catch to let it down. I yelled, and whoever it was didn't stop to argue. I was soon through![28]
>
> Petty Officer George Morgan, HMS *Ocean*

Again there were not many casualties as the shepherding destroyers flocked round to rescue the crew. The *Ocean* was finally abandoned at 19.30.

As the Allied ships withdrew from the Straits, their crews began to come up on deck and take stock. Many of them had been stuck at their action stations far below decks with little or no idea of what had been going on other than vague noises off.

Everyone crowded out on to the upper deck to get a breath of fresh air. By looking at a man's face you could tell if he had been stationed below as ammunition supply, or engine room, or stokehole, or in opposition, those who had been at the guns. The latter were full of fight, whereas those who had been below were white-faced and showed their nerve-wracking experience. They had not the excitement of fighting, or the knowledge of what was going on. From 9 a.m. to 5 p.m. they had heard nothing but the crash of shells striking our ship and the sound of our own guns firing. Rumour passed from one to another often enlarged on the damage done by the enemy fire.[29]

Corporal Fred Brookes, Royal Marines, HMS *Triumph*

After the excitement of the battle there came the sober assessment of what had been achieved. With three of their sixteen capital ships sunk and three more severely damaged the Allies had effectively lost a third of their available force. But what, if anything, had been achieved for these griev-ous losses? One, somewhat sardonic officer, Lieutenant Geoffrey Ryland of the *Ark Royal*, put it succinctly.

There is considerable uncertainty though as to how much damage the forts suffered. It is true one cannot make omelettes without breaking eggs, but it is bad if the eggs are broken and the omelette is not made. The question is have we done three ships' worth of damage to the forts?[30]

Lieutenant Geoffrey Ryland, HMS *Ark Royal*

Apologists ever since have tried to recast the stunning success of the Turks on 18 March as an Allied victory that was only thrown away by a refusal to push on hard the next day. They have claimed that the Turks were teeter-ing on the edge of defeat, their batteries beaten into submission and all but denuded of shells. This despite the torrents of shells that lashed the sinking *Irresistible* as night fell. The reputed shortage of shells is a classic example of hope masquerading as fact. Research in Turkish archives has revealed that they had plenty of shells left – not as many as they may have wanted, perhaps, but enough to face a renewed Allied attack. The forts were battered but still standing, the main Narrows minefield had not been reached, the howitzers were still plying their trade, the torpedo tubes were undisturbed and the *Goeben* still waited for any ship lucky enough to have broken through – her designated conqueror the *Inflexible* already run aground and out of action. There was surely no hope here for a naval attack on 19 March.

3

GATHERING OF THE FORCES

I am being most reluctantly driven to the conclusion that the Straits are not likely to be forced by battleships as at one time seemed probable and that, if my troops are to take part, it will not take the subsidiary form anticipated. The Army's part will be more than mere landings of parties to destroy Forts, it must be a deliberate and progressive military operation carried out at full strength so as to open a passage for the Navy.[1]

General Sir Ian Hamilton, Headquarters, MEF

WITH THE FAILURE of the attack on the Dardanelles on 18 March, the Royal Navy had well and truly shot its bolt. Although the initial reaction of Vice Admiral John de Robeck had been to try again, his ardour soon cooled off and at a conference aboard the *Queen Elizabeth* on 22 March he took the decision to switch to combined operations with the army. He duly informed the Admiralty. Although his Chief of Staff, the energetic Commodore Roger Keyes, was still convinced that the Straits were there for the taking he was an increasingly isolated figure. Older, wiser, more pragmatic officers were conscious that the eternal disadvantages of ships combating forts and mines had been demonstrated with rather too much clarity to allow another attempt. Still scared by the perceived threat of floating mines, they were all too aware of the untouched lines of mines that lay in wait for them in the Narrows. Even if they were able to rush the

Straits with their destroyers modified to carry minesweeping equipment, they feared being cut off if they advanced into the Sea of Marmara. After the events of 18 March few believed that the Turks would necessarily surrender on the arrival of an Allied fleet off Constantinople. There seemed no point in pursuing such desperate measures when, thanks to the change of heart in the War Council, there was already a sizeable number of troops arriving in the eastern Mediterranean who would be ready for possible military operations in support of the navy by mid-April 1915. Churchill was still keen to push on but found that his professional advisers in the Admiralty War Staff Group sided with de Robeck. The navy would try again, with their destroyer minesweepers, *once* the army had seized Kilid Bahr Plateau behind the forts on the European side of the Straits. This was a postponement, not a cancellation; no one considered that the army might fail. Yet there were plenty of professional observers who were already seriously concerned, especially among the High Command watching askance from the Western Front.

> Colonel Hankey, Secretary of the Committee of Imperial Defence, arrived to see me. He is over in France for three days. He states Lord Kitchener is more hopeful as regards the ammunition. As to the Dardanelles operations I asked why the naval bombardment had taken place before the military part of the expedition was on the spot (to take advantage of it and co-operate). He quite agreed with my view, and said the 'operation had been run like an American cinema show' – meaning the wide advertisement which had been given to every step long before anything had actually been done.[2]
>
> General Sir Douglas Haig, Headquarters, First Army

The designated commander of the Mediterranean Expeditionary Force (MEF), General Sir Ian Hamilton, had arrived on 17 March, just in time to see the navy fail the next day. He was polite about the navy's performance, but he too was of the opinion that a military landing in strength would be essential to suppress the fire of the forts, and in particular the mobile batteries.

Born on 16 January 1853, Hamilton was a Scottish soldier who had seen much active service during his distinguished career. A trim, slightly effete figure, he had already fought in the Second Afghan War of 1878–80, the First Boer War of 1880–81 and the Nile Expedition of 1884–5, before a period of service in Burma and India during which he was involved in the Chitral Expedition of 1895 and became a brigade commander in the Tirah Expedition of 1897–8. Unlike many British generals he had had a 'good' Boer War (of 1899–1902), managing to maintain his reputation despite being involved in much fighting before his appointment as Kitchener's Chief of Staff and promotion to lieutenant general. A stream of senior appointments followed, including: Quartermaster General, 1903–4; British observer during the Russo-Japanese War, 1904; Southern Command, 1905–9; Adjutant General, 1909–10; and finally Mediterranean Command and Inspector General of Overseas Forces from 1910 to 1914. In a sense the war had come a little too late for him as he was already sixty-one in 1914, and although appointed as Commander of the Home Forces he had been hitherto sidelined from the action. Hamilton was widely respected for his stream of well-written and thoughtful publications, but his quite dreadful habit of dabbling in poetry and slightly dilettante manner meant that he was considered a little unconventional by many of his peers. Now Kitchener had recalled him from the wilderness, trusting in his old Chief of Staff and wanting to capitalise on his relatively recent experience in the Mediterranean theatre.

As soon as he arrived, Hamilton was locked in conference with Lieutenant General Sir William Birdwood, the commander of the ANZAC Corps. Birdwood was born in 1865 and had served as a subaltern with the cavalry in India, seeing some degree of action on the North-west Frontier. On promotion he had had the good fortune to serve as the military secretary on Kitchener's staff during the Boer War, after which he continued to pursue his career within the Indian Army. Promotion was rapid and he became a major general in 1911, whereupon he took on the role of Secretary of the Indian Army Department. Then, in December 1914, his old benefactor Kitchener selected him to command the newly formed ANZAC Corps, made up of the Australian Imperial Force (AIF) and the New Zealanders Expeditionary Force (NZEF). Soon Hamilton was given the chance to examine the widely disparate divisions that made up the MEF.

The 1st Division and the 1st Light Horse Brigade of the AIF were both volunteer formations that have attained a legendary status. These men were widely pictured as being of a superior breed to the allegedly decadent products of the British industrial towns. Contemporary observers and popular historians have made much of their manly stature and tough outback origins. This romantic image seems little affected by claims that 27 per cent of the volunteers in the first contingent of the AIF had actually been born in Britain.[3] Furthermore, a fair proportion of them hailed from cities as well as the outback of legend. Motivations for the massed Australian recruitment covered the usual spectrum ranging from a desire to serve King and Country, support for poor little Belgium and perhaps, most potent of all, the simple lust for adventure. As the first to volunteer they had excellent potential as soldiers.

The 1st Division was commanded by Major General Sir William Bridges, who had been born in 1861 and raised in Britain and Canada before emigrating to Australia in 1879. His military career, which began in 1886, included brief service in the Boer War, and periods as the Chief of General Staff and as the Australian representative on the Committee of Imperial Defence in London. Nevertheless, he was perhaps best known as the first commandant of the Royal Military College of Australia at Duntroon from 1911 to 1914. The Australians did not have the strength to raise two divisions so early in the war and, as New Zealand had the same problems in raising a whole division, the formation of the combined New Zealand & Australian Division (NZ&A Division) was an excellent compromise. Initially made up of just the New Zealand Brigade, and the 4th Australian Brigade, it would be commanded by Major General Alexander Godley, a British career officer who had served with the British Army until Kitchener had sent him specifically to command the embryonic New Zealand Defence Forces in 1911. At this stage New Zealand lacked a strong national identity and was essentially a collection of provinces with prominently local allegiances; however, there was still an eager response to the call for volunteers. Like the Australians, many New Zealanders, buoyed up by their passion for outdoor pursuits and sporting activities, thought of themselves as natural soldiers. But they still had much to learn as training began to create the four infantry battalions of the New Zealand Brigade and the corresponding mounted rifles regiments which would follow on later.

On 1 November the AIF and NZEF sailed for further training in Britain prior to their deployment on the Western Front. However, Britain declared war on Turkey while they were still at sea and it was decided to halt the divisions in Egypt, where they could help ensure the safety of the Suez Canal while completing their training locally. They disembarked at Alexandria on 3 December and set about a vigorous schedule, marching through the soft sands, digging trenches and carrying out mock attacks. They worked hard but they soon showed the capacity to play even harder if given the slightest of opportunities.

> We had our first pay day on Christmas Eve and leave was general, and everybody went straight into Cairo. Our own party of four really disgraced ourselves, AWOL for three days, finally and very ignominiously dragged out of the Eden Palace Hotel in the early hours of the morning by the picket and made to walk it home and into the guard tent – with quite a lot of others I might add! I was spokesman before the C.O. and tried the excuse that it was Christmas. 'Damn it man, it was Christmas for all of us, seven days confined to barracks and loss of pay!'[4]
>
> Private George Scott, 4th (New South Wales) Battalion, 1st Brigade, 1st Division, AIF

The Australian (and to a far lesser extent, New Zealand) indiscipline is often seen as nothing more than typical 'larrikin' behaviour, but the more serious consequences were shown in numerous incidents of excessive drunkenness, high VD rates and nasty outbreaks of violence against the Egyptians and Military Police which culminated in the infamous 'Battle of the Wozzer' in the Haret al Wassir red light district of Cairo on 2 April. On 4 April the main body of the ANZAC Corps left Cairo sailing for the Mudros harbour at Lemnos Island. The 3rd Brigade, selected as the covering force for the landings, had already reached Lemnos back on 4 March.

> As we steamed quietly to our anchorage we passed numerous British and French warships, battleships, cruisers, destroyers, submarines and store-ships. Being the fastest vessel ours was the first of the troopships to enter the harbour, the others coming in the afternoon and next morning. The harbour was an excellent haven of rest from the rather choppy seas outside, being practically surrounded by hills. The Island seemed mostly given to pasture and there was an absence of trees and bushes. Two or three small villages were in view, the houses looking very old, small and very close together, and in the following weeks we found that this was so, as we had the pleasure of marching through about six or seven different towns or villages. We were ashore nearly every day doing route marches, etc. The inhabitants of the island were nearly all Greek and seemed very hardy folk, quite the typical peasant. Pasture for sheep seemed the chief mode of making a living, and

agricultural work was done in the real old-fashioned way, a wooden plough with oxen pulling, or perhaps a donkey and an ox paired. Business men of the place with a bit of push came to us with their wares, nuts, oranges, figs, hard-boiled eggs, and a white cheese which none of our fellows could stomach.[5]

Private Herbert Fildes, 12th (South & Western Australian and Tasmanian) Battalion, 3rd Brigade, 1st Division, AIF

Also completing their training in Cairo was the 42nd Division from East Lancashire. In September 1914 this had been the first territorial division to go overseas, its troops largely based in the old barracks of Cairo and Alexandria. They too were training hard in the desert but much of what they were taught was unrealistic or irrelevant.

Every day in Egypt our pattern of training was the same. A long gruelling march in the desert under the hot sun to build up our stamina. Then open-order skirmishing, each section in turn dashing forward some 50 to 100 yards, and their advance covered by the supporting fire of the other sections – lots of exhilarating blank cartridges being fired madly by us. Then finally a bugle call, a fixing of nice well polished and shiny bayonets on the end of our rifles and a dashing charge of glory-mad young boy-soldiers towards a mythical and non-existent enemy, who presumably fled terrified at the very sight of the legendary British bayonet. Then the bugle would sound the recall and we'd gather together again – like children do after an exciting picnic 'tired but so happy' – and take about half-an-hour's rest before setting out for the tiring march back to barracks.[6]

Private Charles Watkins, 1/6th Lancashire Fusiliers, 125th Brigade, 42nd Division

While the 42nd Division was standing by as possible reserves for the MEF, the 29th Indian Brigade was also ready for deployment to Gallipoli if necessary.

The 29th Division was the last of the British regular divisions, created by recalling garrison troops from far-flung reaches of the British Empire. With its headquarters in Leamington Spa, it was only formed in January 1915, its constituent units spread liberally across the Midlands area. As a result there was a serious lack of brigade and divisional training, which must have impacted on the efficiency of staff work and communications within the division. This would indeed prove a problem when the division was flung into action just months later. Unaware of the tussles that surrounded their deployment, the troops sailed for Alexandria on 16 March. They then spent a considerable period disembarking and re-embarking in readiness for the proposed landings, before sailing for Mudros on 7 April. Although inexperienced in modern warfare and lacking in training as a combined unit, the 29th Division was a confident formation of soldiers excellently trained in individual military skills and it was regarded by Hamilton as the backbone of the MEF.

Although the French were not overly keen to get embroiled in the Gallipoli land operations they were none the less determined to keep an eye on the Middle East adventures of their allies. They therefore hurriedly created a new division from units left in the depots in France and North Africa. This was henceforth to be known as the 1st Division of the Corps Expéditionnaire d'Orient (CEO) and consisted of the Métropolitaine Brigade (the French 175th Régiment & 1st Régiment de Marche d'Afrique) and the Coloniale Brigade (the 4th Régiment Mixte Coloniale & 6th Régiment Mixte Coloniale). It was thus a cosmopolitan mixture of various French, Senegalese, Foreign Legion and Zouave battalions. Although hastily raised, the CEO was composed of well-trained troops, accustomed to the privations of soldiering and blessed with a full complement of artillery – largely, the much-admired rapid-firing 75mm guns. It should perhaps be equated to the 29th Division as regards military efficiency. In command was General Albert d'Amade, an officer who had already demonstrated his ability to work effectively with the British during the 1914 operations on the Western Front.

The French convoys from North Africa and Marseilles were brought together at Malta where they also first encountered their allies. It would prove an emotional meeting.

> The English cheered us! Frenzied 'Hurrahs' were exchanged by both sides. The 'Marseillaise' was sung by the English; we replied with 'God Save the King', the two anthems are frenetically applauded by one and all. A trumpet sounds; it is applauded. Then numerous trumpets and bass drums make an incomprehensible noise which we applauded anyway![7]
>
> Sergeant D'Arnaud Pomiro, 3rd Battalion, 175th Regiment, 1st (Métropolitaine) Brigade, 1st Division, CEO

Pushing on, they arrived at Mudros on 11 March. There the usual training was soon in full swing. It was noticeable that some of their more experienced veterans were not quite as cheerfully tolerant as the Australians in their dealings with the local Greeks. Private Cornelius Jean de Bruin noted his comrades' abrupt reaction to a case of suspected profiteering.

> We had now been without tobacco for a month and so a right royal welcome was accorded to an old Greek who turned up with a whole cartload of cigarettes. Guided by his native knowledge of the laws of supply and demand and in blissful ignorance of the ways of the Legion and the Système 'D', he expected to make his fortune. The price of the tobacco rose, so did the old Greek, who was lifted bodily and dropped splashingly into the harbour. The battalion enjoyed its first smoke for a month.[8]
>
> Private Cornelius Jean de Bruin, Légion Étrangère, 1st Régiment de Marche d'Afrique, 1st (Métropolitaine) Brigade, 1st Division, CEO

The French made their base at Mudros, although in late March and early April most of the force was required to make the long detour to Alexandria to reorganise transports for the proposed landing.

The most unconventional of all the forces assigned was the Royal Naval Division (RND), a strange combination of barely trained troops with next to no artillery provision. It had been formed by Churchill as a useful home for the 20,000–30,000 Royal Navy reservists and eager new recruits who were excess to the fleet's immediate requirements in 1914. They were originally intended for home defence or deployment to seize an advanced naval base as required. Although their military training had barely started they were flung into action to secure the Channel port of Antwerp in October 1914. Disaster ensued when nearly 1,500 troops of the 1st Naval Brigade strayed into the neutral Netherlands, where they were all promptly interned for the duration of the war. This has been satirised as the result of a minor confusion of port and starboard, but in truth the RND were simply not yet trained to a high enough standard. The rest returned to Britain where their training resumed and the ranks were replenished by further drafts.

The Plymouth and Chatham Battalions, RMLI, had been despatched to assist in the fleet operations against the Dardanelles forts in early February 1915. The main body followed at Churchill's instigation towards the end of the month, bound for the eastern Mediterranean. At this stage there is no doubt that the RND officers were an eclectic bunch recruited from here, there and everywhere on the basis of possessing talents that were not specifically military. Most gilded, most gifted of all was Sub Lieutenant Rupert Brooke, who at 27 years old was already an acclaimed poet. Aboard a troopship in convoy, in his letters home Brooke showed an exaggerated sense of the classical romance of it all, while at the same time retaining a refreshing ability to laugh at himself and his literary predilections.

> I'm filled with confident and glorious hopes. I've been looking at the maps. Do you think *perhaps* the fort on the Asiatic corner will need quelling, and we'll land and come at it from behind, and they'll make a sortie and meet us on the plains of Troy? It seems to me strategically so possible. Will Hero's Tower crumble under the 15" guns? Shall I loot mosaics from St Sophia and Turkish Delight and carpets? Should we be a turning point of history? Oh God! I've never been quite so happy in my life, I think. Not quite so pervasively happy; like a stream flowing entirely to one end. I suddenly realise that the ambition of my life has been – since I was two – to go on a military expedition against Constantinople. And when I *thought* I was hungry, or sleepy, or aching to write a poem – *that* was what I really, blindly wanted![9]
>
> Sub Lieutenant Rupert Brooke, Hood Battalion, 2nd Naval Brigade, RND

Meanwhile, Sub Lieutenant Patrick Shaw-Stewart cheerfully welcomed the addition of Charles Lister, formerly of the British Embassy in Constantinople, to the officers of the Hood Battalion. Lister had given up on the world of diplomacy and, as he put it, 'The date of my birth determines that I should take active service.'[10]

> At Port Said Charles introduced himself by most subterranean methods into the Hood. He pulled as many strings to get off the staff as others to get on to it – and in about three days he had a platoon. The four subalterns of the company were then Charles, Rupert Brooke, Johnny Dodge and me. I had dysentery all the time at Port Said, so I missed the spectacle of Charles drilling stokers on Yeomanry lines – an entrancing one, I have been told. There is one particularly circumstantial story of how he marched a body of men on to the parade ground before the eyes of the Brigade, and in his resonant parade tone ordered them to

halt in words more suited to the evolutions of quadrupeds. It became a very jolly family party on board ship.[11]

Sub Lieutenant Patrick Shaw-Stewart, Hood Battalion, 2nd Naval Brigade, RND

There was a general laxity in disciplinary matters and a great pride in being different, which reflected the lack of proper military training among these officers. But they had brains, they had courage, and above all they were good company.

Our party goes on happily. Charles Lister is a great gain even to those who don't understand him. He has the kindest heart imaginable, hasn't he? We laughed a good deal over the divisional notes on the character of the Turks, particularly at one which said they did not like night attacks because they hated the dark and invariably slept with a night light. Charles parodied them inimitably.[12]

Lieutenant Denis Browne, Hood Battalion, 2nd Naval Brigade, RND

While they were in Egypt, Rupert Brooke went down with an unfortunate combination of sunstroke and diarrhoea, but he was desperate to stay with his battalion.

While I shall be well, I think, for our first thrust into the fray, I shall be able to give my Turk, at the utmost, a kitten's tap. A diet of arrowroot doesn't build up violence. I am as weak as a pacifist.[13]

Sub Lieutenant Rupert Brooke, Hood Battalion, 2nd Naval Brigade, RND

On 17 April the division arrived at the small Greek island of Skyros, where the men began a final series of exercises, practising landing drills and mad dashes into the hills. One significant skill possessed by the New Zealand officer Bernard Freyberg was noticed by Lister.

My Company Commander Freyberg was a superb swimmer and we on several occasions did long distance swims in very cold water. I was defeated on one occasion of a two-mile swim I had set myself in Freyberg's company and came into the boat after a mile and a half in bitterly cold water, deep and blue as a turquoise, but as yet unyielding to the sun's rays. It was the coldness of the water and the relative poorness of my circulation which beat me – not weariness of flesh or muscle.[14]

Lieutenant Charles Lister, Hood Battalion, 2nd Naval Brigade, RND

Freyberg's swimming abilities would be put to practical use in just a matter of days. For the most part these privileged young men had a rather admirable determination to do their best, and at the same time a growing realisation that they were no longer the centre of the universe. Lister, as ever, encapsulated it rather neatly.

> I am every day happier at having left the Staff, and the sight of one's own men lying down in line among the stones and scrub of these jolly hills warms the blood. I hope I shall be brave; I am sure they will.[15]
>
> Lieutenant Charles Lister, Hood Battalion, 2nd Naval Brigade, RND

Sadly, on 20 April, during the same exercises, Rupert Brooke succumbed to severe blood poisoning, apparently caused by an insect bite on his lip. His temperature rocketed and soon nothing could be done. He died on Friday, 23 April, and was buried by a grieving party of his friends in an olive grove high on the side of the island. They never forgot Brooke. When his friend Denis Browne passed Skyros en route to Gallipoli on 2 June, he wrote a rather sad little note.

> We passed Rupert's island at sunset. The sea and sky in the east were grey and misty, but it stood out in the west, black and immense, with a crimson glowing halo round it. Every colour had come into the sea and sky to do him honour, and it seemed that the island must ever be shining with this glory that we buried him there.[16]
>
> Sub Lieutenant Denis Browne, Hood Battalion, 2nd Naval Brigade, RND

Poor Denis Browne would himself be killed just two days later in a hopeless attack on the Turkish lines. Few of that uniquely talented band of brothers from the RND would survive Gallipoli.

So it was that Hamilton's army came together: troops from all over the world, thrown together with no planning or forethought, as symbolised by the packing of the transports with the various units broken up on different ships and their equipment randomly intertwined below decks. A diversion via the Egyptian ports was essential so they could sort themselves out in a more logical fashion. All this took time. With most of the men barely trained as individual soldiers, collectively they had no experience of working together in the higher military formations of battalions, brigades and divisions. Many of the divisions were short of the artillery that was so essential in the Great War; ammunition was terrifyingly scarce. Most of the senior commanders were inexperienced in modern warfare; their staff had little practical experience to enable them to deal with the appalling administrative, communication and logistical problems that would face them on a daily basis. This was a disaster waiting to happen.

4

PLANS: COUNTDOWN TO DISASTER

At once we turned our faces to the land scheme. Very sketchy; how could it be otherwise? On the German system plans for a landing on Gallipoli would have been in my pocket, up-to-date and worked out to a ball cartridge and a pail of water. By the British system (?) I have been obliged to concoct my own plans in a brace of shakes almost under fire. Strategically and tactically our method may have its merits, for though it piles everything on to one man, the Commander, yet he is the chap who has got to see it through. But, in matters of supply, transport, organisation and administration our way is the way of Colney Hatch.[1]

General Sir Ian Hamilton, Headquarters, MEF

THE BRITISH OFTEN FORGET that there are two sides in every conflict and have the particular habit of assuming that the actions of their generals are somehow the prime factor in deciding the outcome of any campaign or battle; that the overall situation, tactics and qualities of their enemies are all but irrelevant. This leads to excessive praise of generals benefiting from the egregious blunders of their opponents, or, far more often, undeserved opprobrium for those facing a dismal outlook, a competent opposing general and well-trained troops. Sadly, during the Gallipoli campaign it was the Turks who had the upper hand from the outset. They occupied the ground that the British required. Unless the British were able to get inside the loop of the Turkish command decision-making process, causing them to recast their plans spontaneously and thereby triggering chaos, then the Turkish High Command would be setting the agenda in the battles to come. As long as they occupied the high ground on either side of the Narrows, they were winning the battle. Nothing else was at issue; there was no merit to the British wearing down the strength of the Turkish armies, no bonus points for a close run race or the apposite use of classical quotations in despatches. Physical dominance of the Dardanelles was the only factor that would decide the outcome of the campaign.

General Otto Liman von Sanders, appointed to command the new Turkish Fifth Army, was given responsibility for the defence of the Straits. His command was made up of the III Corps (the 7th, 9th and 19th Divisions and the Chanak Fortified Area Command) and the XV Corps (the 3rd and 11th Divisions) with the 5th Division and a cavalry brigade as reserves. Liman was born in Prussia on 17 February 1855. He had risen steadily to the rank of lieutenant general in 1911, whereupon, not being considered quite up to taking command of an army corps, he had eventually been despatched to lead the German Military Mission in Constantinople in December 1913. Having reached the port of Gallipoli on 26 March 1915 and set up his headquarters, Liman was faced with the challenge of how to distribute his forces.

> The important question was where the hostile landing should be expected. On it depended the grouping of the troops, which were rather inconsiderable in comparison with the great extent of the coast. Technical feasibility for the landing of large bodies of troops existed in many parts of the coast. All could not be occupied. The decision therefore must be made on tactical grounds. The positions of the five existing divisions up to March 26 had to be altered completely. They had been posted on different principles and distributed along the entire coast, somewhat like the frontier detachments of the good old days. The enemy on landing would have found resistance everywhere, but there were no reserves to check a strong and energetic advance. I ordered the divisions to hold their troops together and to send only the most indispensable security detachments to the coast within their sectors. Whatever might be in store, in view of our weak forces, our success depended not on sticking tight, but on the mobility of our three battle groups.[2]
>
> General Otto Liman von Sanders, Headquarters, Fifth Army

The strength of the Turkish Army in 1914 was a moot point critical to the outcome of the imminent campaign. It was undoubtedly large, with thirty-six cadre divisions with a peacetime strength of just over 200,000 men and 8,000 officers but which could be expanded to a wartime mobilised strength of approximately 500,000 and had the capacity to expand to about 800,000 after six months. However, the army was woefully ill equipped with a lack of modern artillery, machine guns and even rifles. Munitions of every form were also in short supply. Yet this distressing catalogue hid some solid military virtues. The ordinary Turkish soldiers, used to a hard-grafting civilian existence where life was cheap, coped well with the privations of military life and were hammered into shape by a draconian disciplinary system. The appointment of Enver as the Minister of War in 1913 had also brought a much-needed cull of old, incompetent or over-political officers. This increasing professionalism of the officer corps was enhanced by a whole generation of carefully trained staff officers. The harsh lessons of the Balkan Wars had been to some extent assimilated and their training emphasised, at least in theory, mobility, the value of achieving superiority in the fire fight that preceded any battle, the necessity of digging trenches to consolidate features of tactical importance, and the advantage of immediate counter-attacks to regain lost ground. There was also a grim determination among the Turks not to be beaten again.

> A year earlier we had the Balkan Wars and we were defeated very badly, but on the other hand we had the practice of fighting. In this war at Gallipoli we were facing two great forces in the world – the French and British people. They had great armies, but they were lacking practice.[3]
>
> Captain Ashir Arkayan, Artillery, Fifth Army

The Turkish Army was organised into infantry divisions, each consisting of three regiments of three battalions. This triangular structure would prove extraordinarily resilient under the pressures of war and would eventually be adopted by most of the combatants in the Great War. Although the Balkan Wars had been a disaster due mainly to overambitious operational plans, the troops themselves had fought with considerable grit and determination. All told, the raw materials of the Fifth Army at Liman's disposal were far better than either the British or the Germans realised.

One often unappreciated problem Liman faced was the topography of the Gallipoli Peninsula. It was for the most part rough terrain lacking in the shelter, water or easy supply routes that would allow the maintenance of thousands of men there for months at a time. This meant that large units could not be situated far from the few centres of population that existed. Of course these problems would also be faced by the Allies once they had landed.

With all this in mind Liman identified three main possibilities for large Allied landings. The first was on the Bulair Isthmus at the neck of Gallipoli, which he seems to have considered crucial, although misgivings as to the rationality of this preoccupation have surfaced ever since. As a result he based the 7th Division in the town of Gallipoli and had them occupying the Bulair Lines, with the reserves of the 5th Division also concentrated near the Bulair Isthmus, while the independent cavalry brigade guarded the coast of the Gulf of Saros. A further identified risk was a landing on the Asian side, with Kum Kale and Besika Bay being seen as possible landing sites from which an Allied advance could take the Asiatic Straits batteries from the rear. To counter this perceived threat the 3rd Division had one regiment forward covering Kum Kale and Yeni Shehr, while the other two waited close to the ruins of Troy. Similarly, the 11th Division had pushed forward one regiment to watch Besika Bay while the main strength was at Ezine. Finally, Liman thought any invasion of the Gallipoli Peninsula itself was likely to be launched either at Helles, on the southern tip, or on either side of the Gaba Tepe promontory, which lay directly opposite the town of Maidos and the Kilid Bahr Plateau. The whole area was the responsibility of the 9th Division, under the command of Colonel Sami Bey, who stationed the 27th Regiment to guard the Gaba Tepe sector, while the 26th Regiment was set to guard the coastline all the way from just south of Gaba Tepe down to Helles. The 25th Regiment was the divisional reserve positioned at Serafim Farm up on Kilid Bahr Plateau, to be deployed elsewhere or defend the plateau as required. The 19th Division, under the command of Lieutenant Colonel Mustafa Kemal, was the army reserve, based centrally at Boghali, not far from Maidos, and ready to be committed wherever Liman wished.

The concept of centralised reserve units marching swiftly to the landing points required a considerable amount of hard work and preparation if it was to have any chance of operating smoothly in the disorder of battle.

The chief issue was to so arrange matters as to be able to reach landing-places with fighting forces as quickly as possible. Such a fluid condition of the reporting elements, and rapid mobility of the troops, could only be attained by constant practice. This required time. On the 27th March, the Marshal, who was hurriedly surveying his whole zone shortly after assuming command, said to me, 'If the English will only leave me alone for eight days.' Actually four weeks passed.[4]

Colonel Hans Kannengiesser, Headquarters, Fifth Army

The Turks were granted the time they craved for training exercises, and they were also able to improve their defence works on the most likely looking landing sites, particularly the beaches at Helles and south of Gaba Tepe. Lacking material resources and further hampered by the threat of naval bombardments, they would have to rely on their ingenuity.

For the improvement of the field fortifications of the most endangered stretches of the coast all available men were put to work and mostly at night. The available Turkish means of obstruction were as short as were the tools, but we did the best we could. Torpedo heads were used alongside with the regular land mines and the fences of gardens and fields were stripped of their wood and wire. At places particularly suitable for landings barbed wire was stretched under water.[5]

General Otto Liman von Sanders, Headquarters Fifth Army

Liman is often regarded as the architect of everything sound in the Turkish plans for the defence of Gallipoli, but it seems possible that his Turkish subordinates had already begun to move to a light screen and central reserve system before his arrival.[6] The Bulair Lines had already been dug and strengthened to keep the Bulgarians and Greeks out of the Peninsula, while the fortifications dug on Kilid Bahr in 1913 indicate that the Turks had a firm understanding of what were the key geographical features of the area. It would hardly be unusual for a general to put himself more at the centre of events in his memoirs than might be justified. More pertinently, had Liman, as some of the Turkish officers feared, depleted the coastal detachments too much in his desire to bolster the flexible reserves? Were they left too weak to perform their designated function of holding the Allies until the reserves could arrive? By late April the Turks had made their dispositions, rehearsed their plans and prepared their fortifications as best they could. They held the ground they needed to hold; the question now was could the Allies throw them out?

AS GENERAL SIR IAN HAMILTON considered his options for the military operations it was apparent that the Allies had broken another important principle of waging war successfully: surprise. The desired objective of securing the Dardanelles Straits was obvious. Any chance of a strategic shock had been surrendered when the fleet bombarded the entrance forts way back in November 1914, thereby drawing the eyes of the world to the Straits. Tactical surprise was to some extent still possible, but only if the Allies could come up with a plan that could isolate the disparate elements of the Turkish forces. Hamilton had to blind and confuse the Turkish commander as to his real intentions.

> The first and foremost step towards a victorious landing was to upset
> the equilibrium of Liman von Sanders, the enemy commander of
> the Fifth Army. I must try to move so that he should be unable to
> concentrate either his mind or his men against us.[7]
>
> General Sir Ian Hamilton, Headquarters, MEF

In trying to achieve this, Hamilton had considerable advantages, for the Straits themselves already divided the Turkish forces, while the marching distance between Helles at the tip of the Peninsula and Bulair could be measured in days rather than hours. Even local reserve forces would be delayed by the rough ground when marching to the landing sites. There was therefore the potential for Hamilton to cause Liman the very greatest difficulties.

In making his decision as to where to land Hamilton had to consider the trade-off between unexpected landing points and the best locations to allow a rapid advance to secure the Narrows. The obvious approach of landing at either the most suitable beaches or close to his objectives would find the Turks ready and waiting, thereby threatening excessive casualties; a more indirect route might allow the troops to come ashore safely, but the inappropriate nature of the beach, the distance to be travelled, or the rough terrain would give the Turkish reserves ample time to block the approach to the main objectives.

The question of forcing the Dardanelles or landing on the Gallipoli

Peninsula was not new; it had been discussed time and time again over the past fifty years. Indeed, both British and French forces had occupied the Peninsula for a time during the 1850s and the 1870s. A series of reports on the possibilities of a naval attack, with or without military support, on the Dardanelles had been carried out for the War Office in 1906. In general, these recommended against a solely naval attack and commended both the virtues of prior practice landings and of achieving surprise. Subsequent reviews conducted in 1907 and 1908 were contradictory, illustrating the confusion as to whether it was, or was not, a feasible act of war to force the Straits. It seems that Hamilton did not have a copy of the 1906 paper but he was almost certainly in possession of the Anglo-Greek plan, which had only been prepared in 1914 by Vice Admiral Mark Kerr. The absence of any General Staff scheme can be attributed to delays in confirming that any large-scale military operations were being planned. Indeed, the poor communications between the War Council, the Admiralty, the General Staff, the Eastern Mediterranean Squadron (EMS) and the MEF make it difficult to work out when exactly a major landing on the Gallipoli Peninsula became inevitable, or indeed when the planning should have started – the only certainty was that it *should* have been begun earlier. The disarray was made worse by the dispersal of most of the General Staff to the BEF on the Western Front in August 1914. This may have stemmed from the understandable enthusiasm of career officers to take part in active service, but it represented an abrogation of their true responsibilities as key staff functions then had to be fulfilled by officers brought out of retirement. Such 'dugout' officers were almost totally ignored by Kitchener, who tended to act as Commander in Chief of the army rather than Secretary of State for War. The prevailing military culture was such that Hamilton could not make the entirely reasonable demand for a set of fully evaluated combined operations plans conditional to his accepting command of the MEF. Hamstrung by his long-subservient relationship with Kitchener, Hamilton was not the man to kick up a fuss – or not until he wrote his memoirs, by which time it was far too late.

> Where are your well-thought-out schemes for an amphibious attack on Constantinople? Not a sign! Braithwaite set to work in the Intelligence Branch at once. But beyond the ordinary text books those pigeon holes were drawn blank. The Dardanelles and Bosphorus might be in the

moon for all the military information I have got to go upon. One text
book and one book of travellers' tales don't take long to master.[8]

General Sir Ian Hamilton, Headquarters, MEF

However, the truth seems to have been very different. Although the maps
in Hamilton's possession were not good, they were at least adequate for the
purpose of operational planning. He had a 1:63,360 map which had been
prepared in 1908 (based on an older 1:50,000 map from a French survey
made during the Crimean War in 1854), while additional information had
been incorporated to create a 1:40,000 enlargement in March 1915. There
were inadequacies in the methodology of the original French survey and
the subsequent British redrawing with contours shown at intervals of 100
feet suppressed many of the topographic details revealed by the original
10 metre intervals. However, nothing much had changed on the Peninsula in the last sixty years and while the lack of an accurate large-scale map
was unfortunate, what could be done if the requisite topographic survey
had not been carried out? After all, the main features were present on the
maps. The acidic comment of a naval officer is perhaps pertinent here.

> The military history refers to the surprise of many soldiers at the
> unexpected sharpness of the many ravines; but on looking at my copy
> of the map, which I have kept, the contour lines seem to have indicated
> this fairly clearly. As a matter of fact good map-reading is not common,
> and many army officers are, or were, bad at it.[9]

Captain Bertram Smith, HMS *Vengeance*

In addition, while there were no maps accurate enough to be relied on
to allow indirect artillery or naval fire 'shooting off the map' at Gallipoli,
they were not available for the Western Front either in 1915. In any event,
this kind of indirect fire using distances and angles worked out from a map
was not then quite as important as it would become with the benefit of
years of intensive artillery development and the associated detailed map
survey work undertaken over the course of the war in France and Flanders.
The Gallipoli maps would be improved only as and when the Allies either
carried out their own survey, or captured copies of the better Turkish maps
based on a 1:25,000 survey carried out in 1912–13.

In planning the landing on an occupied coast, intelligence therefore
took on a vital importance. The sea approaches, the physical character of

the beaches, the presence or otherwise of defence works, the numbers of opponents likely to be met, the nature of the beach exits, the state of the roads, the exact topography of the ground to be encountered in between the landing place and the objective – these were all crucial to the planning process. For over a hundred years naval hydrographers, consular officials, military and naval attachés, intelligence officers, even civilian yachts-men had channelled intelligence, by open or clandestine means, back to Britain. In 1876, one naval officer had even prepared a 4-inch-to-the mile map with accompanying comprehensive notes covering the direct route between Gaba Tepe and the Kilid Bahr Plateau. What prescience! Indeed, it is noticeable that several of these reports settled on the Gaba Tepe sector as the best landing spot, as it had roads leading directly to both Maidos and Kilid Bahr. These various reports were all collated as secret documents by Naval Intelligence (1908) and the War Office (1909), but the process of intelligence acquisition certainly did not stop then and there were regular updates. Nearly all of this material, it has been convincingly argued, was made available to Hamilton and his staff, if not in London, then at the early briefing meetings out in theatre.[10]

In total these resources provided an excellent picture of the Gallipoli Peninsula and its possible landing places. This layer of detail was then supplemented by further intelligence reports from a variety of sources on the strength of the Turkish forces at Gallipoli. There were also personal observations carried out from the sea augmented by a series of beauti-fully drawn panoramas of landing sites which were duplicated and made available. Finally, there were the efforts of 3 Squadron, Royal Naval Air Service (RNAS), who were able use their aircraft to conduct a series of pioneering photographic reconnaissance missions which recorded with considerable accuracy the locations and ongoing changes in the Turkish defensive dispositions. Whatever Hamilton might claim, the information he required to make his plans was available; the more relevant question was how would he use it?

Right at the start of the belated planning process one decision that had already been provisionally taken by Birdwood was swiftly endorsed by Hamilton and his Chief of Staff, Major General Walter Braithwaite: they would eschew the amateur strategist's favourite ploy – and indeed Liman's main fear – of landing at Bulair. As far as Hamilton was concerned there were several flaws to this superficially attractive idea. Firstly, any landing would have to be on the northern, or Constantinople, side of the Turkish defence lines across the isthmus. These trenches and forts dated back to the Crimean War, but had recently been modernised by the Turks. Furthermore, any troops landing there would be vulnerable to attack from both sides. Secondly, the occupation of these lines would not cut off Turkish supplies and reinforcements to the Peninsula as their sea routes would be unaffected. Thirdly, Bulair was nowhere near the Narrows. Fourthly, the increased distance from the only feasible base at Mudros would have stretched an already strained line of communications to breaking point. Finally, and not insignificantly, there was the presence of the two Turkish divisions specifically placed there by Liman to thwart any such landing.

The British High Command also decided to abandon the option of serious operations on the Asiatic side of the Straits. Opinions as to the feasibility of such operations were mixed. While some thought that the openness of the ground would offer relative freedom of manoeuvre (impossible on the cramped Gallipoli Peninsula), others feared that the expeditionary force would be exposed to full-scale continental operations once the Turks mobilised their forces. As the Allies advanced towards Chanak and their objectives they would be leaving their right flank and communications terribly exposed to counter-attack. In any case, Hamilton had been advised by Kitchener that no such operation should be attempted.

That left the Gallipoli Peninsula itself. A glance at any map would reveal that domination of the Straits meant that the Kilid Bahr Plateau immediately behind the European forts would have to be secured to achieve Hamilton's aims. There were several obvious-looking landing beaches, but they all had some disadvantages. Suvla Bay was lightly guarded, but the line of march would entail crossing, or passing either side of, the Sari Bair range, rising to 971 feet. Hamilton also knew that there were strong Turkish forces in the Boghali area which could intercept the British well before they neared Kilid Bahr. A far better proposition was Gaba Tepe. This was where Hamilton determined to strike, making a night landing of the ANZAC Corps on the beaches north of Gaba Tepe, which were not yet well defended. Although to secure their beachhead the covering force would also have to gain a measure of control of the Sari Bair range, they would have every opportunity to do so before the Turkish reserves could arrive. The main force could then push on to seize the conically shaped Mal Tepe hill feature before launching an attack on Kilid Bahr itself the next day.

I would like to land my whole force in one – like a hammer stroke – with the fullest violence of its mass effect – as close as I can to my objective, the Kilid Bahr plateau. But, apart from the lack of small craft, the thing cannot be done; the beach space is so cramped that the men and their stores could not be put ashore. I have to separate my forces and the effect of momentum, which cannot be produced by cohesion, must be reproduced by the simultaneous nature of the movement.[11]

General Sir Ian Hamilton, Headquarters, MEF

This was to prove a fatal decision, the logic of which is debatable. There were many beaches stretching out on either side of Gaba Tepe and down towards Suvla which could have been used, once the covering force had secured the landing areas. Most or all of Hamilton's MEF could have been landed here for a concerted push on Kilid Bahr – this would have been the real hammer stroke. However, Hamilton also resolved to divide his force and make a series of supposedly coordinated landings all round the Helles tip of the Peninsula. Here, although the likely main landing beaches were well guarded by the Turks, it was felt that the navy would be able to pour in supporting fire from all three sides, pounding the Turks into a state of submission. The main beaches identified were V Beach, in front of the Sedd el Bahr fort and village, and W Beach, further round the Helles Cape. Hamilton also planned surprise subsidiary flanking assaults at the less likely landing points of X Beach, near W Beach, and S Beach in Morto Bay, just below De Tott's Battery. Hamilton also decided to place a force on the isolated Y Beach at the bottom of a very steep gully further up the western side of the Peninsula between the Turkish forward positions and their local reserves, with the intention of breaking their communications. These multifarious Helles operations would be the responsibility of the 29th Division augmented by the Plymouth Battalion of the RND. Their ambitious timetable involved the capture of the dominating height of Achi Baba behind the small village of Krithia by dusk on the first day, followed by a determined push next day in concert with the ANZAC Corps to sweep the Turks from Kilid Bahr. To counter the possible impact of the Turkish Asiatic batteries firing into the back of the landing forces at S and V Beaches it was decided to land a French force at Kum Kale, which would have the additional advantage of confusing the Turkish High Command as to whether the landing was real or not. Finally, Hamilton also approved diversionary operations without any actual landings by the French off Besika Bay and by the RND in the Gulf of Saros to threaten the Bulair Lines.

It is often thought that the only role of the Royal Navy in the operation was to carry out and support the landings. This was of course true on the first two days, but on the third day, with Kilid Bahr having been captured, the intention was to launch a naval attack to finally crash through the Narrows. The navy would also immediately begin a submarine campaign. On 25 April the *AE2* submarine managed to break through the Straits' underwater defences and into the Sea of Marmara. From then on the navy was able to maintain a strong presence behind the Turkish lines. Classic commerce raiding operations were used to disrupt Turkish sea routes to such an extent that by June 1915 most of the larger ships had all but disappeared and resupply was left to the ferries and small sailing craft. Eventually the Turks considered it far too dangerous to transport troops by sea. This forced them to use their land routes, which were in a shocking state of disrepair. Reinforcement units were brought as far as was possible by rail to then face a tiring three-day march on primitive roads before they even got to the Peninsula. Supplies and munitions had to be painstakingly brought in in small loads by pack animals and carts. Although the sea communications were never actually severed, the Allies' submarine operations would form a continual harassing backdrop for the Turks throughout the whole campaign.

Unfortunately, in drawing up his plans for the landings, Hamilton cast aside any slim opportunities that were set before him. Instead of forming a cohesive focused plan and sticking to it, he adopted, at least in part, almost every option on offer. He needlessly overcomplicated everything: like a sentence bespattered with clauses, subclauses and tangential meandering syntax, his plan layered main landings, support landings, diversionary landings and distracting demonstrations one upon the other. He had intended to confuse Liman to prevent him from concentrating the Turkish forces against the landings, but in doing so he failed to concentrate his own forces, which left them vulnerable to defeat in detail, thus mirroring the mistakes of his masters in London. The operations were also predicated on a belief that once the British came ashore the Turks would cut and run. They were not regarded as a 'European enemy' in the terminology of the time; like many senior British Army officers at the time, he underestimated his enemy and felt he could take risks that he would not have attempted against the German Army.

Many of his divisional commanders, however, were worried by the scale of the Turkish defences, the numbers of Turkish troops available, the hostile terrain and their own lack of reserves. Of these the most forthright was Major General Aylmer Hunter-Weston, commander of the 29th Division responsible for the Helles landings. Born in 1864, Hunter-Weston had been commissioned into the Royal Engineers and had seen active service and been wounded on the North-west Frontier of India. Subsequently, like so many of the senior officers at Gallipoli, he had served on Kitchener's staff, in 1896 before service during the Boer War. The usual round of staff postings had followed and he had commanded the 11th Brigade on the Western Front in 1914 before his late appointment on 13 March 1915 to the command of the 29th Division. Although often caricatured as a fool by critics unable to see beyond his bristling manner and imposing military moustache, Hunter-Weston fully recognised the scale of the problems that faced his division. After reviewing the reports of Turkish defensive preparations and the MEF's artillery weakness he considered it likely that they would end up stuck in an extended line across the Peninsula in front of the Kilid Bahr trenches, at which point they would be, in his delightful phrase, 'Up a tree!'[12]

> No loss would be too heavy and no risks too great if thereby success would be attained. But there is not in present circumstances a reasonable chance of success. The return of the expedition when it has gone so far will cause discontent, much talk, and some laughter; but it will not do irreparable harm to our cause, whereas to attempt a landing and fail to secure a passage through the Dardanelles would be a disaster to the Empire. The threat of invasion by the Allies is evidently having considerable effect on the Balkan States. It is therefore advisable to continue our preparations; to train our troops for landing, and to get our expedition properly equipped and organised for this difficult operation of war; so as to be ready to take advantage of any opportunity for successful action that may occur. But I would repeat; no action should be taken unless it has been carefully thought out in all its possibilities and details and unless there is a reasonable probability of success.[13]
>
> Major General Aylmer Hunter-Weston, Headquarters, 29th Division

Unhappily for their men, if one thing was certain in the British Army of 1915, it was that when put under pressure the 'can do' mentality would surface among senior officers. They would buckle to, make the best of a bad situation and muddle through. Hunter-Weston swallowed his doubts and determined to overcome the challenges. He was not alone. When further coastal reconnaissance revealed what was facing them at Helles, Brigadier General Steuart Hare remained undaunted, even though he was commanding the 86th Brigade who would be the first ashore.

> They have made it very strong all round the extreme end but I don't see how they can hold it in the face of the bombardment. Here the sailors will be shooting at what they can see. I do not anticipate much opposition to the actual landing except from long range artillery fire. It will be in our further advance that we shall catch it.[14]
>
> Brigadier General Steuart Hare, Headquarters, 86th Brigade, 29th Division

The main Helles landings would be made in daylight, as Hunter-Weston was vehemently against landing at night in uncharted waters with possible strong currents, and feared the confusion that might result. Hamilton favoured a night landing, as at Anzac, but deferred to his subordinate, whom he considered had the executive responsibility and must therefore be allowed to take the key decisions.

The apparent confidence of Hamilton and his senior staff utterly bemused some of their subordinates when they realised what was to be attempted. The results of recent aerial and naval reconnaissances seem to have been ignored, to the chagrin of those who had spent considerable time collecting that intelligence.

> During the past few weeks we were instructed to show on the chart of the peninsula all places where landing was deemed to be difficult or impossible owing either to defensive measures by the Turks or the unsatisfactory character of the beach, including exposure to bad weather. This was completed and forwarded through the usual channels. We received the operation order for the landing and were amazed to find that the Army had decided to land at nearly all the places which we had reported as being either difficult or impossible. So I was convinced that if the landing was successful it would only be at the expense of very heavy casualties.[15]
>
> Lieutenant Geoffrey Ryland, HMS *Ark Royal*

This choice of landing sites already identified as well defended is best exemplified by the choice of V Beach where there were trenches and lines of barbed wire. Given that the only method of landing was from open rowing boats towed in lines by steam launches, the likely problems were evident. Two weeks before the landings a staff meeting was held aboard the *Arcadian* to discuss the plans. Attending this meeting in a minor capacity was Commander Edward Unwin, a sailor with considerable experience in both the Merchant Marine and the Royal Navy. Although he had retired in 1909, he had been recalled on the outbreak of war and was placed in command of the *Hussar,* an old torpedo boat which had been converted to act as a communications yacht for the Eastern Mediterranean Squadron. Unwin arrived at the meeting with an open mind, but what he heard of the formidable nature of the Turkish beach defences at V Beach both concerned and inspired him. He was not a man to hold back when an idea occurred to him.

> It seemed to me that if the beach was properly defended by an enemy at only 200 yards, who reserved their fire till the boats were about 100 yards from the beach, not many would get ashore. I said, 'My idea would be to land the men in a specially prepared ship, right on the beach.'[16]
>
> Commander Edward Unwin, HMS *Hussar*

Unwin's thinking was straightforward. The ship would carry in relative safety a large number of assault troops who could then be rushed ashore in a matter of moments, then the ship would be used as a makeshift forward base, giving support fire to the attack while providing cover for command functions and shelter for the wounded. There was the additional advantage that it could carry huge quantities of ammunition, food and water and thereby act as a resupply depot in the days immediately following the landing.

Commander Unwin's suggestion was seized upon and he himself was placed in command of the project, using men from the *Hussar* as crew. The ship selected to run aground at V Beach was the 4,000-ton collier the *River Clyde*. She was British built and owned but at the time was under charter to the French. Once the French military supplies had been unloaded a rapid conversion project was commenced. Midshipman George Drewry, also from the *Hussar*, was involved from the start.

He gave me thirty Greeks and told me to clean her. Well, she was the dirtiest ship I've seen. She was in ballast and had just brought French mules up from Algiers, they had built boxes and floors in the 'tween decks and carried the mules there without worrying about sanitary arrangements. We knocked the boxes up and cleaned her up for the troops.[17]

Midshipman George Drewry, *River Clyde*

Eight large holes were then cut in the sides of the ship, four on each side, at the level of the lower decks where the troops could be carried in relative safety and comfort. Drewry then rigged up planking stages stretching along both sides and thereby linking the exit ports to a platform at the bow.

Early on, Unwin realised that the *River Clyde* might run aground too far from the beach to allow for easy disembarkation. Arrangements were therefore made to tow alongside it a steam hopper and three additional lighters which would fill any gap between the *River Clyde* and the beach. Meanwhile it had also been decided to use the machine guns of the RNAS Armoured Car Division to provide a huge concentration of fire to cover the disembarkation and support the attack. Lieutenant Commander Josiah Wedgwood was soon busy carrying out his own vital modifications to the *River Clyde*.

We made casemates for our guns, and have also got eighteen motorcycles aboard so that we can run our guns, or other people's ammunition, up to Krithia if all goes well. Today, this afternoon, 2,400 Munsters, Dublins and Hampshires come on board and conceal themselves in the holds of the Wooden Horse – we are in sight of the windy plains of Troy. In the ship's sides great ports are cut. As soon as the crash comes and we grind ashore, these dragons' teeth spring armed from the ports.[18]

Lieutenant Commander Josiah Wedgwood, No. 3 Squadron, Royal Naval Armoured Car Division

Wedgwood was not the only one to seize on the romantic affectation of regarding the *River Clyde* as a modern-day Trojan Horse being launched forth to bring doom to the Turkish defenders. For many officers who had enjoyed the benefits of a public school education, the story of the fall of Troy was very familiar. This was of little comfort to Unwin, who was finding his personal accountability for the success or failure of the V Beach landings beginning to weigh down on him.

> I have never spent such a time in my life as I did before the landing, the awful responsibility, for I wasn't just carrying out orders, but carrying through a scheme of my own in which if I failed the consequences might be awful. The thousands of thoughts that flash through one's head at such a time as to what might happen and how to meet them. And on top of it all the wonder as to how one will behave one's self, as I don't believe any man is quite sure of himself.[19]
>
> Commander Edward Unwin, *River Clyde*

One enigmatic character caught up in the *River Clyde* plans was Lieutenant Colonel Charles (known as Dick) Doughty Wylie, a staff officer attached to the 29th Division. Born in 1868, he had seen considerable military service before spending periods as first a military consul and then as Director in Chief of Red Cross Units in Turkey during the Balkan Wars. His wife Lily Doughty Wylie was working – in her husband's view overworking – in a hospital in France. Dick Doughty Wylie was a dashing, tall, blue-eyed literary soldier and there was much speculation about his strange quasi-affair with the famous Arabist archaeologist Gertrude Bell. However, he also cared deeply for his wife and worried what would happen to her if he was killed.

> Lily would feel intolerably lonely and hopeless after her long hours of work, which would tell on anybody's spirit and vitality. She talks about overdoses of morphia and such things. I think that in reality she is too brave and strong minded for such things, but still the saying weighs on my spirits. If you hear I'm killed go over at once to France and seek her out; don't lose any time, but go and look after her. Don't take her away from the work, for it will be best for her to work, but manage to stay somewhere near and see her through. I haven't told her yet of this wrecked ship because I don't want her to know till it's over. This is a very interesting show from every point of view – but it runs a great many chances however one looks at it. It may be a success and is certainly bold enough in idea. Don't be unduly anxious over this business – it's all in the day's work as far as I am concerned.[20]
>
> Lieutenant Colonel Dick Doughty Wylie, Headquarters, 29th Division

There was pandemonium in the crowded Mudros harbour in the final few days before the invasion fleet set off. The final prerequisite for a successful operation was not in the Allies' hands – fair weather. The original intended landing date was 23 April, but a gale on the morning of 21 April forced a postponement of forty-eight hours. The date was finally set for 25 April. The ships set off in carnival atmosphere on 24 April. As each transport moved away the cheers rang out. They were heading for their preliminary rendezvous off the islands of Tenedos (for the Helles force) and Imbros (for the Anzac force).

As they moved slowly across the Aegean an air of tension built up that afflicted almost everyone aboard the *River Clyde*. For the most part Commander Unwin acted as the officer of the watch on the bridge, although he briefly allowed Midshipman Drewry to stand a turn.

> At 2 a.m. or thereabouts the Captain turned over to me and I found myself on the bridge very sleepy with only the helmsman, steering towards the Turkish searchlights on a calm night just making headway against the current, shadowy forms of destroyers and battleships slipping past me. Visions of mines and submarines rose up before me as I thought of the 2,500 men in the holds and I felt very young.[21]
>
> Midshipman George Drewry, *River Clyde*

After just an hour or so, Unwin came back on to the bridge and ordered Drewry, accompanied by Seaman George Samson, to board the steam hopper.

As the *River Clyde* made her slow journey to Helles time weighed heavily for these young men about to risk all for their country. Although they knew that they should get some rest, that it might be their last opportunity for a couple of days, their circumstances prevented easy slumbers.

> The night was bitterly cold. The holds were crowded and uncomfortable. Some of the officers went up on to the deck. I tried to get some sleep but the cold and hard iron decks were not congenial to sleep. I did find a warm sheltered spot near the engines, but as I was dozing off a heavy sea boot was planted firmly on my face – I had overlooked the fact that I was lying across the doorway to the engine room![22]
>
> Second Lieutenant Reginald Gillett, 2nd Hampshire Regiment, 88th Brigade, 29th Division

Whatever their commanders may have thought, many of the men realised that they were about to undergo a severe ordeal that might well be their last. It was not a cheery prospect.

> I felt we were for it. That the enterprise was unique and would demand all I was possible of giving, and more. That it was no picnic but a desperate venture. I just longed to get on with it and be done with it. I felt I was no hero and that I had not the pluck of a louse. My nerves were tense and strung up, and yet I never doubted that we would not win through, because I knew the splendid fellows at my back, highly trained, strictly disciplined, and they would follow me anywhere.[23]
>
> Captain Guy Geddes, 1st Royal Munster Fusiliers, 86th Brigade, 29th Division

So the Allied convoys moved with grim purpose to their various landing points scattered up and down the Peninsula. Nothing could stop them, so the soldiers were told. But all the same, they could not help but worry.

5

25 APRIL: LANDINGS AT ANZAC

Almost all parts of this plateau were bombarded with high explosive shells and shrapnel. This bombardment proclaimed that a bitter, hard-fought wrestling match was about to begin between the brave stubborn Australian soldiers and the warlike sons of Turkey who were filling the pages of world history.[1]

Lieutenant Colonel Mehmet Sefik,[2] Headquarters, 27th Regiment, 9th Division, Fifth Army

THE ANZAC CORPS was inexperienced and had undergone the bare minimum of training, yet it had been given a task under Hamilton's plans which, in clichéd military parlance, would have daunted Napoleon's Old Guard. They were to make a night landing on a hostile shore, overcome an ill-defined opposition, take control of the high ground surrounding the landing beaches and then push across the Peninsula to seize Mal Tepe, thereby severing Turkish communications. All that in one day before the even more daunting task of launching a joint attack with the British advancing from Helles on the imposing bulk of the Kilid Bahr Plateau on the second day. Presumably the third day would be devoted to rest, the sanctifying of their labours and watching the fleet sail through the Narrows. What the Turks might do in response – the delaying tactics of their screens near the landing place, the possibility of ferocious counter-attacks by their concentrated battalions – were treated as irrelevancies in the great British scheme of things.

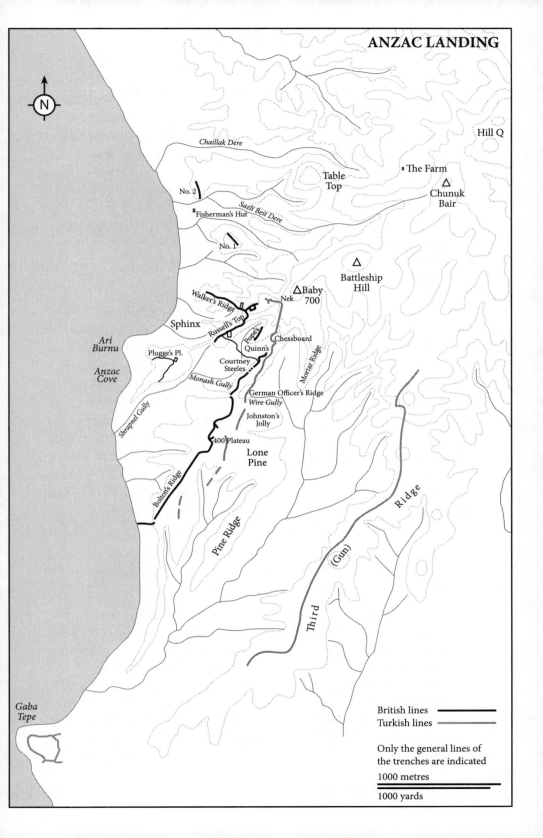

Even before the fighting started, many of the Anzac officers were well aware that this was an ambitious programme.

> Tomorrow must be the most eventful day of my life; cannot feel flurried or excited but tomorrow will tell a different tale. We are to drive a wedge into the Turks, who are also being attacked by the British at the point. If we are successful we will get the beaten Turks on us on one side trying to get home, and the relieving Turks on the other, trying to get down to help. I pray that God will bless and guard all those near and dear to me and that time in its mercy will wash away all memories of these anxious times for the dear ones at home waiting news.[3]
>
> Captain Carl Jess, Headquarters, 4th Australian Brigade, NZ&A Division, AIF

Above all, their own personal fears were intertwined with their duties to those around them. The higher the rank, of course, the greater the responsibilities and so the more sinking the awareness of the manifold pitfalls that could lie ahead of them. First ashore would be the 1st Division, commanded by Major General Sir William Bridges; but the most worried of all – and with good reason – was Colonel Ewen Sinclair-MacLagan in command of the 3rd Brigade, the force that would be first ashore and charged with the vital task of taking up positions along the Third Ridge feature that stretched from Battleship Hill on the main Sari Bair range, though Scrubby Knoll and extending right down as far as Gaba Tepe. Once *in situ* they were to cover the disembarkation of the main body. The next ashore would be the 2nd Brigade under Colonel James M'Cay, who had the task of securing all of the Sari Bair range right up to Hill 971. The 1st Brigade, commanded by Colonel Henry MacLaurin, was to act as the 1st Division reserve. Only when the NZ&A Division was safely ashore would the ANZAC Corps begin its advance on Mal Tepe.

> The commander of the destroyer *Colne* gave me his bunk, but I simply could not sleep. Although I knew that all the orders for the operations had been clear and most carefully thought out, had we, the Brigade Staff, provided for any and every eventuality? How was Brigade Headquarters to keep in touch with the units of the Brigade scattered over a 4,000 to 5,000 yard front and on foot? If opposition was even only moderately serious, could units keep touch with one another? Was the reserve battalion placed in the right position? Were the 'poor' maps issued to us accurate enough to be depended on, especially for the naval

covering fire? If that was wire-entanglement in the water, on the north shore of Gaba Tepe, could the men get through it, or would they be drowned and so leave my right flank open? How could I replace them from the reserve? These and many other thoughts of a similar nature kept me wide awake until we got into the boats for the last few yards to shore.[4]

Colonel Ewen Sinclair-MacLagan, Headquarters, 3rd Brigade, 1st Division, AIF

He was by no means the only man to find sleep difficult that night.

The first wave would be just 1,500 men, made up of two companies each from the 9th, 10th and 11th Battalions of Sinclair-MacLagan's 3rd Brigade, who were to land from twelve tows each consisting of a steamboat and three rowing boats. They were to land across a broad front with the right flank string of tows about a mile north of Gaba Tepe and the left flank tows some 1,600 yards further to the north. This meant that they were intended to land between a point halfway along Brighton Beach to somewhere near Hell Spit at the south end of what would become known as Anzac Cove. There was an assumption that, except at the aforementioned Gaba Tepe, there were very few Turks in the immediate area and that wherever they landed, and indeed whatever happened, the Anzacs would be able to achieve their objectives with relative ease. The possibility of a virile Turkish opposition was not really considered.

Facing the 3rd Brigade was the Turkish 2nd Battalion, 27th Regiment scattered in various outposts all along the five and a half miles of coastline from Aghyl Dere, north of Fisherman's Hut, to Semerely Tepe, well south of Gaba Tepe. The 4th Company was most directly involved with the ninety men of 2nd Platoon under the command of Second Lieutenant Muharrem directly facing the invaders at Anzac Cove on Ari Burnu and Plugge's Plateau. Further to the north were the sixty to seventy men of the 1st Platoon under Second Lieutenant Ibrahim Hayrettin, based on the hills around Fisherman's Hut. The reserve 3rd Platoon was back on Second Ridge along with company commander Captain Faik. The regimental headquarters was well dug in on Gaba Tepe, armed with two old multi-barrelled Nordenfelt guns with further small outposts trickling along Bolton's Ridge looking down on Brighton Beach. The weakness of this screening force worried many Turkish officers who would have preferred to have tried to prevent the British from landing in the first place rather than to contain them prior to counter-attacks, as demanded by Liman.

> Thinking that the Battalion was in a difficult situation and that in the event that they were hard pressed by, for example, a sudden enemy landing by night, it might not be possible to reinforce them, I consulted orally with Divisional Command with a view to understanding the reason for the remaining forces of the regiment being stationed at Maidos and, if possible, to have the Regiment located closer to the above mentioned Battalion. Formerly a large part of 27th Regiment was positioned immediately behind Ari Burnu and this was intended to intervene at once in the event of a landing.[5]
>
> Lieutenant Colonel Mehmet Sefik, Headquarters, 27th Regiment, 9th Division, Fifth Turkish Army

But, despite such concerns, Liman's policy of offering a mere trip wire defence remained in place. The Turks had gained from the Germans' energy and drive, but they also had to fall in with the German solution to the defence of the Peninsula.

THE NAVAL SHIPS of the covering force crept in early on the morning of 25 April. It was a tricky business as they had to time their approach to avoid both the light of the moon, which would set at 02.56, and the onset of dawn at around 04.00.

> At 1 a.m. on going on deck one found that we were proceeding very slowly. The reason for this was the brilliance of the moon. The sailors' friend in peace has become one of his worst foes in war and on this occasion she was at her best and brightest, so much so that one could see for miles. In consequence we were a little late at the rendezvous, but very little, and the transfer of the boats took place without incident. Immediately prior to falling in, the men were given a tot each to keep the cockles warm during their cramped and tedious passage in the boats. The embarkation took nearly 40 minutes, and it was some little time longer before the order, 'Go on!' was given by megaphone.[6]
>
> Commander Charles Dix, HMS *Majestic*

As this was going on, the soldiers in the second wave of the 3rd Brigade were transferring from the troopships to the destroyers from which they would be landed. Maintaining silence was difficult and there were idiots at every level.

> They clambered out as quickly as their ridiculously heavy kit would allow, and the going on a rope ladder was slow. Commander Godfrey of HMS *Beagle* was of an impatient nature, and as time was getting on he got more and more snappy at the troops. The strictest silence was the order and it was pitch dark, of course. You can imagine our feelings when the Commander said sternly through his megaphone, in an undertone, 'Hurry up down that rope ladder there!' And a big raucous digger's voice broke the silence of the Aegean with, 'Put a sock in it; d'yer think we're ******* trapeze artists?' The Commander looked livid, but how we enjoyed it. It seemed to relax the tension.[7]
>
> Captain Arthur Ross, Headquarters, 3rd Infantry Brigade, 1st Division, AIF

As quietly as they could, the assembled forces began to close in on the Peninsula. At 03.30 the battleships halted and the twelve tows were sent forward alone into the stygian darkness. As they moved slowly towards the shore there was considerable uncertainty among the relatively junior naval officers as they struggled to locate the correct landing site. Their orders were somewhat opaque, with room for confusion, especially as the tows were unable to see each other at the specified space between them of 150 yards and so, not unnaturally, began to crowd together, thereby also reducing the width of shoreline upon which they would eventually land. Only the senior officers, Commander Charles Dix in the northernmost tow and Lieutenant Commander John Waterlow in the southernmost one, actually knew where they were intended to land. At the first glimmerings of dawn Midshipman John Metcalf, in the second-most-southerly tow, felt that they were sailing too close to Gaba Tepe. Rightly or wrongly, on his own initiative, he began to steer away to the north.

> I realised that we were heading very close to the north side of Gaba Tepe which, because of its height, is very conspicuous. Knowing that there were Turkish troops there and we would get an enfilading fire all along the starboard side as well as from ahead, I was confident that we must be heading for a wrong place. There was no one to consult and I felt the lives of the men I was towing were my responsibility. Without any delay I altered course two points to port to get away from Gaba

Tepe. After a quarter of an hour, finding that the tows to the port of me had conformed, I again altered course a point and a half to port.[8]

Midshipman John Metcalf, HMS *Triumph*

These were not small course changes – a single point is 11.25 degrees, so in total he had ordered a change of three and a half points or about 40 degrees. The knock-on effects of this radical adjustment soon became obvious. As the senior officer in charge of the flotilla, Dix was horrified when he found the effects of Metcalf's initiative radically influencing the whole approach path.

> At first all seemed to be going well, but when three-quarters of the way ashore the right wing was seen to be steering across the bows of the centre, who were conforming to the movement, thus crowding the left wing: away to port. By this time some of us were awake to the fact that we were already some way to port of our objective and so, in order to save as much ground as possible, the left wing went on at full speed and held their course, only altering to starboard to avoid collision. It was instinctively felt that as soon as the first boat got ashore every other boat would at once put her helm over and do the same, and that the quicker we got there the less would be the error. The first approach of dawn was another reason for speed. Everything was absolutely quiet as we approached the shore and there was nothing to lead one to suppose that the surprise had failed, but as the first boat touched the shore a single shot broke the stillness, almost immediately followed by others, and the firing became general.[9]

> Commander Charles Dix, HMS *Majestic*

Dix's actions ensured that the twelve tows would not only land bunched up together, but also were no longer in sequential order – meaning that the landing parties would be disorganised from the off. They were no longer near Gaba Tepe – that was one blessing – but most of the men came ashore clustered around the lesser promontory of Ari Burnu at the north end of the shallow beach that would forever be known as Anzac Cove. It was 04.30: the battle had begun.

THE STEALTHY APPROACH of the Allied fleet to the coast of Gallipoli was detected fairly early on by Turks stationed above Anzac Cove.

At about 02.00 that night the moon was still shining. The patrols on duty from my reserve platoon reported having sighted many enemy ships in the open sea. I got up and looked through the binoculars. I saw, straight in front of us, but rather a long way off, a large number of ships the size of which could not be distinguished. It was not clear whether or not they were moving.[10]

Captain Faik, 2nd Battalion, 27th Regiment, 9th Division, Fifth Army

By 02.30, Faik had sent his reports to his company commander, Major Ismet, and to the divisional headquarters. Told to keep on the alert, he roused his reserve platoon for action. At this stage it was still thought that any landing party attacking the 2/27th Regiment would be in the Gaba Tepe sector. Shortly afterwards the moon disappeared and all was dark. The question for the Turks was: where were the Allies heading for?

At the southern end of Anzac Cove was Private Adil Sahin, a local man recruited from the village of Buyuk Anafarta. That fateful morning he was fast asleep in one of the shallow tents when he was rudely awoken by the sentry.

He shook us and pointed down the slope to the water below. He said he thought he could see shapes out there on the water. We looked out and strained to see in the half-light and then we heard noises and saw shapes of boats with soldiers coming ashore. We were ordered to start firing. Some fell on the beach and I wasn't sure whether we'd hit them or they were taking shelter. They made for the base of the rise and then began climbing. We were outnumbered, so we began to withdraw. It was very confusing. We didn't know anything about this invasion. We were very scared and retreated to the second ridge, firing as we went. I was very frightened.[11]

Private Adil Sahin, 2nd Battalion, 27th Regiment, 9th Division, Fifth Army

Scared or not, most of the Turks did their duty, holding on as long as they could before falling back under discipline.

The smattering of bullets on the first boats during the landing caused very few casualties – entirely concomitant with undirected rifle fire in the dark. The Turks had held their fire until the boats actually pulled in and thus lost their opportunity to hit the Anzacs while they were at their most vulnerable, sitting packed and helpless in the rowing boats. Indeed, photographs taken later that morning but still in the early stages of the landing show a beach nearly clear of casualties. Just one corpse lies by the waterline, which seems to be that of an engineer killed in a subsequent wave. It is questionable whether anyone was killed in the rush across the narrow beach, which would have been obscured from the defenders on the surrounding hills. Nevertheless the outbreak of gunfire added a certain impetus to the ongoing disembarkation of the second wave of soldiers from the destroyers into their attendant boats.

> The outburst was so sudden, that our men were momentarily checked, when a most cheery very English voice from the bridge called out, 'Go on lads, get into the boats, these fellows can't shoot for tawfee!' A regular laugh went up at the 'tony' accent. I looked up and saw the Lieutenant Commander, his arms folded on the bridge, leaning over, smiling, pipe in hand, as if he was looking on at a sports meeting. It was the right note to strike.[12]
>
> Captain Dixon Hearder, 11th (Western Australia) Battalion, 3rd Brigade, 1st Division, AIF

However, the isolated 2/27th Regiment had no machine guns – contrary to the mixture of rumour and confused reports that have insisted ever since that there were Turkish machine guns not only at Gaba Tepe but on Ari Burnu, Plugge's Plateau, Russell's Top and Fisherman's Hut. The ubiquity of these reports seems persuasive, until it is recalled that there were many other factors that might account for the confusion. The naval picket boats had machine guns mounted in their bows which provided the character-istic rattle when they fired. It is also an acknowledged phenomenon that inexperienced troops cannot distinguish exactly who or what is firing at them in the heat of battle. Finally, exaggeration by the men present of the problems they had to overcome was both understandable and part of the romantic image of war that still existed in 1915. For it is a certainty that the whole of the 27th Regiment had only the one machine gun company of four guns which was held with the reserve 1/27th and 3/27th Battal-ions back near Maidos; held ready to be deployed only when the point of danger had been determined. This made good sense; for to place such pre-cious assets close to the shore was simply asking for them to be over-run in the initial confusion. Shooting down from hills on to a narrow overlooked beach would have allowed them but scant moments of effective use.[13] It is instructive that no Turkish machine guns were captured, despite their supposed proximity to the beach and the impossibility of moving such heavy weapons during a scrambled retreat across rough country. They were not captured simply because they were not there in the first place. The real Turkish machine guns can be tracked in their movements and their arrival was recorded much later that morning. The Turks had one artillery battery of four guns on 400 Plateau but they refused to open fire when asked by Captain Faik as he lacked sufficient authority – the guns were intended to help defend the beaches next to Gaba Tepe.

Meanwhile Captain Faik had moved up on to Russell's Top. From there he could see the destroyers moving in with the second wave.

> We arrived at Yuksek Sirt [Russell's Top] and occupied the trenches opposite the northern beach of Ari Burnu. I ordered firing to be opened from 1,300 metres. The 2nd Platoon in the Haintepe [Plugge's Plateau] trenches a little way in front of us had been drawn into the fighting from the start. Torpedo boats towed the enemy craft and as they approached the shore they slipped the tow rope and quickly abandoned the craft which they had been towing. The torpedo boats then withdrew, firing continuously. The craft at which we were firing remained far from the shore because the coastal waters were shallow. Some of the enemy troops were hit and stayed in the craft. Those who were not hit jumped into the sea and only five or ten men escaped by getting into our 'dead' area.[14]
>
> Captain Faik, 2nd Battalion, 27th Regiment, 9th Division, Fifth Army

The subsequent waves of Anzacs would come under somewhat heavier fire than the first, simply because visibility was improving by the minute and not all the Turks hidden on the surrounding hills had been cleared away. The Nordenfelts and the indirect fire from field guns located behind Gaba Tepe also began to take their toll. Despite these unwelcome attentions the second wave of troops approached the shore, landing across a much wider front stretching from just north of Ari Burnu to Brighton Beach and with the companies in the right order. Among them was Captain Dixon Hearder.

> The pinnace went aground 36 yards from the shore and the men in the boats were packed absolutely closely. We had to get out oars and row ashore under heavy fire. It took no end of a time to get the oars out, as they were 18 foot oars and the men were sitting on them. Five men

were hit in the boat. At last our boat grounded and I jumped out as I thought into 2 feet of water. It was up to my neck, and under I went![15]

Captain Dixon Hearder, 11th (Western Australia) Battalion, 3rd Brigade, 1st Division, AIF

He got up and stumbled ashore, followed by his men. They were only about ten minutes behind the first wave and in some cases made more rapid progress inland.

We climbed up the beach and lay doggo for a few seconds while everyone took off his pack and got a breather, then round a winding precipitous path, up, up, up we charged. Not a rifle had been loaded (by strict order) and our boys did not waste their breath cheering until we got to the top, then a wild 'Cooee!' and the bayonet. I think the uncanny silence, and the fact that not a soul fired a shot, got on the Turks' nerves in the dim light, anyway, very few waited to give an exhibition of bayonet fighting, and in an hour the first ridge was won, save for some snipers concealed in bushes, who lay doggo, and got quite a few of the main body as they came on.[16]

Captain Dixon Hearder, 11th (Western Australia) Battalion, 3rd Brigade, 1st Division, AIF

The complex nature of the terrain meant that in the confusion both sides were continually being enfiladed or in danger of being caught unawares by fire from unexpected quarters – as Captain Faik was to find up on Russell's Top.

We came under fire from the enemy who were climbing up to the ridge where we were from a slope 100 metres to our left. We began to engage them on this side. In this fighting Sergeant Suleyman was wounded. Some of the private soldiers were also hit. I too received a severe wound in the groin and was reduced to a state where I could no longer command the platoon.[17]

Captain Faik, 2nd Battalion, 27th Regiment, 9th Division, Fifth Army

Sensibly, these small isolated parties of Turks, outnumbered as they were, did not wait to cross bayonets with the Anzacs. They had another, far more effective method of resistance. Falling back into the tortured landscape of gullies behind First Ridge, they melted into the scrub ready to carry on the fight as the invaders advanced, to painful contact in more ways than one. For the scrub that sheathed the hills and gullies came in many forms, but they all seemed to be prickly, tearing at uniforms and flesh, insinuating bristly spiked clusters and spores deep inside uniforms to rub soft skin red-raw. The breath rasped from the attackers' lungs as they strove to climb up the sides of jagged ridges, physically forcing their way through tangled undergrowth. Their legs may have been strong enough from their training marches across the desert sands of Egypt, but few of the Anzacs had the aerobic capacity to cope with near-vertical climbs while carrying heavy rifles, their nerves already scraped bare by the extreme tensions of their first action. As the Anzacs moved forward, the Turks continued to fall back, taking advantage of the fact that they knew where they were going, and sometimes taking up impromptu skirmish lines. Elements of the 9th, 10th and 11th Battalions all found themselves on top of Plugge's Plateau, where Major Edmund Drake-Brockman of the 11th Battalion tried to sort them into some kind of order. Corporal Thomas Louch and his party from the first wave had already climbed Plugge's Plateau when they were ordered to cross the valley in front of them and climb up on to Second Ridge in the area that would become known as MacLaurin's Hill.

> We slid down the sheer, sandy slope of Plugge's on our backsides, still clutching our box of ammunition, crossed the floor of Shrapnel Gully and with difficulty climbed the ridge where Major Denton directed us to a position on the forward side covering Wire Gully. We were soaking wet, very uncomfortable and enfiladed by fire from our left. We could see no enemy and did not seem to be doing any good where we were.[18]
>
> Corporal Thomas Louch, 11th (Western Australia) Battalion, 3rd Brigade, 1st Australian Division, AIF

There was still much bewilderment when the machine gun section under the command of Captain Dixon Hearder arrived atop of Plugge's Plateau.

> The first 11th man I fell in with was Brockman. We joined forces and proceeded towards the left, when suddenly across a gorge and on the top of a ridge, about a mile away, arose an awful rattle of musketry and at once 'D' Company of the 11th under Major Denton semaphored through for reinforcements and I hurried off to his assistance. Down we went, slipping and scrambling and sliding, following the track of a stony gorge, while our friend the enemy poured in rifle fire and shrapnel. Here one man of mine got a scalp wound and I was struck at

the back of the knee. We pushed on without one man and got to the top of the next ridge where I had last seen 'D' Company. I halted just short of the ridge, to enable all my men to catch up, as they had strung out a good deal. Bear in mind we had only advanced a mile as the crow flies, but we had at a conceivable estimate marched three miles, so high and so steep were the hills we had to traverse. Then I found we were two men short and a Corporal. However we dashed over the ridge, carrying our guns, tripods, belt boxes of ammunition, when to my dismay there was no sign of the Company I had come to reinforce. We got under cover of some scrub and set up our guns and opened fire, immediately a terrific fire opened on us, but we were lying pretty close to the ground and they could not actually see us, I think.[19]

Captain Dixon Hearder, 11th (Western Australia) Battalion, 3rd Brigade, 1st Division, AIF

Hearder's experience was fairly typical of that of the first Anzacs feeling their way forward under harassing fire and then digging in. There has been a long-held belief that the Anzacs charged too far inland, that they became isolated by going way beyond their objectives. Rather, the bulk of the 3rd Brigade dug in on the seaward side of Second Ridge, instead of pushing across Legge Valley in order to occupy Third Ridge as they should have done in their role as the covering force. This was not through the effectiveness of the sniping of the Turkish screen as it fell back before the vastly superior Australian numbers, but rather through the conscious decision of Colonel Ewen Sinclair-MacLagan, who seems to have decided almost from the off that Third Ridge was a ridge too far. In doing so he was abrogating his responsibility to cover properly the landing of the main body. The fact that the 3rd Brigade might have found themselves under pressure on Third Ridge was irrelevant; it was their job to soak up that pressure as best they could and so allow the 2nd Brigade behind them freedom of action so that they would not get sucked haphazardly into battle. That way the 2nd Brigade could then move purposefully to seize control of the Sari Bair high ground stretching from Chunuk Bair right up to Hill 971 and thereby establish a solid northern flank before the lunge forward to Mal Tepe.

Despite this clear responsibility, as early as 05.30, Sinclair-MacLagan ordered the advance to be reined in. This was despite the fact that small parties of Australians had already gone forward and found nothing other than localised Turkish opposition beyond Second Ridge. But the hapless Sinclair-MacLagan was constrained by his fear of being left exposed to counter-attack from the right if he extended too far forward. Through his caution, he lost several hours that could have enabled the Anzacs to define the perimeters of a much larger bridgehead; for the Turkish reserves did not appear on Third Ridge in any strength until after 08.00. This crucial change in the original plan was compounded when Sinclair-MacLagan encountered Colonel James M'Cay, the commander of 2nd Brigade, some time just after 06.00. He successfully pressed M'Cay not to push on to the north up the Sari Bair Ridge in accordance with his orders, but instead to move south and take up positions on 400 Plateau, the continuation of Second Ridge. In essence he reversed their geographical positions in defending Second Ridge without assigning any units to push on. This effectively paralysed the Australian 1st Division *in situ* and gave the ANZAC Corps operations for the rest of the day a distinctly defensive flavour.

Meanwhile, members of the 2nd Brigade were coming ashore from 05.30 onwards. Most of them landed in Anzac Cove, but one group of four boats carrying men from the 7th Battalion directly approached Fisherman's Hut. Here, a small group of Turks, under Second Lieutenant Ibrahim Hayrettin, were preparing a vigorous reception.

> We faced them with our few weapons and our faith, and thanks to the devastating fire we rained down upon them, within an hour's time we had felled and destroyed so many invading soldiers that the shores were covered with their bodies. Following this, and respecting the dictates of war whereby one must strive to hold the high ground, we went up to the hill of Chunuk Bair, which dominated the positions held by the enemy, and then after having left some of our men there, we pretended that reinforcements had come from the rear and surged forward towards the enemy, getting close enough so that our weapons would be effective and stopping them by engaging them with our intensive fire. In this way we managed to gain time in favour of the main forces which were following behind us.[20]
>
> Second Lieutenant Ibrahim Hayrettin, 2nd Battalion, 27th Regiment, 9th Division, Fifth Army

The nature of Liman's defensive plan meant that any time gained – whether it be through effective defensive actions or the hesitancy of

Sinclair-MacLagan – was crucial. Wherever the British landed the Turks would have to first assess the situation and then physically deploy the troops from the 9th and 19th Divisions held in reserve in the Maidos area on the other side of the narrow peninsula. When the first reports from Gaba Tepe were received they caught Lieutenant Colonel Mehmet Sefik, commanding the 27th Regiment, somewhat at a disadvantage as he and his 1/27th and 3/27th Battalions had been carrying out a night exercise in the Gaba Tepe sector the previous night. His tired men had only returned to their Maidos base shortly after midnight, upon which they had fallen asleep. Nevertheless, when the alarm came Sefik immediately rousted them out, called an order group to brief the officers and began harassing his divisional commander for orders to send forward his two battalions and attached machine gun company to support their beleaguered comrades in the 2/27th Regiment. His superiors hesitated, unsure whether this was merely an Allied diversion, but eventually at 05.45 the orders came and they began marching across the Peninsula. As they crossed the narrow plain between Maidos and Gaba Tepe, their greatest fear was a deluge of naval shells.

> I knew Ari Burnu and the country behind it very well. My purpose in the march was to occupy, before the enemy, Third Ridge which dominates the Ari Burnu ridge and all around. Our situation on the march was precarious and dangerous for the sun had risen and was beginning to get high in the sky. Over the whole plain from Boyun we were exposed to attack by naval gunfire and bombing attacks from aircraft. One reason for the battalions being ordered to march along different roads was in order to pass quickly over the dangerous area. Another reason was to reduce the depth of columns, since the enemy was not far away, and to deploy quickly if necessary for battle.[21]
>
> Lieutenant Colonel Mehmet Sefik, Headquarters, 27th Regiment, 9th Division, Fifth Army

By dint of a combination of good fortune, their taking practical measures such as avoiding the main road, and the inability of the Royal Navy observation officers to penetrate the morning haze, the Turks passed through their moment of greatest vulnerability unscathed. The Allies had thus missed a great chance to disrupt the Turkish reserves before they even reached Anzac. Conversely, it was a very good start for Sefik, who then marched his men up on to Third Ridge behind Scrubby Knoll, arriving some time after 08.00.

> We guessed that the enemy was advancing slowly and cautiously in order to capture the ridge where we were which dominated all sides – namely Chunuk Bair to Gaba Tepe. We set about our task of throwing the enemy and we felt a moral force in ourselves for performing this task. All the signs indicated that opposing our 2,000 armed men was a force of at least four or five times that size – or even bigger. We had to prevent the enemy from reaching and occupying the dominating line of Chunuk Bair–Gaba Tepe and had to gain time until the 19th Division arrived.[22]
>
> Lieutenant Colonel Mehmet Sefik, Headquarters, 27th Regiment, 9th Division, Fifth Army

Although the exact timings of events are unclear, one thing that is certain is that Colonel Aker's appreciation of the ground, the situation and the role of his troops put that of Colonel Sinclair-MacLagan to shame.

Over the next few hours the 1/27th and 3/27th Battalions slowly developed their attack on a wide front across Legge Valley towards Second Ridge covered by the fire from Scrubby Knoll of not only the four guns of his machine gun company but eventually of the battery of guns which had been sent to reinforce them. From Scrubby Knoll (height 540 feet) the Turks looked down on 400 Plateau (so-called as it was mostly about 400 feet above sea level). The small parties of Australians that had reached Third Ridge or its spurs were harried back, step by step, by the Turks, who were pressing hard on hasty positions dug in on Second Ridge itself. During the campaign the Australians would never again set foot on Third Ridge, except as prisoners. Then the Turks attacked Pine Ridge running to the south and the Lone Pine section of 400 Plateau, with the intention of not only hurling the Australians back but more specifically of recapturing their three mountain guns that had been over-run in the first advance. The Australians continually reinforced Second Ridge and 400 Plateau, seemingly oblivious to the fact that, although there was plenty of scrub cover, this offered little protection against the Turkish bullets and shrapnel that sprayed liberally across them.

> Four of us lay under shrapnel, machine gun and rifle fire, not daring to lift our heads the whole while; if we had budged we would have been

killed dozens of times over. The bullets were streaming so thick over our heads. My rifle, which I had placed just a bit ahead of me to protect my head, was chipped two or three times and the dirt was plugged on either side of me. Our officer said he'd never seen anything like it and he's an old soldier. I was jolly tired, too, and as a matter of fact I went to sleep twice. It made no difference whether I got hit sleeping or waking as I couldn't shoot from the position I was in. The only thing to do was to lie low until the fire slackened. It was about 3.30 p.m. when I got hit.[23]

Private Herbert Fildes, 12th (South & Western Australian and Tasmanian) Battalion, 3rd Brigade, 1st Division, AIF

Fildes was hit three times in the legs before he could get back to the beach. Men were wounded time and time again. Captain John Milne, positioned on Bolton's Ridge, just south of 400 Plateau, had already been wounded three times when he was hit again.

A man lying next to me got killed, and I put out my left hand to take his rifle and have a shot. Just as I did so a shell burst right overhead and hit me across the fingers, smashing the stock of the rifle to splinters, so I didn't have a shot that time. I got out my field dressing and tied them up and carried on, but very soon after a 6" shell got to business and a piece of it ripped through the back of my upper left arm.[24]

Captain John Milne, 9th (Queensland) Battalion, 3rd Brigade, 1st Division, AIF

Through his binoculars Lieutenant Colonel Sefik had brief glimpses of the deadly combat, including one skirmish at the north-east corner of Lone Pine.

All of a sudden, among the thickets, a closely packed line of soldiers were seen to rise to their feet. This line moved through the thickets in front of them and rushed upon our riflemen in a bayonets attack. When our riflemen saw this attack of the Australians, they immediately jumped to their feet, all together, and rushed in retaliation at the Australians. Most of the Australians who saw the counter-attack of our men suddenly stopped. While a few of them engaged in a bayonet and rifle duel with our men, the others ran away and got lost among the high brushwood. Our men pursued them with rifle fire.[25]

Lieutenant Colonel Mehmet Sefik, Headquarters, 27th Regiment, 9th Division, Fifth Army

Meanwhile, on Sefik's right, isolated elements of the 3/27th Regiment were fighting hard to prevent the Anzacs from pushing up further towards Chunuk Bair. Second Lieutenant Mucip Bey was on Mortar Ridge, a spur stretching down from Baby 700.

> I went 40 to 50 paces in front of our skirmish line. When I got above the ridge line I could see the Australians advancing among the bushes. A line was also advancing behind them. Without letting the enemy see, I selected a position and had our men moved into it. Suddenly from 200 metres we opened heavy fire. The Australians were shaken by the casualties they suffered. Some heroes appeared amongst them – disregarding death they worked to improve their situation.[26]
>
> Second Lieutenant Mucip Bey, 3rd Battalion, 27th Regiment, 9th Division, Fifth Army

Throughout that long day, whenever the Australian and New Zealand soldiers tried to move forward to reinforce their foremost positions, they faced a quandary. If they moved along the high ridge lines, where they had the chance to see the layout of the landscape, they would be shot down; if they hastily dived down into the gullies then they would soon be lost, climbing up and down the intervening ridges, while still risking instant death every time they allowed themselves to be briefly sky-lined. Whether teetering down near-vertical slopes or tortuously climbing back up the other side, they were slow moving targets. It was all too easy for the waiting Turks to pick them off: first, the officers, their rank insignia clear to behold on their shoulders and sleeves; then the NCOs, cajoling and directing their men as was their duty; and finally, the men of characer would step forward – men willing to risk their all to drive forward. In effect the Turks were able to scythe down the leaders from the advancing Anzacs.

One half company of 11th Battalion, commanded by Captain Eric Tulloch, had pushed determinedly up towards Chunuk Bair in one of the very few forward movements made after the first couple of hours. With them was Signaller Corporal Herbert Hitch. By about 09.30 they had managed to advance on to the Incebayor Spur of Battleship Hill but found themselves more or less isolated, with the bulk of 3rd Brigade still stalled back on Second Ridge.

I was supposed to keep in touch with any unit on the flank, any unit in the front or the rear as we advanced through the scrub. Whenever I reached any vantage point I waved the flag – a small flag white with a blue stripe through it. I was watching out for answering signals, I didn't get any – we were out of touch. It was quite a distance between us and the next unit on the right as far as I know. By that time our numbers were down to about twenty, perhaps thirty.[27]

Corporal Herbert Hitch, 11th (Western Australia) Battalion, 3rd Brigade, 1st Division, AIF

He was finally receiving a signal when he got a terrible shock.

The Turkish artillery had opened up and were firing salvos, dropping the range 100 yards at a time, searching the ground. I was right in the line with two bursts. I thought, 'My goodness, the next one will catch me!' It burst behind me and the whole contents of the shell went round me. I had the rifle leaning against my crutch and that spun to the ground. The pellets flew past and they sounded like a flight of parrots and puffs of dust rose here and there where the pellets struck the ground. I fell down thinking I must have been hit; twitching my muscles. When I picked the rifle up it had three hits on the barrel. Two close together on a hand guard knocking the woodwork away, leaving the springs on the barrel and one on the hand guard casing above the barrel. I also had one through my clothing, I found later on. That was remarkable because there were about 300 odd bullets in a shrapnel shell.[28]

Corporal Herbert Hitch, 11th (Western Australia) Battalion, 3rd Brigade, 1st Division, AIF

Over on Mortar Ridge, Second Lieutenant Mucip Bey and his small squad were desperate for reinforcements.

The battle started showing its effect on our side, too. The commander of the battalion, Major Halis Bey from Uşak, appeared at that moment. I felt that the weight of the responsibility, which had been unbearable for several hours, was being lifted from my shoulders. I took a deep breath. There couldn't have been a bigger support than this for a 20-year-old subaltern. The battalion commander complimented me and then started studying the position of the enemy. I was trying to make sense of his face which was turning yellow, and of the fading light in his eyes.

But I didn't need to reflect much or to search for a clue, for the left arm of his khaki jacket started to turn red and drops of blood gathered at his finger tips. 'You are wounded!' I said. 'Not now! Don't let the men know.'[29]

Second Lieutenant Mucip Bey, 3rd Battalion, 27th Regiment, 9th Division, Fifth Army

Only when he was convinced that his young officer had the situation in hand did Major Halis Bey go back for treatment.

It was evident that the 27th Regiment had little more to give; but the promised reinforcements had still not arrived. The Turks were being overwhelmed by sheer numbers. Lieutenant Colonel Sefik had been told that the men of the 19th Division were on their way. But where were they?

LIEUTENANT COLONEL MUSTAFA KEMAL, the commander of the 19th Division, had had a much longer wait for orders than Sefik. With news of landings flooding in from all sides the Turkish High Command had hesitated to commit its reserves and it was only at about 08.00 that Kemal finally received his orders. His dramatic reaction – crucial to the outcome of the whole day's fighting – was witnessed by Major Zeki Bey.

My battalion was on parade when the news of your landing came to us. It chanced that there had been ordered for that morning an exercise over the ground, especially towards Koja Chemen Tepe [Hill 971]. The Commander of our Division had received about dawn a report that a landing had occurred at Ari Burnu. The Turkish staff and commanders concerned did not expect a landing at Ari Burnu because it was too precipitous. The message then asked the Commander of the 19th Division to send one battalion from Boghali against Ari Burnu. The Regiment was assembled when the order came. Mustafa Kemal came himself, and ordered the Regiment and a Battery of artillery – mountain guns – to intercept the 'English' who had landed. He reasoned, 'If this force has gone in the direction of Koja Chemen Tepe, the landing is not a mere demonstration – it is the real thing, the landing of a main force.' For that reason he took, not one Battalion, as the Commander of the 9th Division had asked, but the whole Regiment. They went at once straight across country towards the south of Koja Chemen Tepe towards Chunuk Bair – Kemal himself leading.[30]

Major Zeki Bey, 1st Battalion, 57th Regiment, 19th Division, Fifth Army

Mustafa Kemal was truly to make his mark on the ANZAC Corps over the next hours, days and months of the Gallipoli campaign. Born in 1881 in the port of Salonika, which was then in Turkish Macedonia, from the age of twelve he had attended military schools before entering the Staff College. He was commissioned as a captain in 1905, but his mushrooming political activities meant that he often found himself in conflict with the authorities and he was posted away to the backwater of Syria and then to a staff position in Salonika. By this time his political group had been subsumed within the much more influential Young Turks. When the revolution came in July 1908 Kemal had been left a peripheral figure and, in his frustration, he had reacted badly, openly criticising the Young Turks. The brief counter-revolution of April 1909 made him militarily useful and he was given a staff appointment during the Tripolitanian War with Italy. Then, during the First Balkan War, Kemal had the unpleasant experience of watching from afar as his Macedonian homeland was over-run by the Greeks. As a staff officer, he was sent to help organise the defence of the Gallipoli Peninsula. By the end of the Balkan Wars Kemal had risen to the rank of lieutenant colonel, but then he was despatched out of the way as a military attaché to Bulgaria. When the Great War broke out in 1914 he had not been in favour of entering on the German side; he feared that Turkey would decline into a satellite state if Germany won, and lose everything if Germany lost. Kemal had wanted to wait and see for as long as possible, but on balance favoured joining the Allies. Nevertheless, despite his past politicking, he remained at heart a loyal Turkish officer and he was appointed to command the 19th Division in Gallipoli with his headquarters in Maidos. This, then, was the complex and driven man who faced the Anzacs on 25 April 1915.

The ground we had to traverse consisted largely of scrub and rocky valleys. I detailed the artillery commander to find a road and to point it out to the units. Kocacimen Tepe [Sari Bair] is the highest hill on the Peninsula, but as Ari Burnu is in dead ground it cannot be seen from here. From there I could see nothing at all except the battleships on the sea. I realised that the enemy infantry which had landed were still some way off. Our men had got very tired crossing that difficult ground without any halt and the line of march had become very strung out. I told the Regimental and Battery commanders to close their men up and give them a short halt. They were to halt there for 10 minutes out of sight of the sea and then follow me.[31]

Lieutenant Colonel Mustafa Kemal, Headquarters, 19th Division, Fifth Army

Kemal moved down towards Chunuk Bair, taking with him a few of his staff. At about 10.00, he saw a detachment of Turkish troops running back.

Confronting these men myself, I said, 'Why are you running away?' 'Sir, the enemy!' 'Where?' 'Over there!' they said, pointing out Battleship Hill. In fact a line of skirmishers of the enemy approached Battleship Hill and was advancing completely unopposed. Now just consider the situation. I had left my troops, so as to give the men 10 minutes' rest. It meant that the enemy was nearer to me than my troops were, and if the enemy came to where I was, then my troops would find themselves in a very difficult position. Then, I still do not know what it was, whether a logical appreciation or an instinctive action, I do not know, I said to the men running away, 'You cannot run away from the enemy!' 'We have no ammunition!' 'If you haven't got any ammunition you have your bayonets!' I said. And shouting to them I made them fix their bayonets and lie down on the ground. When they fixed their bayonets and lay down on the ground the enemy also lay down. The moment of time that we gained was this one.[32]

Lieutenant Colonel Mustafa Kemal, Headquarters, 19th Division, Fifth Army

At the same time Kemal sent back his orderly officer to bring up his men as quickly as possible. Every minute counted but it took a considerable time. As the 57th Regiment arrived they first formed a firing line and were then sent in to attack the tentative Australian positions on Baby 700 and Tulloch's men on Incebayor Spur. It is at this point that Kemal is reputed to have given the order that has gone down in history.

To my mind there was a more important factor than this tactical situation – that was everybody hurled himself on the enemy to kill and to die. This was no ordinary attack. Everybody was eager to succeed or go forward with the determination to die. Here is the order which I gave verbally to the commanders: 'I don't order you to attack – I order you to die. In the time which passes until we die, other troops and commanders can take our places.'[33]

Lieutenant Colonel Mustafa Kemal, Headquarters, 19th Division, Fifth Army

The Australians, partially dug in on Battleship Hill, were caught unawares by Kemal's onslaught. Some had never guessed that the Turks would counter-attack; they imagined that, once a position was taken, it was only onwards and upwards to success. Now they found themselves suddenly outnumbered. There was no command and control at all; indeed, at one point there were isolated portions of seven different battalions in the sector. With no communications, no common plan and no integrated defence system, they were ripe to be overwhelmed by the more purposeful Turks. A rapid swelling in the level of Turkish small arms fire indicated the arrival of their reinforcements. Tulloch's men were unable to do anything more than cower down in small folds in the ground. Retreat was unavoidable if they wanted to live.

Then the order came, retire in sections from the right and being on the right flank I jumped up to run. As soon as I jumped up the air was alive with bullets, most of them going overhead. We ran back about 200 yards, but by the time we reached the top of the next ridge all the rest were in motion. We opened fire and we fired about six or seven rounds each just to keep the enemy from coming on too quickly and then we all ran back together for about another 150 yards and the order was passed along, 'Reform left, Turks advancing on the left!' They were a fine looking body of men. They weren't running but were walking very quickly. As they came under our fire they ran back and I had two shots at a running man and missed him each time – I thought my rifle must have had the barrel bent. Then suddenly down from the sky as if by magic came the shells – their artillery observer had put them on to us. Providentially they were bursting late and the shrapnel was shredding the scrub behind us.[34]

Corporal Herbert Hitch, 11th (Western Australia) Battalion, 3rd Brigade, 1st Division, AIF

Back they tumbled during a gap in the shell fire. In all the confusion Hitch lost touch with his comrades.

I burst through the scrub suddenly and found myself on the edge of a steep ravine. I broke through so suddenly I had to grasp a sapling to save going over. There seemed no way of getting out from there. I thought, 'I'm going to get across here somehow!' and I threw my rifle down into this ravine and jumped. I sailed through the air about 25 feet and landed on a slope of 1 in 1. As I jack-knifed I felt as though I had landed on a couple of bayonets. I pitched over head first and seemed to be heading for a precipice, but I was lucky enough to grab a root with my left hand and swing round and go down feet first. I went over two or three vertical falls of about 8 to 10 feet and landed like a sack of spuds each time until finally I reached the breakaway with a drop of about 30 feet and I managed to stop there with about 6 feet to the next drop. As I stopped the earth I had dislodged came tumbling after me.[35]

Corporal Herbert Hitch, 11th (Western Australia) Battalion, 3rd Brigade, 1st Division, AIF

Battleship Hill fell to the Turks and still they pushed on, driving down on to Baby 700. The fighting surged backwards and forwards, but overall the Anzacs were falling back towards The Nek and Russell's Top.

It was becoming evident that Kemal's intervention could not have been better timed if it had been entirely deliberate. From the Australian perspective the 27th Regiment under Lieutenant Colonel Mehmet Sefik appeared first, threatening their right flank and developing a strong counter-attack, sucking in reserves. All the while, hidden behind the various ridges, the 57th Regiment was marching straight for the key high ground that would determine once and for all the fate of the ANZAC Corps landing. When the 57ths suddenly appeared and began to push home their counter-attack in the afternoon it was already too late. The Anzacs did not have enough reserves left; what minimal chances they had of success had been eroded by the unilateral actions of Colonel Sinclair-MacLagan, first in stopping the advance on Second Ridge and then in deploying most of the available reserves on to 400 Plateau, leaving the left flank open. Since that fateful decision, the 1st Division's commander, Major General Sir William Bridges, had failed to take any determined action that might have changed the course of the battle. Even the battalions of the 1st Brigade, his divisional reserve, had been assigned to the bitter fighting on 400 Plateau – indeed, elements of ten of the twelve 1st Division battalions ended up fighting there on 25 April. Worse still, when the New Zealand Brigade of the NZ&A Division, temporarily commanded by Colonel Harold Walker, began to come ashore from 10.45 with orders to reinforce the left flank, they too ended up dispersed randomly along Second Ridge. The Auckland Battalion was ashore by 12.30 but it had been decided – not unreasonably – that the direct route off the beach via Walker's Ridge was too precipitous and they were redirected through the bottleneck of Shrapnel and Monash Valleys.

> There seemed to be no organisation. The officers were all away on a reconnaissance and we found that it ended up with a whole stream of men going up the gully and the only thing to do was to carry on. We carried on up the gully being pushed from behind and we found it rather tough going. We soon got warm. There was a little water in the bottom of the gully but there was very sticky mud and this dragged on our feet so that a number didn't seem able to keep up the pace that I was setting and I was forever urging them to hurry along. We passed streams of Australian wounded going down the gully and they were all urging us to go to this place, or that, as reinforcements were wanted. I think really what happened to the Auckland Battalion was that they went to a number of different places just as their inclination took them, but as far as I was concerned, I ended up far up on the left on Walker's Ridge.[36]
>
> Sergeant R. H. Harris, Auckland Battalion, New Zealand Brigade, NZ&A Division, NZEF

Just two companies made it on to Baby 700. Among these was a platoon led by Lieutenant Spencer Westmacott, who encountered a frantic Australian officer.

> 'For God's sake push on!' he shouted as he came. I signalled my men to, 'Halt – lie down!' and the officer also stopped, panting. I sat down and he did, too. It seemed no place to stand about. He sat there, beating the ground with his hand, his breath coming in great gasps. When he recovered a bit I said, 'Now, what's the matter?' 'For God's sake push on!' he replied. 'They are getting hell in front and I am going back for reinforcements!' This between gasps. 'All right,' I said.[37]
>
> Lieutenant Spencer Westmacott, Auckland Battalion, New Zealand Brigade, NZ & A Division, NZEF

The image of panicking Australians and imperturbable New Zealanders is overdone, for when Westmacott arrived forward he was horrified at what he found.

> Their firing line had almost ceased to exist. There was no trench. Lying on the forward slope without protective cover, every man there had been killed or wounded. They had fought on there, unsupported, rather than retire, and I saw at once that the same fate awaited me and the few of my men who had got so far forward. We could not retire, of course, nor could we advance until reinforced. Nothing remained but to stay where we were and hope something would happen to ease the pressure on us. What could happen we weren't quite sure.[38]
>
> Lieutenant Spencer Westmacott, Auckland Battalion, New Zealand Brigade, NZ&A Division, NZEF

The troops, whether they were Australians or New Zealanders, had little idea of what was going on around them. The ANZAC Corps was facing an invisible enemy that punched hard while giving little opportunity for retaliation. This was especially the case on 400 Plateau.

> The officer ordered a bayonet charge – we lined the ridge, and with a shout doubled over it in a long line, expecting to find the enemy at close quarters. We were now in a scrub-covered plain, fairly in the open. No Turks were to be seen, but the air was literally full of bullets and the sound was deafening. The point-blank explosion of rifles and the concealed snipers firing on us at close quarters. The bayonet charge had failed, and the men became disorganised: some ran about distractedly, poking in the bushes for Turks; others fell on their faces, rendered nerve-racked by the terrible fire. I ran forward into a slight depression in the ground, where several men were lying, and found myself beside one of my Mena tent mates. Some of the men were wounded, others dead. Still no Turks were to be seen and there was no target for our rifles. Some fired a few shots aimlessly into space, but were warned that they might easily be firing on their own men; others were hit in attempting to assume the firing position.[39]
>
> Lance Corporal Eric Moorhead, 5th (Victoria) Battalion, 2nd Brigade, 1st Division, AIF

The capture of Baby 700 allowed the Turks to dominate both First and Second Ridges. Indeed, if the Turks had broken through The Nek and on to Russell's Top then the whole of the ANZAC Corps position would have been fatally undermined. Lieutenant Robert Cowey was with one of the small parties that fell back from Mortar Ridge on to Second Ridge.

Our casualties were very heavy and included two out of the three officers present. Ammunition ran short. We began to wonder if there were other than enemy troops left on the Peninsula, for we had seen none of our force. Towards evening the few survivors of our party straggled back to the head of Monash Valley, leaving too many good friends lying dead. Things were better here until the Turks again connected with us. We had a short respite during which to look at and think about things. We could now look down that long valley which led to the sea and the ships – and in those ships was safety. To stay seemed to make certain of death, of oblivion, of the loss of all those earthly things one had looked forward to. But to cede our position to the Turks meant that no living thing could enter that valley without being shot to death. We appeared to be occupying a key position. To leave it surely meant the loss of the whole enterprise. We stayed.[40]

Lieutenant Robert Cowey, 3rd (New South Wales) Battalion, 1st Brigade, 1st Division, AIF

Throughout the fighting on 25 April the Anzacs desperately needed artillery support, but they found it extremely difficult to organise the disembarkation of the guns and locate feasible gun positions in the minute bridgehead. Colonel Joseph Talbot Hobbs, the divisional artillery commander, went ashore and climbed up on to Plugge's Plateau in search of suitable gun positions for his flat trajectory 18-pounders. It was to prove a fruitless task.

The enemy resistance began to stiffen all along the line, and his counter-attacks commenced. Worse still, his artillery, now in considerable force, opened a most galling fire from various dominating positions and as the afternoon wore on his fire, controlled from close observation, became murderous. From late in the afternoon urgent and repeated requests had been made to the ships for more guns and hours were spent in patrolling the beach to receive them. None, however, arrived. Looking backwards, I confess I was terribly worried and bitterly disappointed at the inability of the Divisional Artillery, through no fault of its own, to give the infantry the assistance and support to which it was entitled. In the first place it was most difficult – nay, almost impossible – to find suitable gun positions and very difficult to get guns up the steep and rugged hillsides to them.[41]

Colonel Joseph Talbot Hobbs, Headquarters, AIF

They managed to get the 26th Indian Mounted Battery ashore and into action supporting the troops on 400 Plateau by about noon. The Indian gunners performed sterling work but their positions were cripplingly exposed and they were eventually forced back to the beach area.

As the Australians tried to scratch out trenches they suffered numerous casualties, but getting the wounded back to the beach was a dangerous task.

A lad got a smack in the thigh, and I managed to get it dressed, and with him gripping on to my boots I dragged myself along to the slope of the hill on my stomach and then was going to give him a roll down the side and chance what happened, when we saw the gun that was firing at us. Next thing I knew was that the lad had some more wounds. That put the wind up us properly, and we absolutely fell down the side of the hill to safety. I came through with a few torn clothes and a few scratches, but my man was not so well off; he had fallen into a small stream in the valley and was knee-deep in mud. After much struggling we managed to land him, my mate secured a stretcher, we dressed his wounds and made for the Casualty Clearing Station. Everything went well until we were nearly at the beach, near the mouth of Shrapnel Gully, when shrapnel began to burst all round us, and just as we rounded a corner one burst over us, one piece passing between my mate's back and the wounded man's head, and another piece just missing the side of the stretcher. We moved on more quickly and were turning round the next corner when we heard another shell coming. We dropped down to the ground, stretcher and all, and the shell buried itself in the soft earth not six feet away from us. Fortunately it was a dud and did not burst.[42]

Private Vincent Williams, 9th (Queensland) Battalion, 3rd Brigade, 1st Division, AIF

A casualty clearing station had been established in the lea of Hell Spit at the south end of Anzac Cove. But even here no one was safe.

The beach here was not wider than a cricket pitch and was crowded with wounded, waiting to be evacuated by lighters. Colonel Howse and his officers were working hard, and we joined them. Although we had been told to conserve our water supply, our water-bottles were soon empty. It was impossible to turn a deaf ear to the cry of the badly wounded men for 'A drop of water, mate!' Every minute the numbers of wounded increased; newcomers staggering down the hillside, or being carried there by their mates. Shrapnel burst incessantly over us, but the cliff gave comparative shelter. Many of the wounded, however, were hit a second time as they lay on the beach and one fine Australian whom I was dressing received a bullet through his knee. He said angrily, 'I've been hit once **** you Turks! Can't you leave a chap alone!'[43]

Lieutenant Colonel Percival Fenwick, Headquarters, NZ&A Division, NZEF

The casualty evacuation arrangements were dangerously haphazard and the wounded had a world of pain and danger to endure before they were delivered safely aboard the hospital ships. Midshipman Edwin Clark of the *Prince of Wales* was in charge of a pinnace.

We were towed in by a picket boat, she slipped us and I ran on the beach. Our bows were very high so we bagged a plank and lashed it on as a gangway. The Australians staggered up the wobbly plank and they were too dizzy to know what they did with their rifles which they used as crutches. One did go off and I narrowly escaped being shot. The stretcher cases were easier, but we couldn't make them comfortable and it must have been agony for them when we shoved off, dragging along the rocky bottom. It was terrible having to refuse so many wounded lying there who begged to be taken. If there had been a landing place we could have taken a lot more, but we could only just shove off as it was. The picket boat which had towed us in had gone off and I had only two men to pull, so we made fast to a lighter which was at a buoy not far off and tried to attract the attention of a steamboat. At last we got the *Bacchante*'s steamboat to give us a tow. The shrapnel burst in the water round us, but did us no harm.[44]

Midshipman Edwin Clark, HMS *Prince of Wales*

It was at this point that the failure to judge correctly the likely number of casualties took effect. There were just two hospital ships for all the landings that were to take place on 25 April. Even when the wounded were got aboard a ship at either Anzac or Helles it was often a makeshift arrangement: filthy dirty, remarkably overcrowded, with nowhere near enough doctors or medical orderlies, a shortage of medical supplies and few beds. Then there was the voyage of 600 miles with little or no treatment before they could get to Alexandria. One such temporary hospital ship was the *Dongola*.

> All they had on was either nothing, or a first field dressing. Everybody had to do a job of work. Two naval doctors and a parson came to us from a boat that had been sunk and my C.O. told me to go and help them. We put up a couple of sheets to block off a companionway, got a table and that's where we did our operations. The padre and I acted as anaesthetists. All we had to do was to put the mask over their face and using the chloroform drop bottle, just keep dropping, dropping and when the doctor said stop we stopped! We did smaller things, nothing very serious. I hadn't had any training except my first aid in the Scouts! I saw a man who had a bullet wound through his upper thigh straight through his scrotum which it tore and out through the left thigh and it didn't touch an artery, a bone or his testicles. The doctor cleaned right through the wound, tied him all up, and he said, 'What a marvellous thing.' The only thing was that he had wiped the inside of his scrotum with iodine and he said, 'That'll sting him when he comes round!' [45]
>
> Bugler John Ford, 15th Stationary Hospital, Royal Army Medical Corps (RAMC)

The wounded suffered dreadful privations and many who might have survived succumbed to the effects of gangrene or suppurating wounds before they got to a proper hospital in Egypt.

The beach was not only flooded with the wounded but also with an increasing number of leaderless men who had drifted back. Private Charles Duke was among them, although in his case he had badly sprained his ankle and had been ordered back by his officer.

> It was getting dusk and conditions on that narrow over-crowded strip, owing to the influx of wounded, seemed to be chaotic. In addition to the hundreds of wounded there were many whose duty it was to be there, but I also quickly noticed there were many stragglers – some perhaps who had used the excuse of helping a wounded cobber down or for other less legitimate reasons had just faded from the firing line. In the disorder they had become detached from their own officer and nobody worried about them. It was so much easier to lie doggo in a possie on the beach than to go back and face the hellish music that was being played on those hilltops. A shell burst just above us – already over-strained nerves reacted and I remember muttered relief being gained by a chap at my side, 'I wish I had the motherless bastard of a

Turk who sent that **** shell over!' Just what he would have done to him was entirely unprintable! [46]

Private Charles Duke, 4th (New South Wales) Battalion, 1st Brigade, 1st Division, AIF

Not all were guilty of dereliction of duty, but some were very close to malingering. There were as many as a thousand soldiers milling on the beach and at 17.50 Major General Bridges was forced to accelerate the landing of the 4th Brigade from the NZ&A Division to help bolster his front. As the reinforcing battalions of 4th Brigade came ashore they were funnelled into the lines at random, more in response to the immediate concerns real or imagined, of local commanders than in any concerted tactical initiative to take control of the battlefield. Among the 16th Battalion were Lance Corporal Percy Black and Private Harry Murray of the Vickers machine gun section. This was to be the first experience in battle for these legendary soldiers; men who would come to define much of the popular image of the Australians in the Great War.

At last the order came to move. It ran through all ranks like an electric impulse. There was an instant movement. Forward! Colonel Pope led the way up Shrapnel Gully and when we reached Monash Valley we received the welcome order to 'Dump packs!' No questioning that order – they weighed 60 to 70lbs apiece. It was now nearly dark. We proceeded up Monash Valley to where it forked and climbed a steep hill afterwards christened Pope's Hill. The continuous flashing of rifle fire came into sight. No shells now, but those snapping rifles kept up a frightful din, the air being simply saturated with noise. Near the top we halted. There was some confused shouting and a few shots in front, and then a sharp order to man the hilltop and open fire. A rather serious blunder had been made – the Turks having been mistaken for Indian troops – Colonel Pope, the adjutant, another officer and a man were captured, but the colonel escaped by knocking his would-be captors down, throwing himself over the steep edge of the hill and rolling back to his men! We rushed forward, scrambling, slipping and falling, till we reached the top, a plateau, and now, at last, our long bottled-up impatience found vent, as we poured out a tremendous fire into the blackness ahead. The enemy response soon died down, while our own slackened to a steady, controlled effort. Percy Black mounted his gun on the extreme left of the hill, the other gun being placed about a hundred yards to the right. It was impossible just then to see what field of fire we had, but we were all 'set' and began to dig in like fury. The long night dragged on and for me it was a very cold one as, owing to my plunge into the sea, I was still very wet from feet to waist, and I felt absolutely numb.[47]

Private Harry Murray, 16th (Western Australia and South Australia) Battalion, 4th Brigade, NZ&A Division, AIF

Behind them elements of the Wellington Battalion had landed. Its gruff commander, Lieutenant Colonel William Malone, was shocked by the chaos that lay before them.

There didn't seem much organisation on the shore, in fact it was disorganisation. We evidently haven't got a Kitchener about. On paper it was all right, but in practice no good. Still Britishers always muddle through somehow or another. The 'Heads' like General Birdwood and Godley *plan* all right, but the executive officers in the main are no good – have no idea of order, method, etc. They as I put it 'hang up everything on the ground'.[48]

Lieutenant Colonel William Malone, Wellington Battalion, New Zealand Brigade, NZ&A Division, NZEF

As night fell it became evident that those 'heads' were, quite rightly, worried as to the tenability of the bridgehead. The key to holding the position was, as Kemal had grasped so adroitly, gaining the high ground. The Turks had pressed right down from Chunuk Bair and had only just been held at The Nek.

Birdwood had been ashore late in the day and made a reconnaissance. Although he noticed the presence of stragglers, all claiming to be the last survivors of their units, he considered the situation still fairly satisfactory when he returned aboard the *Queen*.

I was horrified, about an hour later, to receive a message from Bridges asking me to return at once, as the position was now critical. I went ashore again and was met by Bridges and Godley, with several of their senior officers. They told me that their men were so exhausted after all they had gone through, and so unnerved by constant shell fire after their wonderfully gallant work, that they feared a fiasco if a heavy attack should be launched against us next morning. I was told that numbers had already dribbled back through the scrub, and the two

> Divisional Commanders urged me most strongly to make immediate
> arrangements for re-embarkation. At first I refused to take any action. I
> argued that Turkish demoralisation was in all probability considerably
> greater than ours, and that in any case I would rather die there in the
> morning than withdraw now.[49]
>
> Lieutenant General Sir William Birdwood, Headquarters, ANZAC Corps

Nevertheless Birdwood felt it his duty to send Hamilton a letter informing
him of what was going on.

> Both my Divisional Generals and Brigadiers have represented to me
> that they fear their men are thoroughly demoralised by shrapnel fire
> to which they have been subjected all day after exhaustion and gallant
> work in the morning. Numbers have dribbled back from firing line and
> cannot be collected in this difficult country. Even New Zealand Brigade,
> which has been only recently engaged, lost heavily and is to some
> extent demoralised. If troops are subjected to shell fire again tomorrow
> morning there is likely to be a fiasco as I have no fresh troops with
> which to replace those in firing line. I know my representation is most
> serious but if we are to re-embark it must be at once. [50]
>
> Lieutenant General Sir William Birdwood, Headquarters, ANZAC Corps

Although intended for Hamilton, through staff incompetence Birdwood's
letter was not addressed to anyone in particular. Hence, in somewhat
farcical circumstances, at about 23.00 it was passed to Admiral Sir Cecil
Thursby, who thought it was for him.

> I was quite taken back, as I had no idea that things were in such a
> critical state on shore. A moment's consideration convinced me that
> to re-embark under the conditions which then prevailed would be
> disastrous and could not be thought of, especially as I did not know yet
> what had happened at Helles. The night had turned dark and stormy,
> our men were tired and disorganised, and the confusion of any attempt
> to re-embark then would have been indescribable. Our losses would
> have been appalling. Besides which, I felt confident that when daylight
> came I could, with the guns of the fleet, hold back the enemy while our
> men dug themselves in and re-organised, either for a further advance or
> for an orderly re-embarkation under the guns of the fleet.[51]
>
> Admiral Sir Cecil Thursby, HMS *Queen*

Thursby set off for shore to meet Birdwood, but on sighting the *Queen Elizabeth* he took the letter aboard to consult with Hamilton and de Robeck.

> I was dragged out of a dead sleep by Braithwaite who kept shaking me by the shoulder and saying, 'Sir Ian! Sir Ian!!' I had been having a good time for an hour far away somewhere, far from bloody turmoil, and before I quite knew where I was, my Chief-of-Staff repeated what he had, I think, said several times already, 'Sir Ian, you've got to come right along – a question of life and death – you must settle it!' Braithwaite is a cool hand, but his tone made me wide awake in a second.[52]
>
> General Sir Ian Hamilton, Headquarters, MEF

After consulting with the anxious Thursby, Hamilton took the decision to 'stick it out', writing, famously, to Birdwood:

> Your news is indeed serious. But there is nothing for it but to dig yourselves right in and stick it out. It would take at least two days to re-embark you as Admiral Thursby will explain to you. Meanwhile, the Australian submarine has got up through the Narrows and has torpedoed a gunboat at Chunuk. Hunter-Weston, despite his heavy losses, will be advancing tomorrow which should divert pressure from you. Make a personal appeal to your men and Godley's to make a supreme effort to hold their ground. P.S. You have got through the difficult business, now you have only to dig, dig, dig, until you are safe.[53]
>
> General Sir Ian Hamilton, Headquarters, MEF

Thursby rushed back ashore carrying the letter to Birdwood. From then on there was no doubt: the ANZAC Corps would fight it out where they stood. This was the only possible decision, as any attempted impromptu evacuation would have surely ensured a far worse disaster.

THE TURKS HAD THEIR OWN PROBLEMS. As Lieutenant Colonel Mustafa Kemal succinctly put it: 'I could not get any clear information from anywhere. Owing to the darkness I could not get a picture of the battle situation.'[54] Their biggest problem lay with the 77th Regiment, which seemed to be disintegrating as it was ordered forward into the line in support of the 27th Regiment. As an Arab unit recruited from outside the Turkish heartlands, its soldiers had much less commitment to the cause than the native Turks. Perhaps as relevantly, they also had much less experience and training. That evening Lieutenant Colonel Mehmet Sefik moved forward into Legge Valley to check the situation.

> We went amongst the brushwood – from the right and left we heard a series of separate rifle shots. Without doubt these shots could have endangered our forward troops. Three or four men were talking in Arabic. It seemed that they and all those who had fired the rifle shots were Arabs belonging to the 77th Regiment which had gone forward for battle. They were men who had deserted, hidden among the bushes and fled. They spoke Turkish mixed with Arabic. It was impossible to overpower them because they ran away again in the darkness.[55]
>
> Lieutenant Colonel Mehmet Sefik, Headquarters, 27th Regiment, 9th Division, Fifth Army

Sefik felt that the Arab soldiers were unwilling to fight and that the combination of rough ground, copious undergrowth and the darkness of night made it impossible for their officers to maintain order. When he went forward to join his men on the Lone Pine section of 400 Plateau there was no sign of reinforcement by the 77th Regiment. This left the Turkish line very weak. In fact the ANZAC Corps was also so weak that no night attack from them was ever going to be feasible, but the Turks did not know that and so spent the night in considerable trepidation. Lieutenant Colonel Fahrettin Bey,[56] the Chief of Staff of III Corps, recalled their fears and relief as the majority of their men stood firm.

> That was our anxiety on the first day. If, God forbid, our soldiers had given way to panic as in the recent Balkan War and had been pushed back, our situation would have been very bad. Thanks to the Almighty, our officers and men rushed forward with self-sacrifice beyond description. Our troops, especially the officers, performed miracles. A wounded private was being carried from the front line to the rear. I walked with him for a little, holding him by the hand. When I uncovered his face and smoothed his bloody cheeks, he sighed, 'Oh, Sir, I am not grieving over my wounds but because I cannot see those fellows chased into the sea. Perhaps, if I could have stayed a bit longer, I should have seen them!'[57]
>
> Lieutenant Colonel Fahrettin Bey, Headquarters, III Corps, Fifth Army

But of course the men of the 27th Regiment were totally exhausted. They had been on an exercise all the previous night, then a full day of marching and fighting. The nerve-shredding tension of being a few yards from their enemy and not having the slightest clue as to what they were planning – or doing – meant that few could sleep.

Struggling with exhaustion as best they could, both sides spent the night trying to consolidate their positions wherever they had been washed up by the tides of battle. When the next day finally dawned they could at last see where they were. And of course their enemies could share that view. The Turks had succeeded in smuggling several men through the porous Australian lines to take up concealed positions on Russell's Top, which was almost vacant of Anzac troops. From here they could shoot straight into the backs of the men in the trenches on Second Ridge and Pope's Hill.

> Dawn showed at last and all had their rifles ready for a shot. Percy Black grabbed his and, sighting carefully, dropped a Turkish sniper, who had been crawling along the side of a cliff about 90 yards away. The poor wretch fell down the steep side, caught his legs in a low fork and there he hung for days. We all hoped that the shot had killed him and that he did not have to linger in such a position. Our own casualties began to mount up unpleasantly. One by one men hurtled down the steep hill, often shot through the head.[58]
>
> Private Harry Murray, 16th (Western Australia and South Australia) Battalion, 4th Brigade, NZ&A Division, AIF

The Anzac left flank was seriously exposed, but the 16th Battalion machine guns on Pope's Hill played a vital part in defending The Nek and the half-open route to Russell's Top.

> There was no organised attack on us for some hours, but rifle fire was increasing in both volume and accuracy. Black never missed a chance with his machine gun and he was a deadly shot. As the day wore on, the Turks tried to cross some open country and Black caught them in enfilade in lines. They simply sank and died. In one case, when overtaken by that death rain, they hunched together for protection and very few escaped. This drew on Black a concentrated 'hate' from the Turks. A mountain gun shelled him. He got a shrapnel through the ear and another through his hand, both painful wounds which bled

profusely, but still he managed to deliver his lethal spray whenever opportunity offered. His gun casing was now holed with rifle bullets. Suddenly a party of seventy Turks jumped out of a small depression some 80 yards in front. 'Here they come,' roared Percy, and a steady stream of fire roared from his gun. The nearest of them got to within 40 yards of us before collapsing. All were exceptionally brave men, who pushed home the attack in the name of Allah, but none were able to get back. A soldier by intuition, Black pointed out the weakness of our open left flank to an officer and offered to take a few men and line listening posts across the valley, but the officer seemed inclined to disregard the suggestion as being unimportant! Some Turkish snipers later got through the unguarded valley, as might have been expected, and that officer was one of their first victims.[59]

Private Harry Murray, 16th (Western Australia and South Australia) Battalion, 4th Brigade, NZ&A Division, AIF

Many of the Anzacs maintained that the Turks attacked them during the second day, but if that was so the attacks were very localised, for additional Turkish reinforcements did not arrive until the night of 26 April. Only small-scale attacks and counter-attacks were made by both sides.

After a heavy bombardment all the morning, attacks were made in force on our right and left. First the right wing broke and we had the mortification of seeing our boys retire at a double. I ordered my gun to swing round and we checked the pursuit by pouring in a heavy enfilade fire on the pursuing Turks. This broke him up and gave our boys time to collect and take up a fair position which their supports had managed to get ready. Just then we noticed that the new line was in the rear of us, so that our position, which had been isolated all through, was now liable to enfilade on the right. We at once started digging and throwing up a parapet to meet this new danger, when I was thunderstruck to see our left give way and retreat. You can guess our opinion of our chances. There we were, out in front, dug right in, no protection on our right or left and enfilade fire coming on us and our retreating troops. Suddenly, like a bolt from the blue, a 15-inch shell fell fair in among the pursuing enemy; before they could rally another fell, then another, a panic set up and the momentary triumph of John Turco was over.[60]

Captain Dixon Hearder, 11th (Western Australia) Battalion, 3rd Brigade, 1st Division, AIF

It was at moments like this that the awesome power of the British naval guns was felt. If they could catch the Turks in the open they were deadly.

> Turks attacked strongly apparently and attempted a flanking movement on the left flank. Urgent signal from General to shell them which we did – it being visible and not indirect firing: this was about 10 a.m. Nearly all ships fired. We fired rapid 6″ and fore turret and must have flattened out anything living in that square. Signal, 'Cease Firing!' followed by a signal expressing the thanks of the Infantry Brigade for the assistance given. I rather think this heavy shelling saved the left flank.[61]
>
> Lieutenant Chichele Bampton, HMS *Prince of Wales*

There was no effective method of controlling the naval guns and the complex situation on the ground militated against them opening fire except when the Turks were visible from the sea. The closeness of the fighting in hidden gullies or on the reverse slopes of ridges meant that the navy could rarely get involved without risking hitting their own men.

> At a time when every nerve was strained to hold the enemy at bay, one of our warships dropped four great shells into our midst. They buried deep into the earth and blew out tremendous craters, hurling men high into the air, but, fortunately, no one was injured. This made us realise how little damage the spectacular bombardment had wrought among the Turks – howitzers were what was wanted, not naval guns. A distinct note of comedy was supplied by some men as they tried to scramble back to the trench over the loose dirt that was sliding down the steep face of the hill and carrying them like struggling ants with it. Serious as the position was, some of us had to smile. Fortunately, there were no casualties.[62]
>
> Private Harry Murray, 16th (Western Australia and South Australia) Battalion, 4th Brigade, NZ&A Division, AIF

If the individual soldiers did not know where they were, if the navy was struggling to see what was going on, then it was incumbent on the ANZAC Corps commanders and staff officers to find out where their units were located and where exactly the front line, if it existed, ran around the bridgehead. And where were the Turks? There was no easy way to find out. Two staff officers were despatched from the headquarters of

1st Division to track the exact course of the line. This was a difficult and dangerous task.

> A good deal of confusion existed as to the position of the front line.
> General Bridges, therefore, sent Major Duncan Glasfurd to the left
> flank and myself to the right. We were to work towards the centre and
> compile, in the shortest possible time, a joint sketch of the line of the
> most forward positions held by 'our' side. The 'line' at that time was,
> of course, very far from being a continuous one – it consisted of holes
> in the ground of every shape and size, sometimes roughly joined up,
> but frequently a cricket pitch or more apart. I aimed at making a 'pace
> and compass traverse' but the pacing consisted of my bolting as hard
> as I could lick between posts. As far as possible, I signalled ahead that I
> was coming, but in many instances I had to guess where the next post
> was and frequently fell into it – to the great discomfiture and alarm
> of the occupant. The survey was indeed a rough one, but it provided
> a rough and ready solution of the mystery as to the position of the
> forward troops – and the reason for the confusion. It turned out that
> the line did not meet in the middle, but overlapped with obviously
> disconcerting result.[63]
>
> Major Richard Casey, Headquarters, 1st Division, AIF

Once it was known exactly where the front line was the Anzacs could rationalise the scattered outposts and over the next twenty-four hours the Corps managed to establish a continuous line. But it was a dangerous operation. Deadly shots could come from almost anywhere. Straight from the front or from the wide open flanks, and even on 27 April there were still Turkish snipers concealed in the scrub behind them on Russell's Top and in the upper reaches of Monash Valley.

> During the afternoon Colonel MacLaurin and Major Irvine started
> out to go along the line towards the left. Irvine, who could not be
> persuaded to get under cover, got on to the top of the parapet and
> proceeded to take stock of the situation, while the Brigadier kept behind
> the line. After going a short distance Irvine was shot by an enemy
> rifleman and died shortly afterwards. Almost at the same moment
> the Brigadier was shot by a sniper concealed in the undergrowth
> behind our lines and lived but a very short time. At this moment
> Lieut. E. G. Hamilton, our signal officer, was the only officer at Brigade

Headquarters and was therefore temporarily in command of the 1st Brigade.[64]

Corporal Frederick James, Signal Company, Headquarters, 1st Brigade, 1st Division, AIF

Two more senior officers had thrown their lives away; officers who had been trained to carry out the military duties befitting their rank, rather than engaging in dangerous heroics to no good purpose. War was more serious than this. Sharper minds were appalled at the waste and tried to inculcate sensible precaution.

> Such unnecessary exposure not only does no possible good but seriously impairs morale. While it is true that, like everybody else, I have had many narrow escapes, such as, for example, passing a spot where a few minutes after a shrapnel burst, yet I have always insisted on all my people exercising reasonable caution in not remaining stationary in spots which are obviously dangerous, and in doing their observations and reconnaissances from covered places.[65]

Colonel John Monash, Headquarters, 4th Australian Brigade, NZ&A Division, AIF

Sniping was not the only problem. As each hour passed the Turkish artillery was becoming increasingly effective as its gunners worked out where the Anzac lines were located. The batteries situated at Scrubby Knoll on Third Ridge and near Gaba Tepe had excellent fields of fire across the ANZAC Corps' positions. A close escape from a bursting shell could leave its mark on a hitherto exemplary soldier – as Corporal Will Weaver was to discover.

> I saw one shell scatter a bunch of our men. Another, and still another came at brief intervals. More men went up. Then a fourth. I was standing back carrying out some observations. With a scream and a screech it passed by my right side. Some yards further on the great mass rushed in to the earth. I can see the base of the shell now. One great ring and the two big dots in the centre. It only occupied a fraction of a second – the scream, the gouging of the earth and then – all was blank. Later in the day I found myself in Shrapnel Gully, dazed – a silly sort of feeling all over me. Other men were lying about, some wounded, some dead. I suppose the explosion lifted me there. I didn't hear any explosion, though. I believe some of the medical corps found me and took me to the hospital. A week later I came to my senses in a well-

made trench while drinking a cup of coffee. They say I must have left the hospital almost as soon as I was admitted, for I had been in the trench a week, during which time I went about my work in a strangely preoccupied way, but sensibly enough. I remember nothing of the happenings of that week. Gradually I was able to piece things together, bit by bit. I became aware that there was something wrong with me physically. My arms and legs had lost concerted action – when I used my arms my legs refused to do duty, and vice versa. I stayed in the trench for a few days. I wasn't the only madman in that trench. They were scattered here and there in it. One chap was as mad as a March hare. When a shell fell anywhere near him he raced for his life up the trench. If one fell near him there he dashed back again. Quite mad – thought every shell was meant for him.[66]

Corporal Will Weaver, 2nd (New South Wales) Battalion, 1st Brigade, 1st Division, AIF

Although the front line had been located, there were still many isolated parties of men in shallow trenches or folds in the ground clinging on to their positions further out in front. One such party, under the command of Lieutenant Eric Goldring, was dug in on the forward slopes of MacLaurin's Hill overlooking Wire Gully.

Captain Croly was wounded at about this time. He was some distance away to our left, and out of sight; but what he had to say about the Turk could be heard all over the battlefield. In a torrent of invective he traced the ancestry of his assailant through a series of irregular liaisons right back to the time of the Prophet. [67]

Corporal Thomas Louch, 11th (Western Australia) Battalion, 3rd Brigade, 1st Division, AIF

Captain Arthur Croly had his arm badly shattered, but survived his painful injury. Shortly afterwards Goldring decided to edge his men forward to reinforce other Australian outposts clinging on further down Wire Gully. As they ran into the gully itself they came under heavy fire. Most of them never made it.

Goldring was wounded. There was little room in our pot-hole but we dragged him in. He implored us to give him a drink, but we had been told this would be bad for anyone with an abdominal wound, so we refused. He became delirious, but after dark when a stretcher bearer arrived he pulled himself together and walked back. The possie into which we had stumbled was anything but a home from home. It was overlooked from the higher ground of Johnston's Jolly, where there were snipers who fired at any sign of movement. After dark there was a lot of movement in front of us, the Turks were shouting 'Allah, Allah!' blowing bugles like those used by the tram drivers in Cairo, and we stood to expecting an attack. But after a time we fired a few rounds in the direction of the noise and the Turks departed. We were too worked up and tired to get any sleep, and the night wore on. At first light we saw Turks digging in on Johnston's Jolly, about 200 yards away on our right, so we opened up on them. But they were being covered by snipers, and in no time Clayden,[68] in the next pit, was shot in the head and my rifle was knocked out of my hand by a Turkish bullet just as I was about to fire. My face was spattered by steel splinters which drew blood; but, though a sorry sight, I was more frightened than hurt. On Tuesday night the 3rd Battalion man who had been with us went off to try and get some water, and we did not see him again. Since the Sunday morning when we landed Dick and I had had nothing to drink other than the water in our water-bottles. We had had little sleep, so by Wednesday we were so dazed that we hardly knew what we were doing.[69]

Corporal Thomas Louch, 11th (Western Australia) Battalion, 3rd Brigade, 1st Division, AIF

It was only on the evening of 28 April that they made their way back up on to Second Ridge. Desperate with thirst, exhausted and totally disorientated, they were amazed to find a fully fledged system of trenches. It was evident that their comrades had not been idle in their absence and the Anzacs had taken Hamilton at his word. When Louch rejoined 11th Battalion on Shell Green he was given a large tot of rum and he slept for thirty hours. His experience almost exactly mirrored that of Private Harry Murray from the 16th Battalion.

One could see men's heads nodding and drooping – some were sleeping as they stood. Days and nights passed slowly enough. Such sleep as we could get was sauced with wild dreams. But for the continual rifle fire of the Turks, we might have been living in a dream world. Every hour our men were falling; men whom we had just got to know and like would drop suddenly, limbs all aquiver in death, for the Turk seemed always to aim for a vital part. But the boys kept their spirits up, although it was plain that the loss of their mates was affecting them. Two would be chatting together when one would pitch forward, and the expression of the survivor would be eloquent of savage, repressed rage. It was a nerve-racking business and there seemed to be no ending to it all.[70]

Private Harry Murray, 16th (Western Australia and South Australia) Battalion, 4th Brigade, NZ&A Division, AIF

And there they would stay for the next eight months. The shallow Anzac bridgehead had been carved out but what would they do next? Liman sent two more Turkish regiments and additional artillery to Anzac to reach a rough parity of numbers. The avowed intent of the ANZAC Corps to seize control of the high ground around the beach before pushing across the Peninsula to seize Mal Tepe in order to wreck Turkish communications was clearly impossible. And there was no chance of the Corps making a joint attack with the British advancing from Helles on the ultimate objective of the Kilid Bahr Plateau. Instead the Anzacs found themselves pinned back, with their horizons restricted by the enclosing heights of Chunuk Bair, Battleship Hill and Third Ridge. Not far away, but still utterly unattainable. Their landing had been a failure.

6

25 APRIL: LANDINGS AT HELLES

The eyes of the world are upon us, and your deeds will live in history.
To us now is given an opportunity of avenging our friends and relatives
who have fallen in France and Flanders. Our comrades there willingly
gave their lives in thousands and tens of thousands for our King and
Country, and by their glorious courage and dogged tenacity they
defeated the invaders and broke the German offensive. We also must
be prepared to suffer hardships, privations, thirst, and heavy losses by
bullets, by shells, by mines, by drowning.[1]

Major General Aylmer Hunter-Weston, Headquarters, 29th Division

THE BRITISH LANDINGS AT HELLES on 25 April 1915 have always been
the subject of self-congratulatory myth-making. The British knew that
the Turks were expecting them at V and W Beaches and were furthermore
worried as to the reception they might get at X, S and Y Beaches. They
also believed that they were opposed at Helles by a full division of Turkish
troops and indeed continued to believe that throughout the landings and
for the duration of the campaign. In other words, they conceived that
this was a battle between roughly equal forces, with the Turks having
the advantage of prepared defence works, where the British would have
to overcome all the odds. Consider for a moment the nature of Major
General Sir Aylmer Hunter-Weston's address to his troops on the eve of
battle at the head of this chapter. No one could say that his men had not

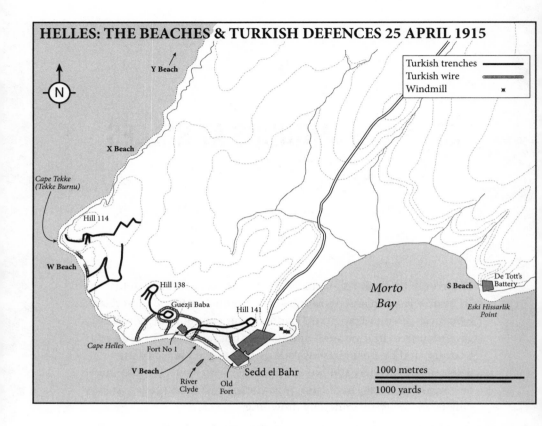

HELLES: THE BEACHES & TURKISH DEFENCES 25 APRIL 1915

Legend:
Turkish trenches ———
Turkish wire ▨▨▨▨▨
Windmill ✕

Y Beach
X Beach
Cape Tekke (Tekke Burnu)
Hill 114
W Beach
Hill 138
Guezji Baba
Hill 141
Morto Bay
S Beach
De Tott's Battery
Eski Hissarlik Point
Cape Helles
Fort No 1
V Beach
River Clyde
Old Fort
Sedd el Bahr
1000 metres
1000 yards

been warned. Yet the truth was that there was just over one battalion of Turkish troops guarding the Helles Peninsula south of Achi Baba. All that faced the British 29th Division was the 3rd Battalion, 26th Regiment of the 9th Division augmented by a very few elements of the 2nd Battalion, 26th Regiment. They had no machine guns, little artillery support, few land mines; but what they did have was good leadership, experienced, well-trained troops and above all they had their rifles.

This British overestimate of the Turkish forces was to dominate the day. Men heard the sound of their own supporting machine guns and thought they were being flayed by Turkish machine guns in improbable numbers; minor platoon or company counter-attacks launched to check the British advance were inflated into thousands of screaming Turks bent on death or glory. These fears hampered the British almost as much as the actual Turkish heroes of the 3/26th Regiment.

The main Helles landings were to be made at V and W Beaches, with flank landings at X, S and Y Beaches. The troops landed at these beaches were to seize tactically significant features before awaiting the general advance of the main force, whose task it was to seize the dominating feature of Achi Baba by the end of the first day. Then the entire force was to advance on Kilid Bahr, mirroring the ANZAC Corps' attack from the north also planned for 26 April. The account that follows will deal with each landing in turn; this is no literary conceit but simply reflects the physical separation of the beaches and the almost total lack of coordination between the forces once the landings had been made. Each fought their own battle. Success at one had little or no impact on any of the others. Failure impacted everywhere.

THE LANDING AT Y BEACH had been at the direct instigation of Hamilton, his intention being for those troops to threaten communications with the Turkish advanced parties at the tip of Helles. The British troops were to advance as far as necessary to attract the attention of the Turkish reserves and deflect them from the main landings at V and W Beaches while threatening the retreat of the Helles garrisons. They were also to make contact with the battalions landing at X Beach while holding their ground before joining the general advance on Achi Baba. Crucially, there was no plan should the main force fail to appear.

As a landing place Y Beach was almost non-existent, a very narrow rocky strip of land at the foot of two narrow gullies that broke the line of scrub-covered cliffs rising above it to about 150 feet. It was completely undefended with the nearest Turks positioned a mile to the south in trenches covering Gully Beach. Another platoon from the 2/26th Regiment was ensconced on Sari Tepe further to the north. As such the first British landing, made by the 1st King's Own Scottish Borderers (KOSB), supported by the Plymouth Battalion (detached from the RND), would be carried out unopposed. Given the terrain it was just as well. As the four tows carrying the KOSB approached the shore at 04.15, Private Daniel Joiner was a worried man.

> At first it appeared to be sheer cliffs with no possible chance of gaining the summit; on closer inspection, however, there appeared to be a

resemblance of a watercourse, which to agile Switzerland mountain climbers might afford a possible ascent. It was too dark to make out anything of the top of the cliffs or background. No beach was visible, it appeared as if the cliffs ran into the sea. We imagined that the boat would go nearly to the beach. A rude awakening awaited us. The water was quite clear, and we began to notice shelves of rock. About 30 to 40 yards from the beach our boat grounded. This had not been in our reckoning, so for a fraction of a second we were at a loss, not so however with those in the know – as soon as the boat touched out they jumped into the water. No further order was necessary, before we realised what had happened we were waist deep. Instead, however, of the water getting shallower, it got deeper. The smaller men having a difficult job to keep their collars dry. The footing was uncertain. The bed was in layers, some higher than others. Floundering was frequent, and when it is taken into account the weight we were carrying, floundering was not a joke. Our rifles were often submerged in our attempts to retain our balance.[2]

Private Daniel Joiner, 1st KOSB, 87th Brigade, 29th Division

Getting ashore had been a wet business, but now a more exhausting challenge awaited.

The main object now was to gain the top of the cliffs. This was easier said than done. The scouts had got there and found it unoccupied. We started. No attempt at order was made, nor was it expected, hand over hand, a pull up here, a jump there, and so on. Seemingly the Turks did not know that we had landed, if they had – well, that is a different story, one Boy Scout on the top of the cliffs could have kept fifty men down with 'Chucky Stones' so treacherous was the foot hold.[3]

Private Daniel Joiner, 1st KOSB, 87th Brigade, 29th Division

When they reached the top of the cliff they had a good view of the surrounding country and companies were sent forward, initially to the deep Gully Ravine that lay parallel to the coast between them and Krithia. Parties of the Plymouths crossed over to the south-east in an unsuccessful search for a reported Turkish artillery piece in that sector. That was the limit of their exploitation and they failed either to press forward or to contact the troops landing at X Beach. There was still no opposition from the Turks.

Command and control problems hampered the Y Beach landing

right from the start. There was confusion on the ground as to whether Lieutenant Colonel Archibald Koe of the 1st KOSB or Lieutenant Colonel Godfrey Matthews of the Plymouths was in charge, but far more serious was the lack of grip at a higher level. Hamilton was delighted with the initial success of his pet project and wirelessed twice to Hunter-Weston asking, 'Would you like to get some more men ashore at Y Beach? If so trawlers available.'[4] Notice that he asked, not ordered; Hamilton adhered strongly to the code that his role was to issue the overall planning outlines, his divisional generals would fight the battles. Only after 10.35 did Hunter-Weston reply saying that to change the plans would be to delay the landing – the off-the-cuff reply of a man under pressure batting off unwelcome interference. Whether an opportunity was missed is now difficult to determine, but the Y Beach force remained frozen in position between the cliff tops and Gully Ravine. Reprehensibly, they failed either to advance or to dig in until late in the afternoon. Eventually Matthews decided to retire to the cliff top and entrench with his battalion holding the flanks while the KOSB held the centre of the position. By this time the British found that they were under ever increasing fire from Turks moving up from Gully Beach, while the newly arrived advance elements of the Turkish reserves from Serafim Farm – the 1/25th Regiment and an artillery battery – also began to make their presence felt.

> The line was formed by the men's packs and with entrenching tools. It never reached what could be called a trench, and was constructed under a most harassing and ever-increasing rifle fire. Although never a serious menace, bursts of gunfire, sniping and threats had accompanied the construction of the frail fort.[5]
>
> Major Alfred Welch, 1st KOSB, 87th Brigade, 29th Division

The front line trenches, barely 18 inches deep covered an unnecessarily long section of cliff top, stretching both north and south of Y Beach. The two battalions had achieved nothing of any military importance, apart from attracting the attention of the Turkish reserves. This they soon came to regret.

> The shrapnel was getting annoying, the high explosives dangerous, the bullets dangerous, the sun hot, the throat dry, the water in our bottles precious and warm, the stomach needed food and the eyes of many

refused to remain open. We still had one company in reserve. Some of
us even tried to make some tea, but no sooner was smoke seen than
bullets began to splutter. No need now for the NCOs to shout as on
manoeuvres 'Keep your head down!' As the sun went down the heat of
the day changed to a very chilly night.[6]

Private Daniel Joiner, 1st KOSB, 87th Brigade, 29th Division

As the main body of the Turkish 1/25th Regiment appeared there was an
increasing perception among the British that they were in danger of being
overwhelmed by sheer numbers, even prior to the first counter-attack,
launched at 17.40.

Shortly after the snipers made their appearance the order was passed
along the line, 'A large body of troops advancing over the skyline!' This
message was followed by another, 'A larger body of troops advancing
over the skyline!' As our platoon had taken up a position about 10 yards
from the top of the cliff it was not possible to see them advancing for
some time after. They were 800 to 900 yards away, advancing in massed
formation, shouting and waving their rifles above their heads. As soon
as they came within a reasonable distance we opened fire upon them.
They still rushed on, until the two cruisers who were supporting us,
HMS Goliath and HMS Dublin, each fired a broadside which completely
scattered them. It was growing dark now and the Turks had taken
possession of the trench 600 yards away. We had prepared ourselves
for the worst. Shortly after dark they made their first charge, as we
expected. They came up within 10 yards of our trench but by keeping
up a rapid fire we held them back. They retired for a short time but
there was a regular hail of bullets hitting the parapet of the trench
and almost blinding us with dirt. The dirt was also getting into the
mechanism of our rifles, which added to the difficulty of keeping up
rapid fire. The noise was awful: the wounded groaning and calling for
stretchers which never came; the incessant rattle of the machine guns
and rifles; the wounded and dying Turks in front calling for Allah. To
make matters more cheerful it began to rain.[7]

Private John Vickers, Plymouth Battalion, Royal Marine Brigade, RND

At about 19.00 Private Joiner's company was ordered forward to reinforce
the sketchy front line. They found there was a dangerous gap in the line
which the Turks were attempting to exploit.

Captain Antrobus called the charge. The Turks were about 200 to 300 yards off, the ground we had to cover was fairly level, covered with the Gallipoli characteristic gorse, and the air was laden with lead, fired from both flanks. However everything happened so quickly we had no time to think. We went at it full tilt. The fire of our supporting flank companies sounded as if each man had a machine gun. The Turks seeing we meant business hastily withdrew to the prepared trenches again. Captain Antrobus who led us through it all selected our fire positions. Had the whole company managed to get into the line it would have been alright, but we had lost half of them in the charge. The result was that instead of having a rifle to every yard, we had about one man to every 5 to 10 yards.[8]

Private Daniel Joiner, 1st KOSB, 87th Brigade, 29th Division

They were desperate for reinforcements and running increasingly short of ammunition, but every box – so quickly fired – had to be hauled up the precipitous cliffs behind them.

The fire from the Turks was now increasing every moment. No guns could support us as our position was so uncertain, we hardly knew where we were. Our only consolation was in fact that our bayonets were kept ready, and would account for something before we said, 'Bust!' About midnight not an officer or man expected to see daylight again, men were going mad, others groaning, others prompted by the officers were conversing about cheerful topics to drive away the thoughts that were rapidly becoming facts and reality. We made some attempt of improving our cover scraping with our fingers and feet. In some cases one man was holding as much as 25 to 50 yards, the remainder being held by dead men.[9]

Private Daniel Joiner, 1st KOSB, 87th Brigade, 29th Division

Under the cover of darkness the Turks managed to come close enough to fling hand grenades.

The bombs came over thick and fast, those that fell short threw the dirt in our eyes, those that fell over set fire to the gorse. Not only did the thoughts of being burned alive cause us to take action, but, the flare being behind us, the Turks opened fire wherever a glare-lit target appeared. We could not retaliate in kind. Firstly we had no bombs and also the position we were in would not allow of us charging or firing at the bombers effectively. As the bombs burst, so men crawled out and put out the flames. We were finally saved from this predicament by the rain.[10]

Private Daniel Joiner, 1st KOSB, 87th Brigade, 29th Division

All night the Turks pressed hard all along the overstretched line. Then, at about 07.00 on 26 April, they launched a final desperate attack.

Down they came in greater numbers than ever, day was just breaking, no preliminaries this time. Line after line: our rifles got hot, wounded men were loading, officers getting us ammunition, what little could be got. It was impossible to miss, it was also impossible to last – something had to give way – it was us. We retired dropping back about 50 yards. Our remaining officers rallied us and we charged. The Turks were dumbfounded, they turned and ran for it. We tried to hold again but again we were forced back. Back and forward we swayed until the Turks had us on the topmost edge of the cliffs, with a sheer drop of 300 feet. The beach was littered with our wounded, in many cases dying comrades. The Turks had the chance of a lifetime. Another push and we would have been over the cliffs. We had turned at bay, every man that could hold a rifle was brought into the line. Holding like this we waited for the last push. No sooner had the Turks shown a hesitation than our remaining officer grasped the situation and ordered the charge. This time everything was in a mix, bayonets, butts, fists, feet, and in fact everything and anyhow. So mad was the rush, the Turks gave way. We got them right back over the position which we had held all night.[11]

Private Daniel Joiner, 1st KOSB, 87th Brigade, 29th Division

By this time both sides were exhausted and a lull had settled over the battlefield. But at Y Beach there was a state of considerable confusion. All night a flurry of messages requesting reinforcements to 29th Divisional headquarters from Colonel Matthews had been ignored. Hunter-Weston still had his eyes firmly fixed on the situations at V and W Beaches and Hamilton was aboard the *Queen Elizabeth* monitoring the situation and giving support fire to the struggling Anzacs. The widely disparate landing forces were too far apart to support each other or to share naval resources. The British had spread themselves too thinly.

Towards the end of the night unsanctioned alarmist messages from unknown individuals on Y Beach caused the navy to evacuate one isolated detachment of the KOSB. They were also doing their best to remove the wounded under difficult conditions.

> We settled down to keep the Turks busy while the stores and wounded were taken off in small boats which the Navy were sending to our aid. The snipers were busy as each boat approached and left the cover of the cliffs. The wounded had to go through the water, up to their necks, in order to reach the boats. Others who were being carried, after getting a ducking as the carriers lost their balance, imagine the conditions of some, blinded, some minus a leg, others a foot or an arm, etc. Each naval boat was ready with its machine gun, the picket boats with 3-pounders. Our battleships were now pounding away at the enemy – we were to advance no more, so they were able to fire without fear of hitting us.[12]
>
> Private Daniel Joiner, 1st KOSB, 87th Brigade, 29th Division

It was not only the wounded who were getting away on the boats. An increasing number of stragglers were drifting back. In the mad confusion many of the men seemed to have thought an evacuation had already begun and in the end the process gained its own momentum. Almost without any conscious decision being made Y Beach was surrendered by default.

> The order to retire was passed from the right of the line. We retired to the extreme edge of the cliffs but as we were short of both stretchers and bearers some of our wounded were left in the trench. We made a counter-attack, driving back their snipers. On regaining our trenches we found they had bayoneted our wounded. Three Scotties near me were in a state of semi-consciousness through loss of blood. They had all been bayoneted through the chest. We got all the wounded away, and not a second too soon, for a large body of Turks made their appearance a few hundred yards ahead.[13]
>
> Private John Vickers, Plymouth Battalion, Royal Marine Brigade, RND

Private Joiner appears to have been one of those holding the clifftop line to give the rest time to get away.

> A rearguard action had to be commenced. We worked them nicely back until we were just near the crest line of the cliffs. There we held, and informed the ships who were keeping the Turks back, that we were ready to clear. By this time the wounded and stores had been taken off. By

prearranged signal, we dropped out of the Turks' sight, below the crest. Many were injured by falling down the cliffs. We were now out of view, but the Turks must have got a shock. No sooner had we got clear the battleships opened fire at the top of the cliffs and intervening ground, and so made it practically impossible for the Turks to follow us. Other ships took up the fire until we had all got into the waiting boats.[14]

Private Daniel Joiner, 1st KOSB, 87th Brigade, 29th Division

The Y Beach fiasco was over shortly after 11.30 when the evacuation was completed. Any brief opportunities that may have existed had been lost through another complete failure of command and control. A lack of clear instructions coupled with a certain pusillanimity on the part of Matthews meant that the troops had been left as sitting ducks awaiting the arrival of the Turkish reserves. Yet it is difficult to say what else they should have done. Advance unsupported on Krithia? Link with the equally static X Beach landing? March towards the sound of the guns at V Beach? In which case why not land as reserves at X Beach, which was considerably nearer? In doing nothing their function had become to act as a lightning rod to attract Turkish counter-attacks and in the end they had not been able to cope with those lethal attentions.

THE X BEACH LANDING would be conducted by the 2nd Royal Fusiliers of the 86th Brigade on a small beach tucked beneath low cliffs which were relatively easy to climb. It was conceived as a supporting affair to the main landings at V and W Beaches, just around the corner of Cape Helles. The pre-dreadnought *Implacable*, commanded by the redoubtable Captain Hughes Lockyer, was shepherding in four tows of cutters. Lockyer had disapproved of the orders for the supporting bombardment which concentrated on the coastal ridges rather than the actual beaches. He was determined to maximise the support to the infantry during the last crucial minutes, so he opened fire with the *Implacable*'s main 12-inch and assorted secondary batteries from close range to blast the cliff tops above X Beach to pieces. After all this effort there was only a small picket of twelve Turks to receive the benefit of his bombardment, but the two four-barrelled Nordenfelts were put out of action. All in all he certainly cleared the way for the Royal Fusiliers as they stormed ashore and straight up the cliffs. By 06.30, the landing had been secured without loss and the whole battalion was ashore by 07.30. As they moved inland the troops encountered a small party of Turks who were on their way to reinforce W Beach. As fighting broke out, the Royal Fusiliers swiftly established a defensive position, before pushing out towards their objective of Hill 114, which was captured by around 11.30, whereupon they established contact with the troops who had landed at W Beach. They were then vigorously counter-attacked by about 250 Turks. This attack had significant effects, for it forced the Royal Fusiliers almost back to the cliffs above X Beach. In the end the 1st Border Regiment was able to stem the Turkish advance and strengthen the screen surrounding the beach pending the arrival of the 1st Inniskilling Fusiliers in the early afternoon. Nevertheless this bold Turkish move had planted the seeds of doubt into the mind of the 87th Brigade commander, Brigadier General William Marshall.

> Heavy firing had started at Y Beach and I was very much tempted to move in that direction, but my hands were tied; because, being divisional reserve, I felt it incumbent to keep the force intact pending an order from the Division. Besides, one never knows. X Beach was now secure from attack and, if all the other landings proved to be failures, everything might have to be transferred there. The fact is, in war, original orders should never go beyond the first stage – eventualities should not be discounted.[15]
>
> Brigadier General William Marshall, Headquarters, 87th Brigade, 29th Division

By the time the requisite orders had come through from divisional head-quarters it was nightfall and Marshall decided to remain where he was. And so the moment of possible reinforcement passed and the men of Y Beach were left to fight on alone. Marshall was probably right to be cautious, for the prospects for a night march against unknown numbers of Turks across unfamiliar terrain featuring the chasm of Gully Ravine were not good.

THE LANDINGS AT S BEACH served a similar function to those at X and Y Beaches. The 2nd South Wales Borderers were to land on the eastern arm of Morto Bay and seize by *coup de main* the old disused De Tott's Battery above the beach and then hold their position pending the arrival of the main force from V and W Beaches. They were to be covered by the pre-dreadnought *Cornwallis*, captained by Captain Alexander Davidson.

> The problem was further complicated for the reason that, instead of there being a beach party and steamboats to assist in landing the troops on this exposed right flank, none were allowed. The trawlers, four in number, each with six transport boats in tow, were to run ashore as best they could; and the battalion had, by their order, to pull ashore, not only in heavy marching gear, but with boats laden with ammunition, water, and provisions. This was beyond the powers of any but highly trained men in pulling against a strong tide, and appeared, on the face of it, certain disaster, as the only chance of success lay in speed, and not giving the enemy an easy target.[16]
>
> Captain Alexander Davidson, HMS *Cornwallis*

The *Cornwallis* would give covering fire for as long as possible, but Davidson decided on his own initiative to try to hurry up the landing by supplying a steam pinnace with two cutters and a naval landing party to bring ashore not only ammunition, water and stores but also the Borderers' kitbags to minimise the amount carried by the men. This naval party would then be responsible for protecting the open left flank of the infantry as they stormed the De Tott's Battery position.

As they moved into the Straits heading for Morto Bay the Borderers found that the Asiatic Turkish batteries were preoccupied with an imminent French attack far nearer to home, at Kum Kale. Thus far everything was going according to plan, but what had not been taken into account was the strength of the current. Delays lengthened and the landing scheduled to coincide with the main Helles landings at 06.00 eventually only occurred at 07.30. The plan of action produced by Lieutenant Colonel Hugh Casson was for two of his companies to land on the beach while another company came ashore on the rocky shore at the junction of Morto Bay and the Straits before climbing straight up the rough cliffs. Sapper James Godwyn was attached to the Borderers as they rowed for S Beach itself.

> I was pulling bow in our boat next to the Corporal. We were rowing with all our might when all of a sudden the bullets began to come. One struck the Corporal's pack, glanced off and hit the man in front in the head. We were the first boat to touch land. As soon as we touched the

bottom, the Corporal and myself lay along the boat and started firing at the Turk. The men were jumping out up to their necks in water; some were killed before they left the boats. I was soon out and wading ashore. One of the Borderers was hit just in front of me, but no one could stop and help him ashore, as it was everyone for himself and get on shore in safety. We reached the first mound alright and got under cover; there we had a breather. Then the order came to rush the first trench, it was soon taken but there were not many Turks in it. Then the rush was made for the top of the hill. The men dug a bit of a trench and began picking off any Turks they could see. My Section in the meantime had to go to and fro to the boats and get the ammunition, biscuits and water. We were fired at all the time but nobody was hit. A Turkish sniper somewhere on the hill was picking off a lot of our men during the day. We had to hold the position till we got relieved; it was a nerve-wracking experience, being shelled and sniped at, not knowing who would be the next, or how soon the Turks would try and rush the position.[17]

Sapper James Godwyn, 2nd London Field Company, Royal Engineers, 29th Division

The South Wales Borderers had performed well in taking De Tott's Battery, but they had grossly overestimated the strength of the Turkish opposition. They claimed they were facing a whole battalion; in fact it was a single platoon from the 2/26th Regiment. Sapper Goodwyn's account also reveals the sad outcome of the S Beach landing. Having successfully gone ashore, they sat around and did nothing; indeed they had been given nothing to do. Perhaps they should have ignored their instructions and moved to take the defenders of V Beach from the rear. But what if it had all gone wrong? What if in their absence the Turks had reoccupied De Tott's Battery, this time in strength? Once again, misplaced fear of the strength of the Turks hamstrung any positive action to link up with the troops on the other beaches.

There was another problem. Captain Davidson's vigorous support of the landing had made him careless of his allotted role in support of the later stages of the V Beach landing. Worse, he went ashore to act as beach master. Here he was effective, liaising well with the infantry and successfully bringing down support fire from the *Cornwallis* to target the Turkish batteries firing across the Dardanelles from Asia. But this was inappropriate behaviour for a man of his rank and should have been carried out by a far more junior officer. This would have allowed the *Cornwallis* to move off earlier without waiting to re-embark her wandering captain. As it was she did not report to V Beach until after 10.00. It is not clear whether bringing in another supporting battleship would have made much difference to the pattern of events at V Beach. But by then it was too late.

W BEACH, KNOWN TO THE TURKS as Tekke Bay, was one of the two main Helles landing places. It was a promising landing site in the sense that it was a spacious 300-yard beach offering a direct route for a concerted advance up towards Achi Baba, picking up the flanking units from X, S and Y Beaches as they went. Unsurprisingly, the Turks had recognised its potential as a landing site and had dug a ring of trenches on the low cliffs at either side and all around the high ground at the back of the beach. On the sands and in the water were a series of ominous barbed-wire obstacles.

The 1st Lancashire Fusiliers had been given the task of taking the beach before moving inland to make contact with the Royal Fusiliers to the north around Hill 141 and to seize Hill 138 before establishing a link with the troops landing at V Beach. Because it was so well fortified, the prospect of making a landing at W Beach was intimidating in the extreme for the Fusiliers. Regrettably, too, the ships supporting their landing had failed to get in close and so when, at 06.00, the tows approached the beach the Turkish wire and trenches had not been properly shelled.

> The morning was dead calm and clear but a bad light for us looking towards our landing place as the sun was about to rise right behind it. The bombardment had begun punctually at 5 a.m. but it did not have anything like the visible effect I had expected. I had expected to see the whole end of the peninsula and especially the surroundings of the beaches one cloud of dust and smoke. As the long semi-circle of tows steamed in towards the shore all was perfectly still except for the booming of the ships' guns – not a sign of life on shore and no one in the boats uttering a sound. Our tows from the *Implacable* cut in just behind the tows from the *Euryalus* with the rest of the battalion. The enemy at our beach never made a sign till the leading boats were close to the beach, 50 yards or so, then they fairly let rip.[18]
>
> Brigadier General Steuart Hare, Headquarters, 86th Brigade, 29th Division

Midshipman Hugh Tate was landed on the far left-hand side of the beach.

The blast from the 12-pounder guns over our heads was most unpleasant, as were the bullets which were now coming down all round like little wasps. The whole Peninsula was a mass of bursting shell and flame. According to plan the picket boat slipped us and we landed our little load. I was on the extreme left and found a sandy patch and got right in, third boat ashore. Nearly all the rest ran on a reef about 20 yards out and the troops had to jump overboard and swim. As we touched land one of our 12-pounder shells hit the cliff just overhead and filled the boat with earth.[19]

Midshipman Hugh Tate, HMS *Implacable*

They had to get the troops ashore as quickly as possible. Leading Seaman Gilligan was in charge of one of the boats.

I told the men to lie down in the bottom of the boat, leaving myself and six oarsmen exposed to the enemy's fire. I then ordered them all to jump out and get under cover as quickly as they could. As soon as we touched the beach we could see wire entanglements. The fire was terrible; just like a hailstorm. I jumped out of the stern up to my arms in water and pushed the boat in. The Sergeant jumped in front of me and got mortally wounded. The cries of the wounded were terrible. By now the Lancashires were ashore. We came off for more men and one man was killed in my crew. He was shot in the ear, and was quite dead when I picked him up.[20]

Leading Seaman Gilligan, HMS *Euraylus*

The Lancashire Fusiliers stayed in the rowing boats as long as they could, but eventually they had no choice but to plunge into the water and make for the beach. It was not an inviting prospect.

They let us off a lot, thank God, as they did not fire until the boats began to ground, and the rifles and machine guns poured into us as we got out of the boats and made for the sandy shore. There was tremendously strong barbed wire where my boat landed. Men were being hit in the boats and as they splashed ashore. I got up to my waist in water, tripped over a rock and went under, got up and made for the shore and lay down by the barbed wire.[21]

Captain Harold Clayton, 1st Lancashire Fusiliers, 86th Brigade, 29th Division

That gallant rush stumbling through the waves, hampered by the unseen obstacles, then up on to the beach was an ordeal by fire. Some, like Major Harold Shaw, were lucky.

> As soon as I felt the boat touch, I dashed over the side into three feet of water and rushed for the barbed wire entanglement on the beach; it must have been only three feet high or so, and three bays, because I got over it amidst a perfect storm of lead and made for cover, sand dunes on the other side, and got good cover.[22]
>
> Major Harold Shaw, 1st Lancashire Fusiliers, 86th Brigade, 29th Division

Most of his comrades found themselves trapped lying on the open sand in front of the wire.

> As ordered the men ran up to the wire and lay down waiting for the wire cutters to get to work. Fatal to many was that order, for Maxims began to play on the serried ranks, an easy target. I shot a sniper who was picking people off from the cliff edge. It was a good shot and I saw him after we got up – hit in the mouth. Under cover of the cliff we started cleaning our rifles which were useless from sand and water and it would have amused you to see men cleaning their bolts with tooth brushes with hell's tornado all around. [23]
>
> Major Richard Willis, 1st Lancashire Fusiliers, 86th Brigade, 29th Division

With respect to the Lancashire Fusiliers, who were lain out along an open beach exposed to coruscating fire, there were almost certainly no Turkish machine guns covering the landing at W Beach. Many historians have chosen to endorse the heated claims of the survivors, but the evidence is not convincing. The Turkish defences consisted of the 12th Company of the 3/26th Regiment which also had detachments on Hill 114 and Hill 138. This left around 100–150 Turkish riflemen ready, willing and more than able to pour concentrated well-drilled rapid fire on to the Lancashire Fusiliers huddled in their boats or lying along the beach, penned back by barbed wire. If there had been even one machine gun few of the Lancashire Fusiliers could have survived and men under concentrated machine gun fire do not usually have the time, inclination or ability to locate and dispose of an individual sniper as Major Willis did. That said, the lines of corpses left along the waterline illustrate all too clearly the terrible scale of the fire the Lancashire Fusiliers faced and there is no need to exaggerate their plight. The details of the story may differ but the outcome remained the same.

Several of my company were with me under the wire – one of my
subalterns was killed next to me and also the wire-cutter who was lying
the other side of me. I seized his cutter and cut a small lane myself
through which a few of us broke and lined up under the only available
cover procurable, a small sand ridge covered with bluffs of grass. I then
ordered fire to be opened on the crests, but owing to submersion in the
water and dragging rifles through the sand, the breech mechanism was
clogged, thereby rendering the rifles ineffective.[24]

Major George Adams, 1st Lancashire Fusiliers, 86th Brigade, 29th Division

Many, like Captain Harold Clayton, despaired of their useless wire-cutters
and simply crawled, rolled or squeezed their way through the wicked
barbs that tore at their uniforms and flesh. Better that than lie out on the
beach waiting for the bullets.

There was a man there before me shouting for wire-cutters. I got mine
out, but could not make the slightest impression. The front of the wire
by now was a thick mass of men, the majority of whom never moved
again. The trenches on the right raked us and those above us raked our
right, while trenches and machine guns fired straight down the valley.
The noise was ghastly and the sights horrible. I eventually crawled
through the wire with great difficulty, as my pack kept catching on the
wire, and got under a small mound which actually gave us protection.
The weight of our packs tired us, so that we could only gasp for
breath.[25]

Captain Harold Clayton, 1st Lancashire Fusiliers, 86th Brigade, 29th Division

As they gathered behind the low sand dunes the Fusiliers looked around
almost for the first time to try to find out what was happening. It was a
terrifying scene of chaos.

On the right of me on the cliff was a line of Turks in a trench taking
pot shots at us, ditto on the left. I looked back. There was one soldier
between me and the wire, and a whole line in a row on the edge of the
sands. The sea behind them was absolutely crimson, and you could hear
the groans through the rattle of musketry. A few were firing. I signalled
to them to advance. I shouted to the soldier behind to signal, but he
shouted back, 'I am shot through the chest!' I then perceived they were
all hit. I took a rifle from one of the men with me and started in at the
men on the cliff on my right, but could only fire slowly, as I had to get

the bolt open with my foot – it was clogged with sand. About this time Maunsell was shot dead next to me. Our men now began to scale the cliffs from the boats on the outer flanks.[26]

Major Harold Shaw, 1st Lancashire Fusiliers, 86th Brigade, 29th Division

It was a dreadful fight, but it was soon over. As Brigadier General Steuart Hare approached with his staff in the second wave, he managed to sum up the situation at a glance and ordered his boat to land just round the corner, to the west of the beach. The Turkish defences were so thin that they could not afford the men to cover this avenue of approach, offering Hare an obvious opportunity to outflank the troops in the trenches overlooking the beach itself.

We started scrambling up the cliff which was a steep earth slope with layers of rock here and there. It was not very steep but was difficult for a man in full kit to climb. There were no Turks on the front edge of the cliff so we were defiladed from the front, but were getting it pretty hot from the trenches on the east side of the mouth of the glen which formed the beach. When we got to the top we could see that the Lancashire Fusiliers were shoving on straight to their front up the glen but must have been losing frightfully from fire from the trenches on both sides. When we got to the top of the cliff we found an empty trench at the very edge. The occupants must have been shot out of it by the bombardment. We collected about a dozen Fusiliers there and an officer, about all who had reached the top, and sent them off to charge a trench which was only about 50 yards off, not facing us but flanking the glen leading up from the beach.[27]

Brigadier General Steuart Hare, Headquarters, 86th Brigade, 29th Division

Hare had reacted to the situation brilliantly. He had seized the moment and used his experience to make a real difference to the course of the battle. But then he got rather carried away and began acting like a junior officer pushing forward at the sharp end rather than as the brigadier general who was ultimately responsible for the whole of the covering force. His intentions seemed admirable but the result was sadly predictable.

I could hear no firing coming from X Beach and, concluding that the Royal Fusiliers had landed without opposition, I thought I would try and work round to meet them and bring them up to make a flank attack on the people who were opposing the Lancashire Fusiliers. The latter had made a certain amount of progress – it was wonderful that they made any – but I did not think they could possibly get far unsupported. I started with Frankland and two signallers and we were just above the top of the cliff not far from Cape Tekke when we found ourselves within about 100 yards of a trench full of Turks. We started to drop over the top of the cliff as they opened fire. I felt a tremendous blow on my calf and just got over the edge of the cliff when I sat down. Frankland and the signallers put on three field dressings without at all stopping the bleeding. If the Turks had had the enterprise to come out of their trench and look for us they could have bagged the lot.[28]

Brigadier General Steuart Hare, Headquarters, 86th Brigade, 29th Division

The wound was a serious one. Hare's campaign was over almost before it had started. He left Major Thomas Frankland and his signallers and started to make his way back to the beach.

I scrambled along the best I could and got about half way back when I was met by Farmar who said a stretcher was just coming. I was very glad of it as I had been feeling pretty lonely. There had been shooting going on just above me and one time the signallers had come back and told me they had been stopped by snipers. They had managed to get a message through. The stretcher bearers turned up and put iodine into the wound and tied me up again.[29]

Brigadier General Steuart Hare, Headquarters, 86th Brigade, 29th Division

Meanwhile, the Lancashire Fusiliers began to move forward, stretched in two different directions by the need to secure both Hill 114 and Hill 138. Although, as we have seen, they were able to link up with the Royal Fusiliers at Hill 114, the attack on Hill 138 and the neighbouring feature of Guezji Baba that blocked the route across the headland to V Beach was held up by a combination of thick barbed wire and a few determined Turks. The Lancashire Fusiliers had suffered heavy casualties and for the moment were thwarted, even though all the Turks could send as reinforcements were two platoons of the 9th Company, 3/26th Regiment.

Behind them the 1st Essex Regiment, having been diverted from V Beach to W Beach, began to come ashore at around 08.30. They threw themselves into an attack on Hill 138 but were held back. Indeed, W Beach itself was still not entirely secure.

Over a hundred dead were on the beach alone, while the sand was all stained red. A derelict cutter full of dead and waterlogged formed a basis for a temporary pier. About fifty Turks suddenly appeared overhead, fired at us then surrendered! Four of our men found a sniper hidden in the cliff, bayoneted him and chucked him over the cliff. All his insides came out. A subaltern and three men tried to locate some other snipers who were firing at us, but each in turn gave little starts and fell down dead. One was wounded and staggered towards us crying.[30]

Midshipman Hugh Tate, HMS *Implacable*

Although the Essex Regiment managed to help stabilise the line, it was soon evident that the 88th Brigade, who should have been pushing on towards Krithia and Achi Baba, were being sucked into the fight that was properly that of the covering force of 86th Brigade. This process continued as the 4th Worcestershire Regiment began to disembark at W Beach at around 12.00. As Napier (commanding 88th Brigade) was dead and Hare (commanding 86th Brigade) had been evacuated wounded, staff officer Lieutenant Colonel Owen Wolley Dod was sent from 29th Division Headquarters to try to bring order to chaos. Having liaised with the navy to secure a stiff bombardment of Hill 138, he ordered the 88th Brigade to launch a two-pronged attack which at last managed to take the position by 15.00, finally ejecting the remnants of two Turkish platoons that had been grimly holding on.

There was more confusion over the presence of a further redoubt on the hill of Guezji Baba that dominated the ground leading to V Beach. This was caused by a lack of precision in the British contour maps, which only recorded the presence of Hill 138. Well protected by barbed wire defences the Turks who manned Guezji Baba fought heroically, holding back the Worcestershires until about 16.00. But still the way was not clear, for as the Worcestershires breasted the hill they came under fire from the Turkish stronghold around the Old Castle on Hill 141. Night was falling and the British troops were unsure whether to advance further. Even though they outnumbered the Turks by 10:1, they were paralysed into inertia by their fears of non-existent Turkish hordes. The men were tired and there were few senior officers left with the experience to lead them forward into battle. All they could do was hold their positions and try to rest.

7

25 APRIL: DRAMA AT V BEACH

The fire changed the colour of the sea with the blood from the bodies of the enemy – a sea whose colour had remained the same for years. Shells and machine gun bullets fell ceaselessly at the points where rifle fire was observed but, in spite of this, heavy fire was opened from all our trenches. In a vain attempt to save their lives, the enemy threw themselves from the boats into the sea. The shore became full of enemy corpses, like a shoal of fish.[1]

Major Mahmut, 3rd Battalion, 26th Regiment, 9th Division, Fifth Army

WORST OF ALL THE 25 APRIL LANDINGS was that attempted at V Beach, known to the Turks as Ertugrul Bay. This was by far the most ambitious plan for, as Commander Edward Unwin observed, the Turks had by no means wasted the time granted to them by the British. Above the beach they had constructed a series of trenches that stretched along the skyline from Fort No. 1 round the natural amphitheatre of the beach to the Sedd el Bahr village. In front were at least two lines of barbed wire, with a gap close to the Sedd el Bahr fort. Throughout their construction work the Turks had been severely hampered, not only by a shortage of the raw materials of wire and stakes, but also by the harassing fire of Allied destroyers.

The beach, which stretched about 300 yards, was fairly narrow, with a low bank bordering it. Here the Turkish garrison was made up of just

250–300 men of the 10th Company, 3/26th Regiment who had relieved the 3/25th Regiment on 22 April. One platoon was positioned in the ruins of the old Sedd el Bahr fort, another in the village and the third in front of Hill 141 and the ruined castle. Sailing towards this death trap was the *River Clyde*. Concealed deep within her cargo holds were the 2nd Hampshires, under Lieutenant Colonel Herbert Carrington Smith (the senior officer aboard), and the 1st Royal Munster Fusiliers, under Lieutenant Colonel Henry Tizard. It was intended that in the later stages of their approach to the beach they would be preceded by the 1st Royal Dublin Fusiliers, who would be the first to land from six strings of rowing boats that were being towed in by steamboats until the last hundred yards. They all knew what they were meant to achieve; the question was: could they do it?

The convoy reached its destination off V Beach and the accompanying warships crashed out their dawn chorus just after 05.00 on 25 April.

> All the other ships joined in, until the noise and the flashes were terrific. Before everything had been so still and the contrast was extraordinary. One could not distinguish between the different guns or ships in the roar and screech of guns and bursting shells. It was like hundreds of gigantic Maxims. The whole of Sedd el Bahr and the surrounding country was shelled and in the half light the bursting shells and the glare of the burning houses spread a reddish glow over everything. It seemed impossible that anything could live in such an inferno: wire entanglements, parts of houses, clods of earth and everything else being blown sky high. It was an extraordinary sight. Above all this away inland a glorious red sun rose and I was quite appalled to see the terrific destruction. The town wasn't there. I've seen ruined towns before but there wasn't a wall standing.[2]
>
> Midshipman Herbert Williams, HMS *Agamemnon*

Although the bombardment undoubtedly made an impressive sight, the high-velocity flat trajectory of the naval shells meant that the results achieved were far less destructive than the navy had hoped. Most of the shells skimmed over the trenches, just missing them. Of course some still hit squarely home and the Turkish troops suffered casualties, but their discipline held up under pressure as their training paid dividends, to the satisfaction of their commander, Major Mahmut.

The enemy was pounding the rifle trenches on the shore. Owing to the bluish-black and greenish smoke which was rising up, the shore was hidden and nothing could be seen. The area was altogether small compared to the weight of fire being put down by the fleet. Many shells were falling side by side and many shrapnel shells exploding one after the other. At this time two of our 37.5mm guns were destroyed and many rifle and communication trenches flattened out. Some of the rifle trenches which had been dug to protect the soldiers' lives instead became their graves. At the same time, wounded who were able to walk began coming into the first aid posts. As the men had been taught in their training on arrival they first of all said, 'I have been wounded and cannot continue my duty; I have given my ammunition to my comrades in the section, here is my rifle – who should I hand it over to?' And then they waited their turn to have their wounds bandaged.[3]

Major Mahmut, 3rd Battalion, 26th Regiment, 9th Division, Fifth Army

The unscathed majority grimly awaited the moment when the bombardment would stop and the landings begin. Then it would be their turn.

The tows of the Dublins were scheduled to land at 05.30 but had been badly delayed by the difficulties of transhipping into the rowing boats, further exacerbated by the current pouring out of the Dardanelles. They were running nearly an hour behind schedule. Confusion ensued when it became apparent that the *River Clyde* would run ashore first.

We slowly steamed towards the beach. The sun was right in our faces and it was very difficult to make things out on shore on account of the smoke from the bursting shells, there being no wind to clear it away. As we got near I was on the upper bridge with Captain Unwin and Lieutenant Colonel Carrington Smith. At that time we could not make out whether the tows had gone in ahead of us or not. As we passed close to a battleship Captain Unwin called out to ask if the tows had gone in, and the reply he got was, 'Don't know, but go on in!'[4]

Lieutenant Colonel Henry Tizard, 1st Royal Munster Fusiliers, 86th Brigade, 29th Division

At this point the army intervened as Carrington Smith warned Unwin that it would dislocate their plans if the *River Clyde* landed its troops before the Dublins got ashore. Unwin therefore decided to mark time by turning a full circle, it being almost impossible to stop the ship while towing the hopper and lighters astern.

I found it very difficult to make this turn, for we were already pointed for the beach and ships were firing on all sides of me. The French were making over to Kum Kale, I couldn't cross their bows, and I didn't want to get between our ships and their targets. I jammed the helm hard-a-port and just managed to clear the stern of the *Agamemnon*, but saw that I could not clear the two destroyers lying on her starboard side with a sweep out between them. So I did the only possible thing and went between them, knowing that they had plenty of time to slack down the wire and let us run over it – if I had attempted anything else certain disaster would have been the result. Well, we got her round and still no tow was in sight. I said to myself, 'Now or never!' And full speed in we went.[5]

Commander Edward Unwin, *River Clyde*

Unable to see properly through the swirling smoke and dust, Unwin used bearings taken on an earlier reconnaissance to guide him into the correct spot. As the *River Clyde* approached the beach it came under harassing shell fire from just across the Straits. It did not have much sea way and ran aground with barely a shudder at 06.22 some eighty yards from shore, a little further out than had been hoped. Despite Unwin's desperate manoeuvrings it still hit the beach a couple of minutes before the first of the rowing boats. Until this time the Turks had not fired a shot. The tows carrying the Dublin Fusiliers slowly approached the beach. Each cutter carried about thirty-six men; four cutters were strung together and towed along by a steam launch.

As soon as the tows got into shallow water the picquet boats cast off and the bluejackets commenced to row. You can imagine how slowly we progressed – six men pulling a heavy boat with about thirty soldiers each carrying over 60-lbs kit and ammunition on his body!![6]

Captain David French, 1st Royal Dublin Fusiliers, 86th Brigade, 29th Division

The beaching of the *River Clyde* seems to have acted as the catalyst for a storm of fire, which lashed across the open boats.

All the men pulling at the oars were either killed or wounded. Able Seaman Leach, though wounded, was the only one still pulling. When we came within 15 yards of the hopper, an RND officer shouted to us to jump out of the boat and swim for it. Weblin and I both jumped out and tried to swim to the hopper, but we found our packs too heavy, and returned to our boat. We hung on to the lifelines for a few minutes, as we could not get into her, she was so high out of the water. However, at last Weblin managed to push me over the gunwale; I then pulled him on board, but with the loss of his pack. While hanging on the lines I got hit, a bullet running under my vest and across my shoulders, just taking some flesh off my shoulder-blade. Also my cap was knocked off. Bullets were flying everywhere, some coming on one side and some the other. The boat was riddled, full of bullet holes, and half full of water. We knew it was hopeless to stay where we were, so we sat at the bottom of the boat in the water and rowed towards the hopper, pulling with our arms above our heads. We got there all right, jumped out, and secured our boat. Here I got another bullet across the back of the hand.[7]

Midshipman Maurice Lloyd, HMS *Cornwallis*

The Turkish riflemen could hardly miss such a target – and they began to wreak a horrifying slaughter.

They opened a terrible fire on us with machine guns and pom-poms, the shells of which contained an incendiary mixture. They began to hit the boat I was in very frequently and killed many of my men as we were rowing ashore. We were also unlucky enough to lose several of the blue jackets who were rowing us in. The men had to take over their oars and as they did not know much about rowing the result was that we often got broadside on to the shore and presented a better target to the enemy. Just before we grounded the boat got hit once or twice with incendiary shells and commenced to go on fire. She was also half full of water from the many holes in her by this time. Several of the men who had been wounded fell to the bottom of the boat and were either drowned there or suffocated by other men falling on top of them; many, to add to their death agonies, were burnt as well.[8]

Lieutenant Cuthbert Maffett, 1st Royal Dublin Fusiliers, 86th Brigade, 29th Division

Trapped in the close confines of the rowing boats the men were utterly helpless and, almost before they knew what was happening, they had been shot to pieces. Captain David French, who was in the last boat of his tow, watched horrified as the Turks methodically dealt with each boat in turn.

> Having practically wiped out those in the other three boats ahead they were now concentrating their fire on us. I jumped out at once into the sea, up to my chest and yelling to the men to make a rush for it and to follow me. But the poor devils, packed like sardines in a tin and carrying this damnable weight on their backs, could scarcely clamber over the sides of the boat.[9]

> Captain David French, 1st Royal Dublin Fusiliers, 86th Brigade, 29th Division

It was a desperate business. The torrent of fire was such that the British have always maintained that there were at least two Turkish machine guns at V Beach, one high to the left and the other in the walls of the castle. Once more this belief seems to fly in the face of Turkish evidence. The 26th Regiment had no machine guns. This controversial matter therefore sets the deepest-held convictions of men who were there against dry documentation. Perhaps some of the confusion at V Beach arises from the admitted presence of four Nordenfelt pom-poms (two of which were knocked out early in the fighting), which had a high rate of fire and might well have been thought of as old pattern Maxim guns by some witnesses. Furthermore, their destructive small shells, coupled with rapid rifle fire and the overwhelming masking roar of the massed British machine guns aboard the *River Clyde*, may have confused men with no time to think coolly about what exactly was shooting at them. They only knew that they were being splattered with bullets from all angles. Certainly the Turkish infantry were well drilled in musketry and able to mimic the deadly effects of machine guns in short concentrated bursts of fire at such easy targets. As at W Beach, the Dublins were the victims of a murderous attack that raked through their ranks. Captain French was one of those who made a dash for the shore, but as he had abandoned his rowing boat well out in the bay he still had a long, long way to go, stumbling through the shallows.

> I had to run about 100–150 yards in the water and being the first away from the cutter escaped the fire a bit to start with. But as soon as a few followed me, the water around seemed to be alive, the bullets striking the sea all around us. Heaven alone knows how I got thro' a perfect hail of bullets. The beach sloped very gently – fortunately! When I was about 50 yards from the water's edge I felt one bullet go thro' the pack on my back and then thought I had got through safely when they put

one through my left arm. The fellows in the regiment had told me I was getting too fat to run, but those who saw me go through that bit of water changed their opinions later – I ran like hell!!!!![10]

Captain David French, 1st Royal Dublin Fusiliers, 86th Brigade, 29th Division

French staggered ashore and took shelter under a low earth bank just five feet high which was his only protection from fire. He was about fifty yards to the left of where the *River Clyde* had grounded. There he lay, helpless, confused and under heavy fire every time he tried to move. There was no chance of an organised attack on the Turks, who remained in complete control of the situation. Meanwhile, the boats that had managed to get further in were still being subjected to the full force of close-range concentrated Turkish fire.

We then grounded, and I jumped out of the bows of the boat and got hit in the head by a machine gun bullet, others going into a pack that I was carrying on my shoulders. I went under water and came up again, and tried to encourage the men to get to the shore and under cover as fast as they could as it was their only chance. I then went under again. Someone caught hold of me and began pulling me ashore, and as I got to dry land a bluejacket joined him. When I recovered a bit I found it was my Platoon Sergeant – Sergeant Willis. I did not see him again that day as far as I remember. Two men got ashore beside me and then two more that were wounded. We took cover under a low sort of bank that was about 10 yards from the water's edge, and bound each other up as best we could. Looking out to sea I saw the remnants of my platoon trying to get to the shore, but they were shot down one after another, and their bodies drifted out to sea or lay immersed a few feet from the shore. I found myself at the extreme left of the beach, and put the men I had around me on the alert for a rush from the enemy: of course we could not have done any good.[11]

Lieutenant Cuthbert Maffett, 1st Royal Dublin Fusiliers, 86th Brigade, 29th Division

Many of the boats carrying the Dublin Fusiliers were marooned, either grounded broadside on to the beach or bobbing about helplessly offshore. Here they stayed, filled with their grim cargo of the dead, the wounded and the few lucky survivors.

There were twenty-five in my boat, and there were only three of us left. It was sad to hear our poor chums moaning, and to see others dead in the boat. It was a terrible sight to see the poor boys dead in the water; others on the beach roaring for help. But we could do nothing for them. I must have had someone's good prayer for I do not know how I escaped. Those who were lying wounded on the shore, in the evening the tide came in and they were all drowned, and I was left by myself on the beach. I had to remain in the water for about three hours, as they would fire on me as soon as they saw me make a move. I thought my life was up every minute.[12]

Private Robert Martin, 1st Royal Dublin Fusiliers, 86th Brigade, 29th Division

The sailors were unable to get the boats away from the lethal reach of the Turks. Every purposeful movement merely attracted the renewed attentions of their tormentors and another lashing of bullets.

I got hit in the right shoulder and of course down I went – anyway we got the boat ashore and the soldiers – those that could – got out. By this time all my boat's crew were either killed or wounded so we had to stop there under a hail of bullets from Maxims and rifle fire. We remained there for about 9 hours. Every time one of us got up to try and get the boat offshore we were met with a hail of bullets.[13]

Able Seaman Dick Rickus, HMS *Cornwallis*

After just a few minutes there was little left of the Dublins. Lieutenant Colonel Richard Rooth had been shot dead on the beach, his second-in-command, Major Edwyn Fetherstonhaugh, was lying mortally wounded in his boat and most of the other officers were either dead or wounded.

The only exception to the general slaughter was the single tow of boats landed at the Camber, round the corner into the Straits and immediately below a step track leading up to the Sedd el Bahr village. This was where the marines had had a rough reception when they had landed there on their raid of 4 March.

About 50 or a 100 yards from the shore the steamboats slowed down, the pulling boats were slipped, and the orders, 'Oars down! Give way together!' were given and we were pulling like mad for the beach. Whiz! A shrapnel burst overhead; everybody ducked. I looked round. Nobody was touched. But going in yet closer we were peppered with the stuff and a lot of balls fell into the boat. We were soon alongside the Camber, which was directly under the wall of the fort, and all the soldiers jumped ashore and took cover under a wall with no casualties. My boat was the first to beach, likewise the first to get away, and as we went out we received a few more words of cheer in the form of shrapnel.[14]

Midshipman Haydon Forbes, HMS *Cornwallis*

The half company of Dublin Fusiliers fought their way up the hill and managed to enter the village. However, here they were gradually out-fought and overwhelmed by the Turks – few escaped.

While the Dublin Fusiliers suffered, the *River Clyde* was getting ready to discharge its hidden cargo. Now was the time for the steam hopper and lighters to move smoothly round from her port side and form a bridge between the platform attached to her bows and the beach. The steam hopper was commanded by Midshipman George Drewry, aided by six Greek crewmen who had been volunteered for the task in all ignorance of what lay in front of them. Let it not be forgotten that Greece was not at war; this was emphatically not these men's fight. When they realised what was happening they reacted badly: they reversed the engines and the steersman violently changed course to port before they all took cover below decks. The steam hopper was left drifting away from the port side of the *River Clyde* until it ran aground at completely the wrong angle to act as a route to the beach. Drewry and Able Seaman George Samson tried their best to redress the situation, but it was hopeless.

Samson and I tried to put a brow out over the bow, the Greeks had run below and two of us could not do it, so I told him also to get out of the 'rain' and I jumped over the bow and waded ashore.[15]

Midshipman George Drewry, *River Clyde*

Meanwhile, Unwin was a desperate man: he could see that his scheme was collapsing. How were the men to get ashore? They could not jump into six feet or more of water and emerge in any fit state to fight. With no time to think of his own safety, he leapt into action, closely accompanied by Able Seaman William Williams. Together the two men were striving to resolve the crisis through their own efforts, even at the likely cost of their lives.

I dashed over the side and got hold of the lighters which I had been towing astern and which had shot ahead by their impetus when we took the beach. These I got under the bow and found Williams with me. I had told him the night before to keep with me and he did so literally. We got them connected to the bows and then proceeded to connect them to the beach, but we had nothing to secure to, so we had to hold on to the rope ourselves. When we had got the lighters close enough to the shore I sang out to the troops to come out.[16]

Commander Edward Unwin, *River Clyde*

Inside the bowels of the *River Clyde* the men of the 1st Royal Munster Fusiliers were ready. Captain Henderson was first away, leading Z Company out of the starboard exit ports and then running down the rickety gangway on to the lighters.

Henderson led his company, ordering me to follow at the end of the first platoon. One by one they popped out, and then my turn. All the way down the side of the ship bullets crashed against the side. On reaching the first barge I found some of the men had collected and were firing. I mistrusted the second barge and the track to the shore so I led them over the side; the water came nearly up to our shoulders. However, none of us were hit and we gained the bank. There I found Henderson badly hit and heaps of wounded. Any man who put his head up for an instant was shot dead.[17]

Captain Raymond Lane, 1st Royal Munster Fusiliers, 86th Brigade, 29th Division

Crouching under a small five-foot bank about ten yards from the water's edge, Captain Lane found himself helplessly pinned down. The barbed wire defences lay inviolate about twenty-five yards in front of him.

The bank we were under had a small nullah running up towards the barbed wire. I worked my way up under the right-hand wall and then tried to cross it, running as fast as I could; a sniper at the top let fly at me, the bullet went through my right ankle and carried on sideways, smashing my left leg to bits. One of my platoon then came out very pluckily and pulled me to safety. I had only been on the beach five minutes and never saw a Turk.[18]

Captain Raymond Lane, 1st Royal Munster Fusiliers, 86th Brigade, 29th Division

Any attempt to break it out of the beach area had minimal chance of success as long as the Turks maintained their concentration and fire discipline. Unwin and Williams, however, seemed to live charmed lives. With bullets splattering all about them in the water, together they clung on to the line that was the only thing anchoring the lighter bridge to the shore. The massed machine guns on the *River Clyde* were their saviours, for they helped to keep the Turks' heads down.

> The Turks seemed to concentrate on the lighters more than on the *River Clyde*, and it was on the lighters and the reef that the greatest number of dead and wounded lay. Of course many of them fell into the water and were drowned – we were literally standing in blood.[19]
>
> Commander Edward Unwin, *River Clyde*

Drewry, meanwhile, was struggling ashore from the steam hopper.

> I waded ashore, meeting a soldier wounded in the water. I and another soldier tried to carry him ashore but he was again shot in our arms – his neck in two pieces nearly, so we left him and I ran along the beach towards the spit.[20]
>
> Midshipman George Drewry, *River Clyde*

On the port side Captain Geddes, leading X Company, was slightly slower in getting his men out through the exit ports, as their gangway jammed. By then he knew what they were about to face when they burst from the dark security of the *River Clyde*. But out they went into a blaze of sunshine and death, watched by the few survivors of the Dublins left huddled along the beach.

> We got it like anything, man after man behind me was shot down but they never wavered. Lieutenant Watts who was wounded in five places and lying on the gangway cheered the men on with cries of 'Follow the Captain!' Captain French of the Dublins told me afterwards that he counted the first 48 men to follow me, and they all fell. I think no finer episode could be found of the men's bravery and discipline than this – of leaving the safety of the *River Clyde* to go to what was practically certain death. I dashed down the gangway and already found the lighters holding the dead and wounded from the leading platoons of 'Z' Company. I stepped on the second lighter and looked round to find myself alone, and yelled to the men following out of the *Clyde* to come on, but it was difficult going across the lighters.[21]
>
> Captain Guy Geddes, 1st Royal Munster Fusiliers, 86th Brigade, 29th Division

Just then, when Captain Geddes and the survivors of X Company were already under heavy fire, the makeshift bridge temporarily broke loose in front of them and their lighter drifted away to port once again. They were left staring at a widening gap of deep water, while the bullets thudded among them. There was no time to lose.

> I then jumped into the sea and had to swim some dozen strokes to get ashore. There is no doubt that men were drowned owing chiefly, I think, to the great weight they were carrying – a full pack, 250 rounds of ammunition, and 3 days' rations – I know I felt it. All the officers were dressed and equipped like the men. There was a small rocky spit jutting out into the sea, which was absolutely taped down by the Turks and few, if any, survived who attempted to land there.[22]
>
> Captain Guy Geddes, 1st Royal Munster Fusiliers, 86th Brigade, 29th Division

Most of the men that tried to follow Geddes were killed or wounded, but his orderly, Private William Flynn, was still close behind him as he jumped out of the lighter.

> He said, 'Well, come on, over we go!' We fall into the sea, of course I lost him! I come up once or twice for fresh air and I drifted to my right and I came up by this strip of rock. It was piled high with dead. Some of the other company instead of running across the gangway which they saw was useless, they must have jumped into the water and managed to get to this rock but eventually got killed – the majority of them. I managed to just crawl on to the rock – I was exhausted – I thought that my knees had bullet holes in them all over where they'd been on the bottom like! They were still pumping lead into all the bodies, any movement. We managed to scramble on to the shore, we had about 8 or 9 feet to go and we got behind a bank about 5 foot high and we were quite safe there.[23]
>
> Private William Flynn, 1st Royal Munster Fusiliers, 86th Brigade, 29th Division

They were going nowhere; the Turks were making sure of that. Just after 07.00, Captain Geddes began to edge his men towards the right to try to gain shelter under the lee of the Sedd el Bahr fort. From here he hoped to either outflank or over-run the Turks. But the Turks were ready and easily thwarted them. Geddes himself was lightly wounded when a bullet struck his shoulder; he would stay ashore for another thirteen hours before finally seeking medical treatment aboard the *River Clyde*.

Meanwhile, Unwin and Williams were reaching the limits of their physical resources as they struggled to hold the lighters together. After about an hour (although the exact chronology is difficult to establish), Williams' luck had run out.

> Thinking I could be more use elsewhere, I asked Williams if he could hang on without me, but he said he was nearly done and couldn't. Just then a shell fell alongside us, Williams said to me, 'Whatever is that?' I told him and almost immediately I heard a thud, looked round and Williams said, 'A shell has hit me!' I caught hold of him and, as I couldn't let him drown, I tried to get him to the lighter.[24]
>
> Commander Edward Unwin, *River Clyde*

In attempting to save Williams by heaving him aboard the lighter Unwin was forced to let go of the rope. He lacked either the weight or the strength to hold the lighters on his own, so it made sense to try to rescue his gallant comrade. However, his efforts, with the assistance of Drewry, would prove in vain, for Williams very soon expired from his wounds and Unwin himself collapsed with exhaustion. It was a miracle that he too had not been hit. He was dragged back aboard the *River Clyde* and placed safely below in his cabin. Meanwhile, Drewry had taken over the thankless task of sorting out the tangled lighters.

> The first lighter was covered with dead and wounded and the spit was awful – the sea around it for some yards was red. When they got ashore they were little better off, for they were picked off many of them before they could dig themselves in. They stopped coming and I ran on board into No. 1 and saw an awful sight – dead and dying lay around the ports where their curiosity had led them.[25]
>
> Midshipman George Drewry, *River Clyde*

Drewry got back into the water and continued to try to create a bridge of lighters between the *River Clyde* and the beach. In this he was greatly assisted by Lieutenant John Morse and Midshipman Wilfred Malleson, who had brought up the third spare lighter, which was being towed on the collier's starboard side. An astonishing sequence of bullets, heroism, snapped ropes, contrary lighters and amazing escapes ensued until at last a viable connection to the beach had been built. At times the confusion was almost farcical, as Midshipman Maurice Lloyd found when he too became involved.

> I saw Lieutenant Morse. He called to me to lend him a hand in securing
> a lighter. So we hauled the lighter astern, giving the stern a kick out
> so as to meet the other lighters. We both jumped into the lighter; but
> as she was moving, Morse said: 'Have you secured the hawser?' My
> reply was, 'No, Sir, I thought you had!' So again I jumped out on to the
> hopper, before the lighter swung out, and secured the hawser round a
> bollard. Just in time, as I got another bullet through my lung, I spun
> round and fell down, managing to get more or less under cover.[26]
>
> Midshipman Maurice Lloyd, HMS *Cornwallis*

In spite of it all they managed to re-establish a passable link with the
beach. Thus, at about 09.00, Lieutenant Colonel Tizard, thinking that
the Turkish fire was dying down, ordered Major Jarrett, commanding Y
Company of the Munsters, to have another try. His wishful thinking was
swiftly exposed as the Turkish fire swelled up in murderous fashion and,
although several Munsters got ashore, it was at great expense as more dead
and wounded swelled the heaps of bodies on the lighters and foreshore.
One last attempt would be made when Carrington Smith, prodded by
Hunter-Weston – who was still unaware of the severity of the situation –
ordered a party of 2nd Hampshires, under the command of Captain Caryl
Boxall, to try to again at around 09.30. Yet again the Turkish fire control
was superb: quiet when nothing much was happening, but bursting into
vicious life whenever a serious attempt was made to resume the landing.
Few of the Hampshires got even as far as the lighters and when the tenuous
bridge on to dry land was once again cut the attempt was given up as suicidal. Boxall himself was mortally wounded. The senior officers on board
the *River Clyde* decided that they must stop this hopeless slaughter.

> I now saw that it was impossible to carry out the original plan of attack.
> My reasons were that the crossfire brought to bear from the fort and the
> village on the right and from the trenches and works on the left was
> so heavy that nothing could live on the ground about the beach. Men
> who left the cover of the bank for an instant were killed. I went back
> to Lieutenant-Colonel Carrington Smith, who was on the upper bridge
> watching the fight, and told him that I considered that we should hold
> on and wait till dark, when I thought we should stand a better chance
> of getting the men out without such heavy casualties. He agreed.[27]
>
> Lieutenant Colonel Henry Tizard, 1st Royal Munster Fusiliers, 86th Brigade, 29th
> Division

But complex military plans, once committed to paper, tend to have a life of their own. Major General Sir Aylmer Hunter-Weston and his staff were marooned aboard the *Euryalus* around the corner off W Beach. They knew there had been a delay, but had no idea of the scale of the disaster at V Beach. Although the 1st Essex were diverted from V Beach to W Beach, this was more to reinforce the efforts of the 1st Lancashire Fusiliers than a reflection of what was happening at V Beach. The bulk of the second wave was still intending to land under Sedd el Bahr as planned, although many of the boats had been destroyed during the first landing. Yet enough survived to allow Brigadier General Henry Napier, his headquarters and elements of both the 4th Worcesters and the 2nd Hampshires to board rowboats, often still reeking with blood, and head for the beach.

> The pinnace has started and is going to run us ashore alongside the *River Clyde*. We were being run in on the right side of this ship, but, had it not been for the Colonel [Carrington Smith] of the Hampshires, we would all have been drowned and never have the chance of getting on land. He shouted from the bridge, 'For God's sake go round the other side!' And we did. You see, the Turks were waiting for the boats just there – and blowing them to pieces.[28]
>
> Private George Keen, 4th Worcestershire Regiment, 88th Brigade, 29th Division

Despite Colonel Carrington Smith's best efforts, Brigadier General Napier still misunderstood the situation and seems to have thought that the men choking the decks of the lighters could be led ashore. He jumped aboard the lighters and into history. Someone shouted down from the *River Clyde*, 'You can't possibly land!' to which Napier replied, 'I'll have a damned good try!'[29] Napier, followed by some of the Worcesters, started to run across the lighters.

> I saw three wounded Irishmen, wounded and hanging on to a small boat; one was shouting, 'Oh, by Jesus save me!' I gave the General a leg-up on to the lighter, then his Brigade Major. Then I was pushed up and the deck of the lighter was covered with dead men. We started over the deck when the General went down, he never spoke. Then the Major went down but he raised himself on one knee and said, 'Carry on, men!' Then he was dead.[30]
>
> Private Cecil Jeffries, 4th Worcestershire Regiment, 88th Brigade, 29th Division

Among those behind them was Private George Keen.

> We were following the General. He got to the third boat and was killed;
> the Brigade Major followed him and he got killed. Our Major said, 'This
> is too risky!' and he got out of the way in the little boat. That caused us
> to stop and we all lay in the lighter, myself lying on another fellow. I was
> sorry for him but he said, 'Never mind!' There we stayed till night came.[31]
>
> Private George Keen, 4th Worcestershire Regiment, 88th Brigade, 29th Division

As the wounded Midshipman Maurice Lloyd lay trapped aboard the steam
hopper he had good reason to curse these newcomers causing an increase
in the damnable Turkish fire. He managed to drag himself to the rear of
the hopper, where he was almost out of sight. Almost, but not quite.

> I saw twenty soldiers making a rush across the hopper from a lighter.
> The Turks turned a machine gun on to them and killed the lot.
> Unfortunately for me, I, too, came under this fire. The only bit of me
> that was exposed was my ankle, which caught another bullet. I was
> rescued by a seaman from the *Hussar* – Able Seaman Samson. He came
> out of the engine-room and carried me below. Here I stayed, knowing
> very little of what was going on, only hearing from time to time the
> sounds of the rushing feet of men who made attempts to get ashore.[32]
>
> Midshipman Maurice Lloyd, HMS *Cornwallis*

In all the mayhem Brigadier General Napier's body slipped overboard,
never to be recovered. His courage was commendable, but his simple
mistake cost the 88th Brigade their commander just when they needed
him most. Shortly afterwards, at 10.21, General Sir Ian Hamilton, a distant
witness from the *Queen Elizabeth* which had joined in the renewed bombardment of the beach defences, signalled to Hunter-Weston to tell him
that there was no hope at V Beach and that all further troops should be
diverted to W Beach.

The situation settled down into one of grim stalemate. The survivors
of the Munsters and the Dublin Fusiliers huddled down behind the low
sandbank where they were partially protected from the Turkish fire, but
with no chance of making a successful advance through the barbed wire
and off the beach area. One of them was Lieutenant Cuthbert Maffett,
who had already been slightly wounded in the head; even so, he was
faring far better than most of his fellow fusiliers.

I lay under cover for the greater part of the morning, and tried to get into touch with some of the others. After a bit I crawled along towards the fort at Sedd el Bahr and there found Captain French. He had been hit in the wrist with a bullet which had driven bits of his wristwatch into him. I lay under cover with him for a time. I then went to the left of the beach to see if I could collect any men there, but all I found were either wounded or dead. At the part almost under the lighthouse I found a boat that was nearly all submerged, and in it were some of our machine gunners under Lieutenant Corbet;[33] they were all dead as far as I could see and the machine guns useless. I then went back to where Captain French was lying and spent the rest of the afternoon under cover beside him. We had a man near us with a pocket periscope, which we put over the top of the bank from time to time to see if the Turks were coming down on us, but there was no move on their part. We had no food or water with us, as the sea water had destroyed it all. The whole beach was strewn with dead and there were very few hale men amongst us. One had to keep down the whole time.[34]

Lieutenant Cuthbert Maffett, 1st Royal Dublin Fusiliers, 86th Brigade, 29th Division

Then the Mediterranean, that supposedly tideless sea, began to demonstrate that there could be a small tidal range that could make a fatal difference.

There were some of our chaps hit while in two feet of water, and could not move, so when the tide started to come in it was awful to see those chaps getting drowned and roaring for someone to save them.[35]

Private Denis Moriarty, 1st Royal Munster Fusiliers, 86th Brigade, 29th Division

By this time, Unwin's enforced rest in his cabin had given him a chance to at least partially regain his strength and he went back on deck. He cut a curious figure, for, with his uniform still soaked from his earlier exploits, he was dressed as if for a day's yachting in a white shirt and flannel trousers. The moaning and wailing of the wounded proved more than he could stand.

I got a boat under the starboard quarter as far from the enemy as I could get. Taking a spare coil of rope with me, I got some hands to pay out a rope fast to the stern of the pinnace I was in, and paddled and punted it to the beach, eventually grounding alongside the wounded. They were all soaking wet and very heavy, but I cut off their accoutrements with their bayonets or knives and carried two or three to the pinnace, but as her side was rather high out of the water, I'm afraid they were none too gingerly put on board. Still they were very grateful. I could not pick up any more, so I got on my hands and knees, they got on to my back and I crawled along to the pinnace. Four more, I managed like this. I found a man in his trousers only, alongside me, he had swum ashore to help me, his name was Russell and he was one of the RNAS. We carried one man down together and then he was shot through the stomach. I tore up my shirt and bound his wound a bit and got him into the pinnace. I was again beginning to feel a bit dickey so I got into the pinnace and told them to haul me aboard. On the way across somebody came alongside in the water and wanted to know why I was going back. I replied because I could do no more – and I really couldn't. I was 51![36]

Commander Edward Unwin, *River Clyde*

The man who questioned Unwin was almost certainly Sub Lieutenant Arthur Tisdall. While the exhausted Unwin collapsed back into his bunk, Tisdall and Petty Officer Geoffrey Rumming carried on the work of rescuing the wounded.

The wounded were still crying and drowning on that awful spit. Tisdall took a boat, one of the *Clyde*'s sailors and one of the men – Rumming. Hiding behind the side of the boat they walked and swam it back. I saw one of the wounded stretch out his hand to stroke Rumming as he hung on to his side, the most pathetic thing I have ever seen.[37]

Lieutenant Commander Josiah Wedgwood, No. 3 Squadron, Royal Naval Armoured Car Division

Leading Seaman James Parkinson was among the men helping the gallant Arthur Tisdall. Eventually they realised that the situation was becoming hopeless.

The boat was leaking very badly and one of the last three was drowned in the boat bottom. We were then called back by one of the ship's officers who stated it was sheer madness to go on, and if we did not return on board and under cover, anything we did would not be recognised. And if we did carry on then we should probably be dead men because the Turks had by now got a machine gun trained on us. We had no alternative than to obey orders and the boat was getting full of water.[38]

Leading Seaman James Parkinson, Anson Battalion, RND

The bobbing rowing boats were also making their way as fast as possible away from that accursed beach. Commanding one of them was Midshipman Forbes, who, after landing the half company at the Camber, had brought a second boatload to the main V Beach. He escaped by the skin of his teeth.

> I made the men sit in the bottom of the boat on stretchers and back for all they were worth, whilst I sat on the bottom of the boat in the stern-sheets and steered. Several bullets passed over my body, and one grazed my right arm. Of the seamen left, one was now hit in the thigh, and another in the arm, so the coxswain took an oar. At last, after what seemed an eternity, we began to glide off the beach, and Harper, who was hit in the arm, now took an oar again, and helped matters greatly; and after being nearly run down by a life-boat, we backed out to where the picket-boat was. The picket-boat came out and picked us up, towing us straight to the *Aragon*, a hospital carrier. I took a comprehensive look round. There were two or three soldiers in the boat, one nearly dead and the others wounded, and with one was a little brown dog, who sat beside his master. Three of my boat's crew were wounded badly and a fourth slightly. Grose was the most severely injured, and he only lived an hour after being hit.[39] Smith was shot in both legs, and I bandaged him up, and did the same for Sawyer, after which I turned my attention to the soldiers. The boat was in a sad state, being about 18 inches deep in blood and water, with eight bullet holes in her bows and the same number aft. When we at last got to the *Aragon* I hunted all over the ship for a doctor, but could not find one for three-quarters of an hour, and it was 2 hours before my wounded were all inboard.[40]
>
> Midshipman Haydon Forbes, HMS *Cornwallis*

So the day wore on. Over a thousand men were still cooped up on the *River Clyde*; while about 200 men were crouching behind the small bank that was all that lay between them and eternity. Their only hope was help from the other landings. Thus it was that in the mid-afternoon, there was a frisson of excitement on board the *River Clyde* as British troops were seen pushing out from W Beach. Unwin was standing alongside Colonel Carrington Smith when they were sighted.

> He cheered and so did the troops. He came up the ladder with me to go to the bridge. I went on to the upper bridge thinking he was following

me and saw him standing on the lower bridge which had no protection, looking towards the beach with his glasses. I shouted to him to come on the upper bridge and I saw him fall shot through the mouth.[41]

Commander Edward Unwin, *River Clyde*

Another senior British officer had paid the penalty for underestimating Turkish marksmanship. It was a lesson that did not seem to penetrate some officers caught up in the drama.

I remained on the upper bridge with Williams and Doughty Wylie staring at the beach, not a Turk did I ever see – I thought I saw one once and took a rifle and fired at it – and an old vulture flew out of a tree. I could not keep Doughty Wylie from unnecessarily exposing himself over the iron screen, so I gave it up at last.[42]

Commander Edward Unwin, *River Clyde*

Upon the death of Carrington Smith, Lieutenant Colonel Henry Tizard of the Munsters took over command of the troops. The brusque Unwin was by no means impressed with Tizard's style of command.

I soon saw he was not the man for the awful position he found himself in. It does not inspire men who don't know what is going to happen to see a little man running about with a papier-mâché megaphone in his hands all day – doing nothing – and he never landed till the show was over. He was no coward, but simply was not the man for the part.[43]

Commander Edward Unwin, *River Clyde*

In Tizard's defence it should be pointed out that far too many senior officers were killed on 25 April through acting as if they were lowly subalterns and taking unnecessary risks. In so doing they were in effect evading their real responsibility to exercise the command and control functions that came with their rank. Tizard, who was an essentially sensible man, was merely trying to wrest some kind of control over a chaotic situation.

I now went to the machine gun stations on the boat to try and locate targets in order to try and keep the enemy's fire under control. It was very difficult to get any definite target – the furthest trenches of the enemy were between 400 and 600 yards distant. Captain Lambert RN assisted me in this and he also directed the gunfire of the supporting ships on to various points of the village and ground commanding the beach. I still considered that our best plan was to hold on till the light failed when the enemy's fire would not be as accurate. However, if I saw a chance when the fire died down, I intended to try and get the men over gradually.[44]

Lieutenant Colonel Henry Tizard, 1st Royal Munster Fusiliers, 86th Brigade, 29th Division

Yet the Turks too were suffering. One message, sent by Lieutenant Abdul Rahman to his commanding officer, Major Mahmut, reflects in its frantic pleas for reinforcements their growing desperation as they realised the numbers that were pressing upon them.

My Captain – the enemy's infantry is taking cover at the back of the Sedd el Bahr gun defences, but the rear of these gun defences cannot come under fire. With the twenty or twenty-five men I have with me it will not be possible to drive them off with a bayonet charge, because I am obliged to spread my men out. Either you must send up reinforcements and drive the enemy into the sea, or let us evacuate this place, because I am absolutely certain that they will land more men tonight. Send the doctors to carry off my wounded. Alas! Alas! My Captain, for God's sake send me reinforcements, because hundreds of soldiers are landing. Hurry up. What on earth will happen, my Captain?[45]

Lieutenant Abdul Rahman, 3rd Battalion, 26th Regiment, 9th Division, Fifth Army

Given the scale of the British attack on the Helles, it was not surprising that the vastly outnumbered Turkish defenders of 3/26th Regiment were approaching the ends of their endurance. There were no significant reserves immediately on hand and Lieutenant Rahman would have to fight on as best he could. All that Major Mahmut could do was to send forward his 11th Company to the Hill 141 sector to try to bolster further the defence of V Beach.

Help and ammunition only arrived 21½ hours after the beginning of the battle. During this 21½ hours, firing had not ceased or diminished. This shows that the fire discipline was perfect. This in its turn was due to the soldiers having been called up at the right time and to the care taken in their training by efficient and capable officers.[46]

Major Mahmut, 3rd Battalion, 26th Regiment, 9th Division, Fifth Army

Darkness brought relief of a kind to both sides. It offered the Turks some respite from the attacks, but it also cloaked the British trapped on V Beach and allowed those cooped up aboard the *River Clyde* finally to start getting ashore. One who took his chance early was Lieutenant George Davidson, a doctor serving with the 89th Field Ambulance Brigade. He could in no conscience wait any longer to try to help the wounded, many of whom had been trapped without help for up to fourteen hours of what must have been the longest day.

> I set off alone over the barges and splashed through the remaining few yards of water. Here most of those still alive were wounded more or less severely, and I set to work on them, removing many useless and harmful tourniquets for one thing, and worked my way to the left towards the high rocks where the snipers still were. All the wounded on this side I attended to, an officer accompanying me all the time. I then went to the other side, and after seeing to all in the sand my companion left me, and I next went to a long, low rock which projected into the water for about 20 yards a short way to the right of the *Clyde*. Here the dead and wounded were heaped together two and three deep, and it was among these I had my hardest work. All had to be disentangled single-handed from their uncomfortable positions, some lying with head and shoulders in the tideless water, with broken legs in some cases dangling on a higher level. At the very point of this rock, which had been a favourite spot for the boats to steer to, there was a solid mass of dead and wounded mixed up together. The whole of these I saw to, although by this time there was little I could do except lift and pull them into more comfortable positions, but I was able to do something for every one of them.[47]
>
> Lieutenant George Davidson, 89th Field Ambulance, RAMC

The troops on the *River Clyde* began to file down the gangplanks, across the lighters and then on to the rocky spit to reach the shore.

> The losses were small then. For 3 hours I stood on the end of the spit of what had been rock in two feet of water helping the heavily laden men to jump ashore on to submerged dead bodies. This is what went on monotonously: 'Give me your rifle!' 'Your shovel!' 'Your left hand!' 'Jump wide!' 'It's all right, it's only kits!' 'Keep clear of that man's legs, can't you?' Trying to persuade the wounded over whom they had

to walk that we should soon get them aboard. Wounded men were brought to the end of the spit and could not be got aboard, because the other stream was more important and never-ending – there they slowly sank and died.[48]

Lieutenant Commander Josiah Wedgwood, No. 3 Squadron, Royal Naval Armoured Car Division

Young Midshipman George Drury had earlier received a slight head wound, but he was still assisting in the collection of the wounded.

I had a party getting wounded from the hopper and lighters and putting them onboard a trawler lying under our quarter. An awful job, they had not been dressed at all and some of the poor devils were in an awful state. I never knew that blood smelt so strong before.[49]

Midshipman George Drewry, *River Clyde*

So it was that by 00.30 on 26 April all the troops were ashore where they would endure a cold and miserable night.

Not far away Major Mahmut visited his men holding the Helles area. By then the 3/26th Regiment had been reduced to about 450 men, having lost something like fifteen officers and about half of the men. They could hear but not see the British troops creeping ashore.

The officers and men of the 9th Company were spoken to. They were told that the fate of the nation depended on us this night, that if we were able to gain time for our army by stopping the enemy's advance, we would have completed our task. It was explained that every hour which we were able to remain here would assist our army in gaining a victory and would result in a crushing defeat for the enemy. We must remain resolute. The battalion officers and men were told that help would come, that on arrival of help a bayonet attack would be made, and that with the grace of Allah the timorous enemy would finally be driven into the sea. The men fired their rifles and awaited the order for the bayonet charge. Not for a moment did they call to mind the comparison between the enemy's strength and their own.[50]

Major Mahmut, 3rd Battalion, 26th Regiment, 9th Division, Fifth Army

Advanced detachments from the 25th Regiment reached Mahmut's headquarters at around 02.30. Accompanied by two of their regiment's four machine guns, they had hoped to re-establish a firm line and then launch a general counter-attack, but this was soon abandoned as impossible, although two companies were sent forward under cover of darkness to help bolster the line. The Turkish forces at Helles were still severely outnumbered.

The British still had their problems. It was soon evident that experienced officers who could motivate the troops were at a premium and would prove crucial to any hopes of success. Their men had suffered great trials either lying helpless on the narrow strip of beach or waiting long hours in the bowels of the *River Clyde*. Some of them were wavering.

> We ought to have been able to seize the crest quite easily, but the men were sticky and lack of officers very apparent; they wanted a good leader.[51]
>
> Lieutenant Colonel Weir De Lancey Williams, Headquarters, 29th Division

The party of divisional staff officers aboard the *River Clyde* decided to intervene directly to sort out the confusion and to lead the troops by personal example. The most powerful personality among them proved to be Lieutenant Colonel Dick Doughty Wylie.

> The Colonel took charge of the situation at once, and after collecting together the whole force, which consisted of the survivors of the Munster Fusiliers, the Dublin Fusiliers and two companies of the Hampshire Regiment under Major Beckwith, he ordered us to charge in one mass into the Castle and occupy it. He led the charge himself with the other officers, whom he ordered to form up in line in front of their respective regiments. The Castle was occupied finally, and the Turkish snipers found in it all bayoneted, with very small loss to us.[52]
>
> Captain Guy Nightingale, 1st Royal Munster Fusiliers, 86th Brigade, 29th Division

By 08.00 the Sedd el Bahr fort was occupied and attention could be turned to breaking the Turkish grip on the beach by ejecting them from the village and older fort which overlooked it from Hill 141.

> The only way into Sedd el Bahr village lay through the Castle, which had two main entrances for this purpose. Each was a stone archway about 15 feet in breadth, but covered by a deadly fire from machine guns and marksmen hidden in the ruins of the village beyond. Anyone attempting to go through, or even walk past the gate, was killed instantly, and invariably shot through the head. Colonel Doughty

Wylie had a very narrow escape here. He was passing some distance in rear of the gateway when a bullet knocked the staff cap off his head. I happened to be quite close at the moment, and remember being struck by the calm way in which he treated the incident. He was carrying no weapon of any description at the time, only a small cane.[53]

Captain Guy Nightingale, 1st Royal Munster Fusiliers, 86th Brigade, 29th Division

Through a potent combination of organisational ability, experience, tactical skills and sheer courage, Doughty Wylie was helping to shake the men from their lethargy and propel them forward.

Meanwhile, Second Lieutenant Reginald Gillett had been given his own rather difficult and dangerous task: to try to encircle the Turks in the village.

Major Beckwith ordered Lieutenant Parker and myself to try and climb along the cliff on the east side of the village and force an entry half way along. The rock cliff was high and almost perpendicular, below was the sea and on the rocks at the foot of the cliff more than one mangled body lay. It must be remembered that we carried very heavy equipment: a full pack which also contained a spare pair of boots, extra water and 200 extra rounds of ammunition in bandoleers slung round the neck. Officers carried exactly the same amount as the men, except that they carried a revolver instead of a rifle. This encumbrance made the climb even more difficult and perilous. One was covered by direct rifle fire, but at one point a large boulder, evidently pushed over by the enemy, came bounding down the cliff straight for me. I thought I was about to be added to the mangled remains below, but the boulder bounced just above my head and again below my feet and I was still safe.[54]

Second Lieutenant Reginald Gillett, 2nd Hampshire Regiment, 88th Brigade, 29th Division

Gillett emerged from his dangerous scramble round the cliffs in time to join in the attack through the village. The numbers of Turks left facing them may not have been large, but their sniping could be deadly.

The village consisted of one straight main street with ruined houses on each side. Slowly we worked our way through the village, but with bullets whizzing down the street, crossing it was something of a hazard. However when necessary we did so one-by-one, somewhat after the fashion of small children daring each other to be last across the road

in front of an on-coming car. One of my men had a nick taken out of
his nose – poor man – but we all thought this rather a joke. When we
got to the last house of the village, Major Beckwith detailed two men
to accompany me and ordered me forward to reconnoitre. I was so
interested in my work that I forgot everything, and for the first time
since the landing felt completely at ease. It was therefore a very great
shock when I received a sledgehammer like blow on the back which
sent me flying up in the air. I thought I was never going to land, but
I did and landed with a thump on my back on top of a large heap of
stones, masonry and rubble. I was helped back to the cover of the last
ruined house in Sedd el Bahr. Soon afterwards the troops advanced and
I was left alone.[55]

Second Lieutenant Reginald Gillett, 2nd Hampshire Regiment, 88th Brigade, 29th
Division

The streets of Sedd el Bahr were full of strange and macabre sights, as witnessed by Lieutenant George Davidson.

The only living things I saw in the village were two cats and a dog. I
was very sorry for a cat that had cuddled close to the face of a dead Turk
in the street, one leg embracing the top of his head. I went up to stroke
and sympathise with it for the loss of what I took to be its master, when
I found that the upper part of the man's head had been blown away,
and the cat was enjoying a meal of human brains.[56]

Lieutenant George Davidson, 89th Field Ambulance, RAMC

When they came to the edge of the village the British looked to their half
left to the last bastion of the Turks, on Hill 141 overlooking the beach.
Once again Doughty Wylie made plans, arranging for the navy to bombard
the redoubt via Tizard, who was still aboard the *River Clyde*. Captain Guy
Nightingale was left in no doubt as to Doughty Wylie's determination to
succeed.

Colonel Doughty Wylie took me up one of the corner turrets of the
old Castle, and pointed out to me the way he intended to carry out
the assault. There was a strong redoubt on the top, but he decided that
the remnants of the three battalions should assault simultaneously
immediately after the bombardment. He was extraordinarily confident
that everything would go well, and the hill be won by sunset, and I
think it was due much to his spirit of confidence that he had been

able to overcome the enormous difficulties with only such exhausted and disorganised troops as he had to deal with. His sole idea and determination was that the hill should be taken that day at all costs. As the time was getting near for the bombardment to cease, the Colonel gave his final orders to the few remaining officers before the assault.[57]

Captain Guy Nightingale, 1st Royal Munster Fusiliers, 86th Brigade, 29th Division

All was ready and the attack went in. Having regained some of their self-confidence, the men were enthusiastic for the fray.

When the order came to fix bayonets the men scarcely waited for any orders, but all joined up together in one mass, and swept cheering up through an orchard and over a cemetery to the first line of wire entanglement, through which was a way out leading past the deserted Turkish trenches to the summit of the hill. On the top was a flat space surrounded by a moat 20 feet deep with only one entrance leading up over it, through which the assaulting troops were led by Colonel Doughty Wylie and Major Grimshaw.[58]

Captain Guy Nightingale, 1st Royal Munster Fusiliers, 86th Brigade, 29th Division

To their left on the beach Captain George Stoney had organised parties of Dublin and Munster Fusiliers ready to join in the attack advancing left of Sedd el Bahr straight up to Hill 141. They were still faced with a formidable barrier of barbed wire. One of the first to reach it was Corporal William Cosgrove, who, at 16 stone and 6 foot 6 inches, was a veritable giant of a man.

The dash was quite 100 yards, and I don't know whether I ran or prayed the faster – I wanted to try and succeed in my work, and I also wanted to have the benefit of dying with a prayer in my mind. Well, some of us got close up to the wire, and we started to cut it with pliers. You might as well try and snip Cloyne Round Tower with a lady's scissors, and you would not hurt yourself either. The wire was of great strength, strained as tight as a fiddle-string, and so full of spikes or thorns that you could not get the cutters between. I threw the pliers from me. 'Pull them up,' I roared. 'Put your arms round them and pull them out of the ground!' I dashed at the first one; heaved and strained, and then it came into my arms the same as you'd lift a child. I believe there was wild cheering when they saw what I was at, but I only heard the screech of the bullets and saw dust rising all round from where they hit. I could not tell how many I pulled up. When the wire was down the rest of the lads came on like 'devils' and, notwithstanding the pulverising fire, they reached the trenches. A machine gun sent some bullets into me, and strange, I was wounded before I reached the trench, though I did not realise it. When I got to the trench I did my own part and later collapsed. One of the bullets struck me in the side, and passed clean through me, took a couple of splinters off my backbone and passed out on my right side.[59]

Corporal William Cosgrove, 1st Royal Munster Fusiliers, 86th Brigade, 29th Division

The men from the beach were joined by those bursting out of the village. Together they surged towards the old fort on Hill 141, racing across the final stretch of open ground.

We did not come under any heavy fire only losing about four men wounded. We rushed the line of trenches and saw the Turks clearing out. Not many getting away alive. The place proved to have been held by only a very few men – certainly if there had been more we could not have got up as easily as we did.[60]

Captain George Stoney, Headquarters, 29th Division

The Turks had been ordered to retire towards Krithia in the late morning, but as this would have left them exposed to fire from the Allied ships, they had decided to try to cling on till nightfall.

Our soldiers were still active and were pinning down the enemy. The enemy was advancing in rushes, he was unable to assault. Many of those who rushed forward were being hit and there were many casualties. But there was no telling in what strength the landing had been made. Not an inch of ground remained which was not shelled either by the shrapnel of the fleet or by the many machine guns of the infantry.[61]

Major Mahmut, 3rd Battalion, 26th Regiment, 9th Division, Fifth Army

The Turks had been fighting for the best part of two days with little in the way of reinforcements. At 13.30 it was decided that, come what may, they would have to retreat. Soon just the few survivors of 10th Company remained on Hill 141. Their position was desperate indeed: trenches smashed, only a few men left on their feet and fast running out of ammunition.

Now even withdrawal was very difficult because the enemy fleet's fire was very intense. There was no information from our units, only enemy could be seen at every hand. It was abundantly clear that the enemy would destroy our soldiers as they retreated with the fire of the fleet, his infantry and his machine guns. In fact our line of retreat had been encircled on right and left. In truth there was no course left but to flee. The distance between us was 500–600 metres.[62]

Major Mahmut, 3rd Battalion, 26th Regiment, 9th Division, Fifth Army

When the final British assault swept up on to Hill 141 at around 14.30 on 26 April, not many Turks made the final stand. Their wounded had to be left, but they were confident that the British would respect them. As they retreated, keeping to ground as best they could, they took every chance to snipe at the advancing British. At least one bullet found its mark.

The men lined round the top edge of the moat firing down on the retreating Turks, who were retiring down their communication trenches in the direction of Achi Baba. It was at this moment that Colonel Doughty Wylie, who had led his men to the last moment, was killed by a shot in the head, dying almost immediately on the summit of the hill he had so ably captured.[63]

Captain Guy Nightingale, 1st Royal Munster Fusiliers, 86th Brigade, 29th Division

Another account of the death of Doughty Wylie exposes the reckless and at times thoughtless nature of his courage.

I was laid down with the company and he was stood up alongside of me, with his orderly. They were shouting to him, 'Get down, sir, you'll get hit!' because there was sniping. He wouldn't and an explosive bullet hit him just below the eye, blew all the side of his face out – and his orderly got killed.[64]

Private William Flynn, 1st Royal Munster Fusiliers, 86th Brigade, 29th Division

That Doughty Wylie had performed a vital role was undeniable. As a senior staff officer he had marshalled his shaken troops and then inspired them in the final assault by his personal example. In this, his performance could hardly have been bettered. But his death was pointless, for though the Turks had been ejected from a defended position they had by no means given up the fight. Hill 141 was hardly Achi Baba, the first day's real objective, and there was much more to be done. Doughty Wylie was desperately needed in his role as staff officer: to help arrange the disembarkation of troops, reorganise scattered formations, and ensure that a logistical framework was in place for the next step of the battle by preparing and distributing coherent plans. But his act of foolish bravado in the moment of triumph cost his own life and apparently also that of his servant, who had little option but to stand by his officer. As a prime example of British overconfidence in the face of dangerous Turkish opposition it is hard to beat.

Shortly after Doughty Wylie's death Lieutenant Colonel Weir De Lancey Williams arrived on top of Hill 141. Immediately recognising the heroism demonstrated by Doughty Wylie, Williams tried to make sure that common decencies were observed in his burial arrangements.

> I found him lying dead inside the castle on top of the hill. As soon as I realised he was dead I took his watch, money and a few things I could find and had him buried where he fell. I had this done at once, having seen such disgusting sights of unburied dead in the village that I could not bear to leave him lying there. This was all done hurriedly as I had to reorganise the line and think of further advances and digging in; we just buried him as he lay and I said the Lord's Prayer over his grave and bid him goodbye. I am firmly of opinion that poor Doughty Wylie realised he would be killed in this war; he was rather a fatalist. I am also convinced that he went singing cheerily to his end.[65]
>
> Lieutenant Colonel Weir De Lancey Williams, Headquarters, 29th Division

Lieutenant Colonel Tizard had only come ashore when Hill 141 was finally captured. He was to be harshly criticised for his performance on V Beach; indeed, he lost the cherished command of his battalion on the morning of 27 April after a somewhat fraught interview with Hunter-Weston. This was the problem: dull proficiency was still regarded as inferior to more eye-catching death-or-glory antics. The British Army of 1915 lacked professionalism in the real business of war; the chaos on the beaches of Helles was testament to that amateurishness.

Nevertheless incompetence on the ground was not the only reason for the British failure at V Beach. Firstly, the outnumbered Turks had fought with a supreme combination of skill and courage. They had stuck to their positions, often holding on beyond the point where surrender was a feasible option and accepting that they might well be butchered when the British finally over-ran them. This was the root cause of the British defeat. Secondly, the British plans had been ludicrously over-optimistic, relying heavily on the Turks not putting up any serious opposition to the naval bombardment. The battleships were stationed too far off the coast for their guns to achieve the necessary accuracy and even when they came in closer their guns' flat trajectory made it almost impossible to hit the Turkish trenches lining the brow of the amphitheatre or tucked away on the reverse slopes. Finally, the commendable imagination shown in the conception of the *River Clyde* scheme had not been matched by an equal attention to detail in its execution. The Trojans of legend had no idea of what lay within the 'gift' left them by the Greeks; that indeed was the whole point. At V Beach the Turks could plainly see the gangways, they knew what would happen when the ship ran aground and they had more than enough time to train their rifles on the exit ports. The British plan, risky at best, demanded a night landing when the Turks would have been unable to discern what was going on. Nor would they have been able to see where to concentrate their fire – important since there were not enough of them to cover all the options. The British High Command had simply not thought the matter through. Hundreds of men paid the price.

8

25 APRIL: KUM KALE AND DIVERSIONS

From the many pale faces among the officers reporting in the early morning it became apparent that although a hostile landing had been expected with certainty, a landing at so many places surprised many and filled them with apprehension.[1]

General Otto Liman von Sanders, Headquarters, Fifth Army

THE TURKISH XV CORPS, commanded by General Weber Pasha, was responsible for the defence of the Asiatic sector on the south side of the Dardanelles, where the main perceived threat was from possible landings at Kum Kale at the entrance to the Straits and in Besika Bay further to the south. The defensive concept was simple: a weak screen would do their best to obstruct the invaders while the main force of the 3rd and 11th Divisions would counter-attack at night, hidden from the naval guns, and throw the invaders back into the sea.

For the Allies, under Hamilton's plans the French, under the command of General Albert d'Amade, were charged with making a landing at Kum Kale in order to protect the Helles landings from the threat of fire from the Turkish Asiatic batteries across the Straits. The 6th Colonial Regiment of the 1st Division would land close to the old demolished fort and the remnants of the village. This was at the tip of what was effectively another peninsula, a low strip of land some two miles long and 500 yards wide running first towards the Orkanie Mound (where Robinson had won

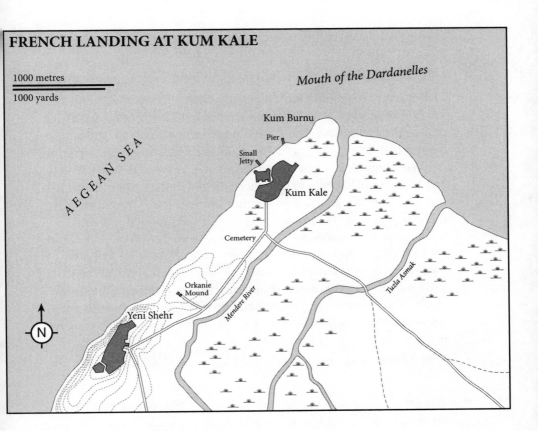

FRENCH LANDING AT KUM KALE

his VC destroying Turkish guns back in February) and then up to the village and demolished battery at Yeni Shehr at a height of 60 feet. On one side was the sea while the other was bounded by the Mendere River. This area was not defended as it was too vulnerable to close-range naval gunfire; instead it was merely patrolled by small detachments, as the Turks planned to hold the line of the river and the high ground at Yeni Shehr. One thing was clear: the French were facing a far more serious conglomeration of Turkish units than the British and Australians. Although their landing place was as unguarded as Anzac, Y Beach or X Beach, the Turkish main lines of defence were fairly close at hand, on the other side of the river. Here, no less than three battalions were waiting, while only a couple of miles further inland were two whole Turkish regiments. Kum Kale was an extremely dangerous undertaking.

The landing was planned for just after dawn on 25 April. As the troopships moved forward the *Jeanne d'Arc* and the Russian cruiser *Askold* began a preparatory bombardment on Kum Kale, while other warships bombarded the surrounding hills.

> The sun pierces the early mist. It emerges above the Gallipoli hills in the hollow of a bay like an enormous globe of blood-red fire. It is a tableau presaging glory. The soldiers on our ship prepare to land and we approach the Asiatic coast. The gunners are at their places. Powerful guns are at our disposal. A first shot is fired. Everybody is dazed. One's ears hurt; the blood goes to one's head. Before we can stuff cotton-wool into our ears a second and a third shot are fired. The outline of the village of Yeni Shehr is now ragged. It is a destruction, certain, methodical, and regular. We see a big house with a red roof. A first shell marks it with a black fountain of smoke, which hides it for a minute from our eyes. It is ruined, and one feels sad; for perhaps it has never sheltered other than peaceful people, perhaps wise and philosophic old men or lovers, only absorbed in themselves and their own passionate embraces. The second shot, hitting it full, disembowels it, scattering it to atoms. The third shell ends its agony.[2]
>
> Medical Officer Joseph Vassal, 6th Colonial Régiment, Brigade Coloniale, 1st Division, CEO

The French landing was dogged by problems. The strong Dardanelles current caused serious delays for the landing tows and it was not until 10.00 that they were able to come ashore at a small wooden jetty near the unoccupied ruined fort of Kum Kale. However, the Turkish coastal detachments had withdrawn to join their comrades behind the Mendere River and the landing was relatively unopposed except for sporadic shell fire from the In Tepe battery further inside the Straits. The fort and village were quickly occupied but the usual confusions and delays inherent in combined operations meant that it took quite some time to get ashore the three battalions of the 6th Colonial Regiment, accompanied by a battery of 75mm field guns from the 8th Artillery Regiment. It was only at 17.30 that an advance was begun on the cemetery and the Orkanie Mound prior to an assault on Yeni Shehr. By this time the Turks had time to react. An ominously stiff resistance pinned the French back into their small beachhead. When at 18.00 an aerial reconnaissance reported the arrival of strong reinforcing columns close to Yeni Shehr, the French attack was abruptly suspended and Kum Kale was readied for defence: trenches dug, loopholes driven through walls, streets barricaded and barbed-wire entanglements put up.

The first of the Turkish counter-attacks burst upon them at 20.30. All that night three battalions from the 3rd Division attacked the French line amid desperate fighting. At one point the French trenches were over-run, only for them to launch a vigorous counter-attack to hurl back the Turks. The situation for the French would have probably been grimmer still but for the fire of the 75mm guns and the supporting fire of the fleet shooting blind into the area of ground in front of their positions.

Off shore Medical Officer Joseph Vassal and his team were hard at work in their makeshift hospital aboard the *Savoie*. Steamboats appeared carrying the masses of wounded men collected from the first aid post established in the lee of the old Kum Kale fort.

> Till the first rays of dawn the next day we are leaning over wounded in an atmosphere of blood, of groans, and of indescribable horrors. We do not stop for a single minute. The wounded still come in. They are mounted on the deck from the bottom of the boats, and from a long line of stretchers. We are able to put six wounded at a time on the big tables of the children's playroom of the *Savoie*. Sometimes not even a groan is to be heard; the silence is impressive. Our fellows are admirable. The wounds of this night are, nevertheless, frightful. A Sergeant Major comes back to us only to die. His chest was crushed by shrapnel; and for a moment we saw his heart, almost bare, still beating. There is a Senegalese with his head torn, a foot missing, and three fingers of a hand gone. Another black, waiting his turn on a chair, is asked, '*Beaucoup malade?*' '*Non, il y en a un peu!*' The doctor looks. Both legs have been torn off by a shell.[3]

> Medical Officer Joseph Vassal, 6th Colonial Regiment, Brigade Coloniale, 1st Division, CEO

Next morning, 26 April, having withstood the Turkish attacks and once more covered by the fire of warships, the French planned to renew their attack on Yeni Shehr. But then, at about 07.00, to their astonishment a party of Turks surrendered.

> The enemy began to wave flags and showed a wish to give themselves up. Eighty Turkish soldiers approached unarmed and were conducted inside our lines. Immediately afterwards many more Turks (several

hundred) arrived in succession but refused to lay down their arms. A parley took place, and Captain Rockel, a very courageous officer, pushed into the middle of the Turks to persuade them to give up their rifles. This officer was surrounded and was not seen again. Others, jostling our men, succeeded in seizing and making off with two machine guns. Our men did not dare to open fire for fear of wounding their own comrades.[4]

Colonel Ruef, Headquarters, Brigade Coloniale, 1st Division, CEO

Private Marius Gondard was one of those caught out when he unwittingly became separated from his platoon.

There were alarms all night long. The Turks were attacking but each time we were able to push them back. And early in the morning they came back, we launched an attack and that's when several Turkish soldiers raised white flags. We stopped firing. The Turks came towards us and a great many surrendered, gave themselves up. We disarmed them as we went along, I don't know how many prisoners there were. And it was then I was taken, because, whilst disarming the prisoners, more Turks arrived and over-ran us. I was taken by both arms by two Turks, with a third walking behind me with a bayonet. I felt surprised. I was ready for anything: I expected I might be injured or killed, perhaps, but certainly not taken prisoner.[5]

Private Marius Gondard, 6th Colonial Regiment, Brigade Coloniale, 1st Division, CEO

It was later realised that this had not been some cunning plot by the Turks but a genuine series of misunderstandings exacerbated by language difficulties. In all the chaos a party of around a hundred Turks managed to slip into the Kum Kale, where they barricaded themselves into some houses. When hostilities resumed the Turks were trapped in the houses, but sold their lives dearly. In the end the 75mm guns were used to blast them away. In view of this desperate resistance it was slightly strange that a further group of about 500 Turks, who were occupying the trenches in the cemetery in front of the village, surrendered at about 15.00. It would seem that the concentrated fire of the 75mm guns ashore and the naval blasting from the flanks had demolished the Turkish trenches and undermined their resolve. From aboard the *Moulouya* transport ship off shore, Second Lieutenant Raymond Weil was watching the fighting.

The Senegalese mounted an attack on the Turkish trenches. We could clearly see the advance of our troops supported by the intense fire from our fleet and a 75mm gun landed ashore. The auxiliary cruiser *Savoie* drew close to the Asiatic coast and opened up a marvellous rapid fire on a covered trench dug by the Turks which we'd just located. It was a veritable bloodbath when the *Savoie* took the trench in enfilade. That ended the battle. Towards the evening a minesweeper loaded with Turkish prisoners passed close by us – what an enthusiastic reaction![6]

Second Lieutenant Raymond Weil, 39th Régiment d'Artillerie, 1st Division, CEO

Meanwhile, at 09.20 on 26 April, orders from Hamilton reached d'Amade requesting that he deploy his Métropolitaine Brigade at Helles to bolster the stalled efforts of the 29th Division. In his acknowledgment of the orders, d'Amade pointed out that his strictly limited remit at Kum Kale had been fulfilled and that he could make no further progress towards Yeni Shehr without reinforcements. An hour later a second order from Hamilton arrived requiring that all remaining French infantry and artillery units be diverted to Helles as soon as possible. As there was now no question of reinforcing his troops ashore at Kum Kale, d'Amade feared for the safety of the isolated detachments and soon after 11.30 asked for permission to withdraw that night, which Hamilton granted. With the sudden mass Turkish surrenders in the afternoon the situation had eased but it was by then too late to reverse the decision. The evacuation could have been tricky but, closely covered by the warships and in the absence of any Turkish night attacks, it all went remarkably smoothly. By dawn on 27 April the Asiatic shore was once again under the complete control of the Turks. The serious nature of the fighting is indicated by the casualty lists: the French had 778 casualties and the Turks 1,730, in addition to having had more than 500 of their men taken prisoner.

HAMILTON HAD INCLUDED TWO purely diversionary operations in his convoluted plans. The first of these was to be carried out by the main body of the RND in the Gulf of Saros, where they were threatening a landing on the Bulair Isthmus. They began operations shortly after dawn on 25 April with a long slow bombardment on the trench lines on the ridges overlooking the flat, swampy isthmus. Then the eleven transports carrying the

RND began their playacting, unshipping their boats, forming up the tows of rowing boats behind steamboats and generally behaving as if an attack were imminent. This had an initial impact, for Liman was pre-occupied with Bulair and indeed rushed there on the morning of 25 April.

> After alarming the 7th Division in the town of Gallipoli and instructing it to march at once in the direction of Bulair, I rode ahead to the heights of Bulair with my German adjutants. On the narrow ridge of Bulair where neither tree nor bush impedes view or gives cover, we had a full view of the upper Saros Gulf. About twenty large hostile ships, some war vessels, some transports, could be counted in front of us. Some individual vessels were lying close in under the steep slopes of the coast. Others were farther out in the gulf or were still underway. From the broadsides of the war vessels came an uninterrupted stream of fire and smoke and the entire coast including our ridge was covered with shells and shrapnel. It was an unforgettable picture. Nowhere, however, could we see any debarking of troops from the transports.[7]
>
> General Otto Liman von Sanders, Headquarters, Fifth Army

This kind of foreplay would not convince for long if it was not followed through. The RND decided to try to add a touch more of a threat by landing a platoon of the Hood Battalion on one of the northern beaches that night to light flares. This seemed likely to be a dangerous expedition and one of the Hood officers, Lieutenant Commander Bernard Freyberg, offered to use his specialist swimming skills to achieve the same result without exposing so many men to risk.

> The boat was painted an angry black, flecked with grey spots, and a Maxim placed at the bows behind the sandbags. The scheme was that Freyberg should be towed out in this ship's boat, escorted by a destroyer to within two miles of the shore. He then should be dropped, swim to the beach and there light some lifeboat flares, while the Maxim on the ship's boat and the guns of the destroyer should make all the noise they could to attract the attention of the enemy. He started out about 9 o'clock and I shall never forget his toilet which consisted of the smearing of his whole person with a black oil-like substance to protect him against the cold of the sea.[8]
>
> Lieutenant Charles Lister, Hood Battalion, 2nd Naval Brigade, RND

The rowing boats were towed by a steam pinnace which set off from the *Grantully Castle* transport ship at 21.00. When they were three miles off shore they slipped their tow ropes and began to head towards shore. Freyberg started his mission from a spot about two miles from shore at 00.40 on 26 April.

> I started swimming to cover the remaining distance, towing a waterproof canvas bag containing three oil flares and five calcium lights, a knife, signalling light and a revolver. After an hour and a quarter's hard swimming in bitterly cold water, I reached the shore and lighted my first flare, and again took to the water and swam towards the east, and landed about 300 yards away from my first flare where I lighted my second and hid among some bushes to await developments; nothing happened, so I crawled up a slope to where some trenches were located the morning before. I discovered they were only dummies, consisting of only a pile of earth about two feet high and 100 yards long, and looked to be quite newly made. I crawled in about 350 yards and listened for some time, but could discover nothing.[9]
>
> Lieutenant Commander Bernard Freyberg, Hood Battalion, 2nd Naval Brigade, RND

Freyberg thought that, although the shore was unoccupied, he could see lights on the surrounding hills. However, he could get no further as he started being afflicted by cramp. He returned to the beach, set off his last flare and swam off into the darkness. In one of the rowing boats bobbing about offshore was Ordinary Seaman Joe Murray, also of the Hood Battalion. Murray gained at least some idea of how cold the water was.

> All of a sudden there was such a flash, such a bloody flash – it was a destroyer setting off a salvo. We couldn't see the sea but we could see the cliffs. As this flash went there was a panic really because it sort of shook us up. Well, we hit something, whether it was driftwood I don't know. We sloped to starboard I know that and I nearly fell out. I was trying to be a sailor – you can't hang on with both hands, you have to do what they do. I went over and my hand was in the water and – oh dear me – it was perishing cold. I don't know how Freyberg survived that swim.[10]
>
> Ordinary Seaman Joe Murray, Hood Battalion, 2nd Naval Brigade, RND

Freyberg was incredibly lucky that, on his return swim, he encountered one of the boats in the pitch dark.

> After swimming for a considerable distance I was picked up by
> Lieutenant Nelson in our cutter some time after 3 a.m. Our cutter, in
> company with the pinnace and the TBD *Kennet,* searched the shore with
> 12-pounders and Maxim fire, but could get no answer from the shore.[11]
>
> Lieutenant Commander Bernard Freyberg, Hood Battalion, 2nd Naval Brigade, RND

Freyberg's was an act of great heroism and physical endurance but, as
Lieutenant Charles Lister regretfully commented, 'The Turks had taken
no notice of their antics.'[12]

The second diversionary operation was a similar demonstration
carried out by six French transports with accompanying destroyers at
Besika Bay on the morning of 26 April. The escort ships began bombarding the local coastline while the transports simulated disembarking their
troops, but the whole affair was short lived. The ships were recalled by
10.00. Yet even that short-lived threat was enough to keep the Turkish
11th Division in location for another day; they would only move off for
deployment across the Straits on 27 April.

FOR ALL HAMILTON'S ATTEMPTS to conceal his intentions, the end
results were unimpressive. Of course Liman was concerned about the situation at Bulair and even at Besika Bay. But the diversions were not serious
enough to maintain Turkish attention for overly long. They only caused a
delay of a day or two in the despatch of divisions to the real landing sites
at Helles and Anzac. Yet Hamilton's scattergun approach of making seven
separate landings and two full-fledged diversionary operations meant that
the Allies did not have sufficient strength of troops landed at any one location to force an emergency response from the Turks. Attacked at almost
every feasible landing site, the Turks were able to hold on for long enough
with local reserves at both Helles and Anzac for Liman to try to work out
what was happening.

> After a while Essad Pasha, commanding the III Corps, arrived on our
> heights and brought some detailed reports. The reports stated that
> British landing attempts at the south point of the peninsula had so far
> been repulsed by the 9th Division, but that the enemy was tenaciously
> bringing up more and more troops. At Gaba Tepe things were going
> well; the enemy had not been able so far to get a footing. But at Ari

Burnu the heights along the coast were in the hands of the British, though the 19th Division was on the march to recapture the former.[13]

General Otto Liman von Sanders, Headquarters, Fifth Army

Once Liman had defined the location and strength of the most serious threats, the diversionary actions ceased to weave their spell. First the 5th and 7th Divisions were put on the march from Bulair towards Anzac and Helles, then a couple of days later the 11th Division was despatched from Asia. At the same time the 15th and 16th Divisions set sail from Constantinople and the 12th Division began the march from Smyrna while as many guns as possible were sent on their way. By the end of April the clock was fast running down for the British invasion force. Meanwhile, on the Western Front there was desperate fighting as the British and French strove to fill the gap in their front line created by the German gas attack which had launched the Second Battle of Ypres on 22 April 1915. The irrelevance of Gallipoli to the outcome of the war could not have been clearer.

9

ANZAC: THE HOLDING PEN

We have been amusing ourselves by trying to discover the longest period of absolute quiet. We have been fighting now continuously for 22 days, all day and all night, and most of us think that absolutely the longest period during which there was absolutely no sound of gun or rifle fire, throughout the whole of that time, was 10 seconds. One man says he was able on one occasion to count 14, but nobody believes him![1]

Colonel John Monash, Headquarters, 4th Australian Brigade, NZ&A Division, AIF

THE ANZAC BRIDGEHEAD was an incredible achievement. Not the winning of it; that had been the meagre results of a thoroughly botched military operation which never had much chance of success. What astounded was that the ANZAC Corps had first secured its fragile lines and then made that small domain all but inviolable, despite the severe pressure exerted by the Turks over the next four weeks. The Anzac line started in the south at the sea, ran up Bolton's Hill, across the 400 Plateau, all along Second Ridge to Quinn's Post, where it petered out, with a gap covered by firepower rather than trenches. The line resumed on Pope's Hill, then, after another gap, over Russell's Top, where it faced the Turkish lines barring The Nek and the route to Chunuk Bair. The line then progressed down the narrow Walker's Ridge to a series of small posts guarding the flank in the foothills by the sea to the north. Just 1,000 yards deep at maximum, only 2,500 yards long and much less than a square mile in total, it was a severely cramped environment.

The Anzacs had taken Hamilton's advice to 'Dig, dig, Dig!',[2] well aware that their own lives depended on disappearing as fast as possible below ground. Day by day the trenches were deepened, dugouts carved out and communications trenches dug. Everywhere was under fire; even rifle bullets could reach the beach and no one was safe. The front line and posts on Second Ridge were just a few yards from their Turkish counter-points and were totally enfiladed from higher up the ridges. Just behind them were the precipitous slopes dropping down into Monash Valley. That and Shrapnel Gully were the main thoroughfares, but they were still under the constant threat of machine gun and sniper fire from the head of the valley, where the grid of Turkish trenches (later known as the Chess-board) barred all routes from Second Ridge on to Baby 700. The whole of the ANZAC Corps had to be supplied from the 300-yard-long shallow beach with makeshift piers that were under intermittent speculative shell fire from Gaba Tepe. Every tin of bully beef, every bullet for their rifles, every drop of water had to be landed under indirect fire, stored somewhere and then carried up to the front lines. The continued occupation of Anzac was a testimony to the hardiness, courage and sheer bloody-mindedness of the men of Australia and New Zealand.

By 28 April the physical exhaustion of the 1st Australian Division was evident and Hamilton had agreed to assign four battalions of the RND, who were returning from their diversionary duties at Bulair, to hold the line while Birdwood's units reorganised and got a little desperately needed rest. The Anzacs, always confident in their own manhood, decried the physical immaturity and callow state of the marines, who were largely wartime recruits and by no means the finished article as soldiers. They were to face a severe challenge when they began to take over the line between Courtney's Post and across 400 Plateau on the night of 28 April. In the pitch dark, with the rain pouring down and contradictory orders being shouted from all sides, they scrambled up the near-vertical scrubby hillside and took over trenches that were often still choked with the dead and wounded. It was a terrifying introduction to warfare at its most basic.

By this time the Turks had also received the reinforcements despatched by General Liman von Sanders following his assessment of the threat posed by the Anzac landing. As a result Lieutenant Colonel Mustafa Kemal was able to launch a major night attack timed for 04.00 on Saturday 1 May to avoid the threat of Allied naval intervention. The Turks poured out of Legge Valley, swirling up Wire Gully and over-running some of the isolated forward posts. However, most of their attacks broke down in the blast of rifle and machine gun fire from the much maligned British marines.

> At dawn the Turks attacked in mass and the situation looked critical, but before arriving at the trench they retired with heavy losses. My machine gun officer was killed; he was using his rifle during the attack and got a bullet through the head. I borrowed a periscope from one of my subalterns to try and spot a machine gun that was worrying us considerably. As soon as I got it in line with the top of the trench a bullet smashed it in my hands. I went to inform the officer, but he had just been killed. Snipers are a menace, they seem to be everywhere and are very clever at concealing themselves. The sun and flies are terrible and one cannot obtain water to quench the thirst. The dead Turks in front and our own fellows lying at the back of us are beginning to smell. The din was terrific: shouting and blowing of bugles and the whole place was lit up with fires that were raging in the scrub. During the attack I caught about thirty of them in a bunch coming towards our gun position. I emptied a belt of ammunition into them at 60 yards range with good effect.[3]
>
> Private Bertram Wilson, Chatham Battalion, Royal Marine Brigade, RND

Both sides were now intent on testing how far they could get at Anzac. Birdwood ordered a night attack on Baby 700 to be carried out by the NZ&A Division, bursting out of Monash Valley at 19.15 after a 15-minute supporting bombardment. In the end everything went wrong. None of the units were properly briefed and the Otago Battalion in particular had nowhere near enough time to get ready to launch a concerted assault. Yet still the 13th and 16th Battalions went into their attack at the head of Monash Valley on either side of the Bloody Angle, just below the Chessboard. With them was the distinctly unimpressed Private Harry Murray.

> Sheer military impossibilities with such troops and munitions as were at our disposal, but one must learn by bitter experience; not that we needed telling, even then. It was a sad and terrible business. The machine gunners advanced with the infantry and as we topped the ridge our men fell like grass before the sweep of an expert mower, but

most tragic of all, one of our own machine guns was firing too low and added to the massacre until we got a message back and stopped it. Disaster on disaster: following fast and following faster.[4]

Private Harry Murray, 16th (Western Australia and South Australia) Battalion, 4th Brigade, NZ&A Division, AIF

The Otago Battalion arrived, some ninety minutes late, at the jumping-off point and at 20.45 lunged forward from Pope's Hill with no artillery support. They too came under heavy fire and their attack was bogged down roughly in a tenuous line alongside the Australians but well short of the Chessboard. That night was a desperate affair but with the coming of the dawn things just got worse, especially when a salvo of their own artillery shells managed to fall smack in the 16th Battalion. The sad remnants were then joined by elements of the Chatham and Portsmouth Battalions who had been moved up in reserve. Private Harry Baker recalled many years later what happened as the Turks launched a sustained counter-attack from the front.

We fired away at all the Turks who kept advancing. They were then about one hundred and fifty yards away and they came up in almost mass formation so we had very easy targets. An Australian came and lay next to me and on his right another man scaled this steep slope and it turned out to be Major Armstrong of the Portsmouth Royal Marines. Captain Richards was next to him and all the way to the right were men shoulder to shoulder lying on the ground. No cover at all, just lying on the ridge.[5]

Private Harry Baker, Chatham Battalion, Royal Marine Brigade, RND

As the Turks attacked from their front the complex nature of the landscape allowed a German machine gun in German Officer's Trench, just north of Wire Gully, to get a clear enfilade shot at the men lying on the open ridge facing the Chessboard.

Suddenly a machine gun crackled away at right angles to us, we were firing ahead and it was even behind us. This machine gun went along and that killed every man on the ridge except the Australian and me. We were the only two left. The Australian said, 'The bastards can't kill me, they've had lots of tries, they can't kill me!' I looked again. The machine gun started barking again behind us. It was knocking the sand up and that covered every man again. Every man, it came right along. I felt the bullets thud into the Aussie and he never spoke again. I felt as though I'd been hit by a donkey and I had a bullet through the right foot. When I saw those bullets coming along and I knew that it would be the end of me if they came along far enough. They say your past comes up but I can say truthfully that I hadn't got much past at nineteen and all I thought of was, 'Am I going to live?' That's all I thought, that's what struck me. 'Am I going to be lucky?' Because I couldn't see how I could be with all these bullets coming along and I waited for it – it was inevitable.[6]

Private Harry Baker, Chatham Battalion, Royal Marine Brigade, RND

Luckily for Baker the machine gun stopped after the bullet had slammed into his foot. However, he wasn't out of trouble yet. Even as they were destroyed from behind, the Turks in front charged forwards to over-run their position.

I lay there and I didn't know what to do. The Turks came and prodded various men with their bayonets, fortunately they didn't poke me, and I could hear them jabbering away and then they moved away again. 'Well,' I thought. 'I must do something!' So I gave myself a push off and went bumpity-bumpity right down to the bottom of the ravine over dead men, rifles, bush, all kinds of things.[7]

Private Harry Baker, Chatham Battalion, Royal Marine Brigade, RND

Baker was eventually rescued and evacuated. The corpses of his comrades lay up on the ridge, rotting and turning black in the hot sun for the rest of the campaign. It became known as Dead Man's Ridge.

The attack merely confirmed that, while the Turks could not break into Anzac, nor could the ANZAC Corps break out. So the digging continued on both sides. It was back-breaking work, though they attained greater security with every shovelful – all this against the backdrop of constant skirmishing that accompanies trench warfare between well-matched adversaries. Small-scale raids, sapping and patrols pushed out into No Man's Land. Along much of the line, patrols were impossible, the trenches being only a cricket pitch or so apart. But to the south there was a relatively open area of ridges and valleys descending from 400 Plateau towards Gaba Tepe. One series of patrols seems to emphasise the spirit of adventurous soldiering that was to become an Anzac tradition. Their ultimate purpose was to try and establish the position of the dreaded 'Beachy Bill' gun, or more likely guns, that were harassing the beach and was believed to be hidden in the Olive Grove sector.

A first patrol was sent out on 9 May and succeeded in locating a source of fresh water not 1,000 yards from the arid Anzac beachhead. They also located two Turkish camps and gained a slightly better impression of what was going on nearer Gaba Tepe. When this was reported to the 1st Division staff it was decided to repeat the patrol on the night of 13 May. This time Sergeant Joseph Will and Bombardier Albert Orchard were sent out, accompanied by Major Thomas Blamey. The Turks had noticed signs of the previous patrol and there seemed far more sentries in evidence.

> To dodge the sentry we turned slightly to our left and passed through the line of sentries, and reached the stream. I made a noise in climbing down the bank and shuffling footsteps were heard on the bank at the far side of the creek. The scrub gave good cover and we were not spotted, although several of the enemy passed within a few feet of the creek. We made our way snake-fashion towards some scrub, crossing a stretch of almost clear ground, when we heard footsteps on our left and a party of men came straight towards us. We were doing the caterpillar act at the moment: myself in front, then the Major, followed by Sergeant Will, with about 10 paces distance between.[8]
>
> Bombardier Albert Orchard, 9th Battery, 3rd Field Artillery Brigade, 1st Division, AIF

The men hugged the ground as closely as possible hidden in the scrub and awaited their fate. The Turkish patrol came up to within fifteen yards of their hiding place.

> I will never forget the many and varied thoughts that passed through my mind during those few minutes of suspense. Had the sentry in the scrub seen us? Was he giving directions to the party of Turks for our destruction? We were like rats in a trap. The Turks moved on towards us. We had quietly fixed bayonets and as they came nearer we realised that they did not know of our presence – surprise on our part was our only chance. They came on an angle – almost like echelon – and would reach me first. There were nine in the party, the sentry having joined the patrol. The leader was within about 5 feet before spotting me. He raised his rifle and bayonet to strike, but Major Blamey fired his revolver and killed him. Will and myself, who were armed with rifles, also fired

rapidly at the Turks, bunched together – making an excellent target for us. Seven of the enemy were down in about that many seconds. One ran towards the scrub and the only other able to run made towards the creek. That being our only line of retreat, we collectively accounted for that one and then closed up to see how we had fared, to find that we had not a scratch between us. In all we had fired about fifteen to twenty rounds. We had raised a hornet's nest around us and had a mile or more of enemy territory to cover before we could hope to be safe. By the time we reached the creek, Turks were running in all directions and the noise they made was terrific, so that we had no need to worry over the noise we made as we ran towards our lines.[9]

Bombardier Albert Orchard, 9th Battery, 3rd Field Artillery Brigade, 1st Division, AIF

On their return they received a soldier's reward – a swig from Blamey's water bottle, which to their delight was not filled with water! But it was obvious that any further patrols would meet with disaster and the efforts to locate 'Beachy Bill' had been thwarted.

At Anzac there was a drip-drip of casualties caused by the close-quarter nature of the fighting. Everyone was at risk; rank or status gave no guarantee of protection. A small mistake in judging dead ground or a second's hesitation in crossing a vulnerable spot could be fatal. Thus it could be no surprise when Major General Sir William Bridges was killed in Monash Valley on 15 May. Captain Horace Viney was on his way to the beach with a working party when he met Bridges coming up the gully to visit the headquarters of the 1st Light Horse Brigade in Monash Valley. As they were not part of his 1st Division it is difficult to justify the dangers Bridges so rashly incurred.

To negotiate Monash Gully safely one had to walk on alternate sides of it according to how the valley twisted and turned. Those who knew it could go up and down it comparatively safely by keeping under cover on one side until a twist in the gully exposed that side to the Turkish fire. It was then necessary to dart across the gully, a distance of from 10 to 20 yards, and gain shelter of the opposite bank. The Turks had marked down the crossing places and had them covered by snipers or machine guns. The worst crossing places had been protected by barricades, but they were neither high enough, nor long enough to give complete immunity. Having been up and down Monash Gully several times I had learned by painful experience just where the dangerous spots were. On several occasions I had beaten the Turkish snipers in my dashes across the gully only by inches and I consequently did not loiter unduly in crossing such places. One of the most dangerous was a distance of about 5 yards between the end of a barricade at the top end of the gully near a gravel pit, where an ambulance collecting post had been established, and a small spur on the opposite side of the gully.[10]

Captain Horace Viney, 3rd (South Australian & Tasmanian) Light Horse Regiment, 1st Light Horse Brigade, NZ&A Division, AIF

After a brief conversation Viney felt it beholden upon him to warn Bridges and his party of the dangers lurking higher up the gully.

I impressed on them that they must keep on the right-hand side of the gully until they came to the ambulance collecting station and also that the only danger spot before they reached Brigade Headquarters was the 5-yard dash across the gully from the end of the barricade there. If they crossed that at speed they would be quite safe. I was very emphatic about the necessity of crossing that spot quickly, and not only because of the machine gun the Turks had trained on it, but also because I had noticed that General Bridges was becoming less and less inclined to dash across the gully at those places where it was necessary to do so. I think that he was of the opinion that I had exaggerated the danger.[11]

Captain Horace Viney, 3rd (South Australian & Tasmanian) Light Horse Regiment, 1st Light Horse Brigade, NZ&A Division, AIF

Bridges reached the barricade and then talked for a while with the medical officers. After parting from them he went to cross the gully but in doing so he seems to have half-stopped and turned his head as if to speak again. A Turkish sniper seized his chance and Bridges was seriously wounded in the right thigh by a bullet which severed the major blood vessels. Only the immediate presence of medical assistance saved his life there and then, but he had lost far too much blood to have a decent chance of survival. Amputation was an option, but his age – fifty-four – militated against that. The result was to be expected: gangrene struck and Bridges took his by then inevitable fate with an admirable sangfroid, saying, 'Anyway, I have commanded an Australian Division for nine months.'[12] He died aboard a hospital ship on 18 May.

Any criticism of Bridges as a military commander has to be tempered by an acknowledgment of the awful confusion of the landing at Anzac, which left him doing little more than fire-fighting the endless calls for reinforcements that poured into his headquarters. On the other hand, although he had made his personal reconnaissance of Second Ridge before 09.00, once he was back in the beach area he did not attempt to seize control of the situation. In particular he allowed *de facto* control of events to pass to Colonel Sinclair-MacLagan; this was an abrogation of his command responsibility. Throughout Bridges demonstrated considerable courage, but, like many British senior officers, he was far too willing to expose himself to unnecessary personal danger, thereby leaving his division leaderless at a crucial time.

The death of Bridges was just one incident among many that encapsulated a strange new way of life for the soldiers of the ANZAC Corps. The low-key but deadly fighting generated a continuous aural backdrop to their existence that could vary from the simple crack of a passing bullet to a veritable cacophony.

> The noises of the battlefield are numerous and varied, and after a little while it is quite easy to distinguish the different sounds. The bullet which passes close by – say, within 10 or 20 feet – has a gentle purring hum, like a low caressing whistle, long drawn out. The bullet which passes well overhead, especially if fired from a long range, has a sharp sudden crack like a whip, and really feels as if it is very close. Our own rifle fire listened to from behind the firing-line sounds like a low rumble or growl. Our machine guns are exactly like the rattle of a kettledrum. The enemy's shrapnel sounds like a gust of wind in a wintry gale, swishing through the air and ending in a loud bang and a cloud of smoke, when the shell bursts. Our own artillery is the noisiest of all, both the discharge of the guns and the bursting of the shells being ear-splitting, with a reverberating echo that lasts 20 or 30 seconds.[13]
>
> Colonel John Monash, Headquarters, 4th Australian Brigade, NZ&A Division, AIF

By mid May what the Anzacs needed were the kind of high-angle howitzers that could fire up over the ridges and drop shells on to the Turks lurking behind. One obviously available spare gun was the 6-inch howitzer that had been fixed aboard the *Prince George* during the naval phase of the campaign. Regimental Sergeant Major David Hepburn and his howitzer were brought ashore and attached to the New Zealanders on the left of Anzac with a makeshift gun detachment of Royal Marines. Hepburn was a gunnery expert but he had never even conceived of the kind of problems he faced at Anzac.

We had to fire over two successive ridges each 400 feet high at a target only 1,300 yards away. We could not see the target. We had the sea at our backs and that was the only direction in which we did not fire. On one occasion we fired in one direction, then turned the gun completely round and fired in the other direction. One afternoon we received a message, 'Engage hostile heavy gun!' Out came the map and from the map we laid our gun. It pointed bang over our own headquarters! It is ticklish work when the shells only just slither over the crests and when our target is only 30–100 yards from our own trenches. I never did get over the idea of firing so close to our own men.[14]

Regimental Sergeant Major David Hepburn, Royal Garrison Artillery

Sergeant Major Hepburn was not alone in having to adjust to the new problems and confusions of operations at Anzac. The front line positions were vulnerable to the slightest advance of the Turks. This would not matter at Helles where there was some room to breathe (though not too deeply). At Anzac a retreat of just twenty or thirty yards at one of the posts along Second Ridge could unlock the whole position. This would prove very tempting to the Turks: just one great heave and surely Anzac would be doomed.

THE TURKS RECEIVED a large reinforcement when their 2nd Division reached Gallipoli on 16 May. The new reservoir of manpower gave them a numerical superiority that reached the dizzy heights of 2 to 1. The temptation was too much and, with Enver's approval, a general night attack was ordered along the line. The 2nd Division was to act as a battering ram in the centre and with the 19th, 5th and 16th Divisions they were to smash through the apparently vulnerable Anzac lines and sweep them into the sea. The mass attack was planned for 03.30 on 19 May. Unfortunately for the Turks, the Anzacs knew they were coming, for it was difficult to conceal such large-scale troop movements from reconnaissance aircraft. When the Turks began a long slow barrage at 17.00 on 18 May, the warning orders went out and the Anzacs ready and waiting.

A deep brooding silence reigned, broken only at intervals by the faintest rattle of accoutrements or a quietly muttered word. The shadowy outline of the head and shoulders of one's neighbour intensified the unreality of the scene, due to the lines of his body being lost in the darkness of the narrow trench which the faint cold light of the morning stars failed to penetrate. At long last word passed from mouth to mouth, uttered quietly as though we were afraid to speak, that the outposts had come in and that 'Jacko' was on the move. One experienced a slight involuntary shiver that might have been due to the chill morning air, a tingling, creeping sensation at the base of the skull which passed down the spine and thoughts which had moved sluggishly now took on a racing pace. Would the impending attack succeed? Would bayonet work be necessary? One tried to picture what was going on out there, seeing in the mind's eye figures creeping, creeping stealthily in the vain hope of catching us unprepared.[15]

Corporal Thomas McNamara, 11th (Western Australia) Battalion, 3rd Brigade, 1st Division, AIF

Private Charles Duke had returned to his unit after spraining his ankle on 25 April and was engaged in digging a sap with a Private Chapman out in No Man's Land on the side of Wire Gully.

I looked over the top of the trench and to my amazement saw a Turk running across the skyline, moving towards our trenches and was quickly followed by others. Almost before I could warn Chapman, all hell seemed to break loose from the Australian trenches. Chapman and I dived through the sap to get through to our mates. All hell had been let loose but that is putting it mildly. We were waist high above the parapet pumping ten rounds rapid into him as quickly as we could fire and reload. Above all the hellish din one could hear their trumpets blowing, shouts from their officers, no doubt exhorting them on and shrill cries of, 'Allah! Allah!' from the men. They got Allah all right![16]

Private Charles Duke, 4th (New South Wales) Battalion, 1st Brigade, 1st Division, AIF

This was the Anzacs' chance for revenge: the waiting was over, now for the slaughter.

From flank to flank the darkness was stabbed with licking flashes of cordite and the stutter of machine guns joined into the harsh discord of the rifle fire and the hard smack of field guns. Shells screamed overhead, and when they burst with a crash the upper darkness was pierced as with fiery breath and with a high pitched, droning whine the shrapnel pellets came to earth. The air was filled with dust and acrid fumes.[17]

Corporal Thomas McNamara, 11th (Western Australia) Battalion, 3rd Brigade, 1st Division, AIF

As the Turks attacked they ran into a storm of small arms fire while the machine guns beat every inch of the ground in front of the vital posts teetering on the edge of Monash Valley. Shells crashed down from the Anzac gunners firing on fixed lines. Perhaps with surprise the Turks might have achieved something, but surprise was always unlikely.

> In the 9th Battalion the fire was so rapid and continuous that the hot rifle bolts began to jam and had to be well-oiled. When rifle oil ran short bacon fat was used. Sometimes the man on the fire-step would borrow the rifle of the support man standing behind him and hand his own rifle down for it to cool, but this did not always suit the support man, for in a number of cases he said to his mate, 'No, you get down and let me have a go!' [18]
>
> Major Alfred Salisbury, 9th (Queensland) Battalion, 3rd Brigade, 1st Division, AIF

In some places the Turks' sheer weight of numbers made it a close-run thing. At Courtney's Post they did, just for a moment, break into the front line, thereby threatening the whole of the Anzac position. Here they encountered the redoubtable Acting Lance Corporal Albert Jacka – a man, it seems, of few words.

> Great battle at 3 a.m. Turks captured large portion of our trench. D Company called into the front line. Lieutenant Hamilton shot dead. I led a section of men and recaptured the trench. I bayoneted two Turks, shot five, took three prisoners and cleared the whole trench. I held the trench alone for 15 minutes against a heavy attack.[19]
>
> Lance Corporal Albert Jacka, 14th (Victoria) Battalion, 4th Brigade, NZ&A Division, AIF

This dry diary note conceals the dreadful confusions of pitch-black night fighting in the complex twists and turns of the trenches at Courtney's Post. Jacka had set a small group of men firing rifles and throwing bombs to create a diversion while he manoeuvred himself behind the Turks to launch the sudden vicious attack that swiftly overwhelmed them. This would earn him the first Australian VC of the war.

Not far away Lance Corporal William Beech of the 2nd Battalion ran back from a forward sap overlooking Owen's Gully which separated Johnston's Jolly and Lone Pine. They had managed to beat off the first attack but now he was requesting reinforcements. One of just two men to respond was Private John Adams. Together they moved gingerly back up the sap.

On reaching the head of it we found five of our men dead shot through the head. Thus a periscope was essential to our very existence and one was found under the bodies. Beech immediately put it up and was alarmed by what he saw. Taking the periscope from him, I, too, received a shock at the sight of what I estimated to be four battalions of Turks forming up for another attack. Bombs were as distant as the moon, our only weapons being rifles and bayonets. Had we attempted to aim over the top we would have exposed our head and shoulders, and have immediately followed our dead pals. Beech, with tears running down his cheeks, momentarily criticised our awful predicament, and remarked, 'It's hell to see this mass of Turks and not being able to aim at them!' With a periscope fixed to a rifle, it would be possible, he said, to fire accurately without personal danger. Beech said that he would return to Captain Dignam and let him know that the Turks were massing for another attack. My mate and I did not think that he should go, because this would weaken the post. However, he left. It looked as though we were doomed, but we decided to stick to our job. Poking our rifles over the top, we pointed them down the gully and blazed away in the direction of the Turks. Occasionally we glanced through the periscope. Officers were shouting excitedly and striking their men across the backs and legs with swords in an attempt to get them into position. A few bugle calls and commands were then made, and on they came until their flanks were exposed to the withering fire of the 3rd Battalion on Johnston's Jolly, and the 2nd Battalion on Lone Pine. The flanks were thus mown down and the attack was doomed. In vain the officers at the bottom of the ravine shouted and waved their arms frantically to the troops in the centre to continue the attack. But the Turks crawled about the scrub bewildered. Some of the Turks came very close to our post without observing it – so close, in fact, that we could almost have prodded them. Somewhere about this time Beech returned with a couple of men, and we all blazed away blindly at the Turks a few feet away.[20]

Private John Adams, 2nd (New South Wales) Battalion, 1st Brigade, 1st Division, AIF

By 05.00 the Turkish attacks had clearly failed, although further sporadic attempts were made throughout the morning. In all the Turks suffered approximately 10,000 casualties. It was later estimated that during this time the Anzacs fired some 950,000 small arms rounds and 1,400 shells.

The true situation was now clear to the Turks. While the Australians' position looked weak, vulnerable to just one mighty effort to throw them into the sea, in fact it had several inherent strengths that were not immediately obvious. It was almost impossible to cross a No Man's Land defended by alert infantry armed with bolt-action rifles and machine guns, with artillery support, unless an artillery barrage had already suppressed their ability to open fire at the crucial moment. This was a universal truth of the Great War that the Allies had discovered often enough on the Peninsula; now the Turks, too, learnt that lesson.

> The line which they held was a bent line with indentations and salients which defended each other by flanking fire. Besides the front firing line there were trenches, suitable for giving support fire, close behind this line. Immediately behind this second line it was very suitable for positioning the enemy reserve in safety. It was a perfect defensive position with ammunition and bomb dumps; arms, especially machine guns; perfect and completely adequate manpower; with naval aid immediately to the rear.[21]
>
> Lieutenant Colonel Mehmet Sefik, Headquarters, 27th Regiment, 9th Division, Fifth Army

The Turks would never again try a general attack; instead, they would concentrate on more localised assaults intended to improve their tactical position.

Meanwhile, one Australian had also learnt a lesson from the fighting on the morning of 19 May. Lance Corporal William Beech was not a man to let inspiration fade and he at once set to work to design and construct a viable periscope rifle. When Major Blamey, a staff officer of 1st Division, was touring the trenches a few hours later he found Beech grimly struggling with assorted bits of wood, glass and wire trying to adapt a rifle so that the upper periscope mirror looked straight along the rifle sights, which view was then reflected in the lower mirror to allow the rifleman to take aim while staying safely under cover. Blamey recognised the brilliant simplicity of the idea and within a few days Beech was supervising a veritable factory churning out periscope rifles. Over the coming months these rifles would allow the Anzacs to establish a superiority of fire which made it death for a Turk to look over the parapet. The Turks would not get their own periscope rifles until late August.

One after effect of the failed Turkish attack was soon evident to everyone at Anzac. The piles of dead bodies sprawled in their thousands where they fell soon made it unbearable for the living as the blazing sun unlocked their putrid secrets and spread the stench of death all over the area. In the end, after a period of negotiations in which neither side wished to betray any weakness, an armistice was arranged to clear No Man's Land of its grim harvest. The arrangements were complex, as neither side could take risks of treachery or subterfuge. A line was marked out with wooden sticks and white rags, along the middle of No Man's Land. On one side the Turks would bury the dead; on the other the Anzacs would be responsible. At 07.30 on 24 May the fifty-strong delimiting parties from each side crossed the wire and moved into No Man's Land. They spread out the whole length of the line, one man from each side about every 100 yards. Every Anzac was provided with two packets of cigarettes, one to smoke and one for the nearest Turk. Lieutenant Colonel Percy Fenwick, a senior New Zealand medical officer, was appointed as delimiting officer during the armistice.

> The Turkish dead lay so thick that it was almost impossible to pass without treading on their bodies. The stench was awful. The Turkish doctor gave me some pieces of wool on which he poured some scent and asked me to put them into my nostrils. I was glad to do so. The awful destructive power of high explosives was very evident. Huge holes, surrounded with circles of corpses blown to pieces, were scattered about the area over which we walked. Everywhere lay the dead – swollen, black and hideous – and over all a nauseating stench that made one feel desperately sick. As we moved along the plateau the trenches became closer and closer together. In one place I calculated the distance between the Turks and ours was only 17 feet. I made this calculation from the fact that four Turks lay head to heel; the front Turk had his hand actually on the side of our trench; the back one had his feet touching his own trench. He had been killed as he leapt over the trench wall.[22]

Lieutenant Colonel Percy Fenwick, Headquarters, NZ&A Division, NZEF

Up on Pope's Hill, Brigadier General John Monash was watching the scene with Major General Alexander Godley. The politeness with which the truce was observed was almost surreal.

We noticed a Turk about 100 yards away trying to repair a loophole in a Turkish trench. We signed to a Turkish officer pointing to it, and he at once understood and ran over to the man and gave him a sound belting with a stick. He then returned to us and still in sign language, with a polite salute, expressed his regrets at the stupidity of the soldier, and then very politely intimated that he would esteem it a favour if we refrained from using our field glasses, because, of course, doing so would give us an unfair advantage.[23]

Brigadier General John Monash, Headquarters, 4th Australian Brigade, NZ&A Division, AIF

And, as ever, the individual soldiers found it all but impossible not to identify with the Turks they encountered. They may have been their enemies, but if anyone understood the privations and horrors of Anzac then it was their opposite numbers, trapped on the same small battlefield.

We stood together some 12 feet apart, quite friendly, exchanging coins and other articles, and in some cases were able to communicate. A Turk gave me a beautiful Sultan's guard's belt buckle made of brass with a silver star and crescent embossed with the Sultan's scroll in Arabic. All I had to give him in exchange were a few coins. Our troops carried the dead Turkish bodies over the dividing line and the Turkish troops did the same for our dead. We also handed their rifles back to them. These rifles were lying around the ground, but we first removed their bolts. The armistice lasted until approximately 6 p.m. and almost immediately the Turks opened fire on our parapets. We were once again enemies.[24]

Corporal Charles Livingstone, 6th (New South Wales) Light Horse, 2nd Light Horse Brigade, AIF

THE SITUATION AT ANZAC may have been static, but elsewhere the war was changing. The ANZAC Corps presence was underpinned by the Royal Navy. The warships' guns protected the soldiers, but even more important the navy maintained the supply chain that stretched right back to Blighty. Any break in the integrity of that chain was a mortal threat to Anzac. What the men most dreaded was the arrival of German submarines in the eastern Mediterranean. It was not long before they were facing exactly that. The U-21, under the command of Captain Otto von Hersing, had set off from Germany on 25 April and reports of her progress had been tracked by the Admiralty with considerable trepidation. When it became evident that her arrival off Gallipoli could shortly be expected a series of anti-submarine precautions was introduced.

A first step was to expedite the return home of the *Queen Elizabeth*, but measures were also taken to keep the pre-dreadnoughts safe as far away as possible while they carried out their support bombardments. At a stroke the number of pre-dreadnoughts on station off Anzac was reduced to just one, but they were still trusting to the efficacy of the torpedo nets that were hung out from their long booms. In addition, all watertight doors below decks were closed tight and anyone not actually on watch below decks was kept on the upper deck in an effort to try to reduce casualties should the torpedoes strike home.

Meanwhile, the U-21 had reached Helles on 25 May. Her early attacks had been thwarted by a combination of alert destroyers and the adroit evasive manoeuvring of the battleship *Vengeance*. Now von Hersing moved off Anzac Cove looking for easier prey. He arrived just after noon and immediately began stalking the *Triumph*, coolly evading the accompanying destroyer *Chelmer*.

> We dived to seventy feet and headed toward the monster, passing far below the lines of patrol craft. Their propellers, as they ran above us, sounded a steady hum. For four and a half hours after I caught sight of the ship I manoeuvred the U-21 for a torpedo shot, moving here and there and showing the periscope on the smooth surface of the sea for only the briefest moments. In the conning tower my watch officer and I stood with bated breath. We were groping toward a deadly position – deadly for the magnificent giant of war on the surface above. 'Out periscope!' HMS *Triumph* stood in formidable majesty, broadside to us, and only 300 yards away. 'Torpedo – fire!' My heart gave a great leap as I called the command. And now one of those fearfully still, eventless moments. Suspense and eagerness held me in an iron grip. Heedless of all else, I left the periscope out. There! And I saw the telltale streak of white foam darting through the water. It headed swiftly away from the point where we lay, and headed straight – yes, straight and true.[25]
>
> Captain Otto von Hersing, U-21

Corporal Fred Brookes was in charge of the two starboard 14-pounder guns in the waist of the ship. At about 12.30 a periscope was sighted.

I gave the order to fire to my two guns but the shells dropped over. I reduced the range but before I could fire the second salvo a torpedo was speeding towards us. My foremost gun tried to depress and hit the torpedo in a forlorn effort. The torpedo struck the ship just below my foremost gun. The explosion shook the ship and she heeled to starboard and then she righted herself before heeling again to starboard and turning turtle in 12 minutes. The explosion blew off all the bunker lids and covered everyone on the starboard side in coal dust. The water cast up by the explosion came down in torrents and I hung on to a stanchion to prevent myself being washed over the side. When it subsided I missed the Private whose duty was beside me and I surmised that he had been washed overboard. I had often rehearsed in my mind what route I should take under such circumstances. The subconscious voice was saying, 'Over to the fore-and-after bridge, along the bridge and on to the after shelter deck, out on the after torpedo boom and drop into the "ditch".' As the voice directed so I took that route and dropped into the sea and swam clear of the ship. I watched the ship heeling over and the torpedo booms on the port side rising up with the nets hanging down from them, and, caught in the meshes of the net by their fingers and toes, were men who had attempted to climb down them.[26]

Corporal Fred Brookes, Royal Marines, HMS *Triumph*

Trawlers and destroyers raced towards the *Triumph* to pick up the survivors who were bobbing about in the sea. The speed of their response meant that they only lost some seventy-three men. Meanwhile, Captain Otto von Hersing was trying to escape the scene.

A huge cloud of smoke leaped out of the sea. In the conning tower we heard first a dry, metallic concussion and then a terrible, reverberating explosion. It was a fascinating and appalling sight to see, and I yearned with every fibre to keep on watching the fearful picture; but I had already seen just about enough to cost us our lives. The moment that dread white wake of the torpedo was seen on the surface of the water, the destroyers were after me. They came rushing from every direction. 'In periscope!' And down we went. I could hear nothing but the sound of propellers above me, on the right and on the left. Why hadn't I dived the moment after the torpedo left? The two seconds I had lost were like years now. With that swarm converging right over our heads, it surely seemed as if we were doomed. Then a flash crossed my brain. 'Full speed ahead,' I called, and ahead we went right along the course the torpedo had taken, straight toward the huge craft we had hit. It was foolhardy, I admit, but I had to risk it. Diving as deeply as we dared, we shot right under the sinking battleship. It might have come roaring down on our heads – the torpedo had hit so fair that I rather expected it would. And then the U-boat and its huge prey would have gone down together in an embrace of death. That crazy manoeuvre saved us. I could hear the propellers of destroyers whirring above us, but they were hurrying to the place where we had been.[27]

Captain Otto von Hersing, U-21

As a result of the sinking of the *Triumph* the reassurance of permanent battleship support had gone for good; now they would only appear on special occasions.

THE SUMMER SAW a steady series of refinements added to the defences at Anzac. As it became evident that the troops would be there for a while, makeshift expedients carried out in the first few days were gradually replaced by more permanent solutions to the problems. Tunnels replaced dashes across the open or enfiladed communication trenches and dugouts became ever more sophisticated. One of the best examples occurred at Quinn's Post right at the sharp end of the whole position. Quinn's Post had become a feared death trap. Overlooked from all sides, it was considered fatal to even peek over the top for fear of the Turkish snipers. Sapping by both sides had reduced No Man's Land at some points to a few yards or a sandbag barricade. Bombs rained down, with only wire netting to stop them from landing in the trench alongside the long-suffering garrison. Sleep was almost impossible and in just a few days the defenders were haggard wrecks of men. That was the situation when the New Zealanders of the Wellington Battalion were assigned the defence of Quinn's on 9 June. There could have been no better choice. Lieutenant Colonel William Malone was a soldier of the old school with a veritable mania for bringing order out of chaos.

There is an awful lot of work to do. Such a dirty, dilapidated, unorganised post. Still I like work and will revel in straightening things up. Quite a length of the trench unoccupiable, owing to bomb-throwing superiority of Turks. No places for men to fall in. The local reserve is posted too far away and yet there is at present no ground prepared on which they could be comfortably put. I selected a new headquarters shelter for myself, and gave orders that every rifle shot and bomb from the Turks was to be promptly returned at least twofold. We can and will beat them at their own game.[28]

Lieutenant Colonel William Malone, Wellington Battalion, New Zealand Brigade, NZ&A Division, NZEF

Working to a clear plan, with the inner steel to take his officers and men with him, Malone made a huge difference.

We soon got the upper hand of the Turk riflemen and bomb-throwers, and have completely changed the position. We have terraced the ground so that the troops in reserve are together instead of being dotted about in all sorts of holes. We have made roads to the top of the hill at the back so that we can counter-attack. Fire positions have been fixed for the supporting troops and in less than a minute we can sheet the hillcrest with lead from 200 rifles, the men being side by side in lines under their NCOs and officers. I got two machine guns mounted to sweep half of our front which before had to depend on some fifty rifles to stop the Turks who had only some 15 yards to cross to get from their trench to ours. Above all the men are inspired with the conviction that they have superiority over the Turks and are getting a fair run for their lives. We have so wrecked and racked the Turks' trenches that they now have the 'dread' and have almost abandoned their front trenches opposite us. Improvements made every day, overhead cover erected over terraces, making them sun and shrapnel and bomb proof. Blankets nailed along west fronts keep out the glare and heat of the westerly sun and can be rolled up at night, out of the way. The post has become absolutely the best in the defence and the safest.[29]

Lieutenant Colonel William Malone, Wellington Battalion, New Zealand Brigade, NZ&A Division, NZEF

Malone was a partisan New Zealander who was not afraid of expressing his biased views on the nature of the Australian soldier.

There is no question but that the New Zealander is a long, long way the better soldier of the two. The Australian is a dashing chap, but he is not steadfast, and he will not or would not dig, work. He came here to kill Turks, not to dig, and consequently, we have suffered. There are lots of good men and good officers among them, but they are not disciplined or trained like our men. The New Zealander is a long way the better soldier, more steadfast, better disciplined and a worker. I don't like the average Australian a bit, in fact I dislike him.[30]

Lieutenant Colonel William Malone, Wellington Battalion, New Zealand Brigade, NZ&A Division, NZEF

The efforts of the Wellingtons were mirrored up and down the tiny beachhead. Every innovation, every piece of hard graft made Anzac that much more secure and reduced the flow of casualties to a trickle.

Meanwhile, another form of warfare had made its presence felt. In a compact battlefield where a small advance could make all the difference, the value of mining operations was understood by both sides. Here the ANZAC Corps had an advantage in that the men of the 1st Field Company Engineer had a great deal of practical know-how from their civilian experience as miners back in Australia. One such was Lieutenant Henry Bachtold, who was pushing out underground tunnels from Courtney's Post.

It was the crudest bit of digging one could imagine but it was done to the best of our ability. First of all from the front line every 200 or 300 feet we ran an incline tunnel. Timber as far as I was concerned was unattainable; fortunately the ground was semi-rock. We had 8 hour shifts. I discovered that we got more progress done if we worked 6 hours and everybody came out for 2 hours and let the place cool down. Then after we had run these main tunnels perhaps 100 feet or thereabouts we connected them altogether. From that underground tunnel we probed forward then with various other kinds of tunnels. Of course the Turk was doing the same sort of thing but I decided on working with 16 foot of cover. Consequently, the Turks always were above me and as soon as they were getting too close I used to pop them off with a mine.[31]

Lieutenant Henry Bachtold, 1st Field Company Engineers, 1st Division, AIF

Such tunnels soon formed an underground maze that began to rival the complexity of the trenches on the surface. The Turks had a lot to learn as they lacked a mining industry from which to draw experienced engineers. Yet they too started mining and gradually an underground war developed, with both sides creating underground trench lines and listening posts to try to detect the exact location of their opposite numbers' shafts. At times they were so close that they could hear each other digging. Then it was a race for the Anzacs to lay and detonate a tamped camouflet mine to direct the power of the explosion in order to smash up threatening Turkish galleries; on other occasions mines were carefully laid and preserved for use in a planned infantry operation.

> After the chamber had been cut out I then prepared all the explosive charges myself. The explosive was in square canisters, something like a gallon oil tin. I used to stack these in the form of a wall, sometimes a double wall and then I drew out two tins. Unscrewed them and into one I put in the ordinary detonator into which you push a piece of fuse and crimp the thing together. Well, then the thing was to start off putting a certain amount of instantaneous fuse hooked on to the detonator and that went into one of the tins and the place where it went into was carefully sealed and then as a safeguard we had electric detonators. They had two wires and the thing was to connect those wires and bring them through to an exploder. When I was satisfied that I had connected them up properly I asked the boys to pass me the sandbags. We had to build back at least 10 to 15 feet of bags then the leads were taken to a suitable place – in this case the Battalion headquarters.[32]
>
> Lieutenant Henry Bachtold, 1st Field Company Engineers, 1st Division, AIF

The mine was now ready to explode. Soon both sides were at it, detonating mines and then engaging in vicious skirmishes to control the resulting craters.

The Turks occasionally could not resist testing out the Anzac defences. The Nek was a particular focus of their interest as by pushing forward a mere 300 yards they could burst through to Russell's Top and crack open the whole ANZAC Corps position. The recent addition of the 18th Regiment to Kemal's 19th Division gave him the chance to try his luck with another night attack on 29 June. A thunderstorm added to the febrile atmosphere and both sides were nervy. The Anzacs noticed the stealthy final preparations for the attack and were fully prepared when the Turks charged across The Nek under cover of darkness at 00.15 on 30 June. The result was a dreadful slaughter.

> They attacked by getting out of their trenches and trying to charge us with the bayonet. You ought to hear the roar of rifles during an attack.

It is something tremendous and you can hardly realise how anything can live through the hail of bullets, as for the machine guns it is something wonderful to hear them when a few get going properly. Our men sat right up on the parapets of our trenches and when not firing were all the time calling out for the Turks to come along and hooting and barracking them. In fact most of our chaps took the whole attack as a real good joke. As soon as they stopped the first rush they jumped out of the fire trench and sat up on the parapets and yelled and cursed at the top of their voices calling out to the Turks to come on they would finish them.[33]

Trooper Ernie Mack, 8th (Victoria) Light Horse, 3rd Light Horse Brigade, AIF

War had never seemed more pleasurable than it did to the men of the 8th Light Horse as they shot down the attacking Turks that night.

It was much more satisfactory than the infernal pot-shooting through loopholes, though this is fair sport now as we are only about 60 yards apart at the widest and in some places much less than that. To drop so many in that narrow space is not bad, is it, and speaks rather well for the alertness of everyone concerned as it was a night attack.[34]

Lieutenant Ted Henty, 8th (Victoria) Light Horse, 3rd Light Horse Brigade, AIF

When they had finished enjoying themselves there were some 260 Turkish corpses lying in the narrow strip of No Man's Land. The Light Horse would be back at The Nek in early August.

One interesting minor tactical operation occurred at 22.16 on 31 July, when the 11th Battalion launched a carefully planned attack from Tasmania Post to push the Turks out of their line clinging precariously to the edge of Holly Ridge above the drop into the poignantly named Valley of Despair. The greater purpose was to keep Turkish attention focused on the southern end of the Anzac positions in preparation for the August Offensive. Four tunnels had been sapped forwards with a mine at the end of each ready for detonation. The attack was under the command of Captain Raymond Leane. Tempted by the rumoured possibility of a commission, Corporal Thomas Louch had tossed for the privilege of leading the party from his company. He had won. The attack was made in fairly strong moonlight.

At the right time the mine on our front went up, and we dashed forward while clods of earth were falling all round us. The Turks were demoralised and most of them fled; so we successfully accomplished our part of the show. The people on our right had more difficulty. Two of the mines were late in going up, and one did not explode at all; consequently the Turks were not shaken, and put up a stronger fight before the whole of what was later known as Leane's Trench was in our hands. Our instructions were to set about improving the Turkish trench, but this had no traverses and gave no shelter from enfilade fire. With no Turks left on Holly Ridge I anticipated that we should be plastered with shells as soon as it became light. So instead of improving the Turkish trench I urged my party on to dig fire bays which would give shelter from the bombardment when it came. This meant more and harder work, but it was worth it. When the expected shelling came the fire bays gave the necessary cover and we suffered no casualties from it.[35]

Corporal Thomas Louch, 11th (Western Australia) Battalion, 3rd Brigade, 1st Australian Division, AIF

Corporal Louch had done well and he was commissioned on 4 August 1915. Private William Pheysey did not share Louch's good fortune. He was on the extreme left of the attack and separated from the main body and could find only a dry watercourse in which to position himself. Here he was soon wounded.

I heard a rifle bang just below me in the darkness and the use went out of my legs. I sat down abruptly. I felt no pain at all and I knew I was hit. Then I could feel warm blood on my legs and feeling gingerly I found that the bullet had gone clean through the calf of my left leg and the fleshy part of my right leg above the knee on the top side. I began thinking – I am a great thinker these days! 'If I stay here I should get hit again!' So I crawled back to the gully and watercourse. I thought, 'Has that bullet cut an artery, there seems to be plenty of blood about?' So I cut up my pants and took off my putties, put a dressing on and lay down. It was impossible to get back to our own trenches, the Turks saw to that. The ground between us was just cut to pieces with machine gun bullets. The captain in charge decided to occupy the gully as well as the trench, to defend it in case the Turkish counter-attacked and then to build up parapets of sandbags. I felt very useless but found that I could hold the bags open for other men to fill and it occupied my mind and I was glad of it. I had to stay in the gully till it was connected to the trench which happened 3 a.m. Sunday morning. The sap through was not wide enough to allow them to carry me out as my legs had stiffened and I could not crawl at all. At 3 p.m. they got me out.[36]

Private William Pheysey, 11th (Western Australia) Battalion, 3rd Brigade, 1st Division, AIF

The operations had been a success, although at the cost of thirty-six killed and seventy-three wounded. The tactical position on Holly Ridge had been improved and at the same time a possible source of flanking fire into any future Australian attack on Lone Pine had been removed.

AS THE SUMMER WORE ON, Anzac became as safe as it would ever be. The interconnecting fields of fire threatened bloody destruction to any Turkish attack that would merely swell the number of corpses in No Man's Land. The only problem was that the Turks had mirrored their industry, their deadly artistry. Any Anzac assault looked likely to reap only the same dreadful harvest in between the lines. The original aim on 25 April had been clear: to seize the Third Ridge, capture Mal Tepe and join in the attack on Kilid Bahr. All this was now impossible. So why were the Anzacs there? They were not engaged in operations designed to secure their objectives. Rather, they were standing fast, watched closely by an equivalent Turkish force. The fighting that went on was to defend themselves, or minor skirmishes that merely explored the practical limits of their domain. It had been a fantastic achievement to carve out this tiny enclave, but now the Anzacs were in a state of stasis. It seemed impossible to evacuate the area until the stalemate was broken. What else could the troops do but cling on? This was in stark contrast to the situation at Helles, where for three months the British and French troops would fling themselves time and time again against the Turkish lines in an effort to gain Achi Baba and then push on to Kilid Bahr. Anzac had become a backwater; the real fight for Gallipoli was raging at Helles.

10

HELLES: THE REAL FIGHT FOR GALLIPOLI

You were never free from something while you were in the Peninsula, no matter where you were: on the earth or in it, on the sea or in it, or in the air. If it wasn't bullets, it was shells. If it wasn't shells, it was colic. If it wasn't fever, it was chill; and often it was both. And the fleas we had always with us.[1]

Captain Albert Mure, 1/5th Royal Scots, 88th Brigade, 29th Division

THE AFTERMATH OF THE LANDINGS at Helles on 25 April 1915 was a pervading, almost tangible atmosphere of exhaustion among the men of the 29th Division. By their own account they had achieved miracles in getting ashore, yet the Turkish defence had not folded as expected. The capture of Hill 141 was not the spur to an advance on Achi Baba, but rather the precursor to a period of reorganisation and consolidation. The process of landing a whole division with all its goods and chattels across open beaches was also taking far more time than expected – apparently beaches were not ports after all. Major General Sir Aylmer Hunter-Weston was also keen to wait for the arrival of the French 1st Brigade (Métropolitaine) before attempting further progress but they did not even begin to land until the evening of 26 April. Among the troops landing at V Beach was Private Cornelius Jean de Bruin of the French Foreign Legion. As was traditional he was serving under an alias – his real name was Dick Cooper. His story illustrates the chaos that was enveloping the Allied forces.

Very soon the Turks started shelling from Fort Chanak. It was my
first experience of shellfire and I did not like it very much. We started
marching straight away. There was no camping; that night we rested
on a hilltop. We had no idea where the enemy was. It was pitch
dark and raining in torrents. The 1st Company was lost and Captain
Rousseau detailed me, with four or five other men, to go out in different
directions to find them and lead them back to the Battalion. I walked
for about half an hour through the rain and darkness, stumbling over
rocks and dead bodies, and, at last, scrambling up a hill, I saw a dim
silhouette at the top. I was glad to see any living human being and
went right up to him and spoke in French. With a yell the man dropped
his rifle and fled, calling on Allah in Turkish. The best part of it that I
was so startled that I did the same thing; that is, I dropped my rifle and
ran.[2]

Private Cornelius Jean de Bruin, Légion Étrangère, 1st Régiment de Marche
d'Afrique, 1st (Métropolitaine) Brigade, 1st Division, CEO

Once ashore the French were assigned the position to the right, next to
the Straits. This was a significant move which, while giving the French the
traditional position of honour on the right of the line, also condemned
them for the rest of the campaign to the very worst of the fire from the
Asiatic batteries and the as-yet-unseen horrors of the Kereves Dere Ravine
that lay across their path. Adjoining the French was the 29th Division,
with the 88th Brigade in the centre, the 87th Brigade on the left and the
remnants of the 86th Brigade as reserves. It was only at 16.00 on 27 April
that the advance began. This was not the planned bold push towards Achi
Baba, merely a general move forward over uncontested ground with the
intention of forming a line from just above S Beach diametrically across
to Gully Beach. There was some progress, although the left lagged behind
and was still some 500 yards from Gully Beach. While the Allies fiddled
about at Helles, the Turkish reserves marched purposefully towards the
battlefield.

Hunter-Weston planned for greater things on 28 April. Achi Baba was
now deemed out of reach, as he was very short of artillery, so instead he
decided to perform an ambitious wheeling manoeuvre pivoting on the
right flank, which was to firm at Hill 236 (near De Tott's Battery) while
everyone else moved forwards to take up a line stretching up through
Krithia to Yazy Tepe a mile to the north. Here they would be facing Achi

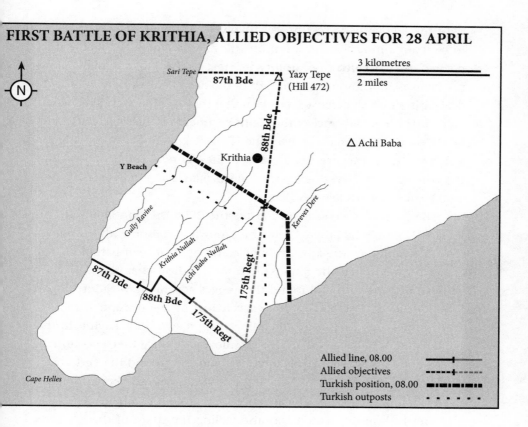

FIRST BATTLE OF KRITHIA, ALLIED OBJECTIVES FOR 28 APRIL

Baba ready to advance another day. Although his orders were issued at 22.00 on 27 April, the staff work was severely hampered by all the recent casualties. As a result many battalions did not get their orders in sufficient time for them to go through their own command processes before the hour of attack was upon them. The plans were also sketchy in the extreme, taking scant notice of factors such as the state of the assaulting troops, the nature of the terrain, distances to be travelled, length of the line to be occupied, or indeed the dispositions and numbers of the Turks facing them. This was unfortunate, for by now the Turks had not only been reinforced, they had begun to dig in, although at this stage they had dug few new trenches, merely augmented natural cover, using ditches, folds in the ground or old defence works in front of which they had placed a series of advance posts.

The First Battle of Krithia commenced at 08.00 on 28 April. On the right the French were keen to get involved. Although they were meant to be maintaining their position on Hill 236 on which the whole force pivoted, they decided to push forward next to the Straits, moving along the Kereves Spur towards the mouth of the deep Kereves Dere in order to deal with a Turkish defensive position that they rightly considered would enfilade the main advance of the 175th Regiment on their left. This attack failed, so when the main body of the 175th Regiment began moving forwards at 10 a.m. they were vulnerable to fire from the Turkish posts along the Kereves Spur. Nevertheless the French managed an advance of some 1,000 yards towards Kereves Dere.

The problems were mounting for the 29th Division alongside the French. Not only had there been a breakdown in liaison with the French over the timing of the advance, but many of their own battalions had either not registered the requirement for a radical change in direction or mistimed the turn and found themselves advancing without support on either flank. This was further exacerbated by the disruptive effect of three gullies running through their line of approach: Gully Ravine, Krithia Nullah and Achi Baba Nullah. For the most part, once they encountered opposition, any wheeling was forgotten and the ground the Turks occupied became the objective. Affecting everything was the bone-numbing exhaustion of the troops. The advance soon ground to a halt.

The Turkish opposition was also feeling the strain of the last three days. The remnants of the 26th Regiment were in the line alongside the 25th Regiment, who had come up from Serafim Farm. Most were worn out and some elements seem to have fallen back without much resistance as the British approached. Indeed, at one point the Turks were considering a full-scale retreat.

> The Regimental Commander gave an order that withdrawal should take place to Soganlidere, but upon this I replied that we should gain time and that the slopes of Achi Baba were important. So he said that we should go together and tell this to the 25th Regimental Commander – and this we did. Just then the 9th Company from the reserve companies arrived. The enemy was then confronted with the 9th and 12th Companies who took up a position to the left, and the remains of the 10th and 11th Companies to the right – and his superior forces were stopped. This situation went on for 3 or 4 hours. Thus, although the second in command of the 10th Company and many of our men

were put out of action, the enemy were prevented from taking a commanding bit of ground like the slopes of Achi Baba. Four hours later our left was extended and our line of battle was reinforced by the 19th Regiment of the 7th Division.[3]

Major Mahmut, 3rd Battalion, 26th Regiment, 9th Division, Fifth Army

It should be remembered that a tactical retreat *was* a feasible option, as the ground that lay between Achi Baba and Kilid Bahr was probably even better suited to defence. Yet Major Mahmut was surely right: Achi Baba was a valuable position, overlooking as it did the whole of Cape Helles, and as such it should be surrendered only as a last – and certainly not the first – resort. In the end the Turks held on to it long enough to break the will of the physically shattered troops before them.

As the British and French advance stuttered to a halt, one of the fresh Turkish battalions counter-attacked the French. They began to fall back and as the 88th Brigade conformed – a word that hides a multitude of sins – many of the gains made at such effort were cast away. At the end of the day the front line stretched from Hill 236 straight across to a point about a quarter of a mile short of Y Beach. Casualties were high, the British losing 2,000 and the French around 1,000. The Turkish reserves had arrived and the road to Achi Baba was now firmly closed off; taking Kilid Bahr had always been a fantasy.

By the end of April the Turks had amassed a force of some twenty-one battalions, or 17,000 men, at Helles. According to the Turkish plan this should have been the moment to launch the counter-offensive to peremptorily eject the invaders from the Helles sector. This was indeed ordered by Enver on 30 April, but Liman was well aware that any daytime troop movements would expose his men to potentially damaging fire from the Allied ships that surrounded the tip of Helles. This meant that attacks had to be at night. That same evening the orders were passed on to Colonel von Sodenstern, commanding the Helles sector, for the 9th and 7th Divisions to attack that night. The Turkish tactics were extremely straightforward; they simply charged out of the night at 22.00 on 1 May.

They crept right up to our trenches, they were in thousands, and they made the night hideous with yells and shouting, 'Allah, Allah!' We could not help mowing them down. Some of them broke through in a part of our line but they never again got back as they were caught between the two lines of trenches. Some of the best men in the Regiment were killed. When the Turks got to close quarters the devils used hand grenades and you could only recognise our dead by their identity discs. My God, what a sight met us when day broke this morning. The whole ground in front was littered with dead Turks. To my left where the attack was strongest, I think there are at least 500 and there is no chance of burying them as anybody who shows themselves outside is bound to be brought down by one of their snipers.[4]

Sergeant Denis Moriarty, 1st Royal Munster Fusiliers, 86th Brigade, 29th Division

The exhausted British and French troops were hard pressed.

My regiment alone got through 150,000 rounds, and they were only 360 strong. The Turks were simply driven on to the barbed wire in front of the trenches by their German officers, and shot down by the score. At one point they actually got into the trenches, but were driven out by the bayonet. They must have lost thousands. The fighting is of the most desperate kind – very little quarter on either side. The men are absolutely mad to get at them, as they mutilate our wounded when they catch them. For the first three nights I did not have a wink of sleep and actually fell asleep once during the big night attack.[5]

Lieutenant Henry O'Hara, 1st Royal Dublin Fusiliers, 86th Brigade, 29th Division

The myth of the omnipresent German officers malevolently controlling the Turkish troops, so common in British veterans' recollections, is surely nonsense given their very restricted numbers, and indeed relatively high rank. It can probably be explained by the better quality and cut of the uniform of the Turkish officers, which provoked unwarranted assumptions that they were German.

These Turkish counter-attacks were launched with maximum intensity against the French on the right of the line. By this time the Colonial Brigade had come ashore and slotted into the line between the Métropolitaine Brigade and the 29th Division. Here there was a real problem for they had had little time to dig in properly. A night attack by massed screaming Turks was a terrifying ordeal and it is unsurprising that many of them bolted. Groups of Turks pushed on, over-running Zimmerman's Farm, some even reaching Morto Bay. This was not the result of colonial troops simply failing to keep up to the mark but rather of a vicious, well-executed attack carried out on exhausted men. The Turks got almost as far as threatening Sedd el Bahr, where Lieutenant Henri Feuille was encamped even though his 150-mm guns had still not been disembarked.

> Fanatical Turks, good brave soldiers, were killed without mercy by our bayonets, in the hand-to-hand struggle. In the course of the night, they broke through almost to the cypress trees not far from our village. We could hear their shouts, their joyful cries in the certain belief that they were close to victory. We retreated, forced back by their savage efforts and heavy sacrifice of human lives. To cover the area of ground in front of us and above the cypresses, and to give the Turks the impression that the hill was occupied, I fired volleys of rifle fire. None the less, the Senegalese were overwhelmed and fell back in disorder. To show their advance, so that their artillery could fire in support, the Turks lit red flares. Green flares marked out the trenches they had recaptured and they also had white flares, which they lit to illuminate our defeat, hopeful that at any moment, if their all-powerful Allah so wished, we would be thrown without mercy into the sea. The night passed in an agonised anxiety as to the outcome of hand-to-hand fighting in which every life is in doubt. The dawn came at last, lighting up a scene of carnage and the Turks retired to their trenches accompanied by salvos of 75mm shells. We have held the line but the dead and the wounded are legion.[6]
>
> Lieutenant Henri Feuille, 52nd Battery, 30th Regiment, CEO

In the end a motley crew of gunners and hastily scraped-together reserves had managed to halt the Turkish attacks.

At night there was little that the Royal Navy could do to support the French, but once it was daylight again they were perfectly placed to cause devastation to the Turkish troops caught in the open.

> Weighed; went up to assist. Could see nothing. Asked French for information. Reply only call for help. Fired blind. Beach officer reported French running, re-embarkation likely. Moved down close in to De Tott's in case, to cover re-embarkation. 4.30: daylight. Moved up. French advanced. Fired 12-pdr at their shrapnel bursts. Found ourselves 1,500 yards on flank, in view of both sides. Saw Turks retreating. Gave them 6-inch: they went back over brow of hill. Hedge on brow. Moved to see behind hedge. 10 minutes later, 5.15, saw reforming again behind hedge. Saw them signal advance. Let them get well started then let rip. They gave up at once and fell back. Hose-piped trench and waited.

6.25. Another try: got them properly and finished them with 6-inch shrapnel.[7]

Captain Bertram Smith, HMS *Vengeance*

Helped by the British Navy, the French counter-attacked vigorously on the morning of 2 May, managing to regain the ground they had lost. Alongside them were the 2nd Naval Brigade of the RND who had hitherto been held back in reserve since being put ashore on the night of 29 April. With no detailed knowledge of the situation or indeed where they were, the Hood Battalion began their advance. It was utterly futile and they soon attracted shrapnel fire. With no time to dig in and unsupported on either flank, they were hopelessly exposed and soon had to retreat. As they did so Lieutenant Charles Lister was wounded in somewhat undignified circumstances.

My company being in the second line retired last, and by the time we were moving the whole of our front was being searched with terrible effect. One of the shrapnel burst on the ground about thirty yards behind me and a pellet ricocheted the ground and struck me in the off-buttock. I thought it was a piece of stone at first. I had already been hit by several spent pellets without any effect. One went through coat and shirt and hardly marked my skin; another knocked in my water-bottle. However, this third one found its billet, and I was soon bleeding like a pig and walking indifferent well – I never fell down. It was an irritating moment, as I should have been there to rally our boys after the retirement. They did well, considering the trying circumstances and their relative rawness. I never saw a Turk within shooting distance. My return to the beach was easily accomplished for me on a stretcher, not so easily perhaps for the poor orderlies who had to carry me, and I had a feeling of great peace as I lay on my back and looked at the blue overhead. I should like to get back quick, because I have seen just enough to tantalise. It is rather like love-making in this.[8]

Lieutenant Charles Lister, Hood Battalion, 2nd Naval Brigade, RND

Lister had tried to conceal his wound, but was given away when his trousers filled with blood. He may not have been a professional soldier but he was brave enough. He would be back. Overall the Allied counter-attacks achieved little except more casualties.

On the night of 2 May there was a heavy outbreak of firing all along the line but no Turkish attack. Meanwhile, Second Lieutenant Raymond Weil came up to the initial battery position of the 39th Régiment d'Artillerie in the orchards on the outskirts of Sedd el Bahr village. The guns were blazing away into the dark but Weil took the opportunity to try to get some sleep.

> I bedded myself down in a hole where another Lieutenant from our Battery was sleeping the sleep of the just! The moon rose and the gunfire quietened down as if enchanted; I profited from this to get a little sleep. I managed to lean my head on something more or less soft. But I was freezing so I got up to try to get warm. I decided to wait till dawn. The bombardment was intermittent and we didn't fire for longer and longer periods. The sky began to light up the precise outline of the Asiatic coast, and I saw appearing at my feet the magnificent panorama of the bay, the Sedd el Bahr castle half destroyed by the bombardment, the encampment on the beach, and finally what remained of the village of Sedd el Bahr with its picturesque orchards. But then I had a disagreeable surprise when I noticed that my pillow was simply a corpse![9]
>
> Second Lieutenant Raymond Weil, 39th Régiment d'Artillerie, 1st Division, CEO

On the night of 3 May the Turks launched another strong night attack utilising their newly arrived 15th Division to augment the fast-fading 9th and 7th Divisions. By this time Weil's guns were ready for action.

> In the pitch dark we immediately let go a furious barrage; the fusillade carried on at the same pitch. It was a dreadful uninterrupted racket. We fired without a break all out! I had to yell in the middle of the din to make myself heard. All the neighbouring batteries were firing without respite. The Turkish batteries replied. The Asiatic coast, behind us, sprayed us copiously with shells. We were perpetually dazzled by the flashes so we couldn't see and we were deafened. Up to 1 a.m. it was a veritable furnace; the gunfire never stopped for a second.[10]
>
> Second Lieutenant Raymond Weil, 39th Régiment d'Artillerie, 1st Division, CEO

Later when Weil arrived at a forward observation post he got the chance to see what he and the dreaded French 75mm guns had achieved; but he was all too aware of a potentially fatal weakness.

> We had massacred the Turks, but we also had a lot of casualties.
> And I was aware of one terrible fact: we had no more shells left. The
> artillery park was exhausted; all that remained at the batteries were
> empty limbers but that was it! If the Turks attacked that night we were
> doomed.[11]
>
> Second Lieutenant Raymond Weil, 39th Régiment d'Artillerie, 1st Division, CEO

During this tense period, rumours of knavish Turkish tricks spread like
wildfire. Everyone knew someone who had seen something untoward;
few, if any, had experienced anything themselves, but still the rumours
proliferated.

> We learnt why the Senegalese had fled. A Captain had given the order
> to withdraw. The same Captain accompanied by two officers claiming
> to be English had passed through all the French lines, giving orders
> everywhere. He passed behind us and ordered us to fire higher and then
> not to fire at all under the pretext that there was nobody in front of us.
> We continued to fire stronger than ever; this was towards 5 o'clock in
> the morning. The three so-called officers were German spies who helped
> the Turkish advance. They were arrested during the day and will be
> judged as they deserve.[12]
>
> Sergeant D'Arnaud Pomiro, 3rd Battalion, 175th Regiment, 1st (Métropolitaine)
> Brigade, 1st Division, CEO

Such stories passed up and down the lines; there was rarely, if ever, any
truth in them. In the end the Turkish attacks failed as comprehensively
as the previous Allied attempts. The narrow front at Helles restricted the
possibility for manoeuvre and raw courage counted for little in the face
of modern weapons.

> In each case daybreak brought an overwhelming fire from the ships
> which compelled the Turks to withdraw to their positions. Only a part
> of the captured machine guns could be carried off. Painful as it was for
> me, I now had to give orders to abstain from further attacks on the Sedd
> el Bahr front and to remain on the defensive. But not an inch of ground
> was to be yielded as the enemy was not far from Achi Baba ridge, his
> next great objective. I ordered the Turkish troops of the first line to
> entrench themselves as close to the enemy as possible. A distance of a

few paces between the hostile lines would inhibit the fire from the ships which would now equally endanger the troops of both sides.[13]

General Otto Liman von Sanders, Headquarters, Fifth Army

Even as the last of the Turkish night attacks was failing, a small party of Germans arrived carrying precious machine guns donated from the *Goeben*.

> Lieutenant Bolz reported with a landing party of marines, eight machine guns and thirty-two men, a most heartily welcomed support. He was at once sent to the front line, where he did extremely well in spite of the difficult position, the pitch-black night, without knowledge of the country, in the midst of troops whose language he did not know and whose uniform he did not wear. The Turks naturally took the German sailors for the English, and a terrible catastrophe was only just prevented by the lucky arrival and intervention of Major Mühlmann. The news of the arrival of German machine guns in the front line gave new life to the defenders.[14]
>
> Colonel Hans Kannengiesser, Headquarters, 9th Division, Fifth Army

Now the British really would be facing massed Maxim firepower; on a front as narrow as Helles this made a genuine difference. But the failure of the Turkish night attacks led to Colonel von Sodenstern being replaced as the commander of the Helles force (henceforth to be known as the Southern Group) by Brigadier General Weber Pasha. Although its theoretical strength had risen to thirty-one battalions, the excessive casualties suffered in the wild counter-attacks had reduced its effective manpower to just 15,000 rifles. Prompted by Liman, the Turks had finally committed to standing where they were, in front of the village of Krithia, defending every yard and counter-attacking wherever possible.

THE SITUATION AT HELLES was by this time highly unfavourable to the Allies. It was evident that the MEF could not possibly advance without significant reinforcements. The 29th Division was exhausted and near demoralised; the RND, an inexperienced formation further hampered by a lack of the proper artillery element, had been split up. The French 1st Division had suffered severe casualties and had already called for reinforcements. The 2nd Division of the CEO, under the command of General Maurice Bailloud, had been despatched by the French but would not arrive at Helles until 6 May. Hamilton needed a substantial injection of troops to have any chance of reaching Achi Baba. Speed was also vital, for it was evident that every day that passed would allow the Turks to further strengthen their defences. He had already sent for the 29th Indian Brigade from Egypt; now he had to swallow his pride and send for the 42nd Division, which had been earmarked by Kitchener as a possible reinforcement from Egypt. These were inexperienced territorial troops, many of whom had only enlisted on the outbreak of war. One young officer, Lieutenant George Horridge, fretted as to how he might respond to the challenges that lay ahead.

> On arrival off Cape Helles in daylight it dawned on one more forcibly that this was it. Everyone wonders what will happen when one actually arrives at the war. Will it be horrible, will one be afraid, will one be able to carry out one's duty, will one be killed or maimed or perhaps only mildly wounded.[15]
>
> Lieutenant George Horridge, 1/5th Lancashire Fusiliers, 125th Brigade, 42nd Division

As only the 125th Brigade could arrive before the next intended assault it was temporarily attached to the 29th Division, as was the 29th Indian Brigade. It was also decided that, as the situation at Anzac appeared to have stabilised, they could afford temporarily to move the New Zealand Brigade and the 2nd Australian Brigade down to Helles to augment the potential assault force for what would become known as the Second Battle of Krithia, beginning on Thursday 6 May.

The plans prepared by Hunter-Weston for this attack were totally unrealistic given the circumstances at Helles. The French would advance to capture Kereves Dere, and then act as a pivot as the British troops wheeled round to take Krithia and Yazi Tepe before attacking Achi Baba. Although some more guns had gone ashore there were still not enough to create a heavy barrage, even when augmented by naval gunfire. In any case, no one had yet been able to locate the Turkish positions accurately and hence this would still be an advance to contact – one of the most difficult battlefield manoeuvres. All would stand or fall depending on French success on the right, advancing between Achi Baba Nullah and

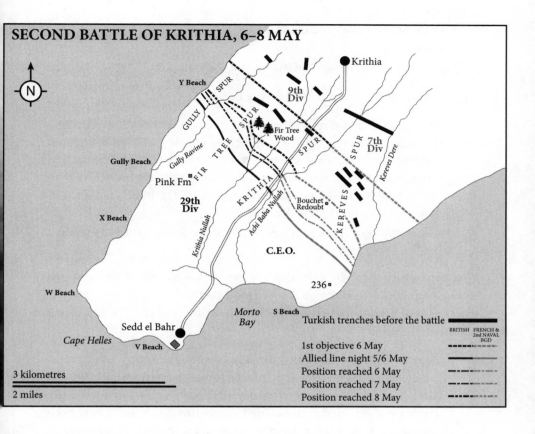

SECOND BATTLE OF KRITHIA, 6–8 MAY

N

Krithia

Y Beach

9th Div

GULLY SPUR

SPUR

Fir Tree Wood

SPUR

7th Div

Gully Ravine

Gully Beach

FIR TREE SPUR

SPUR

KEREVES SPUR

Kereves Dere

Pink Fm

29th Div

KRITHIA

Achi Baba Nullah

Bouchet Redoubt

X Beach

Krithia Nullah

C.E.O.

236

W Beach

Morto Bay

S Beach

Turkish trenches before the battle

Sedd el Bahr

BRITISH   FRENCH & 2nd NAVAL BGD

Cape Helles

V Beach

1st objective 6 May

3 kilometres

Allied line night 5/6 May

Position reached 6 May

2 miles

Position reached 7 May

Position reached 8 May

the sea. The desultory bombardment began at 10.30 and although the troops were meant to attack at 11.00 they would be some forty minutes late in setting off. Lieutenant Henri Feuille, who was observing for his heavy guns (which had finally been brought ashore on 4 May), had a close view of the attack.

> In perfect order our troops shook themselves out and set out to climb up the long spur which separated them from their enemies – No Man's Land. They advanced as on exercise, our brave troops, no gaps in the ranks, punctuated by flashes of bayonets and blue glint of the rifles reflecting the rays of the mid-day sun. You would think they were on a training ground. But what is there to say? This wall of steel stops, hurls itself at an obstacle that it can't breach, hesitates, immobile for an instant. Then, all the geometric lines fall apart. Groups running right, left, thrown into confusion. All the while Turkish machine

guns, rattling away, tearing at the air, ceaselessly firing into a wall of palpitating flesh.[16]

Lieutenant Henri Feuille, 52nd Battery, 30th Regiment, CEO

It was a slaughter, but not all the attacks failed entirely.

Towards midday we reached our designated objective. All of a sudden we become diggers, each one with his entrenching tool hollowing out his trench to defend himself: you've got to believe that this doesn't take long. A few minutes suffice to get shelter from the bullets. While I'm digging the fire continues from both sides. The bullets pass over my head; but they don't scare me at all.[17]

Sergeant D'Arnaud Pomiro, 3rd Battalion, 175th Regiment, 1st (Métropolitaine) Brigade, 1st Division, CEO

Meanwhile, to their left, the British began their advance. There was immediate confusion. To the men of the Hood Battalion, who were advancing up the Achi Baba Nullah, the Turks were invisible, but their bullets seemed to be everywhere.

There's no sign of the French. It was a beautiful morning. We got to a farmhouse, what was left of it, knocked about but serviceable. We were lying alongside the corner of a vineyard, a bush hedge 3 or 4 feet high, a little ditch on the side. We started numbering. There must have been at least 50–60 men there. Then we were told to swing round behind the house and move forward. We found ourselves alongside another hedge of the vineyard. There was a big gap, about 12 feet wide, it looked like the roadway into the farmhouse. We lay there for a little then we were told to bear left, we were at the junction between the French and the British and we tried to keep connection with both flanks. We kept losing so many men we couldn't do it. We could never locate these snipers. There were no trenches; it was open fighting. We had to rush along the front of the house and go through this gap. Only four people got through, we had to climb over the dead and the wounded. We got about 10 yards in front, and down we went. The bullets were hitting the sand, spraying us; you were spitting it out of your mouth.[18]

Ordinary Seaman Joe Murray, Hood Battalion, 2nd Naval Brigade, RND

All along the line the advance staggered to a halt or recoiled before the Turkish line was reached. Overall, with the exception of trivial French gains, the attack was a failure. Hunter-Weston responded by ordering a repeat performance of his master plan on 7 May. This resulted in no advance of any importance and another swathe of casualties. By now it should have been obvious that the French were entering a death trap. As they drew ever nearer to Kereves Dere they found themselves facing a precipitous ravine, while a series of increasingly mature Turkish defence works barred their way as they tried to push along the near-bank.

With hindsight it seems incredible that after two such clear-cut failures another attempt should be ordered. But Hamilton had little choice. He could either attack again or accept defeat. And every day that passed allowed the Turks to improve their defences and move up more reserves. The Allies simply had to try again. Thus a third attack was ordered for 10.30 on 8 May.

This time the New Zealand Brigade was flung into the equation, launching an unsupported attack through the 29th Division positions and along Fir Tree Spur. This attack was carried out in some confusion. Earlier that morning the brigade had been moved forward in preparation, in broad daylight across open ground. Private Cecil Malthus was with the Canterbury Battalion when they left a support trench occupied by the Dublin Fusiliers and the Munsters.

> 'New Zealanders prepare to advance!' Where on earth were the enemy and what were our objectives? Hastily we threw off our packs and piled them in heaps – which were promptly looted by the Irishmen – and it was only in the act of springing over the parapet that we were told of another line of British still lying 100 yards ahead of us. We sprinted the distance all abreast, in fine style, and thanks to our smartness it was only in the last few yards that the enemy woke up and loosed his fire. The tragedy of it was that from that moment he remained awake, and we were left with the certainty, in our next advance, of having to face a living stream of lead.[19]
>
> Private Cecil Malthus, Canterbury Battalion, New Zealand Brigade, NZ&A Division, NZEF

The New Zealanders had now reached the British front line occupied by the Worcesters. At 10.30 it was time for them to make their attack. The Wellington Battalion was on the left, the Auckland in the centre and the Canterbury on the right. Private Malthus was with the scouts who went over first.

For 200 yards we sprinted, thinking oddly how beautiful the poppies and daisies were, then from sheer exhaustion we rushed to ground in a slight depression and lay there panting. We had kept about 10 yards apart, but soon the spaces were filled by those of our mates who managed to get so far. Now the storm was let loose, and increased every moment in fury, until a splashing, spurting shower of lead was falling like rain on a pond. Hugging the ground in frantic terror we began to dig blindly with our puny entrenching tools, but soon the four men nearest me were lying, one dead, two with broken legs, and the other badly wounded in the shoulder. A sledgehammer blow on the foot made me turn with a feeling of positive relief that I had met my fate, but it was a mere graze and hardly bled. Another bullet passed through my coat, and a third ripped along two feet of my rifle sling. Then the wounded man on my right got a bullet through the head that ended his troubles. And still without remission the air was full of hissing bullets and screaming shells.[20]

Private Cecil Malthus, Canterbury Battalion, New Zealand Brigade, NZ&A Division, NZEF

Eventually they managed to dig shallow pits and gained some measure of safety. The New Zealanders had been slaughtered advancing in isolation.

Hamilton then intervened to order a general advance timed for 17.30 that afternoon, as a very last throw of the dice. All along the line units tried to respond but for most it was either physically impossible or they made minor advances that achieved nothing but cost a lot. In a morass of failure the Australian 2nd Brigade, which had been ordered out of reserve, attacked in splendid isolation along the bare slopes of Krithia Spur. The mistakes made during the failed assault of the New Zealanders that morning were repeated: a lack of any coherent planning or organisation; an advance under fire before they had even got to the front line; slaughter as they tried to locate the Turkish front line.

The noise was terrific and shells burst in hundreds over the enemy's position. Then came the order, 'Prepare to advance in 10 minutes!' We were to advance in 'fighting order', each man taking a pick or a shovel. Spent bullets began to drop and men were hit before we began to move. The bombardment ceased and we began the mad rush across the open, pelted by rifle and machine gun fire and shrapnel. No formation was kept and our objective appeared to be utterly unknown to officers and men alike.[21]

Lance Corporal Eric Moorhead, 5th (Victoria) Battalion, 2nd Brigade, 1st Division, AIF

The Turks were ready for them and on the bare, open spur they presented an easy target.

Well, we charged, but what we charged goodness only knows – I never ran so much in my life. Then the machine guns started. That stopped our charging. We advanced by short rushes to within striking distance, but were too decimated to complete the attack. Captain Heron and I happened to be alongside each other and there was a wretched Turk enfilading us with stray shots. It was dark by this time. Heron and I took turns with the rifle and entrenching tool until Heron got an enfilading bullet over the right eye; I then had to dig for the two of us. We got down to cover without any further mishap. Why the Turks never counter-attacked that night and wiped the lot of us out – God alone knows. Think of it, a little band of men, not more than 300, stuck right out in front of the army with nothing to the right or left.[22]

Sergeant Cecil Eades, 7th (Victoria) Battalion, 2nd Brigade, 1st Division, AIF

In the end they had been stopped by the Turkish outpost line. Here was a truly futile attack and the casualties suffered were appalling. And any ground gained could have been occupied with minimal losses under the cover of darkness. As Hamilton told Kitchener:

The result of the operation has been failure, as my object remains unachieved. The fortifications and their machine guns were too scientific and too strongly held to be rushed, although I had every available man in today. Our troops have done all that flesh and blood can do against semi-permanent works and they are not able to carry them. More and more munitions will be needed to do so. I fear that this is a very unpalatable conclusion, but I can see no way out of it.[23]

General Sir Ian Hamilton, Headquarters, MEF

Next day he followed up with a more confident missive, stressing the value of hammering at the Turks until they gave way and expressing confidence that he could make progress with the addition to his force of two more divisions. With a logic that perhaps only he could have explained,

Kitchener replied saying that he would send out just the 52nd Division as a reinforcement; surely a half-cocked response. Trenches and all their devilments had come to Helles. Only a total breakthrough could bring back open warfare. And on the upper slopes of Achi Baba the Turks were watching and waiting for the Allies' next move.

AFTER THE SECOND BATTLE OF KRITHIA both sides took to trench warfare in earnest. There was one imaginative tactical initiative on the night of 12 May, when the 29th Indian Brigade launched an audacious attack on the Turkish defensive positions that surrounded the old Y Beach landing site. Eschewing a frontal attack the 1/6th Gurkhas instead crept under cover of darkness along the foot of the cliffs, behind the Turkish lines, and then climbed stealthily up the nullahs to surprise the Turks, who withdrew some 500 yards, allowing an advance to secure what would henceforth be known as Gurkha Bluff, just to the north of Y Beach. It had been a magnificent achievement, but the Turks were warned of the possibilities of such seaward outflanking moves and their defences soon reached right down to the waves. Front lines were solidified, support and reserve lines were carved out of the earth and communications trenches snaked between them.

> I sometimes think that this war should go down in history as the 'War of Spades'! Certainly the Dardanelles campaign was fought with that homely garden tool. I once heard a woman name forty-six things she could do with a hairpin. It was a poor soldier that couldn't do sixty-four with a spade after a month in Gallipoli![24]
>
> Captain Albert Mure, 1/5th Royal Scots, 88th Brigade, 29th Division

Behind the infantry the artillery were well dug in, tucked as far out of sight as possible of their Turkish opposite numbers perched up on the heights of Achi Baba. The rest camps were no safer nor comfortable than the front lines. They were still under fire and every man found what shelter he could, taking over or digging a grave-like hole in the unyielding ground. Then he would fix in place a waterproof sheet or blanket to provide a little shade and at least the illusion of cover should one of the Turkish shells drop in the vicinity. It was just a matter of luck.

Fortunately for the British and French, the Turks were desperately short of shells. But the British batteries were in the same predicament and were only allowed to fire at obvious targets or during attacks.

> Life has been, on the whole, pretty dull here, enlivened only by an occasional fight. Whenever enough ammunition arrives we arrange a battle and push the enemy back a bit. The amount of ground we gain depends entirely on how much ammunition, particularly high explosives, we have to expend. There is no doubt that if we had sufficient to fight for, say, seven days on end at the outside, we should get the Turks on the run and be right through at once.[25]
>
> Captain Herbert Lush Wilson, Y Battery, 15th Brigade, Royal Horse Artillery

Lush Wilson was in one sense entirely correct: in trench warfare conditions it was almost impossible for infantry to progress without support from the massed power of the guns. Yet at the same time he was misunderstanding the situation at Helles. The absence of shells was not a mysterious or avoidable situation; it was absolutely inevitable, given the munitions crisis that had enveloped the British Empire in 1915. Indeed, even if they had access to unlimited ammunition they would not have had the guns or gunners to fire them. There was never the slightest possibility that this state of affairs could be changed at the behest of Kitchener, Hamilton, Hunter-Weston or Captain Lush Wilson. And of course the reverse argument was equally true: if the Turks had all the ammunition and guns they wanted they too could have swept all before them, but they did not have the artillery resources either. Only the French were properly equipped for modern warfare.

Although artillery was key to dominating the battlefield, another old weapon had been reborn in the desperate fighting that followed the landings. It had become apparent that, as on the Western Front in December 1914, hand grenades were essential for the rough and tumble of close-quarter trench fighting. Yet their use did not form part of the basic training given to the fresh drafts of recruits that had flooded the barracks and depots in England; most of the British soldiers had never seen a grenade, let alone thrown one. Nor indeed had the army authorities yet settled on a standard design for the weapon. The most common bomb in use at Helles was the 'jam tin' bomb. This was not some elliptical army term!

We made our bombs or hand grenades out of used jam tins. This contained stones, a piece of gun cotton to explode it, various wads and a circular wooden piece wired to the top of the jam tin as a lid. Through this lid a detonator was inserted. To prime this grenade a piece of fuse about 2 inches long was cut and inserted into the detonator. Theoretically, this was fired by laying a match head against the top of the fuse and rubbing a match box against it. In fact it was invariably fired by a lighted cigarette. Once the fuse was lit the grenade exploded in 7 seconds. So in action one held it for 3 seconds and then threw it. If it was thrown too soon it could be picked up by the enemy and thrown back as sometimes happened.[26]

Lieutenant George Horridge, 1/5th Lancashire Fusiliers, 125th Brigade, 42nd Division

When new battalions or replacement drafts arrived at Helles they were given an ominous introduction to the battlefield that would make, break or destroy them. During their night approach in small minesweepers or drifters they would have been able to discern the dim outline of Sedd el Bahr fort. Most came ashore passing through the *River Clyde*, now acting as a jetty. Few were unaware of the awful, recent bloody history of the V Beach landing. Now they were treading where heroes had passed before. But most of them felt tremors to their very souls as they heard the deep boom of the guns, the rattle of the machine guns, the sharp random crack of rifles. Every so often they could see a Very light flare splutter its way across the night sky. As they marched away from V Beach they passed by the cemetery full of the men who had died on 25 April and in the fighting that had followed. To nervous young soldiers it was as if the very gates of hell lay open before them.

Overall the countryside had begun to show the strain of having a whole army corps encamped in it. In late April and early May it had looked so very different.

The flowers were growing in rich profusion – poppies, marigolds, dog daisies, and blue flowers, something like violets. They were all wild and presented one glorious mass of colour, most gorgeous and lovely to behold.[27]

Private Ridley Sheldon, 1/6th Manchester Regiment, 127th Brigade, 42nd Division

Now, in late May, most of the flowers were long gone. In fact vegetation of any sort was becoming rare. It was as if a horde of locusts had passed across the Peninsula. The plants were not the only things to disappear.

> The frogs began as soon as it was dark and kept it up for hours, making it impossible to sleep. Rumour had it that the Frenchmen ate the whole lot, but I think that is a slander – it was the drying up of the bogs that caused the frogs to disappear.[28]
>
> Corporal Thomas Rowatt, Headquarters, Royal Artillery, 29th Division

Helles was fast becoming unrecognisable. The beaches were huge store depots, roads were cut into the sides of cliffs, villages were razed almost to the ground, trees disappeared over night. This was not the moonscape of the Western Front battlefields; there was not enough artillery on either side to scene-shift to that extent. But it was becoming a dull and desolate vista.

> You know the pictures in the papers of such and such a place after German occupation? Well, this place was a perfect garden when we first came. Already the ground is cut up into trenches and the horses have stamped the grass away: engineers have put long wooden troughs where the old walls stood before and the trees are torn to pieces to make screens for guns. By the time fresh troops arrive behind us it will be bare as a rock.[29]
>
> Lieutenant Patrick Duff, 460th Battery, 147th Brigade, Royal Field Artillery

Unfortunately it was not rock but bare earth, which was then stirred up by the coastal winds and the endless marching feet to cover everything with a thick layer of choking dust.

Newcomers to this increasingly bleak environment soon found that to show oneself above ground was to risk sudden death at the hands of the Turkish snipers, who soon gained a fearsome reputation for accuracy.

> Johnny arrived in our sector of the trench, bursting with eagerness and curiosity; wouldn't even wait to divest himself of his full pack but must needs stick his head over the parapet, 'I must take a look at these Turks!' Too late to hear the warning cry of one of our chaps, 'Get down, tha' silly young bugger, get down!' Before you could count three his forehead was neatly drilled. These Turkish snipers are terrific.[30]
>
> Private Charles Watkins, 1/6th Lancashire Fusiliers, 125th Brigade, 42nd Division

Just a moment's loss of concentration, allowing an inch or two of head to show above the parapet, was enough to end it all. There were few second chances.

> There was one of our fellows lying on the floor of the trench, apparently asleep; so thinking he might be trodden on when darkness came on, for there is no twilight out there, I called to him to get up. He took not the slightest notice; upon this, I went to him and pushed him with my foot, but there was no response whatever. Then stooping down, I saw to my horror and dismay that the back of his head had been blown away and his brains lay scattered under him. It was a sickening sight.[31]
>
> Private Ridley Sheldon, 1/6th Manchester Regiment, 127th Brigade, 42nd Division

Soon the dead were all around them: lying in No Man's Land, built into the parapets, dug into the floor of the trench. Second Lieutenant Fred Jones wrote home describing the problem:

> I had to dig a dugout for protection from the shells. I had only gone down about three feet when I saw a piece of cloth, which I tried to pull out of the way but I found it was part of a dead Turk who had been buried there. However, there was no time to waste, so my sergeant and I slept on the Turk that night. I felt awfully afraid that first night or two, when the shells were screaming all over and the bullets were 'ping-ponging' all around. But I am quite used to them now. Expect me home safe and sound as soon as we have finished off the Turks. Within the last few hours two Turks' shells here have burst within 20 yards of me, but I am bullet-proof, you see if I am not![32]
>
> Second Lieutenant Fred Jones, 1/9th Manchester Regiment, 126th Brigade, 42nd Division

His luck ran out just eleven days later. No dramatic scene; Jones died almost unnoticed.

> We were standing in Shrapnel Gully from which our trenches branched off. Lieutenant Jones and two other officers were stood at the top talking. Suddenly, Lieutenant Jones fell down. One of the officers said, 'Have you slipped, Jones?' but when they looked at him he was dead.[33] They carried him away on a stretcher and buried him in the gully.[34]
>
> Corporal T. Valentine, 1/9th Manchester Regiment, 126th Brigade, 42nd Division

The snipers made it extraordinarily difficult and dangerous to retrieve and bury many of the corpses, and so they lay there, rapidly decomposing in the summer heat.

> One gets used to anything in war, but I think that the acrid, pungent odour of the unburied dead, which gets into your very mouth, down your tortured throat, and seems even to taint and taste your food, is really the worst thing you have to face on active service. Before long you grow quite inured, if not indifferent even, to the sight of the unburied dead. But to the death smell no one can grow used or callous. Rot and decay and the stench of putrefaction are the supreme and the final degradation of our flesh. And the uncontrollable nausea that the smell of the dead too long unburied must cause the living is not, I believe, solely a physical nausea. But, except through one's nostrils, one grows steeled, if not dense and heartless. You see horrible sights which in peace-time would make your gorge rise uncontainably, and you take them, in the swelter of war, as a matter of course. I have seen men in the trenches making a fire and cooking their bacon close to the corpse of a comrade who had 'gone west' not a yard away, not an hour before, and who had shared their last meal with them.[35]
>
> Captain Albert Mure, 1/5th Royal Scots, 88th Brigade, 29th Division

This amazing ability to carry on despite the carnage was not unique to any nation; it simply reflected a battlefield necessity. Men had to become hardened to the horrors that surrounded them or they would go mad. Some hardy, or possibly insensitive souls seemed to do more than take it all in their stride. As an example, what passed for a joke in the French Foreign Legion would certainly have aroused critical comment in most social circles.

> One of our greatest needs was cigarettes, and after a battle certain of us used to volunteer to creep out and search the dead Turks for tobacco, of which they seemed to have plenty. One night I found a nice big packet of tobacco in the coat pocket of a dead Turk. On the way back to our lines I rolled myself a cigarette but at the first puff I was nearly sick. God knows how long that Turk had lain out there but the tobacco had become tainted by his decaying body and was putrid. I rolled about twenty cigarettes and distributed them to the men in my company, who were duly grateful – until they tried to smoke them! Our jokes were a

bit on the gruesome side, but then so were the conditions in which we were living and dying.[36]

Private Cornelius Jean de Bruin, Légion Étrangère, 1st Régiment de Marche d'Afrique, 1st (Métropolitaine) Brigade, 1st Division, CEO

The men of the Foreign Legion certainly had the capability to extract the best from their situation.

Along the beach were buried the enemy corpses. They had been hurriedly buried just under the sand and pebbles. The crabs swarmed about them in their hundreds. If you knocked over one of the Turkish boots their hideous living contents came scuttling out – terrifying! The Legionnaires quickly harvested this veritable larder to make delicious bouillabaisse – we certainly didn't eat it – although they said it was delicious![37]

Lieutenant Henri Feuille, 52nd Battery, 30th Regiment, CEO

But not everyone could maintain such sangfroid when surrounded by horrors and under nerve-racking stress. As Captain Mure inspected his men one morning he encountered a distressing case of complete mental collapse.

I saw a chap lying on the ground. He was moaning and whimpering, and seemed to be partly comatose. I asked if he was hit, but no one seemed to know, or to know what was wrong with him. I lugged him up on to his feet, but he just fell down again. I hoisted him up again. He lay down. As fast as I pulled him up, he threw himself or fell back on to the ground. I tried to walk him up and down. I might as well have invited Achi Baba to come and waltz with me. He would lie down and groan and weep, and he would do no other thing. I tried to buck him up, to cheer him to sanity, to goad him to courage. It was no good. So I sent him off to the doctor, who told me, when I asked that afternoon, that the poor fellow was off his head, and probably would not recover.[38]

Captain Albert Mure, 1/5th Royal Scots, 88th Brigade, 29th Division

With the putrefying corpses came the flies. Buzzing around them in swarms, they provided an extra torment for the living. As May passed the weather grew ever hotter and the soldiers' movements were restricted.

We were invaded by millions of flies. There was no escape from these beastly insects. They swarmed around everywhere. Drinking and eating was a real nightmare and I avoided no matter how hungry I was rice pudding, which was served up frequently, mixed with currants and dehydrated fruit. It was difficult to distinguish currants from flies. They looked alike in this repulsive mixture. Immediately the lid was taken off the dixie the flies would swarm down and settle on the rim in a cluster and many of them would fall into the pudding. The spreading of jam on to a hardtack biscuit was indeed a frustrating exercise. Driven by the pangs of hunger, the hated apricot jam was tolerated of sheer necessity. A concerted effort by at least three of us to transfer the jam from the tin on to the biscuit was necessary, one to open the tin, another to flick away the flies and a third to spread the jam and cover up. The ceilings of our bivouacs, a waterproof sheet, were black with flies crawling over each other and falling on top of one as you tried to rest.[39]

Gunner Dudley Meneaud-Lissenburg, 97th Battery, 147th Brigade, Royal Field Artillery

The flies were an irritation buzzing around the soldiers' faces, but even more seriously they were feeding on the liquid faeces that filled the open latrines. No fewer than 500 flies could breed from a single deposit of human excrement and the latrines were consequently fertile breeding grounds. It was estimated by one medical handbook that one female fly could be the originator of some 5,598,720,000,000 descendant adult flies in just six months![40] 'Millions of flies' was not an exaggeration.

Latrine discipline was regarded – in theory – as paramount and the latrines were meant to be covered over and fly-proof. The army was well aware of the theory and practice of camp sanitation: in the sanitary manuals a multiplicity of carefully drawn diagrams of Heath-Robinson constructions seemed to cover every possible combination of disastrously malfunctioning bodily functions. But this was not a camp, it was a battle-field every inch of which was under fire. At Gallipoli there was not the wood, the ground space, the disinfectants, or the time to cope with the sheer scale of the problem that overwhelmed the sanitary men. With toilet paper a treasured luxury, the loving letters sent from home often met an unfortunate fate. Men were forced to wipe themselves on vegetation and eventually just used their hands and then wiped them clean as best they could in the dirt or on their filthy uniforms. Hygiene became non-existent.

As a result, the flies that landed on Gunner Meneaud-Lissenburg's food would have been carrying a cocktail of all the infectious agents that made dysentery so widespread. And even as he and his mates were releasing their insides into the crude open trench latrines, there was no respite.

> Seated on a pole placed horizontally on, and supported by trestles on either side of and over a deep, narrow trench swarming with flies, surrounded by a low and inadequate screen, could be seen the incumbent armed with a bunch of leaves, or a rolled piece of paper, striving to keep away the flies. Bouncing up and down on the pole, and smacking the leaves against his backside he looked like a jockey riding his hardest to win a race whilst we in the stands cheered lustily.[41]
>
> Gunner Dudley Meneaud-Lissenburg, 97th Battery, 147th Brigade, Royal Field Artillery

But dysentery was no joke. Both the amoebic and, even worse, the bacillary varieties of dysentery took a heavy toll of the Allied forces. Men were racked with gripping abdominal pains. Often there was nothing but slimy blood-stained mucus for all their straining efforts and soon their backsides were rendered red raw from their endlessly repeated visits to the latrines. In severe cases they could suffer a prolapsed bowel. Men in the throes of dysentery did not have the time, the strength or the opportunity to make it to the latrines and fouled themselves, further undermining the sense of self-worth that is so vital to maintain morale on active service. There were also water shortages at Helles, making dehydration a curse that would eventually hollow out men from within, reducing them to mere shadows of their former selves. Conventional treatment, which centred on a special diet, was all but impossible at Gallipoli.

Other diseases spread rapidly among the weakened soldiers. Paratyphoid went hand in hand with dysentery, so patients often had both complaints at the same time. The symptoms varied greatly in severity but included a fever, head and stomach aches, retching or vomiting, shivering fits, a severe bronchial cough, diarrhoea, vertigo, deafness, aching limbs, rose spots on the torso and in some cases, perversely, constipation. The sheer number of possible symptoms made diagnosis difficult. The conventional treatment of aspirin and a liquid diet was again fairly irrelevant to conditions on Gallipoli. Malaria was a problem specific to those soldiers from the 29th Division who had contracted the disease during their sojourn in the east and who found themselves suffering feverish relapses. Meanwhile, sandfly fever preyed mainly on the French troops, spread by the bites of a tiny hairy fly that seemed to breed in the cellars and old battlements of their base at Sedd el Bahr fort. In this world of misery, the main symptoms of jaundice, as typified by a yellow staining of the skin and the whites of the eyes, were the least of the soldiers' worries. In any case jaundice was seen more as a symptom of men suffering from liver complaints or anaemia rather than a specific disease.

Even if they were not actually ill, nearly all the Allied soldiers were reduced to a frenzy of sweaty itching by the attentions of lice. The female louse would lay about sixty whitish pinhead-sized eggs in the fibres of their uniforms, usually in the seams or natural folds. These would hatch in about ten days and the young lice would almost immediately begin to suck blood from their unwilling soldier hosts, soon infesting every hairy part of their bodies. As the lice strolled about their domain they caused excessive itching exacerbated by their bites, which created tiny puncture marks within an area of inflammation. On the Western Front when the troops were out behind the line they could visit delousing centres, where their uniforms would be heat-sterilised or even replaced. This was impossible at Gallipoli. As a result thousands of men spent hours stripped of their shirts and trousers burning down the seams with matches or candles to destroy the eggs nestling there.

In these conditions very few soldiers were in good health and most had one or more of the common complaints. Some were so weakened by their ordeal that their major body functions began to close down, resulting in complaints like 'soldier's heart', which left men breathless at the slightest exertion. The strength of the army was literally being leached away.

EVEN AT SEA THE ALLIES were beginning to suffer. The great pre-dreadnoughts sitting off shore like enormous tethered goats made obvious targets, but until the German U-boats arrived they seemed safe enough. Or at least they did until early on the morning of 13 May, when a Turkish torpedo boat, the *Muavenet-i Milliye*, crept out and launched an audacious attack on the *Goliath* which was on duty guarding the right flank of the French position just inside the Straits. On board was the youthful Midshipman Wolstan Weld-Forester.

CRASH! Bang! Cr-r-r-ash! I woke with a start and sitting up in my hammock gazed around to see what had so suddenly roused me. Some of the midshipmen were already standing on the deck in their pyjamas – others, like me, were sitting up half dazed with sleep. A party of ship's boys crowded up the ladder from the gun-room flat, followed by three officers; one of these, a Sub-Lieutenant, called out: 'Keep calm and you'll all be saved!' Up to that moment it had never dawned upon me that the ship was sinking, and even then I thought it improbable until I noticed that we were already listing to starboard.[42]

Midshipman Wolstan Weld-Forester, HMS *Goliath*

Weld-Forester made his way up on to the quarterdeck.

The ship was now heeling about 5 degrees to starboard and I climbed up to the port side. It was nearly pitch-dark. A seaman rushing to help lower the boats charged into me and I turned and swore at him. Gradually a crowd gathered along the port side. 'Boat ahoy! Boat ahoy!' they yelled; but, as the ship listed more and more, and there was no sign or sound of any approaching vessel, the men's voices seemed to get a bit hopeless. Inside the ship everything which was not secured was sliding about and bringing up against the bulkheads with a series of crashes. She had heeled over to about twenty degrees, then she stopped and remained steady for a few seconds. In the momentary lull the voice of one of our officers rang out steady and clear as at divisions: 'Keep calm, men! Be British!'[43]

Midshipman Wolstan Weld-Forester, HMS *Goliath*

Again the ship heeled rapidly and, realising she was going down, Weld-Forester decided he would have to jump for it if he was not to be caught up in the ferocious undertow that would be generated when the ship sank.

Raising my arms above my head I sprang well out board and dived. Just before I struck the water my face hit the side of the ship. It was a horrid feeling sliding on my face down the slimy side, and a second later I splashed in with tremendous force, having dived about 30 feet. Just as I was rising to the surface again a heavy body came down on top of me. I fought clear and rose rather breathless and bruised. I swam about 50 yards away, to get clear of the suction when the ship went down. Then, turning round and treading water, I watched her last moments. The noise of crashing furniture and smashing crockery was continuous.

Slowly her stern lifted until it was dimly outlined against the deep midnight sky. Slowly her bows slid further and further under until, with a final lurch, she turned completely over and disappeared bottom upwards in a mass of bubbles. She had been our home for nearly 10 months – she was gone – vanished – in less than 4 minutes.[44]

Midshipman Wolstan Weld-Forester, HMS *Goliath*

After a terrifying battle with the currents that raced through the Straits he was eventually picked up by a naval cutter and taken aboard the *Lord Nelson*. Three of his fellow young midshipmen had been lost. On hearing the alarms they had rushed to their action stations in the after torpedo room deep down in the bowels of the *Goliath*. Midshipman Christopher Tennant later heard of their fate.

Perhaps they did not hear the clang of the shutting of the bulkhead hatches and doors, or the bugle sounds of 'Abandon Ship!' as she foundered and the lights went out. They were trapped in the torpedo room alone and in the dark. Soon it must have been all so quiet and still as the ship came to rest on the bottom of the sea some 100 feet below. Three days later we heard that one of them, MacLeod, had been picked up dead but with air still in his lungs.[45] It might, I think, have been just possible to enter the torpedo tube while the outer door was closed and then the inner door could be opened, using the manual controls. As the outer door opened, the water would rush in with tremendous force but perhaps MacLeod could have struggled out. If so, how did they decide who should have the chance? How long did they wait in silence and the dark before the attempt was made?[46]

Midshipman Christopher Tennant, HMS *Lord Nelson*

In all, some 570 of the total crew of 750 were killed.

This was bad enough, but once the U-21 arrived and sank the *Triumph* off Anzac on 25 May, the situation became entirely hopeless. Still the old *Majestic* was left sitting alone and unguarded off W Beach. Two days later, the U-21 carefully manoeuvred into position to launch a pair of torpedoes at 06.45 on 27 May. The U-21 was spotted too late and the twin explosions and sudden cataclysmic inrush of water doomed the *Majestic*. Aboard the ship was one of the official journalists covering the campaign, Mr Ellis Ashmead-Bartlett.

I was aroused by men rushing by me and someone trod on, or stumbled against, my chest. This awoke me and I called out, 'What's the matter?' A voice replied from somewhere, 'There's a torpedo coming!' I just had time to scramble to my feet when there came a dull heavy explosion about 15 feet forward of the shelter deck on the port side. The hit must have been very low down, as there was no shock from it to be felt on deck. The old *Majestic* immediately gave a jerk over towards port and remained with a heavy list. Then there came a sound as if the contents of every pantry in the world had fallen at the same moment. I never before heard such a clattering, as everything loose in her tumbled about. You could tell at once she had been mortally wounded somewhere in her vitals and you felt instinctively she would not long stay afloat. The sea was crowded with men swimming about and calling for assistance. I think that many of these old reservists, who formed the majority of the crew, had forgotten how to swim, or else had lost all faith in their own powers.[47]

Ellis Ashmead-Bartlett, *Daily Telegraph*

Thanks to the swarms of small vessels that rushed in to rescue the crew, only forty-three of the 700 men died.

The arrival of the U-boats recast the balance of forces at Helles. As at Anzac the great ships of war could no longer prowl night and day off the beaches; now they could only appear in special circumstances. Lesser ships – destroyers – would take up much of the work of supporting the troops. Many of the troops ashore felt deserted after the big beasts had gone. This was a not unnatural reaction. For they were almost totally isolated, sitting at the end of a tenuous supply chain open to disruption and disaster every link of the way.

The United Kingdom was some 2,000 miles away and the nearest fully functioning naval base was Alexandria, in Egypt. This undoubtedly possessed everything required from a port, equipped as it was with spacious quays, cranes, lighters, tugboats, plentiful labour and of course capacious storage areas. Yet it was nearly 700 miles from Gallipoli. The advanced base of Mudros on the island of Lemnos was sixty miles from Helles, but it was by no means the complete article. Mudros Bay offered a good natural anchorage, but that was all – a phenomenal amount of work was required to build it up into a military supply base. Piers soon snaked out into the bay, a decent water supply was secured, camps set up and huge stores established with interconnecting roads and light railways. Two large freighters were retained to act as floating supply and ordnance depots, while the liner *Aragon* acted as headquarters for the multifarious supply and communications staff. Mudros may have been remote but back in the 1840s detailed harbour charts had been prepared by a Royal Navy party under the command of one Captain Corrie, who was commemorated, certainly without his knowledge, as follows by one of his team:

> The somewhat fantastic names of the jagged peaks took our fancy. They ran thus: 'DEN, MAD, EBEIR, ROC'. And then one day some bright lad read them backwards and discovered that they spelt, 'Corrie be damned!'[48]
>
> Brigadier-General Sir George MacMunn, Headquarters, MEF, Mudros

Even though the British had been there over seventy years before, everything had to be built from scratch. Over the length of the campaign the British and French succeeded in establishing a fully fledged Supply and Horse Transport Depot at Mudros, with all the attendant camps, hospitals and necessary infrastructure. A little further forward, at Imbros, was the Advanced Supply Depot, but there was still fifteen miles of open sea between there and the Peninsula. Once the U-boats had announced their unwelcome arrival in the Aegean there was no possibility of unloading directly from large ships off the beaches, so thousands of tons of stores had to be transhipped at night from Mudros or Lemnos by much smaller 500-ton steamers to V Beach, W Beach and Anzac Cove. It was only with great difficulty and much manpower that the foodstuffs, munitions and plethora of daily stores were unceremoniously deposited on these open beaches.

True there were piers constructed and eventually blockships put in place to try to protect the harbour areas. But these were never ports in any conventional sense. And the piers were ephemeral in the face of the raw power of the sea. There was certainly no safe harbour here in the event of a storm, while manmade destruction was always threatening from the Turkish shells that crashed down in random fashion. Despite this, at Helles huge supply depots were constructed. A teeming anthill of activity held stores and munitions to last the troops for at least a month in case the tenuous supply chain was broken, whether by U-boats, storms at sea, or by the destruction of the flimsy piers. Even when the stores arrived at the beaches they still had to be taken up in stages to the units in the line. The campaign was a logistical nightmare that would make any responsible staff officer despair. As a method of waging warfare it was insanity; but the Allies had left themselves no alternative.

Yet even the finest supply arrangements devised by man could not solve the most intractable logistical problem that faced the troops here. The grievous shortage of artillery shells on the Western Front meant that the Gallipoli sideshow, quite rightly, was starved of these most precious of resources. This can be presented as a mere issue of priorities, but it was in fact a sober recognition that the war on the Western Front, like the naval stand-off in the North Sea, was crucial to the survival of the British Empire. It was here that the war would be won or lost. Until this priority changed the MEF would simply have to make do.

IN LONDON THE WAR COUNCIL had met on 14 May to discuss the progress of the campaign that it had been responsible for initiating. Against a backdrop of bad news from both Gallipoli and the Western Front it was clear that serious decisions would have to be made. Was the campaign to be abandoned? Should massive reinforcements be sent to help Hamilton win through? Or was it better to send moderate reinforcements and rely on steady progress towards the ultimate objective? Kitchener was vehemently against any idea of an evacuation, believing the consequences would be politically disastrous in the Balkans and reduce British prestige across the Islamic world. However, he was equally certain that there were not many more reinforcements to be spared. There was also confusion among the committee members as to exactly how many divisions might be required to achieve success. It was therefore decided to check with Hamilton before coming to a decision. Kitchener cabled:

> The War Council would like to know what force you consider would be necessary to carry through the operations upon which you are engaged. You should base this estimate on the supposition that I have adequate forces to be placed at your disposal.[49]
>
> Secretary of State for War Lord Kitchener, War Council

Hamilton responded by asking for three divisions, in addition to the 52nd Division that he had already been promised. However, in the three days it took for him to reply the whole political situation in London changed drastically.

The Liberal government had never been strong. Now, in May 1915, it was crippled by two serious crises that were eventually to bring it down. The first was the shortage of munitions on the Western Front. The terrible casualties there were at least partially attributable to the paucity of the artillery bombardments and the grieving British population was no longer prepared to listen to excuses. The problem was augmented by the resignation of Admiral Sir John Fisher from his position as First Sea Lord. This was predictable: Fisher was too old for the pressures of the job and ground down by its responsibilities. However, he was still adored by the public. On 15 May he finally resigned, citing the drip-drip of new naval reinforcements to the Dardanelles as his reason for going. He accompanied his resignation with leaks to opposition politicians and the press to try to whip up a scandal that would overwhelm Asquith's government.

Although the government fell, Asquith was able to continue as prime minister by negotiating an agreement with the Conservatives, to form the First Coalition Government on 25 May 1915. Many key figures in the previous government survived but Churchill did not. Fisher's departure, the failures in the Dardanelles and the general opprobrium felt by the Conservatives, from whom he had defected to join the Liberals in 1904, meant that Churchill's tenure as First Lord of the Admiralty was terminated. He was reduced to the nominal position of Chancellor of the Duchy of Lancaster, leaving him in effect a Minister without Portfolio and with a much reduced Cabinet status. He was replaced at his beloved Admiralty by the veteran Conservative former prime minister Arthur Balfour. Asquith would have liked to have dispensed with Kitchener's services as Secretary of State for War, but that was politically impossible in view of his continuing popularity with the public.

The War Council was recast and renamed, significantly, the Dardanelles Committee. This new body consisted of six members of the original War Council, five Conservatives and Kitchener. Both service representatives were dropped. Amidst all this political manoeuvring the Dardanelles Committee would not actually meet until 7 June and so no decisions were made. For the moment Hamilton would have to make do with the 52nd Division.

MAY HAD BEEN A SALUTARY MONTH for the Allies at Helles. Their plans had been stymied at every turn by the Turks and they were now facing a prolonged period of trench warfare without the troops, the artillery, the munitions or the logistical structure to succeed. Their Turkish opponents were well dug in, present in strength, had a superior tactical position and better logistics. Their only weakness was an equally chronic shortage of artillery and munitions. Yet somehow Hamilton and Hunter-Weston managed to convince themselves that a successful general assault could be launched all along the line from the Aegean to the Straits. True the British forces had been augmented slightly. Some badly needed replacement drafts had restocked the depleted ranks of the 29th Division, the Royal Marine Brigade fresh from its detachment to Anzac had been reunited with the rest of the RND, while the arrival of the 126th Brigade had completed the 42nd Division. The 52nd Division was also on its way. Nevertheless the only substantive change since the debacle of 8 May was that the Turks had become a lot stronger. Hamilton favoured waiting for the 52nd Division but Hunter-Weston was conscious that every day that passed strengthened the Turkish defences. General Albert d'Amade had been recalled to France on 15 May but his replacement, General Henri Gouraud, was equally keen to make progress. The commanders were also conscious of increasing impatience from London and Paris for tangible progress. The eventual decision to launch a general attack at Helles on 4 June in what would become the Third Battle of Krithia tactically mirrored the strategic mistakes made at the start of the campaign. Resources have to be concentrated and then deployed where there is a realistic chance of success. The decision not to await the arrival of the 52nd Division was an egregious blunder.

Once the sheer madness of making an assault at all is discounted, the operational plans conceived by Hunter-Weston's headquarters staff of what was now known as VIII Corps (29th Division, 42nd Division and RND) were by no means stupid. They at least tried, despite the inadequacy of their artillery and ammunition resources, to destroy the enemy defences with a four-hour preliminary bombardment. They even introduced a cunning plan whereby the guns would suspend firing at 11.20 to encourage the Turks to man their positions before the bombardment resumed for another half hour. As a further innovation they unleashed the Rolls Royce armoured cars of the RND to drive along the small roads that led to Krithia. As no one knew what they were capable of their orders were vague. When the infantry went over the top at 12.00 they would advance in two waves, with the intention of taking the first three Turkish lines to a depth of about 800 yards before consolidating ready to resist the inevitable counter-attacks. The French 1st and 2nd Divisions would assault the Haricot Redoubt which barred their progress at Kereves Dere; on their left the RND would launch an attack between Kereves Dere and Achi Baba Nullah; the 42nd Division would advance between Achi Baba Nullah and Krithia Nullah along Krithia Spur; while the 29th Division would push forward between Krithia Nullah and the sea. Facing them in the Helles lines were the 9th and 12th Turkish Divisions, with most of the 7th Division in reserve. As ever, the Turks could bring up reserves as required. The two forces were approximately equal in strength, an equation that promised failure for the attacking forces in trench warfare conditions on any front in the Great War in 1915.

In anticipation of the offensive, great efforts were made to secure jumping-off positions that were within easy striking range – about 200–250 yards – from the Turkish front line. This involved men being sent on local operations designed to straighten the line, sapping forwards by degrees or creeping out at night to dig new trenches right under the noses of the Turks. The night before the assault the troops made their final preparations. On the 42nd Division front, the 127th Brigade (the 1/5th, 1/6th, 1/7th and 1/8th Manchesters) had the dubious honour of leading the attack.

> We are sending out parties to cut our wire in front of us to-night, the 3rd, so that we can get through. Every man has 200 rounds in his pouches, ten in rifle magazine and a loose bandolier with 100 rounds making 310 altogether to carry with him. Each man is given a gas mask and two empty sandbags. The latter are for filling if necessary, to strengthen any position that we take, then a number of red screens are issued, myself having one to carry. These we have to fix in the ground at the farthest point of enemy ground gained so that our artillery can see them and so lengthen their range beyond the screens to avoid shelling our men advancing: the screen is a piece of red canvas a yard square nailed between two stakes 4ft long to be driven in the ground. We are busy all night preparing scaling ladders and making steps in the side of the trench ready for going over at noon.[50]
>
> Private Jack Gatley, 1/7th Manchester Regiment, 127th Brigade, 42nd Division

To their left the gnarled veterans of the 29th Division felt at least a tinge of hope as they discussed the artillery preparations.

> The way the coming bombardment was spoken about gave one the impression that it would be almost impossible for a Turkish trench to be left whole, and as for the men who would be occupying them, they were as good as dead already, according to the whys, wherefores and therefores! We all said we hope so, as it is better for them to do the killing, than us, when they could do it from such a safe distance.[51]
>
> Private Daniel Joiner, 1st KOSB, 87th Brigade, 29th Division

Friday 4 June 1915 was a beautiful, almost idyllic summer's day where every prospect pleased and only man was vile. The bombardment opened at 08.00, concentrating on the main Turkish redoubts, before it became a general barrage of the whole Turkish lines at 11.05. On the right of the line the French artillery pounded the Haricot Redoubt and the Turkish trenches.

> In a moment fire blazed up all across the Peninsula. All the batteries opened fire at the same time. I noticed with pleasure that several battleships just arrived from Lemnos at the exact hour to cooperate in the attack – that gave us confidence! For quarter of an hour there was an infernal din, although we had to fire with parsimony. What's going to happen now? 11.15. An abrupt end to the explosions. Absolute silence! This silence certainly made a great impression on the Turks after our previous similar bombardments, because they guessed we had finished and opened an intense musketry fire to which our troops, following orders, did not reply. 11.30. The bombardment resumed. This time if the Turks understood anything it was that we had a degree of malevolent cunning![52]
>
> Second Lieutenant Raymond Weil, 39th Régiment d'Artillerie, 1st Division, CEO

The wind was blowing a thick plume of smoke and dust towards the British and French lines, obscuring their view. Colonel Hans Kannengiesser was watching from his vantage point behind the Turkish lines. To him it was an awesome display of gunnery as he watched the British and French shells crashing down on his front line.

> From here one saw how accurately the English bombardment had come down on our front line. Crater lay alongside crater. A continual

thick cloud of dust, which continuously blew into the air at various points like a volcano in eruption, marked our front line more clearly and accurately than I had ever seen it before. Shrapnel fire coming from the flank pierced the cloud of dust streaming upwards and raked along the trenches. 'The poor fellows there forward!' I thought. It was, however, impossible to help them; they must simply endure in their dugouts directly behind the front line, ready to spring out and occupy immediately the trenches, or what was left of the trenches, the moment the artillery fire lifted and the enemy infantry began to storm. We here in the rear received no shells; neither did the batteries around us. The whole artillery might of the enemy lay quite definitely on the front line trenches.[53]

Colonel Hans Kannengiesser, Headquarters, 9th Division, Fifth Army

So the clock ticked down and the last hours, minutes and seconds of hundreds of men's lives trickled away. All along the line men were alone with what might be their final thoughts.

We can see through periscopes that their front line is bristling with machine guns. Meanwhile we are issued with extra iron rations, also a triangular piece of polished tin to fix on our backs so that the sun flashing on these shows where we are to the artillery and staff observers in our rear, and enables them to follow our advance and also distinguish us from the Turks who wear uniforms the same colour as ours – only the headwear is different. Nearer and nearer creeps the Zero Hour and everyone is in a nervous state of excitement which shows in various ways. The waiting is a terrible strain, we are given our usual tablespoonful of rum; we have still half an hour to wait for the whistle. Our guns now increase their fire, again the enemy follow suit until there is only 5 minutes to go then our guns lengthen their range to behind and between the Turks' first and second lines, 3 minutes to go and I whisper a short prayer and feel quite calm now, and many farewells and promises are made to inform each other's wives or mothers in case anything happens. One minute to go and an order to get ready and the whistle goes, we scramble up and over the top into a withering machine-gun and rifle fire with shrapnel bursting overhead.[54]

Private Jack Gatley, 1/7th Manchester Regiment, 127th Brigade, 42nd Division

Finally, the moment had come. On the left of the British line the 29th Indian Brigade stormed forward on the stroke of noon along Gully Spur and up the narrow channel of Gully Ravine. The result was a slaughter, for, whatever the success of the bombardment elsewhere, it had utterly failed to disturb the coherence of the Turkish defences in this sector. Second Lieutenant Reginald Savory was attacking with the 14th Sikhs in near hopeless circumstances.

> Those last few minutes before Zero Hour made no deep impression on me, except possibly the familiar feeling of waiting for the pistol before a sprint with a void in the pit of one's stomach and anxiety as to the result. And, then twelve noon – blow the whistle – scramble over the top – off you go! From that moment, I lost all control of the fighting. The roar of musketry was so intense as to drown all other sound, except for that of the guns. To try to give an order was useless. The nearest man to me was a yard away and even then I could not see him. I was fighting a lone battle. The sooner I could get across No Man's Land and reach the cover of the enemy's trenches the better. And then, before I could realise it, I found myself standing on the parapet of a Turkish trench and looking down at a Turk inside it. He seemed an ordinary person. There was none of the 'Terrible Turk' about him. He was not even firing, but was leaning against the back of his trench. Yet, if I had given him time, he would have shot me and there were others on either side of him. I jumped in and skewered him to the back of his trench with my bayonet. Poor devil! I can see his grimace to this day.[55]
>
> Second Lieutenant Reginald Savory, 14th Sikhs, 29th Indian Brigade

Shortly afterwards he was knocked out and slightly wounded. When he awoke he found that he was one of the very few surviving officers. His subsequent comments on the battle have a bitter note.

> Methods here seem to be based on a theory that all tactics are rot and that the only way to do anything at all is to rush forward bald-headed, minus support, minus reserves, and in the end probably minus a limb or two. We had as our own special task, to advance up a nullah (a thing which one has always learned should never be done until all the ground commanding it is first seized) against the Turks who were in a wired trench at the end, and also on both sides and at the top, and their machine guns took us in front and rear and from practically every side. Needless to say we had no supports whatever! Not a damned thing![56]
>
> Second Lieutenant Reginald Savory, 14th Sikhs, 29th Indian Brigade

Alongside them the 88th Brigade, augmented for the occasion by battalions from the 86th and 87th Brigades, was attacking along Fir Tree Spur and they too encountered fierce resistance. The 1st KOSB and 4th Worcesters suffered severe casualties but they managed to gain a good deal of ground. On reaching the Turkish front line they charged on for the second line. This line had not been under bombardment; the British had neither the guns nor the shells for a deep bombardment.

> Turks were jumping the parados and running for it. Others were throwing away their arms and surrendering. Led by Captain Ogilvy we all gave chase, however as the Turks had discarded their equipment and arms and were trying to beat the world's record in sprinting, they soon widened the gap. After getting to the fourth trench Ogilvy called a halt, as we had lost our first wind. However the Turks were fleeing in all directions, the inclination to follow so strong that hardly had we got into the trench, and told off escorts for the prisoners, than we were off again. There was no more resistance, the trenches were only occupied by dead or wounded.[57]
>
> Private Daniel Joiner, 1st KOSB, 87th Brigade, 29th Division

It had been a fantastic performance against the odds, but could they consolidate and hold their gains when the Turks reorganised and brought up their reserves? Behind the Borderers were the 1/5th Royal Scots. Captain Albert Mure had a first-class view of the pathetic performance of the RND armoured cars as they were thwarted by a combination of trenches and Turkish road blocks.

> An armoured car came with them, spitting and puffing and lumbering along. Nothing so ugly or so awkward ever was seen outside of a zoo! The very amateur bridge that the Engineers had tossed up for them was just beside my phone. The car made for it. She got on to the planks all right; then her off hind-wheel slipped over the side, and down she came on to the axle, and pretty well on to my head. Nothing could be done, so the naval officer in charge and the gunner climbed out. In getting out the naval petty officer was seriously wounded.[58]
>
> Captain Albert Mure, 1/5th Royal Scots, 88th Brigade, 29th Division

Armoured warfare seemed a very long way in the future. Soon the ditched armoured car attracted the shell fire of the Turks and Mure had a remarkable escape.

I had just written out two messages and given them to two orderlies.
I felt restless, and got up, turned about aimlessly, and moved away
some 10 yards. That restlessness saved my life. At that moment a shell
crashed into the trench and exploded precisely where I had been
sitting. Frankly, it made me feel peculiar. I remember that I stumbled a
bit as I walked on, thinking that if I had stayed where I was, or gone the
other way, I should, by now, have been blown to little bits. I finished
what I wanted to do and went back to the trench. I met one of my
orderlies, who, fortunately for him, had left immediately with the first
message I had written. He had bits of shrapnel in his jaw, in his elbow,
and in his back. I bound him up and packed him off. I got back into the
trench, and saw what I had not seen before, for the smoke had cleared
now. My other orderly lay dead with my message still in his hand. His
body and his head lay 4 or 5 feet apart. Two of my signallers were killed
also, and mutilated so horribly that to describe their condition would
be inexcusable. I stood for a moment and gazed at the wreckage: wreck
of trench, wreck of phone, wreck of men, and then I sat dully down on
the mud floor of the trench.[59]

Captain Albert Mure, 1/5th Royal Scots, 88th Brigade, 29th Division

To the right of the 29th Division was the 42nd Division. The Lancashire territorials had been rank amateurs when they had landed at Helles
just four weeks before. Frightened by the noise of battle, afraid of the dark,
terrified by the sight of mangled human remains, unable to perform even
the simplest of military tasks, they had been all but useless. But they had
matured in the trenches, learnt to control themselves under fire, and now
they were ready for battle. The attack was carried out by the Manchesters
of the 127th Brigade.

I shall never forget the moment when we had to leave the shelter of
the trenches. It is indeed terrible, the first step you take – right in the
face of the most deadly fire, and to realise that any moment you may
be shot down; but if you are not hit, then you seem to gather courage.
And when you see on either side of you men like yourself, it inspires
you with a determination to press forward. Away we went over the
parapet with fixed bayonets – one line of us like the wind. But it was
absolute murder, for men fell like corn before the sickle. I had not gone
more than 20 yards beyond our first trench, about 60 yards in all, when
I was shot through the left leg about 5 inches above the knee. At once
I realised what had happened, for it seemed as though someone had

taken a red-hot gimlet and suddenly thrust it right through my leg. I dropped immediately and could not go any further.[60]

Private Ridley Sheldon, 1/6th Manchester Regiment, 127th Brigade, 42nd Division

Private Jack Gatley was more fortunate and made it through to leap down into the Turkish front line, where he became caught up in hand-to-hand battle.

It was a shambles and the slaughter was terrible on each side, and here we were at a disadvantage as the enemy were using bombs with deadly effect and we were being blown to pieces. This drove us into a frenzy of rage and we went at them like madmen, they nearly drove us out as they were three to one, but we rallied and at last we drove them out and had captured the trench and many prisoners as they were scrambling out. I caught hold of one that was carrying a flag on a long stick, he was almost over when I jumped at him and grabbed the end of the stick and tried to pull him down, suddenly he broke away and dropping his flag levelled his rifle straight at my face, I thought I was done for but I got the first shot in and he fired as he fell with the flag under him, I took the flag as a memento. It was a near thing for me.[61]

Private Jack Gatley, 1/7th Manchester Regiment, 127th Brigade, 42nd Division

They would now hold this trench while the other two companies followed up the retreating Turks.

The 127th Brigade managed to break through to a depth of between 1,000 and 1,200 yards, thereby taking the last organised Turkish trenches visible before the outskirts of the Krithia village in front of them. It was a considerable achievement that marked the coming of age of the 42nd Division.

Next in line were the RND, who launched the 2nd Naval Brigade into the attack. This previously ramshackle formation had gained an impressive variety of military skills over the past month, but the blast of fire after the temporary suspension of the bombardment had let them know that the Turks were well and truly ready for them. Still, over the top they went.

Off we go and up we went over the ladder. The moment we started to leave the trench at this traverse, 10–12 feet long, where we were, there were men falling back into the trench or on the parapet. There was dead all over the place. My Platoon Commander got through, I followed him up there. Parsons had already been killed. We got into dead ground. The Petty Officer said, 'Well, come on, lad! C'mon!' We moved again and then lay down to get a breather. He was an old reservist, his bald head glittering in the sun – he'd lost his helmet. He was up on the trench with his rifle and bayonet, 'C'mon! C'mon!' Around his head he'd got a white handkerchief and blood pouring down his face just like the pictures in the *London Illustrated*. He was bleeding dreadfully. I wanted to keep up with him but he was now 20 yards ahead of me. I got to the trench and in I go – it was 10 feet deep! There was one or two dead, nobody alive.[62]

Ordinary Seaman Joe Murray, Hood Battalion, 2nd Naval Brigade, RND

They had succeeded in taking three trenches but had suffered severe casualties. And their attack was faltering. Sustained success would depend on the rapid arrival of reserve troops.

On the far right of the line the French were faced by the Haricot Redoubt that still barred their progress along the western bank of Kereves Dere. The Turks had retaliated in devastating fashion with their own artillery. And then the dreaded rattle of the machine guns and massed small arms tore into the French poilus.

They weren't able to advance a step. I was informed by telephone: on the English side they had made a little progress towards Krithia, but on our front it was a disaster. Our poor foot soldiers were slaughtered in the middle of the Turkish fortifications put up just the night before as if they had guessed our intentions. The enemy had benefited from the pause in our fire, and the moment of hesitation by our infantry (who were wondering if it had really finished) to reoccupy the front lines, that were hardly damaged and to get in place all their machine guns. The result was that our poor poilus, caught up in the barbed wire and *chevaux de frise*, were slowed in their tracks and then literally mowed down by the machine guns.[63]

Second Lieutenant Raymond Weil, 39th Régiment d'Artillerie, 1st Division, CEO

The French assault had been a disaster. It was not their fault: it was almost impossible for them to make progress against well-dug-in Turks, covered on one flank by the chasm of Kereves Dere. The consequences for the British would be dire. As the French attack broke down, the RND began to experience enfilading fire from their right flank. The Collingwood

Battalion was slaughtered as they advanced in support of the Hood attack at 12.15, losing hundreds before they even reached the original British front line.

The battle now appeared to lie in the balance. Hunter-Weston and Gouraud had a choice whether to use their last reserves to support the success of the 42nd Division in the centre or order a renewed effort by the French and the 29th Indian Brigade. Historical commentators present this as a stark choice between supporting success or failure, with victory the reward for the right option, but this view ignores the Turkish position. For the Turks had plentiful reserves and the faltering Allied attack threatened little that firm resistance and counter-attacks could not contain. Hunter-Weston and Gouraud chose to try again on the flanks. A renewed attack was ordered. The French reserves were deployed on the right alongside the RND, while the reinforced 29th Indian Brigade were to try again on the left. In the event, almost nothing happened as the French were simply unable to mount another attack in the dreadful circumstances that still prevailed in front of the Haricot. The gallant efforts of the reinforced 29th Indian Brigade only added to the slaughter. Nothing had changed since the attack scant hours before.

The consequences of the French failure were now working their way across the battlefield as the Turks viciously counter-attacked, pressing into the right flank of the RND who had little chance to consolidate or dig vital communication trenches back across No Man's Land. Sometime after 12.30 an ignominious retreat to their old front line began. It was a process fraught with danger. Ordinary Seaman Joe Murray was in a fairly dazed state in the Turkish second line.

> I remember seeing two officers away to my left – Denis Browne was one – taking about fifty men going forward. We went forward about half a dozen of us to a bit of a ditch – that was considered to be the third trench. All of a sudden the right flank started retiring, the Anson Battalion. We were forced to retire, hopped back, jumped over the second trench; then we scampered back to his first trench. I thought, 'Well now, if we can stop here we can hold them here!' I kept on turning round and firing, but there wasn't much opposition from the front, I couldn't understand why we were retiring, we weren't being pressed at all. We were almost near his first trench. I was out of puff, so tired and I thought, 'One more trot and I shall be in the trench!' But

when I got there it was full of Turks! So instead of stopping over the trench I leapt over the top and I was helped over by a bayonet stuck right in the posterior – right in the nick!!!! I went falling right in front of the trench into a shell hole, lying flat in there.[64]

Ordinary Seaman Joe Murray, Hood Battalion, 2nd Naval Brigade, RND

Murray had to stay there for hours with a Turk, oblivious to his presence, firing a rifle through a loophole just above his head. He only managed to get back to the British front line when night fell. With the chastened men of the RND back in their jumping-off trenches the pressure shifted to the right flank of the 42nd Division. Private Jack Gatley was busy in the old Turkish front line when the Turks began to push along the trench.

We are consolidating our position and securing dugouts and take many more prisoners that are hiding in them. The whole trench is a shambles with dead and dying, limbless trunks are lying all over the place and the whole bottom of the trench is running with blood which we have to move about in, arms, legs and heads are strewn about and being added to every minute by shells from the front and bombs from the right. We searched for the dead and wounded and took all bombs from their haversacks, and used them on the right. Wounded were lying about groaning in pain until taken away to the dressing station.[65]

Private Jack Gatley, 1/7th Manchester Regiment, 127th Brigade, 42nd Division

If they had given way then his comrades who had advanced into the Turkish second and third lines would have been totally cut off. The old No Man's Land lay like an open wasteland behind them, preventing reinforcement.

We are parched with thirst, the position here is terrible, what few men are left are spaced out at some distance apart with less chance of being hit. Lieutenant Hamilton and a few men started to fill all the spare sandbags we carried and with these built up the gap making a barrier between us, but a lot of men were lost in doing so. It eased the strain for a while. But they started lobbing bombs over amongst us and did terrible damage as we had no more to reply with, so we caught some bombs as they came over and returned them. A fellow named Rawlinson was hit by a bomb, it exploded under his chin and blew the whole of his face off from ear to ear and it hung down on his chest, the poor chap walked about groping his way and making an awful groaning noise, until someone placed an empty sandbag over his head and lead him away, he died before night, it is a sight that lives in my mind still.[66]

Private Jack Gatley, 1/7th Manchester Regiment, 127th Brigade, 42nd Division

The Manchesters just about managed to hold on and the Turks never got past their crude ramshackle barricade. During the night the shortage of men meant that the survivors had no choice but to fall back. Among them was Private Jack Morten.

We then got the order to retire to the first trench we had taken, which was about 500 yards to the rear, so we started off at the double. It seemed an awfully long 500 yards, as after advancing about 1,000 yards we were pretty jiggered. On I ran with the bullets whistling past and men on either side of me dropping down shot. I fell twice from sheer exhaustion and finished up walking. At last I reached the trench and dived over the parapet like a shot rabbit, none the worse, thank God, but absolutely jiggered.[67]

Private Jack Morten, 1/7th Manchester Regiment, 127th Brigade, 42nd Division

It was on 5 June that it became apparent that the Allies were no longer directing the course of the Third Battle of Krithia. The Turks were fully in control and at dawn launched a series of vigorous counter-attacks that not only threatened the remaining gains of the day before, but sought to undermine the entire Allied front.

There was a heavy sea mist hanging over everywhere and it was not properly light yet, they were almost on us before we realised they were coming. We poured a continuous rapid fire into the Turks, we had only two machine guns in our line and these joined in, we simply mowed the Turks down in front but they still came on yelling, 'Allah! Allah!' They were trying to drive us out and so link up with the Turks on our right and recapture all their own line back. We kept up rapid fire all the while they advanced on us and our rifle barrels are almost red hot and burnt our hands as we gripped them. Still they came on, and nearer, until it looked as though we should be swamped out by overwhelming numbers, still we kept up the fire and our slightly wounded men replenished our stacks of ammunition as we used them up. Then our artillery took a hand and set up a barrage on the advancing enemy with shrapnel and did terrible havoc. This was the turning point, they retreated and were chased by rapid fire.[68]

Private Jack Gatley, 1/7th Manchester Regiment, 127th Brigade, 42nd Division

The aftermath of battle proved too much for Captain Mure of the 1/5th Royal Scots. Suffering from a form of shell shock, he could not control either his body or his nerves.

> I felt that there was something very wrong with me. I couldn't quite diagnose what it was. My spine seemed to be misplaced, and to be made of glue rather than of bone; yet I could walk all right. I went back at about half-past seven, and started my usual evening's work. But I was listless. I could neither rest nor really work. Nothing interested me – nothing! I gave it up and lay down, but I couldn't sleep. At half-past seven I struggled down to the gully for breakfast. It was torture to walk. It was torture to think. It was double torture to be. I remember chatting quite cheerfully with someone, I cannot recall with whom, as I began to eat, and then something suddenly snapped, and I collapsed into a sort of maudlin, weeping condition. I was all in. I felt that I was going silly, and that I *must* have a rest, if only for one day. I had been under fire for forty-two days.[69]

Captain Albert Mure, 1/5th Royal Scots, 88th Brigade, 29th Division

In a daze of confusion Mure was evacuated from W Beach, at least for the moment a broken man; one among many.

Over the next two days there was some desperate fighting. The Turkish counter-attacks were so vigorous that at times they threatened to break through themselves, there were so few Allied reserves at hand to plug gaps in the line. The desperation can be judged by the award of the VC to the 18-year-old Second Lieutenant Dallas Moor who, despite his youth, was acting commanding officer of the 2nd Hampshires when, on the morning of 6 June, there was a dangerous outbreak of panic in the salient left by the partial retirement of the 42nd Division. Terrified of being cut off, the troops occupying the front line trench (known as H12) ran back, promoting equal chaos in the second line (H11) whose garrison also fell back in terror. The Turks were threatening a complete breakthrough. Moor rushed across and stemmed the retreat by the abrupt action of shooting up to four of the fleeing soldiers. He managed not only to stop the rout, but to rally his men and lead them forward to retake H11, although still leaving H12 in Turkish hands. This level of chaos and panic was not an isolated incident as the Turks pushed down the gullies, seeking to penetrate as far as they could out of sight as they probed the weak points in the line. Key to breaking up the Turkish attacks was the artillery. Australian Gunner Ralph Doughty of the 2nd Battery, 1st Field Artillery Brigade was among those who played a vital part in keeping back the rampaging Turks on 6 June.

> Very rowdy morning. Got action before breakfast and kept a warm fire for an hour. Immediately afterwards got to it hot and strong. Our gun was detailed to keep reinforcements from getting to the firing line, via a small nullah. And it did. We just waited for them to come over the far crest and they got it. We had them on toast alright. Couldn't advance or retreat and our guns cut off flanking movements by spraying each side with shrapnel. The only thing for them to do was to take cover in a bit of light scrub which they did and we got on to that scrub and searched every inch of it for two solid hours. I've just been to the observation station and had a look at it with the glasses. Not a man came out of it alive. The ground is packed thickly with them. I am as deaf as a mule in the right ear and both hands burnt a bit. We're having another go in a few minutes.[70]
>
> Gunner Ralph Doughty, 2nd Battery, 1st Field Artillery Brigade, AIF

After the main battle petered out there was a series of minor attacks to straighten the line or to counter the equivalent activities of the Turks. Thus it was that Second Lieutenant Bartle Bradshaw found himself faced with an acute dilemma on 10 June.

> The Company Commander asked Platoon commanders for a list of subalterns and men from Platoons who would volunteer for an attack on a Turkish sap which is getting perilously near 'B' Company's lines. It means a DCM for men who get through. It is hardly fair to ask for volunteers, work of this [kind] should be done by rota. I have volunteered of course, and I expect the rest of the subalterns will do also. Out here one does everything that comes one's way. Trusting in God.[71]
>
> Second Lieutenant Bartle Bradshaw, 1st Border Regiment, 87th Brigade, 29th Division

Led to his fate by his sense of duty, poor Bradshaw was killed in the attack that followed.[72]

THE BRITISH AND FRENCH OFFENSIVE had ground to a halt, not with them positioned astride Achi Baba poised for an untroubled advance on Kilid Bahr, but clinging on to their meagre gains and with no hope of a successful advance. A French staff officer realised the gravity of their situation.

> Theoretically our situation is untenable. I'd say that if we were on peacetime manoeuvres the exercise umpires would have adjudicated that we were all dead. That is the logical consequence of our troops living under the cross fire of Turkish batteries firing from Achi Baba to our front and the Asiatic coast to our rear. Happily, practice and theory are two different things. In practice our situation is tenable because from current military experience it takes ten times a man's weight in steel to kill him! Also the Turkish bombardment, even on their best days, is far inferior in intensity to the deluges of shells that the Germans fire on the Western Front.[73]
>
> Captain François Charles-Roux, Headquarters, CEO

The British and French sat in their trenches, their every move obvious to the Turkish artillery observation officers high up on the slopes of Achi Baba. The failure of the attack meant that instead of augmenting their force the 52nd Division, which had begun to disembark during the final stages of the Turkish counter-attacks, was merely restocking depleted ranks.

The story of Helles was not a tale of defensive actions, skirmishes, patrols and small-scale company attacks, as at Anzac in May and early June. At Helles the real battle for Gallipoli had been fought out as whole divisions hurled themselves at each other time and time again on a front of about 5,000 yards from the Aegean to the Straits. Now the British and French horizons had closed in. Their aspirations were no longer Kilid Bahr or Achi Baba, or even Krithia, but merely the unprepossessing vista of the next in an endless sequence of trenches. The British had suffered 4,500 casualties and the French 2,000 at the Third Battle of Krithia; the Turks had lost about 9,000 men. Would a Fourth, Fifth or Sixth Battle of Krithia offer anything but more deaths?

11

HELLES: WRITING ON THE WALL

We were afraid of being attacked, but, believe me, we were even more afraid of attacking ourselves. In scarcely three months my regiment has lost 1,700 men. And it isn't over yet.[1]

Private Jean Leymonnerie, 1st Battalion, 175th Regiment, 1st (Métropolitaine) Brigade, 1st Division, CEO

SOMETHING HAD TO GIVE. The Allies could not keep battering themselves senseless against the Turkish trenches at Helles. When the members of the Dardanelles Committee met for the first time on 7 June to discuss the progress of the campaign it was evident that nothing much had changed in the three weeks since their last meeting as the War Council. They had still to steer between the rocks of evacuation and the expense of massive reinforcements. Although after the fall of the Liberal government Winston Churchill was no longer at the Admiralty, he had nevertheless retained his membership of the committee, and he contributed an influential memo recommending giving General Sir Ian Hamilton all four divisions he had asked for on 17 May to push on for a rapid success. Kitchener had also submitted a paper urging caution, but by the time of the meeting he had already changed his mind, buoyed up by a renewed assertion from Hamilton that he really could deliver on his promise to take Kilid Bahr. The decision was finally made and the committee consented to sending out three more divisions to join the 52nd Division. A week later, bad news from Russia triggered another offer at the Dardanelles Committee meeting of 17 June of a further two divisions to try to use success in the Balkans and the capture of Constantinople to bolster their failing ally. This caused no little consternation to the generals engaged in fighting the Germans on the Western Front.

> I still think it is fatal to pour more troops and ammunition down the Dardanelles sink. The whole British Expeditionary Force here if added to the Force now there cannot clear the two sides of the Dardanelles so as to make the Straits passage safe for ships and ensure the fall of Constantinople.[2]
>
> General Sir Douglas Haig, Headquarters, First Army

Such protests, well grounded in experience and the study of war, fell on deaf ears.

To accelerate the transportation of troops to Gallipoli in order for them to participate in a new offensive planned for August, it was decided to use specially chartered commercial liners. Ships like the *Mauritania* and the *Aquitania* could carry 6,000 men each. Capable of travelling at 25 knots, they could also complete a trip in just a week – all but invulnerable to the slow-moving U-boats.

In the meantime, at Helles the generals and their men seemed to be locked into a campaign without hope. Yet, as they still believed that continuous pressure must be exerted on the Turks, Hunter-Weston and Gouraud came up with an alternative to the discredited idea of a general advance. They decided to concentrate all possible artillery resources to support strictly localised attacks, with the aim of biting off small chunks of the Turkish line and then using a wall of shells to assist the infantry in holding off the Turkish counter-attacks. The French were given the honour of trying out the new tactic. On 21 June they would launch an attack on the Turkish lines between the Ravin de la Mort offshoot of Kereves Dere and the Haricot and Quadrilateral Redoubts that dominated the Kereves Spur. They would attack on a very narrow front of just 650 yards, but it contained three objectives of excessive difficulty in not only the Haricot and Quadrilateral Redoubts but also the trenches overlooking the Ravin de la Mort. The crucial artillery support centred on the deployment of seven batteries of French 75mm guns, two batteries of 155mm howitzers, trench mortars and seven British howitzers to shatter the Turkish defences. At the

Mustafa Kamel: On 25 April 1915 he was the Colonel commanding the 19th Division. Sidelined in the political fighting that had preceded the Great War, he proved the man of the moment, acting with great decisiveness to stem the advance of the ANZAC Corps. He built on this well-earned reputation throughout the war and used it as a springboard to seize power as President Kemal Attaturk in the post-war years. (IWM Q 101744)

2. General Otto Liman von Sanders: the German General appointed to command the new Turkish Fifth Army given the responsibility for the defence of the Dardanelles Straits. Liman was proved a sound general, deploying his troops to cover the various possibilities for invasion and reacting calmly to despatch his centrally controlled reserves to contain the Allied threats. His ennobled title of 'von Sanders' was a creation that reflected his deceased Scottish wife's name, Sanders. (IWM Q 95324)

General Sir Charles Monro: The man given the poisoned chalice of replacing Hamilton and ordering the evacuation of Gallipoli. He had served on the Western Front and was convinced of the primacy of that front; what he saw of the situation at Gallipoli appalled him. (IWM Q 68187)

4. Lieutenant General Aylmer Hunter-Weston: the commander of the 29th Division and then VIII Corps responsible for operations on the main battlefront at Helles. Often caricatured by his critics he was no fool when it came to recognising the scale of the problems that faced his men on 25 April. (IWM Q 13289)

3. General Sir Ian Hamilton: the 'Happy Warrior' appointed to command the Mediterranean Expeditionary Force. A distinguished soldier who had lived his life to the full, he was brought down by his own willingness to attempt, and keep on attempting, to achieve the impossible dream at Gallipoli. It destroyed his career and he never held a meaningful command again before his death at 94 in in 1947. Here he is leading the cheer in front of an RND detachment at a medal ceremony. (IWM Q 68187)

6. General Maurice Bailloud and General Henri Gouraud pictured by one of the dismounted Turkish guns at Sedd el Bahr. These French officers had terrible problems facing not only the chasm of the Kereves Dere in front of their lines but with shells crashing down into their backs from across the Dardanelles Straits. (IWM Q 13300)

7. A picture that sums up not only the insouciance of the jolly Jack Tar but also the sheer size of the mighty 15" guns of the Queen Elizabeth. They fired a shell weighing 1,920-pounds over 32,000 yards. The problem was hitting a worthwhile target. (IWM Q 13240)

. V Beach, 25 April 1915. A moment in time frozen forever. The view from the River Clyde during the stalled landings. Some of he Munster Fusiliers are sheltering in the lighters and there are Dublin Fusiliers sheltering behind the five foot bank on the beach. WM Q 50473)

. The teeming store depot established by the French at V Beach. Thousands of tons of munitions, food and general supplies had o be brought thousands of miles, transhipped and brought ashore in the makeshift harbour, all under the constant threat of shell re from Asiatic Annie from across the Dardanelles Straits. (IWM Q 13857)

10. Landing at Anzac, 25 April 1915. The second wave move in moving away from the destroyers towards the Anzac shoreline. (IWM Q 99270)

11. The senior officers of Turkish 27th Regiment who won the day at Anzac on 25 April. Sitting in the centre of the front row is Colonel Sefik Bey while sitting beside him on the left is Major Halis Bey. (Serdar Halis Collection)

2. The front line at Anzac. This gives a superb indication of claustrophobia in the trenches. Notice the chap with the periscope, looking for unwary Turks while the man on the right is ready to fire his periscope rifle once the exact location of a prospective victim has been identified. (IWM Q 13428)

3. The miracle of Anzac Cove: The men on the beach were by no means safe and were constantly under risk of Turkish shell fire. They honeycombed into the hills, in terraces and despite all the problems managed to establish a supply depot for the whole ANZAC Corps. (IWM Q 13603)

14. The King's Own Scottish Borderers go over the top during the Third Battle of Krithia, 4 June 1915. (IWM Q 70701)

5/16. The Manchesters of 127th Brigade, 42nd Division go over the top Krithia, 4 June 1915. These once callow soldiers ⋅earned a great deal about war during their few weeks at Helles – if they survived. (IWM Q 81454/81452)

17. Gully Beach and the entrance to Gully Ravine. The headquarters of the 42nd Division was based here for most of the campaign. Dugouts burrow into the hillside and the horse lines can be seen just inside the gully. (IWM Q 13400)

18. Gurkhas of 29th Indian Brigade inside Gully Ravine. Gallipoli was a true multinational campaign. (IWM HU 105665)

9. 'Splinter Villa' a makeshift dugout and its proud owners at Anzac. (IWM Q 13797)

. Cheerful in adversity: just a hole in the ground and a groundsheet for 'cover' at W Beach, September 1915. (IWM Q 13803)

21. French infantry manning the line within thirty yards of the Turks. (IWM Q 13502)

22. French soldier carrying his wounded comrade back through the communications trenches. (IWM Q 13489)

23. A French soldier cautiously looking over the side of a communication trench at Helles. (IWM Q 13491)

. Support troops of the 4th Australian Brigade wait behind Quinn's Post, 29 May 1915. (IWM HU 50622)

. Stretcher cases on their way back through a crowded narrow communication trench. For the badly wounded, bumped and
ed about, their life's blood leaching away, broken bones grating, this could be a journey through hell. (IWM Q 13325)

26. A grainy view of the Yeomanry of the 2nd Mounted Division advancing under shell fire across Suvla Bay towards Chocolate Hill on the afternoon of 21 August 1915. (IWM Q 70704)

27. British soldier offering water to Turkish prisoner. (IWM Q 13255)

Turkish prisoners being marched back by Zouave escort at Helles. (IWM Q 13245)

29. Field Marshal Lord Kitchener, Secretary of State for War during his whistle stop visit to the front lines at Anzac Cove in November 1915. He is accompanied by Lieutenant General William Birdwood commanding the ANZAC Corps. (IWM Q 13595)

). Happier days before the storm. Men of the A&NZ Division aboard the *Lutzow* from which they landed at Anzac on 25 April ⁊15. (IWM Q 13798)

.. An iconic view of the store dumps ablaze photographed from the *Cornwallis* after the evacuation of Suvla on the night of 19 ₂cember. (IWM Q 13679)

32. The grave of Lieutenant Colonel Dick Doughty Wylie VC, buried on Hill 141 where he was killed on 26 April 1915. (IWM Q 13709)

same time six more batteries of 75mm guns were assigned to fire into the rest of the Turkish lines facing the French, while other French long-range batteries, accompanied by the pre-dreadnought *Saint-Louis*, attempted to suppress interference from the Turkish guns on the Asiatic shore. In all it worked out at one gun or howitzer for every ten yards of front to be assaulted. In the days leading up to the attack the level of French fire increased as they tried to eradicate the Turkish trenches. Second Lieutenant Raymond Weil was in a forward observation post.

> All along the French front the artillery raged. For our part we made our range corrections with a slow deliberation. Then we proceeded to methodically mop up every last fragment of the Turkish trenches which had to be completely destroyed. Each of our guns had its own pre-determined task.[3]
>
> Second Lieutenant Raymond Weil, 39th Régiment d'Artillerie, 1st Division, CEO

As ever, not all the infantry were overly appreciative of the gunners' efforts. The trenches were close together and there was little margin for error. If the artillery played safe then the Turkish line might survive and the casualties would once again be heavy. But if they dropped their range to ensure eradicating the Turks in the front line, then some shells would surely drop short and hit the French lines. This led to some recriminations.

> Today we had a powerful bombardment. Was this the sign of an imminent attack? A 155mm shell, one of ours, passed over us and burst a few metres in front of our trenches. The result: panic and energetic protests, as we were showered with soil and stones of all sizes, and the appearance of a cloud of stinking yellow smoke. A mortar shell fell not far away at the same time. Later an idiot artillery adjutant believed that it was this mortar bomb and not his shell that caused our scare.[4]
>
> Private Jean Leymonnerie, 1st Battalion, 175th Regiment, 1st (Métropolitaine) Brigade, 1st Division, CEO

The final bombardment, opening at 05.15, lasted for just forty-five minutes. At 06.00 the 176th Regiment lunged for the redoubts, while to their right the 6th Colonial Regiment tried to clear the Ravin de la Mort. The French had plentiful ammunition and would expend over 30,000 shells during their attack on that narrow front. The British looked on with something approaching awe.

The 75s were going like machine guns and every now and again great columns would rise up and then a dull rumble, some gun about the size of our 6" firing HE. There were some wild shots, but on the whole the shooting was magnificent. Some bursts were too high and you saw a long chain of 'spurts' from the ground extending across two lines of trenches. There was a battleship lying off Sedd el Bahr with her usual escort of destroyers. She was hurling shells into batteries in Asia or trying to do so anyway. The bombardment went on till 6.10 a.m. and then suddenly ceased and there was a moment's oppressive silence. There was a cloud of smoke hanging over the trenches and running right back to the beach. Till then I had not seen a man and had only heard an occasional rifle speak. And then a glorious sight – the French advancing through the smoke, a long line extended for the most part, but composed of extended groups of six or seven men. On they came out of the smoke and then rifles and Maxims began to make music, but it struck me the Turkish artillery was very slow, perhaps they could not see for the covering black mantle of smoke. Then they came but the French were very near the first trench and only a few fell – as they got into it shrapnel and 'Black Marias' ploughed up the ground behind them.[5]

Second Lieutenant Angus McCracken, 368th Battery, 147th Brigade, Royal Field Artillery

The attack was going well and the dreaded Haricot was swiftly over-run by the 176th Regiment, then the Turkish second line, although the Quadrilateral behind it remained inviolable. Corporal Charles Thierry had been engaged in digging a sap when at 15.00 he was sent forward with extra ammunition to the newly captured Turkish front line.

The men go in threes: Legeay gets a shell fragment in the back, Legèndre is wounded – many men fall! Our turn to go, a little shiver up the spine! I pass through a small communication trench, treading on the corpses of dismembered men, dry arms, one can no longer find anything human in these corpses. Only 25 metres across the open. At last I am in the first Turkish trench at the side of a wounded captain. We are subjected to a short bombardment. Surrounded by corpses we occupy the trench – I am almost alone in more than 100 metres of front, all the men are wounded. At every moment reinforcements are called for but none come; ammunition is also demanded but nothing arrives. I attend to a wounded Turk in the trench. In gratitude he kisses my hand and lifts it twice to his forehead. I want him to write something in my pocket book but there is nothing to be done. The heavy shells from the Asian side rain down: Brumel is hit, Henriot as well. At about 6 p.m. an intense and well-directed bombardment from their lines warns us of a counter-attack, besides the situation demands it. But we enfilade them and they retreat swiftly. It is a veritable manhunt with our bullets. We throw our kepis in the air with shouts of joy. The bombardment is terrible; the shrapnel rains down. I lie down in the trench but a few moments later I am hit in the left hand. At last the bombardment stops.[6]

Corporal Charles Thierry, 176th Regiment, 3rd (Métropolitaine) Brigade, 2nd Division, CEO

Thierry was safely evacuated to the French lines, despite the close attentions of the Turkish machine guns. This time the French, aided by their massed artillery, threw back the Turkish counter-attacks and the Haricot was finally captured.

The 6th Colonials were also successful in taking the Turkish front line but could get no further forward. The newly captured line had been severely damaged by the French bombardment and what remained was choked full of dead and dying Turks. There was little effective shelter and, as Turkish fire lashed across the trenches the 6th Colonials commander, Colonel Noguès, was badly wounded. Confusion set in and by 07.00 the 6th Colonials had fallen back in disarray to their start line. At 14.15 they tried again, with no success. A final attempt was made at 18.45 when the Régiment de Marche d'Afrique recaptured and this time held the line overlooking the Ravin de la Mort.

The results of the hard fighting represented a considerable achievement, but even a successful battle has its melancholy harvest and Second Lieutenant Weil was not alone in carrying out a grim task the next day.

This morning we had to bury the two under-officers killed yesterday at the Projecteur Observation Post. Captain Michel made me the battery representative. It was a very sad task. The poor devils yesterday were in full health; sadly they fell so far from France with no chance for their families to have the consolation of another day with them. In descending down the gully, the Turks, as if forewarned of what we were doing, fired across several 105mm shells of the highest quality. The explosions followed us from top to bottom as if drawn by an invisible hand. It was next to Morto Bay that we found the cemetery, unhappily filled with numerous graves. The ceremony was quick; terrible in its simplicity. The chaplain intoned the usual prayer. We rendered the honours in front of the two graves into which we would lower the unlucky pair. Captain Sainpère made a short address interrupted at every moment by the explosion of 105mm shells very nearby. But no one turned a hair. Yet each of us was thinking that at any moment he could be rejoining those that had gone to their last resting place. The prospect of mouldering away under 2 metres of Turkish soil beside the sea, 900 leagues from France, was not a prospect to rejoice in![7]

Second Lieutenant Raymond Weil, 39th Régiment d'Artillerie, 1st Division, CEO

At least the two Frenchmen were decently buried. Far too many were missing and would never receive the consolation of any kind of individual burial. Their collected anonymous remains now lie in three large ossuaries in the French Cemetery. Despite over 2,500 killed and wounded, the French attack on 21 June had been a great success: the Haricot had been taken at last and the Turks had suffered nearly 6,000 casualties. Yet the Quadrilateral remained in their hands, meaning the Turks still had the potential to fire into the right flank of any advance by the RND in line next to the French.

NOW IT WAS THE TURN of the British to try a narrow frontal attack. On 28 June they were to attack along Gully Spur to capture a series of five trenches numbering back from J9 to J13. At the same time they would push up Gully Ravine, hoping to move forward to where the Nullah tributary joined the main gully, while on Fir Tree Spur an attack would be made on the formidable Boomerang Redoubt and the H12 trenches. They would be supported by some seventy-seven guns and howitzers. In the course of the battle, they fired just over 16,000 rounds, or nearly half the total British ammunition supply at Helles. Yet that still fell short of what was required, for most of the guns were concentrated on the Gully Spur and Gully Ravine sectors. The attack on the H12 trenches on Fir Tree Spur was an afterthought as far as gun allocation was concerned.

Before the action the Corps Commander sent for me to say that he did not consider that enough guns and ammunition had been allotted to this portion of the Turkish trenches. I replied that I agreed, but that there were no more available, and that to reduce the bombardment of the hostile trenches on the left of our front would gravely prejudice the success of the 29th Division in that quarter, and that I understood success there was more vital than on our right flank. After consultation with the GOC 29th Division, the Corps Commander agreed with my allotment of the artillery. We then did our utmost to obtain the loan of more guns from the French without success.[8]

Brigadier General Sir Hugh Simpson Baikie, Headquarters, VIII Corps

From 06.00, prior to the main bombardment special attention was devoted by borrowed French trench mortars to eradicating the Boomerang Redoubt. Although the redoubt was on the right of Gully Ravine it was in a position which would allow it to enfilade any attack up Gully Spur. Then the main bombardment opened at 09.00. The concentration of artillery paid dividends when the 1st Border Regiment successfully attacked the Boomerang at 10.45 some fifteen minutes before the main assault. As they consolidated they could see the main attack going in across Gully Ravine at 11.00.

Wave after wave of khaki clad troops sweep over their trenches and rush one Turkish trench after another. Behind come the supports marching in a steady unwavering line with sloped arms, their bayonets glittering in the sunlight. It is a fine sight and we give them an encouraging cheer as they pass our position. The enemy artillery now switch their artillery fire on to this advancing line but with little effect. Gaps occur here and there as the shrapnel mows its way through them but they close up as if on parade and steadily advance onwards.[9]

Private Sydney Evans, 1st Border Regiment, 87th Brigade, 29th Division

Private Daniel Joiner was in the second wave, with the 1st KOSB, as they joined the attack.

While waiting underneath the parapet, it was torture! Hell! The sensations felt, going over the parapet, expecting to be hit anywhere, awful, but as soon as you realise you are over safe, you lose all such thoughts and feelings – mad! Men are falling right and left, they are hardly noticed – one thought only exists – the first trench! It is almost impossible to remember afterwards whether you walked, ran, crawled, or flew over the intervening ground. The South Wales Borderers have reached the first line and are engaging the enemy, we are soon with them and materially assist them – 'Allah, Allah!' the Turk cries as he puts his hands up, while another tries to bury himself in the ground out of reach of our bayonets. Others kneel and fire, until their magazine is discharged, then try to run away. They are soon all accounted for and the first line is ours.[10]

Private Daniel Joiner, 1st KOSB, 87th Brigade, 29th Division

On their left flank the 29th Indian Brigade was attacking along the cliff side. On they pushed, charging up Gully Spur, capturing several Turkish lines and reaching as far as Fusilier Bluff.

It was a very different story for the 156th Brigade facing the H12 trench line on Fir Tree Spur. The fate of one battalion reveals the scope of the tragedy as they charged forward without adequate artillery support. Major James Findlay had only taken command of the 1/8th Scottish Rifles a week before, but now he had the responsibility of leading his inexperienced battalion into action on the right of the brigade front.

I do not think that many of us got much sleep – I know that to me the night was slow in passing – but dawn came at last, cool and beautiful, with a hint of the coming heat, and the dried-up sparse scrub had been freshened by the night's dewfall. One was impressed by the good heart of all ranks, but, whether it was premonition or merely the strain of newly acquired responsibility, I could not feel the buoyancy of anticipated success. I remember going round the line in the early morning and finding that there was some difficulty about the planks which the support and reserve companies had to put across the front trenches to facilitate passage, but these eventually arrived in time. The artillery bombardment which took place from 09.00 to 11.00 was, even to a mind then inexperienced in a real bombardment, quite too futile, but it drew down upon us, naturally, a retaliatory shelling. How slowly these minutes from 10.55 to 11.00 passed! Centuries of time seemed to go by. One became conscious of saying the silliest things, all the while painfully thinking, 'It may be the last time I shall see these fellows alive!' Prompt at 11.00 the whistles blew.[11]

Major James Findlay, 1/8th Scottish Rifles, 156th Brigade, 52nd Division

Over the top went his men, to be met by a deadly stream of fire from all sides. Findlay soon realised that the attack was breaking down in No Man's Land. He sent back to his brigade for reinforcements and moved forward up a sap with his adjutant, Captain Charles Bramwell, and his signal officer, Lieutenant Tom Stout, trying to establish a forward head-quarters. They did not get far; rank was no defence against bullets.

> Bramwell and I then pushed our way up the sap, which for a short distance concealed us, but got shallower as we went along, until first our heads, then our shoulders, and then most of our bodies were exposed. We soon arrived at Pattison's bombing party, which I had sent up this sap.[12] He had been killed, and those of his men that were left were lying flat; they could not get on as the sap rose a few yards in front of them to the ground level, and the leading man was lying in only about 18 inches of cover. In any case they were still some 50 yards from the enemy trenches. Bullets were spattering all around us, and we seemed to bear charmed lives, until just as we arrived at the rear of this party Bramwell fell at my side, shot through the mouth. He said not a word, and I am glad to think that he was killed outright.[13] I made up my mind that the only thing to be done was to collect what men there were and make a dash for it. I told this to Stout, and stooping down to pick up a rifle I was shot in the neck. At the moment I didn't feel much, but when I saw the blood spurt forward I supposed that it had got my jugular vein. I stuck a handkerchief round my neck and tried to get on, but I was bowled over by a hit in the shoulder. I tumbled back over some poor devil, and for a minute or two tried to collect myself. Up came young Stout and said, 'I am going to try to carry you back, Sir!' but I wouldn't let him.[14]
>
> Major James Findlay, 1/8th Scottish Rifles, 156th Brigade, 52nd Division

It was obvious to everyone around him that his wounds were serious, but Findlay was obsessed with the idea that he had to establish his forward headquarters and coordinate the next stage of the attack. In the end Lieutenant Tom Stout simply ignored him.

> I told Stout to send another runner for reinforcements. A few minutes later he came back and took me by the shoulders and some other good fellow lifted me by the feet, and together they got me back some 10 yards, and though a bullet got me in the flesh of the thigh, I was now comparatively sheltered while they were still exposed. It was then that

a splinter of shell blew off Tommy Stout's head, and the other man was hit simultaneously.[15] Gallant lads! God rest them![16]

Major James Findlay, 1/8th Scottish Rifles, 156th Brigade, 52nd Division

Findlay finally managed to stagger back to his own lines, either very lucky or unlucky depending on one's viewpoint, having suffered seven major wounds as well as a liberal sprinkling of minor scrapes from bomb fragments. His battalion had suffered over 400 casualties and 25 of its 26 officers had been hit. The attack of 156th Brigade had resulted in a massacre, with nothing achieved militarily but a few insignificant gains on the left. Further attempts to advance during the day resulted in nothing but more slaughter.

At the same time the Turks were counter-attacking on Gully Spur. The series of trenches running across the spur and into the Nullah tributary were the scene of murderous fighting as the Turks used their superior bombs to try to blast the British and Indian troops out. Attempts by the 1st Dublin Fusiliers to attack up Gully Ravine met with little success and eventually a new front line was constructed that bent back from Fusilier Bluff to link across Gully Ravine with those small segments of the H12 trench that had been captured on the left of Fir Tree Spur. The men of the KOSB were then ordered to clear Gully Ravine of the tangled detritus of war. It was to prove an unforgettable task.

Both sides of the Gully were lined with what had been Turkish shelters – they were in appearance like a farmyard outhouse. They were still shelters, but not for live Turks. As we proceeded down the Gully, we had to drag the dead bodies into them, to make room for the traffic. Farther down, pools of stagnant water, with green, evil-smelling slime, had to be passed. Often the skeleton of some unknown soldier floated on top. The dead had to be disposed of. There were too many to bury, and not sanitary. Cremation was decided on. Each sergeant with twelve men was instructed to prepare a fire from the wood of the Turkish shelters. The bodies after being searched were then put on. What a nice pleasant job. Count had to be kept of the number cremated. One head, two arms, one body and two legs to count as one man. The sun was already having its effect on them. Respirators had to be worn. All scruples had to be laid aside, and get on with it, 'Steady there, don't lose that leg it is only hanging up by the trousers. Bring that head here; that completes another man! Yes, bring that leg – we only want a body now to make another man!' The fires blazed upon the ground of Gully Ravine. So hot did the fires get, we were forced to put sand on. It is too hot now to place them on, we throw them on. We have luckily forgotten we are human beings.[17]

Private Daniel Joiner, 1st KOSB, 87th Brigade, 29th Division

Careless of casualties, careless of anything, the Turks continued to launch massed attacks out of the Nullah across Gully Spur and down Gully Ravine. Private Joiner and his company were ordered forward to support the South Wales Borderers in the front line.

On they came crowd after crowd. The machine guns were mowing them down. Those who managed to gain the open were under fire from the infantry of either flank. The Ross Battery was paying attention to the Turkish reinforcements, which were being hurried up. They persevered with this mad attack until 4 a.m. next morning. What had they gained? Nothing but a small trench they had succeeded in digging about 200 yards in front of us. At what cost? To them 1,000 lives! To us, an enormous amount of ammunition, a night's sleep and a few lives.[18]

Private Daniel Joiner, 1st KOSB, 87th Brigade, 29th Division

Shortly afterwards Private Joiner was wounded in the leg and he was evacuated, his campaign over. All night the fighting raged. Among the killed was Sergeant Victor Rathfelder, a South African serving with the 1st Munsters.

Sergeant Rathfelder came along to me and asked in a voice harsh with thirst, 'Can I go and get water, Sir?' The Turks attacked twice more and then about 3 a.m. Rathfelder returned, a pick handle over one shoulder. From it dangled nine water bottles filled with water. He put them beside me saying, 'The boys will be glad of that, Sir.' 'Thanks, Rathfelder, now get some rest behind the parados.' He turned away and as he did so I saw two more men shot down in the trench and shouted out, 'Send two more men into the trench!' The sergeant halted to catch the order which rose faintly above the surrounding din, and then pitched forward, shot through the head, splattering me with his blood and brains.[19] To this day I blame myself bitterly for having spoken those words![20]

Second Lieutenant Roy Laidlaw, 1st Royal Munster Fusiliers, 86th Brigade, 29th Division

The Turks were very concerned by this advance on their right flank and ordered the 3rd and 5th Divisions to regain lost ground without fail. The final effort was made at dawn on 5 July after a weak preliminary bombardment. On that dreadful day the Turks would find that bravery was useless against a combination of artillery, machine guns and rapid fire from well-aimed rifles. It is difficult to determine the exact number of Turkish casualties in the Gully Ravine area over the week of 28 June–5 July, but the Turks themselves reckoned that they suffered losses of some 14,000. Certainly the ground in front of the British trenches was covered with a huge number of rotting Turkish corpses. There they would stay for the rest of the campaign as the British steadfastly refused Turkish requests for an armistice for mass burials. It was imagined that the Turks might be less willing to attack over a No Man's Land sprinkled with their own rotting dead and Hunter-Weston decided his men would just have to endure the awful stench.

The lessons of 28 June seemed simple: the Allies should focus their attacks but, above all, they needed more artillery, more howitzers, more high explosive shells and more bombs to help counter the Turkish counter-attacks. The success of these tactics seemed to be further confirmed when the French managed to capture the infamous Quadrilateral in an attack on 30 June.

> As on 21 June we preceded the attack with a slow and deliberate destructive bombardment. We had at our disposal shells with the new instantaneous fuses which exploded on impact, which were much more efficient in destroying the trenches and fortifications. The result was that in our sector the trenches were utterly destroyed and when the assault went in at 5.30, it allowed our troops to over-run the Turkish first lines almost without casualties. Carried away in their enthusiasm they didn't stop there but putting improvised bridges over the captured trenches, they continued to push forwards. I soon learnt over the telephone that our men had gone on so far that we could not follow their progress as they were masked by the crest of a ridge. We even had to stop our fire in order not to hinder their movements. At 8 p.m. the gunfire, which had died down a bit, suddenly swelled up violently. It seemed that our troops were falling back in disorder across the crest. They had clashed with several fresh Turkish battalions arriving to the rescue, who had almost surrounded our advanced elements. Without

any communications, waiting for reinforcements that never arrived and now lacking artillery support, they hastily had to withdraw.[21]

Second Lieutenant Raymond Weil, 39th Régiment d'Artillerie, 1st Division, CEO

It was becoming increasingly apparent that artillery was the dominant force on the battlefields of Gallipoli, as on the Western Front. If the guns succeeded in their primary task of smashing the Turkish trenches, then a successful assault could be made, but even then artillery was needed to cover any gains achieved, or they would soon be lost. The more sophisticated gunnery tactics of using concentrated counter-battery fire, creeping barrages and the whole concept of suppressing one's opponent's ability to fire while the troops were exposed in No Man's Land lay two years in the future. But by concentrating their artillery resources the French had once again inched forward and the Quadrilateral, so long their bête noire, had been captured – and this time it was held.

One French problem had been removed but the harassing fire from across the Straits was still giving them considerable grief. On 30 June, even in his moment of triumph, General Henri Gouraud had been badly wounded by a shell crashing down from the Turkish Asiatic batteries; he was evacuated but would lose an arm. Gouraud had been a competent and energetic leader and would be sorely missed. His replacement was General Maurice Bailloud who, although 73 years old, was already at Helles commanding the French 2nd Division, and was hence well aware of the state of the campaign. The loss of Gouraud typified the relentless threat posed by the Asiatic guns. Captain Ashir Arkayan was one of the Turkish officers responsible.

I was appointed to command the 10.5-centimetre battery on the Anatolian coast. The battery had been removed from one of our warships and remounted. My duties were as follows: 1) To harass the flank and rear of the enemy in front of our lines at Sedd el Bahr and to destroy the gun position in this sector. 2) To keep the enemy's landing stages at Sedd el Bahr and at Tekke Bay under fire, to stop him using his jetties and to harass him. I carried out these duties with much success. In order to knock me out the enemy stationed two monitors off Kum Kale, but, while they tried for days with 34-centimetre guns to neutralise me, they were unable to do so.[22]

Captain Ashir Arkayan, Artillery, Fifth Army

This process was watched with detached Gallic amusement by Lieutenant Henri Feuille on 25 July.

> Two English monitors fired their big guns on Kum Kale, Yeni Chehir and Eren Keui. If it didn't do any good, it couldn't do any harm! It was a lot of noise for nothing! They fired at long intervals on the Asian coast. Connected to land by a telephone line, we did our best as observers to try and range their fire. At last! By a miracle a shell seemed on target. It exploded, shaking the very Straits close to the Batterie des Cochons. To encourage the monitor's gunners we said, 'Direct hit!' Half an hour, an hour passed: nothing occurred, complete silence! What had happened? We telephone the monitor which after numerous calls answered. "Le shooting has finished, all right, fini! We've hit the target, killed the pigs! Nous buvons le champagne! Au revoir!'[23]
>
> Lieutenant Henri Feuille, 52nd Battery, 30th Regiment, 1st Division, CEO

Happy in their work, the monitors weighed anchor and left the puzzled French to ponder the wonders of alliance warfare.

For all their problems, for just a moment the Allied commanders could dream of making real progress, one bite at a time, until they could take Achi Baba and start again. It was evident that the Turks were indeed alarmed by the partial success of the British and French 'bite and hold' tactics. The heavy shell fire had shaken some of their troops and the commander of the 11th Division tried to stiffen their resolve with well-placed threats.

> Henceforth, commanders who surrender these trenches, from whatever side the attack may come, before the last man is killed will be punished in the same way as if they had run away. I hope that this will not occur again. I give notice that if it does, I shall carry out the punishment. I do not desire to see a blot made on the courage of our men by those who escape from the trenches to avoid the rifle and machine gun fire of the enemy. Henceforth, I shall hold responsible all officers who do not shoot with their revolvers all the privates who try to escape from the trenches on any pretext.[24]
>
> Colonel Rifaat, Headquarters, 11th Division, Fifth Army

To relieve the divisions of the Southern Group, plans were made to move in the Second Army, made up of the V Corps (8th & 10th Divisions) and the XIV Corps (13th & 14th Divisions), under the command of General

Wehib Pasha. Yet the Turks showed no signs of giving up the fight. They may have wavered under heavy artillery fire, but that would have applied to most troops of all nationalities. The Turks were still providing a determined opposition to the Allies.

LIEUTENANT CHARLES LISTER had returned to the trenches and rejoined the Hood Battalion ready once more for the fray. Both his delicate sensitivities and his underlying sense of humour were considerably tickled by the arrival of the 155th and 157th Brigades of the 52nd Division.

> Trench life means a good deal of repose but very little sleep. This is not so much due to the enemy as to the torrents of raw levies coming up to do working parties or to relieve pals or to look for their proper places in the line, and so on. I have had my toes trodden on by every officer and man of a Scotch Territorial Division. They come up in driblets, carrying the most weird cooking utensils, and with every sort of impedimentum. They never know how many of them are coming, and if you ask them each man says he is the last. Then after about 10 seconds' interval fresh men come up, carrying what appear to be portions of bagpipes. They are always getting lost and held up. Last night I had to get them out by dint of jumping on the top of the communication trench parapet and kicking dust on to their heads, and at the time using the most violent language. The humours of trench warfare are really delicious.[25]
>
> Lieutenant Charles Lister, Hood Battalion, 2nd Naval Brigade, RND

One of the dark jokes beloved of the veterans of the trenches was recalled by the newly arrived Lieutenant John Millar of the 1/5th KOSB.

> Sergeant Johnstone stopped and said, 'Now, Sir, I want to introduce you to our mascot, especially as this is your first tour in the firing line!' He pulled aside an empty sandbag covering an alcove in the wall of the communication trench. Sticking out from the earth horizontally was the stiff forearm and hand of a dead Turkish soldier. The hand was leathery and wrinkled; the clutching fingers were stark and stiff. 'Shake!' said my Sergeant. I hesitated, then grimly took the hand.[26]
>
> Lieutenant John Millar, 1/5th KOSB, 155th Brigade, 52nd Division

It was these young inexperienced Scots of the 52nd Division that were earmarked for the next offensive.

HUNTER-WESTON AND GOURAUD had intended an attack in the centre to follow the advances on the flanks achieved on 21 and 28 June. The idea was for the right-hand British division to make an attack in the Achi Baba Nullah sector supported by the combined strength of the British and French artillery. Meanwhile the French were to try to take the remaining Turkish trenches on the western bank of Kereves Dere. This project had been made easier by the French success in capturing the Quadrilateral on 30 June, which removed a potent source of enfilading fire. The 52nd Division was brought up into the line to replace the haggard remnants of the RND, while the French prepared their artillery for the attack set for 12 July. A sophistication introduced into the plan was the idea of splitting the 52nd Division attack into two parts to try to maximise artillery usage in two separate barrages. Thus the 155th Brigade would attack alongside the French at 07.35, while the 157th Brigade to their left would attack separately at 16.50.

The bombardment opened at 04.30 and the French troops on the right went over the top at 07.35. Among them was Sergeant D'Arnaud Pomiro of the 175th Regiment.

> Without exception, we leapt out at an athletic pace, under a thin rain of bullets and a few shrapnel shells. We were advancing towards the second trench objective. The left got there a bit before me because I had a few metres further to go. Got there all the same; didn't find any Turks. But at the base of the ravine I saw at least three hundred of them swarming about under terrible sustained fire from us. For my part I fired eight rounds, I slaughtered four Turks including an officer; I threw a grenade at a group of four who were creeping up to within 20 metres. Then I passed out. Coming to myself, I made my way to the rear.[27]
>
> Sergeant D'Arnaud Pomiro, 3rd Battalion, 175th Regiment, 1st (Métropolitaine) Brigade, 1st Division, CEO

Pomiro had been knocked out by a splinter of stone thrown up by a Turkish bullet or shell. The French had done well but were then drawn into an attritional battle to hold their gains against the usual intensive Turkish counter-attacks.

However, alongside them, the 155th Brigade attack met considerably more resistance.

I remember putting my head down and going all I could, barely conscious that at any moment I might be laid out. It seemed like running against a hailstorm. Bullets sputtering – showers of shrapnel across the ground we were crossing – HE shells exploding all around, raising clouds of dust and making the air reverberate with their explosion. The air was dark with dust and smoke and dimly I remember men falling at intervals.[28]

Lieutenant James Harrison, 1/4th Battalion, KOSB, 155th Brigade, 52nd Division

As the brigade pushed on to secure the first and second lines of the Turkish trenches, there was an awful confusion as they charged the third line which was their final objective.

About 150 yards away, we could see the parapet of what looked like another trench. Accordingly, we doubled across in that direction, and on getting up to this third trench we found it to be untenanted and only a couple of feet deep. However, it afforded us some cover, and in we scrambled – the order immediately coming along for every man to fill his two sand bags and build up the parapet. The ground was like flint, and we could make little headway with our entrenching tools. To the left from where I found myself, this shallow trench ran up towards a wood and there seemed to be a great deal of rifle and machine gun fire coming in our direction from this wood. In front of us, however, there appeared to be no enemy at all. After about half an hour, during which time we suffered numerous casualties, word was passed along to extend towards the wood. I got out and doubled across the open until I came to a very comfortable-looking shell hole, into which I very contentedly jumped. Very shortly after I heard shouts of, 'Retire! Retire!' I got back safely, crawling most of the way, as a shell burst very close and I found I had lost the power of one of my legs.[29]

Corporal Tom Richardson, 1/4th KOSB, 155th Brigade, 52nd Division

By this time, the fog of battle had descended, but it was decided to continue with the second attack. The 157th Brigade attack, made at 16.50, was an almost identical performance: bombardment, advance facing some resistance, confusion over the absence of the third trench and a fallback to consolidate, where they came to rest alongside the 155th Brigade in the Turkish second line. During the battle medical officer Lieutenant George Davidson had a strange meeting with Hunter-Weston.

Most of the day I had been watching the battlefield from the Observation Hill, then at 5 p.m. went to tea in the mess where I was alone. General Hunter-Weston entered in a few minutes, and sitting opposite me said, 'What an extraordinary thing war is!' The progress of the day had greatly satisfied him, I could see, and he was in great glee. 'Yes!' I said. 'But I wish to goodness it was all over!' 'My dear sir,' he replied, 'we'll have years of it yet!' I asked if he thought there was any possibility of its ending this year. 'Absolutely none!' [30]

Lieutenant George Davidson, 89th Field Ambulance, RAMC

Overnight there were some panicky withdrawals here and there among troops that were, not unnaturally, terrified at the prospect of imminent Turkish counter-attacks. The new front lines were not yet secure and the men knew that they needed time to consolidate their positions.

As a result of these fears the 1st Naval Brigade of the RND was first called up into reserve and then committed to an attack next day alongside yet another French effort towards Kereves Dere. They were meant to go over the top at 16.30 on 13 July. But just about everything that could go wrong on that unlucky day duly did so. Appalling staff work meant that one battalion did not receive its orders in time and eventually the depleted Portsmouth and Nelson Battalions were forced to go forward on their own. A fairly good barrage was fired but the troops were late in arriving at their allotted jumping-off positions and went over the top some twenty minutes late, at around 16.50. With no idea of what was happening they advanced in the open from the old British front line and were greeted by the forewarned and well-armed Turks. Once again there was confusion over the location of the third Turkish line. The Drake and Hawke Battalions were then ordered forwards in order to further bolster the line. When they reached the former Turkish front line they found themselves in a manmade hell, yet one of the old guard of RND officers could still raise a smile.

It was indescribable, just hundreds of men wandering about in the captured trench system in the burning sun, with corpses blackened and stinking lining the old Turkish firing steps, the sinister symmetry of their position being the only sign of any method at all. The redeeming feature of that occasion was A. P. Herbert's instruction to the sentries on his platoon frontage, 'Remember, regard all Turks with the gravest suspicion!' [31]

Lieutenant Douglas Jerrold, Hawke Battalion, 1st Naval Brigade, RND

Dehydrated by their recent physical exertions, their throats coated with the powdery dust that filled the air and their parched tongues sticking to the roofs of their mouths, the dominant thought of the men clinging to their newly captured trench was a craving for water. Yet there was no safe way back to the water points, for communication trenches were either non-existent, half blocked by bursting shells or choked with corpses and, worse, the former No Man's Land was still being raked by Turkish snipers. Even if water bottles or biscuit tins full of water reached them there was only a tablespoon or so per man; not even enough to wet their parched lips.

> Our water bottles were now empty and thirst increased with the increasing heat of the day; yet we had to carry on without water until the following day, when the Battalion Chief Petty Officer arrived with a large skin bag which looked for all the world like a diseased bagpipe minus the chanter. For a measure he carried a Wills tobacco tin, which normally contained two ounces of tobacco, and from this tin each man received two rations of water. Unfortunately it was found impossible to get forward to an isolated Company of the Drakes, who set to dig for the precious liquid; but as soon as they reached moist earth they stuffed their mouths with it in order to relieve their torment.[32]
>
> Able Seaman Thomas Macmillan, Drake Battalion, 1st Naval Brigade, RND

When the counter-attacks came it was up to the artillery to protect the front line troops as best they could. As they sweated blood, loading the guns time and time again, carrying out their practised drill like automatons till the guns glowed red, it was a question of which would collapse first, the guns or the gunners.

> Up at 4 a.m. this morning. Turks counter-attacked in force and gave us particular hell with vengeance. We've just stopped firing for the third time this morning and, as far as we can find out, the ground gained yesterday has been held by our chaps. Had a glorious time – started at 6.30 a.m., stopped firing at 9.10 p.m. Worked the old gun till the springs broke and the piece itself was so hot that the bearings expanded with the heat and stopped the recoil. We fired 1,160 rounds. My hands are burnt beautifully. Can hardly close my left. Got a whack on the knee which put me off the gun for half an hour but it's OK again. Heavy fighting all night. What a day. One of the hottest and best we've had.

Have just repulsed a mass attack by the Turks. Can't close my right hand, agony to write. We're all like niggers. Absolutely black with cordite smoke and dust. Like Mater to see me now. Gee, these Turks are some fighters – they counter-attacked all night.[33]

Corporal Ralph Doughty, 2nd Battery, 1st Field Artillery Brigade, AIF

In the end the gains were secured and locked firmly into the Allied defensive system. Turkish losses had been serious – in the region of 9,800 – but their reserves were nearer to hand and those losses were soon made good. Over the next few days the four relieving divisions of the Turkish Second Army would take over the Helles lines. But the cost to the Allies was far more hurtful: it was apparent that the 52nd Division had been largely destroyed by its involvement in the attacks, while all residual energy in the RND had drained away. The British suffered some 3,100 casualties and the French a further 840. This seemingly relatively low loss by the French concealed a greater predicament. Over the previous ten weeks or so they had driven themselves into the ground. The Asiatic fire that had smashed into their right flank, coupled with the mordant chasm of Kereves Dere, had finally defeated them. They would do little more for the rest of the campaign than hold their line. They had fought hard, backed to the hilt by their splendid artillery, but they could give no more.

COMMENTARY ON THE ATTACKS made on 21 June, 28 June, 30 June and 12–13 July has often been coruscating, as the attacks had little or no chance of making significant gains. Also, when they launched them, Hamilton and all the other senior generals were well aware that the new divisions were on their way as a result of the decisions of the Dardanelles Committee meetings of 7 and 17 June. As we shall see, Hamilton had already decided that the main effort would be launched from Anzac – there was therefore no prospect of taking Achi Baba or Kilid Bahr even by means of the much-vaunted 'bite and hold' tactics. It would take them years at the current rate of progress. Concentrated artillery support could achieve small-scale advances, but the very nature of limited front attacks caused severe problems once the Turks realised what was happening.

Attacks on a limited front tended to be much more costly to the attackers, in that they allowed the concentration of the fire of a large proportion of enemy guns on the area attacked. Further, attacks on a limited frontage simplified, for the Turkish commander, the problem of the handling of his reserves (always the most difficult problem for the defenders), and facilitated the delivery of counter-attacks, not merely by reason of the early movement of reserves towards the threatened point, but also of the short distance from each other of flanks that were not being attacked and were therefore ready points for support to counter-attacks.[34]

Colonel John Anderson, 1/6th Highland Light Infantry, 157th Brigade, 52nd Division

But surely the most damning criticism comes from Major General Granville Egerton, commander of the 52nd Division. Although often dismissed with faint contempt as a man too old and infirm for active service on such an enervating battlefront, he was none the less an experienced officer and his analysis of the fighting on 12–13 July is persuasive.

It seems to me that the fighting of this battle was premature and at the actual moment worse than unnecessary – I submit that it was cruel and wasteful. The troops on the Peninsula were tired and worn out; there were only two Infantry Brigades, the 155th and the 157th, that had not been seriously engaged. It was well known to the higher command that large reinforcements were arriving from England and a grand attack was to be made at Suvla. Was it not therefore obvious that the exhausted garrison at Helles should be given a fortnight's respite and that the fresh attacks from that position should synchronise with those at Suvla and Anzac? I contend that the Battle of July 12–13th was due to a complete want of a true appreciation of the situation. If the conception of the battle was wrong the tactics of the action were far worse. The division of the attack of two Brigades on a narrow front into two phases, no less than 9 hours apart, was positively wicked.[35]

Major General Granville Egerton, Headquarters, 52nd Division

Shortly after the battle finished Hunter-Weston began to suffer from the effects of sunstroke. On 25 July he was evacuated home and was forced to hand temporary command of VIII Corps to General William Douglas. Often cruelly caricatured as a buffoon, Hunter-Weston was capable of moments of piercing insight and not resistant to tactical innovation. Nevertheless he had entirely failed to master the endemic problems of 1915 trench warfare against a determined enemy of roughly equal number, and without the superior artillery power that would have offered the only chance of success. This in itself is not surprising, for generals all along the Western Front were encountering exactly the same challenges and they too were failing with horrendous losses. But Hunter-Weston's readiness to carry out orders, his willing acceptance of severe casualties and his stubborn persistence against the odds were not the right qualities for the hopeless situation he faced. Yet the overall responsibility for the disaster was not his: Helles was a doomed front and the unnecessary attacks in June and July 1915 were a terrible indictment of the man in overall command. The real burden of guilt should rest on the slim shoulders of General Sir Ian Hamilton, a man whose mind had long turned to the new horizons of Anzac and Suvla.

12

NEW BEGINNINGS: HAMILTON'S PLANS

A battle is a swirl of 'ifs' and 'ands.' The Commander who enters upon it possessed by some just and clear principle is like a sailing ship entering a typhoon on the right track. After that he lives from hand to mouth.[1]

General Sir Ian Hamilton, Headquarters, MEF

THE CUMULATIVE DECISIONS of the Dardanelles Committee meetings on 7 and 17 June had assigned the 10th, 11th and 13th Divisions to the Gallipoli campaigns. These were all New Army divisions raised under the famous recruitment campaign spearheaded by Lord Kitchener in the first year of the war. In addition the 53rd and 54th Divisions, both Territorial Army formations, were despatched to Hamilton. This was all strangely haphazard as it seemed to depend far more on the availability of troops than on a realistic assessment of the overall strategic situation and the paramount needs of the Western Front. There had also been no proper consideration of the readiness of these divisions for war. Their training was woefully inadequate: although willing in the sense that they were all volunteers, these men were still civilians in uniform rather than soldiers. Their regimental officers were all either older men recalled to the colours from retirement, or young callow officers with little suitability for command other than their class status.

The question was, what would Hamilton do with this huge addition to his forces? A whole range of options lay before him: a new Asiatic landing, the siren call of a landing on the Bulair Isthmus at the neck of the Peninsula, more attacks at Helles, or a renewed assault at Anzac. Most of these were swiftly dispensed with. The arguments against a landing on the Asiatic side of the Straits or at Bulair had not changed, while the summer battles at Helles had dimmed enthusiasm for frontal assaults on a narrow front against layered trenches. Anzac, though, was different; success there would allow a swift march to the promised land of Kilid Bahr. The only problem was that Anzac had so small a bridgehead that there was not physically enough room there to take the number of troops required. But then, as luck would have it, Birdwood hatched a plan that seemed to offer an attractive solution.

Lieutenant General Sir William Birdwood, commanding the ANZAC Corps, had long been monitoring the situation to the north of Anzac, beyond his outposts in the foothills and looking towards Suvla Bay.

> Soon after our landing I had made up my mind that we must eventually attack at Suvla, beyond my left. With this possibility in view I had given the strictest orders that no demonstration or attack of any kind should be made in that direction, though the country there was easier. I wanted to let the Turks think that we entirely ignored it, and that any breaking out we might contemplate would come from my right – in conjunction, perhaps, with the force at Helles.[2]
>
> Lieutenant General Sir William Birdwood, Headquarters, ANZAC Corps

The idea of a breakout away from the Anzac trenches was obviously an attractive one and there was little sign of a Turkish presence in the tangled inhospitable mass of gullies and ridges visible from Walker's Ridge. It seemed that the Turks were relying on the sheer slopes to guard their northern flank. Birdwood and his staff despatched scouts to find out exactly what the situation was. Major Percy Overton of the Canterbury Mounted Rifles played a leading role.

> The first time I took Corporal Denton and we had a great day together and gained a lot of valuable information for which General Godley thanked me. The last time I was out for two nights and a day and I took Trooper M. McInnes and Corporal Young. We had a most exciting and interesting time dodging Turkish outposts. I was able from what I saw of the country to make a map and gain much information as to the

movement of the Turks and would not have missed the experience for the world.[3]

Major Percy Overton, Canterbury Mounted Rifles, New Zealand Mounted Rifles Brigade, NZ &A Division, NZEF

Overton found no serious Turkish presence; it did indeed seem that there were opportunities for exploitation. Gradually the vision of a left hook out of Anzac dawned: moving into the valleys and then pushing up the ridges to seize the key heights of the Sari Bair range – thereby evading all the main Turkish defences.

Birdwood's first outline proposals were presented to Hamilton on 30 May. The plan was for a night attack to burst out of Anzac and overwhelm the Turks on Hill Q and Chunuk Bair, then sweep down next day to take the Turks on Battleship Hill and Baby 700 from the rear. To achieve this he asked for the assistance of the 29th Indian Brigade and a further British division for the advance across the Peninsula and attack on Kilid Bahr. This, then, was the scheme that had reached the top of Hamilton's agenda as he pondered his options. Next he considered the feasibility of a fresh landing in the Suvla Bay area, to overcome the problem of lack of space at Anzac. This would allow more divisions to be brought ashore with room to breath and then be deployed forward in good order. Suvla had been considered as a landing site in April but had been rejected as too far away from the ultimate objectives. The Royal Navy was therefore brought into the planning process to achieve a simultaneous landing with the Anzac breakout.

The Royal Navy had one innovation to offer the army. Prompted by Fisher – always a pacesetter when it came to new types of ship – the navy had ordered a number of armoured motor lighters in February 1915. These shallow-draught craft were each capable of carrying 500 soldiers and were known colloquially as 'beetles' – a reference to the shape of their prominent prows, from which a ramp would be dropped to facilitate the troops getting ashore. They represented a great advance from the towed strings of rowing boats used on 25 April and offered the chance to mimic the intended impact of the *River Clyde* without the disadvantage of grounding eighty yards from shore. However, these were not sophisticated craft and they still had some drawbacks, in particular they were slow and difficult to manoeuvre, rather like the Thames barges they resembled.

The navy also tried to find beaches in the Suvla Bay area suitable for a landing. The conclusions were that while the beach stretching south from Nibrunesi Point was ideal for a landing, there were probably shoaling waters in the bay itself. No detailed survey could be done, as it would undoubtedly attract the attention of the Turks, but this sound practical advice was ignored.

Hamilton intended to form the divisions landing at Suvla into the new IX Corps, and there was considerable debate as to who should take command. The first suggestion emanating from Kitchener was Lieutenant General Sir Bryan Mahon, then leading the 10th Division and therefore already on his way to the Peninsula. He was probably the most realistic choice, but Hamilton did not rate Mahon highly enough for a corps, believing he had reached his peak as a divisional commander. It was this decision to reject Mahon for promotion that triggered the disastrous sequence of events that followed. Hamilton boldly asked for either Lieutenant General Sir Julian Byng or Lieutenant General Sir Henry Rawlinson, both of whom were attracting much admiration for their performances on the Western Front. For that very reason Hamilton's request was curtly rejected and Kitchener in turn not only refused to remove Mahon from his divisional command but stipulated that whoever commanded IX Corps must be senior to him. The British Army still made a shibboleth of seniority which could sometimes get in the way of the appointment of younger, more competent men. This was especially problematic when most of the more promising generals were already fully engaged on the Western Front. The intransigence of both Kitchener and Hamilton left only two feasible candidates: Lieutenant General Sir John Ewart and Lieutenant General Frederick Stopford. But Ewart was too physically frail for Gallipoli, which meant Stopford was the last man standing. It was not the ideal method of selecting a leader for a complex operation of war demanding excellent leadership qualities, proven military command skills and steely determination. What they got was a 61-year-old man who was in semi-retirement as the Lieutenant of the Tower of London. He was a career soldier, but his career had been of the sort that had not featured the command of troops in action and his expertise had been largely in staff work – valuable, but not the skill set required at Suvla Bay. Mahon would have been a far better choice.

Meanwhile, there had been an update on the Anzac plans. Birdwood's schemes went through the usual process of conception and review as he attempted to keep pace with the changing situation. The availability of additional troops led him to add Hill 971, the highest peak of the Sari Bair range, to the list of objectives, while his requirement for the suppression of Turkish batteries believed to be in the Chocolate Hill and W Hills sector of Suvla was passed over to Stopford. After due consideration was given to the need for moonless nights during the build-up of forces at Anzac, the attack was eventually fixed for 6 August.

The plan for the ANZAC Corps' operations was drawn up largely by their Chief of Staff, Brigadier General Andrew Skeen. A key element was a series of diversionary operations, of which the first was to be a full-scale attack at 17.30 on 6 August on Turkish positions on Lone Pine on the southern half of 400 Plateau. After dark, while the fighting was still raging at Lone Pine, hopefully distracting all Turkish eyes, the left hook would be launched in a series of four columns marching out from Anzac and along North Beach. These would be divided into covering forces and assaulting columns. The Right Covering Force was to seize the series of Turkish outposts in the foothills commanding the valleys leading up to the Sari Bair Ridge. This done, the Right Assaulting Column was to advance through Sazli Beit Dere and Chailak Dere before climbing to Rhododendron Ridge, then up to their objective of Chunuk Bair. The Left Covering Force was to advance further along the beach, then up Aghyl Dere before securing the left flank by over-running Damakjelik Bair. Meanwhile, the Left Assaulting Column would continue further along Aghyl Dere before climbing Abdul Rahman Spur leading up to Hill 971. These plans for a night attack were excessively ambitious, given the extreme complexity of the terrain, the weak physical state of many of the troops and the distances that would have to be covered before the objectives could be attained. Although plans had been made to distract the Turks the timetable was so rigid that there would be no scope for mistakes, or the Turks would surely be on top of Sari Bair and waiting for them. Almost as a throwaway GHQ endorsed the idea of a major holding operation to be launched by VIII Corps at Helles in order to prevent Turkish reserves from marching north to reinforce Anzac.

The GHQ staff produced the initial plans for the Suvla landings. The original concept was for a *coup de main* whereby the covering force of the 11th Division would land on the night of 6 August on the beaches to the south of Nibrunesi Point and overwhelm the Turkish outposts on the Lala

Baba hills and Hill 10 before moving swiftly inland to seize the Kiretch Tepe and Tekke Tepe ranges that dominated the whole Suvla Bay area. One complication was the defence works and artillery positions that it was suspected existed on the southern slopes of Chocolate Hill and W Hills, the foothills lying below the main Tekke Tepe range. It was decided to attack these from the rear and hence the troops would skirt the northern shore of the Salt Lake behind Suvla Bay to attack them before dawn on 7 August. One thing was certain: the high ground must be seized as soon as possible, thus allowing the 10th Division to come ashore and then co-operate, if necessary, in the ANZAC Corps' advance on Hill 971 and the Sari Bair range. But the main intention was to establish a secure supply base for the future push forward across the Peninsula after the success of the Anzac breakout.

The plans were communicated to Stopford and his formidable Chief of Staff, Brigadier General Hamilton Reed, VC, who was fresh from service on the Western Front. Stopford's initially favourable reaction was soon eroded by the pessimistic council of Reed, who considered that attacks on prepared positions were impossible without proper artillery support. This he had learnt through bitter experience. But were his warnings appropriate to the situation facing the IX Corps at Suvla? Were they facing quite such formidable trench works? Or was speed more important, in order to catch the Turks before they could reinforce the sector? Lieutenant Geoffrey Ryland gained an insight into the pessimistic mindset of the senior officers of the IX Corps during an offshore naval reconnaissance.

Towards the end of July the Captain received orders to send me on board the destroyer *Arno* to point out to various Generals salient features of the landscape north from Gaba Tepe, round Suvla Point into the Gulf of Xeros. I was informed that it was essential these officers should be thoroughly acquainted with the nature of the country since a new landing was projected. When I arrived on board the *Arno* a number of Generals were already there and almost immediately we weighed anchor and left Kefalo Bay and set course for Gaba Tepe. On the way across it occurred to me that if all this array of 'Red Tabs' was observed by the Turks on the deck of a destroyer steaming close inshore in the neighbourhood of Suvla Bay, it would not need great imagination on their part to conclude that another landing was to be made. I therefore reported to the Captain of the *Arno* and suggested that we might induce the Generals to put on white working rig. He agreed and the Generals also fell in with the suggestion. The result was rather comic since elderly Generals, several of whom had large drooping moustaches, looked odd in sailor suits and caps, in most cases the latter being too small for them. I suppose at the age of 25 most people over 45 look old, but I was shocked at the apparent age of some of these officers and wondered how they would be able to stick the very unpleasant and unhealthy conditions on the Peninsula. I pointed out to them all the features which we knew so well like Chocolate Hill, W Hills, the Anafartas, the Salt Lake, Kavak Tepe, Kiretch Tepe and Ejelmer. One of the Generals asked me where the Turkish trenches were and seemed surprised when I told him there weren't any. I do not think he believed me![4]

Lieutenant Geoffrey Ryland, HMS *Ark Royal*

This was at the root of the problem: the generals simply could not believe that the Turks were not well dug in and present in force. As these tremulous doubts multiplied at IX Corps headquarters, a series of changes was introduced into the original GHQ plans. The first was to land a brigade inside Suvla Bay, from which it would take less time to march round the northern boundary of the Salt Lake. This was unfortunate in view of the navy's justifiable fears of shoaling waters inside the bay. It was also totally unnecessary as the Salt Lake had completely dried out during the long hot summer of 1915 and there was thus no need to march round it. Secondly, the capture of Chocolate Hill and W Hills was now considered problematic without the support of howitzers and so could no longer be contemplated until after dawn on 7 August. When Stopford produced his orders for the landings they had lost all sense of purpose. Now all reference to the urgency of the 11th Division rapidly seizing the Kiretch Tepe and Tekke Tepe ranges had been expunged and the 10th Division was no longer charged with any particular responsibility to push out and assist the attacks from Anzac. This process of dilution was continued by Stopford's subordinates. Major General Frederick Hammersley, in command of 11th Division, was hamstrung by his own fears. His orders stating that the capture of W Hills was to be attempted only 'if possible' were a clear abrogation of responsibility. The whole process of command and control within IX Corps was a disaster; the intent of the landings was being submerged by conditional inanities that left no one responsible for the attainment of Hamilton's defined objectives. But Hamilton and his staff also bear a great deal of blame for failing to properly direct and control their subordinates – indeed, Stopford subsequently claimed that he had never had even a one-minute conversation with Hamilton prior to the Suvla landings.[5]

Anzac, though, was at the heart of the matter. The left hook swinging up to the heights of Sari Bair was to be the apogee of the complex series of attacks, diversions and holding operations that had been commissioned by Hamilton. But were the Turks really so unprepared? It seems certain that well before the August operations began Lieutenant Colonel Mustafa Kemal was worried by the perceived weakness of the northern flank of their Anzac positions.

> I believed that the new attempts would be made by an extension of
> the Anzac front to the north in pursuit of his aim of dominating the
> Sari Bair range. These ideas and opinions I passed on to the regimental
> commanders of the 19th Division and also to my staff. Sometimes even,
> on quiet nights when there was no action, I used to carry out with my
> regimental commanders short war games on the map regarding these
> points.[6]
>
> Lieutenant Colonel Mustafa Kemal, Headquarters, 19th Division, Fifth Army

Fortunately for Hamilton, Kemal's superiors did not share his fears and, despite his repeated written and verbal protests, did little to strengthen either the northern borders of Anzac or indeed the Suvla Bay defences.

The great open spaces of Suvla Bay, despite Stopford's and Reed's fears, were only weakly defended by the Anafarta Detachment under the command of a German officer, Major Wilhelm Willmer. He had control of just three battalions: the Broussa Gendarmerie Battalion, the Gallipoli Gendarmerie Battalion and the regular 1/31st Regiment. As artillery he had two batteries stationed up on the heights of the Tekke Tepe range, with two 8-year-old mountain guns available for more immediate support. His plans were simple; they had to be, as he did not have sufficient men or resources to prepare major fortifications or continuous trench lines. Instead he selected certain key points for defence on the coastal hills of Lala Baba, Hill 10 and the Karakol Dagh continuation of Kiretch Tepe. Here there were localised trenches and he managed to lay a few mines. The troops at these outposts were to act as tripwires, causing maximum disruption, before they fell back to join the rest off his forces dug in as best they could on Chocolate Hill, Green Hill, W Hills and Kiretch Tepe, where a far more determined resistance was intended. In the meantime it was expected that the Turkish reserves from the Bulair sector would be making their way to the rescue.

THE BRITISH PLANS HAD BEEN MADE. When complete, they bore all the distinctive imprimaturs of Hamilton and his staff. They were not stupid, in the sense that considerable imagination had been shown and there had been a commendable attention to detail in their construction. The problem lay in the overcomplication that was the hallmark of a Hamilton plan. Just as on 25 April, there was a rash of schemes stretching from end to end of the Peninsula. Too many elements were supposedly dependent on each other's success, but as physically separate entities they were unable to help each other achieve that success. Once again there were diversions that were major operations in themselves. The forces assigned to the various operations were also often unsuited to the operations that lay before them: the ANZAC Corps charged with the main responsibility for breaking out of Anzac was a husk racked by disease and suffering from an underlying exhaustion; the British units which were to make the new landings at Suvla were totally inexperienced; the VIII Corps at Helles was experienced enough but worn down by their ordeals in continually attacking trench lines between themselves and Achi Baba. Taken as a whole the scheme was utterly unrealistic. It demanded feats of endurance from the assaulting columns climbing to Sari Bair which would have made Hannibal think twice; it asked raw troops to perform like veterans and sickly veterans to put their illnesses behind them; it required leadership from incompetents; it sought to create diversions by attacks that bitter experience had already shown were bound to fail. And worst of all it assumed, despite all the evidence so far accumulated, that the Turks would fight badly.

13

AUGUST: HELLES SACRIFICE

The omens from the Helles sacrifices had not been propitious.[1]

Colonel Cecil Aspinall, Headquarters, MEF

THE DOG DAYS OF SUMMER brought little hope of respite for the VIII Corps at Helles. The remorseless sun blazed down upon them, the Turks were as implacable as ever, their trench system rivalling anything to be found on the Western Front at that stage of the war. Front lines, support lines and redoubts faced the VIII Corps in front of Krithia, while behind them reserve line trenches snaked their way up and along the contours of Achi Baba. And behind that more fortifications barred the way to Kilid Bahr. Under Hamilton's plans the VIII Corps was required to pin the Turkish Helles garrison while the main offensives progressed at Anzac and Suvla. The initial plans were remarkably similar to the disastrous attacks made on 12–13 July: there were to be two highly localised attacks in order to use limited artillery resources for maximum effect. On 6 August the freshly replenished 88th Brigade of the 29th Division was to attack the Turkish lines north of Krithia Nullah and push up Fir Tree Spur. Next day it was the turn of the 125th and 127th Brigades of the 42nd Division to attack along Krithia Spur and up Krithia Nullah itself. The aim was to pinch out the Turkish salient in the centre. That was as far as their intended role went, but the VIII Corps, under the temporary command of Major General William Douglas pending the arrival of Lieutenant General

Sir Francis Davies, was optimistic. For some unfathomable reason success was more or less assumed and the capture of both Krithia and Achi Baba was confidently anticipated.

The prevailing character of the Helles fighting at the start of August was one of routine trench warfare. The men lived in their trenches day in, day out, with little or nothing to do or look forward to. Second Lieutenant Hugh Heywood of the 1/6th Manchesters found that, although he could have been killed at any moment, his life was one of mind-numbing tedium.

> Our existence here has been more monotonous than anything I have ever endured before. We have been stuck in the same place in the same trenches, doing the same thing – nothing! Our programme every day is as follows: 3 a.m. 'stand to' till 4 a.m., then sleep again (if the flies will let you) till 8 a.m. when you rouse up again and prepare for one's breakfast at about 8.15. Breakfast has to be rushed otherwise the flies get too numerous in the vicinity of the jam. After breakfast you settle down as comfortably as you can and start to do nothing, interrupted at 10.20 by inspecting your platoon lines, but once that is done you can really get going and go on doing nothing till 8 p.m. with short interruptions for food.[2]

> Second Lieutenant Hugh Heywood, 1/6th Manchester Regiment, 127th Brigade, 42nd Division

Every so often there would be a sudden flurry as one side or the other tried to improve its tactical position. Small, almost unnoticeable features of the landscape could provoke vicious spasms of fighting. Lieutenant Charles Lister was involved in one such skirmish over some disputed barricades.

> The artillery shelled the advanced Turkish post for about 20 minutes while we massed, with a covering party of men with bombs and bayonets and a main body of men with sandbags, in the trench, ready to rush out up the old communication trench and push our sandbag barrier still farther forward. We realised the importance of rushing in immediately our shelling ceased. But as it turned out we were rather too close, for a shell fell among our people and buried six of them, who were, however, dug out unhurt or only slightly wounded. The shell luckily did not burst. This was followed by a Turkish shell which fell right in the middle of us as we were all crouching for the rush, hit

Freyberg in the stomach, killed another man, and covered me with small scratches, which bled profusely at the moment. We had by now got to our original barrier, so I got our covering party out and rushed them up the trench over quite a number of dead Turks. We stopped our men just short of the Turkish advanced post: threw bombs and at once started the new barrier – not a Turk in sight. The snipers, however, soon came back and made work at this point difficult, so we moved back and contented ourselves with a gain of about 40 to 50 yards on our old position. I have been hit in about six places, but all tiny little scratches.[3]

Lieutenant Charles Lister, Hood Battalion, 2nd Naval Brigade, RND

Lister was evacuated for medical treatment on Imbros. Behind him the VIII Corps was getting nowhere fast.

THE DIVERSIONARY ATTACK on Friday 6 August would be supported by the 1/5th Manchesters who would attack in order to protect the right flank of the advancing 88th Brigade. In addition they would be supported by the massed machine guns of the 127th Brigade. The British bombardment opened up at 14.20 but the Turkish response was almost immediate. They had been expecting an attack.

Our own bombardment started and I've never seen or heard or smelt anything like it; the shells were bursting wherever you looked, there was a hellish din and overall a dense cloud of pungent, sickly yellow smoke, through which nothing could be seen distinctly. Bits of shell were flying about in every direction; either from Turkish shells or from the 'blow back' from ours. This went on for nearly 2 hours.[4]

Second Lieutenant Hugh Heywood, 1/6th Manchester Regiment, 127th Brigade, 42nd Division

Lieutenant General Sir Francis Davies, who had arrived fresh from service on the Western Front, was 'horrified at the total inadequacy of the British bombardment'.[5] Warfare on the Western Front had danced to the rhythm of the guns for most of 1915. Bombardments there were measured in hundreds of thousands of shells; soon millions of shells would be expended in a single day. The barrage offered in support of the infantry on 6 August was totally insufficient. As the infantry would find soon enough when they went over the top at 15.50.

All the line on the left to the Krithia Nullah got over the parapet and went for the Turks. As soon as our fellows got over an absolute hellish rifle and machine gun fire was opened on them. They fairly dropped and it was a vile sight, but the dust soon got too thick for us to see further than 30 or 40 yards from the trench. We who had to stay behind could only listen and hope.[6]

Second Lieutenant Hugh Heywood, 1/6th Manchester Regiment, 127th Brigade, 42nd Division

There was little hope for the men in No Man's Land. The result was abject failure and the slaughter of another generation of the 'Immortal' 29th Division. The collective spirit may have been willing but thousands of men were paying the penalty for wishful thinking. Buoyed up by optimistic reports that lacked foundation in reality, Major General Henry de Beauvoir de Lisle, commanding the 29th Division, ordered a night attack to be carried out by the 86th Brigade at 22.30. After protests from some of his officers the attack was cancelled. As it was, Heywood and his machine gunners of the 1/6th Manchesters were on the *qui vive* all night in expectation of a Turkish counter-attack.

One or two wounded began to crawl in: one poor fellow crept back very slowly under a heavy fire and rolled fainting into our arms over the parapet. When we came to clean him we found he had three huge holes in his stomach and half his insides were outside.[7]

Second Lieutenant Hugh Heywood, 1/6th Manchester Regiment, 127th Brigade, 42nd Division

It took five field dressings to staunch the flow of blood, after which he was given morphine and stretchered back. His chances of survival would have been meagre.

The Turks did not, however, counter-attack; they remained firm in their positions. Indeed, Liman was so confident of the ability of his Helles divisions to withstand further onslaughts that he ordered the reserve 4th Division based at Serafim Farm to march towards Anzac early on 7 August. This illustrated the total failure of the Helles operations designed to pin the Turkish garrison. Yet the plan remained the same and that morning the badly under-strength 127th and 125th Brigades of the 42nd Division attacked along Krithia Spur.

The preparatory barrage commenced at 08.10, with the massed

machine guns standing ready to create a rainstorm of bullets on vulnerable points behind the Turkish lines.

> The only difference was that the Turk hardly replied at all. It lasted till 9.40 and the job for which my machine gun section had been detailed was to fire for the last half hour, i.e. from 9.10 to 9.40, at aiming marks which we had previously put up and set so as to carry us on to certain of the Turkish trenches. The object was to try and get any Turks who might be being sent up to support the firing line. In the half hour the three guns got through about 6,000 rounds so I hope we did some damage. At 9.40 the line charged and got a dreadful time from shrapnel and the enemy's machine gun and rifle fire. We could see the line being simply mown down; it was a very nerve-trying sight.[8]
>
> Second Lieutenant Hugh Heywood, 1/6th Manchester Regiment, 127th Brigade, 42nd Division

The aftermath of the Manchesters' charge was terrible; the evidence of their failure soon lay in No Man's Land for all to see. Alongside them the Lancashire Fusiliers of the 125th Brigade initially had slightly more success breaking through on Krithia Spur, even getting men through into the Turkish support lines. Private Arthur Kay was in the second wave of their attack.

> Suddenly the guns ceased and afterwards we heard the shouts of our boys over the parapets. Some of them did not run a yard before they were hit. Our 'C' Company advanced – we suffered the worst, for the Turks were ready for us. I am sure I was half-mad when I saw my mates dropping as I was running. I did not get to their trench for I was hit through the neck – a narrow shave for me. It came right through. The blood spurted out, of course. I dropped down but managed to crawl back to our old trench. I rolled into the trench. One poor fellow was moaning; he had been hit in the back with shrapnel. You could put your arm through the hole it had made. I got his field-dressing and did the best I could for him, whilst I myself was growing weaker.[9]
>
> Private Arthur Kay, 1/7th Lancashire Fusiliers, 125th Brigade, 42nd Division

The Turks soon threw them back; their only remaining gain was in the Vineyard sector. Here some of the worst fighting was experienced by the 1/9th Manchesters when they moved up to relieve the Lancashires. A key figure in the defence of the north-west corner of the Vineyard was Captain William Forshaw.

> I and about twenty men were instructed to hold a barricade at the head of the sap. Facing us were three converging saps held by the Turks, who were making desperate efforts to retake this barricaded corner, and so cut off all the other men in the trench. The Turks attacked at frequent intervals along the three saps from Saturday afternoon until Monday morning, and they advanced into the open with the objective of storming the parapet. They were met by a combination of bombing and rifle fire, but the bomb was the chief weapon used both by the Turks and ourselves.[10]
>
> Captain William Forshaw, 1/9th Manchester Regiment, 126th Brigade, 42nd Division

Alongside Captain Forshaw at the head of the sap was Sergeant Harry Grantham.

> There were all sorts of bombs. Round bombs and bombs made out of jam tins and filled with explosives and bits of iron, lead, needles, etc. It was lively while it lasted. We could see the Turks coming on at us, great big fellows they were, and we dropped our bombs right amidst them. Captain Forshaw was at the end of the trench. He fairly revelled in it. He kept joking and cheering us on, and was smoking cigarettes all the while. He used his cigarettes to light the fuses of the bombs, instead of striking matches. 'Keep it up, boys!' he kept saying. We did, although a lot of our lads were killed and injured by the Turkish firebombs. It was exciting, I can tell you.[11]
>
> Sergeant Harry Grantham, 1/9th Manchester Regiment, 126th Brigade, 42nd Division

The bombs used by both sides lacked potency. They could of course kill but, not having much explosive power or a proper fragmentation casing, they were far more likely to wound, or bespatter the victims with cuts from hundreds of minute fragments. That is not to say that they were not dangerous if you were unlucky or over-ambitious.

> Bombs were bursting all around us. Some of the boys in their excitement caught the Turkish bombs before they exploded, and hurled them back again. They did not always manage to catch them in time

and three of them had their hands blown off. What made the position worse was that as soon as we had entered the trench a bomb laid out six of us. I was one of them. I bandaged up my leg, bandaged the others and sent them back – I carried on.[12]

Lance Corporal Thomas Pickford, 1/9th Manchester Regiment, 126th Brigade, 42nd Division

The fighting continued for the best part of two days. Even when the 1/9th Manchesters were relieved, Forshaw insisted on staying on to lead the defence.

I was far too busy to think of myself or to think of anything. We just went at it without a pause while the Turks were attacking, and in the slack intervals I put more fuses into bombs. I cannot imagine how I escaped with only a bruise from a piece of shrapnel. It was miraculous. The attacks were very fierce at times, but only once did the Turks succeed in getting right up to the parapet. Three attempted to climb over, but I shot them with my revolver. All this time both our bomb throwing and shooting had been very effective, and many Turkish dead were in front of the parapet and in the saps. The attack was not continuous, of course, but we had to be on the watch all the time, and so it was impossible to get any sleep. Fortunately, we had no fewer than 800 of those bombs, but we got rid of the lot during the greatest weekend I have ever spent.[13]

Captain William Forshaw, 1/9th Manchester Regiment, 126th Brigade, 42nd Division

The physical and nervous exhaustion that followed their eventual relief took its toll on Forshaw, despite his apparent insouciance.

Myself, a few men and the Captain held a trench which was almost impossible to hold, but we stuck it like glue, in spite of the Turks attacking us with bombs. I can tell you I accounted for a few Turks. Our Captain has been recommended for the VC and I hope he gets it because he was very determined to hold the trench till the last man was finished. But we did not lose many. Our Captain has not got over it yet, but it is only his nerves that are shattered a bit.[14]

Lance Corporal Samuel Bayley, 1/9th Manchester Regiment, 126th Brigade, 42nd Division

Forshaw would be awarded the VC for his reckless disregard for his personal health and would for ever be known as the 'Cigarette VC'. The fighting over the Vineyard – an area of ground just 200 yards long and 100 yards wide – continued for several days as the British strove to incorporate it into their lines and the Turks tried to eject them. Here was the chance for revenge as the Turks counter-attacked. The moment the Turks charged out of their trenches they too were massacred. The Australian gunners of 1st Field Artillery Brigade once again sweated in the blazing heat as they poured shells into easy targets over the next few days.

> Heavy fighting all day. A few monitors with 14˝ guns came up and helped to paint the landscape hideous. Towards evening the Turks attacked in massed formation. Every available gun was turned on to repelling them, which they did with terrible effect. Not one Turk succeeded in getting within striking distance of our fire trench. The shrapnel just tore long lanes in the advancing lines, and their well-planned attack came to a sticky end. Fighting all night ... Very hot day. Heavy fighting up in the infantry trenches all day. Chas and I up to the first line this afternoon. Had a good screw around. The heaviest fighting during the last four days has been in a vineyard. The vines are trampled down and torn about with HE and shrapnel and interspersed with bodies. Our fellows got it pretty heavy in one corner, but Johnny Turk got it hot, too.[15]
>
> Corporal Ralph Doughty, 2nd Battery, 1st Field Artillery Brigade, AIF

How many more futile attacks would be launched, how many more men would die on both sides before their commanders grasped that an advance was impossible for either side at Helles? The fighting finally shuddered to a halt on 13 August. The losses in this most ineffective of diversions were huge, with the British losing over 3,300 in their attacks and the Turks sacrificing 7,500 to their crazy obsession to regain control of a few blasted vines that were of no use to either side. This was fighting for the sake of it: it wasn't strategy; it wasn't tactics; it was legalised manslaughter. When the second British attack failed, Liman had the confidence to order another of his Helles divisions, the 8th Division, to march north. Now everything had changed – indeed, the positions had reversed: Helles had become the backwater where little or no progress was likely; any remaining hopes for tangible success had shifted to the new offensive planned to burst out of Anzac.

14

AUGUST: ANZAC, DIVERSIONS AND BREAKOUT

To take on the responsibility for a new task, with troops I did not know and in a completely vague and unknown situation, was no mean task. It was responsibility for a battle that had been going on for three days and which had resulted in the defeat and disorder of every commander and unit taking part – a battle which was a life and death struggle for the nation begun by others and ending in bloody defeat. I however accepted the responsibility with pride.[1]

Colonel Mustafa Kemal, Headquarters, 19th Division, 5th Army

THE BREAKOUT FROM ANZAC was the centrepiece; the very heart of the August Offensive that was the last chance for the Gallipoli campaign of 1915. There were three main elements of the operational plans as prepared by Lieutenant General Sir William Birdwood and Brigadier General Andrew Skeen. The first was a major diversion centred on the assault by the 1st Division on Lone Pine in the late afternoon of 6 August; then the main event was the dramatic breakout from Anzac, intended to seize the key heights of Chunuk Bair and Hill 971 by dawn on 7 August; and finally concerted attacks to be launched on The Nek and Chessboard. Depending on your viewpoint, this was either a brilliantly imaginative programme that left little to chance, or a farrago that substituted optimism for realism. Brigadier General John Monash considered it to be a new beginning.

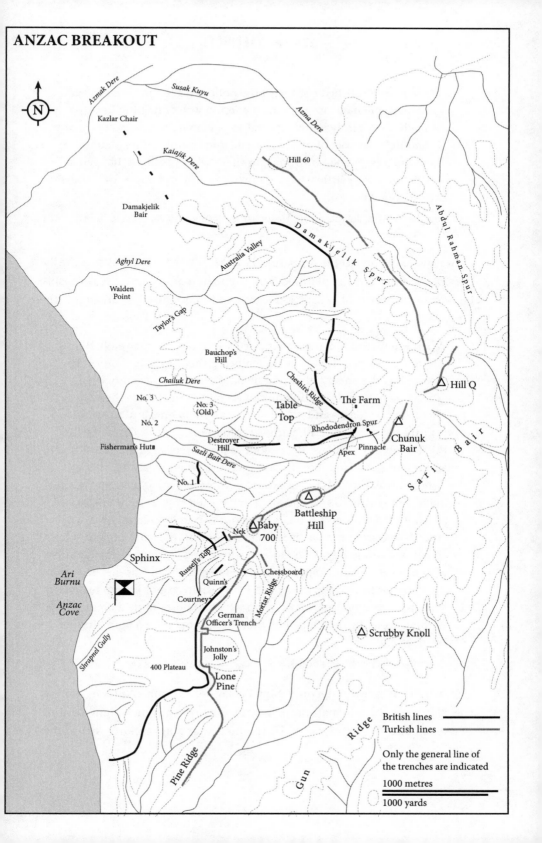

I am very well satisfied both with the policy and the progress of our operations. We have dropped the Churchill way of rushing in before we are ready, and hardly knowing what we are going to do next, in favour of the Kitchener way of making careful and complete preparations on lines which just can't go wrong. For that's what's going to happen in Gallipoli in a very little while, and what's going to happen in Flanders and Belgium later on.[2]

Brigadier General John Monash, Headquarters, 4th Australian Brigade, NZ&A Division, AIF

Others were deeply sceptical, particularly as to whether it was physically possible to carry out the planned flanking march at night in the unhospitable country north of Anzac. One such was Major Cecil Allanson of the 1/6th Gurkha Rifles.

When the method of attack was disclosed to me confidentially that afternoon I gasped. It is to be remembered that Anzac is completely invested by the enemy; that no one has been able to reconnoitre the ground outside and that no one can absolutely guarantee the map. There are no villages and no inhabitants to help one, and the whole country seemed to be stiff, with very sharp rocky cliffs, covered with thick scrub. I have a few ideas about night marches, their great difficulty and the need of careful reconnaissance; but when I was told that we were to break through the opposing outpost line at 10 p.m. on the 6th, march along the sea coast for three miles then turn at right angles and attempt to get under this big ridge about two miles inland, by dawn, and covered from the sea by innumerable small hills and nullahs, I felt, 'What one would have done to a subaltern at a promotion examination who made any such proposition?' The more the plan was detailed as the time got nearer, the less I liked it, especially as in my own regiment there were four officers out of seven who had never done a night march in their lives. The one hope was that the scheme was so bold it might be successful.[3]

Major Cecil Allanson, 1/6th Gurkha Rifles, 29th Indian Brigade

The delightfully curmudgeonly New Zealander Colonel William Malone was also a sceptic. His natural penchant for maintaining a tight control of any situation was threatened by the many variables lurking within the plan.

I do not like this job, it will be night work. We have to wait on the Maoris and our Mounted Rifles clearing some hills and trenches over or by which we have to tackle the high ridge and none of our troops are trained enough for night work in very rough country. We shall possibly mistake the Maoris for Turks and the confusion in the dark will be terrible. If we could only start fighting at dawn and have the day before us, we should have a real good fight, artillery support and seeing what to do and when to go would be a treat. Still it is not for me to decide. If, and a big if, the Maoris and Mounted Rifles do their job properly then unless we get lost, ours ought to come off all right. And if too the Otago and Canterbury people do theirs – I wouldn't be surprised if the Wellington Battalion gets up alone the first and has to dig in and stick it out.[4]

Lieutenant Colonel William Malone, Wellington Battalion, New Zealand Brigade, NZ&A Division, NZEF

Malone could see the risks inherent in the operations they were about to undertake. It would indeed be a dangerous business.

THE TASK OF THE 1ST BRIGADE in launching their diversionary attack on a front just 140 yards wide across eighty to 130 yards of bare, open ground to reach the Turkish trenches on Lone Pine was also daunting. The Turks had tried their best to make their trenches impregnable, carefully layering pinewood logs and earth to provide head cover and, where possible, they had put out barbed wire. Major General Harold Walker, commanding the 1st Australian Division, was worried and he seems to have strained every sinew to improve the chances of his men by a series of measures designed to get them across the killing zone as quickly as possible. After all, the more successful they were the more effective the diversion would be. A series of shallow tunnels were dug, pushing out into No Man's Land to within just forty to sixty yards of the Turks. Some of the men could burst out of these but, perhaps more importantly, the roofs could then be pulled in to create readymade communication trenches for reinforcements if the attack went well. As a diversion they were meant to draw attention to themselves, so a leisurely three-day bombardment was opened up to gradually destroy the Turkish wire defences. At 14.00 on 6 August, three mines would be detonated in No Man's Land in order to create a degree of cover from the disturbed earth. For the men there were more mundane preparations. In the last half hour the bombardment would be increased in weight in the hope of smashing holes in the covered trenches and forcing the Turks to take shelter in deep dugouts.

> White patches were sewn on the back of the men's tunics and around the sleeves as distinguishing marks. Dry rations, ammunition, picks and shovels were carried by all ranks. Officers carried rifles, ammunition, packs, etc., and in addition each platoon commander carried two artillery indication flags and a large percussion bomb. Lieutenant Cradick's last advice to me was to fix a certain sandbag in the enemy's parapet, make a bee-line for it and run my hardest when the whistle went.[5]
>
> Second Lieutenant Charles Lecky, 2nd (New South Wales) Battalion, 1st Brigade, 1st Division, AIF

These were no longer the green, unsophisticated troops that had landed on 25 April. Collectively they had become far more tactically adept and no longer needlessly exposed themselves to fire when there was good cover to be had. Equally, they knew the terrors that lay ahead of them. Finally the whistle blew and the three waves of men went over the top, running as fast as they could. Among them was Lieutenant Lecky.

> I followed the advice and ran for one of the black sandbags in the Turkish line. I cannot remember hearing a sound, although the Turkish machine guns and rifles must have been firing. Neither can I remember having seen anything except that sandbag until I crashed into a deep hole about halfway across. Captain Pain was in the hole busily trying to plug a bullet hole in his arm. He requested me to help him out, as it was too deep for him to scramble out with an injured arm. I tried to get out but toppled back under the weight of my equipment. Captain Pain pushed me up with his good arm and I then pulled him out. Captain Pain, despite his wound, and I then raced on and reached the Turkish line. Many of the men, exposed to and suffering casualties from machine gun fire, were firing through the logs with which the front line was covered. I called to them to jump into a communication trench which I saw and jumped in myself.[6]
>
> Second Lieutenant Charles Lecky, 2nd (New South Wales) Battalion, 1st Brigade, 1st Division, AIF

Over to the left, Major Iven Mackay and his men of the 4th Battalion had been ordered to vault over the Turkish front line and run a further fifty yards before entering the support trenches and sending parties back towards the front line to mop up any remaining Turks.

> Our sudden attack took them by surprise, but nevertheless I have a distinct recollection of little puffs of dust appearing at every loophole as we ran across No Man's Land. As 'A' Company ran beyond the front line we found the Turks running beneath us in the communication trenches whilst we ran along the top. We shot a number of these men, firing our rifles from our hips.[7]
>
> Major Iven Mackay, 4th (New South Wales) Battalion, 1st Brigade, 1st Division, AIF

They ran on and dropped into the next Turkish trench before turning back to clear out the Turks in between. Lance Corporal Joseph Aylward was lucky enough to pick a relatively quiet spot.

> Where I landed in the support trench, no great opposition was met with. Picking up with two other members of the battalion, the three of us moved along the trench until we came to a cross-trench leading to the front line. On the other side of a bend were a number of Turks, who, however, gave way as we charged round it, shouting as loudly as possible. Reaching the front line we were again temporarily held up. At this stage, Lieutenant Seldon, with his eye shot away, came round from the support trench and ordered us to advance along the front line and clear out the enemy.[8]
>
> Lance Corporal Joseph Aylward, 4th (New South Wales) Battalion, 1st Brigade, 1st Division, AIF

Seldon's eye was a macabre sight, the mangled remnants hanging down his cheek. He nevertheless refused treatment and pushed on with his party down the parallel support trench. As ordered, Aylward charged along the front line.

> We hunted around and found a few bombs, which we threw into the trench, shouting and cheering as we followed them up with rifle fire. The ruse succeeded, the Turks retreating across the communication trench into the Jolly. On arrival at the point where the Pine ended in the trench across Owen's Gully, we found Lieutenant Seldon's body lying across the head of it.[9] Peering round the edge of the trench, I saw

a large body of Turks, apparently waiting to repulse an attack down the communication trench. I therefore cut a niche in the side-wall of this trench, and engaged the Turks with fire, while the others proceeded to drag the sandbags from the top of the old front line, in order to block the trench. The sun, glistening on my bayonet, soon gave our position away and the Turks poured in a hot fire. By this time the sandbags were ready to place in position, and when they had been built high enough I crawled across to Lieutenant Seldon, but found that he was quite dead. I therefore took possession of his revolver and we buried his body in the sandbag barricade. There was no sign of any of his party. While we were thus engaged numbers of the enemy had taken advantage of the absence of firing to crawl towards the barricade, but they were discovered in time and driven off by fire. The trench at this point was about 9 feet deep, but had no fire-steps on the side facing the Jolly. Setting the others to cut fire-steps, I proceeded along the front line to establish touch with the rest of the battalion.[10]

Lance Corporal Joseph Aylward, 4th (New South Wales) Battalion, 1st Brigade, 1st Division, AIF

He had done a splendid job helping to secure the northern flank of the advance on to the Lone Pine position. Somewhere nearby was Private Charles Duke.

I was trying to get my breath when from the right end of the traverse a big fellow of a Turk came bolting along the trench. He took no notice of me because close at his heels were two Aussies and as he passed me I raised my rifle and let him have it fair in the middle of the back, almost at the same time as the other two. He went down like a pole-axed bull and the three of us then followed on down the trench to be met by some Turks who came at us suddenly and savagely. I lunged at the nearest, but my bayonet stuck in his leather equipment and for the moment I was helpless. Instantly he raised his rifle to shoot me, but before he could there was an awful bang alongside my ear and he crumpled up at my feet. My mate behind had put his rifle over my shoulder and had shot him but that discharge nearly blew my head off.[11]

Private Charles Duke, 4th (New South Wales) Battalion, 1st Brigade, 1st Division, AIF

The battle had broken up into hundreds of vicious skirmishes. All along the front the Australians were creeping through the network of covered trenches. The cramped tunnels were dark and dust-filled, with the threat of a Turk behind every corner.

> We proceeded to penetrate with misgiving into Turkish territory. As each bend in the trench was reached I placed my cap on the end of my bayonet and if nobody shot at it I poked my head round and went on until I thought we had gone more than a mile. As a matter of fact, we were only a couple of hundred yards away from the captured Turkish position. The men who followed were ordered to block up the trench with sandbags and unremitting hard work was carried on to try and secure the position before the counter-attack arrived.[12]

Second Lieutenant Charles Lecky, 2nd (New South Wales) Battalion, 1st Brigade, 1st Division, AIF

By about 18.00 the front lines had been over-run. Despite the preliminary bombardment, the Turks had been taken by surprise and it took them a while to react. Kemal ordered forward the 1/57th Regiment.

> From the regimental headquarters at the back of Mortar Ridge you could see clearly. There was a lot of dust raised by the shells at Lone Pine. I could not see through it, but when the bombardment there ceased we heard infantry fire – like after thunder you hear the rain beginning; and the observers beside us said, 'The English are getting into our trenches!' Our observation of this bombardment had given us the impression that the trenches subjected to it would not be in a condition to repel the attack – there had been much damage, and heavy loss. At that moment an order arrived by telephone lines from Mustafa Kemal Pasha, 'The battalion of reserve will move at once to Lone Pine!' The battalion was ready to go. I gave the order to move as fast as possible to Lone Pine. On the way, we fixed bayonets. The moment we turned into that valley we came into fire, from your men at the head of it. Near there I met the commander of one of the battalions which had been holding the centre of the Lone Pine front. I asked, 'What has happened?' But he was clearly very shocked. He kept on saying, 'We're lost; we're lost!' I saw it was useless to ask for information from him, and I didn't want to lose time.[13]

Major Zeki Bey, 1st Battalion, 57th Regiment, 19th Division, Fifth Army

Major Zeki launched his men into the counter-attack. The Turkish onslaught was presaged by a flurry of bombs: the shattering detonations and slicing fragments brought sheer terror to the Australians trapped in the confined trenches.

> A dark head appeared round the traverse. I immediately let fly with my rifle from my hip and missed. In reply came two cricket ball bombs. One was kicked by one of my mates round a corner, but the other was behind us. I had a moment or two of uncontrollable paralysing fear – to be utterly helpless with that thing sizzling within a few feet of me. I flattened myself in the side of the trench, clawing at it with my fingers and certainly thought my last moment had come. By some miracle none of us was seriously hurt.[14]
>
> Private Charles Duke, 4th (New South Wales) Battalion, 1st Brigade, 1st Division, AIF

Not too far behind the bombs would be the glittering bayonets and, not surprisingly, they fell back. Further along, Second Lieutenant Lecky struggled to hold his swiftly built barricade as the Turks raged up against them.

> Then the bombing attack started. We had no bombs to retaliate with: Harkness and Cox were killed, among scores of others. Despairing appeals were made to Company Headquarters for bombs, but none were to be had. The men caught the enemy's bombs as they fell and hurled them back before bursting. Many were killed, hands and arms being blown off as bombs exploded in the act of being thrown back at the Turks. The trench was now packed with dead and wounded. The wounded had no hope of rescue and when the Turks finally drove us out of this section I am quite sure no survivors were left.[15]
>
> Second Lieutenant Charles Lecky, 2nd (New South Wales) Battalion, 1st Brigade, 1st Division, AIF

The Turks threw their local reserves into the battle with a grim determination to retake every last inch from the Australians. By this time Private Duke had been forced back and found Lieutenant Giles, who was organising the defence.

> From the trench less than 30 yards away I saw the Turks emerging and gave the warning to Giles who ordered us to line the parapet to shoot at them. We did so but almost before we could get our rifles into position our appearance above the parapet was greeted with an appalling burst of

Turkish supporting rifle fire. There was an almighty crash right in front of my face which knocked me reeling back into the trench. I knew I was hit as blood was streaming from my forehead into my eyes and over my glasses. I was not knocked out and took my glasses off so that I could wipe them and my eyes sufficiently to look round. Imagine my horror to see every one of those lads who had lined the parapet with me lying still and dead in the bottom of the trench – six of them all hit clean in the head – which left Giles and I the only survivors. It had all happened in less than one minute. Fortunately for us the attacking Turks had been wiped out by rifle fire from our chaps further up the trench.[16]

Private Charles Duke, 4th (New South Wales) Battalion, 1st Brigade, 1st Division, AIF

It was obvious that the 1st Brigade could not hold out for long under this kind of pressure and more Australian battalions were moved forward to reinforce the line. By now some of the trenches were all but blocked by the dead and the helpless wounded.

The elaborate overhead cover prepared by the Turks was in many places intact and gave one the impression of passing through a tortuous tunnel, the gloom being accentuated by leaving the bright sunshine. The Turkish dead had not yet been removed and so thickly carpeted the ground that there was no alternative but to tread along a line of bodies. On arrival in the firing line, the Company moved along to the left of this sector, where the Turks during the morning had counter-attacked and effected a lodgement. The trenches here were extremely narrow and not well traversed. Our own and Turkish dead lay anywhere and everywhere, and in some instances our own wounded were still lying at the bottom of the trench.[17]

Major Denis Lane, 12th (South & Western Australian and Tasmanian) Battalion, 3rd Brigade, 1st Division, AIF

The former communications trenches were barricaded off by both sides, but the contested space between was choked with even more bodies as the battle swayed to and fro. But in the midst of all that death and destruction there were moments of humour, as evinced by one Sergeant Campbell.

A sniper's bullet removed the whole of his front top teeth, which protruded beyond his upper lip as if they had been taken off with a fretsaw. Recovering from the shock, the 'bullocky' in Campbell asserted itself and there followed the best exhibition of cursing in between the gulping and spitting of mouthfuls of blood it would be possible to imagine. I don't know what the Turks thought, but the dozen or so men left in that trench roared with laughter as the eloquent Campbell beat it for the beach. I was told later that Campbell hadn't exhausted his vocabulary by the time he had reached the hospital ship.[18]

Sergeant Major Paul Goldenstedt, 3rd (New South Wales) Battalion, 1st Brigade, 1st Division, AIF

The situation grew more and more fraught as the Turks refused to accept the loss of their trenches at Lone Pine. For almost four days the fighting raged before building up to a spluttering crescendo amidst mutual exhaustion on 9 August.

The rifle, bomb and machine gun fire just after daybreak was something never to be forgotten. Our men were swept off the parapets like flies. General Smyth, VC, who commanded the 1st Brigade, issued an order for every man to step down off the parapet and prepare to meet the Turk on the floor of the trench. I was then near Lieutenant Percy Woods – Percy and I had been sergeants together. He took out a pencil and wrote a few words to his wife on a field service post card. Having no wife and few relations that I could think of for the moment, I scribbled a few lines to her as well, and Percy fixed a bayonet to his rifle. I preferred my revolver. The feeling at that moment must be something like what a condemned man feels when the hangman is tying the rope. Anyhow, of a sudden there was a wild cheer and before we knew where we were the Turks had beat it for their trenches.[19]

Sergeant Major Paul Goldenstedt, 3rd (New South Wales) Battalion, 1st Brigade, 1st Division, AIF

Never had an anti-climax been more welcome. An hour or so later they were relieved and their ordeal was over. It was estimated that in the fighting the Australians lost approaching 2,000 men while the Turks' relentless counter-attacks took their losses to as high as 5,000. The Australians had triumphed, but the gain of the trench and a hundred or so yards of blood-drenched ground, however much it was regretted and disputed by the Turks, meant little. Tactically, the situation at 400 Plateau remained much the same. But had the fighting at Lone Pine distracted the Turks' attention sufficiently from the great left hook launched from Anzac?

THE ASSAULTING COLUMNS had been hidden in the valleys of Anzac waiting patiently for their moment. Now their time had come and as soon as night fell the four columns began to file their way slowly out of Anzac. In front were the Right Covering Force, composed of the New Zealand Mounted Rifles Brigade and the attached Otago Mounted Rifles. Their crucial task was to overwhelm any Turkish posts guarding the various routes up to the heights of Sari Bair. The most significant of these was the Old No. 3 Post (on a lower extension of Rhododendron Ridge), which guarded the entrance to Sazli Beit Dere. A cunning ruse was employed and, for once, it worked. Every night the navy had sent the destroyer *Colne* to shell and illuminate the post with searchlights between 21.00 and 21.10, then again from 21.20 to 21.30. This time it was no different, except that the bombardment concealed the approach of the Auckland Mounted Rifles, who stormed the post catching the Turks in their shelters. The Turkish posts on Destroyer Hill and Table Top were overwhelmed by the Wellington Mounted Rifles, and the way was clear for the New Zealand Infantry Brigade which made up the Right Assaulting Column to move through Sazli Beit Dere and Chailik Dere and up on to Rhododendron Ridge. Further along, the Otago and Canterbury Mounted Rifles were forced to endure a brisk fight to capture Bauchop's Hill standing guard over the entrance to Aghyl Dere, up which would advance the Left Assaulting Column under the overall command of Brigadier General Vaughan Cox and made up of his 29th Indian Brigade and the 4th Australian Brigade led by Brigadier General John Monash. Meanwhile, the Left Covering Force, made up of two battalions of 40th Brigade, was clearing Damakjelik Bair in order to secure firmly their left flank.

> Try to imagine that long column of silent men stealthily making its way through the black night, not knowing what was to happen next! Every bayonet was wrapped in hessian to obviate glint, every nerve was tense through the uncertainty. Overhead were the searchlights of the destroyer – the shafts of light did not appear to be more than 20 feet above our heads – and the illuminated heights were being subjected to a terrific fire from the *Colne*'s guns. Under this the brigade wriggled along like a huge snake until a right-wheel took us into the blackest of valleys, surrounded by steep, rugged hills covered with prickly bushes.[20]
>
> Lieutenant Hubert Ford, 13th (New South Wales) Battalion, 4th Brigade, NZ&A Division, AIF

A night march over unfamiliar ground under constant fear of attack by the Turks was a true test of their nerve.

> The regiments in front never waited for us, not giving one time to collect the men, and I had to go off on my own. After half an hour of deadly funk as to where I was, I ran into the rest of the column halted. It was now 12.15 midnight and we were two hours behind our programme time. There was a feeling of panic and doubt in the air as to where we were and where we were going. It was a pitch black night. Suddenly I heard a rush in front – I thought it was the Turks and drew my revolver – and was almost at the same moment knocked down. Dallas behind me fixed bayonets and stopped the rush. It was only a panic of a few men in the regiment in front.[21]
>
> Major Cecil Allanson, 1/6th Gurkha Rifles, 29th Indian Brigade

The Australian 4th Brigade had been at Gallipoli since 25 April and were now highly experienced soldiers, but at Gallipoli that meant that they were also riddled with dysentery and in an enfeebled state. As the long march dragged on they fell further and further behind the optimistic predictions of their progress. Constant halts by the head of the column to check the route made the line concertina wildly behind them and at times the overall pace was almost funereal. This was exacerbated when the local Greek guide took them on a disastrous 'short cut' through Taylor's Gap between Bauchop's Hill and Walden Point. The scrub-filled gully narrowed, allowing only single file, and, harassed by Turkish sniper fire, the Australian columns slowed almost to a halt. It took three hours for them to get through the 600 yards of Taylor's Gap before they finally arrived at Aghyl Dere at about 02.00. According to the plan, the 4th Brigade was to climb up Abdul Rahman to Hill 971 while the 29th Indian Brigade headed south towards Hill Q. Increasingly disorientated and still plagued by Turkish marksmen, the 4th Brigade found that in the dark one ridge looked much like another. Soon they were totally lost. Eventually they thought they had reached Abdul Rahman Ridge, but they were in fact on a continuation of Damakjelik Bair. Hill 971 was a very long way off, much of it a steep climb. To reach it that night would be a physical impossibility for the exhausted troops. Monash became convinced that they could do nothing more and ordered a halt at daylight. Behind him the 29th Indian Brigade was not doing any better. It too had got lost in Aghyl Dere and, although the battalions had moved up various likely looking spurs, they were still well below their objective of Hill Q. But where were the New Zealanders?

The New Zealand Brigade, commanded by Brigadier General Francis Johnston, had not had so far to travel and on the map their task looked deceptively simple: the Canterbury Battalion was to push up Sazli Beit Dere while the Otago, Wellington and Auckland Battalions moved up Chailak Dere. All four battalions were to rendezvous on Rhododendron Ridge between 01.00 and 02.00, at which point they would make the final thrust up the ridge and on to Chunuk Bair ready to attack down Battleship Hill towards The Nek. But the terrain was horrendous. The gullies, so innocent-looking on a map, were totally confusing in the dark. Which was the main course? Which was the best route by which to climb out on to the right ridge? They were surrounded by ridges! There were no signposts and the guides were equally disorientated. Here again delays doubled and redoubled, but at last the Wellington Battalion managed to get out past Table Top and up on to Rhododendron Ridge itself from about 04.30. They were already badly behind schedule. But then Johnston made the fateful decision to wait until his whole force was assembled. The Canterbury Battalion had not yet emerged from Sazli Beit Dere.

> After we had been advancing some hours I was astounded to get a message from Stewart that the guides had lost their way. Here was a dilemma, the whole success of the push depended on us doing our job on time. I was up against it and on my own, having to decide quickly. To obey orders and occupy the hills, I thought would do no good to anyone. I felt also that the tail of my battalion, where the machine guns were, must be far in the rear, as we had been moving, practically in single file, owing to the narrow ravine, for some hours and it's easy to lose touch in the dark. Therefore, to give the order to occupy the hills, would, I felt sure, leave my men thinly extended over much country and easily mopped up by the enemy at daylight. I decided to disobey orders and take the battalion back to the beach, and so save it intact to fight another day. I knew I would be broken for it and thought of the disgrace to my family in New Zealand, but felt it was the only way to save the men. I gave the order to retire. At the spot where I had halted, the ravine was so narrow that the advance guard, now the rear guard, had to pass me in single file.[22]
>
> Lieutenant Colonel Jack Gethin Hughes, Canterbury Battalion, New Zealand Brigade, NZ&A Division, NZEF

Hughes' decision would not have mattered much if Johnston had not sat still with his three battalions vainly waiting for the Canterbury Battalion to appear. Johnston had serious health problems (which are alleged to have included alcoholism) but this was a criminal neglect of his responsibilities as clearly laid out in Birdwood's orders: he was not to wait on delays but must push on, regardless of the size of his force, to capture Chunuk Bair before dawn and then press down through Battleship Hill before 04.30, when the 3rd Light Horse Brigade were due to attack across The Nek. It may have been that they were already too late and it certainly seems that the influential Malone, the most senior of Johnston's battalion commanders, was against pushing on regardless. However, there was considerable personal animosity among the senior staff of the New Zealand Brigade, so no clear picture emerges from their accounts by which posterity can apportion the blame.[23] Whoever's fault it was, they did not resume their advance until 06.30.

This loss of time would prove crucial, as the Lone Pine diversion had only been partially successful. It had succeeded gloriously in sucking in the local reserves of the 5th Division, located around Kojadere village behind Gun Ridge, and away from Chunuk Bair. But the very success of the Lone Pine attack had caused the 9th Division, commanded by Colonel Hans Kannengiesser, to be despatched from further south and, when the dangers threatening Chunuk Bair became clear, the Turkish High Command merely ordered them to keep marching up to the Sari Bair heights. Thanks to Johnston's dilatory performance, Kannengiesser reached the summit of Chunuk Bair at 07.00, from which he could look down on groups of New Zealanders moving to occupy the Apex some 500 yards away.

> The English approached slowly, in single file, splendidly equipped and with white bands on their left arms, apparently very tired, and were crossing a hillside to our flank, emerging in continually increasing numbers from the valley below. I immediately sent an order to my infantry – this was the twenty-strong artillery-covering platoon – instantly to open fire. I received this answer, 'We can only commence to fire when we receive the order of our battalion commander!' This was too much for me altogether. I ran to the spot and threw myself among the troops who were lying in a small trench. What I said I cannot recollect, but they began to open fire and almost immediately the

English laid down without answering our fire or apparently moving in any other way. They gave me the impression that they were glad to be spared further climbing.[24]

Colonel Hans Kannengiesser, Headquarters, 9th Division, Fifth Army

At about 08.00 Johnston held a further meeting with his senior commanders. It seems that Malone again urged caution, fearing the consequences of an isolated attack in daylight on such a strong position. This led to yet more delay as the New Zealanders consolidated their positions at the Apex instead of pushing up Rhododendron Ridge to Chunuk Bair. Yet as every minute ticked by more of Kannengiesser's men were reaching the crucial spot and adding their weight to the defending force. When this decision was communicated to Major General Alexander Godley, commanding the NZ&A Division, he was furious at the hold-up and ordered an attack at once on Chunuk Bair. At last Johnston acted, but perversely, given all the problems caused by waiting for the Canterbury Battalion, he sent just one battalion – the Auckland Battalion – into the assault, accompanied by two companies of the 2/10th Gurkhas who were in effect stragglers from the 29th Indian Brigade Column further north. They attacked at 10.30. But by this time there were approximately 500 Turks waiting for them on the summit.

Another short climb and we were halted and lined up in three or more rows, bayonets fixed. Here we waited. To one end stood the Brigadier, casually swinging his stick and gazing around. Finally he glanced at his wristwatch and gave a blast on his whistle, 'Go along, Colonel, lead your men and charge!' The first line swept up and over, and the Turks, who up to then had been practically silent, let loose a murderous hail. A few survived that withering blast and ran on, over the rough sloping hillside. The second row went and then followed the remainder. Where we were going, God only knew, we didn't! A trench was the objective, but it was no time to stop and take bearings. There seemed to be no covering fire and the enemy did as he liked. Finally, three of us plunged to earth in a shallow depression which afforded just sufficient cover and none to spare. Each move brought a burst of machine gun bullets. After a very careful survey of the surrounding few yards, the trench was spotted some 40 feet ahead. A wild spring and a rush, and two reached it and jumped in. The parapet being on the wrong side for us, the Turkish bullets hailed along the stones, but willing hands dragged us down. The trench, only about four feet deep, had been empty and was under the complete control of the Turks higher up.[25]

Private Eric Lewes, Auckland Battalion, New Zealand Brigade, NZ&A Division, NZEF

By then it was too late and the result was failure, with serious casualties. They advanced just a hundred yards or so before taking shelter in the unoccupied Turkish trench at the Pinnacle, where the attack broke down. At this point Johnston ordered Malone to send his Wellington Battalion on another charge up towards Chunuk Bair. Malone stoutly refused, stating that he would not send his men over to commit suicide but would wait for darkness. Just then orders arrived from Godley that all offensive operations were to cease for the time being. And that was that. The great night attack had failed; none of the objectives had been achieved. But what of the attacks from Anzac that were meant to coordinate with the New Zealanders? How had they fared?

AS WELL AS LONE PINE there was another series of operations planned at Anzac for 6 and 7 August. The first of these was the attack to be launched at midnight on 6 August by the 6th Battalion from Steele's Post on German Officer's Trench, which was designed to remove the flanking threat to the further attacks planned on The Nek and Chessboard at 04.30. This episode has almost been forgotten but it is a classic war horror story. Here, as at Lone Pine, tunnelling was central to success.

Three tunnels, 3–4 feet wide and 7 feet deep, had been dug, leading from our front line for a distance of about 30 yards. These were linked up by another tunnel, which was roughly parallel to our front line. A thin crust of earth, from 6 to 12 inches thick, was left as a roof to the tunnels. And from the forward tunnel a number of narrow saps were dug, leading to small posts, each capable of accommodating three or four men. These saps were just wide enough for a man to crawl through. The attack was to be launched by the 6th Battalion from these fire posts at midnight. The roofs were to be removed just after dark and the men were to charge across the intervening 20 yards to the enemy trench. The attack was to be preceded by three mine explosions: at 11 p.m., 11.30 p.m., and 11.40 p.m. These mines, it was hoped, would destroy a portion of the enemy trench, with its garrison, and completely demoralise the rest of the troops holding that section of trench.[26]

Major Henry Gordon Bennett, 6th (Victoria) Battalion, 2nd Brigade, 1st Division, AIF

The assaulting troops did not dare occupy the forward tunnels from which their attack was to be made until the last mine had been detonated, in case the reverberations caused the tunnels to collapse around them.

As 11 o'clock approached everyone waited anxiously to see yards of the enemy trench go skywards. But instead there was a low muffled rumbling and a slight earth tremor. We peered over the parapet, expecting to see the flash of the explosion and tons of earth and a few Turks hurled into the air. But nothing happened. The mine was too deep to be effective. A minute or so later we were all crouching low hoping to dodge the shells the enemy poured on us in retaliation. Shell after shell landed in and around the trench, tearing great rents in the communication tunnels. At 11.30 the next mine was blown, with even less effect. This brought another hurricane of shells on Steele's Post. We were beginning to feel depressed. We realised that the enemy, instead of being destroyed or, at least, demoralised by them, had been made alert and ready. Then the third mine was blown at 11.40, with no better result.[27]

Major Henry Gordon Bennett, 6th (Victoria) Battalion, 2nd Brigade, 1st Division, AIF

Still, orders were orders, so they moved down the tunnels to the underground front line ready to break through the crust of earth and charge the twenty yards to the Turkish front line at midnight. It soon became apparent that the Turkish counter-bombardment had been far more effective than the Australian mines.

The party moving by one tunnel groped its way forward in the pitch-black darkness, stumbling over the heaps of debris caused by the bombardment. Movement was difficult and slow. One tunnel was completely blocked and impassable, while another was almost as bad. The party that had been detailed to use one tunnel was forced to retrace its steps along the crowded trench and to find its way to its position by an unknown route. To make matters more difficult, commands could only be given in whispers and this made control almost impossible.

Instead of reaching their position in 10 minutes, as anticipated, it took almost an hour. The time for the attack was well passed and the troops had not arrived at their posts.[28]

Major Henry Gordon Bennett, 6th (Victoria) Battalion, 2nd Brigade, 1st Division, AIF

It was an utter shambles. Finally, at 00.35, the men were in position to attack.

The signal for the assault was given – a blast of a whistle. Men in the fire-posts jumped out and rushed forward. The moment they did, the enemy raked No Man's Land with machine guns, rifles, and bombs. The thin line melted away. Some were hit before they left the posts. Those who followed fell back wounded, blocking the saps and preventing the rest of the attacking force from leaving the tunnel. The wounded crawled back out of the inferno into the safe refuge of the tunnel and before many minutes it was realised that the attack had failed.[29]

Major Henry Gordon Bennett, 6th (Victoria) Battalion, 2nd Brigade, 1st Division, AIF

The attacking troops were under a shattering fire, not just from German Officer's Trench immediately ahead of them, but also from machine guns and rifles in the Turkish trenches at Quinn's Post on their left, Mortar Ridge to the front and Johnston's Jolly to their right. The attack was a total failure.

I telephoned Brigadier Forsyth telling him the result of the attack: the impossibility of attacking from the congested tunnels; the failure of our mines; with the result that the enemy trench was strongly held by an alert enemy. After consulting with the Divisional Commander, the Brigadier ordered another attempt to be made as soon as practicable.[30]

Major Henry Gordon Bennett, 6th (Victoria) Battalion, 2nd Brigade, 1st Division, AIF

Communications were bad and, despite Bennett's report, the brigade and divisional staff were unsure what was really happening. The capture of German Officer's Trench was essential to avoid the threat of devastating fire into the southern flank of the planned morning attacks on The Nek, the Chessboard and from Quinn's Post. There was also a degree of unwarranted scepticism about whether the 6th Battalion had tried as hard as it might.

Bennett rang up and said that as we left recesses and started to cross intervening ground the fire increased to hellish extent and many were wounded in the recesses which were now filled with the dead and wounded who had crowded back into them, and that the assault was impossible. The Brigadier rang up Colonel White and told him that attack had failed. Colonel White very put out and said they were to be put at it again and that trench must be taken. The CO of 6th accordingly instructed to reorganise and go again.[31]

Captain Carl Jess, Headquarters, 2nd Australian Brigade, 1st Division, AIF

Major General Walker and his Chief of Staff, Colonel Brudenell White, could not accept that this failure was irreversible. Captain Jess went forward to see what was happening for himself. When he got there he found the outlook worse than his darkest imaginings.

The scene in the tunnel I shall never forget – men leaning against the walls in the darkness without a word, and what their thoughts must have been God only knows, but they must have been a hundred times worse than mine, and I knew how hopeless was the job – with no chance of surprise in it. However it had to be tried. I found Bennett in the forward firing line doing his best to reorganise his men, who were more or less stunned. The groans of the wounded still in the recesses, and the awful blackness and silence, were enough to take the heart out of anyone. Bennett himself wanted to lead the first line in the new attack as he felt it his duty. I would not agree as I pointed out it was his duty to feed with reinforcements the daring men who went out first. We eventually got the wounded and dying out, which I shall never forget as they nearly all had three or four wounds, but seldom a groan as they were pulled out of the recesses and along the bumpy dark tunnel floor.[32]

Captain Carl Jess, Headquarters, 2nd Australian Brigade, 1st Division, AIF

Major Bennett had no choice but to set about reorganising his men for the second attempt. He knew it was a waste of lives, but, despite having tried to get the assault cancelled, he was not willing to disobey a direct order.

The tunnels were cleared of wounded; officers were given fresh orders for the attack and a commencement was made to reorganise the men ready for the charge. In the dark and crowded tunnels this took two hours to accomplish. But at last everything was ready. Everyone in those tunnels knew they were embarking on a forlorn hope. They knew the Turks were waiting to mow them down the moment they showed themselves. Still, they decided to give the best that was in them to make a success of the venture. The signal was given.[33]

Major Henry Gordon Bennett, 6th (Victoria) Battalion, 2nd Brigade, 1st Division, AIF

There had been countless frustrations and delays, but at last they were ready. So it was that Bennett watched his men go to their deaths when the new attack was finally launched at 03.53.

The enemy answered it with a hail of lead from the trench 20 yards away. Our men scrambled from the posts, only to be shot down. A few survived, to find themselves alone on reaching the enemy trench. As they essayed to return, they too were hit. For the second time the assault had failed, not because the men were unwilling to face the danger, but because it was physically impossible to succeed.[34]

Major Henry Gordon Bennett, 6th (Victoria) Battalion, 2nd Brigade, 1st Division, AIF

This time it was Captain Jess who rang brigade headquarters, at 04.10, to tell Brigadier General John Forsyth that the attempt had failed. Jess then found himself trapped in a circular nightmare as Walker and Brudenell White at divisional headquarters still refused to accept defeat.

Forsyth informed Divisional Headquarters who I believe nearly went mad. Anyway he was ordered to come round and reorganise the Battalion and supervise another attack personally. When he arrived I shall never forget his face. He knew as well as I did that the men were by this time unnerved, had been for about 36 hours without sleep, and that to attempt such an attack in daylight was slaughter. However he was ordered to do it and we had to try. We had no idea of our losses and could only withdraw right out of the trench and reorganise. The sight on the terraces in rear of Quinn's Post would make anyone's heart bleed to see the weary nerve-strained men moving listlessly into their places and alongside them the dressing place with scores of badly wounded men, two in particular writhing about in the death throes.[35]

Captain Carl Jess, Headquarters, 2nd Australian Brigade, 1st Division, AIF

Yet for a while it seemed that, come what may, the 6th Battalion would again be put to the sword.

At about 8 o'clock Major Glasford came round from Division and I put it to him that the men were not fit and it would be sheer murder to put them at it in daylight. To make matters worse, with the dawn No. 3 Section attempted to attack the Chessboard, and this with our big breakout on the left brought a hell of an artillery fire on to our already shattered trenches. At about 9 o'clock we received word from General Walker that no further effort would be required of the 6th that day but we were asked if any other Battalion was better fitted for the job – as if any men in the world could have done more. Forsyth replied and said that all Battalions of the Brigade were the same type of men. Forsyth took it much to heart.[36]

Captain Carl Jess, Headquarters, 2nd Australian Brigade, 1st Division, AIF

All in all, the 6th Battalion lost eighty killed and sixty-six wounded. It was a dreadful episode, now largely forgotten, but surely worthy of remembrance.

The failure of the 6th Battalion would have terrible consequences for the interlinked assaults planned to follow on The Nek, the Chessboard, Dead Man's Ridge and from Quinn's Post. These attacks were already heavily reliant for their success on the New Zealand Brigade capturing Chunuk Bair and then launching a simultaneous attack down through Battleship Hill on to Baby 700. Indeed, unless the New Zealanders took the Turkish positions from the rear, these attacks were doomed to fail. At ANZAC Corps headquarters Birdwood and Skeen considered the situation reports: they knew the New Zealanders were well behind schedule and still struggling up Rhododendron Ridge. It was a difficult decision. As Skeen put it: 'It is not the Light Horse I am anxious about. I think they will be all right. What I hope is that they will help the New Zealanders.'[37] Birdwood decided to proceed on the grounds that the frontal assault would prevent the Turkish garrison from moving reserves to block the New Zealanders. This surely was a sacrifice too far.

So it was that the 3rd Light Horse Brigade went over the top at The Nek and into legend. They would go over in four waves, 150 men in each, and with the 8th Light Horse having the dubious honour of going over the top first. The slow preliminary bombardment blazed into life at 04.00 with shells pouring down on to the Turkish trenches at both The Nek and the Chessboard. As ever, the barrage appeared more destructive than it was and its effect was further diminished when it ended prematurely at 04.23. Controversy surrounds this issue, but the relative inaccuracy of timepieces in 1915, coupled with some inadequate synchronisation, are the most likely reasons for the curtailment. In all probability it made little difference to the outcome. Forewarned, the Turks cocked their rifles, put their machine guns into position and waited for the assault. In a courageous gesture, Lieutenant Colonel Alexander White insisted on leading his men over the top; however, by so doing he was neglecting his primary role of providing tactical leadership. Perhaps the Light Horse should have attacked immediately the barrage stopped, but the confusion was too great, the time too short to react quickly enough. The first wave leapt over the parapet at 04.30; in front of them lay The Nek, just twenty-five yards across at its narrowest point, with sixty bare yards to cross to the Turkish trenches.

> They were waiting ready for us and simply gave us a solid wall of lead. I was in the first line to advance and we did not get 10 yards. Every one fell like lumps of meat. All your pals that had been with you for months and months blown and shot out of all recognition. I got mine shortly after I got over the bank and it felt like a million ton hammer falling on my shoulder. I was really awfully lucky as the bullet went in just below the shoulder blade round by my throat and came out just a tiny way from my spine low down on the back. It was simply murder.[38]
>
> Sergeant Cliff Pinnock, 8th (Victoria) Light Horse, 3rd Light Horse Brigade, AIF

Fire poured in from right, left and straight ahead. No question about the presence of machine guns this time: the open ground of The Nek was alive with bullets. The whole wave was down in the dust and dirt in thirty seconds. The gallant White and all the officers who attacked with him were killed in seconds.[39] In the chaos one of the yellow and red signal flags intended to indicate progress had been reported briefly fluttering in the Turkish front line on the right flank of the attack. This meant nothing – whoever was carrying it had surely been butchered – but the report would engender false optimism in higher authorities, with fatal consequences for the men in the third wave. Meanwhile, the second wave went over the top just two minutes after the first. With them was Lieutenant Andrew Crawford.

There was the din of rifles, machine guns and bombs. On mounting the parapet just in front of us was a double row of Turks with bayonets fixed, firing at us. Most of the first wave were down: either killed, wounded, or had taken cover. I was soon laid out with a couple of bullet wounds in my body and a graze on my head. I could not move and was eventually dragged back into our trenches, while the Turks seemed to pause for a few minutes, realising that they had stopped the attack.[40]

Lieutenant Andrew Crawford, 8th (Victoria) Light Horse, 3rd Light Horse Brigade, AIF

Trooper Alex Borthwick was already shot through the buttocks when he was badly menaced by the bombs lobbed by the Turks into No Man's Land.

It hurt for a moment but I thought to myself, 'I am wounded and have a good excuse to retire!' But finding it was nothing I had to continue to lie there while the Turks from their trenches 10 yards away were throwing bombs on to the top of my ridge. How I escaped being killed I don't know. The bombs are round like a cricket ball and one rolled over my neck, bumped alongside my body and burst a little lower down the hill. The bombs killed a lot of men that day. They make frightful, ghastly wounds.[41]

Trooper Alex Borthwick, 8th (Victoria) Light Horse, 3rd Light Horse Brigade, AIF

The charge had been a complete failure and Lieutenant Colonel Noel Brazier of the 10th Light Horse, whose men would form the third and fourth waves, rushed back to brigade headquarters to try to get the attack abandoned. But now the question of the cursed signal flag briefly seen in the Turkish front line obscured all reason, for Brazier was ordered to follow up this supposed success by the 8th Light Horse. And of course Colonel White could not support his efforts as he was dead. In the absence of Brigadier General Hughes, it fell to his brigade major, Lieutenant Colonel Jack Antill, brusquely to order them to push on. So it was that the third wave went over at 04.45. By now they all knew it was hopeless.

I was in between the Sergeant and the Sergeant Major. The Sergeant said to me, being the youngest fellow in the regiment, 'Now listen to me lad, there is no hope for us, so as soon as you get over the top lie down!' I was pushed down – I wasn't allowed to lie down! Fortunately we got into a groove in the land and we laid there all day until night came and we crawled back into the trench.[42]

Trooper Charles Williams, 10th (Western Australia) Light Horse, 3rd Light Horse Brigade, AIF

Brazier tried his best to stop the fourth wave charging and indeed had angry confrontations with both Antill and Hughes. Tragically, while he was arguing back at the brigade headquarters, in all the uncertainty the fourth wave went over without clear orders at about 05.15. With them was Sergeant Sanderson of the 10th Light Horse.

The rhododendron bushes had been cut off with machine gun fire and were all spiky. The Turks were two-deep in the trench ahead. There was at least one machine gun on the left and any number in the various trenches on the Chessboard. The men who were going out were absolutely certain that they were going to be killed, and they expected to be killed right away. The thing that struck a man most was if he *wasn't* knocked in the first 3 yards.[43]

Sergeant William Sanderson, 10th (Western Australia) Light Horse, 3rd Light Horse Brigade, AIF

Trooper James Fitzmaurice did slightly better than that – he got about twenty yards before he took cover.

As soon as we went over we went to ground and kept your nose to the ground – never moved, if you lifted your head at all you would have got it. We were fortunate; we were in a little depression. You were just waiting for orders, listening. We were there about three-quarters of an hour and then we got the order to retire. That was passed along the line several times and we retired, turned round on our bellies and crawled back with our noses that close to the ground, you know you couldn't get any closer! And fell back into our trenches.[44]

Trooper James Fitzmaurice, 10th (Western Australia) Light Horse, 3rd Light Horse Brigade, AIF

A secondary follow-up attack by the 8th Royal Welsh Fusiliers, planned to burst out of Monash Valley between Russell's Top and Pope's Hill, was entirely conditional on success at The Nek. In the confusion, however, at 05.10 the go-ahead was given by the staff of the 3rd Light Horse Brigade. The result was a predictable failure as the Turks threw bombs down the steep slopes to deadly effect. The attempt was soon abandoned. There was no way through The Nek on 7 August.

Meanwhile, the 1st Light Horse were launching an audacious but suicidal attack from Pope's Hill across Waterfall Gully and directed against the Turkish trenches on Dead Man's Ridge, with the Chessboard immediately behind it. Lieutenant Geoffrey Harris and his men had set off to climb stealthily up Waterfall Gully at 03.30 in an effort to be in position at Zero Hour at 04.30. Against all the odds they had some initial success.

> I fell in my little party of twelve bomb throwers and twelve riflemen with fixed bayonets in support. The latter had orders not to fire a shot without orders, but to use the cold steel. We marched silently down our communication trenches to the gully, where we waited 10 minutes while the engineers opened the barbed wire entanglements for us to get through. Then up to the waterfall, which we scaled, to be met by a shower of Turkish bombs before we had time to get into any sort of order. I immediately gave the order to charge and we quickly took the first two lines of trenches in our course bombing the Turks out. Our bombers went on and took the third line trenches on a narrow front and we could just see the Turks getting back along their communication trenches. It was just breaking daylight when we went over the hill to be met by the crescent trench, full of Turks, half out their trench, waiting for us. Machine guns were barking on three sides of us. Seeing that we could get no further, I gave the order 'Down!' and went to earth just as a bullet hit my shoulder. Sergeant Ellis went down on my right – killed instantly, riddled with bullets at close range. Luckily, I fell in a small depression out of sight of the Turks.[45]
>
> Lieutenant Geoffrey Harris, 1st (New South Wales) Light Horse, 1st Light Horse Brigade, AIF

Harris managed to get back safely. All over Dead Man's Ridge the scattered parties of the 1st Light Horse tried to consolidate their tenuous position clinging to the steep slopes.

> At present I am lying on the side of the hill trying to keep under a bit of cover. Bombs are terrible. Dead all around. God keep and protect me. I am not scared but it's hell. Could not hold position. Bombed out of it. I was dodging bombs all the time. Writing this as I rest on the way back. Suppose we will have another go again later on. It's hell right enough. Where I was lying on the hill there were four dead chaps beside and

in front of me. No one living – bombs, I think. Don't think we ran when we retreated. We damned well walked. Most of us, especially the survivors of the charge, are very weak and feel sore and bruised all over the body where stones hit us as they were chucked up by exploding bombs. Four or five of our wounded chaps are still lying out under the Turks' trenches. I would volunteer to go and have a cut for them but it's sheer suicide and I could no more carry a man at present than fly. I'm too sore and feel very weak.[46]

Corporal David Lindsay, 1st (New South Wales) Light Horse, 1st Light Horse Brigade, AIF

At one point some of them managed to gain a foothold on a couple of bays in the Turkish trenches. This just triggered more slaughter on both sides.

Notwithstanding the great losses they suffered, eight or ten of their men managed to penetrate a covered area of our trench. All the same very few of them, and of those who came to their aid, managed to escape, with the remainder being toppled. The battle ended at 07.00 and, as it was a very violent battle, we suffered 52 dead and 166 wounded. I submit also the information that the artillery fire on our trenches, following the repulse of the enemy, resulted in the partial destruction of our trenches and caused most of our casualties.[47]

Major Halis Bey, 3rd Battalion, 27th Regiment, 9th Division, Fifth Army

In the end the 1st Light Horse were forced to retreat with nothing achieved. The attempt by the 2nd Light Horse surging out from Quinn's Post towards the Chessboard was also repulsed as the fifty men in the first wave were cut down by machine guns not only from directly in front of them, but from German Officer's Trench and Dead Man's Ridge on either side. Their commanding officer, Major G. H. Bourne, had the strength of mind to call off the attack, thereby avoiding further pointless slaughter.

All of these attacks had been failures: they had been pursued with the utmost gallantry, but as serious operations of war they represented unprofessional madness. Men cannot advance against massed machine gun fire; courage alone cannot win through. Furthermore, utter failures effortlessly dealt with by local garrisons, do not divert reinforcements. The sacrifice of the 8th and 10th Light Horse at The Nek (372 casualties, of which 234 were dead) has attained a particular notoriety due to populist Australian attempts to link the slaughter there with the British failure to progress as planned at Suvla. This is a red herring: their slender hopes of success on The Nek rested on the New Zealanders' capture of Chunuk Bair and had nothing whatsoever to do with the British at Suvla. Moreover, the Gallipoli campaign had many similar disasters that few now choose to recall. Who now remembers the Turkish attack with an almost identical butcher's bill on the very same ground on 29–30 June? On that occasion it was the self-same Light Horsemen that revelled in dealing out the death and destruction; war is full of tragic ironies.

THE NEXT CHAPTER in the saga of the great Anzac breakout would take place on 8 August. The assaulting columns had failed to achieve their objectives by dawn on 7 August, but there was still hope that they might yet prosper before the Turkish reserves could arrive in force next day. As part of a general advance the Wellington Battalion, supported by the 7th Gloucestershires and 8th Welsh Regiment, were to spearhead a renewed attack on Chunuk Bair after an artillery bombardment and massed machine gun fire commencing at 03.30. To general surprise, this seems to have caused the Turks temporarily to withdraw from the summit.

> Each Company was approximately 200 strong and this solid phalanx of men emerged from the Apex just before the shelling ceased. It was expected that stiff opposition would be met with at the top. The orders were that immediately the ground permitted, Companies were to open out to a frontage of 100 yards each and to fix bayonets, but to keep well closed up; that no shot was to be fired, but the position was to be carried with the cold steel. Some distance had to be traversed before the leading platoons were able to open out at all and it was less than 150 yards from the top of Chunuk Bair, where bayonets were fixed on the move. The two leading Companies swept in line in a final rush to the top, to find to their amazement the position was unoccupied. Certainly a small Turkish picquet was overwhelmed, without firing a shot, in a small trench on the seaward slope some distance from the top. But where were the Turks who had shattered the Auckland attack?[48]
>
> Major William Cunningham, Wellington Battalion, New Zealand Brigade, NZ&A Division, NZEF

Still, the Wellingtons were hardly complaining and they tried to consolidate their position. Behind them the 7th Gloucestershires and 8th Welsh

Regiment suffered far more as they were exposed to a deadly enfilade fire in reaching the summit where the remnants took up positions on the flanks of the Wellingtons. Malone split his companies between the forward and reverse slopes of Chunuk Bair, but they soon encountered serious problems.

> For the best part of an hour the Wellington Battalion was unmolested in its digging operations, but owing to the hard and stony nature of the soil, and the fact that the majority of the men had only entrenching tools, progress was very slow, and the trenches were not more than 2 feet deep when the Turkish counter-attack started. Preceded by showers of bombs, the Turks worked their way up until they were able to fire into the gun-pits where our advanced covering parties had been placed. These pits soon became untenable and the survivors of the covering parties returned to their companies in the new front line. By now all digging had ceased and the front line companies, taking what cover their shallow trench line afforded, were engaged in a deadly musketry duel with the Turks, who were crowding up from the valley to recapture the hill. Enfilade machine gun fire from the old Anzac position made matters most unpleasant and soon the shallow front line trenches were filled with the killed and wounded. No longer able to hold the forward line, a few unwounded men were able to dash in safety to the reverse or seaward slope of the hill.[49]
>
> Major William Cunningham, Wellington Battalion, New Zealand Brigade, NZ&A Division, NZEF

That retreat meant the Turks could creep forwards. The Wellingtons were able only to cling to their shallow trenches on the reverse slope, losing control of the brow of the hill. Some meagre reinforcements arrived but never as many as were replenishing the Turkish ranks.

> Odd Turks began to work into a position from which they could fire into the reverse slope of the hill. When the forward trenches had been abandoned the Turks crept up close enough to the crest line to hurl showers of egg bombs among the men on the reverse slope. These had long fuses and were promptly thrown back before they exploded. Bolder and bolder, the Turks essayed a bayonet charge, but were promptly stopped by a few well-directed volleys at point-blank range. Several times the Turks gallantly repeated their attempts to charge over the top, but always with the same result. Ammunition was running short, and

had to be collected from the dead and wounded. As the day wore on, still the defenders of the hill stuck stubbornly to their ground. In the afternoon a Turkish battery searched the slopes where our men were with accurately timed shrapnel. This shelling ceased about 4 p.m., but Colonel Malone fell a victim to the last salvo. He stood up in the trench where his headquarters were thinking the shelling had ceased and practically the last round fired killed him instantly.[50]

Major William Cunningham, Wellington Battalion, New Zealand Brigade, NZ&A Division, NZEF

The shattered remnants of the Wellingtons, (just 70 unwounded were left of the 760 men who had originally occupied the crest), the 7th Gloucester-shires and the 8th Welsh were relieved after dark on the night of 8 August by the Otago Battalion and the Wellington Mounted Rifles. With more Turkish divisions marching purposefully towards the Sari Bair heights, the chances of such exposed positions being held were minimal.

Meanwhile, the 29th Indian Brigade was strewn across the ground below Hill Q. The general chaos can be seen in the combination of problems facing the ebullient Major Allanson commanding the 1/6th Gurkha Rifles:

Unfortunately the operation orders for the attack next day on the hill at dawn did not reach me till 1.30 a.m. and I had to get them all out to the outpost line. We had been heavily shelled that evening and I had been much frightened. We had no blankets and no coats, and when I got the orders I was so shivering with cold (fright!) that I could with difficulty read them. My regiment was ordered to make a frontal attack, leaving at 2.45 a.m., supported by two British battalions, and I arranged to send the outposts direct to the position of assembly allotted. The officer who issued the orders had never seen the country, he never had had a chance, and the point of assembly was the junction of two nullahs, each 2 feet wide. The confusion was, of course, awful, and as I could not get into touch with either the North Staffordshire or South Lancashires, to get on was all important. I started off to the attack on my own, asking the other regiments by note to follow. We were then two and a half hours behind the scheduled time for the attack.[51]

Major Cecil Allanson, 1/6th Gurkha Rifles, 29th Indian Brigade

If anything, it was even worse for Second Lieutenant Reginald Savory who, as acting adjutant of the 14th Sikhs, was ordered to distribute the orders to the widely scattered companies of his battalion.

> I took an armed orderly with me and set out across the Aghyl Dere in almost pitch darkness. It was then about 2 a.m. It took me an hour and a half to find MacLean, only about half a mile away, through thick scrub and dried-up river beds. I was challenged now and again, but no one could tell me where he was. I was in a fever. Here I was, with very urgent orders, and I could not find the man for whom they were intended. At half-past three I stumbled on him, fast asleep. I went through the orders with him, they were in indelible pencil on thin paper and difficult to read by the doused light of an electric torch. We were to assault Hill Q in company with the 5th Gurkhas, and with the 4th Australian Brigade on our left. Neither he nor I knew where Hill Q was. It was not marked as such on the map; nor had it been pointed out to us. All we did know was that within three-quarters of an hour or so we were to capture it. It was still dark and the men were fast asleep.[52]
>
> Second Lieutenant Reginald Savory, 14th Sikhs, 29th Indian Brigade

Notwithstanding the problems facing the 29th Indian Brigade, Major Allanson seems to have been a determined officer and once he got his men moving he found they made surprisingly good progress.

> The ground was covered by a horrible scrub, all nullahs with very steep sides. I advanced in more or less open formation of company columns, and got forward to within 500 yards of the objective without any trouble at all: this I decreased by 200 yards by short rushes. I recognised that reconnaissance and knowledge of the position was so important that I decided to be with the firing line in front, and left the Adjutant to control behind. Dallas and Underhill both came up, each with about 15 men, but all the rest of their double companies were close. They were working slowly up, picking their way splendidly. Suddenly Dallas went down, hit through the head;[53] shortly after Underhill fell,[54] and I saw reinforcement was essential.[55]
>
> Major Cecil Allanson, 1/6th Gurkha Rifles, 29th Indian Brigade

Thus it was that Allanson managed to get his troops into a promising position perched just under the crest of Hill Q.

Unsurprisingly, Monash's 4th Brigade failed to make any impact on 8 August. The exhausted Australians erroneously believed that they were advancing along Abdul Rahman rather than their actual position, further back on a spur of Damakjelik Bair. The Turks soon stopped them in their tracks and nothing whatsoever was achieved.

While the British were unable to take control of the battle, the Turks were moving with purpose. By this time elements of the 4th, 8th and 9th Divisions had reached Anzac, while the 7th and 12th Divisions under the command of Colonel Feizi Bey were on their way to Suvla. Yet there was still much confusion. It was at this point that Mustafa Kemal came up with the ideal person to weld together the forces dealing with the threat to the Sari Bair heights and the Suvla landings. It could only be one man, as he modestly revealed to Liman's Chief of Staff.

> Unified control of operations was necessary to take into account the large enemy forces which had landed at Anafarta – and which were still landing – and to adopt overall measures as demanded by the situation. I said that there was no other course remaining but to put all available troops under my command. 'Won't that be too many?' he said. 'It will be too few!' I replied.[56]
>
> Colonel Mustafa Kemal, Headquarters, 19th Division, Fifth Army

Kemal may have been saying this for effect, but he was putting his reputation on the line. His replacement commanding the 19th Division was the redoubtable Lieutenant Colonel Mehmet Sefik.

By nightfall on 8 August British plans for the left hook had already failed, but they could hardly just give up. As at Helles, there was a tendency to keep trying, recycling plans and shuffling units in order to try to achieve success. This time the benighted Australian 4th Brigade was left to consolidate its positions as there was clearly no chance of pushing up Abdul Rahman to take Hill 971: that avenue had been firmly closed by the Turkish reinforcements. The main effort on 9 August would be made by the scattered elements of the 29th Indian Brigade and the 39th Brigade, who were to seize Hill Q. To their right a Composite Brigade, made up of battalions from the 13th Division and under the command of Brigadier General Anthony Baldwin, would attack the northern shoulder of Chunuk Bair. The New Zealand Brigade would consolidate its hold on the southern shoulder of Chunuk Bair before moving down on to Battleship Hill. A bombardment would begin at 04.30, with the assault timed for 05.15. In the event almost everything went wrong. Baldwin's force got totally lost and was consequently nowhere near the start line at Zero Hour. That failure forced the cancellation of the attack by the already badly weakened New Zealand Brigade.

The only remaining hope lay with the 1/6th Gurkhas, who by this time had been reinforced by three companies of the 6th South Lancashires under the command of Major Geoffrey Mott. This was a weak force for a supremely difficult challenge. It may not have been far to the top of Hill Q, but the cliffs were steep. At least Allanson was pleased with the artillery barrage.

> I had only fifteen minutes left: the roar of the artillery preparation was enormous; the hill was almost leaping underneath one. I recognised that if we flew up the hill the moment it stopped we ought to get to the top. I had my watch out: 5.15. I never saw such artillery preparation; the trenches were being torn to pieces, the accuracy was marvellous, as we were only just below. 5.18, it had not stopped and I wondered if my watch was wrong. 5.20, silence! I waited 3 minutes to be certain, great as the risk was. Then off we dashed all hand in hand, a most perfect advance and a wonderful sight. I left Cornish with 50 men to hold the line in case we were pushed back, and to watch me if I signalled for reinforcements. At the top we met the Turks: Le Marchand was down, a bayonet through the heart.[57] I got one through the leg and then, for about 10 minutes, we fought hand to hand, we bit and fisted, and used rifles and pistols as clubs; blood was flying about like spray from a hairwash bottle. And then the Turks turned and fled, and I felt a very proud man: the key of the whole peninsula was ours.[58]
>
> Major Cecil Allanson, 1/6th Gurkha Rifles, 29th Indian Brigade

In the excitement of the charge, Allanson and his men dashed off down the other side of Hill Q. It was then that they were hit by shells fired either by the artillery at Anzac, the naval ships or the Turks. Allanson blamed the navy, but whoever was responsible it made little difference to the outcome.

> All was terrible confusion: it was a deplorable disaster, we were obviously mistaken for Turks and we had to get back. It was an appalling sight: the first hit a Gurkha in the face; the place was a mass of blood and limbs and screams. We all flew back to the summit and to our old position just below. I remained on the crest with about 15 men. It was a wonderful view: below were the Straits, reinforcements coming

over from the Asia Minor side, motor cars flying, we commanded Kilid Bahr, and the rear of Achi-Baba and the communications to all their army there.[59]

Major Cecil Allanson, 1/6th Gurkha Rifles, 29th Indian Brigade

Allanson was an effective officer but he was being carried away here by his emotions. Hill Q was an important tactical position, but only in tandem with control of the overlooking heights of Hill 971 to the left and Chunuk Bair on the right – without them it was a death trap. The reality was that there were far too few men to hold the summit against even a weak Turkish counter-attack. Major Mott took over the command shortly after Allanson had been wounded.

There was no question of our seeing the Narrows owing to the bursting of shells – supposed to have been fired by our battleships, but as I heard afterwards fired by our field artillery. Unfortunately, I was compelled to order a return owing to an enormous number of Turkish reinforcements appearing in sight. The retirement was carried out successfully, although casualties were severe.[60]

Major Geoffrey Mott, 6th South Lancashire Regiment, 38th Brigade, 13th Division

The men fell back to their jumping-off positions, where they beat off further Turkish attacks before retiring still further under the constant pressure. Meanwhile, the wounded Allanson, his leg painful and stiffening, made his way back through the gullies.

The nullahs on the journey back were too horrible, full of dead and dying, Maoris, Australians, Sikhs, Gurkhas, and British soldiers, blood and bloody clothes, and the smell of the dead now some two days old. I gave morphia (I always carry it) to ever so many men on my way down who could get no further and were obviously done. On arriving down I reported to the General, looking like nothing on earth, my clothes and accoutrements in ribbons, filthy dirty and a mass of blood. I told him that unless strong reinforcements were pushed up, and food and water could be sent us, we must come back, but that if we did we gave up the key of the Gallipoli Peninsula.[61]

Major Cecil Allanson, 1/6th Gurkha Rifles, 29th Indian Brigade

It was already too late. A brief glimpse of the Straits prior to a shambolic retreat is nowhere near victory; incontrovertibly, the abruptness with which the Turks ejected the 1/6th Gurkhas and 6th South Lancashires showed how far from success they were. The Anzac offensive was all but over. The only remaining question was whether they could retain their lodgement on just one small shoulder of the Chunuk Bair summit.

The Turks, under the command of Kemal, were now ready to launch their counter-attack with the best part of three regiments at dawn on 10 August. Although they perhaps could not have known it, the odds were firmly in their favour. The British plans had fallen into disarray and in the chaotic landscape between Walker's Ridge and Damakjelik Bair there were the remnants of multifarious units of various nationalities commanded for the most part by men who had no idea where they were or what they were meant to be doing. On Rhododendron Ridge and Chunuk Bair itself there were some 2,000 soldiers, representing four different brigades and three different divisions. The New Zealanders had been relieved over-night and the Chunuk Bair positions were now the responsibility of the 6th Loyal North Lancashires and the 5th Wiltshires. Many of the British soldiers were already exhausted, thirsty and demoralised. Their Turkish opponents were unstoppable as they poured over the ridge line at 04.45 that morning. On Chunuk Bair they overwhelmed the British defenders in an instant before throwing themselves down the precipitous slopes in pursuit. Charging down Rhododendron Ridge, they over-ran the Pinnacle and were only stopped by the massed machine guns of the New Zealand-ers at the Apex. North of the ridge the Turks swept down over the Farm Plateau some 300 feet below and slaughtered those defending troops that had not run for their lives.

> The sheer terror of some men, the bewilderment of others; none of whom had slept for four days; all of whom were at the end of their physical tether; all mixed up together; with strange officers trying to control men whom they had never seen before; with men looking for officers they could not find; with shouted orders merely adding to the uproar; with some unashamedly running away; with others trying to slip past, as if on some duty or errand, but intent only on putting as much distance as possible between themselves and the enemy; it was like the bursting of a dam. Yet, as the waters of a flooded river eventually spread out, slow down, and come to a trickle, so, in due course, the rush was stopped and the men led back. All this was only

on a very narrow front, and for a very short time, but it was nasty while it lasted. Those like us who were in trenches on the sides of the ravine, watching their front and facing the enemy, were the lucky ones; not only did the torrent miss them, but they were dealing with the tangible and could see that the Turks were not following up. It is the fear of the 'unknown' that matters. Most of those who had run, when the panic started, were not at the time engaged directly with the enemy, but were in reserve in the clefts and gullies behind.[62]

Second Lieutenant Reginald Savory, 14th Sikhs, 29th Indian Brigade

The retreat would end, the Turkish troops would run out of steam and their advance would grind to a halt, but the damage was done: Chunuk Bair was once more firmly back in Turkish hands.

The planning, the secrecy, the courageous attacks, the heroic resistance – in the end the attack from Anzac had been for nothing. In the four-day battle the ANZAC Corps had lost 12,500 men, that is, 33 per cent of the total. By far the highest casualties had been suffered by the 13th Division, who lost 5,500 men, but the 1st Australian Division and NZ&A Divisions had lost a further 5,800 between them.

The torrents of casualties all but overwhelmed the medical arrangements back near the beaches. The wounded were soon lying all around the dressing stations, out in the open under the blazing sun, still under occasional fire. The doctors, the medical orderlies and, above all, the stretcher bearers were exhausted beyond measure. But they worked on, conscious of their duty to the shattered men all around them and plagued by a familiar pest.

One of the most horrible features for the wounded lying in the hot sun, with bloodstained dressings and filthy clothes, was the plague of flies. Great blue bottles swarmed over every dressing and when one had sometimes to change a dressing or move one for any purpose, the wounds were already crawling with maggots. When there were hundreds of stretchers in a line stretching far back into the scrub from the pier it meant that anyone far back was likely to remain there anything up to 36 hours or more. Many wounded were without jackets or distinguishing clothing but an orderly called my attention to the fact that one man far back in the queue was a Brigadier-General. At the time I didn't know his name but later learned it was Brigadier-General Cooper (29th Brigade). His arm was shattered and in a tourniquet. I told him I had not known sooner who he was and offered to get him quickly to the pier. He asked me how many were in front and how long would he normally have to wait. I told him, 'Hundreds!' and probably over 24 hours' wait. He said firmly that I was to give him no advantage and everyone in front must be moved before him. I do not know whether he lived or not but it was quite 24 hours before he was moved to the hospital ship and the wound by then would be crawling with maggots and the limb probably gangrenous.[63]

Lieutenant Norman Tattersall, No. 13 Casualty Clearing Station, RAMC

For Lieutenant Norman King-Wilson aboard the hospital ship *Caledonia* it was a ghastly experience. Lighter after lighter pulled up loaded with the wounded. Soon there were some 1,350 men crammed aboard and the doctors and nurses were unable to cope.

We worked, one and all, until we could no longer tell what we were seeing or doing, dressing, dressing, dressing, hour and hour on end, all day and all night, picking out the cases where the dreaded gas gangrene had set in, where immediate and high amputation was the only hope of saving life. Even the clean open decks stank with the horrid smell of gangrenous flesh, and the holds, dark, hot and ill-ventilated, were just like cockpits of the fleet in the days of Nelson. The operating room was a veritable stinking, bloody shambles, where patients were brought up on a stretcher and left waiting for their predecessor to be taken down, then rapidly chloroformed, placed on the table, a leg or arm whipped off in a couple of minutes, by a circular incision, one sweep of the knife and the bone sawed through, the limb thrown into a basket with many others, awaiting incineration. No sutures were used, just a huge moist dressing applied to the stump. Then McCasey, bloody and perspiring, in the muggy, tropical night, would await the next poor victim of German ambition, who, in his turn, would be rendered a maimed testimonial to his life's end, of the brutality and savagery of war. Modern war? Perhaps, but does the limb shattered by a bullet look as brutal as the limb half cut through by a sword? Does the chest through which a half pound of jagged shell has ploughed its way appear less brutal than that pierced by a rapier or even a spear? Assuredly, since the days when men killed with club alone, no warfare has produced such savage wounds, such shattered wrecks, once human bodies, as the war surgeon of today has to deal with.[64]

Lieutenant Norman King-Wilson, HMHS *Caledonia*

The journey to Alexandria took four long days, the daylight hours filled with exhausting work and every night the grim ritual of the burials at sea.

The Parson every night, at midnight exactly, would appear in surplice and cassock on the main deck, aft, and there by the flickering light of a solitary candle lantern, would read aloud the burial service. It was the most weird ceremony one could possibly imagine – lying on the deck, bound tightly up in sailcloth, with a weight at the feet, anything from three to near a score of silent motionless figures. Three placed at a time on the gangway board from the ship's bulwark, lying feet pointing seaward, the Union Jack spread over all three, the hundreds of dark figures watching from the decks, sailors and soldiers, silent and awed for once at the sight of the last rites of those chaps who so lately had been cheery lusty comrades. The few words of the Chaplain soon over, the Union Jack is whipped off the bodies by a sailor and three bells are heard in the engine room, the great engines stop their roar and the ship glides on in silent darkness. The board is elevated and with a swish, followed by a dull splash, those three join Britain's countless dead, deep down in the Aegean Sea, far from home and those who hope for their return. Once again the Chaplain reads over three more, again the splash, and so on, until it is over and the watchers disperse to their rest or their work, but in each brain, be it ever so dull, an impression must linger until their life's end.[65]

Lieutenant Norman King-Wilson, HMHS *Caledonia*

15

AUGUST: SUVLA BAY LANDINGS

The success of the operation depended upon the progress made by the new troops landing at Suvla Bay. At daybreak, those of us with glasses eagerly scanned the country where we expected the Suvla troops to be. Gradually the country was searched with our glasses from right to left, finally resting on Suvla Bay itself, where we found the landing force had not advanced beyond the beach. To the best of our knowledge there was little to stop the new force straddling the Peninsula almost without opposition and it is describing it mildly to say we were bitterly disappointed.[1]

Lieutenant Colonel Leslie Tilney, 13th (New South Wales) Battalion, 4th Brigade, NZ&A Division, AIF

THE BRITISH IX CORPS OPERATIONS at Suvla Bay were never the main event in the August offensives and the common Australian perspective, as typified by the quote above, is simply wrong. The plan at Suvla was to secure a safe harbour and army base for future combined Suvla and Anzac operations. As such it was secondary to the ANZAC Corps operations. Although the initial plans had been diluted down from the *coup de main* conceived by General Sir Ian Hamilton due to the escalating caution of Lieutenant General Sir Frederick Stopford influenced by his domineering Chief of Staff Brigadier General Hamilton Reed, none the less the idea was still to seize the heights that enclosed the Suvla Plain, namely the Kiretch Tepe and Tekke Tepe ridges. The main flaw in this plan lay in its reliance

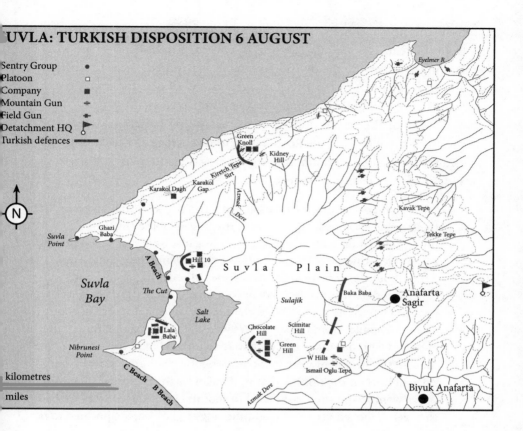

on a faulty interpretation of prior intelligence reports and a failure to adapt to later aerial reconnaissance. This created an obstacle out of the dry Salt Lake, exaggerated the scale of the Turkish defences on Chocolate Hill and, perversely, underestimated the strength of the Turkish outpost on Hill 10. As a result Hamilton's headquarters had vetoed any thoughts of a direct advance by the 11th Division from B and C Beaches to thrust either directly across or around the southern shore of Salt Lake to capture Chocolate Hill, Green Hill and W Hills. Instead the 34th Brigade was to land at A Beach on the northern side of Suvla Bay, capture Hill 10 and then send a battalion to secure the entire length of the Kiretch Tepe Ridge running along the north of the Suvla Plain. Meanwhile, the 32nd Brigade was to land on B Beach and, having first captured the Lala Baba hills north of the beach, was to move north, join with the rest of 34th Brigade and march all the way round the shores of Salt Lake to attack Chocolate Hill from the north, thereby taking the largely imaginary Turkish defences from the rear. The 33rd Brigade was to cover the right flank of the whole landing and provide the divisional reserve as required. Once the artillery and baggage of the 11th Division were safely ashore, the landing craft would be reused to land the men of the 10th Division.

Many of the senior officers of the assaulting battalions were given the chance, courtesy of the Royal Navy, to take a look at the landing sites and terrain that faced them. Among them was Lieutenant Colonel Bashi Wright of the 11th Manchesters.

> I first heard of the projected landing at Suvla Bay a few days before the landing was made, when I, with the Brigadier and the three other commanding officers of the 34th Brigade, were sent on board a destroyer which was leaving Imbros on patrolling duty. Before we left harbour we were disguised as marines in order to prevent our being recognised as soldiers. We moved slowly along the coast of the Peninsula, from Anzac to the north of Suvla Bay at a distance of about one to two miles from the shore. We were able to see something of the land and with our maps ready we were told the plan of the landing. The Manchester Regiment were to move along the coast and clear the high ridge of hills on the north – that is, Karakol Dagh and Kiretch Tepe Sirt. As we went round the coast I tried to spot the lie of the country we had to cover. It looked very rough and the ridge to be cleared appeared to be a very strong position.[2]
>
> Lieutenant Colonel Bashi Wright, 11th Manchester Regiment, 34th Brigade, 11th Division

With minimal knowledge of what awaited them, many junior officers, NCOs and men of the Suvla battalions were confident that they were superior to the Turks. The disasters at Helles and Anzac were flukes. This time all would be well.

The 11th Division sailed from Imbros at 19.45 in the early evening of 6 August in ten destroyers and ten 'beetle' lighters. The landings of the 32nd and 33rd Brigades on the long sandy sweep of B Beach north of Nibrunesi Point went near-perfectly. There was no opposition and the battalions quickly sorted themselves out ready for action. The 7th South Staffordshire and the 9th Sherwood Foresters moved off to the south to dig a system of flanking defences covering the beach landing places, while the 6th Yorkshires moved forward to attack the Turkish positions on Little Lala Baba, Lala Baba and to clear Nibrunesi Point. This would be the first attack made by a unit of Kitchener's all-volunteer New Army and they were very raw troops. Indeed on the Western Front the New Army would not go into offensive action until the Battle of the Somme nearly a year later. Following up well behind the 6th Yorkshires was Second Lieutenant Edmund Priestman of the 6th York and Lancasters, a devoted former Scoutmaster. He could not help but be nervous as they approached the beach.

> What was waiting for us? What had the first landing party found? You can picture us standing at the rail with our pulses doing tattoos as we strained our eyes into the darkness. Slowly our boat comes to a stop, and the absence of the rushing waves under her bows leaves a silence that can be felt hanging over the waters of the little bay in which we find ourselves. Only away on our right comes the distant rattle of a volley and the dull boom of an occasional gun at Anzac. So the Turkish picquet has been driven in by the Yorkshires and the land is clear. A lighter glides alongside us out of the shadow of the beach and as it draws near, 'Crack, crack, r-r-r-r-rattle, crack!!!' From among the black mounds inland a sharp crackling of rifles and then silence again. As the echo dies away over the still water all our conjectures return. If the Turks are driven back, whose is this firing? What's happening beyond there, among the shadows?[3]
>
> Second Lieutenant Edmund Priestman, 6th York and Lancaster Regiment, 32nd Brigade, 11th Division

Having come ashore, they advanced up the main Lala Baba hill.

> So we are nearing the introduction we have all had in our minds so long: the introduction to war as it is. As we push on, through sweet, sickly smelling scrub now, the darkness in front takes the form of a peaked hill and we meet the first slopes of its flank. And then, to our straining ears, there comes a voice from the blackness on our right. Almost inaudible at first, it swells up into a shrill, wordless whine, quavers for a moment and then dies again into silence. Then again, 'Ah-h-h-h-h-h.' This time it halts and inflects as though trying to frame some word, then, almost as though it would sing a few quivering notes, it sinks down the scale into the night and the shadows again.[4]
>
> Second Lieutenant Edmund Priestman, 6th York and Lancaster Regiment, 32nd Brigade, 11th Division

By midnight the 32nd Brigade had a firm grip on Lala Baba. Then all urgency vanished and no push was made, as planned, to join up with the 34th Brigade for the advance on Hill 10. Firing could be heard ahead and it was considered that to avoid confusion the troops should wait until dawn illuminated the situation. Precious hours were squandered.

Meanwhile, the landing of the 34th Brigade on A Beach actually within Suvla Bay was a disaster. The men's experiences sum up those of all the soldiers who fought in the first two weeks at Suvla Bay, so it is fortunate for future historians that the collected memories of their surviving senior NCOs and officers were collated in April 1916 to answer criticism of their performance. Seen through the prism of their memories, then, Suvla seems a far more threatening and deadly battleground than it is conventionally portrayed; their response not quite so pusillanimous and rather more pragmatic in the face of complete chaos and a threatening Turkish opposition. Their misadventures began when the 'beetle' lighters were brought to the bay towed by the three British destroyers *Beagle*, *Grampus* and *Bulldog*.

> Considerable difficulty was experienced at times by the breaking away of the towing ropes and it was imminently expected by those on board that we would either cut adrift and capsize, or be wrecked against the side of the destroyer. On one occasion the rope broke away, taking with it the rail. Regarding the troops, in some cases sleep had come as a welcome relief, but in the majority of cases former gaiety had given way to anxiety as to the ultimate issue of the enterprise, especially when the orders of strict silence and no smoking were given by the commander of the destroyer. The engines of the destroyer stopped and a whisper went round that we were 'There!' The destroyer had stopped, the towing ropes were unfastened and we were sent forward under our own steam. The commander of the destroyer, who was standing on the bridge, wished us 'Good Luck!' as we moved off.[5]
>
> Sergeant William Taylor, 11th Manchester Regiment, 34th Brigade, 11th Division

Packed tightly aboard one of the lighters were a company of the 11th Manchesters, a further company of 9th Lancashires and the two headquarter companies. They cast off from their destroyer about a mile from shore, but as the destroyers had anchored some 1,000 yards to the south of their intended positions in the north of the bay, the lighters were heading straight for the area already identified by the navy as being likely to shoal rapidly.

Midshipman Henry Denham was aboard the small picket boat which accompanied a lighter as it chugged slowly into Suvla Bay. With his senses heightened by anxious anticipation, every sound they made seemed to echo round in his head.

> Everything here seemed unbelievably quiet, and at last the destroyers let go their anchors, making sufficient noise to rouse every drowsy Turkish sentry in Suvla Bay. Our landing craft, heavily laden with troops, headed for the shore closely followed by my picket boat. Apart from the throb of the landing craft's diesel engine the night was still and inky black.[6]
>
> Midshipman Henry Denham, HMS *Agamemnon*

Then, as had been feared, the lighters ran aground on sandbanks or reefs between fifty and 100 yards from the shore. There was much more noise in almost farcical circumstances.

> The officer in charge of the lighter gave out some orders to a junior officer who was standing at the gangway ready to lower it for disembarkation. Up to this point we were all inwardly congratulating ourselves that we had a very easy task and that we would not be discovered landing. We had a very rude awakening! The officer gave his orders in a fairly low tone, but owing to the elements they had to be repeated several times, until his voice developed into a loud bawl. He continually bawled out the name of Robertson; simultaneously with this came the enemy's fire which seemed to come from the right.[7]
>
> Sergeant William Taylor, 11th Manchester Regiment, 34th Brigade, 11th Division

Whether the Turks heard the confusion and shouting, or had already been alerted by the lighters' throbbing engines and were merely biding their time, the result was the same.

> A heavy rifle fire was opened on us from our right at a range of about 200 or 300 yards and shrapnel burst over us. Then I knew that we had been taken to the wrong beach and were close to Lala Baba, about two miles south of where we should have been. We tried to take soundings with a stick, but could not reach bottom, and I was not going to disembark my men in deep water and drown them. The weight of the

ammunition and kit they were of necessity carrying was such that a man would have little chance of getting ashore in deep water.[8]

Lieutenant Colonel Bashi Wright, 11th Manchester Regiment, 34th Brigade, 11th Division

They were facing a beach some 200 yards to the south of the Cut, a dried-up channel running from the Salt Lake to the sea. And there they were, packed together in the lighters, static targets well within rifle range, hopelessly stuck aground on the sandbanks. Soon they began to suffer casualties. Something had to be done. But what?

The moment the firing started we all lay down in the lighter and the bullets came pretty close; I heard several men say they were hit. We were now stuck pretty fast and a somewhat heated altercation took place between our CO and the naval commander. The latter said here we were and here we must disembark; my CO said he would not disembark at a place where every man would be out of his depth, and would probably drown. Some rough soundings were taken which varied from 5–12 feet which shows how 'rough' they were. As a final expedient the men were pushed and packed back in the stern to take the weight off the bows and so get off the obstruction, but this proved futile. Finally it was decided for a few men to go over the end with a rope attached to the lighter and take this to shore and that the remainder should get to shore as best as they could hanging on to the rope and pulling themselves along by it. The CO called for tall men and I being about 5 feet 11 inches stepped forward. Our Second in Command, Major Sillery, was going over first. He turned to me and said, 'I advise you to take off all your equipment like me!' I did so and jumped in after him. I went clean under and could not touch bottom. However, I struck out and in about 5 yards I found my depth. The CO of the 9th Lancashire Fusiliers[9] followed and when we three got to the shore Major Sillery, the Colonel and I hung on to the rope and kept it as taut as we could.[10]

Captain Geoffrey Meugens, 11th Manchester Regiment, 34th Brigade, 11th Division

Back on the lighter, Lieutenant Colonel Wright kept order, marshalling his men down the gangway and into the sea. It was a tricky, nerve-racking business and therefore imperative that the officers kept control of their inexperienced men, checked their fears and tried to keep them under tight military discipline. Otherwise they would soon degenerate into a rabble before they had even landed.

The majority of the men were under fire for the first time, it was a nerve trying moment and they received that kind of shock that stagnates action and they simply lay down on the deck undecided what to do, but a few words from Lieutenant Hart brought them to their senses and then all made tracks for the sea. Personally I groped my way through, my sole thought being to get away from the lighter, being under the impression that they were only firing at the lighter.[11]

Sergeant William Taylor, 11th Manchester Regiment, 34th Brigade, 11th Division

Many of the men of the Manchesters and Lancashire Fusiliers took considerable strength from the sight of their officers struggling up to their necks in the cold water, helping them one by one to safety.

We had a warm time of it whilst we were on board as there is very little cover on board these lighters, so we had a lot of our chaps put out of action. I can tell you I said my prayers more than once. Well, the skipper dived overboard with a rope so that we could have something to assist us to get ashore, as a great many could not swim. I was one of them – so I thought my time had come! We got orders to get ashore and when I got to the bottom of the gangway our CO was in the water helping all that came off the boat. He was wounded while he was doing this, but he stuck to his guns like a hero.[12]

Lance Sergeant Thomas Dolan, 9th Lancashire Fusiliers, 34th Brigade, 11th Division

As the troops slowly struggled ashore the lighter drew less water and was washed over the offending sandbar closer to the beach, before grounding again. This time she was in an even worse position, as she was caught between the sandbank and rocks projecting out from Nibrunesi Point. The level of Turkish fire from the north side of Lala Baba was gradually increasing and Colonel Wright detached a company under the command of Major Harry Bates to deal with the threat. They moved off in skirmishing order in four platoon lines.

The order was given, 'Fix bayonets!' and not a shot to be fired – everything was to be done with the bayonets. All the time the Turks were firing at random at us, and we had to move very cautiously. We made a zig-zag course up the slopes of the hill under very trying circumstances, as most of our men were having their first baptism of fire and everybody dripping wet.[13]

Sergeant W. Jones, 11th Manchester Regiment, 34th Brigade, 11th Division

They were perhaps fortunate that the Turks were fatally distracted by the tempting targets in the lighters still trapped on the shoaling sandbanks below them.

> We moved towards it in four lines quite safely as the firing was all directed towards the ship and lighter. We reached the bottom of the hill and got to within about 30 yards of the enemy trench before they realised our presence and they had scarcely fired a round at us before Major Bates gave a shout and the whole Company picked this up and charged the trench.[14]
>
> Company Sergeant Major Charles MacDonald, 11th Manchester Regiment, 34th Brigade, 11th Division

The Turks were soon overwhelmed; indeed most of them evacuated their trench as soon as they saw the dark shapes charging up the hill towards them.

> We had very few casualties going up, and judging from the amount of rifle fire I should say the Turks had no more than thirty or forty men on the north side of this position. On nearing the top we came across one long trench which the Turks were hastily evacuating. We cleared this with the bayonet killing about a dozen of the enemy, the remainder getting away under cover of the darkness.[15]
>
> Captain Edward Hartley, 11th Manchester Regiment, 34th Brigade, 11th Division

When the over-excited men showed signs of losing discipline and charging off into the darkness after the Turks, their senior NCOs and officers intervened swiftly. It was perhaps just as well that they managed to retain order, for a minor incident then occurred which reveals the risks of changing plans even for the best of motives. Lala Baba was not the objective of the 34th Brigade, who had been landed in the wrong place, but rather of the 32nd Brigade. The confusion that ensued could have been disastrous as the Yorkshiremen charged up and across the hill.

> It was a blessing that orders had been given previously that not a shot was to be fired, because the East Yorks Regiment evidently taking us for a force of Turks came for us with fixed bayonets and totally un-English yells. We lined up and prepared to receive the supposed enemy. The mistake was not discovered until they were on top of us. If orders

had been given to fire one shudders to think of what might have happened.[16]

Company Quartermaster Sergeant F. L. Eaton, 11th Manchester Regiment, 34th Brigade, 11th Division

One way or another, Lala Baba had been secured.

Back on the beach, Captain Geoffrey Meugens had been charged with collecting and sorting out the other companies of the Manchesters as they slowly pieced themselves together in the sand dunes along the shoreline. No sooner had the problem of flanking rifle fire been dealt with than another emerged.

The old gun at Ghazi Baba started firing and we saw the shells going over us and bursting about 200 yards to our right front. The men I thought here were very good, lying still and trying to clean their rifles, which were soaked of course and nearly all choked with sand. Being unarmed, I picked up a rifle, but the bolt simply stuck fast and I could not open it. I gave it to a private who had lost his.[17]

Captain Geoffrey Meugens, 11th Manchester Regiment, 34th Brigade, 11th Division

Meanwhile, Wright was trying to refocus on his designated mission to advance along Kiretch Tepe Ridge.

There was a good deal of firing going on and we were being peppered pretty freely from all directions, but we did not reply for two reasons: our rifles, by order, were not loaded, and we could see nothing to shoot at. I had previously given my Company Commanders orders as to the order of march, objective and also compass bearings. These latter were now of no use as we had been landed two miles south of where we should have been. We were all fearfully cold as it was a cool night, we were in thin khaki drill and soaked to the skin. The men were wonderfully cheerful and keen. We could dimly see the outline of the [Suvla] Point and Karakol Dagh, so I gave the company commanders a line to march on, more or less guessing the direction.[18]

Lieutenant Colonel Bashi Wright, 11th Manchester Regiment, 34th Brigade, 11th Division

Wright was demonstrating a robust determination to push forward to secure his objectives, overcoming problems as they arose, without being deflected from the ultimate aim.

After we had gone a few hundred yards we crossed a muddy kind of dyke which I put down as the cut from Salt Lake to the sea. During the march, we were fired at a good deal from the front and flanks, but could not see any of the enemy. After about a mile or more I heard the men shouting and several screams, so I knew that they had got into a body of Turks. I could see nothing of the three companies in front, but could hear them, and was quite sure that a pretty good scrap was going on.[19]

Lieutenant Colonel Bashi Wright, 11th Manchester Regiment, 34th Brigade, 11th Division

For the less well briefed men, tramping along the beach and across the low sand hills, there seemed no logic to their movements and the persistent Turkish sniper activity tore at their nerves. It was also very difficult to maintain a coherent formation, especially when they began to ascend the foothills and then the heights of Karakol Dagh that formed the western end of Kiretch Tepe Ridge. Here they encountered serious opposition from the Turks.

Instead of two or three sentry posts we ran into several strongly held, well-entrenched picquets. I hope I am not going too far in saying that I shall always consider that the order 'not to load rifles' had a very disheartening effect. I know that it would have bucked our fellows considerably if they could have taken a few pot shots at the retreating enemy and brought a few down. We were discovered then and nothing was gained by silence. The whole thing was a beastly nerve-racking experience in the dark.[20]

Captain Geoffrey Meugens, 11th Manchester Regiment, 34th Brigade, 11th Division

Behind Meugens' men, R Company, having helped the 6th Yorkshires clear Lala Baba, was dutifully following on along the beach, before cutting further inland across the ridged foothills and gullies of the southern face of Karakol Dagh to catch up with the rest of the 11th Manchesters.

Once on the ridge it was exceptionally hard going. The narrow, jagged ridge was covered in prickly scrub and fell away steeply on both sides; indeed it was at times precipitous to the north. Meugens was sent to check the progress of the men advancing along the broken north face of the ridge, but on his return he made a near-fatal error.

I made a perfectly fatuous mistake. Immediately below me I saw No. 2 Platoon in line halted – they were very dimly outlined and about 50 yards in front two small groups of scouts. A good way in front of these I thought I saw bayonets flashing. I decided that these must be my Company who I had understood were pushing on and I made a bee-line for the bayonets. After a bit I got into a hollow but pushed on knowing I should come to them over the next spur. Now I was alone I began to feel extremely tired and it is to that I ought to attribute my mad act in walking over a skyline on this next spur without any precautions whatever. I was thinking about my Company and not about Turks as I did so, but I very soon woke up when I saw about 20 yards away a small trench and realised that the bayonets really belonged to a picket of about fifteen Turks. They all started yelling and firing at once and I decided to bolt for it. As I turned something hit me on my right shoulder and knocked me over. I thought then the best thing to do was to lie still and they kept it up for what seemed a horribly long time. Suddenly I heard Major Sillery's voice calling out to the men to come on and the Turks stopped firing. I nipped back over the spur and found about a platoon of our fellows. When I had persuaded them not to bayonet me, I told them to come on and clear out the trench. When we came in sight of it, however, the Turks made up their mind to leave it. I reached the trench at one end as the last Turk left it at the other.[21]

Captain Geoffrey Meugens, 11th Manchester Regiment, 34th Brigade, 11th Division

The Turks occupied a series of both prepared and impromptu positions: sangars of piled-up rocks, natural breaks in the rock formations and narrow gullies.

As the light grew clearer we got badly sniped, officers in conspicuous uniforms being the first to suffer. Up to this time none of our rifles had been fired, and we found that most of them were badly jammed owing to their bath the night before. Another reason that we could not get a large volume of fire to bear on the enemy was the limited amount of frontage and cover on the crest of the ridge. The Turkish snipers shot very effectively – no doubt we made good targets for them.[22]

Lieutenant Allan Norbury, 11th Manchester Regiment, 34th Brigade, 11th Division

Although wounded, and feeling increasingly exhausted from loss of blood, Meugens continued to lead his men forward as best he could.

As far as I could make out there were a lot of these trenches all over the hill and the result of our people meeting them was that though the Turks did not hold them for long, they sufficed to make our columns break up and in the dark the men got rather scattered. The time was now about 03.30 and very soon it began to get light. Our fellows were scattered all over the place in little groups and one had a great job trying to get them together. We were still being fired on, and the fire increased, while our fellows were practically all unable to return it owing to their rifles being still clogged with sand. I got someone to tie me up – rather ineffectually – and we pushed on. By the time we got up to the third line of defences it was broad daylight and the firing was very hot indeed.[23]

Captain Geoffrey Meugens, 11th Manchester Regiment, 34th Brigade, 11th Division

The bayonet might be useful at close quarters, but bullets were needed to deal with the Turkish snipers. At last they began to get their rifles working again.

Urinating on the bolts seemed to be the only way to open them, and it was a big relief to be able to fire upon the enemy, who, skilfully concealed behind the rocks and bushes, were picking off our officers and NCOs with uncanny certitude. Major Bates, our Company Commander, was wounded in the wrist and stomach, but with heroic disregard of pain and discomfort he still kept on leading us. The sun was boiling hot, and what with the heat and the salt water we had inadvertently swallowed we were suffering untold agonies from thirst. The wounded were indeed a pitiful sight, with swollen tongues and lips.[24]

Company Quartermaster Sergeant F. L. Eaton, 11th Manchester Regiment, 34th Brigade, 11th Division

Nevertheless the Manchesters continued to press forward until they reached the junction with the main body of Kiretch Tepe, the Karakol Gap.

We were brought up by a heavy fire from the opposite side of the gap, where the majority of the Turks had collected. We could see very few Turks, as there was good cover for them in the broken ground. We were also very much worried by rifle fire from the right flank which appeared to come from the low ground, which was covered with scrub. I was unable to clear this with the men at my disposal. At this spot I lost in killed and wounded seven officers and about 50 to 60 men. I estimated the numbers of the Turks at this time to be about 300 and judging by the volume of fire, they were receiving reinforcements rapidly. We could not go on without covering fire of some sort, were in a most exposed position and the Turks had begun to shell us from two guns somewhere to our right front. It was an unpleasant situation.[25]

Lieutenant Colonel Bashi Wright, 11th Manchester Regiment, 34th Brigade, 11th Division

The attack across the Karakol Gap was made at about 10.00 on the morning of 7 August. Crucially, despite his machine gun having been dropped to the bottom of the sea during the landing, Lieutenant John Lithiby stripped it right down and achieved a veritable miracle.

Lithiby came up. He told me that he had got the machine gun close behind in working order and asked me what he should do. I told him to try to find cover on the top of the hill, to open fire on the Turkish position and that I would try to get the men across the gap under cover of his fire. Lithiby and Sergeant Pickles got the gun to the top but could find no cover. In spite of this, under heavy fire, they mounted the gun and let off belt after belt into the Turks. I was watching and saw a few Turks get up and run back and hoped more would go. Whether they did or not it was our only chance, so I ordered the advance. The officers and the whole battalion got up and walked across the gap. This sudden movement seemed to surprise the Turks as they drew back from the crest and I had very few casualties during this advance.[26]

Lieutenant Colonel Bashi Wright, 11th Manchester Regiment, 34th Brigade, 11th Division

But the Turks had merely fallen back to the next defensible point. And the further the Manchesters advanced up Kiretch Tepe the more it broadened out on either side of the sharp ridge line. Soon it became apparent that the Manchesters would be swallowed whole if they attempted to continue their advance.

I saw that we should not get far without reinforcements: the Turks were getting round us on both flanks, I had nobody to attend to my wounded, and at the rate we were going on our ammunition would not last. I wrote two messages to this effect and sent them off by separate messengers with orders to try and find Brigade Headquarters. One of them got through eventually, but was delayed through having fallen into a nullah and injured his knee. The other did not reach his destination. There were no signs of any troops on the plain and we seemed to be alone and to be gradually being surrounded. We managed to get on a bit further and were finally held up about 3 miles from the sea a few hundred yards in advance of a high point in the ridge which was afterwards known as Jephson's Post. The officers and men behaved most gallantly and made several desperate efforts to take the next hill without success. The forward slope of the hill was without cover and under a very heavy rifle and machine gun fire, shrapnel was bursting over us from two guns on our right front and the men were worn out with hard work and heat. They were fainting with thirst as they had given up any water they had in their water bottles to keep the machine gun going. At about noon my leading companies were about half-way to the next hill – the Benchmark – and could not move, machine gun ammunition had run out, my Second in Command and two Company Commanders had been killed and a third wounded – we were suffering heavily. I was hit myself and there were no signs of our being reinforced. Anxious as we were to take the Benchmark, it was impossible and there was nothing to do but hang on as best we could and hold the ground we had taken.[27]

Lieutenant Colonel Bashi Wright, 11th Manchester Regiment, 34th Brigade, 11th Division

Captain Meugens had struggled on as best he could having been wounded, but he was now utterly exhausted. Reluctantly, he made his way along the ridge to the beach.

We saw no British troops at all advancing on our right and our Battalion seemed absolutely isolated. It is a curious fact that we were sniped all the way down from the plain, which seemed to be alive with Turks. We found Captain Oliver there and Sergeant Hall, bleeding badly from a severed artery in the arm. There were about fifteen of us and the Turks sent about six shrapnel over and then left us in peace. Sergeant Hall's condition was serious and we used frantic endeavours to get into semaphore communication with all sorts of boats in the bay. But the hours went on and no boat of any kind came near us or anywhere near the north end of the bay. The bay was crowded with transports loading into lighters but the lighters never seemed to move.[28]

Captain Geoffrey Meugens, 11th Manchester Regiment, 34th Brigade, 11th Division

What they could see was the Suvla plan falling apart. The three brigades of the 11th Division had been hours behind schedule when, at 04.30, the forward elements of the 10th Division appeared off Suvla Bay. It had been planned that they would land at A Beach following in after 34th Brigade and then reinforce the push along Kiretch Tepe. The shoals seemed to render this impossible so it was decided to land the 31st Brigade and half of 30th Brigade on C Beach round Nibrunesi Point and just north of B Beach, where the 32nd Brigade had landed. Here, under the overall command of Brigadier General William Sitwell of 34th Brigade, they would be temporarily attached to the 11th Division and assist in the capture of Chocolate Hill. This of course weakened the force devoted to the capture of Kiretch Tepe. More disorder followed when the navy discovered a feasible landing place at West Beach on the northern side of Suvla Bay and the other half of 30th Brigade were landed there. As the 10th Division was already lacking the 30th Brigade, which had been detached for deployment with the ANZAC Corps' left hook, the changes in landing plans left Lieutenant General Sir Bryan Mahon's forces split into three, with a devastating effect on command and control. The brigade and battalion commanders had no idea what to do. All these changes caused delays. Time was trickling away.

At last Captain Meugens saw the Irish troops of the 6th Munster Fusiliers beginning to land at West Beach.

Captain Oliver and I went over to see them and they turned out to be the Munsters – 10th Division. I asked their CO the time and he said 12.30. He then informed Oliver, as far as I can remember the exact words, that he had no orders what to do except to 'Get on shore and reinforce the troops at present fighting!' He asked the direction he should go and whom he was to reinforce. Captain Oliver then begged him to go and help the Manchesters, who were held up alone on the ridge. He agreed to do his best. At this point the sporting pinnace from the *Chatham* arrived with a Doctor who told us I am glad to say that he was just in time to save Sergeant Hall. The poor fellow was nearly dead through loss of blood.[29]

Captain Geoffrey Meugens, 11th Manchester Regiment, 34th Brigade, 11th Division

It would still take several hours before the Irish battalions of the 10th Division could organise themselves to undertake the steep climb to reinforce the Manchesters struggling on Kiretch Tepe.

About 5 p.m. the Munsters reinforced us and went through us to the attack. They lost so heavily however that we were ordered to join them in the firing line. We then advanced as far as the Pimple, part of which we occupied, but were again held up by the Turks who appeared to have been strongly reinforced. At this point about fifty of the Munsters, who seemed to have lost all their officers and most of their NCOs, retreated through us in disorder, but were afterwards sent back again by our officer.[30]

Captain Edward Hartley, 11th Manchester Regiment, 34th Brigade, 11th Division

In the end the Manchesters and the Munsters charged into the attack together.

We advanced in extended order down the slope on to the enemy position. Major Bates took charge of the combined Battalions, and with a cry of 'Come on Manchesters, show the Munsters what you are made of!' we made a charge. Unfortunately he was hit again and was instantly killed.[31]

Company Quartermaster Sergeant F. L. Eaton, 11th Manchester Regiment, 34th Brigade, 11th Division

Major Harry Bates had already been badly wounded, but had been determined to stick it out. His grit was all in vain, for they could get no further and the Pimple remained in Turkish hands. The Manchesters could do no more: they had been fighting hard all day, and they had no water, so thirst had become an overwhelming obsession. They were replaced in the line by the 5th Inniskilling Fusiliers. When the roll calls were taken the Manchesters were found to have suffered some 215 casualties.

But what of the rest of the 34th Brigade? The other three battalions found themselves trapped in a situation that they could neither understand nor control. The 9th Lancashire Fusiliers had eventually managed to get ashore, sending out patrols towards the dried up Salt Lake and probing both flanks to try and determine their position. Just after 03.00, as the first rays of dawn filtered above the horizon, the already lightly wounded Colonel Harry Welstead and Major Cyril Ibbetson were brusquely briefed by Major Lionel Ashburner, the senior staff officer of 34th Brigade.

'Look, do you see that hill, over there on the left? That is the hill we want – Hill 10. If you can take all the men you have got, and carry that hill between those two trees on the horizon we shall be all right, otherwise we shall probably be driven into the sea!' We started in three lines in extended order, the men going forward splendidly, led by their Platoon Commanders, in the most superb manner imaginable, with shells and bullets coming thicker and thicker, every man being eager to get to the objective. There was a check just before we got to the foot of the hill. Then in one mad rush we carried the hill at the point of the bayonet. A terrific fire was opened on us from a fieldwork facing us, from some trenches on our right which enfiladed our position and from some guns high up in a valley above us. Realising that we could not hold this position, unless the trenches were cleared of the enemy, I ordered an attack on these trenches. There was much confusion, so I was unable to get orders to the whole of my command, but I got a good lot together and soon we took those trenches, but the casualties were very heavy and I was wounded too. I soon found that the fieldwork, which I had ignored, enfiladed to a nicety these trenches and if anybody moved he was immediately hit. I ordered everybody to make cover for themselves and attend to the wounded. Nobody was allowed to show himself. Suddenly, to our horror, we saw Hill 10 evacuated by the troops which had come up to reinforce us and we watched them retire right back in the direction from whence we had come. We were now isolated. Our casualties increased and we made a desperate fight of it for hours until the West Yorks appeared on Hill 10 again. I shall not forget that trench.[32]

Major Cyril Ibbetson, 9th Lancashire Fusiliers, 34th Brigade, 11th Division

Worse still this was *not* Hill 10. The low hill erroneously identified by Major Ashburner was just a large sand dune occupied by a small Turkish detachment. The real Hill 10 was some 400 yards further north. The bulk of the Turkish forces in the sector were still firmly dug in and their positions had not yet been located by the Lancashire Fusiliers.

Behind the first wave of the 34th Brigade troops came the 8th Northumberland Fusiliers and the 5th Dorsets, who had been left aboard the destroyers until the lighters could refloat themselves and then get back to take them ashore. They had to guess what was happening and wait patiently; there was no effective means of communication. When the lighters eventually picked them up they were again caught on the infuriating shoals of Suvla Bay. And despite the efforts of those that had gone before them, snipers were still firing at them from concealed positions. As a result many of the Northumberland Fusiliers and Dorsets had become unnerved by their prolonged exposure to a nasty combination of tedium and danger without the compensating opportunity of returning fire, or indeed of doing anything at all. At least the navy had eventually sent small tows of boats to help land the men from the stricken lighters, but the delays just kept multiplying. When they at last arrived on shore they were met by chaos.

> We had only advanced a short distance when we fell into a hopeless confusion, Lancashire Fusiliers, West Yorks and others getting mixed up with us. It was at this point I lost my Company, but pushed straight on until I came to a bog. The men I had with me were inclined to look for a way around it, but shouting, 'Follow me!' I waded straight through it and the others followed. It was a good job we did so for we came under cover on a sand hill. I crept up the side and saw some of the enemy trying to take some of the Lancashire Fusiliers prisoners. I called on my men to hurry up into position and open fire, having first shouted to the Lancashires to lie down, which they did. The enemy left a few dead behind them and then retired as fast as possible. We followed them up and whilst doing so one of my men trod upon a land mine, blowing him up. The force of the explosion lifted me off my feet.[33]
>
> Corporal Daniel Burns, 8th Northumberland Fusiliers, 34th Brigade, 11th Division

By this time the Turkish artillery had begun to fire towards the beach areas. The combination of land mines and shells was intimidating.

> We came in contact with some very marshy ground, which was very difficult to pass, and on which several of our men fell wounded or killed. As I got near the edge of the marsh, I heard another explosion in front of me and to the right, which I soon learned was the bursting of a mine. Still we pushed on, and within a very few minutes there

was another mine exploded close by my right side. This affected
the advance, but through some encouraging remarks made by my
Company Commander we kept pushing forward, until we could find
cover behind a short hedge. Just then a shell dropped in front of me on
the other side of the hedge and I felt something strike my helmet which
carried me about 2 yards on my back. However, it was only some of the
earth that had been blown up from in front, and, apart from the shock,
I was little the worse.[34]

Sergeant Peter Thompson, 8th Northumberland Fusiliers, 34th Brigade, 11th
Division

Hill 10 was eventually located and captured shortly after 06.00. By
this time all semblance of command and control had disappeared. No
one had any idea of what was happening, or indeed any apparent grasp of
their objectives. Soon the orders and counter-orders began, draining the
energy of the men and frustrating their officers.

Apparently we were too much to the right, because we got the order
to move about 500 yards north, which we did, and then lay down
extended. About an hour later, we got orders to close in to the right.
During this closing in, Platoons and Companies became somewhat
muddled, as some men made longer rushes than others, making for
cover behind the sand dunes as much as possible. The next orders I
received were from Colonel C. C. Hannay personally, who told me that
we were to advance, changing direction half-right. This would bring
us facing south-east towards Chocolate Hill – the original idea. When
the sun had about half-risen the advance began and I found that the
remainder of the Battalion in sight were swinging half-left, or towards
Karakol Dagh, so I came to the conclusion that fresh orders had been
issued and not reached me, so I followed suit. A short way further on I
came across about 50 men of different companies, taking cover behind
a large sand dune, apparently without a leader and uncertain what to
do. I took charge of them and told them to wait where they were while
I went round the forward side of the sand dune to see exactly what was
happening and how I could best get them extended again, preparatory
to continuing the advance. I had hardly gone about 5 yards when
three shells landed on the forward slope of the sand dune without
any appreciable effect; but by the time I went back to fetch the men I
found they had scattered, evidently thinking the locality unhealthy. I

collected what men I could and with them advanced towards Karakol Dagh.[35]

Lieutenant Donald Drysdale, 5th Dorsetshire Regiment, 34th Brigade, 11th Division

With the sun beating down on them the men became increasingly tired as they sweated uphill and down across the fringes of the Suvla Plain. With the rudimentary communications equipment available in 1915, controlling the men was almost impossible once they were out of earshot. Wireless sets were far too heavy and unwieldy to be portable and it was extremely difficult to run out and maintain telephone lines, even if it was known where they should be laid, while runners were sniped at mercilessly. Yet even allowing for this severe handicap, Brigadier General William Sitwell, now in command of both the 34th Brigade and part of 10th Division, was incompetent – in which he was typical of most of the senior officers and staff officers of the 11th Division. While the Turks undoubtedly provided a more robust defence than had been expected, nevertheless what was needed from Sitwell was a determined resolution to push ahead to the overall objectives. But paralysed by his own fear of failure and unwillingness to take a chance, he did nothing. Attacks were ordered and cancelled; troops were marched backwards and forwards and the strength of their formations was leached away to no constructive end. He was the senior brigadier general, but he constantly sought to defer to higher authority. Worse, the commander of 11th Division, Major General Frederick Hammersley, was already exhausted and unable to cope with the responsibility. He had suffered severe psychiatric problems before the war and lacked the mental resilience to wrest control of the situation in the face of his negative-minded subordinates. He too looked to a higher authority: but Lieutenant General Sir Frederick Stopford remained hopelessly out of touch offshore, aboard the headquarters yacht *Jonquil*. General Sir Ian Hamilton, the ultimate authority, had his eyes fixed on the Anzac breakout and at this stage was paying little attention to Suvla. The end result was a command vacuum.

All that long, boiling afternoon Chocolate Hill, Green Hill and the W Hills remained in Turkish hands. It was not until shortly after 19.00 that elements of the 11th Division joined in the attack launched by the 10th Division. Only then were the twin Chocolate and Green Hills finally captured. As darkness fell units were scattered all over the northern sector of the Suvla Plain and Kiretch Tepe Ridge.

I was separated from the Company and found myself among some of the Lincoln Regiment and, together with stragglers of the Royal Irish, a handful of the Munsters and others of the 10th Division, I took part in a skirmish and an advance against Chocolate Hill. We gained the summit of the hill and took a ring of trenches round the top of it. By this time I was thoroughly tired and slightly nervy as we had very little artillery support – all the work in that direction seemed to be done by the enemy![36]

Sergeant Cyril Johnston, 8th Northumberland Fusiliers, 34th Brigade, 11th Division

Up on Kiretch Tepe, the 5th Inniskillings had overnight relieved the valiant 11th Manchesters.

There was no one in front of us but the enemy of whose whereabouts or number we had no knowledge and we must try to dig in, as the staff were of the opinion that we should be shelled in the morning. That night was one of the most arduous and uncomfortable I have ever spent. The soil was hard and rocky; our only digging implements were entrenching tools. We dug all night and when dawn broke had little to show for our labours. Most of the men had succeeded in digging shallow graves with a parapet of loose earth and flints, but some who had struck rocks had not even that. It was indeed fortunate that we were *not* shelled in the morning.[37]

Second Lieutenant Ivone Kirkpatrick, 5th Royal Inniskilling Fusiliers, 31st Brigade, 10th Division

The Irish troops found it indeed a harsh environment to cope with. The bare rock reflected back the heat of the August sun, baking them alive or dead as they lay in their sangar trenches. When the wind blew from the sea there was some slight relief, but on the landward side of the ridge there was no respite. All around them various insects went about their business oblivious to the war that had come to their world. Lizards scurried and even the occasional snake could be seen basking in the sun. The men, completely exposed to the broiling sun, had to make do with a pint or so of water a day. And even obtaining that was a trial.

I took a party of some thirty men one afternoon to 'A' Beach to draw water for the company. It was considered a great treat to be selected for these fatigues since it meant that we could have a hearty whack at the water on the beach. It took us well over an hour to cover the three mile journey. On arrival I paraded the men in front of a large iron tank the shape of a trough into which water had been pumped by a hose from a ship. Each man advanced in turn, filled the water bottles he was carrying, and then put his head into the tank to drink until he could drink no more. Of course the water was quite warm from exposure to the sun and was almost black from the dirt off the unwashed faces and hands of the countless soldiers who had used the tank. Our return to the line took longer even than the outward journey. The men weighed down with the weight of their water bottles could do little more than crawl up the rocky paths and gullies which led back to the Battalion.[38]

Second Lieutenant Ivone Kirkpatrick, 5th Royal Inniskilling Fusiliers, 31st Brigade, 10th Division

Many of the men suffered agonies of thirst, unrelieved by the constant sight of the salty seas from their vantage point on the ridge.

I suffered less than most, for instead of drinking my ration of water I spat it back into a small collapsible tin mug and kept rinsing my mouth at constant intervals, always spitting what remained back into the mug. Even so I must admit that I had a perpetual craving for a drink and envied the people at home who have only to turn on a tap to get as much as they want.[39]

Second Lieutenant Ivone Kirkpatrick, 5th Royal Inniskilling Fusiliers, 31st Brigade, 10th Division

Soon, for most of the troops at Suvla, the water shortage began to dominate their waking thoughts. Unlike Kirkpatrick, few had any concept of water discipline, of keeping some water back for possible worse shortages to come.

After turning the enemy off the hill we posted sentries and tried to get what rest we could, but we were continually being fired on and firing back on our part. At this period I parted with my last drop of water to a wounded comrade of the Munster Fusiliers and I'll never forget how grateful he was for that drop of water – for being young soldiers they had drunk all their water earlier in the day whereas I, benefiting from other campaigns, had nursed my water, therefore not feeling the want as much as they did.[40]

Corporal Daniel Burns, 8th Northumberland Fusiliers, 34th Brigade, 11th Division

Under the pressure the arrangements for water supply collapsed completely. Near the beach there was a breakdown in discipline as men fought to get at the water lighters as soon as they pulled into harbour. Nothing could be more counter-productive, but these men were desperate beyond reason.

> Some 20 tons of water comes in and the troops, in their frightful anxiety to get at something to drink, slit the pipes conveying the water from the barge to the shore with their jack knives in order to get the first drink. Thus the barge is rendered useless and I am sent down to keep order as well as possible and see what can be done. I arrive to find a perfect Babel of chaos. Two or three engineers on the barge are struggling with the men, the intervening space between the boat and shore is thick with struggling humanity, swimming backwards and forwards and carrying strings of water bottles over their heads.[41]
>
> Lieutenant Frank Howitt, Army Service Corps, 11th Division

The official history remarks insouciantly that many of the battalions had not been seriously engaged, but that does not match the perceptions of the men of the 34th Brigade in their after-battle reports written eight months later. They could still well remember the heat and thirst, the confusion, the deadly Turkish sniping, the harassing artillery fire, the aimless marching and counter-marching.

The British performance at Suvla has often been pilloried yet the brilliance of the Turkish defence led by Major Willmer is often ignored. His original defensive positions had been well chosen and his men were well briefed, fighting hard then withdrawing at the last moment to the next defensible positions. All the time their accurate sniping drained the strength from the British troops floundering in front of them. Although the British leadership was appalling, credit must also be given to the superior quality of the Turkish opposition. Whatever it may have looked like from the heights of Anzac there was plenty of fighting across the Suvla Plain on 7 August.

The race for the heights surrounding Suvla Bay was triggered by the landings. Liman reacted fairly quickly, sending one regiment from the Bulair sector when the first reports of the landings reached him at about 01.40 on 7 August. Once he was sure that Bulair would not be the focus of attack he despatched the 7th and 12th Divisions, commanded by Colonel

Feizi Bey, to Suvla at 07.00. These units had already undergone heavy fighting at Gallipoli, but they gamely marched down the thirty or so dusty miles to Suvla. It was once thought that they did not reach the area until the night of 8 August, but it has now been established that the 7th Division reached a position to the east of Tekke Tepe at about 22.00 on 7 August, with the 12th Division following a few hours later.[42] On arrival, Feizi Bey asked for time for his exhausted men to recover before launching a counter-attack, at which point he was (as we have seen) abruptly replaced as Commander of the Northern Sector of Anzac and Suvla by Mustafa Kemal. Yet the replacement of commander had no discernible impact on the exhausted troops, incapable of offensive action until the morning of 9 August. So the British gained another day.

The British had lamentably failed to achieve their objectives on 7 August. Perhaps that was never likely given the unnecessary complexities of their battle plan, the vigorous Turkish reaction, the British troops' inexperience and the lack of push displayed by their generals. But there was still time. A quick reorganisation during the morning of 8 August, followed by a concentrated assault focused on seizing the rest of Kiretch Tepe, Scimitar Hill, the W Hills and the Tekke Tepe Range, could yet achieve success with time to secure the key tactical positions before the Turks could effectively deploy their recently arrived but physically fatigued divisions. But that depended on everything going right and the collapse of the Turkish opposition. When Lieutenant Cuthbert Llewelyn Allen arrived with the reserves for the 11th Manchesters on 8 August he found ominous signs all around.

> I noticed General Hammersley strolling on the beach with Brigadier-General Sitwell, and his Brigade Major Ashburner. General Hammersley did not seem at all excited, but judging from appearances looked rather bewildered and worried, and I concluded all was not going well with us.[43]
>
> Lieutenant Cuthbert Llewelyn Allen, 11th Manchester Regiment, 34th Brigade, 11th Division

Hammersley and his brigadiers were already broken men, unwilling to do anything but allow their troops to rest and reorganise – and their own frailties were being projected on to the men they commanded. Their priority was to consolidate what they had already captured and any meagre offensive gestures during the long summer's day were limited to trying to forge a link across the Suvla Plain between Chocolate Hill and Kiretch Tepe. The 32nd Brigade moved forward, but, exhausted by the last two days, they found the going tough, although the 6th East Yorkshires managed to take Scimitar Hill unopposed. Nor could Mahon see much hope of further advance for the elements of his 10th Division up on Kiretch Tepe without considerable artillery support. So he too did next to nothing. By this time GHQ had belatedly become aware that the dash for the hills was stalled and a visit to Stopford from Hamilton's Chief of Staff, Colonel Cecil Aspinall, soon confirmed that rapid executive action was needed if another day was not to be wasted.

Hamilton, whose eyes were mainly fixed on Hill 971 and Chunuk Bair, finally realised that in the case of IX Corps no news was not good news. Belatedly horror-struck at the lack of positive action he rushed over to Suvla in the late afternoon of 8 August to try to persuade Stopford to launch an attack that evening. He met Stopford aboard the *Jonquil* and then, after a brief consultation, rushed ashore. At about 19.00 he found Hammersley immersed in the process of planning an attack by the 33rd and 32nd Brigades on the W Hills and the Anafarta Spur for the morning of 9 August. This was not soon enough for the distraught Hamilton, who broke his usual habits to interfere directly in a subordinate's command. He ordered forward the 32nd Brigade and the divisional pioneers the 6th East Yorkshires that very night, with the focus not on the W Hills but on the imposing mass of Tekke Teppe. Although Hamilton had the right end in mind, this was madness: there was no time for the distribution of orders; no one knew where anyone else was; it was not possible within the timeframe to get the right units in the right place to launch the attack. The 32nd Brigade was scattered across the Suvla Plain and soon runners were struggling through the night trying to sort out the disarray. Catastrophically, as part of the rushed preparations, the 6th East Yorkshires were withdrawn from their position on Scimitar Hill to the 32nd Brigade rendezvous behind them at Sulajik. It was not until 04.00 on 9 August that the advance began, led by the 6th East Yorkshires. Until recently, historians thought that one exhausted company managed to reach the top of Tekke Tepe before being ambushed by the Turks sweeping over the heights.

We reached the point where the ravine ended, and in the scrub ahead of us we saw a number of men who fired upon us. For a moment we thought they were our own, firing in ignorance. Then we saw that they were Turks. We had run into the back of an enemy Battalion which held the lower slopes against our supports. They had crossed the range at a point lower than that we had attacked and had cut in behind our climbing force. We could do nothing but surrender. When we held up our hands some dozen or more of the enemy charged towards us with fixed bayonets. The man who took possession of me searched my pockets and annexed everything of military use except my revolver, which had fallen out of my hand a minute before, when I had been knocked down by a bullet that glanced off a rock on to my leg. Of those taken with me, one was not molested; one was fired at from 5 yards' distance, missed and quietly captured; one was beaten and fired at. Thank God the man who fired at him hit the man who was beating him and broke his wrist. The fourth, my Colonel, was bayoneted. Then, for the moment their fury ceased. I was permitted to tend the Colonel. He did not seem to suffer pain at all, only to be intensely thirsty. He drank the whole of the contents of my water-bottle as well as his own. They even allowed me to carry him on my back; and on my back the Colonel died.[44]

Lieutenant John Still, 6th East Yorkshire Regiment, 11th Division

Local Turkish sources, who have analysed the location of discovered fragments of British equipment, coupled with the simple lack of marching time available to the East Yorkshires after their late start, would seem to indicate that they were probably ambushed far lower down on the slopes of the Baka Baba foothills, in front of Anafarta Sagir.

This relatively minor incident has been attributed disproportionate importance – the IX Corps had *tried* to launch a brigade attack but proved unable to generate sufficient force to take or hold Tekke Tepe against the Turkish reinforcements. The less well publicised fate of the rest of the 6th East Yorkshires demonstrates the futility of it all.

We were supposed to attack before dawn, but owing to orders being late it was broad daylight. The attacked position had not been reconnoitred, the men were dead beat, having had no sleep since we landed, and were utterly done. We were allowed to march half way up the slope by the Turks – then received it in the neck. The Turks were strongly entrenched – we were [outnumbered] four to one. They also had a machine gun enfilading us from our left and a party of men enfilading us on our right. They had us in a trap pure and simple. The regiments that were supposed to be on our left and right flanks had gone somewhere else. We lost officers and 300 men in half an hour. Human nature could stand no more. One Company was captured all together and the rest turned and ran. I don't blame the men for it was their first time under fire and really men could not be expected to endure it. I collected a few men and we made a bit of a stand further back, but eventually had to retire back to the reserves who were a mile and a quarter back instead of 400 yards. The staff work was damned rotten and nearly all the staff officers are incapable and inefficient. They take no interest in anything at all – if they are safe it doesn't matter about the rest of us.[45]

Lieutenant Eric Halse, 6th East Yorkshire Regiment, 11th Division

When the 32nd and 33rd Brigades eventually began their move forward they were soon pressed back away from the hills and could not even recover Scimitar Hill. They had certainly tried, but they had been found wanting and had failed.

Although embittered officers such as Lieutenant Halse blamed staff officers for much of the disaster, this was not altogether fair. There had been a systemic malfunction that individuals could do little to prevent – a lamentable disintegration in the whole process of generating, issuing and carrying out orders, whether at the headquarters of IX Corps or within its divisions and brigades. Orders were issued, cancelled and reissued. The results were often vague or even contradictory in nature. There was little or no coordination between neighbouring brigades, which, having no sense of being part of a coherent plan, often acted independently of each other in a vacuum. The sheer scale of the Suvla operations and the relatively large distances involved exaggerated the communication problems, so that when it came to the further dissemination of orders to the battalions there was yet more confusion. Most received them far too late to plan their attacks properly, and some never received them at all. Also, hastily cobbled-together headquarters were staffed by officers with little relevant experience – although of course this statement could apply to most British formations in 1915, wherever they were serving, it was especially relevant to those that made up the benighted IX Corps. Almost no one knew what they were doing – not just the generals. All the Turks had to do was hold their ground.

The situation on 9 August grew increasingly threatening for the British brigades strewn across the Suvla area. Any advantage of surprise they may have had had been dissipated and it was evident that the Turkish rearguard action had achieved its aim of buying time for reinforcements to arrive. Worse still, a gap had opened in the British line in the plain and foothills to the north of Sulajik. Furthermore, as Lieutenant Cuthbert Llewelyn Allen discovered when he moved forward with his party of reinforcements for the 11th Manchesters, morale was deteriorating and there were many stragglers.

> The country through which we advanced was very open, small scrub and trees being dotted here and there. These afforded excellent places for snipers and very soon we began to receive their attention. This, together with land mines, which had to be watched for and avoided, also stray bullets coming across from every direction, made things somewhat unpleasant. Heavy firing was going on to our front and on both flanks. We met a continuous stream of wounded being helped or, in the case of those who could walk, making their way back to the dressing station. One thing I noticed here was that in a great number of cases, and especially of men who were not too seriously wounded and could walk, two or three men would accompany them: one carrying his rifle and equipment and the others helping him. This meant that for every actual casualty inflicted on us by the Turks, our fighting strength was reduced by two or three men. Naturally anything of that kind had to be stopped at once and orders were given that no one, unless actually wounded, would be allowed to pass back through our lines.[46]
>
> Lieutenant Cuthbert Llewelyn Allen, 11th Manchester Regiment, 34th Brigade, 11th Division

By 10 August the 10th and 11th Divisions were showing all the signs of being exhausted. Behind them the 53rd Division had begun landing on the night of 8 August but had been split up when some battalions were fed into action piecemeal on 9 August. Even worse, the 53rd Division was not really a division at all. Many of its best original battalions had already been sent to the Western Front and it had been despatched to Gallipoli without its allotted artillery – an absurd measure in a war in which artillery dominated the battlefield. Now the 158th and 159th Brigades were ordered to attack Scimitar Hill and the W Hills at 06.00 on the morning of 10 August, with neither rhyme nor reason shown in the manner of their deployment. Whatever potential the half-trained territorials may have had as soldiers was lost in attacks which took place in an atmosphere of complete disorder. One seething staff officer summed up the disaster as the battalions tore themselves to pieces on the Turkish defences:

> Orders for attack at 6 a.m. received at 4 a.m. Had a frightful rush to give our orders even to the 4th Cheshires and 4th Welsh commanding officers. None of them knew where their battalions were and we never saw anyone of the 7th Cheshires at all. At 6 a.m. the attack began in a very ragged sort of way and passed through the trenches held by the 34th and 32nd Infantry Brigades. The attack progressed very slowly and there was little cohesion. It was finally held up by about 8.35 a.m. About noon the 4th Welsh bolted and rout was stopped by me and some men on our left and right. Another assault ordered for 5 p.m. in spite of contrary opinions of Brigadiers of the 159th, 34th and 158th Infantry Brigades. It was quite impossible to do any more than tell the leading line to advance at 5 p.m. and leave the rest to luck. Cowan and I had to lead the firing line. The attack was badly supported and eventually failed. The troops occupied their original trenches held by the 32nd Infantry Brigade. Failure was caused by entire lack of organisation of the attack – hurry which was quite unnecessary – exhaustion of men who had no food and worst of all no water.[47]
>
> Captain Arthur Crookenden, Headquarters, 159th Brigade, 53rd Division

The result was the needless destruction of a division that should not have left Britain until it was ready for action. Given another six months' proper training it might have become a valuable formation in the battle against Germany on the Western Front. Instead it was cast away in just a day. The 53rd Division would henceforth be regarded as 'sucked oranges', as Stopford put it in discussions with Hamilton on 11 August;[48] a negligible force, largely discounted in the planning of future battles.

On the night of 10 August, the next division of inexperienced troops arrived for the slaughter – this time the 54th Division. They were moved forward to fill the large gaps in the British front line to the south of Kiretch Tepe. After another day had been wasted it was decided that the 163rd Brigade of the 54th Division would advance across the plain at 16.00 on 12 August to secure the ground and prepare the way for a major assault on the Tekke Tepe Range at dawn the next day. By now the story should be familiar.

> We suddenly got word about 3.30 p.m. that we were to move at 4 p.m. We had no water and very little food but a little extra came along with some rum which we all took neat. I enjoyed my share. Then the advance took place, our regiment in part of the front line. Talk of the fog of war. Nobody knows what is happening on their right or left and very soon all connection is lost. Our chaps did awfully well. As for my platoon, I absolutely love them and some of my men would insist on keeping with me. Well, a group of us got to a place in the advance which we decided to organise for defence. At first there were not many of us but driblets of men of all regiments in the brigade came and reinforced us. You should just hear us cheer and wave our helmets when two machine guns came up – entirely manhandled. Although under a decent fire everybody was as cool as a cucumber, cigarettes and thirst quenchers were passed round without distinction of rank, for on the battlefield the lot of officer and man are one. Oh it was fine. I had some narrow escapes. A shrapnel shell burst above and a pellet went right through the toe of my right boot and out at the side without so much as holing my sock. A bullet also just hit my finger and drew a little blood but that was all. I did not forget to thank God for my deliverance. Well then we had to dig ourselves in to escape the effects of the shrapnel which might be expected next morning. This digging is in reality 'scraping' with the entrenching tools which each man carries with him.[49]

Lieutenant Hubert Wolton, 1/5th Suffolk Regiment, 163rd Brigade, 54th Division

In the course of the advance a small party of men of the 1/5th Norfolk Regiment were cut off, chose to fight to the death and found the Turks more than willing to oblige. It was this incident that over the years created a ludicrous legend of the 'missing Norfolks' who were supposed to have mysteriously disappeared 'into a cloud'. The failure of the 163rd Brigade attack meant that the main action planned for dawn on 13 August was cancelled. Perhaps it was just as well, as none of the IX Corps divisions thrown together at Suvla were in a fit state for offensive action. If anything there was a threat that the Turks might breach the British line and imperil the whole operation. It was evident that a pause was needed before the next attack. Major General Walter Braithwaite passed on Hamilton's orders to Stopford.

Chief has decided that he will not call upon corps to make general attack at present. Therefore you must with utmost energy reorganise your troops and consolidate your present line. Take every opportunity to make as forward a line as possible and make that line impregnable. Chief relies on you to expedite by every means in your power the process of reorganisation and the thorough preparation of trenches, communications etc.[50]

Major General Walter Braithwaite, General Headquarters, MEF

Of course this gave the Turks yet more time to bring up reinforcements, consolidate their units and dig trenches. But there was no alternative.

So another couple of days passed. The important questions had been answered. The major hills and ridges surrounding the Suvla Plain would be under the control of the Turks. All that now remained to be resolved was the exact position of the trench lines weaving their way across the foothills and plains below them.

The next major attack by the IX Corps would take place along the knife-edge ridge of Kiretch Tepe. At last most of what remained of the 10th Division had been reassembled, with the 30th Brigade on the northern face of the ridge and the 31st Brigade on its southern slopes. Perversely, Stopford seems to have interpreted the words, 'Take every opportunity to make as forward a line as possible' to mean that Mahon should launch a full-scale assault on the Turkish forces on Kiretch Tepe and Kidney Hill, which ran down as a spur from the main ridge. But what would have been a laudable initiative with some hope of success a couple of days earlier was near suicide when the 10th Division attack went in supported by the 162nd Brigade of the 54th Division at 13.00 on 15 August. The Turks had been reinforced by several battalions from the 19th and 127th Regiments.

The exact strength of the enemy was not known, but there was abundant evidence that he had recently been substantially reinforced and that the bulk of his strength was on our southern side of the hill where he was not subjected to direct fire from HMS *Grampus*. It was believed that his trenches were located on the near slope of Kidney Hill, but it was impossible to be certain owing to the thickness of the scrub. The preparations for the attack having been completed, there was nothing to do but to sit down and wait. In order to fill in the time the company mess had a large meal at 11 a.m. – my first on the Peninsula – out of a Fortnum and Mason hamper which had just arrived. Tinned fruit, bottled asparagus, potted meat, dates, biscuits and so on; everything was devoured with the utmost celerity. During the meal we discussed the coming attack and arranged what was to be done with our effects if we were killed or wounded. I estimated for three casualties but was hooted down as a prophet of evil. No one guessed that by evening no survivors would be left to carry out our complicated testamentary dispositions.[51]

Second Lieutenant Ivone Kirkpatrick, 5th Royal Inniskilling Fusiliers, 31st Brigade, 10th Division

The attack was presaged by a bombardment, the effects of which were derisory.

If the fire had any effect it must have been to warn the Turk to rise from his siesta. At 1.15 we started off at a brisk walk. My platoon was on the extreme left, that is to say the highest up and nearest to the crest on our side of the hill. In front of us the ground undulated downwards for some 200 yards; then came an even stretch of some 800 yards running up to the foot of Kidney Hill. Gullies of irregular shape and size ran at right angles to our line of advance and the ground was covered with scrub, very thick and prickly in places, whilst here and there were bare patches of sand and rock. We came under fire at once. Owing to the invisibility of the enemy it was not practicable to retaliate with rifle fire and our only course was to push on. My chief care and anxiety was to convey this to the men and to keep my platoon in line with the rest of the company. This was not so easy as it sounds. In the first place the scrub and the broken nature of the ground made it impossible often to see more than two or three men on either side of one. Secondly the rate of advance varied necessarily in various parts of the line. Whilst a section were racing across a bare sandy patch, the men on each side of them would be slowly pushing their way through dense clumps of scrub. It was only by dint of much labour and running hither and thither that it was at all possible to keep in touch with one's platoon let alone the rest of the company.[52]

Second Lieutenant Ivone Kirkpatrick, 5th Royal Inniskilling Fusiliers, 31st Brigade, 10th Division

They had been advancing for about thirty minutes and had almost reached Kidney Hill, but the Turkish fire seemed to be increasing and it was at this point that Kirkpatrick ran out of luck.

Suddenly I felt a terrific blow on the left shoulder blade, as if someone had driven a golf ball into me at close range. I thought I had been shot from behind and looked round angrily for the careless fool, but I saw nobody. I was unable to go on, so I sat on the ground to examine the damage. I found that I had a puncture in front above my heart and concluded that the bullet had gone right through my lung. I had hardly sat down when I noticed that I seemed to be in an unhealthy spot and I started to crawl up the hill to my left. At once what seemed to be a heavy projectile struck me in the stomach and I sank to the ground. For a moment I felt weary and discouraged; it seemed the last straw and I thought all was up.[53]

Second Lieutenant Ivone Kirkpatrick, 5th Royal Inniskilling Fusiliers, 31st Brigade, 10th Division

Kirkpatrick already had two serious wounds, either of which could have proved fatal, and he was in an isolated position in the middle of a battlefield far from help. He had nothing to lose.

On further reflection I decided that it would be folly to give in and I cast about for means of escape. I remembered that our Medical Officer had warned us on no account to move if hit in the stomach, but it seemed certain death to stay where I was and I preferred to take my chance. As a preliminary I crawled into a hollow and tried to dress my wounds. The attempt was not a success, partly because my hands were shaking, but chiefly because it requires a high degree of skill to bandage one's own chest and stomach. I managed, however, to get a little iodine into the wounds.[54]

Second Lieutenant Ivone Kirkpatrick, 5th Royal Inniskilling Fusiliers, 31st Brigade, 10th Division

He believed that he had been hit by a Turkish sniper whom he imagined would be watching and waiting for a further chance to finish him off. He was in a truly awful situation.

It was quite hopeless to go back the way we had come. The whole area was swept with bullets and I should have been lucky to get through even if I had the strength. My only chance seemed to be to make for the crest of the hill on my left and hope that there were no Turks on the other side. A few yards from me lay a wounded soldier of my platoon. He started to crawl back to our trenches and I asked him to get me a stretcher later, if he could. He soon disappeared and I began my slow and painful journey to the top of the hill some 100 yards away. As I crawled over the rough ground I became weaker and weaker. Sometimes a bullet would hit the sand beside me and thinking that my sniper was after me I would scurry behind a rock or bush. These sudden efforts cost me so much that I could scarcely move. Soon I discarded my precious glasses, then my revolver, this very reluctantly, but I did not feel up to carrying it. It seemed that I would never reach the top; eventually I did so and had to face the problem of getting over the sky line. It would be a dangerous operation if my sniper friend was still watching me, but I decided to try it. After a rest I crawled the last few yards very slowly, then at the last moment got up, jinked quickly to the right and scrambled over. As I did so, I fancied I heard a bullet whistle by, but in the general din I was not sure. I laid down on a soft spot and waited.[55]

Second Lieutenant Ivone Kirkpatrick, 5th Royal Inniskilling Fusiliers, 31st Brigade, 10th Division

Kirkpatrick was eventually picked up by stretcher bearers from the Dublin Fusiliers who carried him back to the regimental aid post.

A Sergeant looked at my wounds. I asked him whether he thought they were mortal and he cheerfully replied that they were nothing at all. I was carried through the ranks of a whole battalion of Dublins waiting to attack. I tried to say a few words of encouragement to them, but I don't think that my 'speech before battle' sounded very convincing. After a short walk I found myself at a field dressing station half way down the hill in a little hollow, behind a rock. The stretcher was put down and the doctor examined my wounds. By this time I was in acute pain. A sort of violent cramp convulsed my stomach and I was unpleasantly conscious that all was not well with my left lung or shoulder. The doctor cut away most of my clothes and dressed the wounds; after which he gave me an injection of morphia and left me.[56]

Second Lieutenant Ivone Kirkpatrick, 5th Royal Inniskilling Fusiliers, 31st Brigade, 10th Division

The morphia did not seem to reduce significantly Kirkpatrick's bodily pain, but he found himself drifting off into unconsciousness which provided its own relief. Then began the long and painful journey along the benighted ridge of Kiretch Tepe.

I was awakened by hearing the Doctor say, 'He must take his chance!'
Two stretcher bearers took hold of my stretcher and carried me away.
It must then have been about 5 p.m. The journey was something of an
ordeal. On we went over the rough ground: sometimes a bearer would
stumble, sometimes let the stretcher drop. Occasionally they would
fail to clear a boulder which would hit the bottom of the stretcher. On
the way I was violently sick, all over my chest, as I could not move. My
wounds began to bleed again and I lay in a pool of greasy blood which
covered me from my helmet to my boots. It was over an hour before I
reached the beach.[57]

Second Lieutenant Ivone Kirkpatrick, 5th Royal Inniskilling Fusiliers, 31st Brigade,
10th Division

But he was still not safe. The beach areas were all under sporadic shell fire
and the medical arrangements were strained beyond breaking point by
the torrent of casualties pouring in for treatment. There was little time for
the doctors to do anything but basic triage: sort those who could benefit
from medical assistance from those for whom it was likely to be a waste of
time. The prognosis did not look good for Kirkpatrick.

I was placed in a marquee already filled with wounded. A doctor came
to look at me by the light of an oil lamp, tied a label on my coat and
ordered me to be evacuated. I was carried out and placed on the beach.
All around me were men on stretchers, groaning, shouting and cursing.
It was now dark. A Methodist chaplain with a white shaggy mane asked
me my religion. When I told him, he replied that it didn't make much
difference. 1 was getting rather short-tempered by then and said I
thought he was mistaken. He shook his head sadly and disappeared.[58]

Second Lieutenant Ivone Kirkpatrick, 5th Royal Inniskilling Fusiliers, 31st Brigade,
10th Division

But the good chaplain was wrong. Kirkpatrick was to be safely evacuated
aboard the hospital ship *Assaye* and would survive his ordeal. Behind him
the attack had spluttered out in abject failure. Initial gains by the Irish
battalions on the crest of the ridge were counterbalanced by the lack of
progress at Kidney Hill and, when the Turks vigorously counter-attacked
on 16 August, they were able to smash them back to the old front lines.
As at Helles and Anzac the front lines were not moving.

Hamilton realised the hopelessness of his position and on 17 August sent a cable to Kitchener detailing the course of operations up to that point and confessing failure. It finished up with a plea for yet more reinforcements that threw the future of the whole campaign into harsh relief.

> Unfortunately the Turks have temporarily gained the moral ascendancy over some of our new troops. If, therefore, this campaign is to be brought to an early and successful conclusion large reinforcements will have to be sent to me – drafts for the formations already here, and new formations with considerably reduced proportion of artillery. It has become a question of who can slog longest and hardest. Owing to the difficulty of carrying on a winter campaign, and the lateness of the season, these troops should be sent immediately. My British Divisions are at present 45,000 under establishment, exclusive of about 9,000 promised or on the way. If this deficit were made up, and new formations totalling 50,000 rifles sent out as well, these, with the 60,000 rifles which I estimate I shall have at the time of their arrival, should give me the necessary superiority, unless the absence of other enemies allows the Turks to bring up large additional reinforcements.[59]
>
> General Sir Ian Hamilton, Headquarters, MEF

It is noticeable that even this request has a caveat, showing that Hamilton had finally realised that the Turks found it far easier to reinforce their forces. Unless Kitchener responded quickly and positively then the Gallipoli adventure was drawing to a close. On the Western Front the Allies were in the throes of preparation for their autumn offensives, of which the British contribution was to be an attack on Loos commencing 25 September 1915. It is not therefore surprising that decisions were delayed and Hamilton only received an interim promise of 13,000 replacement drafts and 12,000 new troops. The writing was on the wall.

When judging the performance of the British at Suvla it is best to ignore the Australian perspective, which has been warped by their own awful trials in the August fighting and magnified by the great shibboleth of the attack at The Nek. The Australians looked down from the heights at Anzac and cruelly caricatured the British efforts as nothing more than sea bathing and drinking tea by the beaches. Some of the British units did mill about without purpose, but many others were engaged in vicious fighting against an invisible enemy who cut them down in swathes. The conditions they faced were a dreadful trial for barely trained soldiers caught up in a situation that was far beyond them. They often found themselves isolated in mere scrapes in the ground that provided minimal cover. It was too cold at night and far too hot during the day. Ravaged by a permanent thirst exacerbated by their physical efforts and the leaching effect of the cordite smoke, they were pinned down unable to move in the sweltering sun, with dust caked on their faces, their cracked dry lips black with blood. The IX Corps was thrown into battle long before it was ready, with incompetent commanders and preposterously optimistic plans which, despite the experience of the last four months, seemed to ignore the possibility of a potent Turkish resistance. And the IX Corps was not alone in its failure: the ANZAC Corps had also fallen short in its thrust from Anzac, while the VIII Corps had encountered disaster at Helles.

Above all when assessing the failure of IX Corps it is essential to ignore the self-serving assessments made by Hamilton and his senior staff officers such as Major Guy Dawnay:

> Our plans all succeeded, and worked out beyond expectation satisfactorily. But the task set to the New Army divisions was, as it turned out, rather beyond their powers, owing to the fact that their officers were not sufficiently trained. It is no one's fault – but officers can't be made good company leaders even after nearly a year. The result was that, though the New Army divisions were not opposed by any great force, and though they had practically no artillery against them, they could not get on quickly enough, and their advance hung fire.[60]
>
> Major Guy Dawnay, Headquarters, MEF

Dawnay after all had a vested interest in defending the integrity of the plan. Hamilton himself attributed failure to the combination of the incompetency of Stopford and his senior generals and the rawness of the troops that made up IX Corps. His assessment was cutting: 'Just as no man putteth new wine into old bottles so the combination between new troops and old generals seems to be proving unsuitable.'[61] From his perspective the 'old' generals lacked the guts and gumption that were required at Suvla. At the same time the young and inexperienced soldiers did not have the training, the knowledge or the self-confidence to push on regardless; easily dispirited, they were not tough enough to cope with the physical challenges.

As far as Hamilton and his staff were concerned they had nothing to reproach themselves about. Yet even well-led élite battalions in the peak of condition would have had trouble carrying out the operational orders issued by Hamilton's staff in the face of the Turks' robust opposition at Suvla. Ultimately, the plan was Hamilton's responsibility, but he found plenty of scapegoats and there was consequently a veritable cull of IX Corps senior officers. On 15 August Kitchener gave his sanction for the dismissal of Stopford himself and shortly afterwards arranged for Lieutenant General Julian Byng to come out from the Western Front to take over command of IX Corps. In the meantime Major General Henry de Beauvoir de Lisle was to take temporary command, having been replaced at 29th Division by Major General William Marshall. Lieutenant General Sir Bryan Mahon predictably objected to the appointment of de Lisle, who was junior to him, and he was therefore temporarily replaced by Brigadier General Felix Hill in command of 10th Division. Shortly afterwards Major General John Lindley gave up his command of the 53rd Division to be replaced by Major General Herbert Lawrence, while Major General Frederick Hammersley was replaced in command of the 11th Division by Major General Edward Fanshawe. Many of the brigadiers who had been found to lack the necessary qualities of command were also replaced. There is no doubt that these changes were justified, that the incumbents had failed, but was it really fair? The ultimate architect of their failure and disgrace, Sir Ian Hamilton, remained in command of the Mediterranean Expeditionary Force.

16

21 AUGUST 1915: A USELESS GESTURE

The battle of the 21st was a complete failure, except as proof that the
British race is not yet played out.[1]

Captain Stair Gillon, author, *The KOSB in the Great War, 1930*

A POINTLESS BATTLE is always tragic. Soldiers on both sides are killed,
maimed or mentally shattered, their families left distraught, but overshad-
owing everything is the depressing realisation that it was all for nothing.
And if there was ever a futile battle it was the assault at Suvla by IX Corps
on 21 August. All the issues of the August Offensive had already been
resolved. The British had secured a large base to facilitate their logistical organisation; but the Turks had confined them to the lower foothills
and remained inviolate on the high ridges that surrounded them. Given
the balance of forces available to the two sides, that was not going to
change whatever happened on 21 August. In these circumstances it was
perverse that Major General Beauvoir de Lisle decided on one last attack
with the intention of seizing the foothills of the Scimitar and W Hills,
thereby further securing the tentative British line snaking across the Suvla
Plain. These were in themselves worthwhile objectives; but did the plan
have any realistic chance of success? Hamilton should have stopped him,
but instead he stoked the fire and sent the 29th Division from Helles to
augment the forces available for the attack.

The plan, such as it was, was simple: the 29th Division would storm

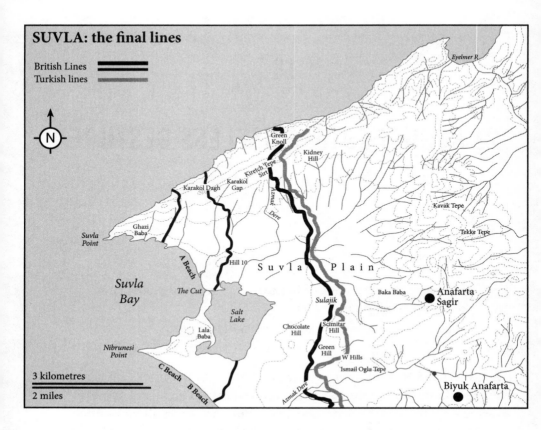

SUVLA: the final lines

British Lines
Turkish lines

N

Eyelmer R

Green Knoll
Kidney Hill
Kiretch Tepe Sirt
Karakol Dagh
Karakol Gap
Azmak Dere
Kavak Tepe
Ghazi Baba
Suvla Point
Tekke Tepe
Hill 10
Suvla Plain
Suvla Bay
A Beach
The Cut
Salt Lake
Sulajik
Baka Baba
Anafarta Sagir
Chocolate Hill
Scimitar Hill
Lala Baba
Nibrunesi Point
Green Hill
W Hills
C Beach
B Beach
Ismail Oglu Tepe
Azmak Dere
Biyuk Anafarta

3 kilometres
2 miles

Scimitar Hill while the 11th Division would attack the W Hills. These were two divisions in name, but both were shattered from their recent experiences. The 29th Division had been fighting without a break since 25 April, with few of its original regulars left, while the 11th Division had been flailing around Suvla Bay for the last two weeks, experiencing constant frustration and ever-mounting casualties. Meanwhile, to the south of the plain a composite brigade from the ANZAC Corps was to launch an attack on the diminutive Hill 60 feature which, despite its minimal height, was in a critical position standing guard over the junction between Anzac and Suvla. Kept safe behind Lala Baba would be the final reserves to arrive for the denouement of the summer campaign, the 2nd Mounted Division, made up of members of the dismounted territorial Yeomanry Regiments, of whom none apart from a few old Boer War hands lurking within their ranks had seen active service.

The preliminary bombardment commenced at 14.30 and lasted for just half an hour in order to try to limit the time available to the Turks to move up their reserves. There were a mere eighty-five guns and howitzers firing in support of IX Corps, with the assistance of the pre-dreadnought *Swiftsure*, three cruisers and a couple of destroyers. They had a severe shortage of ammunition, but they still managed to make an impact on the Turks, as exemplified by the experiences of Lieutenant Ismail Hakki Sunata of the 2/35th Regiment.

It was after one in the afternoon. Two howitzer shells whined over our heads. They fell on the 5th Company a little to our left. One shell fell in front of the trench, and another behind it. There was a tremendous explosion that filled the air with dust and smoke. Howitzers are different from other guns. We can't hear the gun fire. It's coming from somewhere on the right flank. The shells make a strange whistling noise as they pass over our heads. Then they land and explode with a great noise. They destroy where they land. May Allah help those who happen to be there. They are using Mestan Tepe as a sighting point. The trenches on the other side of it are under heavy artillery fire. This is turning into a major battle. The shelling goes on and on. Ismail Efendi says, 'Things are getting bad, I had better go!' He needs to be with his unit. The howitzer shells are coming so fast they seem like a constant thunder. Fortunately very few are falling in my area. The closest is about 30 metres away, on the far end of my platoon. From there to the left is dust, smoke, noise, confusion and terror. Nothing can be seen for the dust and smoke. I cannot see how far the bombarded area extends. A while later the 3rd Battalion companies who were in reserve began to arrive. They are sent to fill the gaps in the shelled trenches, but the shelling is still going on, so they pack into our trenches. There is hardly room to move. With great difficulty I was able to get some of them out and moving. Anyway, it is pointless to send more troops to be killed there. They can wait in readiness a little in the rear. If Allah was on the Muslims' side he would stuff the British guns with straw and their guns could not fire. He doesn't stuff them, and they fire as they wish. We don't have as many guns to fire as they do. With prayers and paeans the firing does not stop. Well, prayers are from desperation, what can we say?[2]

Lieutenant Ismail Hakki Sunata, 2nd Battalion, 35th Regiment, 12th Division, Fifth Army

In fact the British shelling appeared much worse than it was. Great sections of the Turkish lines were left relatively untouched, nothing hit the rear lines and the massed reserves went unscathed. Not enough guns, not enough shells – the situation was hopeless, as the assaulting British troops were to find out when they went over the top at 15.00.

> The air is full on every side with invisible death. 'Whizz! Phutt!' A bullet kicks up a little spray of dust from the dry grey earth underfoot, another and another to left and right. The sensation of terror is swallowed in an overwhelming conviction that the only possible course is forward – forward at any cost. That is what we have been telling ourselves all through the long waiting, and that is our only clear impression now. Forward – and we instinctively bend as one does to meet a hailstorm – and rush for it. Beyond the rough ploughed ground over which we are advancing lies a low, thick belt of brambles and bushes. Here, for a time, we can lie under cover and regain our breath for a second rush. The man on my left stumbles and comes down with a crash and a groan. Only an instinctive catch of the breath and the old conviction – forward at all costs – swamps all other sensations. Down we go behind the kindly shelter, and the bullets fly over us. Telling the men to be quiet, I crawl through the brush to try and find our direction for the next rush. Satisfied of our direction once more, our line bursts through the bushes and rushes over the open for the next hedge. A few piteous bundles behind us tell of our lessening strength – and now a new horror discloses itself, 'Boom! Whirrrr-crash!' On every side the ground is torn up by the heavy leaden pellets as the shrapnel bursts above us. And to left and right of me fresh sounds break out – dreadful human sounds which I won't describe.[3]

> Second Lieutenant Edmund Priestman, 6th York and Lancaster Regiment, 32nd Brigade, 11th Division

From the Turkish perspective it was a desperate fight, but a fight that they could win.

> Suddenly the howitzers shelling the trenches fell silent. The naval guns and shrapnel shelling the rear continued. When the howitzer fire stopped the dust and smoke over the trenches slowly began to clear. From the right the word was passed by mouth: 'The enemy have risen to the attack, let the left flank take care!' The news came from Kiretch Tepe. Indeed, behind the slowly clearing dust and smoke, from our

position we began to see masses of British advancing. We immediately opened fire on them from the flank. The enemy is not attacking our front, but that of the units to our left. Our flanking fire is very effective. As the dust and smoke cleared from over them the units to our left also opened fire. Now it's up to the infantry. All the reserves and other idle forces began to move in that direction, towards the area under attack. The infantry fire is getting stronger and stronger. At this time I heard that Rustem's Company Commander had been seriously wounded. A howitzer shell landed next to a squad's trench and exploded. All the soldiers in the trench were buried. The excitement mounts, and we are consumed by anxiety and worry. I doubt the enemy can succeed when all is up to the infantry rifles. But I don't know how much damage the artillery fire did. The British keep coming. We see this and fire incessantly.[4]

Lieutenant Ismail Hakki Sunata, 2nd Battalion, 35th Regiment, 12th Division, Fifth Army

To the south of the 11th Division, the 29th Division was collectively demonstrating in front of Scimitar Hill that experience counted for little in such a doomed set of circumstances. The 1st Royal Inniskilling Fusiliers and 1st Border Regiment had between them managed to gain a tentative foothold on top of Scimitar Hill, only to find themselves under severe enfilading fire from the Anafarta Spur. Backwards and forwards went the battle, momentary triumphs followed by chastening retreats back down the hill when the pressure became too much. At 16.00 de Lisle decided to send forward his last reserves, the 2nd Mounted Division. They had been relatively safe behind Lala Baba, but now the foolishness of that deployment was laid bare. To get forward to Scimitar Hill they would have to advance across the wide open spaces of the Salt Lake in full view of the Turkish artillery. These Yeomanry soldiers' conversion into infantry had been hasty; indeed, they had only been issued with infantry pattern webbing and equipment a few days before. The 1st County of London Yeomanry (Middlesex Hussars) would lead the advance. At least the men set off with a jaunty tune.

In my troop we had been rather proud of a mouth organ band which had produced some amazing orchestral effects and we had set our hearts on going into action on the first occasion to its music. Unfortunately, having to act as Adjutant, I was unable to march with my men, but when the regiment was drawn up to take the lead as the first line of the reserve to sweep on towards Chocolate Hill, I was delighted to hear the sound of the familiar mouth organ. The *chef d'orchestre* was a certain trooper who rejoiced in the name of 'Gunboat Smith' and enjoyed no small reputation in the regiment by reason of the fact that he had acted as trainer to the famous boxer of that name. 'Gunboat' accordingly struck up, and it was positively to the sound of music that this troop of the Middlesex Hussars went for the first time into battle.[5]

Captain William Wedgwood Benn, 1st County of London Yeomanry, 4th Brigade, 2nd Mounted Division

Of course many of the men were nervous. This was their first time in action. Initially nothing much happened as they trudged slowly across the dried lake bed.

After about half-an-hour's progress we reached the enemy's shrapnel, through which, of course, we were bound to pass if we were to attain Chocolate Hill. Casualties began, but our orders were strict, and forbade us to stop for anyone. When men fell they had to be left for the stretcher parties which were following. Suddenly I saw with horror my troop hit by a shell and eight men go down. The rest were splendid. They simply continued to advance in the proper formation at a walk, and awaited the order, which did not come for another quarter-of-an-hour, before breaking into the double. Some men exhibited extraordinary calm. I remember one picked up a tortoise, surprised to see it running wild, and another, an NCO, observing a man drop his rations, bent and gathered them up for him – an act which just brought him in reach of a splinter which wounded him![6]

Captain William Wedgwood Benn, 1st County of London Yeomanry, 4th Brigade, 2nd Mounted Division

Visually the scene resembled a Napoleonic battlefield, with the men laid out in vast formation walking slowly to an all too obvious fate as a mass of exploding shells engulfed the head of the column. For the Turkish artillery officers the British presented a ridiculously easy target. First they ranged on the head of the column but then they redoubled their efforts to create a wall of shells that every squadron following had no choice but to walk through. The open plain was devoid of cover; once they had started the troops had no option but to plod on.

The first shell I remember seeing burst a little over to my left nearly smashing an ambulance party with stretchers – the next thing I saw was one of our staff captains double up then run towards the ambulance to be attended to – then our Colonel dropped with a bullet through his jaw. After that shells and bullets began to burst and spit amongst us properly and we knew we were copping it hot and strong. First one poor fellow would double up and fall then another poor chap would collapse all in a heap. I suddenly found that we were all at the double though as far as I had heard, no order had actually been given. There are one or two more incidents which still stand out in my mind – one was the bursting of a shell a little to my right scattering bullets right through us. It was from this shell that most of the casualties in my troop were made and I distinctly remember ducking under a piece of it which ricked from the sand, sang just over me hitting someone on the left flank and smashing his rifle which was held up in front of his face to protect him – he came through unhurt. Another thing I remember was getting caught with some part of my equipment in some bushes and how bad tempered I got (to say the least of it) because I thought it would prevent me keeping up with my pals. I also remember how fearful the desire seemed to want to lie down behind each bush or tuft of grass to take useless cover. In fact most of us did start to get down in one place where the shells were falling thickest but I think it was more through fatigue than anything else. However we had hardly touched the ground when our Adjutant, running up from the rear, yelled, 'Come on boys, it's worse if you lie down!' So off we went again until we reached the safety under cover of Chocolate Hill. This was our baptism of fire which had to be done in cold blood because the enemy were absolutely invisible and we had no chance to get our own back in any way.[7]

Lieutenant Harold Davis, 1st Royal Gloucester Hussars, 1st Brigade, 2nd Mounted Division

Finally, as the Yeomanry approached Chocolate Hill, they received the orders to advance at the double. This was easier said than done.

No confusion or shouting, just a grim determination on everyone's face, dripping with sweat and not a few with streams of blood. Now and again a hoarse shout from our officer to extend and not to get bunched up. The running with our pack was difficult. Across ploughed fields we went, jumping over ditches and trenches, almost falling exhausted on the other side amongst the dead and wounded.[8]

Corporal Colin Millis, 2nd County of London Yeomanry, 5th Brigade, 2nd Mounted Division

When they reached the cover and respite offered by the bulk of Chocolate Hill they rested for a brief while before launching attacks round either side of the hill. The 1st County of London Yeomanry were directed to the right, with Scimitar Hill and then the W Hills their ambitious objectives.

Up to that moment I can remember nothing but wild excitement and supreme buoyancy as of one living in oxygen. During the next advance we had no shell fire to meet, only rifle and machine gun – a new experience for us, and one which inspired more fear than it really merited. We ran across the first field and jumped into a line of trenches – supports of our own, then out again and forward into the next trench, leaping in on top of the men of the Division ahead of us, whose reserves we were. They nearly all, I recollect, shouted to us as we approached to take cover and get down, but almost always tried to wave us away from the particular part they themselves were occupying. The fact was they were packed tight, I should say one man to every 15 inches.[9]

Captain William Wedgwood Benn, 1st County of London Yeomanry, 4th Brigade, 2nd Mounted Division

They made a break forward advancing on to the slopes of Scimitar Hill. Here they completely misjudged the situation.

As far as we could see it provided good cover, for there appeared to be a number of reserves lying there in perfect quiet and safety. Out we sprang with a shout and ran forward to the selected spot, only to find that it was under brisk machine gun fire. The reserves were quiet indeed – for they were dead! We lay down flat, and then crawled a little higher up the hill, hearing all the time the terrifying rattle of a Maxim which we, of course, thought was the cause of all the killing. We assured one another for our better comfort that it must be one of our own guns covering the advance, and this, in fact, turned out to be true. We saw nothing for it now but to get up and shift our position. For one thing, the bushes in front of us were alight and the fire was steadily advancing on to the corpses at our side.[10]

Captain William Wedgwood Benn, 1st County of London Yeomanry, 4th Brigade, 2nd Mounted Division

The burning hills brought a whole new horror to a battlefield that was already full of terrors.

> A long belt of gorse and scrub had caught alight with the shells which very quickly spread. There was no help for it but to push through and chance to luck, which I did, but came out the other side like a nigger and almost choking with the smoke. An awful death trap this was and it claimed many victims, the poor devils simply dropped in dozens and were speedily burnt with the flames – a sight that I shan't forget.[11]
>
> Corporal Colin Millis, 2nd County of London Yeomanry, 5th Brigade, 2nd Mounted Division

That desperate night saw much confusion. It was extremely difficult for officers and NCOs to maintain good order with men tried beyond endurance in a situation for which their meagre training had not prepared them. Soon panic set in as the Yeomanry tumbled back on to Green Hill.

> A young officer ran along the trench shouting that the orders were to retire at once. I can remember how foolish I thought his conduct, for the effect on our troops under fire for the first time and completely fatigued by ten hours of fighting, was of the worst. However, I had to carry the order to the regiment on our left, and gradually the whole of what remained of the brigade was withdrawn, and began to form up in a road some two or three hundred yards to the rear. I was then sent back to inform whatever troops I could find on our right that the brigade was moving. For me this was the most unpleasant hour I had had during the day. The moon seemed suddenly to be extinguished, and the rifle fire to redouble in vigour and the flashes all to become visible, though up to then I had hardly noticed them. I was suddenly convinced that the Turks now were actually coming on. I found the regiment on our right, and shouted out my instructions in much the same style as the officer I had been blaming! I was pulled together by the conduct of a very young person in charge, who rose from the trench and most strenuously damned me for giving orders direct to his men, adding that as they did not belong to our brigade he intended to ignore the orders and remain where he was. I shall always admire that exhibition of grit.[12]
>
> Captain William Wedgwood Benn, 1st County of London Yeomanry, 4th Brigade, 2nd Mounted Division

But the night was terrifying for the Turks too. Not sure what was going on, they feared a renewed night attack, or perhaps a British breakthrough.

It is getting dark. With the ceasing of the artillery fire some calm has descended on the scene. But the infantry fire continues. The sound of the artillery has given way to other sounds. From our left come shouts, moans, groans and screams, and orders are given. The rear of the trenches is full of wounded and moaning men; there are dead also. In the twilight some are coming, some are going, total confusion. Nothing can be understood of what is happening. A medical orderly has been raked across the stomach at the level of his navel by a machine gun, his wounds are exposed. Sergeant Hakki, whom I first met in the 6th Company, is badly wounded. I went to him at once. 'Don't forget me, avenge me on the British, I am going. Give me your blessing!' he said. I immediately sent him with some soldiers from his company to the aid station. Will the poor fellow survive, I wonder? I doubt it. A clean, innocent, honourable soldier of this army. What a pity. There are many dead and wounded. The enemy wounded are also calling out in front. The enemy was completely repulsed. The night passed with carrying the wounded and burying the dead. We were all awake. The day's events had made us so nervous we had forgotten even what sleep was.[13]

Lieutenant Ismail Hakki Sunata, 2nd Battalion, 35th Regiment, 12th Division, Fifth Army

Of the 14,300 men who had taken part in the Allied attack, 5,300 were killed, wounded or missing. Ultimately, the 11th Division, the 29th Division and the 2nd Mounted Division had, like so many divisions before them, been sacrificed on the Suvla Plain for nothing.

Only in the battle for Hill 60, near the tenuous junction with Anzac, was there the possibility of a worthwhile gain. But even here the name of the hill indicates to what a low ebb British ambition had sunk. For Hill 60 was a mere hillock that had gone unnoticed in the early planning of the Suvla landings. Now that everything else had turned to dust, that small eminence seemed crucial. The remnants of numerous battalions were therefore scraped up from the battered brigades of the ANZAC Corps to launch an assault which would begin at 15.30 on 21 August, half an hour after the main attack. The task of the depleted 4th Australian Brigade, reduced to just 1,400 men, was particularly eye-catching. They had to attack from Damakjelik Bair, across the shallow valley of Kaiajik Dere and up on to Hill 60 itself, all the while enfiladed from the Turkish trenches on

Hill 100 at the head of the valley. Although they would be assisted by elements of various British, Indian and New Zealand units, the experienced Australians were not impressed.

> On August 7 we could have taken Hill 60 and Hill 100 almost without a casualty. Now that the Turks had thoroughly entrenched Hill 60, garrisoned it strongly and arranged machine guns to sweep every foot of its surface, we were to storm it. What chance would the Turks have had of taking Hill 92 from us by direct attack? None whatever; just as much chance as we had of taking Hill 60 from them. The Australian attacking force – consisting of 250 men each from the 13th and 14th Battalions – was to make a sortie from the left of the 13th's line, form up behind a bushy hill which partly masked our line from Hill 60, and charge over the crest of this hill in three waves. The distance to be covered varied from 200 to 250 yards. While this would have been an impossible task for troops 'in the pink', four out of five of those chosen for the attack were sick and weary men.[14]
>
> Captain Henry Loughran, 14th (Victoria) Battalion, 4th Brigade, NZ&A Division, AIF

When the time came to launch the attack at 15.30 it was Lieutenant Ford of the 13th Battalion who led the first wave of 150 men, with the cry of 'Come on!' as he leapt over the parapet.

> The men rose as one and rushed to the attack. The severity of the naval bombardment led us to believe that no Turk would be left alive on the position; but as soon as we topped the rise a merciless hail of rifle and machine gun fire met us, and men fell quickly. A rush down the slope, over a dry gully and up the other slope, I found myself at the first objective, a ridge, with six men. I sent Sergeant Norman McDonald to the right and another to the left to see if any more had got over – one could not see for the scrub and broken ground. McDonald found ten on the right, and about 24 reported on the left – 40 of us out of 150 in about a 200 yards rush. The Turks kept up a very heavy fire, making it impossible to advance with so few.[15]
>
> Lieutenant Hubert Ford, 13th (New South Wales) Battalion, 4th Brigade, NZ&A Division, AIF

All they could do was wait for the reserve waves – but then again could they get across that awful open ground? As it was, very little had changed, with the Turks on Hill 100 still enfilading their line of approach to Hill 60.

Major Sydney Herring, in command of the third wave, had watched the
first two waves go over. Now it was his turn.

> We were heavily laden, this made a quick dash impossible and we only
> got half way across when we were held up by enemy machine gun fire.
> I decided to stay where we were for half an hour to give the machine
> gun fire a chance of dying down and then make a surprise dash for our
> objective. This wait was one of the worst I have ever experienced. There
> we were crouched behind some very indifferent cover in No Man's
> Land, half way between our front line and our objective. Our dead
> and wounded were lying around us in all directions, and to add to the
> horror of the situation our shells had set fire to the scrub and some of
> our wounded were being burnt to death before our eyes. After half an
> hour had elapsed I said, 'Come on, we will give it a go!' and dashed out.
> There were two slight depressions leading towards Hill 60 and by lucky
> chance I chose the one nearest to the Turks and it so happened that this
> particular depression was slightly sheltered from their fire. Of those that
> took this route the majority reached their objective, whilst the ones
> that took the other route nearly all became casualties. I managed to
> reach the position our first wave had captured with all that was left of
> the third wave – about fifty in all.[16]
>
> Major Sydney Herring, 13th (New South Wales) Battalion, 4th Brigade, NZ&A
> Division, AIF

They could go no further. They began digging in. And there they stayed.
A volunteer died trying to take back a message to Hill 92 to report their
parlous position. That night Captain Henry Loughran went out looking
for wounded.

> The Turks were now shelling the hill and soon the scrub was alight in
> several places. This was an advantage from the point of view of the
> medical personnel, for it gave us a smoke screen behind which we could
> work, even on the frontal slope, though there was a fair amount of risk
> from chance bullets. It was, however, by no means an advantage to
> those wounded who were unable to crawl away from the flames and for
> some time all that my stretcher bearers did was to carry away wounded,
> as rapidly as possible, from this zone. Dead men we left where they
> were and, as the flames reached them, the cartridges in their pouches
> popped off and occasionally a bomb exploded. If any living wounded

were burnt, they were unconscious, as we heard no cries of pain from the flames.[17]

Captain Henry Loughran, 14th (Victoria) Battalion, 4th Brigade, NZ&A Division, AIF

They had gained a small footing on their objective but the Turks merely fell back to another line of trenches. They still controlled the top of Hill 60. That night the calls for reinforcements grew so insistent that the 18th Battalion of the newly landed 5th Australian Brigade was thrown into action early on the morning of 22 August. These men were fresh, but correspondingly untested. Most of them had no idea until the last minute that they were going into an attack but thought they were merely taking over a section of the line. Corporal Rex Boyden found it difficult to forget his traumatic experiences as they attacked Hill 60.

> We were moving along through a Gurkhas' trench and were ordered to fix bayonets, so we knew that there was to be a charge. Having been marching from 12 o'clock we were extremely tired and thirsty, for we had had nothing to eat or drink from the evening before, so we did not feel much like charging. Well, about 6 o'clock the charge was ordered, and we all rushed forward. We captured two trenches and were charging forward to capture the third when I was hit.[18]

Corporal Rex Boyden, 18th (New South Wales) Battalion, 5th Brigade, 2nd Australian Division, AIF

Boyden would lie out in the open for a day and a half, rendered immobile by a severe stomach wound, but miraculously he suffered only a few slight grazes as bullets splattered all around him, even ripping through his clothes.

> It was simply wonderful how God watched over me. I could realise His presence so strong with me that all fear was taken away, although shells and shrapnel were bursting within a few yards of me and bullets flying everywhere. I couldn't possibly move at the time, and it was fortunate I didn't, for I was behind a dead man and he was sheltering me from the deadly fire of the Turks. I could hear the bullets pelting him while I was lying there. All day long I was looking forward to the night when I thought it would be dark enough to allow the stretcher bearers to come for me. But it was not to be, for it was bright moonlight, and none came to fetch me, so I lay there until the moon went down, about an hour before daybreak next morning. I managed to crawl about 25 yards, which took me nearly an hour, and brought me near to a part of our trench. I

couldn't go any further but shouted out for a stretcher bearer, and one of the New Zealanders pulled me over the parapet into the trench.[19]

Corporal Rex Boyden, 18th (New South Wales) Battalion, 5th Brigade, 2nd Australian Division, AIF

For all their efforts, the junction between Anzac and Suvla was still under threat. It was decided to make one last effort on 27 August. A scratch force of Australians, New Zealanders and the 5th Connaught Rangers charged forward once again at around 16.00. These battered units made varying degrees of progress, some managing to get into the Turkish lines and press them back from the southern slopes. In desperation the 10th Light Horse were called forward. They were still suffering the aftereffects of their disastrous charge at The Nek and had just under 200 men when they charged forwards at 01.00 on 28 August. Against all the odds they gained a little more ground, but could they keep it?

The Turks made a very determined counter-attack from the right and right rear of our position. They came in waves, crying, 'Allah, Allah!' and at one time we could see a German officer standing on the parapet of their trench urging the men on, but he was soon put out of action. They came right up to the muzzles of our rifles, and were only kept out by rapid rifle fire and bomb-throwing. They managed to smash down our first barricade, but another one was built at the next traverse and a stand was made from there. Fortunately many of the enemy bombs had long time fuses, and we had time to catch a number of the bombs and throw them back before they exploded. Of course some were missed, exploded among our men and did a great deal of damage.[20]

Corporal Henry Macnee, 10th (Western Australia) Light Horse, 3rd Light Horse Brigade, AIF

In charge of blocking off the communication trench leading to the rest of the Turkish trenches was Second Lieutenant Hugo Throssell. He stood watch in the inky darkness while his men hurriedly filled sandbags to create a barricade. Before they could finish the job the Turks made their first tentative move, creeping along the trench to try to locate the Australian position. Throssell is reputed to have calmly shot the first five to appear. Then the real fighting began.

The Turks are fine fighters and extremely brave men, and all that night they stood one side of this barrier within five yards of us trying to bomb us out. The Turks counter-attacked three times; that does not sound very much, but I can assure you that with the Turks within five yards of you with only a couple of feet sandbag barrier between, and with hundreds of them coming at you with fixed bayonets in the front, the chances of coming through that ordeal alive are very remote.[21]

Second Lieutenant Hugo Throssell, 10th (Western Australia) Light Horse, 3rd Light Horse Brigade, AIF

The Turks were determined to regain their viewpoint and attacked throughout the night. It was a desperate fight with no quarter given by either side. Sergeant John McIlwain was sent forward with the meagre reserves of the 5th Connaught Rangers.

I take my party over the top in rear and with about twenty men occupy portion of trench nominally Australian as many wounded Anzacs are there. Not long there when Turks bomb us from front and left flank, also snipe us along the trench from left. My men with few exceptions panic-stricken. By rapid musketry we keep down the bombing. My rifle red almost with firing. By using greatcoats we save ourselves from bombs. Turks but 10 yards away drive us back foot by foot. I have extraordinary escapes. Two men killed beside me in the narrow trench and I am covered head-to-foot in blood. Casualties alarming and we should have fought to the very end but for the 18th Australian Battalion, a party of whom jumped in amongst us and held the position until reinforced. When able to look about me I find but two Rangers left with me. The rest killed, wounded, or ran away before or after the Anzacs had come. Struggling all night: consolidating, firing, and looking out. Anzacs abusive for the Rangers having lost trench. The most awful night of my life.[22]

Sergeant John McIlwain, 5th Connaught Rangers, 29th Brigade, 10th Division

So many bombs were thrown by both sides that the Turks would later call the Hill 60 feature 'Bomba Tepe'. One of Throssell's men, Corporal 'Sid' Ferrier, caught a bomb which exploded in his hand before he could hurl it back. He is reputed to have then continued throwing bombs using his other hand before walking back to the aid post. Throssell managed to hold out, but just before dawn the Turks made their final great effort.

Then they crawled out of the trenches and came straight at us. In the dim light we could see them against the skyline. I passed the word to our fellows, and when the first Turks got within 10 yards we cheered and shouted, and, standing up in the trenches, started firing as fast as we could. There was no thought of cover. We just blazed away until the rifles grew red-hot and jammed, then we picked up the rifles the wounded or killed men had left.[23]

Second Lieutenant Hugo Throssell, 10th (Western Australia) Light Horse, 3rd Light Horse Brigade, AIF

Corporal Ferrier had his shattered arm amputated, but would die of tetanus on the hospital ship and was buried at sea on 9 September. Throssell would be awarded the VC. The long-awaited dawn, however, brought bitter disappointment. Although they had captured the Turkish trenches, thereby depriving them of the ability to observe closely the junction of Anzac and Suvla in the Susak Kuyu sector, the morning light revealed that the Turks were still in control of a trench system on the slightly higher round summit which in turn overlooked the Turkish lines on the northern slopes. The attacks had drained the last of the offensive vitality from the ANZAC Corps. Further attacks would not happen – at least in the short term. As it was, both sides could look out over their own lines but could see little of their opponent's hinterland. Both sides, therefore, had good reason to want to advance just a little further so Hill 60 would remain a bitterly contested battleground.

THESE LAST AUGUST ATTACKS on the foothills of Scimitar Hill, the W Hills and Hill 60 were never likely to result in significant gains. The Turks had plenty of troops, access to reserves, adequate artillery support and a clear line of retreat to ranks of trenches stretching back up the hills and ridges that surrounded Suvla. As localised tactical objectives their capture made sense, for that would strengthen the British positions. Scimitar Hill and the W Hills would certainly also provide a better launching point for the next offensive – in the unlikely event of tens of thousands more troops being assigned for the Gallipoli campaign. However, the desirability of limited objectives should not have been the impetus for launching attacks with minimal chance of success – all that was achieved was an inflated casualty list. These were pointless attacks and if they typified any British trait it was a lunatic persistence in the face of the obvious.

17

SHOULD THEY STAY OR SHOULD THEY GO?

We have four enemies to contend with – the Bosches, the Turks, the Bulgars and His Majesty's Government – and the last is the most deadly. It is deplorable that it should be so.[1]

Major General Sir Charles Caldwell, Director of Military Operations, War Office

THE TRADITIONAL ANALYSIS of the Anzac and Suvla operations of August 1915 has presented the fighting as a near-run thing, in which the British were only thwarted by a mixture of bad luck, poor command and control at Suvla and the genius of Mustafa Kemal. This ignores clear evidence that once again blind optimism had stood in the place of realistic operational planning.

We have already examined and found wanting the plans for the night operations out of Anzac on 6 August; we have also commented on the confused planning process that fatally blurred the focus of the Suvla landings and on the poor standards of leadership that helped stall the operations. But these operations only represented the first stage of a four-stage campaign, in which every phase needed to be successful in order to justify the deployment of so many men and resources away from the fulcrum of the war on the Western Front. Remember: the overall objective of the campaign was nothing less than the removal of Turkey from the war. The capture of Sari Bair Ridge was just a stepping stone; from there the Allies would have to take control of the Third Ridge and Mal

Tepe. Somehow, then, enough troops would have to be found to storm the Turkish defences on the Kilid Bahr Plateau which guarded the Narrows. Then the fleet would have to penetrate the Sea of Marmara – something for which there seems to have been no realistic advance planning. Next the *Goeben*, the *Breslau* and the Turkish fleet would have to be summarily despatched, before Constantinople itself could be threatened. Would the Turks surrender? If not, and they prolonged the fight, then the fleet would soon find itself isolated, possibly even condemned to a humiliating retreat.[2] The truth is that the whole campaign was ill-conceived, with minimal chances of success, whether there was an attack on 25 April, 4 June or 21 August. Given that, perhaps the major criticism of Sir Ian Hamilton should be for his refusal to accept the military logic of the situation and for his willingness to push on regardless. One thing is certain: the failure of the August Offensive made the likelihood of a clear-cut military success in Gallipoli an impossibility. Second Lieutenant Raymond Weil pondered gloomily on grimness of the situation at Helles.

> The whole terrain was scored, mined, criss-crossed with traps, barred with skilfully concealed barbed wire; air reconnaissance photographs revealed to us new earthworks, lines of defence and recently established gun batteries, while we just stayed put where we were. Systematically sprinkling with shells the trenches and works of the enemy and in counter-battery fire on irritating Turkish batteries without managing to muzzle them completely. Our infantry dug saps on saps, moving forward bit by bit the front lines, every day getting closer to the Turkish lines until they were almost touching. As a result our barrage fire was almost impossible. In all, although we had confidence in our High Command we felt that we were no longer being directed; that there was a total lack of unity of purpose and as a result of all this our expedition was dormant.[3]
>
> Second Lieutenant Raymond Weil, 39th Régiment d'Artillerie, 1st Division, CEO

The darkening scene was greatly complicated by the wavering of the French government, which promised four divisions of reinforcements for a possible Asiatic landing and then reversed the decision. General Joseph Joffre, the Commander in Chief of the French Army on the Western Front, had insisted that no further troops could be sent until after his September offensives there. The French commitment to Gallipoli began to ebb away as they switched their focus to countering the threat to Serbia, under attack from a combined Austo-Hungarian and German Army and further threatened from the rear by the mobilisation the Bulgarian Army in September 1915. This, coupled with the failure of Greece to enter the war in accordance with its treaty obligations to Serbia, meant that it would fall to Britain and France to provide an expeditionary force to defend Serbia. Suddenly Gallipoli was no longer a priority. Reinforcements must be sent to Salonika, forming a new front. Kitchener reacted quickly, ordering two divisions to be sent from Gallipoli. Thus the French 2nd Division and the 10th Division left the Peninsula for good in late September. In October hostilities commenced against Bulgaria. As in Gallipoli, there would be much confusion over the purpose, level of commitment and leadership of the Salonika force. Nothing had changed in the irrational strategic policy directions emanating from the respective governments of Britain and France in 1915. Hamilton railed against the decisions, but to no effect. He had had his chance.

THE TROOPS ON THE PENINSULA had lost any remaining faith in the future of their campaign. All they could do was sit in their trenches and think of what might have been. Many of their suppositions were disturbingly unrealistic, showing that they had not learnt any lessons on the superiority of the Turkish tactical position, the hardiness of their troops, the solidity of their leadership and their ease of access to reserves that could quickly reduce any small success of the Allies to dust with one well-timed counter-attack. Major Cecil Allanson was one such; his views combine a depressing realism with pure fantasy.

> Generally, it would look now as if things were at a standstill and deadlock. It will cost us thousands if we are to break through the Turkish trenches which now envelop us and it will cost them more considerably, I trust, if they try to break through us. Winter is approaching: the weather at night is getting very cold, we hear no breath of fitting us out for the winter, and we shall have terrible sickness if they do not. I have no idea what the future holds forth, what our subsequent movements may be. I can only speak of the narrow front we hold, and one knows little of what goes on elsewhere. We have had our chance here, and we have missed it. Towering above us is the

Sari Bair Ridge, on which we should be safely ensconced and are not, and had we held it Achi Baba and Krithia must have fallen. I never look up to those rugged heights without a sigh of bitter regret.[4]

Major Cecil Allanson, 1/6th Gurkha Rifles, 29th Indian Brigade

It is tempting to see the fate of Lieutenant Charles Lister as somehow symbolic of the campaign history: stationed at the British Embassy in Constantinople, he was present at the genesis of the war; then he was one of the happy band sailing to adventure with the RND in March 1915; he was wounded three times during the fruitless trench warfare at Helles; now as all hope faded he was fighting his own final battle aboard the hospital ship *Gascon*. Lister was as chipper as ever when he wrote home to his father, Lord Ribblesdale, on 26 August to tell him of his latest wounds.

Just think, I have been wounded once more, the third time. We were in a trench, observing the Turkish trenches, when suddenly they fired some shells into our trenches. I went along to see what had happened, got my people back into a bit of a trench they had had to leave, then went down the trench, thinking the show was over, and then got it, being struck in the pelvis and my bladder being deranged, and slight injuries in the legs and calves. I have been operated on, but am sketchy as to what has been done. I am on a hospital ship, comfy enough, but feeling the motion of it a good deal, and I have to be in bed and cannot change my position. The hours go slowly, as one does not feel very much up to reading. However, I got to sleep all right. I feel this will be a longish job, and I don't know where I shall do my cure – perhaps Alexandria. My doctor is quite happy at the way things are going. The shell that hit me killed one man and wounded the others. Forgive this scrawl, but it's not easy to write.[5]

Lieutenant Charles Lister, Hood Battalion, 1st Naval Brigade, RND

Sadly, the next letter to his father was from the hospital ship chaplain on 29 August.

He had very skilled attention and very careful nursing while on board, and was, I know, a wonderful patient. He never complained or even spoke of his wound, and if he had pain he bore it very bravely and patiently. But I believe that he did not have too much pain. We talked together sometimes, but he was easily tired, and one could not stay with him long. My great regret is that I did not know yesterday that he was so much worse until rather late, and when I went to see him he was unconscious. It is seldom comparatively that one sees a man in such command of himself, and so controlled. The books at his bedside spoke for his literary taste and the day before he died I lent him a copy of the poems of Rupert Brooke whom we both knew. As I write we are waiting for the boat to take his body ashore at Mudros, where the burial will take place tomorrow. He will lie almost within sound of the heavy guns.[6]

Chaplain Mayne, HMHS *Gascon*

The chaplain responsible for that burial was none other than Ernest Raymond, the man who would subsequently become the high priest of Gallipolian romanticism with the publication of his much-acclaimed novel *Tell England* in 1922. Here he had to perform the last rites as he supervised the burial of one of the *beaux sabreurs* he so revered.

As burial officer I went down to the little wooden jetty to receive them. They were lifted from a steam pinnace on to the jetty, each wrapped up in a grey army blanket which, holding tight to his figure, gave him the shape of an embalmed Egyptian. Each had pinned on to his breast some available scrap of paper, giving his name, regiment and religion, and no more. The Corporal in charge of my burial party said, 'One of 'em's an officer, Sir!' and pointed to the longest figure of all; officers having to be buried in a different part of a cemetery from Other Ranks; so retaining their class distinction beyond the grave. With my record book in my hand I went to the officer's body to enter his name. The paper pinned on to his breast chanced to be an envelope snatched in an orderly room or other office; and I read, 'On His Majesty's Service. Lieut., the Hon. Charles Lister.' For Charles Lister and his companions in death a GS wagon drawn by two mules waited by the jetty. I sat with them in the wagon, and so did the Corporal and his burial party, as we jolted to the cemetery. We and the dead were the whole company. Our little army cemetery on Mudros East lay far behind the hills that rolled up from the great Lemnos harbour and held the white-tented hospitals in line abreast. It was a bare and lonely little acre on a stony plain within a fence of barbed wire. Of course there was no firing party or Last Post; only a silence among the empty hills.[7]

Chaplain Ernest Raymond, HMHS *Gascon*

And there Charles Lister remains to this day, buried in East Mudros Military Cemetery, his manifest potential cut short well before his prime.

WHETHER AT HELLES, SUVLA OR ANZAC the situation was fundamentally the same. The Turks occupied the high ground and the Allies sat sullenly below them, surviving as best they could and pondering the injustice of their fate.

> This is the dullest war that ever was! So far none of the triumphs
> and victories that make wars so wonderful, so dramatic, so splendid.
> The events I have seen have been but boundlessly sanguinary. What
> suffering! What misery! What pathetic patience! Mechanism is
> destroying humanity. It is a pitiful spectacle! Out of the brain of man has
> sprung this monster that devours his genius! Genius has been engineered
> out of existence. An aeroplane is a miserable substitute for the mighty
> imagination of a Napoleon and vastly less efficient. And the reward of
> great courage is in ninety-nine cases out of a hundred – death![8]
>
> Major Claude Foster, 9th Worcestershire Regiment, 39th Brigade, 13th Division

All too aware of the lethal hidden dangers of the battlefield, many found it difficult to motivate themselves to do anything that might add to their troubles and, like Lieutenant George Hughes, they had learnt through bitter experience to keep their heads down, both literally and metaphorically.

> All night long I would hear the ping of bullets against the sandbags
> which sometimes becomes a crack like a whip if it gets a stone. The first
> sensation is that one would not be the other side of those sandbags
> for all the threats of all the generals in the British Army. But one gains
> courage for the first week as a rolling stone gains impetus; after that
> one's courage gradually oozes away again. But once volunteer to go
> out on patrol and the next night you are ordered to go and bomb the
> disused Turkish trench from one end to see whether there were any
> Turks in the other.[9]
>
> Lieutenant George Hughes, 5th Dorsetshire Regiment, 34th Brigade, 11th Division

Gradually, as weeks turned into months, it became evident that survival was the only attainable goal at Gallipoli. For many this took the most practical of negotiations in their prayers: 'Oh God, not in the belly or the balls!'[10] as one soldier was heard to say while going over the top. All ranks at Gallipoli were vulnerable as everywhere was within range of shells.

> At present I am ensconced in my dugout as there is a nasty strafe going
> on. Commanding Officers don't cower they 'ensconce' but I don't mind

confessing that my ensconcement is just about as close to the front part of my dugout that I can jam myself.[11]

Major Norman Burge, Nelson Battalion, 1st Brigade, RND

Life at Gallipoli was nasty, brutish and often short. The conditions of service were such that everything seemed to conspire to make men ill.

I felt so very depressed and low spirited, I hardly knew what to do with myself. Somehow or other, I had developed an attack of influenza which made me very weak, and I had also contracted a cough, with a splitting headache. All this, combined with the reaction, made me feel right down ill and I would have given anything to have been at home just then, for there was not a single soul to sympathise with me, or to say one loving word to me, I had to bear it all alone. Ah! No one can possibly realise what this means, unless they have gone through it all; it is an awful experience. This is one of the great drawbacks in military service; it may be all right when you are strong and well, able to rough it; but when you are feeling so bad, and longing for some gentle hand to be laid upon your burning brow, and a soothing voice to speak words of sympathy and love, *then* is the time you miss your home and dear ones.[12]

Private Ridley Sheldon, 1/6th Manchester Regiment, 125th Brigade, 42nd Division

Lieutenant Norman King-Wilson was by this time the Medical Officer in charge of an advanced dressing station at Suvla. As he gazed at the queues of invalids lining up in front of him he was mortified to realise that he could not minister to them all or soon there would be no one left to fight.

They all looked so ill, poor devils, that it required a heart of stone to send the lighter cases, say of simple diarrhoea, back to duty. However, one had to remember the military exigencies, and my heart used to bleed as I watched some poor, diarrhoea-stricken, emaciated skeleton, with sunken lack-lustre eyes and unsteady gait, accept without murmur my decision that he must return to duty, pick up his kit and slowly return to the stinking, pestilence-stricken, ill-constructed trenches.[13]

Lieutenant Norman King-Wilson, 88th Field Ambulance, RAMC

Some men could stand it no longer and a few were driven to take matters into their own hands.

A rifle shot went off behind some bushes beside us, followed by howls from someone in agony. A soldier lay on his back with his rifle beside him, his left foot merely held on by his puttee. His comrades, I see, are convinced that this was an intentionally inflicted wound. I have never before seen a man shoot off more than a finger or toe, carrying off a foot shows that the man has plenty of pluck of a sort.[14]

Captain George Davidson, 89th Field Ambulance, RAMC

Out at sea were the hospital ships with their bright lights twinkling as a promised land of safety, comfort and hope for the future. All Gallipoli had to offer was unending misery, disease and the threat of death.

A thin, bright silver strip of moon hung in the transparent blue just over the hospital ship, which lay about a mile from the shore. Out of the darkness her lights shone with piercing radiance. You could not see the ship: only a high white light at the bow and stern, a row of green lights along her side, like a string of emeralds, with a great cross of red flaming in the centre, all reflected in gleaming streaks wavering in the water. It gave one the impression of a great fairy lantern, hung on the moon, shining with almost unearthly beauty.[15]

Chaplain John Ewing, 1/4th Royal Scots, 156th Brigade, 52nd Division

One of those evacuated was Private John Gallishaw of the 1st Newfoundland Regiment. His departure had a bitter postscript that soured his relief to have escaped from Suvla with his life intact.

The stretchers were laid across the boats, close to each other. Soon all the boats were filled. I could see the man on the stretcher to the right of me, but the one on the other side I could not see. I tried to turn my head but could not. The eyes of the man next to me were large with pain. I smiled at him, but instead of smiling back at me, his lip curled resentfully, and he turned over on his side so that he could face away from me. As he did, the blanket slipped from his shoulder, and I saw on his shoulder strap the star of a Second Lieutenant. I had committed the unpardonable sin: I had smiled at an officer as if I had been an equal, forgetting that he was not made of common clay. Once after that, when he turned his head, his eyes met mine disdainfully. That time I did not smile. I have often laughed at the incident since, but there on that boat I was boiling with rage. Not a word had passed between us, but his expression in turning away had been eloquent. I cursed him and the system that produced him.[16]

Private John Gallishaw, 1st Battalion, Royal Newfoundland Regiment, 88th Brigade, 29th Division

Increasing criticism and unhappiness spread among the troops as they realised that everything had gone wrong. Some soldiers blamed their own High Command for what they saw as gross incompetence.

We failed purely through bad management and the fat overfed headquarters people in their comfortable quarters on Lemnos and Imbros know nothing – or at any rate do nothing – to prevent what looks like an awful catastrophe facing us. I can't help being a bit pessimistic tonight, but I feel as do all the others here that the mismanagement is criminal, and yet it is all smoothed over and the people in England are told nothing of it. If their eyes were opened, they would raise hell for some of our complacent superiors who get all the honours and put all the blame on the poor chaps who live like pigs here to cover up the mistakes of the authorities. So much for our English methods. We will probably muddle through in the end, but at what cost?[17]

Lieutenant Norman Tattersall, No. 13 Casualty Clearing Station, RAMC

These disillusioned feelings were exacerbated when news reached the Peninsula of strikes led by the trades unions back in Britain. Whatever the merits of the workers' case there was little sympathy for them exhibited among the soldiers suffering such awful conditions and risking their lives for minimal wages.

We are fed up with the shirkers, at home. They earn more than a subaltern gets, and they can live in comfort and do their work without risk except of the recognised kind. Here one has to sweat and carry on, no matter what is happening, and the hours of work are anything up to 24 per day. It would do them good to be put in a bunch for 24 hours and be well shelled at a halfpenny a day, with no regular meals, no regular rest, and no roof over their heads – like our Tommies.[18]

Lieutenant Charles Cooke, Army Service Corps, 29th Division

The strikes awoke some of the deep political and class-based tensions that lurked just beneath the surface of British society.

I was awfully sick with the accounts in a speech by Lloyd George of the way 'workers' are hindering the production of munitions. English people really manage to produce some first-class swine without effort. These obstructers are every bit as bad as the Welsh miners. I hope Lloyd George's pathetic references to his working-class home will have the desired effect. In the end I suppose it will be necessary to bribe the obstructers not to obstruct. My two co-staff officers are almost as bad – they can't see the wood for the trees. I am becoming a rabid enthusiast for the public school educational system – with all its faults. Really I suppose, no amount of public school education would have turned my two hobble-de-hoys into gentlemen or their ideas – culled from middle-class homes – into those of gentlefolk. On any topic, especially where there is any question of honour and the like, their ideas are those I should have expected from the average monkey. I had no idea that such low standards existed among the manufacturing and town clerking classes.[19]

Captain Arthur Crookenden, Headquarters, 159th Brigade, 53rd Division

Lieutenant Clement Attlee, a prominent pre-war member of the Independent Labour Party and future prime minister, had already been evacuated with dysentery from Helles but had rejoined the 6th South Lancashires at Suvla, where he found that his socialist views made him stand out among his fellow officers. He enjoyed several pleasant evenings discussing the arcane ins-and-outs of union politics with some of his NCOs active in the trades unions during their civilian lives, but he found a far more combative approach in the officers' mess. Never a man to flinch from a challenge, Attlee seems to have thoroughly enjoyed himself.

We used to have a merry time at headquarters where I used to go frequently of an evening. The CO would say, 'Let's have a good strafe, send for Attlee!' and after dinner we would discuss some broad proposition such as, 'All socialists are scoundrels!'[20]

Lieutenant Clement Attlee, 6th South Lancashire Regiment, 38th Brigade, 13th Division

For most of the men, talking was all they could do as they sat in their holes in the ground. One astute observer was drawn to point out the similarities of the crudeness of life on the Peninsula with the imagined habits of Neanderthal man.

Cregan, the doctor, says we get more childish every day and prophesies that if we are here much longer we shall not converse but utter weird noises and snap at our food, hiding the bones in holes in the ground. He drew a graphic picture of Farquhar retiring into the Krithia Nullah and hunting about the country on all fours and occasionally making raids for food to the beaches. All efforts to tame him will be useless and he will revert to the prehistoric man.[21]

Lieutenant Charles Cooke, Army Service Corps, 29th Division

Everywhere they looked the situation was getting worse. The effects of disease were hollowing out units from the inside and, of the 100,000 or so men serving on the Peninsula, it is estimated that half were unfit for duties by the early autumn. A further concern was the continuing paucity of artillery support. Now there was not just a lack of guns and munitions but, like their gunners, the guns were falling sick as barrels wore out, springs failed and one by one they dropped out of action. Most important of all the approach of winter could not be ignored; in fact it was already apparent that the piers and breakwaters would have to be improved on the beaches if they were to withstand the predictably rough weather and storms. Huge store depots would have to be built as insurance against prolonged bad weather. Proper dugouts would have to be constructed and winter uniforms issued. The logistical situation had been bad in summer but the prospects were daunting for the winter months. In these circumstances the idea of evacuation, first whispered but then ever growing, began to dominate the agenda both in London and on the Peninsula.

But Hamilton would still have none of it. When asked by Kitchener on 11 October to estimate how many men might be lost in a possible evacuation, he poured vitriol on the very idea, saying he would lose half his force. 'They would stamp our enterprise the bloodiest of tragedies!'[22] This refusal to consider seriously a retreat from the Peninsula proved fatal to his command. Hamilton had already failed time and time again, silken promises of success being followed with requests for yet more reinforcements, a circle that simply had to be broken in the face of the competing demands of the Western Front and Salonika. It was also unfortunate that the disgraced Stopford had not accepted his culpability for the Suvla disaster and was launching a campaign to restore his reputation, which naturally involved the sustained denigration of Hamilton. When his claims were investigated, the reports were ambivalent and predictably some of the mud stuck to Hamilton. This was exacerbated by the efforts of an Australian journalist, Keith Murdoch, who translated his legitimate concerns over the conditions and tactics he saw at Gallipoli into a letter laced with a considerable degree of exaggeration, addressed originally to the Australian prime minister, but subsequently circulated to the British Cabinet. As a result, on 14 October the Dardanelles Committee decided to dismiss Hamilton and replace him with General Sir Charles Monro. Hamilton quit his headquarters at Imbros on 17 October, leaving Birdwood in temporary command.

Hamilton was livid at both his own dismissal and the appointment of Monro, who was convinced of the primacy of the Western Front. He predicted withdrawal would follow under Monro and he was right. Where he erred was in thinking that an evacuation was strategically the wrong decision and doomed to disaster. But then he had been wrong so many times before. Hamilton's career was finished; he would never hold an active service command again.

Judgement of General Sir Ian Hamilton's performance at Gallipoli is rendered difficult by the effective smokescreen behind which he and his defenders deliberately concealed the lack of success of the operations under his command. Working in tandem with Churchill, his performance at the subsequent Dardanelles Commission was of dubious morality; but then it was inevitable that they would defend themselves as best they could in stressful circumstances. This was followed by the publication in 1920 of his *Gallipoli Diary* which was in fact an emotive memoir. Since then a potent romantic mythology has grown up, of failure by the narrowest of margins and betrayal by those at home, fuelled over the succeeding years by willing acolytes of both Hamilton and Churchill. Rationally, Hamilton's task was all but impossible, given the inhospitable terrain, the vigorous Turkish opposition, the restricted forces available to him and the lack of effective artillery support. Nevertheless his unquenchable optimism, over-complicated plans, inability to make best use of his forces and unwillingness to reflect the gravity of the situation in his reports to Kitchener went a considerable way to turning likely failure into disaster. Yet any criticism has to be tempered by the truism that even had Hamilton's generalship been brilliant, this would probably have resulted in only minor tactical gains which would not have affected the overall outcome of the campaign. Hamilton might have captured Achi Baba, he might even have taken Sari Bair, but the capture of the heights of the Kilid Bahr Plateau and effective control of the Dardanelles were never likely – it was by attempting an impossible challenge that he doomed himself and others.

Hamilton's replacement, Sir Charles Monro, was an entirely different character. No 'happy warrior', he was a hard, practical man who had served in staff positions during the Boer War. He then had a lengthy spell as Commandant of the School of Musketry at Hyde and was promoted to major general in 1911. He had served in command of the 2nd Division on the Western Front, being promoted first to command the I Corps and then, in July 1915, the newly formed Third Army. Now he was given command of the Eastern Expeditionary Force and his Chief of Staff was to be Major General Arthur Lynden-Bell. They were to report on the overall military situation at Gallipoli with particular attention to the ramifications of the alternative possibilities of evacuation and another offensive. Before they left for the Peninsula, the Director of Military Operations, General Sir Charles Caldwell, sent them a warning note:

> Ian Hamilton's failure was to my mind to a large extent due to his disinclination to tell Lord Kitchener unpleasant things and I think he was backed up in this by Braithwaite. They did not insist on having what they wanted and invariably communicated in an unduly optimistic strain. I do not suggest that your Chief and yourself will adopt the same line, but I would urge on you not to hesitate before telling unpleasant truths in your wires to K. Especially I would keep on about the troops being so very short of establishment and the discouragement which this causes them. Remember also the time that it takes to get anything to the Peninsula from this country.[23]
>
> Major General Sir Charles Caldwell, Director of Military Operations, War Office

Although Churchill had lost his position at the Admiralty back in May, the unreconstructed Easterner still made a last effort to influence Monro and Lynden-Bell during their departure from Charing Cross railway station on 22 October, under somewhat comic circumstances.

> Everyone felt a bit under the weather at 6 a.m. and we were not cheered up by the appalling smell of beer exhaled by our servants who had spent the night 'celebrating'. Just as the train was about to start Winston Churchill rushed along the platform, threw a bundle of papers

into our carriage and shouted, 'Don't forget, if you evacuate it will be
the biggest disaster since Corunna!'[24]

Major General Arthur Lynden-Bell, Chief of Staff, Headquarters, MEF

When they reached Imbros, on 28 October, they formally met their headquarters staff. Lynden-Bell was not shy of recording his distinctly unfavourable initial impression.

As we passed between the line of them Sir Charles said to me, 'Did you
ever meet such a down and out lot of fellows in your life?' I agreed and
subsequently discovered the reason why. They were not a united Staff
– or in fact, as they knew, not a staff at all. I found the General Staff
Officers thought themselves miles superior to mere Administrative and
Quartermaster Officers and they were not on speaking terms.[25]

Major General Arthur Lynden-Bell, Chief of Staff, Headquarters, MEF

Harassed from afar by Kitchener not to dawdle, Monro visited Helles,
Anzac and Suvla on a single day: 30 October. His report back to Kitchener
was a coruscating indictment of the situation, which he later summed up:

The positions occupied by our troops presented a military situation
unique in history. The mere fringe of the coast line had been secured.
The beaches and piers upon which they depended for all requirements
in personnel and material were exposed to registered and observed
artillery fire. Our entrenchments were dominated almost throughout
by the Turks. The possible artillery positions were insufficient and
defective. The force, in short, held a line possessing every possible
military defect. The position was without depth, the communications
were insecure and dependent on the weather. No means existed for the
concealment and deployment of fresh troops destined for the offensive
– whilst the Turks enjoyed full powers of observation, abundant artillery
positions, and they had been given the time to supplement the natural
advantages which the position presented by all the devices at the
disposal of the field engineer.[26]

General Sir Charles Monro, Headquarters, MEF

After further commenting on the problems posed by disease, a shortage
of competent officers, the Turks' ability to hold their positions with a
reduced force, and of course the improbability of a successful advance,
Monro's solution was to the point:

Since we could not hope to achieve any purpose by remaining on the Peninsula, the appalling cost to the nation involved in consequence of embarking on an overseas expedition with no base available for the rapid transit of stores, supplies and personnel, made it urgent that we should divert the troops locked up on the Peninsula to a more useful theatre. Since therefore I could see no military advantage in our continued occupation of positions on the Peninsula I telegraphed to your Lordship that in my opinion the evacuation of the Peninsula should be taken in hand.[27]

General Sir Charles Monro, Headquarters, MEF

On 3 November, Monro departed for Egypt to discuss the impact of evacuation, leaving Birdwood in temporary command. Churchill later famously pilloried Monro's approach as 'He came, he saw, he capitulated!'[28] As an epigrammatic sneer it is clever; as a comment on Monro's eminently sensible analysis it merely highlights Churchill's lack of grip on strategic matters.

Perversely, just as the army was at last seriously considering evacuation, so the Royal Navy was studying the possibility of making a dash through the Straits. The impetus behind this was Vice Admiral de Robeck's Chief of Staff, the irrepressible Commodore Roger Keyes, who had always believed that it was a perfectly feasible operation. In support of his case, he pointed to the addition of the long-range guns of the monitors which had joined the fleet, its vastly improved capacity for aerial spotting using aircraft rather than seaplanes and the possibilities inherent in using destroyer minesweepers. Although de Robeck and the French admirals were adamantly against such a risky attempt, Keyes was allowed considerable leeway in promulgating his ideas, even canvassing support in London. Partially motivated by a noble desire to help the army facing a winter campaign on the shores of Gallipoli, the Admiralty wavered a little, but was firmly slapped back into place by the indomitable Monro and Lynden-Bell, who considered the naval theorising a nuisance.

The Navy are giving us a great deal of trouble – I say the Navy but it is really Roger Keyes – by continually trying to urge us to help them in putting forward their pet scheme of forcing the Narrows. This we absolutely decline to do as we cannot see how the operation could possibly succeed, and if it did succeed it would not help the military situation at all. This has been pointed out frequently to the Vice-Admiral and to Keyes, but they still persist, and their last effort has been to wire to the Admiralty and urge that we should make a land attack on Achi Baba. To this we have replied that the operation is quite beyond our powers and would require at least 100,000 men.[29]

Major General Arthur Lynden-Bell, Chief of Staff, Headquarters, MEF

For a month these naval rumblings persisted until eventually the First Sea Lord, Sir Henry Jackson, stamped on the fantasy scheme by pointing out that even if a squadron could get through to the Sea of Marmara it might well be cut off, with disastrous consequences. This whole lingering distraction was described by the splendidly acerbic Lynden-Bell as 'The swan song of the lunatics!'[30]

Yet the ground was shifting elsewhere beneath Monro's feet. Kitchener, as ever obsessed with the question of British prestige in the Islamic world, was terrified of the effects an evacuation might have across the East. At the meeting of the newly constituted War Committee (a slimmed-down body of between three and five ministers which had superseded the Dardanelles Committee) it was decided that Monro's advice could not be accepted at this stage and that Kitchener should be sent out to review the situation in person. Kitchener's mind must have been in turmoil for, early on 4 November, he conceived of an absurd plan for a new landing at Bulair while also giving Keyes his opportunity to charge the Straits. As a result Kitchener despatched an extraordinary telegram transferring Monro to command of the forces at Salonika and placing Birdwood in command of the Mediterranean Expeditionary Force. Wisely, Birdwood suppressed these orders pending Kitchener's arrival at Gallipoli and loyally expressed his confidence in Monro. It was as well he did so. Within a matter of hours Kitchener had been disabused of the feasibility of both elements of his scheme and he cancelled his instructions. This incident demonstrates Kitchener's fading grip on events.

When Kitchener arrived in theatre he was joined by Monro. So began a series of discussions on evacuation and further pondering of the feasibility of a landing near Alexandretta, in Syria, to distract the attention of the Islamic world from the implications of an Allied defeat at the hands of the Turks at Gallipoli. This new scheme was soon dropped when the British government refused to deploy yet more troops on Middle Eastern adventures. Kitchener also completed a three-day tour of the Peninsula. He was evidently shocked at the prevailing conditions and at last realised that, like it or not, Monro had accurately reported the situation. Soon the discussions were centring on exactly what proportion of the forces would be lost in an evacuation and the nature of the plans to be adopted. Finally, on 22 November, Kitchener sent a telegram to the War Committee recommending a partial evacuation: he wanted to retain Helles to assist the Royal Navy in any future operations (they feared that a U-boat base might be established in the Straits with access to dockyard facilities back at Constantinople) while evacuating only Anzac and Suvla. Next day the War Committee accepted the need for evacuation and, indeed, recommended leaving Helles as well. However, at the same time the matter was referred to the Cabinet, which made the final decision in all cases that involved a major change in strategic policy – which this clearly was. A confirmation was anticipated after the Cabinet meeting on 24 November. At this point Kitchener appointed Monro as Commander in Chief of all Mediterranean Forces outside of Egypt, while Birdwood was put in charge of the renamed Dardanelles Army and the now-rehabilitated Lieutenant General Sir Bryan Mahon took command of the Salonika Force. Kitchener set off back for London and, despite his vacillations, everything now seemed settled. Sadly this proved not to be the case. The members of the British Cabinet were appalled at the gravity of the decision and, afraid to take responsibility for ordering an evacuation that could cause the deaths of thousands, they prevaricated. Even as they pondered their fateful decision, 'General Winter' was on the march at Gallipoli.

18

THE BEGINNING OF THE END

Rumours and suggestions that the enemy were going to evacuate Gallipoli naturally swarmed round us on Gallipoli. I, personally, did not believe in such a possibility because, taking into account the English character, I considered it out of the question that they would give up such a hostage of their own free will and without a fight.[1]

Colonel Hans Kannengiesser, Headquarters, XVIII Corps, Fifth Army

EVEN AS KITCHENER SAILED AWAY from the Peninsula, having finally accepted the inevitability of evacuation, there were clear signs that it was not just the Turks that the newly christened Dardanelles Army would have to fear over the winter months. While the government back in London avoided making any irrevocable decisions, the relatively benign Mediterranean climate began to lose sway over the Gallipoli Peninsula to the continental effects of its proximity to central Europe. At first the advent of cooler weather seemed a blessing as the swarms of flies disappeared and there was a slight enhancement to the overall health of the men. This feeling of improved well-being did not last.

About the 15th November the fine weather broke and a period of south-westerly squalls began. It was always quite uncertain what these would lead to. They were warm, terribly dry, shifty winds which blew straight into the shallow bay at Suvla, throwing up a tremendous ground swell, which made the landing of supplies impossible. No bread and half rations of water tomorrow was the inevitable outcome. Sometimes these squalls simply blew themselves out without rain; sometimes the ominous crack of thunder with forked lightning behind [the island of] Samothrace would foretell a hurricane and probably a deluge. The booming of the guns at sea, the swish of the wind, the sudden glare of the searchlights thrown from some big ship on the cliffs at Anzac, the white flash of lightning throwing the shadowy forms of the ships and scrub into relief against the sky and the growling of the thunder made one feel uncomfortably small.[2]

Lieutenant George Hughes, 5th Dorsetshire Regiment, 34th Brigade, 11th Division

If the men in the trenches were to look behind them, they could see the flimsy piers being smashed by the heavy sea, the grounded lighters and the general debris that littered the beach areas. If there was to be an evacuation then whatever scheme the general staff came up with would have to be sensitive to the risk of unpredictable disruption. In particular the number of consecutive nights of good weather they could expect was limited.

There was far, far worse to come. Friday 26 November began much the same as any day but it soon became apparent that something out of the ordinary was brewing up.

The morning was overcast and the wind from the North-East steadily rising, and as the day wore on the cold increased, and by evening every tent was straining at its guy ropes, and men could be heard hammering pegs in all directions. A foreboding of evil seemed to come to all. For weeks we had heard rumours of the dreadful winters on Gallipoli and anxiously we watched the banked up clouds and the ships tugging at their anchors in the Bay.[3]

Lieutenant Norman King-Wilson, 88th Field Ambulance, RAMC

At about 18.00 the rain started. Soon it was pouring down as if from some celestial hosepipe. At first the men seemed snug enough in their dugouts and shelters.

I was just sitting in my dugout when it started raining and as the roof started leaking, I piled all my kit on a box and went up to HQ for refuge, thinking it to be an ordinary drop of rain. I dined there and the rain continuing we asked the lads in the kitchen how they were. They said, 'It's just up to our knees but we'll manage the coffee!' Looking down we saw the water spreading across the floor up to our boots. I went out to see how the men were and found the main communication trench a torrent in which I could hardly stand. It was rushing down from the higher ground. I found our trench and most of the dugouts flooded and collapsing.[4]

Lieutenant Clement Attlee, 6th South Lancashire Regiment, 38th Brigade, 13th Division

Although there were many gullies at both Anzac and Helles, the locations of most of the trenches up on the ridges and spurs meant that they were spared the worst of the floods, though communication through the formerly dry gullies was halted. But at Suvla the wide open spaces of the plain were crossed by several streams that were capable of catastrophic flooding. The 1st Herefords were most unfortunate as they occupied trenches running across the bed of the Azmak Dere. Normally there was only a barely visible trickle of water in the watercourse.

Suddenly, without warning, a brown flood poured in. The water rose as you watched until it was about 3½ feet deep and then stopped. As I didn't want to drown I struggled out of the trench, and met the CO emerging from next door where the same thing had happened. It was quite obvious what had occurred. The very heavy rain, probably still heavier back in the hills, had suddenly transformed the Dere into a river again. The water had poured down from the high ground behind the Turks till it got caught up behind their barricade. This, presumably, had held until there was a respectable weight of water behind it, when it collapsed and the whole tearing flood came rushing down at ours. It didn't gather, or pause for the twinkling of an eye at ours, it simply swept it away as if it hadn't been there, and swept on to the sea, a solid river, 20 yards wide and 8 or 9 feet deep. All our trenches opened out of the Dere, and though their floor level was higher than the bottom of the stream they were still deep enough to take in about four feet of water.[5]

Captain Peter Ashton, 1st Herefordshire Regiment, 158th Brigade, 53rd Division

Ashton struggled through the flooded trenches to try to check on the situation in the front line, which had been cut in two by the Azmak Dere. This left the machine guns vital to their defences marooned on the other side of the torrent.

It wasn't possible to cross anywhere near the front line, so I went down stream about 300 yards, to a wide, pebbly place I remembered, and managed to get across. The water was about waist deep and running very strong. The Royal Engineers' two wooden bridges had absolutely disappeared. On my way down stream I heard something snorting and blowing in the dark in the water, and I found it came from a little Turkish ammunition pony, which had come down stream and got caught in a bush. I put two men on to get him out, and he continued his career in the British Army. When I got across I walked overland to the front line, and found our two precious guns intact.[6]

Captain Peter Ashton, 1st Herefordshire Regiment, 158th Brigade, 53rd Division

They would spend most of the day soaked through, trying to reorganise their positions. But this was just the start. At about 02.00 on 28 November the wind got up and began to blow in from the north. The temperature dropped rapidly below freezing and flurries of snow began to fall. That night the Herefords were relieved and they had moved back into reserve in the barren sand dunes behind Lala Baba.

Dawn, Sunday, 28th November, found it still snowing. We rose with considerable difficulty and started a little circulation back in our frozen limbs. A great many people were unable to get up at all; Holman, for one, was practically unconscious and we thought he was dead. But worse was to follow. Overnight our rations had been sent out to us in a lorry. The folk who sent them out, presumably sorry for those unfortunates in the snow, sent with them a double ration of rum. The wagon drivers, who brought the stuff, apparently before we arrived, finding no one to hand over to, had simply dumped the things by the side of the road and gone home. When morning broke men began wandering about, as men will, and unhappily found the dump. Instead of telling somebody, or even eating the food, which would have been sensible, they broke open the rum jars and started in. The effect on empty stomachs and in that cold was simply devastating. Filled with a spurious warmth, they lay on the ground, and in many cases took off coats, boots, even tunics! Those in the immediate vicinity of the dump were quickly put in the 'bag' but, unfortunately, the majority had filled mess tins and water bottles, and crawled into the bushes to enjoy themselves. We fairly combed those bushes all the morning, but by the time we found them all a certain number were dead. I remember finding one man in particular in only his shirt and trousers, holding out an empty mug with a perfectly stiff arm, quite dead. Coming on top of everything else, it was heartrending.[7]

Captain Peter Ashton, 1st Herefordshire Regiment, 158th Brigade, 53rd Division

Major Cecil Allanson's 1/6th Gurkha Rifles, who occupied the trenches on Hill 60, were exposed to freezing winds. Still handicapped by a slight hand wound received only days before, Allanson was suffering torments.

Lower and lower went the temperature, every bone in my body ached with cold, and my hand wound became most painful. Sleeping and living in miserable dugouts under such circumstances has to be gone through to be appreciated and understood. Think what it was for the men in open trenches. Truly one was learning the necessity of courage. I rarely got a smile out of myself, and as I could neither shave nor wash one probably looked even more miserable than one felt. The cold was just intense, and I have never seen such courage as I saw through this blizzard. Men found at the parapet facing the Turk with glassy eyes and stone dead, who gave up their lives rather than give in. Imagine the death of slow, accepted torture. It is, at such periods, and at such periods only, that one really does not seem afraid of death.[8]

Major Cecil Allanson, 1/6th Gurkha Rifles, 29th Indian Brigade

Men had fallen asleep, or more accurately unconscious; those that awoke could well consider themselves fortunate to be alive at all.

It took us about an hour to make sure that each man had a rifle and to get them on to drier land. When I returned along the trench, which was still unfit to stay in, I found six men had crawled back and were huddled together on a firing step frozen to death. We then found about twenty men lying by a hedge with ground sheets over them more or less frozen stiff; we got them up, after a lot of groaning and complaining, and made them hop round in a circle to restore their circulation.[9]

Second Lieutenant Philip Gething, 9th Royal Warwickshire Regiment, 39th Brigade, 13th Division

Many men were afflicted badly by frostbite, although at first few of them realised what was happening.

I got into the middle of a heap of old blankets and slept for 2 hours. When the sentry woke me to put the next relief on, then I noticed something wrong with my feet, for they ached and burned awful! I suppose it was through being warm with blankets and the reaction had set in. After I had changed the sentries, I took my boots off to see if I could see what was the matter. I was surprised to find my feet nearly black, I thought at first it was dirt and tried to rub it off but I soon gave that up as it was so painful. Then I guessed I'd got a touch of frost bite, so as soon as I could I went and saw the doctor. He said I must rub and wash them in cold water. Well, I got about a pint and did as he said. They seemed easier, but they were still painful and I could not get my boots on again. So I went to the Quartermaster Sergeant and asked him for a dry pair of socks and some boots. After a good deal of arguing I got them![10]

Corporal William Barron, 1/4th Northamptonshire Regiment, 162nd Brigade, 54th Division

Since many of the men were still wearing thin summer kit the freezing conditions and snow were potentially lethal. In such circumstances much depended on the vigour of the response of the officers and senior NCOs. Practical measures carried out with enthusiasm could make the difference between life and death.

Men were brought into HQ in a state of collapse. However a fire was got going and the CO hustled round getting the Doctor to all the men who were bad, moving them into fairly dry dugouts. I made our men who would stand shivering run about and we had fairly frequent issues of rum. I found one line of dugouts fairly dry and, collecting all the men who had been drowned out, I marked our new dugouts for them on a little hill under the trees and set them digging. I also collected a lot of old tins, issued fuel and some petrol and got braziers going. I then had a foot inspection and made all the men with sodden feet rub them with snow. Lindley and I and the batmen got some old sandbags and made a sort of shelter about 6 feet by 6 feet in which he and I and Basepool spent the night. The bullets used to go, 'Plunk! Plunk!' into it just over our heads, but we were too done in to worry.[11]

Lieutenant Clement Attlee, 6th South Lancashire Regiment, 38th Brigade, 13th Division

Many men sank into despairing lethargy. Captain Thomas Watson, who had only returned recently to the front himself after having recovered from wounds received in the August fighting, was a firm believer in using robust methods to get his men moving.

> No possibility of sleep – the men who were unfortunate enough to sleep were mostly frostbitten by morning. It was like slave-driving. The men had to be kept awake – poor beggars, dead tired some of 'em – at the point of a good nailed boot. You simply had to keep stamping or moving in the freezing mud to avoid losing the use of your limbs. The Sabbath dawned, one of the most hopeless days ever dreamed of. Men died of exposure too tired, in some cases too lazy, to make the necessary effort to live. There was one saving grace – the wretched Turks were in a worse plight and small groups of them walked about collecting brushwood to try and make a fire. This afforded sport to those who were warm enough to shoot and we potted several.[12]
>
> Captain Thomas Watson, 6th East Lancashire Regiment, 38th Brigade, 13th Division

For IX Corps, stretched across the open Suvla Plain, this was a disaster. The ground was white with snow and the trenches up to waist deep in icy water. There were over 200 fatalities and the medical officers and their stretcher bearers had the near-impossible task of dealing with over 5,000 men suffering from frostbite and hypothermia.

> Passing on to the aid posts I passed scores of men on their way down to the beaches, hobbling along, their feet tied up in puttees. The nearer to the trenches, the worse the sights grew. At the relief station hundreds of men were having their feet rubbed in oil and being given food. Their poor feet were swollen to double their normal size, blue and stone cold. The pain must have been frightful, but seldom did one hear a groan. The small aid posts in the trenches had some shocking cases brought in. Some frozen and unconscious, some quite drunk, for they had consumed large quantities of rum to keep warm. Some lying prone in the mud, dead. Others lying on top of the parapets, frozen in. Oh God, it was pitiful! As the day wore on, more and more men with frozen feet came hobbling down, some with rifles as crutches, some crawling, others being assisted by pals nearly as crippled as themselves. One officer with frozen feet was making his way slowly across the mud flat to our dressing station. He asked two others who were with him to

go on, and sat down in the mud. They went on sending back bearers. When the bearers reached him, he was dead – of cold and exhaustion.[13]

Lieutenant Norman King-Wilson, 88th Field Ambulance, RAMC

Back at the dressing stations the medical teams were almost overwhelmed by the numbers requiring treatment. By the time the sick could finally be evacuated many of them were in a very poor state.

The majority could only just crawl up the ladder, dozens tried, failed and had to be carried; they came on, mouths open, gasping, faces bluish, grey eyes glazed. Many of those who could stumble had to be led, as they just walked automatically, their clothes frozen stiff. I shall never forget the experience. We got them all below into cots, filled them up hot soups and Bovril and piled blankets on to them. Heaps had badly frostbitten feet which as they warmed up gave them great pain. We had frostbite in all stages. I was going until midnight, wrapping up feet in cotton wool.[14]

Surgeon Lieutenant Commander Albert Gilbertson, HMHS *Reha*

The hospital ship *Reha* had only 214 cots, but there were soon about 600 patients aboard and the decks were covered with mattresses.

The Turks were on higher ground and hence did not suffer quite so much from the flooding, but the later stages of the great freeze were still a tremendous ordeal for them.

Flakes gently float down. Since the temperature is below zero degrees centigrade, snow turns to ice. Though the brazier glows it is unable to dispel the cold in our dugout. Go out and tour trenches. Feel really sorry for my men. If this continues, what condition are we going to be in? Our conclusion is that there aren't many who can take this sort of life. If one has to put up with such conditions, there is no solution but to become as philosophical as a wandering dervish, completely bereft of worldly ambitions and concerns.[15]

Second Lieutenant Mehmed Fasih, 2nd Battalion, 47th Regiment, 16th Division, Fifth Army

A dreamy theoretical idea, but of little practical value to the bulk of his freezing men. The Turks were not immune from bad morale and they too had suspected cases of self-inflicted wounds among men driven to the limit.

Sergeant Ishak from 1st Battalion comes by. Reports a soldier was wounded in the arm by a bullet. Medics took him to the rear. The Doctor who treated him detected traces of gunpowder in the wound and, his suspicions aroused, demanded that we investigate. Together with the man we proceed to the embrasure where he had been posted to investigate the matter. Since the soldier gives a confused account of what happened one does become suspicious; however, no empty cartridge found in his rifle. During lengthy interrogation, he merely repeats his original story. Sent him off.[16]

Second Lieutenant Mehmed Fasih, 2nd Battalion, 47th Regiment, 16th Division, Fifth Army

The weather finally changed at the start of December, taking on a far more benign, almost autumnal feel. But there would be more storms, perhaps even worse.

If anything brought home the brittle status of the Allies' situation at Gallipoli it was the great storm and freeze, underlining as they did that any bad weather during the last few days of an evacuation could leave them stranded with one foot on the Peninsula and the other in mid-Aegean. Clearly, the delays of politicians could cost as many lives as the mistakes of generals. Major General Lynden-Bell raged impotently at the continuing failure of the government to make up its mind.

It is absolutely impossible for us to keep pace with the kaleidoscopic changes of policy which take place at home. One moment we are told that the War Council is for clearing out of here; this is followed by a telegram saying that the Cabinet is strongly opposed to this policy; then we receive no news for some days, and finally are told to clear out partially. Of course, the weather is the great factor here, and, as we have pointed out already, after the 21st December the bad weather almost invariably sets in. If there is a disaster, responsibility for it must rest on the Cabinet and its advisers. Had evacuation been decided on when we recommended it first, there would have been no difficulty and we should have got off in our own time with but little loss. In addition to the weather we now have grave anxiety about the large number of big guns which are being brought down by the Germans to the Peninsula.[17]

Major General Arthur Lynden-Bell, Headquarters, MEF

Of course the weather was still not their greatest enemy. The Turks had by no means given up that cherished status. Bulgaria joining the Central Powers in October had made it much easier for heavier artillery and reliable ammunition to be brought up to Gallipoli from Germany and Austria. The relative paucity of modern Turkish artillery and shortage of reliable shells meant that hitherto the Allies could continue to occupy the bridgeheads even though their rear areas were under the intermittent menace of shell fire. But if the Turks' access to arms and munitions improved then the Allies' logistical difficulties would be magnified significantly.

> At last in November the long coveted German artillery ammunition reached the Fifth Army. Its arrival increased the hope of a successful ending of the campaign. The Turkish artillery was in excellent training and its firing was good, but with its poor ammunition it could not produce more than limited results. From now on it was different. The first troops from the Central Powers arrived in Gallipoli in November 1915 for our active support. It was an excellent Austrian 24-cm mortar battery which was posted on the left of the Anafarta front and soon opened a very effective fire. An equally good Austrian 15-cm howitzer battery, which followed in December, was attached to the south group.[18]
>
> General Otto Liman von Sanders, Headquarters, Fifth Army

Many men on the Allied side commented on the arrival of the Austro-Hungarian mortars, while the introduction of artillery shells that actually exploded further added to the prospective devastation.

> They sent over quite a number of HE shells and, unusually for them, *all* busted and that with terrific violence. I think it is some new toy they've acquired via Bulgaria. Well, only one shell really hit anything that mattered and that was a bay next to our own dugout occupied by nine of my men. With the exception of three, they were all literally blown to pieces and unrecognisable. I've never seen such an awful shambles as that bay presented. All were dead: the first glimpse being a headless trunk. We buried three we could recognise, five trunks and a bag of spare limbs.[19]
>
> Captain Thomas Watson, 6th East Lancashire Regiment, 38th Brigade, 13th Division

All over Anzac and Suvla shells were dropping in areas that had been previously considered relatively safe.

> We were resting in Victoria Gully, till then untouched by Turkish
> shellfire, when I was called away to watch a 'Two-up' game and maybe
> hoping to try my luck as well! Suddenly a newly arrived howitzer
> battery (Austrian, it was said) dropped one amongst the five or six I
> had just left. All died; amongst them I found Sergeant Jack Herbert just
> alive. Before he died he whispered, 'They've got me downstairs, Scottie
> – no more fun for me!' So they had.[20]
>
> Private George Scott, 4th (New South Wales) Battalion, 1st Brigade, 1st Division,
> AIF

There was a general perception among the troops that the Turkish shelling
had increased in both quality and effectiveness. Major Cecil Allanson was
wounded by a shell on 3 December.

> I was standing not far from my dugout giving notes to orderlies, when
> there was a terrific roar; the world seemed to come on the top of me,
> and the next vivid memory I have, though temporarily deprived of
> my sight, was the communion on the hospital ship, *Gloucester Castle*. I
> asked someone in the next bed if I was dying, as I had been given the
> last sacrament, but he told me to be of good cheer, as he had also been
> given it and he was only suffering from jaundice![21]
>
> Major Cecil Allanson, 1/6th Gurkha Rifles, 29th Indian Brigade

Allanson's campaign was over.

BACK IN LONDON members of the Cabinet were still dithering. Many
feared the effect of acknowledging defeat on Egypt and India, but the main
cause of this vortex of indecision was Lord Curzon. The former Viceroy of
India wrote an influential memo that predicted in the most lurid terms
a nightmarish military disaster should an evacuation be attempted. The
strange mood of the Royal Navy, still apparently considering a renewed
assault on the Straits, did not help, as it seemed to offer an alternative
avenue of escape. The decision was debated, put off, reconsidered, post-
poned and then deferred. Days stretched into weeks as incremental delays
mounted up. All possible solutions were considered, ranging from the
vaguely impractical to the frankly surreal. Kitchener too began to wobble
again, now apparently possessed of the belief that Salonika could be closed
down and the troops there sent to Gallipoli to support the putative naval

assault on the Straits. Once again Monro, Byng and Birdwood were asked their opinions of the possibilities and perils of staying on in Gallipoli. The military consensus remained firmly in favour of evacuation. Then, on 4 December, a series of high-level meetings with the French began on the future of the Salonika front. The French wavered but eventually declared that Salonika could not be surrendered; by contrast, they were perfectly happy to evacuate Gallipoli. Finally, on 7 December, a full meeting of all twenty-two members of the Cabinet met: a final decision had to be taken. As it was impossible to conceive of a damaging public split with the French, the politicians made their decision and plumped for evacuation. Even then, influenced by the wishes of the Royal Navy, they decided to retain Helles in order to restrict U-boat usage of the Straits. It had taken just over five long weeks from the despatch of Monro's appreciation to his receipt of the final decision on 8 December. Anzac and Suvla would be evacuated. The final date was set for 19 December. But was it still possible?

Throughout this hiatus the headquarters staff had been making preliminary preparations for the evacuation. Nevertheless the final approval brought home with stunning force a realisation of the manifold difficulties of what they were about to attempt.

> A retirement in the face of an enemy on land where you have plenty of room is a very difficult and critical operation but under the circumstances here, where one is bang up against your enemy, and where you have absolutely no room to sling a cat, and also have to embark in small craft every single man, gun, animals and stores on a beach which is under the enemy's gun-fire, and of which they know the range to an inch – and in the case of Suvla can see from their positions – you can imagine what a difficult anxious job it is. We have not only the enemy to contend with, but at any moment, practically in the twinkling of an eye, a south-west wind may spring up.[22]
>
> Deputy Quartermaster General Walter Campbell, Headquarters, Eastern Mediterranean Forces (EMF)

Somehow the Allies had to evacuate from Anzac and Suvla some 83,000 men, 186 guns and as much equipment and stores as possible. The huge depots were gradually whittled away as the more valuable or esoteric items were re-embarked. However, they were constrained in how much they could take away by the fear that the Turks might notice, or worse still, a resumption of the bad weather might cause a postponement. It was therefore essential to keep ashore sufficient food to feed tens of thousands of men and animals.

> I expect to lose a good deal of food, as I had stocked up each place with about thirty-five days' rations in view of the coming bad weather in January, February and March, as I calculated that during that time there might be frequent periods of about a week or 10 days when no food could be landed at all – so the accumulated stocks meant some 6,000 to 7,000 tons. Of course at such short notice it has been impossible to get all that quantity away.[23]
>
> Deputy Quartermaster General Walter Campbell, Headquarters, EMF

The initial sets of evacuation plans were drawn up by the staff of the ANZAC and IX Corps. The original solution as drawn up by the IX Corps staff under Lieutenant General Sir Julian Byng was to make a fighting withdrawal, falling back in stages to two pre-prepared trench systems close to the beaches on either side of the newly flooded Salt Lake before making a final break for it. But this plan could not co-exist with the secrecy required at Anzac, where they were already effectively in their last-ditch positions. Eventually it was abandoned in favour of the plan produced by Brigadier General Brudenell White, the Chief of Staff of the ANZAC Corps. On the basis that the Turks were fully capable of causing huge casualties by bombarding the beaches and launching disruptive attacks, this plan prioritised deception to try to conceal the evacuation until the very last moment. It was a brilliant piece of work that combined rigorously detailed planning with a considerable imaginative effort to fool the Turks. In the week before evacuation the units holding Anzac and Suvla would be thinned out to the bare minimum required to hold the front. Then, over two nights, the reserve and support units would be evacuated on the penultimate night while on the last night they would thin out the remaining units in stages, before the final parties pulled back, covered by small rearguards. Every effort would be made to maintain the appearance of normality in everything they did.

One clever feature of the plan was the introduction of silent periods in the weeks before the evacuation to try to get the Turks used to the telltale reduction in noise that would become apparent as the Anzac trenches emptied in the final hours. All small arms and artillery fire was to cease unless the Turks attacked or presented an exceptional target. These silent nights clearly confused the Turks. Captain Basil Holmes was in Quinn's Post.

> The Turks did send a patrol across the 15–20 yards to look into our trenches to see whether we were still there or not, as we had suddenly stopped replying to any of their bombs. They were very suspicious, they came over and one brave Turk jumped down into a part of the trench at Quinn's Post. There was no one in it and he started to walk along the trench. He hadn't gone far, no distance at all, when there was a lead off the trench and one of our fellows just shoved the bayonet into him and killed him. No shots were fired. There were four or five other fellows on the bank and they realised that something had happened, that we were there and they headed back to their own trench and left this dead body with us.[24]
>
> Captain Basil Holmes, 17th (New South Wales) Battalion, 5th Brigade, 2nd Division, AIF

Such experiences made the Turks very wary of probing too far, even when they noticed something unusual in the Anzac lines; the silent periods had their intended effect.

As preparations progressed around them, the men of Anzac and Suvla began to realise that an evacuation really was underway. Not unsurprisingly, they were filled with conflicting emotions: relief, a feeling of being thwarted and an underlying sense of guilt over the prospect of abandoning the graves of their dead comrades. And of course, like any soldiers, they speculated – or rather gossiped – as to what would happen next.

> We know nothing as yet and spend all day arguing as to what our final destination may be. In fact we have started a sweep to-day. The horses running are (1) England (2) Western Front (3) Helles (4) Egypt (5) Balkans (6) Townsend's Expedition (7) East Africa (8) The Field which includes any place not mentioned above. If anybody comes back from the orderly room it is correct for him to put on the air of 'knowing a lot, but not being able to tell!' This drives Walter into a frenzy as he jumps at any rumour and works it absolutely threadbare, making himself quite ill and 'highly inflammable' over it.[25]
>
> Lieutenant Alfred Richardson, 1st West Somerset Yeomanry, 2nd Brigade, 2nd Mounted Division

Throughout the last week the garrisons of Anzac and Suvla were reduced in secrecy, night by night, to the bare minimum capable of holding off a surprise Turkish attack.

> We had in round numbers some 75,000 men to take off. Mercifully the elements have been kind. We commenced last Sunday night, the 12th, and we have continued it every night since without interruption. We divided the operations into two spheres. [The first] lasting over six nights, working from two hours after sunset till two hours before daybreak, our object being to withdraw, without giving any indication to the enemy, every man, animal, gun, stores, etc. that we could spare, and at the same time hold our position in case we were heavily attacked. I am glad to say the six nights of the first stage finished last night, and we reduced the numbers to what was considered a safe minimum, i.e., 20,000 men on each beach. Now tonight we begin the final stage; as far as we can gather, the enemy have no inkling that we contemplate withdrawal.[26]
>
> Deputy Quartermaster General Walter Campbell, Headquarters, EMF

They could not take the mounds of food stores away but they could destroy or render unusable as much as possible. It was a mammoth task but they worked away at it with a will and, as might be expected, there were many opportunities for low humour.

> Some wags steam the labels off bully, pierce a couple of neat holes in the tin and replace the label. They hoped that 'Abdul' would eat it and become indisposed, but I think they hoped in vain, because a Turk's anatomical pantry is copper-lined![27]
>
> Lance Corporal William Scurry, 7th (Victoria) Battalion, 2nd Brigade, 1st Division, AIF

The men took a particular pleasure in setting up various booby traps for unwary Turks.

> The men in the trenches spent the last day in turning every dugout into a death trap and the most innocent looking things into infernal machines. The fireplace in General Cayley's dugout was set, but thirty pounds of TNT was fixed to go off whenever the fire had burned down to a fuse. Other dugouts would blow up when the doors were opened. The CRA's drafting table had several memorandum books lying on it,

each with electrical connections to an explosive charge sufficient to destroy a platoon. A gramophone, wound up and with record on, ready to be started, was left in one dugout – so contrived that the end of the tune meant the death of the listeners. Piles of bully beef tins turned into diabolical engines of destruction lay scattered about. In front of the trenches lay miles of trip mines. Really, I never thought the British Tommy possessed such diabolical ingenuity. They entered into it with the greatest zest and enjoyed it – a little practical joke on Johnny Turk![28]

Lieutenant Norman King-Wilson, 88th Field Ambulance, RAMC

What they could not destroy, ruin or pollute, they tried hard to bury and there was considerable ingenuity employed in disguising their actions. One memorable ruse was used by the Australians occupying the Warwick Castle post at the head of Aghyl Dere.

Before the last of us left all available ammunition and bombs were collected. These were buried and on a cross stuck into the ground was the following inscription: 'To the Memory of Private Bullet. RIP.' That was to prevent the Turks from becoming inquisitive and digging up the ammunition and bombs![29]

Company Sergeant Major William Burrows, 16th (Southern and Western Australian) Battalion, 4th Brigade, NZ&A Division, AIF

The first night of the evacuation took place on 18 December. As the men filed silently back to the beach they were packed aboard passenger steamers and spirited away in three batches at 22.00, 24.00 and 01.00 next day. Everything went like clockwork, the Turks seemed oblivious to what was going on and there were no casualties; indeed, ironically, two Turks deserted that night. Truly a case of bad timing. There were now just 10,000 men holding the lines at Suvla, with a further 10,000 at Anzac. Would the Turks notice, come the dawn?

TO HELP DEFLECT TURKISH ATTENTION from Suvla and Anzac, the VIII Corps was charged with launching attacks at Helles on 19 December. Much of the planning for this risky operation relied on harvesting the hard work of the miners who had been long fighting an intensive underground war there. As fighting above ground had died down, the pace of the mining operations had increased right across the Helles front. Sapeur

Gaston-Louis Giguel found himself tunnelling under the Turkish lines in the Kereves Dere sector. But of course the Turks were also burrowing their way towards him.

> In a moonless night the flares never stopped illuminating the ravine. From our trench by means of a microphone we could clearly hear them working. Who would get there first? There are six of us working in our shaft. We are divided into two teams; the work goes on 24 hours a day. One man is digging at the end of the shaft; two others carry out the spoil with the aid of a little sledge that they push right to the entrance to the gallery. All this is controlled by a sergeant and we barely manage in our 24 hours to dig 3 metres of shaft despite working conscientiously. In a mine next to us two comrades were nearly asphyxiated when the miner at the head of the gallery broke into a pocket full of gas left by the previous explosion of a Turkish mine. Our work is particularly tiring – only wine and spirits keep us going! [30]
>
> Sapeur Gaston-Louis Giguel, 1st Régiment du Génie, CEO

Such operations continued all through the autumn and into the winter. It was a murderous game as each side raced to explode their mines first; yet if they blew their mines too early they would not achieve their objective. It was all a matter of judgement and nerve. Now such mines were a ready-made ingredient of a daring set of attacks launched up Gully Ravine and Krithia Nullah on the afternoon of 19 December.

> A pretty big demonstration was made at Cape Helles which included a heavy and long bombardment and an advance at one or two points along our front. We had the privilege of seeing a successful infantry advance on our right, but the grand sight was quickly ended as the men were soon enveloped in smoke from bursting shrapnel. As regards the spectacle of bursting shells in the bombardment it is impossible for me to portray and I can only liken it to an exaggerated Brocks Benefit [fireworks] at the Crystal Palace. During this demonstration the Engineers sprung a gigantic mine on the part of our Gully known as Border Barricade and our Division occupied the crater. [31]
>
> Corporal Godfrey Clifford, 1st West Kent Yeomanry, South Eastern Mounted Brigade, 42nd Division

Following the detonation of the mine, an attack made by the 1/7th Lancashire Fusiliers who with the assistance of the sappers managed to link the new smoking crater to Crawley's Crater in the Gully Ravine sector. The Turkish reaction was not a surprise.

> At night time the Turks counter-attacked. They succeeded in getting back to the trench, but we rushed them out again. My arm is sore with throwing bombs at them. I saw some soldiers with blue uniforms on, and heard they were Bulgarians. I got hit because I was a bayonet man for a team of bombers rushing up a sap. I did not get far before a bullet got me – made a hole in my hat and a flesh wound in my head. It was a lucky hit for me, as it was in my head![32]
>
> Private Arthur Kay, 1/7th Lancashire Fusiliers, 125th Brigade, 42nd Division

The Turks did not give up easily and over the next two days teams of bombers from the Sussex Yeomanry and West Kent Yeomanry were sent up to bolster the hard-pressed garrison in holding on to the new posts.

> What a sight met our eyes. I have never been in a big crater before and only had a slight idea of what they were like. This one was like a huge gravel pit about 50 foot deep and 250 foot in diameter, with great cracks in sides and bottom and huge lumps of earth and rocks scattered about which had been torn out by the explosion. The crater was about 100 yards in front of our firing line and about 10 yards in front of the crater a small gully ran across our front. It was impossible to see down the gully and the Turkish trenches on the opposite side prevented any forward movement on our part. One never knew what this little gully hid from view and it was this fact that made our position so rotten. Lucky for us there was a particularly bright moon that night which made observation by periscope possible. Had it been dark I am sure the first attack would have carried them into our position. We were in an absolutely rotten position for bombing – the explosion of the mine had filled in the trench to such an extent that we were compelled to move about on our hands and knees. To make things worse a machine gun kept flicking the tops of the remaining sand bags so after we got the observer in position we set to work to stock ourselves with bombs and then dig ourselves in. After about 4–5 hours' hard work during which time we were continuously shelled and sniped, our observer noted a movement just in front of us, word was passed along and we were ready. They were making one of their many counter-attacks. We waited for them to get a little nearer then we got the word, 'Go!' The noise was terrific, what with bursting bombs, 'Whiz Bangs', rifle and machine gun

fire – it was necessary to shout in the next man's ear to get an order passed up.[33]

Corporal Godfrey Clifford, 1st West Kent Yeomanry, South Eastern Mounted Brigade, 42nd Division

The storm of fire held back the Turks. There would be many more attacks, but in the end they managed to incorporate the crater into their front line positions. The real measure of their success, however, was whether they succeeded in diverting eyes from events further north.

AT SUVLA THE TURKS WERE WARY, but remained baffled. The earlier quiet periods followed by the vigorous resumption of normal hostilities had created doubts in their minds. Just as they themselves were preparing for winter, so they presumed that the Allies were doing the same, closing down non-essential firing and so quietening down the front. Even on the last day they were completely unaware of what was going on under their very noses.

> Opposite us there was peace with the exception of the usual fire from the enemy. About 11 o'clock in the morning our howitzer battery on Ismail Oglu Tepe [the W Hills], with a field battery, had shelled Lala Baba, as a result of which Ismail Oglu Tepe was immediately shelled by several enemy batteries. The usual picture.[34]
>
> Colonel Hans Kannengiesser, Headquarters, XVIII Corps, Fifth Army

It was of course crucial to manage the staged withdrawal of the artillery batteries. The guns had to be saved where possible, but at the same time if they were prematurely withdrawn and fell silent too early, then the Turks might realise what was happening. Considerable judgement was required.

In the event the evacuation of Suvla proved far simpler than anyone had envisioned. The tension all through Sunday 19 December was evident, but the Turks continued to show no signs of awareness. Once darkness fell the troops filed quietly back with no undue incidents. It was all going very smoothly. Lieutenant Clement Attlee of the 6th South Lancashires had been ordered to hold the last ditch lines around Lala Baba.

> We had 250 men and six machine guns. We went down the still very muddy road in the dark. I despatched Lindley and Wakeford with sixty

men and two machine guns to hold the road between the Salt Lake and the sea, the remainder I disposed in the trenches as previously arranged and took post myself in a dugout with the Company Sergeant Major, signallers and orderlies. I was in telephone communication with General Headquarters. I had four officers of the East Lancashires on duty at the gaps in the wire which had been erected half way to the trenches, one of these was rather barmy and caused Lindley some trouble by his manner of waving his revolver about. We soon began to get reports of parties passing through. This continued at intervals all through the evening and night. About 3.30, word came that the parties holding the wire half way had closed the gaps and were coming through. I warned our men to get ready. There followed a period of waiting. All this time everything was very peaceful though there were occasional shots to be heard from Anzac. Then we got the order to move. The men hustled up the trench, machine guns going first. I brought up the rear and found at the pier a few military police, General Maude and a few of the staff. We went on board lighters which seemed to go round and round. Flames shot up from the dumps of abandoned stores.[35]

Lieutenant Clement Attlee, 6th South Lancashire Regiment, 38th Brigade, 13th Division

They finally bade farewell to the shore of Suvla at 04.00 on the morning of 20 December. Major General Stanley Maude, commanding the 13th Division, was considered to have done a good job, though even his devoted staff regarded him as a strange fish.

In appearance he was not exceptional. He was tall and thin and walked with rather a stoop. He wore a Victorian moustache, which hung rather raggedly over a small mouth. His chin lacked firmness. His high-pitched and sometimes rather querulous voice was unmelodious. At times of stress he had a tiresome habit of whistling out of tune. Nothing, admittedly, could be much less flattering than this description, and yet this was the soldier above all others for whom I have the greatest respect and admiration. Beneath this ordinary exterior, and despite these blemishes, there beat in him the heart of a warrior. His craving for detail would have been a vice in another man, but in him it did not seem to matter. At any rate, he never lost sight of the wood for the trees.[36]

Captain Douglas Brownrigg, Headquarters, 13th Division

As was expected, the main tension on 19 December was at Anzac. Here there was no margin for error, with the trenches often just a few yards apart. If the Turks realised that only a skeleton force was holding the key positions at The Nek, Quinn's, Courtney's, Steele's and Lone Pine, then they could be through and across Russell's Top or 400 Plateau in minutes. From these vantage points they could fire directly down into the throngs of men being evacuated in boats from the beach. It was a terrifying prospect, especially for the men charged with the responsibility of holding the front lines to the end. Each unit in the line was carefully organised. The arrangements revealed to the officers of the 24th Battalion at their briefing were typical:

> The 24th Battalion would hold Lone Pine until the end and for a time would be supported by some of the 23rd in reserve. We left that conference with our feelings too deep for speech. We were stunned and broken in spirit, if not broken-hearted. Subsequent orders divided the battalion into three echelons, to be designated 'A', 'B' and 'C' parties. These groups were subdivided into 'Al' and 'A2'; 'B1' and 'B2'; 'C1', 'C2' and 'C3' parties. 'A' parties, consisting of six officers and 245 men (mostly sick), would leave on the first night. 'B' parties, consisting of six officers and 386 men, would commence to move out at 9.30 p.m. and be clear of the trenches by 11 p.m. on the last night. 'CI' party, consisting of four officers and 26 men, would move at 2 a.m. on the 20th; 'C2' party, two officers and 34 men, at 2.15 a.m.; and 'C3', the last party, of three officers and 34 men, would leave the trenches at 3 a.m. and arrive at Watson's Pier at 3.20 a.m. on December 20. Three volunteers were called from among the officers to remain in charge of the last party and it was clearly indicated that there could be no chance of it getting away. The party was to be the rearguard to cover the final retirement, no matter what happened. [37]
>
> Second Lieutenant Stanley Savige, 24th (Victoria) Battalion, 6th Brigade, 2nd Division, AIF

Every officer volunteered and among those selected were Second Lieutenant George McIlroy and Second Lieutenant Stanley Savige. Their chances of survival relied on competent staff work and an attention to detail.

> A list has been drawn up of the names of each of the last 170 officers and men, showing for each man the time that he has to leave the

front trenches, and exactly what he has to do – whether to carry a machine gun, or its tripod, or its belts, or to throw a bomb, or to start an automatic rifle, or to light a fuse which will blow up a gun-cotton mine, or to complete a previously prepared barbed-wire entanglement on a track which might be used by the enemy. Every one of these 170 officers and men has been given a card, containing all these particulars so far as they apply to himself, and the exact route by which he is to reach the beach. All this means *organisation* and makes all the difference between success and failure.[38]

Brigadier General John Monash, Headquarters, 4th Australian Brigade, NZ&A Division, AIF

As the shortened daylight hours slowly ticked by there was inevitably the occasional false alarm.

We experienced our first scare about midday. A Turkish plane appeared and, dropping to about a hundred feet above the trenches, moved backwards and forwards along their length. Did the airman know anything of our plans? It looked as if he did. If so, our chances were not too bright. As the plane swept along the lines every man was ordered to fire his rifle as rapidly as possible, not at the plane, but simply into the air, hoping to impress the Turkish infantry into believing our line was strongly held.[39]

Second Lieutenant Stanley Savige, 24th (Victoria) Battalion, 6th Brigade, 2nd Division, AIF

The Anzacs did have other strings to their bow, however. A series of mines had been dug and made ready for detonation. At Russell's Top two mines were charged with over 1,500 lbs of ammonal, while a tunnel feeling its way right under the Turkish lines at The Nek was packed with two tons of high explosives by the Australian sappers. Lieutenant James Caddy was left with a small party of the 5th Field Company up on Russell's Top, the last sector to be evacuated.

Right up to the last, men were left in the faces of the tunnels tapping with picks so that the enemy would think that mining operations were still being continued. The day was spent waiting for the end and testing the connections with the mines to ensure that they would explode when required. It was still doubtful whether the mines would be fired or not, so we fixed up an arrangement which, if necessary, would fire the mines some hours after we had left. This consisted of a sandbag suspended by a string and a candle, which, after staying alight for about 2 hours, would burn the string, causing the sandbag to fall on the exploders and fire the mines.[40]

Lieutenant James Caddy, 5th Field Company, Australian Engineers, AIF

Similar devices were used to create self-firing rifles which were left in the front line trenches to fire at irregular intervals when the last of the troops had fallen back. Several designs were created, the best-known of which was the invention of Lance Corporal William Scurry of the 7th Battalion.

It occurred to me that if we could leave our rifles firing we might get away more surely. The sand of the hourglass was the first germ of the idea. If the sand could be made to trickle from above into a container attached to the trigger, the increased weight would finally release it. Next day I started on the idea but it wouldn't work. The sand wouldn't run and the trigger wanted a jerk to pull it. The jerk was easily got over by the cartridge box full of dirt, but water was the only thing that I could think of to replace the sand.[41]

Lance Corporal William Scurry, 7th (Victoria) Battalion, 2nd Brigade, 1st Division, AIF

This was a problem and it took some considerable entreaties to get the three pints he needed for the experiments. The principle was fairly simple, but fiddly to achieve in the conditions. A can of water was perched on a small shelf. This dripped the water down into another tin which in turn was attached by a wire to a cartridge box full of dirt and stones. When the second tin was full enough of water it toppled over the cartridge case which was in turn linked by a wire to pull the trigger. He showed his prototype to his officer and tests were held to prove that the idea had merit. It was accepted and Scurry spent his last few days there explaining his simple construct to hundreds of curious Anzacs up and down their front line.

Shortly after dusk there was an ominous increase in Turkish shell fire, with shells crashing down into the Anzac area. What did it mean?

As the shadows lengthened, the enemy began to register with his heavy artillery the communication trenches leading to the front. Past experience indicated that this ranging was a preliminary to a more serious attack. Nerves were now getting a bit on edge. Would he attack after dark or at dawn? We hoped it would be a dawn attack! [42]

Second Lieutenant Stanley Savige, 24th (Victoria) Battalion, 6th Brigade, 2nd Division, AIF

As everyone else began to make their way as quietly as possible to the beach the men left in the trenches had to create the impression of an undiminished occupancy. Obviously the quiet periods had helped, but it was still best to try to maintain a physical presence for as long as possible.

Each man would take ten to fifteen fire bays as his sector. This demanded great individual activity, as each man, though able to fire from only one bay at a time, must maintain a regular fire from all. This fire must be maintained by firing from irregular bays and not bay after bay in succession. Everything must be done as normally carried out by the full garrison, even to throwing the occasional bomb. These plans were not difficult in making, but extremely difficult in their execution, as the average distance between the lines was only 15 yards, and, at places, considerably closer. [43]

Second Lieutenant Stanley Savige, 24th (Victoria) Battalion, 6th Brigade, 2nd Division, AIF

Midnight came and went and it became apparent that the Turks were not planning to attack that night, nor were they aware of what was going on just a few yards away. Indeed, the intelligence reports they had received had only added to the confusion.

It was reported from the division that thirty enemy transport ships and eight or nine warships were off Imbros, that four of the transports were sailing towards Suvla Bay and that we should be constantly on the alert for an anticipated landing operation by the enemy. [44]

Corporal Huseyin Atif, 1st Battalion, 17th Regiment, 5th Division, Fifth Army

As the hours passed, so some of the Australians began to hope that they might, against all the odds, get away with it.

A still night, with a bright moon overhead casting shadows in the bottom of the trench – a scene so peaceful one could hardly associate it with war. The mind found leisure to wander off to far Australia and imagine something of the surprise which would be caused by the newspaper headlines on the morrow. All quiet in front and everything working so smoothly to schedule, one even began to contemplate the hitherto very remote possibility of our getting away with it altogether. It was a great satisfaction to know that most of the troops were already clear and it was beginning to look like a sporting chance for us, although time enough for quite a lot of things to happen yet.[45]

Second Lieutenant George McIlroy, 24th (Victoria) Battalion, 6th Brigade, 2nd Division, AIF

Yet there were still occasional excitements. Routine Turkish activity, which in normal circumstances would have passed without comment, was suddenly perceived as very threatening.

A little after midnight the officers were sharpened up a bit by a telephone report that a Turkish patrol had been observed pushing up Wire Gully. If this meant a general move forward, we could expect trouble very shortly, while our isolated party might easily be cut off in the rear. Our orders were clear, however, that the position must be held, even though attacked heavily, until 3 a.m. at all costs. Nothing was said to the men, except a warning to be alert and the time arrived for 'C1' and 'C2' parties, including the machine gunners, to retire, while the phone from the rear was cut off, leaving three officers and 34 other ranks doing their best to sound like a whole battalion, although feeling somewhat isolated in the world, for as far as we could tell no other Australian troops were on either flank for some distance. When each officer, precisely at 2.40 a.m., moved along his front with instructions to slip quietly out to the rendezvous in Gun Lane, instead of the frenzied anxiety to depart which one might have expected, the popular idea of the moment seemed to be, 'Just another shot at the old **** before we go!'[46]

Second Lieutenant George McIlroy, 24th (Victoria) Battalion, 6th Brigade, 2nd Division, AIF

McIlroy's men were filing silently out of the trenches while he conscientiously checked the front line to make sure everyone had got clear. To his amused surprise, he found Corporal Edgar Worrall having a final leisurely pot-shot at the Turks.

The Turk could be heard strengthening his barbed wire. I probably fired the last shot at Lone Pine. At last our time to go had come and with blankets tied round our feet to muffle the noise we made our way along the blanket-covered trenches out to the communication trench and then down to the beach.[47]

Corporal Edgar Worrall, 24th (Victoria) Battalion, 6th Brigade, 2nd Division, AIF

Many of them felt an eerie remoteness as they walked down deserted trenches and paths that had previously been packed full of soldiers. The hundreds of dugouts that lined the gullies still had candles burning but there was no one at home. This strangeness was intensified by the muffling effect of the blanketed trenches and swathed boots. Behind them they left the self-firing rifles. Lance Corporal William Scurry must have cursed the harvest of his brainwave as he was, not unnaturally, given the task of setting up the 7th Battalion self-firing rifles.

I was told that I had been detailed to remain with 'C' Party to work the rifles, which were to be fixed – twelve on a battalion front – ready at the loopholes. The nose caps and magazines were removed, back sights bent and any other little idea for making the weapons useless to the Turks was carried out. At the time when the last men would be moving down we were to start operating the rifles. On the left, where I was posted, the Turks were fairly close, so we had the drip set longer there and after I saw the men leave the rifle pit on the flank, I stood alone in that black tunnel for 15 minutes. White moonlight through the entrances to the rifle 'possies' made it all the more gruesome and it was a very frightened lad who at last started to fill the water-cans. Off we started. Orders were to move smartly, but not to run, and it took considerable self-control to stick to the latter part. I wondered then, and often since, if any unfortunate 'Jacko' got hit with one of those bullets, as it would have been the depth of 'stiffness' for him.[48]

Lance Corporal William Scurry, 7th (Victoria) Battalion, 2nd Brigade, 1st Division, AIF

In the pitch dark the route down to the beach was not easy and the officers needed all their motivational skills to keep their exhausted men going.

The strips of blankets around the boots began to unwind and impede progress. There was not time to halt and rectify this. Before we had traversed half the distance we faced our greatest difficulties, difficulties we had not foreseen. The men of the last party had not slept since the night of the 17th. It was now the morning of the 20th. While on the job in the line the excitement of the situation had kept all of us actively awake. Now that we were clear of the trenches, the nervous strain had its reaction. We were all loaded with packs and rifles. Some men began to drop out of line. All they desired was sleep and to be left alone. All the Turks in the world did not interest them. Persuasion was useless and time was slipping by. There was nothing left but to ply the boot to the fleshy part of the anatomy. We literally booted some of them along to, and on to, the last boat.[49]

Second Lieutenant Stanley Savige, 24th (Victoria) Battalion, 6th Brigade, 2nd Division, AIF

Up on Russell's Top, Lieutenant James Caddy and his team of sappers sat in their dugouts waiting for the order to detonate their mines. They stayed there long after the front lines had been abandoned.

Everyone was now clear of the trenches and Major Fitzgerald having received permission by telephone from the Rearguard Commander, Colonel Paton, to fire the mines, instructed me to do so after he had got on top of the dugout to see the effect. At 5.30 a.m. Sergeant Contan pushed down the exploder connected with the mines in L8 and L11, and immediately afterwards I fired the big mine in Arnall's tunnel. The ground vibrated, there was a dull roar and two large craters were formed. Immediately afterwards, heavy rifle fire opened up along the whole of the enemy line. After slabs of guncotton to destroy the exploders had been set off and Corporal Penny had lit the fuse of the mine on the track leading down to the beach, we made as quickly as possible down the hill.[50]

Lieutenant James Caddy, 5th Field Company, Australian Engineers, AIF

Also among the last to leave were the signallers who had been manning a signal station on Plugge's Plateau to monitor the progress of the arrangements. They saw from close range the thunderous detonation of Caddy's mines.

Half way down the hillside a mine in the direction of Russell's Top was fired like a miniature Vesuvius. The Turks, apparently very nervous, instantly opened a furious rifle and machine gun fire. The bullets lobbed among and all round us, but miraculously no one was hit. Breath was not drawn till all were safely aboard the barge. The Turks, contrary to our expectations, appeared to know nothing of our withdrawal.[51]

Private A. H. Edwards, 2nd Divisional Signal Company, 2nd Division, AIF

Meanwhile, the exhausted last ditchers had got back to the beach. Even here they were not safe from some old enemies – the guns from behind Gaba Tepe that had been firing intermittently into Anzac since 25 April. Still McIlroy's luck held good.

> At the beach we found a sentry, who warned us to hurry past, as 'Beachy Bill' was dropping his 'pills' regularly every few minutes. We crowded on to the barge lying alongside the jetty and between decks was soon filled with a mass of unshaven, haggard and dirty looking 'diggers' all talking at once, and the air thick with tobacco smoke. After the recent strain and the prohibition on smoking for fear the lighting of matches might arouse suspicion, one can imagine the clamour which broke out – everybody at once trying to tell the other fellow his experiences. I will always remember those men – probably the pick of the whole Force, and they looked it, despite their ragged appearance; some with full beards, while the lean cheeks of the others were covered with several days' stubble.[52]
>
> Second Lieutenant George McIlroy, 24th (Victoria) Battalion, 6th Brigade, 2nd Division, AIF

As they sailed away from Anzac Cove for the last time there was at least a visually impressive send-off.

> We were taken off to a small transport, from which the Turks could be heard still firing at nothing, and as a grand finale we had a panoramic view of the wholesale destruction of stores on shore. Hundreds of hospital tents had been soaked in kerosene and fired; as the guy ropes burnt through the tents floated up like fire balloons; the tremendous conflagration being reflected in the sky.[53]
>
> Private A. H. Edwards, 2nd Divisional Signal Company, 2nd Division, AIF

The attempted destruction of the stores was a grand sight at both Anzac and Suvla. Huge fires blazed and the ships of the Royal Navy poured shells into the abandoned stores depots. They had done it: not only had Suvla and Anzac been evacuated, but it had been achieved without casualties.

ASHORE THE TURKS were slow to react. In recent days, the Anzacs had gone quiet before, but then burst back into lethal life. Had they really gone? Had the British left Suvla? It is not clear at exactly what time the Turks moved from tentative suspicions to certainty about the evacuation, but there were many factors hampering any response beyond opening up a vigorous artillery barrage and sending out patrols.

> The alarm was sent to all the Divisions, the reserves brought close up and orders issued to immediately send out strong officer patrols to approach the enemy trenches to establish whether they were occupied and report forthwith any evacuation by signal. It was urgently necessary to establish the enemy's intention, and in the case of evacuation to immediately drive forward with all available forces to the seashore. The artillery was to open fire on the coastal area and the landing-stages. It was impossible to do more at the moment. A clearing of the position depended on the resolution with which the patrols advanced towards the enemy lines. Yes, this was the only possible way of clearing up the position, because about three in the morning a steadily increasing mist commenced rising which hid the full moon which so far shone, and clouded the English activities in a curtain which we were neither able to pierce nor penetrate. God had been stronger than Allah![54]
>
> Colonel Hans Kannengiesser, Headquarters, XVIII Corps, Fifth Army

The British have always claimed that they destroyed almost everything, but there were so many thousands of tons of stores squirrelled away in the ANZAC and IX Corps bases that this is not impossible. When the fires had burnt down and the explosions ceased, there was still a cornucopia of valuable supplies left to plunder for the Turks, who were short of almost everything.

> Immense stores of all kinds were abandoned by the British on their withdrawal. Between Suvla Bay and Ari Burnu five small steamers and more than sixty boats were abandoned on the beach. We found large quantities of material for dummy rail lines, telephones and obstacles, piles of tools of all kinds, medicine chests, medical supplies and water filters. A great mass of artillery and infantry ammunition had been abandoned and whole lines of carriages and caissons, hand arms of all kinds, boxes of hand grenades and machine gun barrels. Many stacks of conserves, flour, food and mountains of wood were found. The tent camps had been left standing and sacrificed. This probably served better

than anything else to mask the withdrawal. Several hundred horses which could not be embarked were killed and lay in long rows.[55]

General Otto Liman von Sanders, Headquarters, Fifth Army

The British and Anzac forces had also left behind their dead. As they departed, Private George Scott remembered two of his old comrades, linked together by a long-forgotten misdemeanour on Christmas Day back in Cairo.[56]

There was Company Quartermaster Sergeant Archie Bowers, killed by a shell fragment while shaving in the trench – prior to going down to the beach to be commissioned. He was the NCO who found our AWOL Aussies in the Eden Palace Hotel and marched them ignominiously back to Mena Camp. He would have made a first-class officer. Another grave is that of my great friend, Tom Harness. Shot through the eye, he died in my arms at Johnston's Jolly, conscious just long enough to mutter, 'Can you do anything for me?' He was one of the four marched home by Archie.[57]

Private George Scott, 4th (New South Wales) Battalion, 1st Brigade, 1st Division, AIF

His friends' graves are still there today in the 4th Parade Ground Cemetery at Anzac.

THE QUESTIONS LEFT were fairly simple. Would the Allies really want to continue to hold on to Helles? Would the Turks blast them off the Peninsula with their new, heavier guns? And, if the Allies did decide to evacuate, could they fool the Turks a second time? Or would there be another catastrophic slaughter on the shores of V and W Beaches? The Turks began to move their units south to Helles while the men of VIII Corps watched the weather patterns with considerable trepidation. Some 1,400 miles away at his headquarters in a freezing St Omer, General Sir Douglas Haig, just a few hours after being appointed to replace Sir John French as Commander in Chief of the BEF, received a telegram from Kitchener telling him that Suvla and Anzac had been evacuated. Haig expressed his grim satisfaction at this news in his diary. As well he might. Without any further draining of the Empire's strength into the 'Dardanelles sink', as he called it, he could turn his full attention to the business of winning the war where he and the professional generals had always said it must be won, the Western Front.

19

LAST RITES AT HELLES

There must have been a dead man of ours to pave every yard of that last march. And we were leaving them, lads of our platoon, gallant officers who were merry at mess, who died to win trenches we had left behind us. Trudging past the sombre-brooding cypress trees we remembered our dead and the pity and tragic waste of it all, and tried to hope that someday a British service bugle would once again ring out over those little graves in that lost land of ours.[1]

Sub Lieutenant Ivan Heald, Hood Battalion, 1st Naval Brigade, RND

FOR THE ANZAC CORPS the Gallipoli campaign was over. The operations at Anzac had been a failure, but the responsibility for that failure did not lie with the Australian and New Zealander troops themselves, who had demonstrated remarkable resilience. What they had been asked to do was not a realistic operation of war. But now they had gone; now the VIII Corps was left marooned in its lines at Helles. By this time the Helles garrison, which still numbered 42,000 in late November, was in a dire state. Both the RND and the 42nd Division were played out and needed a lengthy period of rest and recuperation to rebuild their depleted ranks. It was therefore decided that the 13th Division, fresh from their evacuation of Suvla, should be sent to relieve the 42nd Division; the RND would have to wait. An additional complication was the attitude of the French, who were keen to remove their remaining division and artillery contingent as soon as possible. The North African troops were already being gradually withdrawn, to be replaced in the line by the 29th Division, which was also in a terrible condition. The French artillery perforce remained, for not only were they irreplaceable but their departure would be a sure sign to the Turks that an evacuation was imminent. Of their infantry soon only the Colonial Brigade remained perched on the cliffs above Kereves Dere on the extreme right.

The Turks now had the freedom to focus their energies on Helles. More to the point their increasingly effective artillery could move up and blast the British and French to perdition. The Turks were well aware that Helles was likely to be evacuated, but they still had no idea when.

> It was thought possible that the enemy might hang on for some time. That could not be permitted. Hence a plan of attack on the enemy's position at Sedd el Bahr was at once taken in hand, giving due consideration to the technical troops expected from Germany. An attack was prepared on the entire south front by the four divisions there and eight others to be brought up.[2]
>
> General Otto Liman von Sanders, Headquarters, Fifth Army, Turkish Army

The guns were already being stacked up around the shoulders of Achi Baba and their shells crashed down on the Allied lines. The odds in the lottery that decided life or death were getting shorter for the troops left at Helles. On 20 December, Lieutenant Henri Feuille was at his observation post looking out towards Achi Baba. Already several shells had dropped nearby, but Feuille had been ordered to locate a concealed Turkish battery.

> Suddenly, the characteristic roar of another shell approaching rapidly! The whistle grew to a crescendo – was it going to pass over us? To my sorrow the question had no sooner crossed my mind when the answer came: it was a direct hit! It had a terrifying rending effect on the paltry roof protection, just 60 centimetres from my head. The earth seemed to open up like a volcano. In a flash my shelter was overwhelmed as huge stones crashed down on my men and on me! Struck violently all over the left hand side of my body, I was thrown to the ground. My telephonist Dechamboux fell across me and we were covered by an avalanche of building material and rough stones, enveloped in acrid fumes, unbreathable, locked in like the night. A few moments passed following this incredible explosion. The melinite fumes slowly

dissipated. I hadn't lost consciousness, despite the pain I felt. I was buried alive, not able to move, buried in a mass of earth and stones as in a straitjacket. The blood flowed freely from two wounds in my skull, covering my face and blinding me.[3]

Lieutenant Henri Feuille, 52nd Battery, 30th Regiment, CEO

With a supreme effort he managed to shout out and was rescued and evacuated. Besides the head wounds, his left arm was broken in two places and his left leg had been ripped open by a shell splinter. But he was lucky. The other two men occupying the observation post were killed.

This shelling steadily increased as more Turkish batteries arrived from Suvla and Anzac, their gunners determined to make their presence felt at Helles.

On Christmas Eve the Turks put up the heaviest bombardment on our section that I had experienced and inflicted, despite the dugouts, very severe casualties. The disadvantage of deep dugouts is the extreme unpleasantness of leaving them. It is relatively easy to be conscientiously brave when you have no alternative, but excuses for remaining under cover where cover exists are damnably easy to find. Fortunately I was robbed of mine because the telephone to the front line from battalion headquarters was seventy yards away from our headquarters mess, and it had to be answered. I know nothing more unpleasant than walking along a trench which is being shelled by howitzers. The bullet which kills you is inaudible, so they say, but the howitzer which kills you is unmistakable. You can hear it coming down for some seconds and you know whether it is going to be close or not, and no parapet or trench can save you, so you just wait or walk on, feeling extremely curious as to what is going to happen. One's curiosity, I found, is strangely mundane. Curiosity about the next world is rare. And yet perhaps the most interesting thing of all is that no one has any sense of grievance against the enemy for trying to kill him, as he tried so very hard, on that unpleasant Christmas Eve, to kill us. And after it is all over, one has much the same feeling of exhilaration as after a cold bath.[4]

Lieutenant Douglas Jerrold, Hawke Battalion, 1st Naval Brigade, RND

Christmas at Helles was a strange affair. Far from home and in the glowering presence of their enemies the troops found the festive season somewhat depressing.

Christmas Day in the trenches! A fitting title for an ode by Dante! Morning found us wet and cold, without a fire to warm us, without change of clothing or hot food or drink: a Christmas without home, friends or cheer. Somehow the thought was so melancholy, while the fact in itself was so small. Why should the 25th of December be any harder than any other day spent under the same circumstances? The Padre and the men looked so disheartened and sad that I could not resist the temptation to laugh – there was a sardonic humour in it all.[5]

Lieutenant Norman King-Wilson, 88th Field Ambulance, RAMC

As on the Western Front, there was no attempt at a Christmas Armistice in 1915. The war had become a serious business with no room for such sentimentalities.

THE FINAL DECISION TO EVACUATE HELLES was accelerated by the appointment of Lieutenant General Sir William Robertson to the position of Chief of the Imperial General Staff (CIGS) on 23 December 1915. He was replacing General Sir Archibald Murray, who had only held the post for three months, but was already generally regarded as indecisive and unable to exercise a meaningful influence on Kitchener; traits that Murray shared with his partial namesake and predecessor, Lieutenant General Sir James Wolfe Murray. Robertson was a very different beast; he was a career soldier who had risen right through the ranks from private to general. His last posting had been as Chief of Staff to General Sir John French at BEF Headquarters. Before taking up his new role as CIGS, Robertson had taken the precaution to define closely his relationship with Kitchener in an effort to reduce the great man's ability as Secretary of State for War to interfere directly in military operations. It was clear that this would be no mere post-holder. Indeed, Asquith was consciously looking for a source of independent advice on the great strategic issues of the day and in Robertson he got an unbiddable, strong-minded individual who was totally committed to the primacy of war on the Western Front.

It is one of the first principles of war that all available resources should be concentrated at the 'decisive' point – that is, at the place where the main decision of the war is to be fought out. There may be a difference of opinion as to where that point should be, but there should never be more than one such point at a time, and once the selection is made, no departure from the principle just mentioned is admissible except (*a*) when it becomes necessary to detach troops for the protection of interests vital to oneself, for example the Suez Canal; or (*b*) when by detaching them the enemy will be compelled as a counter-measure to send a still larger detachment in order to protect interests which are vital to him. This principle, as old as the hills, had been inexcusably violated in 1914–15, and however much we might afterwards try to mitigate the evils resulting there from they could never be entirely removed.[6]

General Sir William Robertson, Imperial General Staff

Robertson's appointment followed that of another career soldier, General Sir Douglas Haig, to command the BEF. Over the next three years the two men would attempt to apply increasing levels of professionalism to the ramshackle British war strategies. But first Robertson had to sort out the inherited chaos of Gallipoli.

But, after all, the main question was what useful purpose would be served by keeping a detachment at Helles, now that the troops had been withdrawn from Anzac and Suvla? Clearly there was none, and to continue hanging on to the place merely because we were afraid to leave it, was not only a waste of men but would be a constant source of anxiety. On the 28th of December, five days after becoming CIGS, I placed before the War Committee a memorandum drafted for me by Callwell, who was acquainted with my views, advocating the immediate and total evacuation of the peninsula. Lord Kitchener supported the recommendation, evacuation was approved, the necessary orders were despatched the same day.[7]

General Sir William Robertson, Imperial General Staff

Monro and Birdwood, who had been forewarned about a likely evacuation, had already commenced planning and progress was rapid. Logistically they knew what to do. But could they get away with it again with the Turks up on Achi Baba peering down on everything they did?

The plans were all but identical to those used in the evacuations of Anzac and Suvla. There would be a long Intermediate Stage during which the Helles garrison would be thinned down from 35,000 men and 127 guns, followed by a quick Final Stage (the evacuation of the last 17,000 soldiers and thirty-seven guns) planned for the night of 8 January. It was accepted that six old French guns and one British 6" gun could not be removed on the final night and would have to be destroyed.

Once again the ruse of silent periods was employed to trick the Turks into exploring forwards into No Man's Land. Thus in the lead-up to New Year's Eve the Helles garrison deliberately allowed their fire to trickle away to a nothing.

> The Turkish sentries kept on firing occasional shots as usual, but as the night wore on their rifles spoke at longer intervals, and towards midnight scarcely a sound disturbed the still air. One of our guns, stationed not far behind Wigan Road, kept firing for short periods at long intervals. It was always the same gun that spoke, but the Turkish artillery made scarcely any effort to reply to it, and the monotonous sound it made only served to render the silence more acute. Only too ready to fall asleep on other nights when the noise of rifles and shell-fire always prevailed, I found it impossible on this particular night to let sleep steal over my eyelids, and there were many other tired soldiers near me who were in the same state. And so we lay more or less awake the whole night through. The night seemed as if it would never end. In the almost intense stillness the senses became exceptionally acute, and one had the feeling that something was going to happen. As it was, nothing happened. Unable to sleep, I lay and smoked, and several times I went out of the dugout into the trenches and looked around. The darkness shrouded everything and the silence of the great night had clearly cast a curious spell upon the imagination. I was looking up at the stars above me when suddenly a man lying on the firestep of the parapet said in a low voice, which almost startled me, 'Do you think Johnny Turk will come over?'[8]
>
> Lieutenant William Sorley-Brown, 4th KOSB, 155th Brigade, 52nd Division

Nothing happened that night but the next night the British introduced a cunning variation when at 00.25 on 1 January every possible man along the whole line opened fire with five rounds rapid while the artillery blazed out. Unable to discern a clear pattern, the Turks were confused. They were even nervous that the British might be about to launch an attack on their lines.

It had been thought that it would be easier to organise and control the evacuation procedure if the soldiers concerned were all of one nationality.

Thus it was decided that the French would be withdrawn entirely and the Colonial Brigade duly departed on the evening of 1 January 1916. Behind them the French left only their artillery batteries and a small party of sappers engaged in dismantling the Decauville light railway.

> The firing scarcely stopped all night at the front. I was a little afraid. We can no longer receive messages; things are getting desperate. How long must we remain here? We are being well shelled from Europe and Asia; the whistling and rumbling of the shells' passage followed on without a gap, falling more or less everywhere but mainly on the beach from which we must be evacuated. I envy my comrades who have already left.[9]
>
> Sapeur Gaston-Louis Giguel, 1st Régiment du Génie, CEO

After the reshuffle the Helles garrison consisted of the 13th Division on the left, the 29th and 52nd Divisions in the centre, and finally the RND, who had moved across to take over the Kereves Dere sector. This sector had contained some of the worst ground anywhere on the Peninsula. The French casualties in the first four months of the campaign had been horrendous; but it soon became apparent to the new residents that a live and let live attitude had grown up on both sides since the campaign had stagnated back in August.

> In many ways this was a rather weird sector. The lines ran right down to the water's edge at a point where a fair sized and very precipitous gully, the Kereves Dere, opened out into the Straits. Here our lines were at the bottom of the gully with the Turks looking right down over us on the other side. A little further inland the positions were reversed, our lines being on the top of the hillside, whilst Johnny was at the bottom. In both cases the communication trenches running steeply down the hillsides were in full view of the chaps opposite, without any possibility of protection, short of head-cover. By all the rules of the game the locality ought to have been an exceptionally unhealthy one, and a happy hunting ground for snipers and whizz-bang merchants on both sides. Fortunately, however, our predecessors, jointly with Johnny, had devised a brilliant way out of the difficulty. On two trees between the lines, right down near the beach, were two flags – one French; one Turkish. As long as nobody, from either side, ventured beyond those flags, there was to be no rifle fire during daylight hours in this particular

region. The agreement was strictly adhered to with the result that this portion of the line was an absolute rest-cure. Wandering along the line, through an olive grove which it traversed, one found chaps placidly leaning over the parapet, or sitting on it. I succeeded in getting one or two photos of No Man's Land by the simple method of strolling out in front of the line near the afore-mentioned trees. I there and then formed the resolve that if ever I should have occasion to run a private war of my own, I would organise it on similar lines![10]

Sapper Eric Wettern, No. 2 Field Company, Royal Engineers, RND

Overall the situation at Helles was extremely difficult as the opposing trenches were in some places as close as any at Anzac, while the front line troops had further to march back than at Suvla. It was a nasty combination. One solution was to block off as many avenues as possible for any pursuing Turks. Routes back to the beach were carefully marked off while all other communication trenches were blocked with barbed wire. All this had to be achieved under ever-increasing Turkish artillery fire during the first week of January 1916. Among the attached German officers on the Turkish side was Major Senftleben.

I am now commander of the heavy artillery of the southern portion from Kirthedere to the shores of the Dardanelles, and have two old and ten new batteries under my command, among which is the Austrian 24-cm howitzer battery with 1,200 rounds. I also have ample ammunition for the other batteries, so that we are shooting from early till late and somewhat facilitating with German shells the retreat of the enemy. In order to stir things up a bit I have brought my 15-cm quick-firing howitzer battery so far forward that from early morning we can also treat Sedd el Bahr to some of our good ammunition. I await each dawn with impatience to be able to reopen firing, and you can very easily imagine what joy such artillery activity with such good observation affords us.[11]

Major Senftleben, Artillery, Southern Group, Fifth Army

With the Turks deeply suspicious of what the British were up to, Liman finally decided to test the waters by ordering an attack along Gully Spur.

During the first days of January 1916 it appeared as though the fire of the land artillery at Sedd el Bahr was becoming weaker. But one gun was firing from several batteries, frequently changing its position, while the fire from the ships, including the largest calibres, sometimes grew to great vehemence. The removal of guns was observed from the Asiatic side. The scouting parties which were pushed forward against the hostile front at all hours of evening and night invariably met with strong resistance. Of the troops designated for the attack, the 12th Division had arrived to the rear of the south front. The division was designated to capture a section of trenches projecting northward opposite the extreme Turkish right, from which the British artillery could have flanked the great attack we were planning. On 7 January I ordered the 12th Division to carry out the attack planned on the extreme Turkish right after 2 hours of preparation by the heaviest artillery fire and explosion of mines.[12]

General Otto Liman von Sanders, Headquarters, Fifth Army

The shells rained down from about noon, building up to a final climax, before the Turks went over the top following the explosion of two mines on Gully Spur at 16.00 on 7 January. In the end the attack was a damp squib, for the Turkish infantry seemed to lack their usual élan and those that did emerge from their trenches were soon quashed by a combination of small arms fire and the naval support fire tearing into the Turkish flank. Only where they faced the 7th North Staffords in the Fifth Avenue sector did they threaten any progress. Afterwards the adjutant of the North Staffords, Captain John Robinson, had to write to the wife of his commanding officer, Lieutenant Colonel Frank Walker:

During all the bombardment your husband was in the firing line. Then the Turks attacked. Their trenches were, at one corner only, from 10–15 yards away. Some four Turks got on to the parapet of our trench here and Colonel Walker finding the bay empty collected three or four and rushed into the bay, into which the Turks were firing. I believe he shot two with his revolver and was himself shot. But the Turks were driven off. That I think is the plain unvarnished tale. He fell down into the bottom of the trench and two of our men fell dead on the top of him. I feel sure he did not speak and that he felt no pain.[13]

Captain John Robinson, 7th North Staffordshire Regiment, 39th Brigade, 13th Division

Colonel Walker's was a typical painless death; a death of the kind found predominantly in letters of condolence to grieving widows.[14]

The British were enormously relieved that the Turkish attack had not been pushed home. That day their total numbers at Helles stood at only 19,000, with sixty-three guns in support. Any sustained effort by the Turks would have surely broken through. Everyone feared a renewed assault and the tension remained excruciating. That night another 2,300 men and nine guns were evacuated. Still the Turks seemed oblivious to what was going on. Come dawn on Saturday 8 January at least those that remained had the consolation that, one way or another, the situation would soon be resolved. As the long hours passed until their evacuation, many could hardly believe what was happening.

> That last day was rather queer. One would feel very much the same sensation on being left behind alone in a house that had been one's home after the family and the furniture had gone. Two French 75s near our camp were very successfully trying to pretend that they were a battery of four guns. Apart from them, there was hardly a soul to be seen. Having nothing to do, we wandered round the line to have a last look round and take some photos. Ate as much as we could possibly tackle, to use up the surplus grub and spent a happy evening opening bully and jam tins and chucking them down a well, also biffing holes in dixies and generally mucking up any serviceable articles.[15]
>
> Sapper Eric Wettern, No. 2 Field Company, Royal Engineers, RND

Meanwhile, the Royal Navy had been told to keep the Turks busy.

> In order to try and make sure the Asiatic batteries should not shell the beaches that night, which they had been doing, and which we feared they might increase, and so prevent our embarking so many men in one night, the Navy sent out some ships off the Asiatic coast. Our aeroplanes went up and they heavily bombarded all Saturday afternoon – 12", 15" and 6" shells were hurled in a continuous stream to where we thought the hidden batteries were, one ship fired 1,000 shells, another *all* her ammunition and it seemed to have the desired result.[16]
>
> Deputy Quartermaster General Walter Campbell, Headquarters, EMF

Every possible preparation had been made and all they could do now was wait for nightfall. The selected routes back to the beach had been marked out with flour while the others had been blocked with masses of tangled barbed wire. Along the planned exit routes control stations were set up to monitor carefully the passage of each party.

> I'm in charge of the divisional rendezvous and as these small scattered groups come in, I have to sort them out into their own particular units and pack them off to the beach. I don't quite know all details yet but the idea seems to be that I've got to put the last man in on his right road, and once that's done, I can promise you that you won't see my heels for small pebbles! Of course we hope that even if they do discover that we are retreating from our front lines pretty soon after we have commenced to go, that they won't come after us too quickly. In fact we are discouraging little schemes of that kind by leaving large numbers of contact mines behind us and various other little booby traps, which should throw a considerable amount of cold water (otherwise melinite) on any thrusting and inquisitive spirits.[17]
>
> Major Norman Burge, Nelson Battalion, 1st Naval Brigade, RND

Up near the front line the final few men wore sandbags over their boots, while a layer of straw was put down on the floors of the trenches to muffle the sound. There was nothing they could do but wait.

> Never did man listen to sound so anxiously as I did, sitting alone in the old French dugout in the red glow of a charcoal brazier. I was fearful that any moment there might come clamouring in my ears the furious babbling splutter of rapid fire, which would mean an attack. But the hours wore on in a healthy sequence of occasional bombs and steady sniping, and half an hour before midnight I made a tour to the end of my line, where my commander, Freyberg, with Asquith and six men, were holding the chaos of mine craters and trenches which the French named *Le Ravin de la Mort*. They both decided there was time to finish some biscuits they had left in a dugout.[18]
>
> Sub Lieutenant Ivan Heald, Hood Battalion, 1st Naval Brigade, RND

At long last the time came for Heald and his small party to creep away on their fraught journey back to V Beach.

> A touch on the back of the last man and he climbed down from the firing step and touched the next man farther along, and quietly we filed out of the long firing line, and, as we stole away, I could hear the Turks

coughing and talking in their trench 20 yards away. Two or three times, to hide the shuffle of the men's gear against the side of the trench, I jumped on the firing step and let my Webley-Scott bark at Achi Baba, and somewhere on the left someone fired a farewell. Very light, which lit up the sandbags until the blackness came welling up out of the trench again as the rocket died away. So we shuffled past the telephone station at the top of the communication trench.[19]

Sub Lieutenant Ivan Heald, Hood Battalion, 1st Naval Brigade, RND

They left behind them a rather élite little group under the command of Lieutenant Commander Bernard Freyberg, accompanied by Arthur Asquith and F. S. Kelly.

We had the honour of being the very last company to leave the firing line on our sector and your humble was selected along with another two to hold a communication trench while the rest of the company retired. Our officer selected J. Geddie (Byker), J. Raymont (West Hartlepool) and myself as 'three level-headed men' to stay till the last. It was a big strain on our nerves as if the Turks tumbled and made a big attack there was only a thin line to keep them back. The men withdrew from the firing line a few at a time, 'B' Company being the last to leave at 11.20 at night. Us three in a specially constructed fort that commanded *our* firing line, the Drakes and the supports. If the Turks made an attack we had to hold it at all costs. 'Johnny' didn't tumble and after Mr Kelly had destroyed the telephone station I led the way as guide, Mr Kelly bringing up the rear. We couldn't help laughing as we could still hear Johnny sniping away as usual – stray bullets whizzing over our heads.[20]

Private Thomas Goulden, Hood Battalion, 1st Naval Brigade, RND

But they were not the very last to abandon the front line in the RND sector. That honour fell to small detachments of divisional engineers whose task it was to block and booby trap as far as possible all trenches that formed the designated route back to V Beach.

We worked our way down, distributing in our trail umbrellas, crinolines and other just causes and impediments why Johnny should not attempt to follow up too closely. Although we were industriously working down as fast as our various little jobs would permit, for some time we were not getting appreciably further from the line, as that beastly trench ran along the support line, and therefore parallel to the front line, for some considerable distance. We naturally expected to see Johnny bobbing over the top at any moment. However, he didn't![21]

Sapper Eric Wettern, No. 2 Field Company, Royal Engineers, RND

Off they went back down the zigzagging communication trenches. Ahead of them the main body of troops was still plodding along the long road that stretched some three miles back to the beach.

The Turk's own moon was in the sky, a perfect crescent with a star, and a wind rising dangerously from the north. Now and again a wistful sigh of a spent bullet, and ever wheeling behind us the shaft of the great Chanak searchlight. The men talked little among themselves, and I think we were all awed by the bigness of the thing, and saddened by the thoughts of the little crosses we were leaving behind us – the little wooden crosses that were creeping higher every day to meet the crescents on that great sullen hill.[22]

Sub Lieutenant Ivan Heald, Hood Battalion, 1st Naval Brigade, RND

Even when they had reached the beach they knew that they were still extremely vulnerable to fire from the Asiatic batteries.

We toiled on to other parties coming through the roofless village of Sedd el Bahr, all anxious now with the knowledge that a Turkish telephone message would stir Asiatic Annie to pound us with shells. Sure enough one came as we waited on the beach. We saw the great flash blotted out by the night, the warning 'G' on a bugle sounded, and, full of foreboding, we began to count the 27 seconds which Annie gives one to think about one's sins before she drops her shell on the beach. This one squabbed miserably in the sea and none followed. The beach was awesome with the throbbing of motor-launches and the shouts of naval officers making perilous berths alongside the sunken steamers which make the pier. There is a curving yellow cliff here, and the foot of it was one long black line where the battalions were moving slowly on to the pier. The whole place reeked of paraffin, and we guessed that dawn would see the beach ablaze. Over the listed sunken ship we clambered, and a jolly naval petty officer chased us along a gangway to the deck of a pitching black silhouette of a destroyer. Seven hundred and fifty war-weary men covered the deck of that destroyer before she slid out into the night, and I think most of us were asleep before we had lost the shore lights.[23]

Sub Lieutenant Ivan Heald, Hood Battalion, 1st Naval Brigade, RND

The men in the control stations carefully counted off each and every soldier who passed them, then at last they themselves moved off to the beach.

At about 1.30 everyone was through and so even if we – the last 600 – had been collared the evacuation would have been a great success as we formed such a small proportion of the total numbers. But I don't think any of us last folks had any such high and uplifting thoughts. I hadn't anyway. At 1.45 the French blew up two 10" and two 4.7"s which had to be left firing till then otherwise it would have given the show away. The flash and noise was just like the gun going off so the Turks didn't suspect.[24]

Major Norman Burge, Nelson Battalion, 1st Naval Brigade, RND

Still the Turkish lines remained quiet. In the end V Beach was evacuated with little trouble from the Turks; all was going perfectly in that respect. But it was increasingly obvious that the weather was changing for the worse.

The wind was rising pretty rapidly and it was beginning to be nastyish by the time we got down. But the French pier, which we used, consisted largely of an out-of-date battleship, which they sank some time ago to form a breakwater, and so we were able to get from her straight into a destroyer. She was the *Grasshopper*, one of the biggest, and we pretty well filled her up. You see, we few and the 400 beach guard (put out as a last line of defence round the beach) and some others make a pretty good load for a destroyer in bad weather. We got away about 3.30.[25]

Major Norman Burge, Nelson Battalion, 1st Naval Brigade, RND

Just round the headland at W Beach there were far more alarums and excitement in the last few hours. Here the sea was much rougher and the waves were pounding away at the makeshift jetties upon which the lives of hundreds of men depended. A further complication was the huge quantity of ammunition which had been packed into the caves at the back of the beach and fused ready for detonation after the last men had left.

As ever even with the best-laid plans there is always the near-certainty of human error; the only question was how serious its consequences might be.

> About midnight one of the magazines in which was stored fire rockets, flares, fuses, small explosives, etc., was accidentally set alight by a careless man with a candle. For a time things seemed serious, for a very large volume of flame was shooting out of the mouth or entrance to the magazine, and frequent explosions, some of them very heavy, were occurring. There was a danger of it spreading to the other magazines which contained quantities of heavy explosives, shells, etc. – and if such occurred it would not be safe on any part of W Beach. The danger appeared so great at one time that the officer in charge of the magazines advised us to clear out of the PMLO's office. So we gathered up everything, but when moving out got word that the danger was past, though the fire continued to burn during the rest of the night, though with lessening severity.[26]
>
> Lieutenant Owen Steele, Newfoundland Regiment, 88th Brigade, 29th Division

On the beach by dint of constant running repairs to the piers and pontoon bridges, most of the men were able to embark in safety. Then, in the very last stages, there was a complication as the tempestuous waves threatened the evacuation of a relatively small party of troops from the 13th Division who were designated to leave by two lighters from Gully Beach. When one of them ran aground and had to be abandoned there was no room for all the men on the remaining lighter, so a party of 150 men was ordered to make its way to W Beach by the path cut into the shoreline. They set off just after 02.00. Meanwhile, Major General Stanley Maude, who was unwilling to abandon his headquarters kit, decided to make his own way with his immediate staff by the main road using mobile stretchers to carry the load.

> We could not go by the beach route as it was too heavy going, so we started up hill on to the plateau, and very hard work it was. We all puffed and blew like grampuses, especially as we were all warmly clad.[27]
>
> Major General Stanley Maude, Headquarters, 13th Division

Lieutenant Colonel Edward Stretch led the main body by the shoreline path. Neither party had an easy passage.

It was the wire that our troops had put down which delayed us so much as we had to cut our way through and then re-lay it so as to delay 'Johnny Turk' in case he was coming up behind us. When my party reached W Beach the General had not turned up, the two lighters were therefore kept alongside the jetty to wait for him and everyone embarked in the lighter which was ready to depart at a moment's notice. We waited there perhaps half an hour, our surroundings brightly lit up by the burning dump on the cliff above and we wondered whether the General or the Turks would arrive first.[28]

Lieutenant Colonel Edward Stretch, 8th Royal Welsh Fusiliers, 40th Brigade, 13th Division

The military commander at W Beach, Brigadier General James O'Dowda, was unwilling to abandon Maude and his roving eye fell upon Lieutenant Owen Steele, who was peremptorily ordered to track him down.

I went up over the hill and shouted the General's name until I eventually found him and so soon hurried them on board the waiting lighter. This was a dangerous and fearsome undertaking when one considers the following. When I left it was 3.30 a.m. – the fuses in the magazines were lighted at 3.15 timed for 45 minutes – one of the many fires to be lit, among the stocks of supplies etc., was already burning – the Turks had sent over a few shells during the night, though very few, but two at a time, and two were likely to come at any time – and again, our firing line had been empty since just before 12 o'clock – 4 hours – so one might possibly encounter a body of Turks. However we got on board at just 5 minutes to 4.00 and within 5 minutes and before we had even untied from the wharf, the first magazine went off with a very heavy explosion. A great volume of flame shot hundreds of feet into the air, debris of all kinds went everywhere, and as we were only a hundred yards away from it some came our way. It did no damage beyond breaking one man's arm in three places. The second explosion came when we were less than 50 yards off the wharf and flame, noise and everything was greater though nothing reached us. By now there were fires everywhere, and it was really a wonderful sight. Another lighter and a hospital boat went away from the pier when we did – so we were really the last away from the Peninsula.[29]

Lieutenant Owen Steele, 1st Royal Newfoundland Regiment, 88th Brigade, 29th Division

The weather was still deteriorating; the waves were driving in hard, there was a heavy swell running and the strong winds threatened to push the heavily laden lighters back in towards the cataclysmic explosions and the threat of Turkish shells crashing down on the beach. A threat that soon became a reality.

> What a hullaballoo! The Turks thought we were going at last and opened every gun they could on roads, communication trenches, beaches and anything else they could think of. Some of us had thought they wanted to let us get off – but this fire showed they had meant to make it as uncomfortable for us as possible.[30]
>
> Major Norman Burge, Nelson Battalion, 1st Naval Brigade, RND

The very last man left at Helles seems to have been Lieutenant Ronald Langton-Jones of the Royal Navy. He and two seamen had been detached to stay on the sunken hulk, which was only connected to W Beach by a flimsy pontoon bridge, with the duty of making fast the destroyers on to which many of the men would embark. Now he was trapped.

> In the early hours of the morning, the frail bridge connecting us with the shore broke away. However, I managed to get a hurried despatch through to Captain Staveley, advising him of the situation, and he was able to divert in time the few remaining troops due to pass through the hulk. When the evacuation was completed, he passed by the end of the hulk in his picket boat, and shouted above the now howling gale that he would send in a destroyer to rescue us. The main magazine by that time had exploded and blown sky-high the cliff, forming it into a gully. Stores and dumps were burning furiously, and the Turks were really excited. As we stood in the dawn watching and waiting a piece of shrapnel tore off my left shoulder-strap and knocked yet another hole in the hulk's funnel. Just as daylight was breaking HMS *Fury* arrived, and, by a superb feat of seamanship, turned his ship short round on a lee shore and shoved her bows close into the hulk and held her with a bow line. Willing hands then threw us ropes and hauled us on board over her forecastle, one at a time. I was the last man.[31]
>
> Lieutenant Ronald Langton-Jones, Royal Navy

Langton-Jones was taken off at about 04.30 in the morning. Shortly afterwards, as the rescuing *Fury* moved away under a smattering of Turkish shrapnel as a last goodbye, the British warships responded in kind, plaster-ing the mottled slopes of Achi Baba with layers of shell bursts and spurts of flames in one last defiant bombardment.

Despite the tension, it was apparent that the British had escaped all but unscathed, although they had had to abandon a lot of their stores and equipment. The destruction had been impressive; but the scale of the stores held at Helles was such that much remained for the delectation of the Turks.

The booty was extraordinary. Wagon parks, automobile parks, mountains of arms, ammunition and entrenching tools were collected. Here too most of the tent camps and barracks had been left standing, in part with all of their equipment. Many hundreds of horses lay in rows, shot or poisoned, but quite a number of horses and mules were captured and turned over to the Turkish artillery. Here as at the other fronts the stacks of flour and subsistence had some acid solution poured over them to render them unfit for our use. In the next few days the hostile ships made vain attempts to set the stacks and the former British tent camps and barracks on fire. It took nearly two years to clean up the grounds. The immense booty of war material was used for other Turkish armies. Many ship loads of conserves, flour and wood were removed to Constantinople. What the ragged and insufficiently nourished Turkish soldiers took away, cannot be estimated. I tried to stop plundering by a dense line of sentinels but the endeavour was in vain.[32]

General Otto Liman von Sanders, Headquarters, Fifth Army

The British soldiers may have been reluctant to accept the defeat that was confirmed by their withdrawal but it is not in the nature of soldiers to brood for too long on what might have been. Their minds turned swiftly to the challenges to come; some were less serious than others.

Personally I wouldn't mind a winter on the Suez Canal – with a mild engagement in which of course we rout the Turks with no loss to ourselves second and fourth Fridays![33]

Major Norman Burge, Nelson Battalion, 1st Naval Brigade, RND

The tangled strategic policy bequeathed by the blunders of 1915 meant that hundreds of thousands of British and Imperial troops would be caught up in the needless sideshow campaigns at Salonika, Palestine and

Mesopotamia. The best of the Gallipoli divisions were despatched to the Western Front: the 29th Division, the RND and the ANZAC Corps were all serving on the Somme within months. Here, once they had acclimatised to the pace and intensity of real trench warfare dominated by the massed roaring of the artillery, they did well. But their casualties were high: indeed, the insouciant Major Norman Burge, quoted above, would be killed leading his Nelson Battalion into action against the Germans at Beaucourt in November 1916.

The evacuation had been carried out brilliantly, of that there could be no doubt. The Allies had been blessed with good fortune at several points in the process, but they had deserved their luck for the foresight and application used in conceiving and implementing the plans under severe pressure. Yet those who, in pointing to that achievement, have sought to wrest victory from defeat have considerably overstated the case. It was a success; but it was a success forged from the wreckage of defeat. Lieutenant Douglas Jerrold, one of the surviving cynics among the RND officers, was inclined to pour scorn from his lofty pedestal.

> The evacuation, the world has repeatedly been informed, was a
> very skilful operation. The phrase is just stupid. It does not require
> intelligence but merely the instinct of self-preservation to withdraw
> troops quietly by night instead of noisily by day, or to withdraw them
> gradually instead of all at once. Or to hold the front line to the last and
> so conceal your intentions from the enemy. There were no casualties
> because the Turks did not attack, but in no case would there, or could
> there, have been a major disaster. The period of danger was nothing
> like twenty-four hours but in any case there was nothing that anyone
> could do about it. If the Turks had chanced to launch a powerful attack
> on the last day no staff work could have prevented the loss of most
> of the few troops left behind there. But the risk, seeing that the Turks
> never attacked in force, was negligible. It was, as everyone else has said,
> a 'miracle of organisation'. We are good at that sort of thing. When we
> surrender the last defences of our Empire, we may be certain that the
> protocols, like the graves, will be in perfect order.[34]
>
> Lieutenant Douglas Jerrold, Hawke Battalion, 1st Naval Brigade, RND

And there was indeed an element of exaggerated self-congratulation in much of the praise lavished on the evacuation from within the British camp. It was evident that the hubris – that overestimation of their own genius and abilities that had provoked the disaster of Gallipoli in the first place – had not yet been burnt out of them. That casual arrogance would be finally exorcised by the Germans on the gently rolling ridges and valleys of the Somme in 1916.

20

MYTHS AND LEGENDS

Though the bodies recovered from the tragedy have been stripped and laid out in the Morgue, no hand has yet dared remove the masks from their faces.[1]

General Sir Ian Hamilton

THERE ARE MANY POTENT MYTHS relating to Gallipoli. They have had a compelling and long-lasting grip over the imagination due to the power of the emotions unleashed during the course of the campaign and the intoxicating literary prowess of some of the main participants. But towering above all else is the construct of Australian and New Zealand popular opinion that places their two nations firmly at the centre of the campaign, at times ignoring the contributions of the British, French and Indian troops. The truth is that the ANZAC Corps played a very important, but secondary role. The total British and French forces were much larger, the main effort at Gallipoli was firmly centred at Helles, and only during the August Offensive did the emphasis shift to Anzac and Suvla. Even then the larger British numerical contribution was manifest.

Overall the campaign was a huge drain on Allied military resources involving nearly half a million troops across the eight-month campaign, of which 410,000 were from the British Empire with a further 79,000 from France and her North African colonies. Of these the British Empire lost 205,000 (115,000 killed, wounded or missing; 90,000 evacuated sick) while the French had 47,000 casualties (approximately 27,000 killed, wounded or missing, with some 20,000 evacuated sick). This compares with 251,309 Turkish casualties (186,869 killed, wounded or missing; 64,440 evacuated sick).[2] Within this all-consuming bedlam the significance of the ANZAC Corps involvement in the campaign lay not in its actual achievements on the battlefield as an inexperienced formation – the Turks won, after all – but rather in the development of a powerful spirit of comradeship, a determination in battle and a growing military competence which would help create a burgeoning sense of nationhood in both Australia and New Zealand. This would be the real legacy of Anzac Cove.

But the underlying British myth is even more pernicious. It is a far more dangerous construct, riddled with the kind of self-delusion and boastful assumption of racial superiority that had been responsible for the Gallipoli disaster in the first place. The landings of the 29th Division and the ANZAC Corps have been hailed as a military achievement of the highest order. Much is made of the numerous Turkish machine guns, the streams of lead, heroism beyond measure and of struggles against almost insuperable odds. Their heroism *is* undeniable, but at Helles and Anzac on 25 April the insuperable odds were faced by the Turks not the British. It may have been the first landing to be made in the face of modern weapons, but the British could hardly have done worse; or indeed the Turks much better. This was not the view held after the war by General Sir Ian Hamilton and his acolytes. They simply refused to accept defeat; as far as they were concerned they had won.

> When at long last the official history of the Dardanelles comes out we shall learn for the first time how sweeping were the victories won at Anzac as well as Helles by the afternoon of the 25th April 1915. On the reverse of those pages we shall read how the fog of war descended upon the commanders, hiding from them what lay in the hollow of their hands.[3]
>
> General Sir Ian Hamilton

The official histories show nothing of the kind. The British Empire could hardly have survived too many more 'sweeping' victories like those 'won' on 25 April. Throughout the campaign the British exaggerated the numerical and machine gun strength of the opposition while simultaneously underestimating the collective military skill and resolve of the Turkish soldiers. As evidence of failure mounted up, the time-honoured response was to blame everyone else.

> Behind us we had a swarm of adverse influences: our own General Headquarters in France, the Chief of the Imperial General Staff of the War Office, the First Sea Lord of the Admiralty, GQG in France, the French Cabinet and the best organised part of the British press. Fate willed it so. Faint hearts and feeble wills seemed for a while to succeed in making vain the sacrifices of Anzac, Helles and Suvla. Only the dead men stuck it out to the last.[4]
>
> General Sir Ian Hamilton

There is a distinct whiff of 'everybody is mad but me' in this diatribe. Yet it is irrefutable that mistakes *were* made at *every* level of command at Gallipoli: operational planning was woeful and any localised tactical opportunities that arose were routinely missed. This endemic military incompetence at command and staff level was then lethally combined with troops that had little or no experience of modern warfare in 1915. The lesson was clear to those who would heed it: raw courage was not enough to combat bolt-action rifles, machine guns, trench systems, barbed wire and, above all, artillery. Amateurism was doomed and the British Army needed a more professional approach if it was to triumph in the Great War.

Overall the British attitude to Gallipoli has been one of wishful thinking, filtered through romantic classicism; a tragedy acted out by doomed new romantic heroes, as typified by the likes of Rupert Brooke, Dick Doughty Wylie and Charles Lister. But one slightly macabre story concerning the post–war treatment of Doughty Wylie's grave shows the dark comedy that keeps breaking through to undermine any attempt to rewrite Gallipoli as a classical tragedy for our modern age.

> His grave was located on a small knoll just outside of the village. I was requested by the Imperial War Graves Commission to make the site more permanent as his widow had in view building a monument over it. We went to the spot and I instructed my men to make a trench down to solid ground around it, then to pour concrete in it and to cap the whole grave with a 6" slab of concrete. We got started first by removing the tangle of barbed wire over it and then carefully removed the top

soil. Within a few inches his body became visible huddled in a crouched position enveloped in a ragged uniform with belt.[5]

A. E. Cooper, Imperial War Graves Commission

Cooper marked off the precise location of the special foundations he required for the new grave and then rode off on his horse to inspect the other war cemeteries under his jurisdiction. On his return he looked to see how his men were getting on with their task.

I did not know whether to laugh or cry! What had obviously happened is that the trench in the soft soil had collapsed so that my men removed the body from the grave and finished the excavations. Then they had placed his skull at the top of the grave and made a geometric pattern of his bones – even down to the finger bones. I hurried to get the foundations around the bones and waited to put the concrete slab over him. I hope he now rests in peace.[6]

A. E. Cooper, Imperial War Graves Commission

The imagined dignity of death in a righteous cause should always be overlaid with the brutal realities of that forfeit: the sudden end of a life, the hurried burial, the grieving widow or family back in England, but here we have the surrealistic use of the corpse as idle plaything. The scale of Doughty Wylie's sacrifice is not undermined by such sordid realities; but let no one use such heroes as examples to young soldiers without allowing them to consider the whole picture. Death is not glorious; it is almost always squalid, or at least slightly tawdry in its aftermath. The chimera of imperishable fame is the cruellest hoax of all – for no name lives forever and all deeds are ultimately either forgotten or mythologised out of all recognition. Ultimately it must be remembered that the British heroes died for a losing cause in 1915.

In contrast to the British, the French have always rather downplayed the doomed campaign for the Dardanelles. This may seem perverse, as for the most part their troops fought both bravely and with considerable skill against terrible odds. They were backed by their magnificent artillery, which not only had to deal with the Turks in front of them but had to support the British attacks. All this, while engaging and suppressing as best they could the batteries firing into their flank from the Asiatic coast just across the Dardanelles. Yet, to the French, Gallipoli was always a British campaign. Their more pressing concerns were closer to home and, while their losses at Gallipoli were painful, these were dwarfed by the incredible casualties they suffered on the Western Front. Perhaps one day French historians will re-evaluate their role at Gallipoli; one can only hope so.

The Turks too had their heroes, although few of their names have survived. But they too sacrificed their tomorrows for their country. And of course they did emerge victorious in the 1915 campaign. The best remembered, Mustafa Kemal, would rise to become the leader of his country as Kemal Atatürk.

> The English brag about the soldiers and officers who fought gallantly and bravely at Ari Burnu landings and at this front. But think about the enemy which landed at Ari Burnu's shores equipped with the most advanced war machinery and determination, and was, by and large, forced to remain on these shores. Our officers and soldiers who with love for their motherland and religion and heroism protected the doors of their capital Constantinople against such a strong enemy won the right to a status of which we can be proud. I congratulate all the members of the fighting units under my command. I remember with deep and eternal respect all the ones who sacrificed their lives and became martyrs for this great objective.[7]
>
> Kemal Atatürk

Yet we must also beware the potent Turkish mythology centred on their successes at Gallipoli which seeks to forget the denouement of the wider hostilities. For the Turks were to comprehensively *lose* the war, totally defeated when they surrendered on 30 October 1918. There was even a second, totally unopposed and now forgotten, landing of British troops at V Beach on 10 November 1918. By the end of that year all those potent symbols of Turkish resistance – Krithia, Achi Baba, Third Ridge, Chunuk Bair, the Kilid Bahr Plateau, the Narrows forts and even Constantinople itself – were under the iron grip of the Allies. The French were back in occupation of Sedd el Bahr and a British division was encamped in the plain adjoining Maidos. That was the eventual outcome of the war – Allied victory and *total* Turkish defeat. Indeed, no one could have put it more bluntly than Atatürk himself did in his renowned 'Six Day' speech to the Second National Conference in 1927.

The group of powers which included the Ottoman Government had been defeated in the Great War. The Ottoman Army had been crushed on every front. An armistice had been signed under severe conditions. The prolongation of the Great War had left the people exhausted and impoverished. Those who had driven the people and the country into the general conflict had fled and now cared for nothing but their own safety. The Army had been deprived of their arms and ammunition, and this state of affairs continued. The Entente Powers did not consider it necessary to respect the terms of the armistice. On various pretexts, their men-at-war and troops remained.[8]

Kemal Atatürk

In the end Gallipoli was just a small staging post – one of many – in a global conflict that would ultimately be decided on the Western Front. Winston Churchill, the individual most responsible for launching the attack on the Gallipoli Peninsula in 1915, was the same man who cared little how the Turks would react when he 'stole' their battleships from them in August 1914. Yet, when Turkey joined the German side, Churchill suddenly found it vital to knock them out; indeed, he came to believe that the whole secret of beating the Central Powers lay in removing Turkey from the war. But the Easterners were totally wrong in their dangerous fantasies. As the campaign progressed, both Churchill and Hamilton were sucked into the fatal trap of thinking that *their* project was all-important, of failing to consider the far more telling requirements and priorities of other leaders and fronts. Little thought was given to Admiral Sir John Jellicoe, who faced the German High Seas Fleet across the North Sea knowing that a serious naval defeat could lose Britain the war in an afternoon. No consideration at all was given to Field Marshal Sir John French taking on the unfettered might of the German Army on the Western Front. Others who should and did know better failed to rein back the protagonists in their Gaderene rush to disaster. The Secretary of State for War, Field Marshal Lord Kitchener, the greatest British soldier statesman of his age, feared the consequences of a diversion of resources. He also feared the effects on India and the Middle East of a reversal against the Turks, but despite those fears he failed to take any effective restraining action. The First Sea Lord, Admiral Sir John Fisher, knew the importance of concentrating naval resources in the North Sea, but allowed himself to drift along in the reassurances of the charismatic Churchill until it was far too late. And nor should the other members of the War Council escape the blame for failing to pay due care and attention in the decisions they took in January 1915, committing hundreds of thousands of soldiers and sailors to a doomed expedition.

By diverting resources to Gallipoli the Allies exposed themselves to a greater possibility of defeat by the Germans on the Western Front. They also ran the risk of the Turks to soundly thrashing them, with negative consequences for British standing across the Islamic world – exactly what happened and the very result that Kitchener originally dreaded. But beating the Turks would have had no impact if the Germans had triumphed elsewhere. The real battle would be fought on the Western Front where Germany, the driving force of the Central Powers, had to be beaten if the war was to be won. Germany was possessed of the finest army and one of the most robust economies in the world. Millions would have to die before she could be brought to accept defeat. Yet in the end Germany was beaten in the series of gigantic toe-to-toe battles in 1918. Battles in which the much-maligned British generals, under the command of Field Marshal Sir Douglas Haig, employed the sophisticated 'All Arms Battle' tactics collectively developed over the preceding four years. Battles centred on the employment of massed artillery to suppress the ability of defending troops to fire on attacking troops. And yes, battles where the Australian Corps and New Zealand Division, both by then forged into brilliantly led veteran forces, set the benchmark for the Allies in the art of modern warfare. It was these battles that drained the last lifeblood from the German Army. But this was a world away from the irrelevancies of Gallipoli. A *professional* world away from blindly optimistic schemes sketched out without reference to the forces required to beat a dangerous and experienced enemy, the Turks, who had almost everything in their favour.

Crucial to an understanding of the failure at Gallipoli is an appreciation of the short comings of the British Army of 1915. The military technology, staff work, logistics, weaponry and tactics at Hamilton's disposal were inadequate for the task. There were simply not enough guns at Gallipoli for the Allies to have any chance against Turkish troops that were well dug in, with barbed wire, machine guns and artillery support.

There were fifty-six 18-pdrs at Helles when I assumed command on the 29th May, and subsequently they were increased to seventy-two at the end of July. The total amount of ordinary 18-pdr ammunition I could therefore allot justifiably for the artillery preparation before an attack of our four British infantry divisions never exceeded 12,000 rounds. The complete absence of HE was severely felt, as shrapnel was of little use for destroying trenches, machine gun emplacements, etc. During June two batteries and during July two more batteries of 5" howitzers arrived at Helles. Some of these howitzers were very old and worn by corrosion, and were consequently inaccurate. As for heavy artillery, practically speaking there was none! Consequently we had no heavy guns capable of replying to the Turkish heavy guns which enveloped us on three sides, and from whose fire our infantry and artillery suffered severely. My feelings as artillery commander, unable to give them anything like the support they would have had in France or Flanders, may be guessed. In Gallipoli the VIII Army Corps at Helles, which was composed of four British Divisions, never had enough field artillery or ammunition to support more than one Division, and never possessed sufficient heavy artillery to support more than one Infantry Brigade.[9]

Brigadier General Sir Hugh Simpson-Baikie, Headquarters, VIII Corps

There it was in a nutshell. The British Army triumphed on the Western Front because, as a crucial part of the development of the 'All Arms Battle', they eventually won the artillery war. At Gallipoli they never even got started: it was a campaign that needed hundreds of guns that did not exist, fired by gunners not yet trained, using complex artillery techniques that had not yet been invented, firing hundreds of thousands of shells not yet manufactured. It required infantry tactics not yet painfully developed in the heat of battle and support weapons not even imagined. It needed a logistical infrastructure that did not and probably never could exist in the eastern Mediterranean. It needed an experienced body of general and staff officers able to operate in a coherent fashion at all levels of command, who could analyse any prospective operations for practicality and pitfalls before issuing the orders in good time to allow lower echelons to carry out their own operational planning.

But it *was* 1915. Gallipoli shared the failings of every campaign launched in that benighted year. Indeed, it provided a checklist of the defining characteristics common to the other British Easterner military adventures in Mesopotamia, Salonika and East Africa in 1915: a lack of realistic goals; no coherent plan; the use of inexperienced troops; a failure to comprehend or properly disseminate maps and intelligence; negligible artillery support; inadequate logistical and medical arrangements; a gross underestimation of the enemy; easily disrupted communications; incompetent local commanders – all overlaid with lashings of misplaced confidence, leading to inexorable disaster. Gallipoli was damned before it began, and it ended at a level of catastrophe that could only be disguised by vainglorious bluster. Some humorists, even at the time, joked that the campaign was based on 'Lemnos, Tenedos, Imbros and Chaos!';[10] others mythologised themselves as the victims of a tragedy beyond mortal control. Churchill was rightly pilloried in the aftermath of the failure at Gallipoli and his rebirth as a war leader during the Second World War is a testament to both his amazing political skills and the sheer forgetfulness of the average voter.

After the dust had settled, the military view of the Gallipoli campaign was largely negative throughout the inter-war years. Indeed, it was widely considered that daylight assaults on defended shores were little more than suicide and that they should not be considered except in desperation. Yet the complete British retreat from the Continent by June 1940 in the Second World War meant that landing operations against the German-occupied coastline of Europe would have to be considered. As a result, the Combined Operations Command was established to prepare plans for such offensives. By a coincidence the first director would be Admiral Sir Roger Keyes, who had served at the Dardanelles, although he was to be replaced by Admiral Lord Louis Mountbatten in October 1941. Combined Operations developed a methodology that evinced considerable success in North Africa and Italy. But these were still sideshows and the real test would be the D-Day landings on the Normandy coast on 6 June 1944.

The genesis of D-Day was protracted, with plenty of planning time for the staff of the Royal Navy, Army and Royal Air Force. Experts of all kinds were drafted in to hammer out and polish all phases of the operations, with inter-service communications refined to ensure that the results dovetailed into a coherent whole. This entailed the charting of accurate maps and the collection of precise intelligence to give a detailed picture of the topography of the landing beaches. The Allies had to know the exact strength of the German forces and identify the strongpoints that could threaten the beachhead. They also had to locate the position of reserve units that would pour into the battleground once the Allies had landed and complex deception plans were created to try to confuse German High Command.

When it came to the practical aspects of beach landings it was the principles of the 'All Arms Battle', as used by the BEF on the Western Front in 1918, rather than the disasters of Gallipoli that acted as a template for the Allies. Modern landing craft were manoeuvred to crash on to the beach in concert and so minimise the perils of landing under heavy fire. The considerable technical developments in naval gunnery also allowed the Allies to effectively target, eliminate or suppress German batteries and machine gun posts. The whole of the landing area was smothered with plunging fire from rocket ships, while self-propelled guns, floating tanks and conventional guns were rushed ashore to ensure that the landing forces had immediate artillery support. Meanwhile, specialised airborne troops and commandos seized key tactical features. Above them in the skies massed bombers hit German troop concentrations and attempted to cut communications, while the fighters tried to secure the landing areas from German air raids. The main body of the troops was put ashore in the right place, in their correct formations and in a fit state to immediately engage the Germans. Above all, the intention was to seize a viable Normandy beachhead big enough to contain a force capable of fighting face to face with the German Army and with the potential to create a whole new Western Front. Finally, there would be no repeat of the logistical nightmare of Gallipoli. This time the Allies used prefabricated Mulberry harbours, built to make a secure landing place which would allow reinforcements and supplies to be brought ashore during the crucial first phases of the operations while the PLUTO undersea pipe line secured their fuel supplies.

In all of this process the dire experiences of Gallipoli could have been cited as an example of how *not* to carry out combined operations on a hostile shore. For the failure of Gallipoli could not be risked again. However, the planners of the D-Day landings had learnt in a far more organic manner which, although partly drawing on the negative lessons of 1915, was more firmly grounded in the positive experiences and lessons of the combined operations already undertaken during the Second World War. Underpinning it all was the fact that the quality of staff work had improved immeasurably since 1915.

The complex planning and long gestation period that took place before D-Day throw into stark relief the truncated plans and inadequate preparations made prior to the Gallipoli operations. The Gallipoli campaign would never have been launched if a proper staff appreciation of operations had been carried out: of the enormity of the task in hand, the strength of the opposition, the nature of the terrain, the scale of the forces and the logistical back-up required to make it succeed. But thanks to political interference, lethally combined with the bullish optimism of generals who saw only opportunities, the Gallipoli campaign was launched into a void that guaranteed failure.

And yet, and yet, and yet – the enigma of the 1915 campaign, the story of that Allied failure and the comprehensive nature of the Turkish success still inexorably draws people in. The 'terrible ifs', as Churchill put it, may be a fantasy cloaking his personal responsibility for that failure, but the sheer drama of the ferocious fighting is undeniable. The beautiful setting overlaid with the all-pervading stench of rotting corpses; the chivalry demonstrated by individuals on both sides amidst merciless wholesale slaughter; the futility of the cause for which seemingly ordinary men fought with near-superhuman courage and endurance: with these contrasts so evident it is inevitable that the study of Gallipoli will continue for years to come as each generation seeks to resolve the conundrum of how something so stupid, so doomed from the outset, can remain so utterly fascinating.

NOTES

1. Dodging the Issue

1. H. Kitchener, quoted in M. Gilbert, *Winston S. Churchill, Vol. III, Part 1, August 1914–April 1915* (London: William Heinemann Ltd, 1972), p.361.

2. I have generally preferred to use the terms Turkey and Turks to the more technically correct Ottoman Empire and Ottomans.

3. G. Kopp, translated by A. Chambers, *Two Lone Ships: Goeben and Breslau* (London: Hutchinson & Co. Ltd, 1931), p. 108.

4. C. Lister, quoted by Lord Ribblesdale, *Charles Lister: Letters and Recollections* (London: T. Fisher Unwin Ltd, 1917), pp. 170–71.

5. C. Lister, quoted by Lord Ribblesdale, *Charles Lister: Letters and Recollections* (London: T. Fisher Unwin Ltd, 1917), pp. 174–5.

6. C. Lister, quoted by Lord Ribblesdale, *Charles Lister: Letters and Recollections* (London: T. Fisher Unwin Ltd, 1917), p. 172.

7. G. Kopp, translated by A. Chambers, *Two Lone Ships: Goeben and Breslau* (London: Hutchinson & Co. Ltd, 1931), pp. 30 and 48.

8. E. Troubridge quoted by Den van der Vat, *The Ship that Changed the World* (London: Hodder & Stoughton, 1985), p. 85.

9. HMS *Defence* and the rest of 1st Cruiser Squadron were to have the dubious pleasure of encountering German battlecruisers while under a different, far less cautious commander, Rear Admiral Sir Robert Arbuthnot, at the Battle of Jutland on 31 May 1916. The *Defence* was duly despatched in a matter of minutes, lost with all hands, totally outclassed. HMS *Warrior* and HMS *Black Prince* were also sunk during that battle.

10. C. Lister, quoted by Lord Ribblesdale, *Charles Lister: Letters and Recollections* (London: T. Fisher Unwin Ltd, 1917), pp. 172–3.

11. Admiralty telegram, 3/1/1915. See *Lord Kitchener and Winston Churchill: The Dardanelles Commission, Part I, 1914–1915* (London: The Stationery Office, 2000), p. 60.

12. S. Carden, telegram, 3/1/1915. See *Lord Kitchener and Winston Churchill: The Dardanelles Commission, Part I, 1914–1915* (London: The Stationery Office, 2000), p. 60.

13. Minutes of War Council, 13/1/1915, in *Lord Kitchener and Winston Churchill: The Dardanelles Commission, Part I, 1914–1915* (London: The Stationery Office, 2000), p. 78.

14. W. L. S. Churchill, *The World Crisis, 1911–1918* (New York: Free Press, 2005), p. 602.

15. V. Augagneur, quoted by G. H. Cassar, *The French and the Dardanelles* (London: George Allen & Unwin, 1971), p. 60.

2. Navy in Action

1. IWM Docs: H. W. Williams, typescript account, 'Fat's War', p. 61.

2. H. Jackson, quoted by J. S. Corbett, *Naval Operations, Vol. II* (London: Longmans, Green & Co., 1921), p. 124.

3. IWM Docs: H. W. Williams, typescript account, 'Fat's War', p. 52.

4. B. H. Smith, 'Dardanelles Dilemma', *The Naval Review*, vol. 24, no. 1, p. 85.

5. C. R. W. Lamplough, quoted by S. M. Holloway, *From Trench and Turret: Royal Marine Letters and Diaries, 1914–1918* (Portsmouth: Royal Marines Museum, n.d.), pp. 35–6.

6. C. H. Benfell, *Barnsley Chronicle*, 10/6/1916.

7. B. Sinfield, http://www.jackclegg.com.

8. H. A. Williamson, quoted by A. J. Marder, *From the Dardanelles to Oran: Studies of the Royal Navy in War and Peace, 1915–1940* (Oxford: Oxford University Press, 1974), p. 7.

9. IWM Docs: H. W. Williams, typescript account, 'Fat's War', p. 62.

10. J. Waterlow, quoted by E. W. Bush, *Gallipoli* (London: George Allen & Unwin Ltd, 1975), pp. 45–6.

11. B. H. Smith, 'Dardanelles Dilemma', *The Naval Review*, vol. 24, no. 1, pp. 86–7.

12. IWM Docs: A. J. G. Langley, typescript account, p. 20.

13. IWM Docs: A. J. G. Langley, typescript account, pp. 20–23.

14. IWM Docs: D. H. Hepburn, manuscript diary account, 18/3/1915.

15. IWM Docs: L. H. Straw, manuscript letters, 25/6/1915 and 27/10/1915.

16. P. E. Guépratte, *L'Expédition des Dardanelles* (Paris: Payot, 1935), pp. 64–6.

17. P. E. Guépratte, *L'Expédition des Dardanelles* (Paris: Payot, 1935), p. 66.

18. IWM Docs: D. Cemm, manuscript account, p. 2.

19. Brotherton Special Collections Library, Leeds University, Liddle Collection: Ashir Arkayan, TI 01, manuscript transcript of interview, p. 3.

20. IWM Docs: D. H. Hepburn, manuscript diary account, 18/3/1915.

21. S. Payro, quoted by P. Liddle, *Men of Gallipoli* (London: Allen Lane, 1976), pp. 54–5.

22. Brotherton Special Collections Library, Leeds University, Liddle Collection: S. Payro, edited transcript of interview.

23. IWM Docs: G. I. S. More, typescript, p. 48.

24. IWM Docs: D. Cemm, manuscript account, p. 4.

25. IWM Docs: G. Morgan, microfilm memoir, p. 35.

26. IWM Docs: A. J. G. Langley, typescript account, pp. 24–5.

27. IWM Docs: O. Ommanney, 'Midshipman's Journal', 18/3/1915.

28. IWM Docs: G. Morgan, microfilm memoir, pp. 37–8.

29. F. Brookes, quoted by S. M. Holloway, *From Trench and Turret: Royal Marines Letters and Diaries, 1914–1918* (Portsmouth: Royal Marines Museum), pp. 10–11.

30. IWM Docs: G. K. Ryland, typescript diary, p. 9.

3. Gathering of the Forces

1. I. Hamilton, *Gallipoli Diary, Vol. I* (London: Edward Arnold, 1920), p. 361.

2. D. Haig, diary 3/4/1915, quoted by J. Bourne & G. Sheffield, *Douglas Haig: War Diaries and Letters, 1914–1918* (London: Weidenfeld & Nicolson, 2005), pp. 113–14.

3. C. E. W. Bean, *Official History of the War of 1914–1918: The Story of Anzac, Vol. 1* (Sydney: Angus & Robertson, 1921), p. 84.

4. G. L. Scott, 'The First Australian Imperial Expeditionary Force', *The Gallipolian*, no. 11, p. 23.

5.   Brotherton Special Collections Library, Leeds University, Liddle Collection: H. Fildes, letter, 5/5/1915.

6.   C. Watkins, 'If I Touch It with My Stick', *The Gallipolian*, no. 34, pp. 25–6.

7.   A. Pomiro, *Les Carnets de Guerre* (Toulouse: Editions Privats, 2006), p. 49.

8.   A. R. Cooper (enlisted as C. J. de Bruin), http://www.greatwardifferent. com/Great_War/With_the_Foreign_Legion_in_Gallipoli/With_the_Foreign_ Legion_in_Gallipoli_01.htm.

9.   R. Brooke, quoted by M. R. Brooke, *The Collected Poems of Rupert Brooke: With a Memoir* (London: Sidgwick & Jackson Ltd, 1929), pp. 138–9.

10.   C. Lister, quoted by Lord Ribblesdale, *Charles Lister: Letters and Recollections* (London: T. Fisher Unwin Ltd, 1917), p. 129.

11.   P. Shaw-Stewart, quoted by Lord Ribblesdale, *Charles Lister: Letters and Recollections* (London: T. Fisher Unwin Ltd, 1917), pp. 156–7.

12.   D. Browne, quoted by Lord Ribblesdale, *Charles Lister: Letters and Recollections* (London: T. Fisher Unwin Ltd, 1917), p. 157.

13.   R. Brooke, quoted by M. R. Brooke, *The Collected Poems of Rupert Brooke: With a Memoir* (London: Sidgwick & Jackson Ltd, 1929), pp. 138–9.

14.   IWM Docs: C. Lister, typescript account, pp. 52–3.

15.   C. Lister, quoted by Lord Ribblesdale, *Charles Lister: Letters and Recollections* (London: T. Fisher Unwin Ltd, 1917), p. 162.

16.   D. Browne, quoted by M. R. Brooke, *The Collected Poems of Rupert Brooke: With a Memoir* (London: Sidgwick & Jackson Ltd, 1929), p. 159.

4. Plans: Countdown to Disaster

1.   I. Hamilton, *Gallipoli Diary, Vol. I* (London: Edward Arnold, 1920), pp. 42–3.

2.   O. L. von Sanders, *Five Years in Turkey* (Nashville, Tennessee: The Battery Press, 2000), pp. 59 & 61.

3.   Brotherton Special Collections Library, Leeds University, Liddle Collection: Ashir Arkayan, TI 01, typescript transcript of interview, p. 3.

4.   H. Kannengiesser, translated by C. J. P. Ball, *The Campaign in Gallipoli* (London: Hutchinson & Co., 1927), pp. 91–2 & 95–6.

5.   O. L. von Sanders, *Five Years in Turkey* (Nashville, Tennessee: The Battery Press, 2000), p. 62.

6. The similarities between the Turkish plans for the Balkan Wars and 1915 have been noted by E. J. Ericson, *Ordered to Die: A History of the Ottoman Army in the First World War* (Westport: Greenwood Press, 2001), p. 82.

7. I. Hamilton, *Gallipoli Diary, Vol. I* (London: Edward Arnold, 1920), p. 95.

8. I. Hamilton, *Gallipoli Diary, Vol. I* (London: Edward Arnold, 1920), pp. 13–14.

9. B. H. Smith, 'Dardanelles Dilemma', *The Naval Review*, vol. 24, no. 1, p. 87.

10. This section is loosely based on the trail-blazing and much appreciated work of Peter Chasseaud and Peter Doyle in their book *Grasping Gallipoli: Terrain, Maps and Failure at the Dardanelles, 1915* (Staplehurst: Spellmount, 2005).

11. I. Hamilton, *Gallipoli Diary, Vol. I* (London: Edward Arnold, 1920), p. 96.

12. A. Hunter-Weston, quoted by I. Hamilton, *Gallipoli Diary, Vol. I* (London: Edward Arnold, 1920), p. 91.

13. A. Hunter-Weston, quoted by I. Hamilton, *Gallipoli Diary, Vol. I* (London: Edward Arnold, 1920), pp. 92–3.

14. IWM Docs: S. W. Hare, typescript diary, 18/4/1915.

15. IWM Docs: G. K. Ryland, typescript diary, pp. 11 & 15.

16. IWM Docs: E. Unwin, typescript account, 'The Landing from the *River Clyde*', p. 1.

17. IWM Docs: G. L. Drewry, manuscript letter, 12/5/1915.

18. IWM Docs, E. Unwin Collection: J. C. Wedgwood, typescript letter, 24/4/1915–26/4/1915.

19. IWM Docs: E. Unwin, typescript account, 'The Landing from the *River Clyde*', p. 3.

20. IWM Docs: C. H. M. Doughty Wylie, manuscript copy of letter, 22/5/1915.

21. IWM Docs: G. L. Drewry, manuscript letter, 12/5/1915.

22. IWM Docs: R. B. Gillett, typescript account, pp. 33–4.

23. National Archives: G. Geddes, report, Royal Munsters Fusiliers War Diary, WO95/4310.

5. 25 April: Landings at Anzac

1. IWM Docs, Rayfield Papers Collection: S. Aker, 'The Dardanelles: The Ari Burnu Battles and 27 Regiment'.

2. Later known as Sefik Aker.

3. IWM Docs: C. Jess, transcript diary, 24/4/1915.

4. E. G. Sinclair-MacLagan, 'Armada Moves: Egypt to Gallipoli', *Reveille*, 31/3/1932, p. 59.

5. IWM Docs, Rayfield Papers Collection: S. Aker, 'The Dardanelles: The Ari Burnu Battles and 27 Regiment'.

6. C. G. Dix, 'Armada Moves: Efficient Navy', *Reveille*, 31/3/1932, p. 63.

7. A. M. Ross, 'Anzac's Death: Last Message', *Reveille*, 1/4/1933, p. 28.

8. IWM Docs: J. S. Metcalf, typescript account.

9. C. G. Dix, 'Armada Moves: Efficient Navy', *Reveille*, 31/3/1932, p. 63.

10. IWM Docs, Rayfield Papers Collection: Captain Faik, quoted by S. Aker, 'The Dardanelles: The Ari Burnu Battles and 27 Regiment'.

11. A. Sahin, edited from quotes in K. Fewster, V. Basarin & H. H. Basarin, *Gallipoli: The Turkish Story* (New South Wales: Allen & Unwin, 2003), p. 63.

12. IWM Docs: D. Hearder, typescript account, 'Landing of the 3rd Brigade', p. 10.

13. I am indebted to Kenan Chelik, Bill Sellers and Chris Roberts for finally convincing me of the absence of Turkish machine guns at Anzac. The best summation is provided in C. Roberts, 'Turkish Machine Guns at the Landing. Is it Another Myth?', *Wartime*, 2009.

14. IWM Docs, Rayfield Papers Collection: Captain Faik, quoted by S. Aker, 'The Dardanelles: The Ari Burnu Battles and 27 Regiment'.

15. IWM Docs: D. Hearder, typescript account, 'Landing of the 3rd Brigade', p. 11.

16. IWM Docs: D. Hearder, typescript account, 'Landing of the 3rd Brigade', p. 12.

17. IWM Docs: Captain Faik, quoted by S. Aker, 'The Dardanelles: The Ari Burnu Battles and 27 Regiment'.

18. IWM Docs: T. S. Louch, typescript account, p. 15.

19. IWM Docs: D. Hearder, typescript account, 'Landing of the 3rd Brigade', pp. 12–13.

20. I. Hayrettin, quoted by H. Oral, *Gallipoli 1915: Through Turkish Eyes* (Istanbul: Turkiye Is Bankasi, 2007), pp. 49 & 54.

21. IWM Docs, Rayfield Papers Collection: S. Aker, 'The Dardanelles: The Ari Burnu Battles and 27 Regiment'.

22. IWM Docs, Rayfield Papers Collection: S. Aker, 'The Dardanelles: The Ari Burnu Battles and 27 Regiment'.

23. Brotherton Special Collections Library, Leeds University, Liddle Collection: H. Fildes, letter, 9/1915.

24. J. A. Milne, quoted by N. K. Harvey, *From Anzac to the Hindenburg Line: The History of the 9th Battalion, AIF* (London: Naval & Military Press, 2008 reprint), p. 52.

25. IWM Docs, Rayfield Papers Collection: S. Aker, 'The Dardanelles: The Ari Burnu Battles and 27 Regiment'.

26. IWM Docs, Rayfield Papers Collection: M. Bey, quoted by S. Aker, 'The Dardanelles: The Ari Burnu Battles and 27 Regiment'.

27. Brotherton Special Collections Library, Leeds University, Liddle Collection: H. V. Hitch, transcript of tapes 235 & 252 .

28. Brotherton Special Collections Library, Leeds University, Liddle Collection: H. V. Hitch, transcript of tapes 235 & 252.

29. M. Bey, quoted by H. Oral, *Gallipoli 1915: Through Turkish Eyes* (Istanbul: Turkiye Is Bankasi, 2007), pp. 306–7 and IWM Docs, Rayfield Papers Collection: S. Aker, 'The Dardanelles: The Ari Burnu Battles and 27 Regiment'.

30. Z. Bey, quoted in C. E. W. Bean, *Gallipoli Mission* (Canberra: Australian War Memorial, 1948), pp. 131–2.

31. IWM Printed Books: *Atatürk Memoirs*, KO3/1686, pp. 5–6.

32. IWM Printed Books: *Atatürk Memoirs*, KO3/1686, pp. 6–7.

33. IWM Printed Books: *Atatürk Memoirs*, KO3/1686, pp. 8–9.

34. Brotherton Special Collections Library, Leeds University, Liddle Collection: H. V. Hitch, transcript of tapes 235 & 252.

35. Brotherton Special Collections Library, Leeds University, Liddle Collection: H. V. Hitch, transcript of tapes 235 & 252.

36. Brotherton Special Collections Library, Leeds University, Liddle Collection: R. H. Harris, transcript of tape 242.

37. S. Westmacott, quoted by D. Cameron, *25 April, 1915: The Day the Anzac Legend was Born* (Crows Nest: Allen & Unwin, 2007), p. 199.

38. S. Westmacott, quoted by D. Cameron, *25 April, 1915: The Day the Anzac Legend was Born* (Crows Nest: Allen & Unwin, 2007), pp. 200–201.

39. Brotherton Special Collections Library, Leeds University, Liddle Collection: E. W. Moorhead, typescript diary, 25/4/1915.

40. R. O. Cowey, 'Monash Valley', *Reveille*, 1/4/1936, p. 40.

41. J. J. Talbot Hobbs, 'A Gunner's Reflections: Gallipoli Campaign', *Reveille*, 31/3/1932, p. 66.

42. V. H. Williams, quoted by N. K. Harvey, *From Anzac to the Hindenburg Line: The History of the 9th Battalion, AIF* (London: Naval & Military Press, reprinted 2008), pp. 56–7.

43. P. C. Fenwick, 'Reminiscences of Anzac', *Reveille*, 31/3/1932, p. 39.

44. IWM Docs: E. B. Clark, transcript account, p. 2.

45. IWM Sound: J. R. Ford, AC 8172, reel 2.

46. Brotherton Special Collections Library, Leeds University, Liddle Collection: C. R. Duke, typescript account, p. 57.

47. H. W. Murray, 'The First Three Weeks on Gallipoli', *Reveille*, 1/4/1939, p. 60.

48. W. G. Malone, edited by J. Crawford, *No Better Death: The Great War Diaries and Letters of William G. Malone* (Auckland: Reed Publishing Ltd, 2005), p. 163.

49. W. Birdwood, *Khaki and Gown: An Autobiography* (London & Melbourne: Ward, Lock & Co. Ltd, 1941), p. 259.

50. W. Birdwood, quoted by I. Hamilton, *Gallipoli Diary, Vol. I* (London: Edward Arnold: 1920), p. 143.

51. C. F. Thursby, 'Power of the Navy: Made Landing Possible', *Reveille*, 31/3/1932, p. 54.

52. I. Hamilton, *Gallipoli Diary, Vol. I* (London: Edward Arnold, 1920), p. 142.

53. I. Hamilton, *Gallipoli Diary, Vol. I* (London: Edward Arnold, 1920), p. 144.

54. IWM Printed Books: *Atatürk Memoirs*, KO3/1686, p. 10.

55. IWM Docs, Rayfield Papers Collection: S. Aker, 'The Dardanelles: The Ari Burnu Battles and 27 Regiment'.

56. Later known as Fahrettin Altay.

57. Brotherton Special Collections Library, Leeds University, Liddle Collection: F. Altay, manuscript translation of letter, 7/5/1915.

58. H. W. Murray, 'The First Three Weeks on Gallipoli', *Reveille*, 1/4/1939, p. 60.

59. H. W. Murray, 'The First Three Weeks on Gallipoli', *Reveille*, 1/4/1939, p. 60.

60. IWM Docs: D. Hearder, typescript account, 'Landing of the 3rd Brigade', pp. 14–15.

61. IWM Docs: C. K. Bampton, manuscript diary, 26/4/1915.

62. H. W. Murray, 'The First Three Weeks on Gallipoli', *Reveille*, 1/4/1939, p. 60.

63. R. G. Casey, 'First Survey of Anzac Line', *Reveille*, 1/4/1936, p. 6.

64. F. C. James, 'MacLaurin's Ridge, April 26–27, 1915', *Reveille*, 1/4/1939, p. 38.

65. J. Monash, quoted by F. M. Cutlack, *War Letters of General Monash* (Australia: Angus & Robertson Ltd, 1934), pp. 55–6.

66. IWM Docs: W. Weaver, typescript copy of letter, *c.* 1915.

67. IWM Docs: T. S. Louch, typescript account, p. 15.

68. Norman Clayden, aged nineteen, was reported killed on 2 May 1915. There is no known grave for him but he is commemorated on the Lone Pine Memorial.

69. IWM Docs: T. S. Louch, typescript account, pp. 15–16.

70. H. W. Murray, 'The First Three Weeks on Gallipoli', *Reveille*, 1/4/1939, p. 61.

6. 25 April: Landings at Helles

1. A. Hunter-Weston, quoted by S. Gillon, *The Story of the 29th Division* (London: Thomas Nelson & Sons, 1925), p. 17.

2. D. Joiner, 'Y Beach: Memoirs of Soldiering', Book 1, pp. 17–18.

3. D. Joiner, 'Y Beach: Memoirs of Soldiering', Book 1, p. 19.

4. I. Hamilton, quoted by C. F. Aspinall-Oglander, *Military Operations: Gallipoli, Vol. I* (London: William Heinemann Ltd, 1929), p. 204.

5. A. J. Welch, quoted by S. Gillon, *The K.O.S.B. in the Great War* (London: Thomas Nelson & Sons Ltd, 1930), p. 136.

6. D. Joiner, 'Y Beach: Memoirs of Soldiering', Book 1, p. 21.

7. J. Vickers, quoted by S. M. Holloway, *From Trench and Turret: Royal Marines Letters and Diaries, 1914–1918* (Portsmouth: Royal Marines Museum), p. 40.

8. D. Joiner, 'Y Beach: Memoirs of Soldiering', Book 1, p. 22.

9. D. Joiner, 'Y Beach: Memoirs of Soldiering', Book 1, p. 23.

10. D. Joiner, 'Y Beach: Memoirs of Soldiering', Book 1, p. 23.

11. D. Joiner, 'Y Beach: Memoirs of Soldiering', Book 1, p. 24 and Book 2, p. 1.

12. D. Joiner, 'Y Beach: Memoirs of Soldiering', Book 2, pp. 1–2.

13. J. Vickers, quoted by S. M. Holloway, *From Trench and Turret: Royal Marines Letters and Diaries, 1914–1918* (Portsmouth: Royal Marines Museum), p. 47.

14. D. Joiner, 'Y Beach: Memoirs of Soldiering', Book 2, p. 2.

15. W. Marshall, *Memories of Four Fronts* (London: Ernest Benn Ltd, 1929), p. 58.

16. A. P. Davidson, quoted by A. T. Stewart & C. J. E. Pershall, *The Immortal Gamble* (London: A & C Black Ltd, 1917), p. 99.

17. IWM Docs: J. A. Godwyn, typescript memoir, 'My Experiences in the Turkish War on the Gallipoli Peninsula'.

18. IWM Docs: S. W. Hare, typescript diary, 25/4/1915.

19. IWM Docs: H. R. Tate, manuscript diary, 25/4/1915.

20. Leading Seaman Gilligan, letter to the *Bury Guardian*, 16/6/1916.

21. H. R. Clayton, quoted by O. Creighton, *With the Twenty-ninth Division in Gallipoli* (London: Longmans, Green & Co., 1916), pp. 59–60.

22. H. Shaw, quoted by O. Creighton, *With the Twenty-ninth Division in Gallipoli* (London: Longmans, Green & Co., 1916), p. 62.

23. IWM Docs: R. Willis, manuscript letter, 10/5/1915.

24. G. S. Adams, quoted by O. Creighton, *With the Twenty-ninth Division in Gallipoli* (London: Longmans, Green & Co., 1916), p. 58.

25. H. R. Clayton, quoted by O. Creighton, *With the Twenty-ninth Division in Gallipoli* (London: Longmans, Green & Co., 1916), pp. 59–60.

26. H. Shaw, quoted by O. Creighton, *With the Twenty-ninth Division in Gallipoli* (London: Longmans, Green & Co., 1916), p. 62.

27. IWM Docs: S. W. Hare, typescript diary, 25/4/1915.

28. IWM Docs: S. W. Hare, typescript diary, 25/4/1915.

29. IWM Docs: S. W. Hare, typescript diary, 25/4/1915.

30. IWM Docs: H. R. Tate, manuscript diary, 25/4/1915.

7. 25 April: Drama at V Beach

1. IWM Library, Special Collection: Major Mahmut, 'Memoirs of the Battalion Commander Who Opposed the First Landings at Seddulbahr', p. 3.

2. IWM Docs: H. W. Williams, typescript account, 'Fat's War', pp. 70–71.

3. IWM Library, Special Collection: Major Mahmut, 'Memoirs of the Battalion Commander Who Opposed the First Landings at Seddulbahr', p. 2.

4. IWM Docs, Papers of G. B. Stoney: H. E. Tizard, typescript account, p. 6.

5. IWM Docs: E. Unwin, typescript account, '*River Clyde*', pp. 4–5.

6. National Army Museum: D. French, manuscript letter, ref. 72558.

7. M. C. H. Lloyd, quoted by A. T. Stewart & C. J. E. Pershall, *The Immortal Gamble* (London: A & C Black Ltd, 1917), pp. 106–7.

8. C. W. Maffett, quoted by H. C. Wylly, *Neill's 'Blue Caps'* (County Cork: Schull Books, 1996), p. 30.

9. National Army Museum: D. French, manuscript letter, ref. 72559.

10. National Army Museum: D. French, manuscript letter, ref. 72560–72561.

11. C. W. Maffett, quoted by H. C. Wylly, *Neill's 'Blue Caps'* (County Cork: Schull Books, 1996), pp. 30–31.

12. R. Martin, letter, 26/5/1915, http://corcaigh3.googlepages.com/Sedd el Bahr.

13. IWM Docs: E. E. Rickus, manuscript letter, 7/5/1915.

14. H. M. S. Forbes, quoted by A. T. Stewart & C. J. E. Pershall, *The Immortal Gamble* (London: A & C Black Ltd, 1917), pp. 110–11.

15. IWM Docs: G. L. Drewry, manuscript letter, 12/5/1915.

16. IWM Docs: E. Unwin, typescript account, 'The Landing from the *River Clyde*', pp. 5–6.

17. R. Lane, quoted by S. McCance, *History of the Royal Munster Fusiliers, Vol. II* (Aldershot: Gale & Polden, 1927), p. 49.

18. R. Lane, quoted by S. McCance, *History of the Royal Munster Fusiliers, Vol. II* (Aldershot: Gale & Polden, 1927), p. 49.

19. IWM Docs: E. Unwin, typescript account, 'The Landing from the *River Clyde*', p. 6.

20. IWM Docs: G. L. Drewry, manuscript letter, 12/5/1915.

21. National Archives: G. Geddes, report, Royal Munsters Fusiliers War Diary, WO95/4310.

22. National Archives: G. Geddes, report, Royal Munsters Fusiliers War Diary, WO95/4310.

23. IWM Sound: W. Flynn, SR 4103.

24. IWM Docs: E. Unwin, typescript account, 'The Landing from the *River Clyde*', p. 6.

25. IWM Docs: G. L. Drewry, manuscript letter, 12/5/1915.

26. M. C. H. Lloyd, quoted by A. T. Stewart & C. J. E. Pershall, *The Immortal Gamble* (London: A & C Black Ltd, 1917), pp. 107–8.

27. IWM Docs, papers of G. B. Stoney: H. E. Tizard, typescript account, pp. 8 & 9.

28. IWM Docs: G. Keen, manuscript letter, misc. 37, item 682.

29. Quoted by C. F. Aspinall-Oglander, *Military Operations: Gallipoli, Vol. I* (London: William Heinemann Ltd, 1929), p. 240.

30. C. Jeffries, 'Landing on the 25th', *The Gallipolian*, no. 36, p. 23.

31. IWM Docs: G. Keen, manuscript letter, misc. 37, item 682.

32. M. C. H. Lloyd, quoted by A. T. Stewart & C. J. E. Pershall, *The Immortal Gamble* (London: A & C Black Ltd, 1917), p. 108.

33. Lieutenant Reginald Corbet.

34. C. W. Maffett, quoted by H. C. Wylly, *Neill's 'Blue Caps'* (County Cork: Schull Books, 1996), p. 31.

35. D. J. Moriarty, http://ww1.osborn.ws/.

36. IWM Docs: E. Unwin, typescript account, 'The Landing from the *River Clyde*', p. 8.

37. IWM Docs, E. Unwin Collection: J. C. Wedgwood, typescript letter, 24/4/1915–26/4/1918.

38. J. Parkinson, quoted by S. Snelling, *VCs of the First World War: Gallipoli* (Stroud: Sutton Publishing, 1995), p. 41.

39. Able Seaman Ernest Grose.

40. H. M. S. Forbes, quoted by A. T. Stewart & C. J. E. Pershall, *The Immortal Gamble* (London: A & C Black Ltd, 1917), pp. 112–13.

41. IWM Docs: E. Unwin, typescript account, 'The Landing from the *River Clyde*', p. 7.

42. IWM Docs: E. Unwin, typescript account, 'The Landing from the *River Clyde*', p. 7.

43. IWM Docs: E. Unwin, typescript account, 'The Landing from the *River Clyde*', pp. 8 & 10.

44. IWM Docs, Papers of G. B. Stoney: H. E. Tizard, typescript account, p. 12.

45. A. Rahman, quoted in K. Fewster, V. Basarin & H. H. Basarin, *Gallipoli: The Turkish Story* (New South Wales: Allen & Unwin, 2003), p. 75.

46. IWM Library, Special Collection: Major Mahmut, 'Memoirs of the Battalion Commander Who Opposed the First Landings at Seddulbahr', p. 5.

47. G. Davidson, *The Incomparable 29th and the* River Clyde (Aberdeen: James Gordon Bisset, 1920), pp. 53–4.

48. IWM Docs, E. Unwin Collection: J. C. Wedgwood, typescript letter, 24/4/1915–26/4/1918.

49. IWM Docs: G. L. Drewry, manuscript letter, 12/5/1915.

50. IWM Library, Special Collection: Major Mahmut, 'Memoirs of the Battalion Commander Who Opposed the First Landings at Seddulbahr', p. 6.

51. IWM Docs: W. L. Williams, manuscript copy of letter, 22/5/1915.

52. G. Nightingale, quoted by C. H. Dudley-Ward, *Regimental Records of the Royal Welch Fusiliers, Vol. 4* (London: Forster, Groom & Co., 1929), p. 15.

53. G. Nightingale, quoted by C. H. Dudley-Ward, *Regimental Records of the Royal Welch Fusiliers, Vol. 4* (London: Forster, Groom & Co., 1929), p. 15.

54. IWM Docs: R. B. Gillett, typescript account, pp. 38–9.

55. IWM Docs: R. B. Gillett, typescript account, pp. 38 & 40.

56. G. Davidson, *The Incomparable 29th and the* River Clyde (Aberdeen: James Gordon Bisset, 1920), p. 46.

57. G. Nightingale, quoted by C. H. Dudley-Ward, *Regimental Records of the Royal Welch Fusiliers, Vol. 4* (London: Forster, Groom & Co., 1929), p. 16.

58. G. Nightingale, quoted by C. H. Dudley-Ward, *Regimental Records of the Royal Welch Fusiliers, Vol. 4* (London: Forster, Groom & Co., 1929), pp. 16–17.

59. W. Cosgrove, quoted by S. Snelling, *VCs of the First World War: Gallipoli* (Stroud: Sutton, 1995), pp. 82–3.

60. IWM Docs: G. Stoney, manuscript letter, 10/5/1915.

61. IWM Library, Special Collection: Major Mahmut, 'Memoirs of the Battalion Commander Who Opposed the First Landings at Seddulbahr', p. 9.

62. IWM Library, Special Collection: Major Mahmut, 'Memoirs of the Battalion Commander Who Opposed the First Landings at Seddulbahr', p .9.

63. G. Nightingale, quoted by C. H. Dudley-Ward, *Regimental Records of the Royal Welch Fusiliers, Vol. 4* (London: Forster, Groom & Co., 1929), p. 17.

64. IWM Sound: W. Flynn, SR 4103.

65. IWM Docs: W. L. Williams, manuscript copy of letter, 22/5/1915.

8. 25 April: Kum Kale and Diversions

1. O. L. von Sanders, *Five Years in Turkey* (Nashville, Tennessee: The Battery Press, 2000), p. 63.

2. J. Vassal, *Uncensored Letters from the Dardanelles* (London: William Heinemann, 1916), pp. 49–50.

3. J. Vassal, *Uncensored Letters from the Dardanelles* (London: William Heinemann, 1916), pp. 56–7.

4. Colonel Ruef, quoted by C. F. Aspinall-Oglander, *Military Operations Gallipoli, Vol. I* (London: William Heinemann Ltd, 1932), p. 261.

5. Brotherton Special Collections Library, Leeds University, Liddle Collection: M. Gondard, typescript transcript of interview, pp. 5–6.

6. R. Weil, quoted in Association des Dardanelles, *Dardanelles Orient Levant, 1915–1921* (Paris: L'Harmattan, 2005), p. 26.

7. O. L. von Sanders, *Five Years in Turkey* (Nashville, Tennessee: The Battery Press, 2000), pp. 59 & 61.

8. IWM Docs: C. Lister, typescript account, pp. 52–3.

9. National Archives: B. Freyberg, report, WO95/4290.

10. IWM Sound: J. Murray, AC 8201.

11. National Archives: B. Freyberg, report, WO95/4290.

12. IWM Docs: C. Lister, typescript account, pp. 52–3.

13. O. L. von Sanders, *Five Years in Turkey* (Nashville, Tennessee: The Battery Press, 2000), pp. 59 & 61.

9. Anzac: The Holding Pen

1. J. Monash, quoted by F. M. Cutlack, *War Letters of General Monash* (Australia: Angus & Robertson Ltd, 1934), pp. 35–6.

2. I. Hamilton, *Gallipoli Diary, Vol. I* (London: Edward Arnold, 1920), p. 144.

3. Brotherton Special Collections Library, Leeds University, Liddle Collection: B. I. Wilson, typescript diary, 1/5/1915–3/5/1915.

4. H. W. Murray, 'The First Three Weeks on Gallipoli', *Reveille*, 1/4/1939, p. 62.

5. IWM Sound: H. Baker, AC 8721, reels 2–3.

6. IWM Sound: H. Baker, AC 8721, reels 2–3.

7. IWM Sound: H. Baker, AC 8721, reels 2–3.

8. A. A. Orchard, 'In Turkish Lines: Daring Patrols', *Reveille*, 31/3/1932, p. 68.

9. A. A. Orchard, 'In Turkish Lines: Daring Patrols', *Reveille*, 31/3/1932, p. 68.

10. H. G. Viney, 'Fatal Pause: General Sniped', *Reveille*, 1/4/1933, p. 52.

11. H. G. Viney, 'Fatal Pause: General Sniped', *Reveille*, 1/4/1933, p. 52.

12. W. T. Bridges, quoted by C. D. Coulthard-Clark, *A Heritage of Spirit: A Biography of Major-General Sir William Throsby Bridges* (Carlton: Melbourne University Press, 1979), p. 175.

13. J. Monash, quoted by F. M. Cutlack, *War Letters of General Monash* (Sydney: Angus & Robertson Ltd, 1934), pp. 35–6.

14. IWM Docs: D. H. Hepburn, manuscript diary account, pp. 10–11.

15. T. W. McNamara, 'Memories of Gallipoli', *Reveille*, 1/6/1936, p. 28.

16. Brotherton Special Collections Library, Leeds University, Liddle Collection: C. R. Duke, typescript account, pp. 65–6.

17. T. W. McNamara, 'Memories of Gallipoli', *Reveille*, 1/6/1936, p. 28.

18. A. G. Salisbury, quoted by N. K. Harvey, *From Anzac to the Hindenburg Line: The History of the 9th Battalion, AIF* (London: Naval & Military Press, 2008 reprint), p. 70.

19. A. Jacka, quoted by I. Grant, *Jacka, VC: Australia's Finest Fighting Soldier* (Canberra: Macmillan Australia, 1989), p. 25.

20. J. Adams, 'A Gallipoli Invention: Beech's Periscope Rifle', *Reveille*, 1/7/1937, p. 28.

21. IWM Docs, Rayfield Papers Collection: S. Aker, 'The Dardanelles: The Ari Burnu Battles and 27 Regiment'.

22. P. C. Fenwick, 'Reminiscences of Anzac', *Reveille*, 31/3/1932, p. 70.

23. J. Monash, quoted by F. M. Cutlack, *War Letters of General Monash* (Sydney: Angus & Robertson Ltd, 1934), pp. 47–8.

24. IWM Docs: C. H. Livingstone, typescript account, 'Some Memories of Anzac', p. 8.

25. O. von Hersing, quoted by Lowell Thomas, *Raiders of the Deep* (Penzance: Periscope Publishing, 2002), p. 64.

26. F. Brookes, quoted by S. M. Holloway, *From Trench and Turret: Royal Marines Letters and Diaries, 1914–1918* (Portsmouth: Royal Marines Museum), p. 14.

27. O. von Hersing, quoted by Lowell Thomas, *Raiders of the Deep* (Penzance: Periscope Publishing, 2002), pp. 64–5.

28. W. G. Malone, edited by J. Crawford, *No Better Death: The Great War Diaries and Letters of William G. Malone* (Auckland: Reed Publishing Ltd, 2005), p. 235.

29. W. G. Malone, edited by J. Crawford, *No Better Death: The Great War Diaries and Letters of William G. Malone* (Auckland: Reed Publishing Ltd, 2005), p. 236.

30. W. G. Malone, edited by J. Crawford, *No Better Death: The Great War Diaries and Letters of William G. Malone* (Auckland: Reed Publishing Ltd, 2005), edited from pp. 276 & 283.

31. Brotherton Special Collections Library, Leeds University, Liddle Collection: H. Bachtold, transcript, tape 250.

32. Brotherton Special Collections Library, Leeds University, Liddle Collection: H. Bachtold, transcript, tape 250.

33. E. Mack, combined quotes from J. Hamilton, *Goodbye Cobber, God Bless You: The Fatal Charge of the Light Horse, Gallipoli, August 7th 1915* (Sydney: Pan Macmillan Australia, 2004), pp. 236 & 237.

34. T. Henty, quoted by J. Hamilton, *Goodbye Cobber, God Bless You: The Fatal Charge of the Light Horse, Gallipoli, August 7th 1915* (Sydney: Pan Macmillan Australia, 2004), p. 237.

35. IWM Docs: T. S. Louch, typescript account, pp. 20–21.

36. IWM Docs: W. E. Pheysey, typescript account, pp. 7–8.

10. Helles: The Real Fight for Gallipoli

1. A. H. Mure, *With the Incomparable 29th* (London: W & R Chambers Ltd, 1919), p. 142.

2. A. R. Cooper (enlisted as C. J. de Bruin), http://www.greatwardifferent.com/Great_War/With_the_Foreign_Legion_in_Gallipoli/With_the_Foreign_Legion_in_Gallipoli_01.htm.

3. IWM Library, Special Collection: Major Mahmut, 'Memoirs of the Battalion Commander Who Opposed the First Landings at Seddulbahr'.

4. D. J. Moriarty, http://ww1.osborn.ws/.

5. H. D. O'Hara, quoted by H. C. Wylly, *Neill's 'Blue Caps'* (County Cork: Schull Books, 1996), p. 39.

6. H. Feuille, *Face aux Turcs: Gallipoli 1915* (Paris: Payot, 1934), p. 43.

7. B. H. Smith, 'Dardanelles Dilemma', *The Naval Review*, vol. 24, no. 1, p. 84.

8. C. Lister, quoted by Lord Ribblesdale, *Charles Lister: Letters and Recollections* (London: T. Fisher Unwin Ltd, 1917), pp. 168–9.

9. R. Weil, quoted in Association des Dardanelles, *Dardanelles Orient Levant, 1915–1921* (Paris: L'Harmattan, 2005), p. 28.

10. R. Weil, quoted in Association des Dardanelles, *Dardanelles Orient Levant, 1915–1921* (Paris: L'Harmattan, 2005), p. 28.

11. R. Weil, quoted in Association des Dardanelles, *Dardanelles Orient Levant, 1915–1921* (Paris: L'Harmattan, 2005), p. 29.

12. D'A. Pomiro, *Les Carnets de Guerre* (Toulouse: Editions Privats, 2006), p. 107.

13. O. L. von Sanders, *Five Years in Turkey* (Nashville, Tennessee: The Battery Press, 2000), p. 71.

14. H. Kannengiesser, translated by C. J. P. Ball, *The Campaign in Gallipoli* (London: Hutchinson & Co., 1927), p. 133.

15. IWM Docs: G. B. Horridge, 'War Memoirs', p. 3.

16. H. Feuille, *Face aux Turcs: Gallipoli 1915* (Paris: Payot, 1934), pp. 53–4.

17. D'A. Pomiro, *Les Carnets de Guerre* (Toulouse: Editions Privat, 2006), p. 110.

18. IWM Sound: J. Murray, AC 8201, reel 7.

19. C. Malthus, *Anzac: A Retrospect* (Christchurch: Whitcombe & Tombs Ltd, 1965), p. 68.

20. C. Malthus, *Anzac: A Retrospect* (Christchurch: Whitcombe & Tombs Ltd, 1965), pp. 70–71.

21. Brotherton Special Collections Library, Leeds University, Liddle Collection: E. W. Moorhead, typescript diary, 8/5/1915.

22. C. T. Eades, 'Krithia Fight: Turks Stood Pat', *Reveille*, 1/9/1932, p. 31.

23. I. Hamilton, quoted by C. F. Aspinall-Oglander, *Military Operations Gallipoli, Vol. I* (London: William Heinemann Ltd, 1932), p. 349.

24. A. H. Mure, *With the Incomparable 29th* (London: W & R Chambers Ltd, 1919), pp. 98–9.

25. H. G. Lush Wilson, quoted in *The Royal Artillery Commemoration Book* (London: Bell & Sons Ltd, 1920), p. 58.

26. IWM Docs: G. B. Horridge, 'War Memoirs', p. 12.

27. IWM Docs: R. Sheldon, typescript account, p. 40.

28. IWM Docs: T. Rowatt, manuscript account.

29. IWM Docs: P. Duff, typescript letter, 15/5/1915.

30. C. Watkins, 'One Moment in Annihilation's Waste', *The Gallipolian*, no. 14, p. 22.

31. IWM Docs: R. Sheldon, typescript account, p. 44.

32. F. Jones, quoted in the *Ashton Reporter*, 19/6/1915, http://ashtonpals.webs.com.

33. Second Lieutenant Fred Jones's body was recovered and he now lies buried in the Redoubt Cemetery.

34. T. Valentine, quoted in the *Ashton Reporter*, 7/8/1915, http://ashtonpals.webs.com.

35. A. H. Mure, *With the Incomparable 29th* (London: W. & R. Chambers Ltd, 1919), pp. 150–51.

36. A. R. Cooper (enlisted as C. J. de Bruin), http://www.greatwardifferent.com/Great_War/With_the_Foreign_Legion_in_Gallipoli/With_the_Foreign_Legion_in_Gallipoli_01.htm

37. H. Feuille, *Face aux Turcs: Gallipoli 1915* (Paris: Payot, 1934), p. 149.

38. A. H. Mure, *With the Incomparable 29th* (London: W. & R. Chambers Ltd, 1919), pp. 75–6.

39. IWM Docs: D. N. Meneaud-Lissenburg, typescript, p. 125.

40. *Memoranda on Some Medical Diseases in the Mediterranean War Area with some Sanitary Notes* (London: HMSO, 1916), p. 114.

41. IWM Docs: D. N. Meneaud-Lissenburg, typescript, p. 126.

42. W. B. C. Weld-Forester, *From Dartmouth to the Dardanelles* (London: William Heinemann, 1916), p. 152.

43. W. B. C. Weld-Forester, *From Dartmouth to the Dardanelles* (London: William Heinemann, 1916), pp. 153–4.

44. W. B. C. Weld-Forester, *From Dartmouth to the Dardanelles* (London: William Heinemann, 1916), pp. 154–5.

45. Midshipman Torquil MacLeod, HMS *Goliath*, died 13 May 1915, aged fifteen.

46. IWM Docs: C. G. Tennant, typescript account, pp. 8–9.

47. E. Ashmead-Bartlett, *Some of My Experiences in the Great War* (London: George Newnes Ltd, 1918), pp. 130 & 131.

48. G. MacMunn, *Behind the Scenes in Many Wars* (London: John Murray, 1930), pp. 142–3.

49. H. Kitchener, quoted by C. F. Aspinall-Oglander, *Military Operations Gallipoli, Vol. I* (London: William Heinemann Ltd, 1932), p. 365.

50. IWM Docs: J. S. Gatley, typescript diary account, p. 30.

51. D. Joiner, 'Y Beach: Memoirs of Soldiering', Book 2, p. 15.

52. R. Weil, quoted in Association des Dardanelles, *Dardanelles Orient Levant, 1915–1921* (Paris: L'Harmattan, 2005), p. 32.

53. H. Kannengiesser, translated by C. J. P. Ball, *The Campaign in Gallipoli* (London: Hutchinson & Co., 1927), p.174.

54. IWM Docs: J. S. Gatley, typescript diary account, p. 30.

55. R. Savory, 'Some Gallipoli Memories', *The Gallipolian*, no. 10, p. 14.

56. R. Savory, quoted by S. Chambers, *Gully Ravine: Battleground Europe, Gallipoli* (Barnsley: Leo Cooper, 2003), pp. 51–2.

57. D. Joiner, 'Y Beach: Memoirs of Soldiering', Book 2, p. 17.

58. A. H. Mure, *With the Incomparable 29th* (London: W. & R. Chambers Ltd, 1919), pp. 181–2.

59. A. H. Mure, *With the Incomparable 29th* (London: W. & R. Chambers Ltd, 1919), pp. 182–3.

60. IWM Docs: R. Sheldon, typescript account, pp. 47–8.

61. IWM Docs: J. S. Gatley, typescript diary account, p. 31.

62. IWM Sound: J. Murray, AC 8201, reel 9.

63. R. Weil, quoted in Association des Dardanelles, *Dardanelles Orient Levant, 1915–1921* (Paris: L'Harmattan, 2005), p. 33.

64. IWM Sound: J. Murray, AC 8201, reel 10.

65. IWM Docs: J. S. Gatley, typescript diary account, p. 31.

66. IWM Docs: J. S. Gatley, typescript diary account, pp. 31–2.

67. J. Morten & S. Morten, *I Remain, Your Son Jack: Letters from the First World War* (Wilmslow: Sigma Leisure, 1993), p. 70.

68. IWM Docs: J. S. Gatley, typescript diary account, p. 33.

69. A. H. Mure, *With the Incomparable 29th* (London: W. & R. Chambers Ltd, 1919), pp. 182–3.

70. R. D. Doughty, diary, 6/6/1915, http://www.thekivellfamily.co.nz/family_pages/ralphs_diaries/Ralph_Doughty.html.

71. IWM Docs: B. Bradshaw, typescript letter/diary, p. 18.

72. Second Lieutenant Bartle Bradshaw is buried in Twelve Tree Copse Cemetery.

73. F. Charles-Roux, *L'Expedition des Dardanelles* (Paris: Armand Colin, 1919), p. 146.

11. Helles: Writing on the Wall

1. J. Leymonnerie, *Journal d'un poilu sur le front d'Orient* (Paris: Pygmalion, 2003), pp. 107–8.

2. National Library of Scotland: D. Haig letter to C. Wigram, 27/6/1915.

3. R. Weil, quoted in *Dardanelles Orient Levant, 1915–1921* (Paris: L'Harmattan, 2005), p. 35.

4. J. Leymonnerie, *Journal d'un poilu sur le front d'Orient* (Paris: Pygmalion, 2003), p. 106.

5. IWM Docs: A. M. McCracken, typescript account, p. 53.

6. Brotherton Special Collections Library, Leeds University, Liddle Collection: C. Thierry, typescript translation of diary, 21/6/1918.

7. R. Weil, quoted in Association des Dardanelles, *Dardanelles Orient Levant, 1915–1921* (Paris: L'Harmattan, 2005), p. 36.

8. H. Simpson Baikie, quoted by R. R. Thompson, *The Fifty-second (Lowland) Division* (Glasgow: Maclehose, Jackson & Co., 1923), p. 48.

9. S. W. Evans, 'My Gallipoli Story', *The Gallipolian*, no. 46, p. 21.

10. D. Joiner, 'Y Beach: Memoirs of Soldiering', Book 3, p. 8.

11. J. M. Findlay, *With the Eighth Scottish Rifles, 1914–1919* (London: Blackie & Son, 1926), pp. 34–5.

12. Second Lieutenant Robert Pattison. No known grave.

13. Captain Charles Bramwell. No known grave.

14. J. M. Findlay, *With the Eighth Scottish Rifles, 1914–1919* (London: Blackie & Son, 1926), pp. 36–7.

15. Lieutenant Thomas Stout. No known grave.

16. J. M. Findlay, *With the Eighth Scottish Rifles, 1914–1919* (London: Blackie & Son, 1926), p. 37.

17. D. Joiner, 'Y Beach: Memoirs of Soldiering', Book 3, pp. 12–13.

18. D. Joiner, 'Y Beach: Memoirs of Soldiering', Book 3, p. 14.

19. Sergeant Victor Rathfelder. No known grave.

20. R. F. E. Laidlaw, 'Gallipoli, 1915', *The Gallipolian*, no. 32, p. 23.

21. R. Weil, quoted in Association des Dardanelles, *Dardanelles Orient Levant, 1915–1921* (Paris: L'Harmattan, 2005), p. 37.

22. Brotherton Special Collections Library, Leeds University, Liddle Collection: Ashir Arkayan, TI 01, manuscript transcript of interview, p. 4.

23. H. Feuille, *Face aux Turcs: Gallipoli 1915* (Paris: Payot, 1934), pp. 124–5.

24. Rifaat, quoted by R. R. Thompson, *The Fifty-second (Lowland) Division* (Glasgow: Maclehose, Jackson & Co., 1923), pp. 69–70.

25. C. Lister, quoted by Lord Ribblesdale, *Charles Lister: Letters and Recollections* (London: T. Fisher Unwin Ltd, 1917), pp. 209–10.

26. IWM Docs: J. S. Millar, typescript account, p. 17.

27. D'A. Pomiro, *Les Carnets de guerre* (Toulouse: Editions Privats, 2006), p. 183.

28. J. Harrison, quoted by G. Richardson, *For King, Country and the Scottish Borderers* (Hawick: Buccleuch Printers, 1987), p. 48.

29. T. Richardson, quoted by W. Sorley-Brown, *War Record of 4th Battalion KOSB and Lothians and Border Horse* (Galashiels: John McQueen & Son, 1920), pp. 23–6.

30. G. Davidson, *The Incomparable 29th and the River Clyde* (Aberdeen: James Gordon Bisset, 1920), p. 130.

31. D. Jerrold, *Georgian Adventure: The Autobiography of Douglas Jerrold* (London: Right Book Club, 1938), p. 137.

32. IWM Docs: T. Macmillan, typescript account, p. 65.

33. R. D. Doughty, diary 13/7/1915–14/7/1915, http://www.thekivellfamily. co.nz/family_pages/ralphs_diaries/Ralph_Doughty.html.

34. J. Anderson, quoted by R. R. Thompson, *The Fifty-second (Lowland) Division* (Glasgow: Maclehose, Jackson & Co., 1923), p. 113.

35. IWM Docs: G. G. A. Egerton, typescript account, pp. 2–3.

12. New Beginnings: Hamilton's Plans

1. I. Hamilton, *Gallipoli Diary, Vol. II* (London: Edward Arnold, 1920), p. 5.

2. W. Birdwood, *Khaki and Gown: An Autobiography* (London and Melbourne: Ward, Lock & Co. Ltd, 1941), p. 268.

3. P. Overton, quoted by C. Pugsley, *Gallipoli: The New Zealand Story* (Auckland: Hodder & Stoughton, 1984), p. 218.

4. IWM Docs: G. K. Ryland, typescript diary, pp. 21–2.

5. National Library of Scotland: G. Egerton papers, AC 1656 no. 1, p. 51. It was rumoured that Hamilton rebutted Stopford's claim at the Dardanelles

Commission that he used a fake diary entry. Egerton certainly believed Stopford, stating in the margin note on the same source that 'Never was there such a liar in this world as Ian H.'

6.   IWM Printed Books: *Atatürk Memoirs*, KO3/1686, pp. 5–6.

13. August: Helles Sacrifice

1.   C. F. Aspinall-Oglander, *Military Operations: Gallipoli, Vol. I* (London: William Heinemann Ltd, 1932), p. 176.

2.   IWM Docs: H. C. L. Heywood, manuscript account, pp. 94–5.

3.   C. Lister, quoted by Lord Ribblesdale, *Charles Lister: Letters and Recollections* (London: T. Fisher Unwin Ltd, 1917), pp. 211–12.

4.   IWM Docs: H. C. L. Heywood, manuscript account, p. 113.

5.   F. Davies, quoted by C. F. Aspinall-Oglander, *Military Operations: Gallipoli, Vol. I* (London: William Heinemann Ltd, 1932), p. 171.

6.   IWM Docs: H. C. L. Heywood, manuscript account, pp. 113–14.

7.   IWM Docs: H. C. L. Heywood, manuscript account, pp. 113–14.

8.   IWM Docs: H. C. L. Heywood, manuscript account, pp. 116–17.

9.   A. Kay, quoted by N. Drum & R. Dowson, *Hell Let Loose: The 1/7th (Salford) Territorial Battalion Lancashire Fusiliers, 1914–1915* (Radcliffe: Neil Richardson, 2005), pp. 36–7.

10.   W. T. Forshaw, quoted in the *Ashton Reporter*, 16/10/1915, http://ashtonpals.webs.com.

11.   H. Grantham, quoted in the *Ashton Reporter*, 16/10/1915, http://ashtonpals.webs.com.

12.   T. Pickford, quoted in the *Ashton Reporter*, 18/3/1916, http://ashtonpals.webs.com.

13.   W. T. Forshaw, quoted in the *Ashton Reporter*, 16/10/1915, http://ashtonpals.webs.com.

14.   S. Bayley, quoted in the *Ashton Reporter*, 11/9/1915, http://ashtonpals.webs.com.

15.   R. D. Doughty, diary 8/8/1915–10/8/1915, http://www.thekivellfamily.co.nz/family_pages/ralphs_diaries/Ralph_Doughty.html.

14. August: Anzac Breakout

1. IWM Printed Books: *Atatürk Memoirs*, KO3/1686, p. 42.

2. J. Monash, quoted by F. M. Cutlack, *War Letters of General Monash* (Australia: Angus & Robertson Ltd, 1934), p. 59.

3. C. Allanson, typescript diary, 2/8/1915.

4. W. G. Malone, edited by J. Crawford, *No Better Death: The Great War Diaries and Letters of William G. Malone* (Auckland: Reed Publishing Ltd, 2005), p. 295.

5. C. S. Lecky, 'Inferno of Death: 2nd Battalion Losses', *Reveille*, 1/8/1932, p. 29.

6. C. S. Lecky, 'Inferno of Death: 2nd Battalion Losses', *Reveille*, 1/8/1932, p. 29.

7. I. G. Mackay, 'Lonesome Pine: Called after Song', *Reveille*, 1/8/1937, pp. 14–15.

8. J. W. Aylward, 'With the 4th at the Pine', *Reveille*, 1/8/1937, p. 37.

9. Lieutenant Richard Seldon. He is buried in Johnston's Jolly Cemetery.

10. J. W. Aylward, 'With the 4th at the Pine', *Reveille*, 1/8/1937, p. 37.

11. Brotherton Special Collections Library, Leeds University, Liddle Collection: C. R. Duke, typescript account, pp. 99–100.

12. C. S. Lecky, 'Inferno of Death: 2nd Battalion Losses', *Reveille*, 1/8/1932, p. 29.

13. Z. Bey, quoted by C. Bean, *Gallipoli Mission* (Canberra: Australian War Memorial, 1948), pp. 184–5.

14. Brotherton Special Collections Library, Leeds University, Liddle Collection: C. R. Duke, typescript account, p. 100.

15. C. S. Lecky, 'Inferno of Death: 2nd Battalion Losses', *Reveille*, 1/8/1932, p. 29.

16. Brotherton Special Collections Library, Leeds University, Liddle Collection: C. R. Duke, typescript account, pp. 101–2.

17. D. A. Lane, 'Holding On: 12th Battalion at Lone Pine', *Reveille*, 1/8/1932, p. 43.

18. P. Goldenstedt, 'Attack and Defence: 3rd at Lone Pine', *Reveille*, 1/8/1932, p. 26.

19. P. Goldenstedt, 'Attack and Defence: 3rd at Lone Pine', *Reveille*, 1/8/1932, pp. 26–7.

20. H. C. Ford, 'With the 13th Battalion: August in Gallipoli', *Reveille*, 1/8/1932, p. 64.

21. C. Allanson, typescript diary, 6/8/1915–7/8/1915.

22. J. Gethin Hughes, 'Objectives Secured: New Zealand Advance', *Reveille*, 1/8/1937, p. 49.

23. By the end of the war most of the main protagonists were dead. The account left by Major Arthur Temperley reflects his considerable personal animosity towards Malone.

24. H. Kannengiesser, *The Campaign in Gallipoli* (London: Hutchinson & Co. Ltd., 1927), p. 207.

25. E. Lewes, 'Chunuk Bair', *Reveille*, 1/8/1936, p. 10.

26. H. Gordon Bennett, 'German Officers: 6th Battalions Attack', *Reveille*, 1/8/1932, p. 10.

27. H. Gordon Bennett, 'German Officers: 6th Battalions Attack', *Reveille*, 1/8/1932, p. 10.

28. H. Gordon Bennett, 'German Officers: 6th Battalions Attack', *Reveille*, 1/8/1932, p. 10.

29. H. Gordon Bennett, 'German Officers: 6th Battalions Attack', *Reveille*, 1/8/1932, p. 10.

30. H. Gordon Bennett, 'German Officers: 6th Battalions Attack', *Reveille*, 1/8/1932, p. 10.

31. IWM Docs: C. Jess, transcript diary, 7/8/1915.

32. IWM Docs: C. Jess, transcript diary, 7/8/1915.

33. H. Gordon Bennett, 'German Officers: 6th Battalions Attack', *Reveille*, 1/8/1932, p. 10.

34. H. Gordon Bennett, 'German Officers: 6th Battalions Attack', *Reveille*, 1/8/1932, pp. 10–11.

35. IWM Docs: C. Jess, transcript diary, 7/8/1915.

36. IWM Docs: C. Jess, transcript diary, 7/8/1915.

37. A. Skeen, quoted by C. Bean, *The Story of Anzac: The Official History of Australia in the War of 1914–1918, Vol. II* (Sydney: Angus & Robertson, 1924), p. 606.

38. C. Pinnock, quoted by J. Hamilton, *Goodbye Cobber, God Bless You: The Fatal Charge of the Light Horse, Gallipoli, August 7th 1915* (Sydney: Pan Macmillan Australia, 2004), p. 288, and L. A. Carlyon, *Gallipoli* (London: Doubleday, 2001), p. 404.

39. Lieutenant Colonel Alexander White. No known grave.

40. A. Crawford, '3rd Light Horse Brigade on Gallipoli', *Reveille*, 1/8/1932, p. 38.

41. A. Borthwick, quoted by J. Hamilton, *Goodbye Cobber, God Bless You: The Fatal Charge of the Light Horse, Gallipoli, August 7th 1915* (Sydney: Pan Macmillan Australia, 2004), p. 291.

42. Brotherton Special Collections Library, Leeds University, Liddle Collection: C. H. Williams, typescript interview transcript, tape 254.

43. W. L. Sanderson, quoted by C. Bean, *The Story of Anzac: The Official History of Australia in the War of 1914–1918, Vol. II* (Sydney: Angus & Robertson, 1924), p. 619.

44. Brotherton Special Collections Library, Leeds University, Liddle Collection: J. Fitzmaurice, typescript interview transcript, tape 234.

45. G. H. L. Harris, 'True to Name: Bloody Angle', *Reveille*, 1/8/1932, p. 22.

46. D. Lindsay, diary, 6/8/1915–8/8/1915, http://wwi.lib.byu.edu/index.php/The_War_Diary_of_David_Lindsay.

47. H. Bey, quoted by H. Oral, *Gallipoli 1915: Through Turkish Eyes* (Istanbul: Turkiye Is Bankasi, 2007), pp. 274–5.

48. W. H. Cunningham, 'Chunuk Bair Attack: New Zealand Infantry Brigade', *Reveille*, 1/8/1932, p. 87.

49. W. H. Cunningham, 'Chunuk Bair Attack: New Zealand Infantry Brigade', *Reveille*, 1/8/1932, p. 87.

50. W. H. Cunningham, 'Chunuk Bair Attack: New Zealand Infantry Brigade', *Reveille*, 1/8/1932, p. 87.

51. C. Allanson, typescript diary, 8/8/1915.

52. R. Savory, 'Some Gallipoli Memories', *The Gallipolian*, no. 15, pp. 14–15.

53. Captain J. S. Dallas was mortally wounded and died on 12 September 1915. He is buried in Alexandria Military Cemetery.

54. Second Lieutenant H. C. Underhill. No known grave.

55. C. Allanson, typescript diary, 8/8/1915.

56. IWM Printed Books: *Atatürk Memoirs*, KO3/1686, p. 40.

57. Lieutenant J. W. J. Le Marchand. No known grave.

58. C. Allanson, typescript diary, 9/8/1915.

59. C. Allanson, typescript diary, 9/8/1915.

60. G. R. Mott, *The Battle for Sari Bair*, copy supplied by J. Sheldon from the South Lancashire Regimental Archives.

61. C. Allanson, typescript diary, 9/8/1915.

62. R. Savory, 'Some Gallipoli Memories', *The Gallipolian*, no. 18, p. 13.

63. IWM Docs: N. Tattersall, diary, 10/8/1915.

64. IWM Docs: N. King-Wilson, typescript account, 'Jottings of an MO', pp. 3–4.

65. IWM Docs: N. King-Wilson, typescript account, 'Jottings of an MO', p. 4.

15. August: Suvla Bay Landings

1. L. E. Tilney, 'Night March: 4th Brigade Steadiness', *Reveille*, 1/8/1937, p. 47.

2. National Army Museum: B. A. Wright, 34th Brigade Collection, p. 1.

3. E. Y. Priestman, *With a BP Scout in Gallipoli: A Record of the Belton Bulldogs* (London: George Routledge & Sons, 1916), pp. 164–5.

4. E. Y. Priestman, *With a BP Scout in Gallipoli: A Record of the Belton Bulldogs* (London: George Routledge & Sons, 1916), pp. 166–7.

5. National Army Museum: W. Taylor, 34th Brigade Collection, pp. 1–2.

6. IWM Docs: H. M. Denham, typescript account.

7. National Army Museum: W. Taylor, 34th Brigade Collection, p. 3.

8. National Army Museum: B. A. Wright, 34th Brigade Collection, pp. 2–3.

9. Lieutenant Colonel Harry Welstead.

10. National Army Museum: G. E. Meugens, 34th Brigade Collection, p. 2.

11. National Army Museum: W. Taylor, 34th Brigade Collection, p. 4.

12. National Army Museum: T. Dolan, 34th Brigade Collection, p. 1.

13. National Army Museum: W. Jones, 34th Brigade Collection, pp. 2–3.

14. National Army Museum: C. MacDonald, 34th Brigade Collection, p. 1.

15. National Army Museum: E. H. Hartley, 34th Brigade Collection, p. 2.

16. National Army Museum: F. L. Eaton, 34th Brigade Collection, p. 2.

17. National Army Museum: G. E. Meugens, 34th Brigade Collection, p. 3.

18. National Army Museum: B. A. Wright, 34th Brigade Collection, pp. 3–4.

19. National Army Museum: B. A. Wright, 34th Brigade Collection, p. 4.

20. National Army Museum: G. E. Meugens, 34th Brigade Collection, p. 9.

21. National Army Museum: G. E. Meugens, 34th Brigade Collection, pp. 5–6.

22. National Army Museum: A. W. Norbury, 34th Brigade Collection, p. 2.

23. National Army Museum: G. E. Meugens, 34th Brigade Collection, pp. 6–7.

24. National Army Museum: F. L. Eaton, 34th Brigade Collection, pp. 2–3.

25. National Army Museum: B. A. Wright, 34th Brigade Collection, pp. 5–6.

26. National Army Museum: B. A. Wright, 34th Brigade Collection, p. 6.

27. National Army Museum: B. A. Wright, 34th Brigade Collection, pp. 6–7.

28. National Army Museum: G. E. Meugens, 34th Brigade Collection, pp. 7–8.

29. National Army Museum: G. E. Meugens, 34th Brigade Collection, pp. 8–9.

30. National Army Museum: E. H. Hartley, 34th Brigade Collection, pp. 4–5.

31. National Army Museum: F. L. Eaton, 34th Brigade Collection, p. 3.

32. National Army Museum: C. O. Ibbetson, 34th Brigade Collection, pp. 2–4.

33. National Army Museum: D. Burns, 34th Brigade Collection, p. 2.

34. National Army Museum: P. Thompson, 34th Brigade Collection, pp. 3–4.

35. National Army Museum: D. R. Drysdale, 34th Brigade Collection, pp. 3–5.

36. National Army Museum: C. C. G. Johnston, 34th Brigade Collection, pp. 3–4.

37. IWM Docs: I. Kirkpatrick, typescript account, p. 17.

38. IWM Docs: I. Kirkpatrick, typescript account, p. 19.

39. IWM Docs: I. Kirkpatrick, typescript account, p. 21.

40. National Army Museum: D. Burns, 34th Brigade Collection, p. 3.

41. IWM Docs: F. Howitt, manuscript account, p. 34.

42. Credit should be given here to the research carried out on Turkish sources by T. Travers in *Gallipoli 1915* (Stroud: Tempus, 2003).

43. National Army Museum: C. Llewelyn Allen, 34th Brigade Collection, p. 5.

44. J. Still, *A Prisoner in Turkey* (London: Bodley Head, 1920), pp. 29–30.

45. E. A. Halse. This item is from (and copyright of) The Great War Archive, University of Oxford, http://www.oucs.ox.ac.uk/ww1lit/gwa/document/9000.

46. National Army Museum: C. Llewelyn Allen, 34th Brigade Collection, pp. 6–7.

47. IWM Docs: A. Crookenden, typescript letters, 10/8/1915.

48. F. Stopford, quoted by C. F. Aspinall-Oglander, *Military Operations Gallipoli, Vol. II* (London: William Heinemann Ltd, 1932), p. 314.

49. H. C. Wolton, 'Letters from the Front', *Gallipolian Journal*, 110, pp. 14–15.

50. W. P. Braithwaite, quoted by C. F. Aspinall-Oglander, *Military Operations Gallipoli, Vol. II* (London: William Heinemann Ltd, 1932), p. 320.

51. IWM Docs: I. Kirkpatrick, typescript account, p. 26.

52. IWM Docs: I. Kirkpatrick, typescript account, pp. 27–8.

53. IWM Docs: I. Kirkpatrick, typescript account, p. 30.

54. IWM Docs: I. Kirkpatrick, typescript account, pp. 30–31.

55. IWM Docs: I. Kirkpatrick, typescript account, pp. 31–2.

56. IWM Docs: I. Kirkpatrick, typescript account, pp. 32–3.

57. IWM Docs: I. Kirkpatrick, typescript account, pp. 33–4.

58. IWM Docs: I. Kirkpatrick, typescript account, p. 34.

59. I. Hamilton, *Gallipoli Diary, Vol. II* (London: Edward Arnold, 1920), p. 117.

60. IWM Docs: G. Dawnay, manuscript letter, 12/8/1915.

61. I. Hamilton, quoted by C. F. Aspinall-Oglander, *Military Operations Gallipoli, Vol. II* (London: William Heinemann Ltd, 1932), p. 325.

16. 21 August 1915: A Useless Gesture

1. S. Gillon, *The KOSB in the Great War* (London: Thomas Nelson & Sons Ltd, 1930), p. 162.

2. I. H. Sunata, translated by 'Reha', *Geliboludan Kafkaslara*, (Is Bankasi Publications) Axis History Forum: http://forum.axishistory.com/viewtopic. php?f=80&t=153416&start=15.

3. E. Y. Priestman, *With a BP Scout in Gallipoli: A Record of the Belton Bulldogs* (London: George Routledge & Sons, 1916), pp. 181–2.

4. I. H. Sunata, translated by 'Reha', *Geliboludan Kafkaslara* (Is Bankasi Publications), Axis History Forum: http://forum.axishistory.com/viewtopic. php?f=80&t=153416&start=15.

5. William Wedgwood Benn, *In the Side Shows* (London: Hodder & Stoughton, 1919), pp. 25–6.

6. William Wedgwood Benn, *In the Side Shows* (London: Hodder & Stoughton, 1919), p. 26.

7. IWM Docs: H. Davis, transcript letter, 8/1918.

8. IWM Docs: C. C. M. Millis, manuscript diary, 21/8/1915.

9. William Wedgwood Benn, *In the Side Shows* (London: Hodder & Stoughton, 1919), p. 28.

10. William Wedgwood Benn, *In the Side Shows* (London: Hodder & Stoughton, 1919), pp. 28–9.

11. IWM Docs: C. C. M. Millis, manuscript diary, 21/8/1915.

12. William Wedgwood Benn, *In the Side Shows* (London: Hodder & Stoughton, 1919), pp. 31–2.

13. I. H. Sunata, translated by 'Reha', *Geliboludan Kafkaslara* (Is Bankasi Publications) Axis History Forum: http://forum.axishistory.com/viewtopic.php?f=80&t=153416&start=15.

14. H. G. Loughran, '4th Brigade's Inland Movement against the Turks', *Reveille*, 1/8/1932, pp. 36 & 52.

15. H. C. Ford, 'With the 13th Battalion: August in Gallipoli', *Reveille*, 1/8/1932, p. 65.

16. S. C. E. Herring, 'Three Waves: Dash for Hill 60', *Reveille*, 1/8/1932, p. 54.

17. H. G. Loughran, '4th Brigade's Inland Movement Against the Turks', *Reveille*, 1/8/1932, p. 52.

18. R. H. Boyden, 'Family Quotas', *Reveille*, 1/9/1938, p. 32.

19. R. H. Boyden, 'Family Quotas', *Reveille*, 1/9/1938, pp. 32–3.

20. H. M. Macnee, 'Hand to Hand: Heavy Bomb Fight', *Reveille*, 1/8/1932, p. 71.

21. H. Throssell, quoted by B. Manera, 'Hill 60 – The Last Battle: 29 August 1915: http://www.awm.gov.au/events/conference/gallipoli_symposium/manera.asp#34.

22. IWM Docs: J. McIlwain, diary, 28/8/1915.

23. H. Throssell, quoted by S. Snelling, *VCs of the First World War: Gallipoli* (Stroud: Sutton Publishing, 1995), p. 224.

17. Should They Stay or Should They Go?

1. IWM Docs: C. E. Caldwell, letter to A. Lynden-Bell, 2/12/1915.

2. I am greatly indebted to Rhys Crawley who helped me develop this analysis of the August operations. See R. Crawley, 'The Myths of August at Gallipoli',

in C. Stockings (ed.), *Zombie Myths of Australian Military History* (Sydney: UNSW Press, 2010), pp. 50–69.

3. R. Weil, quoted in Association des Dardanelles, *Dardanelles Orient Levant, 1915–1921* (Paris: L'Harmattan, 2005), p. 46.

4. C. Allanson, typescript diary, p. 36.

5. C. Lister, quoted by Lord Ribblesdale, *Charles Lister: Letters and Recollections* (London: T. Fisher Unwin Ltd, 1917), pp. 226–7.

6. Chaplain Mayne, quoted by Lord Ribblesdale, *Charles Lister: Letters and Recollections* (London: T. Fisher Unwin Ltd, 1917), pp. 16–17.

7. E. Raymond, *The Story of My Days* (London: Cassell, 1968), pp. 131–2.

8. IWM Docs: C. Foster, typescript letters, p. 82.

9. IWM Docs: G. R. Hughes, typescript account, pp. 14–15.

10. National Army Museum: V. Coates, typescript letter, 22/9/1915.

11. IWM Docs: N. Burge, manuscript letter, 11/10/1915.

12. IWM Docs: R. Sheldon, typescript account, p. 56.

13. IWM Docs: N. King-Wilson, typescript account, 'Jottings of an MO', p. 19.

14. G. Davidson, *The Incomparable 29th and the* River Clyde (Aberdeen: James Gordon Bisset, 1920), p. 198.

15. J. Ewing, quoted by R. R. Thompson, *The Fifty-second (Lowland) Division* (Glasgow: Maclehose, Jackson & Co., 1923), p. 131.

16. J. Gallishaw, *Trenching at Gallipoli* (New York: A. L. Burt Company, 1916), pp. 199–200.

17. IWM Docs: N. Tattersall, diary, 19/8/1915.

18. IWM Docs: C. A. Cooke, typescript diary, 7/8/1915.

19. IWM Docs: A. Crookenden, typescript letters, 3/10/1915.

20. C. R. Attlee, *War Memoirs*, copy supplied by J. Sheldon from the South Lancashire Regiment Archives.

21. IWM Docs: C. A. Cooke, typescript diary, 11/9/1915.

22. I. Hamilton, *Gallipoli Diary, Vol. II* (London: Edward Arnold, 1920), p. 249.

23. IWM Docs: C. E. Caldwell, letter to A. Lynden-Bell, 22/10/1915.

24. IWM Docs: A. Lynden-Bell, typescript account, pp. 1–2.

25. IWM Docs: A. Lynden-Bell, typescript account, p. 2.

26. C. C. Monro, 'First Despatch', *London Gazette*, 10/4/1916 (3rd Supplement).

27. C. C. Monro, 'First Despatch', *London Gazette*, 10/4/1916 (3rd Supplement).

28. W. L. S. Churchill, *World Crisis, 1911–1918, Vol. II* (London: Odhams Press, 1938), p. 908.

29. IWM Docs: A. Lynden-Bell, letter to C. E. Caldwell, 12/1915.

30. IWM Docs: A. Lynden-Bell, typescript account, p. 7.

18. The Beginning of the End

1. H. Kannengiesser, translated by C. J. P. Ball, *The Campaign in Gallipoli* (London: Hutchinson & Co., 1927), p. 245.

2. IWM Docs: G. R. Hughes, typescript account, p. 53.

3. IWM Docs: N. King-Wilson, typescript account, 'Jottings of an MO', p. 28.

4. C. R. Attlee, *War Memoirs*, copy supplied by J. Sheldon from the South Lancashire Regiment Archives.

5. P. Ashton, quoted by C. H. Dudley-Ward, *History of the 53rd (Welsh) Division, 1914–1918* (Cardiff: Western Mail Ltd, 1927), pp. 47–8.

6. P. Ashton, quoted by C. H. Dudley-Ward, *History of the 53rd (Welsh) Division, 1914–1918* (Cardiff: Western Mail Ltd, 1927), p. 48.

7. P. Ashton, quoted by C. H. Dudley-Ward, *History of the 53rd (Welsh) Division, 1914–1918* (Cardiff: Western Mail Ltd, 1927), p. 49.

8. C. Allanson, 'Gallipoli Diary', *Reveille*, 1/4/1938, p. 80.

9. P. J. Gething, 'The Flood', *The Gallipolian*, no. 11, p. 20.

10. IWM Docs: W. Barron, typescript account, p. 2.

11. C. R. Attlee, *War Memoirs*, copy supplied by J. Sheldon from the South Lancashire Regiment Archives.

12. IWM Docs: T. P. Watson, manuscript letter, 2/12/1915.

13. IWM Docs: N. King-Wilson, typescript account, 'Jottings of an MO', pp. 30–31.

14. IWM Docs: A. J. Gilbertson, manuscript diary, 29/11/1915.

15. M. Fasih, *Gallipoli 1915: Bloody Ridge (Lone Pine) Diary of Lieutenant Mehmed Fasih* (Istanbul: Denizler Jitasbevi, 2001), pp. 139–40.

16. M. Fasih, *Gallipoli 1915: Bloody Ridge (Lone Pine) Diary of Lieutenant Mehmed Fasih* (Istanbul: Denizler Jitasbevi, 2001), pp. 148–9.

17. IWM Docs: A. Lynden-Bell, letter to C. E. Caldwell, 12/1915.

18. O. L. von Sanders, *Five Years in Turkey* (Nashville, Tennessee: The Battery Press, 2000), p. 96.

19. IWM Docs: T. P. Watson, manuscript letter, 13/12/1915.

20. G. L. Scott, 'The Evacuation of Anzac', *The Gallipolian*, no. 16, p. 25.

21. C. Allanson, 'Gallipoli Diary', *Reveille*, 1/4/1938, p. 80.

22. IWM Docs: W. Campbell, typescript letter, 18/12/1915.

23. IWM Docs: W. Campbell, typescript letter, 18/12/1915.

24. Brotherton Special Collections Library, Leeds University, Liddle Collection: B. Holmes, TI 01, typescript transcript of interview, tape 250.

25. IWM Docs: A. T. L. Richardson, typescript manuscript, 'Last Days in Gallipoli', pp. 19–20.

26. IWM Docs: W. Campbell, typescript letter, 18/12/1915.

27. W. C. Scurry, 'The "Pop Off" Rifle: Inventor's Story', *Reveille*, 1/12/1932, p. 30.

28. IWM Docs: N. King-Wilson, typescript account, 'Jottings of an MO', pp. 38–9.

29. W. H. Burrows, 'Private Bullet: 16th Battalion's Last Grave', *Reveille*, 1/12/1932, p. 17.

30. G. L. Giguel, quoted in Association des Dardanelles, *Dardanelles Orient Levant, 1915–1921* (Paris: L'Harmattan, 2005), p. 68.

31. IWM Docs: G. Clifford, typescript account, 'A Night in a Crater', p. 1.

32. A. Kay, quoted by N. Drum & R. Dowson, *Hell Let Loose: The 1/7th (Salford) Territorial Battalion Lancashire Fusiliers, 1914–1915* (Radcliffe: Neil Richardson, 2005), p. 59.

33. IWM Docs: G. Clifford, typescript account, 'A Night in a Crater'.

34. H. Kannengiesser, translated by C. J. P. Ball, *The Campaign in Gallipoli* (London: Hutchinson & Co., 1927), p. 245.

35. C. R. Attlee, *War Memoirs*, copy supplied by J. Sheldon from the South Lancashire Regiment Archives.

36. D. Brownrigg, *Unexpected: A Book of Memories* (London: Hutchinson & Co., 1942), p. 28.

37. S. G. Savige, 'Lone Pine Sector: 24th Battalion's Goodbye', *Reveille*, 1/12/1932, p. 9.

38. J. Monash, quoted by F. M. Cutlack, *War Letters of General Monash* (Australia: Angus & Robertson Ltd, 1934), pp. 98–9.

39. S. G. Savige, 'Lone Pine Sector: 24th Battalion's Goodbye', *Reveille*, 1/12/1932, p. 9.

40. J. P. Caddy, 'The Last Shot at Anzac', *Reveille*, 1/12/1932, p. 38.

41. W. C. Scurry, 'The "Pop Off" Rifle: Inventor's Story', *Reveille*, 1/12/1932, p. 30.

42. S. G. Savige, 'Lone Pine Sector: 24th Battalion's Goodbye', *Reveille*, 1/12/1932, p. 9.

43. S. G. Savige, 'Lone Pine Sector: 24th Battalion's Goodbye', *Reveille*, 1/12/1932, p. 60.

44. Tolga Ornek Collection: H. Atif, diary, 19/12/1915, translated by G. Erginsoy, H. N. Beşe, R. D. Özbay and Y. Demirel.

45. G. S. McIlroy, 'Silent Stunts: Turks Outwitted', *Reveille*, 1/12/1932, p. 54.

46. G. S. McIlroy, 'Silent Stunts: Turks Outwitted', *Reveille*, 1/12/1932, p. 54.

47. E. Worrall, http://www.diggerhistory.info/pages-battles/ww1/anzac/evacuation.htm.

48. W. C. Scurry, 'The "Pop Off" Rifle: Inventor's Story', *Reveille*, 1/12/1932, pp. 30 & 39.

49. S. G. Savige, 'Lone Pine Sector: 24th Battalion's Goodbye', *Reveille*, 1/12/1932, p. 60.

50. J. P. Caddy, 'The Last Shot at Anzac', *Reveille*, 1/12/1932, p. 38.

51. A. H. Edwards, 'The Evacuation of Anzac', *Reveille*, 1/12/1936, p. 44.

52. G. S. McIlroy, 'Silent Stunts: Turks Outwitted', *Reveille*, 1/12/1932, p. 54.

53. A. H. Edwards, 'The Evacuation of Anzac', *Reveille*, 1/12/1936, p. 44.

54. H. Kannengiesser, translated by C. J. P. Ball, *The Campaign in Gallipoli* (London: Hutchinson & Co., 1927), pp. 246–7.

55. O. L. von Sanders, *Five Years in Turkey* (Nashville, Tennessee: The Battery Press, 2000), p. 99.

56. See page 49.

57. G. L. Scott, 'The Evacuation of Anzac', *The Gallipolian*, no. 16, p. 24.

19. Last Rites at Helles

1. I. Heald, *Ivan Heald: Hero and Humorist* (London: C. Arthur Pearson Ltd, 1917), pp. 177–8.

2. O. L. von Sanders, *Five Years in Turkey* (Nashville, Tennessee: The Battery Press, 2000), pp. 100–101.

3. H. Feuille, *Face aux Turcs: Gallipoli 1915* (Paris: Payot, 1934), pp. 173–5.

4. D. Jerrold, *Georgian Adventure: The Autobiography of Douglas Jerrold* (London: Right Book Club, 1938), p. 153.

5. IWM DOCS: N. King-Wilson, typescript account, 'Jottings of an MO', p. 43.

6. W. Robertson, *From Private to Field Marshal* (London: Constable & Co., 1921), p. 248.

7. W. Robertson, *From Private to Field Marshal* (London: Constable & Co., 1921), p. 270.

8. W. Sorley-Brown quoted by R. R. Thompson, *The Fifty-second (Lowland) Division* (Glasgow: Maclehose, Jackson & Co., 1923), pp. 216–17.

9. G. L. Giguel, quoted in Association des Dardanelles, *Dardanelles Orient Levant, 1915–1921* (Paris: L'Harmattan, 2005), p. 70.

10. IWM Docs: E. F. Wettern, typescript account, pp. 25–6.

11. Major Senftleben, quoted by H. Kannengiesser, translated by C. J. P. Ball, *The Campaign in Gallipoli* (London: Hutchinson & Co., 1927), pp. 91–2 & 95–6.

12. O. L. von Sanders, *Five Years in Turkey* (Nashville, Tennessee: The Battery Press, 2000), pp. 101–2.

13. IWM Docs, T. A. Andrus Collection: J. Y. Robinson, quoted in manuscript letter by N. Walker, 14/2/1916.

14. Colonel Frank Walker was buried in Border Ravine close to his dugout, in a grave marked out with empty shell cases and a solid wooden cross edged in black and recording his name. Despite the efforts of his men the location of the grave was lost and he is now commemorated on the Helles Memorial.

15. IWM Docs: E. F. Wettern, typescript account, p. 28.

16. IWM Docs: W. Campbell, typescript letter, 9/1/1916.

17. IWM Docs: N. Burge, manuscript letter, 4/1/1916.

18. I. Heald, *Ivan Heald: Hero and Humorist* (London: C. Arthur Pearson Ltd, 1917), p. 176.

19. I. Heald, *Ivan Heald: Hero and Humorist* (London: C. Arthur Pearson Ltd, 1917), pp. 176–7.

20. IWM Docs: T. C. Goulden, manuscript letter, 16/1/1916.

21. IWM Docs: E. F. Wettern, typescript account, pp. 29–30.

22. I. Heald, *Ivan Heald: Hero and Humorist* (London: C. Arthur Pearson Ltd, 1917), pp. 177–8.

23. I. Heald, *Ivan Heald: Hero and Humorist* (London: C. Arthur Pearson Ltd, 1917), pp. 178–9.

24. IWM Docs: N. Burge, manuscript letter, 10/1/1916.

25. IWM Docs: N. Burge, manuscript letter, 10/1/1916.

26. O. W. Steele, edited by D. R. Facey-Crowther, *Lieutenant Owen William Steele of the Newfoundland Regiment* (Montreal: McGill-Queen's University Press, 2002), p. 123.

27. S. Maude, quoted in Sir C. E. Callwell, *Life of Sir Stanley Maude* (London: Constable, 1920), p. 184.

28. E. Stretch, quoted in 'The Last Man Out', *The Gallipolian*, no. 120, pp. 60–61.

29. O. W. Steele, edited by D. R. Facey-Crowther, *Lieutenant Owen William Steele of the Newfoundland Regiment* (Montreal: McGill-Queen's University Press, 2002), pp. 123–4.

30. IWM Docs: N. Burge, manuscript letter, 10/1/1916.

31. IWM Docs, R Langton-Jones Collection: letter to the *Sunday Times*.

32. O. L. von Sanders, *Five Years in Turkey* (Nashville, Tennessee: The Battery Press, 2000), p. 103.

33. IWM Docs: N. Burge, manuscript letter, 10/1/1916.

34. D. Jerrold, *Georgian Adventure: The Autobiography of Douglas Jerrold* (London: Right Book Club, 1938), pp. 150 & 152.

20. Myths and Legends

1. I. Hamilton, *Gallipoli Diary, Vol. I* (London: Edward Arnold, 1920), p. viii.

2. Exact casualty figures are difficult to determine as different countries define and account for their losses using different methods. However, there is some agreement that the British incurred 29,134 fatalities, the French approximately 9,800, the Australians 8,520, New Zealanders, 2,806 and the Indians, 1,891. Confidence in the French figure is somewhat undermined by the higher number of French remains that seem to be interred in their cemetery at Helles.

3. I. Hamilton, preface to T. J. Pemberton, *Gallipoli Today* (London: Ernest Benn Ltd, 1926), pp. 3–4.

4. I. Hamilton, preface to T. J. Pemberton, *Gallipoli Today* (London: Ernest Benn Ltd, 1926), pp. 7–8.

5. IWM Docs: A. E. Cooper, typescript account, p. 1.

6. IWM Docs: A. E. Cooper, typescript account.

7. M. Kemal, quoted in K. Fewster, V. Basarin & H. H. Basarin, *Gallipoli: The Turkish Story* (New South Wales: Allen & Unwin, 2003), p. 129.

8. T. Ataöv, 'The Principles of Kemalism', http://www.politics.ankara.edu.tr/dosyalar/MMTY/20/2_turkkaya_ataov.pdf.

9. H. Simpson-Baikie, quoted by R. R. Thompson, *The Fifty-second (Lowland) Division* (Glasgow: Maclehose, Jackson & Co., 1923), pp. 42–4.

10. IWM Docs: N. Burge, manuscript letter, 4/1/1916.

Acknowledgments

1. Drink more, and more often!

ACKNOWLEDGMENTS

FIRST OF ALL I must thank the Turkish experts who have done so much to refine my views over the last ten years on the conduct of the campaign, in particular with regard to the landings on 25 April. Kenan Çelik was the first to open my mind as we walked the Peninsula during our combined Imperial War Museum/Australian War Memorial staff study visit in 2000. Since then the quixotic expatriate Australian Bill Sellars, who lives in Eceabat (Maidos), was kind enough to introduce me to Sahin Akdogan and Haluk Oral. Collectively they convinced me that there were no Turkish machine guns on the beaches during the initial stages of the landings. I was also lucky enough to be able to draw on the expertise of Bulent Korkmaz and Aykut Degre during many of my Gallipoli tours with various army groups. I am very appreciative of Ramazan Altuntaş and T. J. himself of T. J. Tours, who have always been most helpful while I have been out in Turkey. I would also like to thank Tolga Örnek, director of the brilliant documentary *Gallipoli, 1915*, who has also been a great help over the years.

I am appreciative of the massed ranks of Australian historians who have long taken a far more mature view of the Gallipoli campaign than many of their compatriots, who are generally still swept up in the emotional power of the nationalistic legend. Prominent among them is Ashley Ekins, whose battlefield stand on the five myths of Anzac was eye-opening. I am also greatly indebted to Chris Roberts, who has thrashed out in detail the sequence of events of the ANZAC Corps landings and the 'mystery' of the Turkish machine guns, while Peter Pederson refocused my thinking on the enduring importance of competent staff work. In addition to this trio I have considerable awe for both the historical expertise and collective drinking stamina of Peter Burness, David Cameron, Rhys Crawley,

Karl James, Matt Maclachlan, Aaron Pegram, the legendary Rick Pelvin, Robin Prior, Peter Stanley and of course the maestro Trevor Wilson. The lone New Zealander, Christopher Pugsley, has a masterly grasp of the campaign and has been generous with his time. The Americans who strangely failed to win the day at Gallipoli have nevertheless given us the wonderful Edward J. Erickson who has made us aware of the very real achievements of the Turkish Army during the Great War.

Of the British Gallipoli historians I regard my old writing partner Nigel Steel as the *éminence grise*. Over the years he has worked continuously on the campaign, both carrying out copious amounts of original research and acting as a tour guide. For the most part our historians have lamentably refused to grasp the enormity of the failure at Gallipoli, or the strategic and tactical realities of the Great War. However, I would like to pay tribute to the work of Steve Chambers, Peter Chasseaud, Peter Doyle, Michael Hickey, John Lee, Jenny Macleod and Tim Travers, all of whom, one way or another, have attempted to move the debate on. Yet overall it is the hard graft of historians more concerned with the primacy of the Western Front which has cast the calamitous conduct of the Gallipoli operations in a realistic light: Chris Baker, John Bourne, Gordon Corrigan, Paddy Griffiths, Bryn Hammond, Chris McCarthy, Charles Messenger, Gary Sheffield, Pete Simkins, John Terraine and the incorrigible George Webster, to name just a few. I have also greatly treasured the input of members of the Western Front Association Forum, the Great War Forum and the Facebook *Gallipoli, 1915* page – all fantastic internet sources of freely exchanged information. The veterans of the Gallipoli Association were an inspiration to know and the recent republication of their magazine, *The Gallipolian*, provides a rich seam of invaluable first-hand accounts.

Nevertheless the best books on Gallipoli are easy to name: *Military Operations: Gallipoli* (1929 and 1932) by C. F. Aspinall-Oglander and *The Official History of Australia in the War of 1914–18: The Story of Anzac* (1921 and 1924) by C. E. W. Bean are both incredible achievements, still the prime sources for facts, and cogent narratives of events, well written and at times wonderfully evocative. I may disagree with some of their conclusions – indeed, both authors were overly close to the campaign to have a truly impartial view – but I recommend their works without hesitation.

As ever I am beholden to the staff of the Imperial War Museum (IWM). Firstly I must acknowledge my debt to Rod Suddaby and his team in the Department of Documents: Wendy Luttorloch, Simon Offord, Tony Richards and Simon Robins, while Phoebe Reed was a great help during her work experience at the IWM in 2008. Thanks also to Alan Wakefield and other members of the Photograph Archive. I am most grateful to the IWM for permission to use the photographs. I fondly recall my colleagues in the Sound Archive: James Atkinson, Margaret Brooks, Richard Hughes, Richard McDonough and Lyn Smith. I have not used their outstanding Gallipoli oral history collection this time as I had assiduously trawled through it previously; but their interviews certainly taught me the importance of dysentery, fatigue and stress in understanding the problems facing soldiers at Gallipoli. It was a lesson I did not forget as I read the more sanitised face of battle as presented in most of the letters, diaries and post-war memoirs. There is nothing like oral history for exposing the sordid nature of war; nothing like contemporaneous written accounts for expunging it! I am particularly grateful to the staff of the Peter Liddle Archive held at the Brotherton Library of Leeds University, the National Library of Scotland and to Simon Moody of the National Army Museum. Indeed, I would thank all my museum and library colleagues for their hard work in ensuring that these voices from the past are not forgotten. Except in rare cases the historian is the beneficiary of their selfless professional dedication and not an intrepid explorer hacking a trail through uncharted undergrowth.

On a practical note I would like to thank my editor Daniel Crewe and all the staff at Profile, particularly Andrew Franklin, the wonderful Sally Holloway and Penny Daniel. Without their skills and easy tolerance of my failings there would be no book to read at all. Then I must thank my chums David Cameron, John Paylor, Chris Roberts and George Webster for reading through the manuscript and helping keep me, as far as is humanly possible, on the straight and narrow. Rob Massey and John Paylor also did me the invaluable service of providing excellent translations of the French sources. I am also greatly indebted to Polly Napper for creating my website which you can visit on http://peterhartmilitary.com/index.html. My lovely Polly also somehow found the time to cherish our two little lovelies, Lily and Ruby Hart, who continue to make our lives ever more interesting! What would I do without them?[1]

This book is by no means intended to replace *Defeat at Gallipoli* (1994), my youthful collaboration with Nigel Steel, which we rather ambitiously intended to become one of the standard histories of the campaign. Instead, this new offering hopes to take a place somewhere near it on your bookshelf. I have of course avoided quoting the same sources, but this has proved no handicap; indeed, I am staggered by the sheer variety of memoirs available. I enjoyed immensely the opportunity to delve deep into the French and Turkish sources to provide a rather more balanced perspective than before. I also had some innocent fun featuring quotes from a future Labour prime minister (Clement Attlee), the father of a famous left-wing firebrand (Tony Benn) and a dilettante socialist (Charles Lister) – all up to their necks in the ordure created by Winston Churchill, the hero of Conservative MP Robert Rhodes James. No more explanation should be necessary!

All in all, I have thoroughly enjoyed writing this book – Gallipoli will always be my primary interest in the Great War. I still love visiting the scenes of this most powerful of human dramas and long may that continue.

Peter Hart
21 August 2010

APPENDIX A
A Gallipoli Tour

Gallipoli Tour Day One: Helles

If you are based at Eceabat (Maidos) or Çaanakale (Chanak), then it is a good idea to start your tour at Kilid Bahr. Here you can look at the recently renovated forts and look out into the Narrows and across to Eren Keui Bay. With a little imagination the constant traffic in giant oil tankers and cargo ships can stand in for the pre-dreadnought behemoths of 1915. If you climb out of the back of the forts and up the side of the Kilid Bahr Plateau you will gain a valuable perspective of why Kilid Bahr was the main British objective.

Next drive to Sedd el Bahr. The castle is fascinating but slightly dangerous to walk around, so be careful. You can climb on to the north wall and get the Turkish viewpoint of the landings from the *River Clyde* on V Beach. If you walk out on to the spit of rocks you can look back across the very spot where so many men lost their lives in the bloody water. The only risk now is from the bow waves of the passing ships!

Now move along the beach, past the V Beach Cemetery, and up on to Fort No. 1 overlooking the beach, which is now a major Turkish tourist site. From here it is a short walk to the Helles Memorial, always a sobering moment as you look at the thousands of names of those killed who have no known grave. From here, though, you can gain a superb perspective of the whole of Helles looking up to Achi Baba. If you have time, search out some of the old heavy guns still lying in the fields nearby.

Then take a short drive round the headland to W Beach where the Lancashire Fusiliers landed. You can walk along the beach on which they were pinned down and slaughtered under heavy fire. There are still traces of the distinctive 1915 piers in the water. At the back of the beach are the remains of the old cave which was stuffed full of ammunition and exploded on the early morning of the final evacuation on 8 January 1916. Stones and boulders that shot up into the air still cover the local area. Then retrace your steps back across the beach to follow the footsteps of Brigadier General Steuart Hare up the cliffs just round the corner on the north side. En route you may notice some of the interconnected dugouts that lie just below the cliff top. On top you can see both the reservoirs left from 1915 and the myriad defensive and communication trenches dug all over the hill.

Next drive round to the path leading down to the beautiful Gully Beach at the exit of Gully Ravine. The remnants of the lighter abandoned on the morning of 9 January 1916 are still there. From here you can explore the lower reaches of Gully Ravine, which was one of the main supply depots for the VIII Corps. Then drive up to the Nuri Yamut Turkish Memorial. This marks the British furthest point and is also a mausoleum for the thousands of dead bodies collected by the Turks in the 1940s. The skulls are supposed to have littered the fields on Gully Spur and the upper Gully Ravine like melons in a field. You can explore the upper reaches of the Gully, a challenging walk which can be quite muddy depending on the season. There are clear traces of the front lines here and human bones can still be found.

Take a break, perhaps, in Alcitepe, as Krithia is now known. A visit to Kereves Dere, where the French sector was, will soon reveal its horrors – it is a dreadful configuration of terrain. Then drive up to the summit of Achi Baba. From the upper slopes of the hill you can appreciate its obvious tactical importance at Helles – it loomed over everything, and from here the Turkish artillery observers could direct the fire of the concealed batteries on the reverse slopes. But there is no view of the Narrows from Achi Baba. This reinforces the point that Achi Baba was just a stepping stone; the Kilid Bahr plateau was the real objective.

Gallipoli Tour Day Two: Anzac

Drive to Anzac Cove and pay a visit to the Ari Burnu Cemetery before walking along the shallow beach where the ANZAC Corps landed and had its base in 1915 – an emotional site for many visitors. At the other end of the beach is the Beach Cemetery on Hell Spit, probably the most beautiful cemetery in the world. Here is the grave of John Simpson, the 'Man with the Donkey', that most Australian of heroes. A larrikin rough diamond of a man, careless of rank or authority, he truly made the difference for a few weeks in Shrapnel Valley, rescuing the wounded with the help of his trusty donkey. Simpson was a man who summed up much of the modern values that army training establishments still struggle to din into recruits. Yet although an Australian, he was born, bred and raised in South Shields, County Durham.

Then climb the path from Shrapnel Valley up MacLaurin's Hill and on to Plugge's Plateau. The views across Anzac are staggering. Scramble down into Rest Gully and ascend to Russell's Top. Here you can still see a communication trench six feet deep. Move on to gaze across Mule Valley at the wonders of the Sphinx. If you feel confident you can teeter carefully down Walker's Ridge, once a scary prospect with sheer drops, but now quite tame.

Having reached the Anzac beach area again, drive up to Lone Pine, a staggeringly small area to be the scene of so much death and destruction on 6 August. The Lone Pine monument recording the ANZAC Corps missing is a sobering sight. Walk along the road which runs parallel with what was No Man's Land – just twenty to thirty feet wide – along Second Ridge. Notice the trenches and tunnels on 400 Plateau. Walk on to Quinn's Post which clung to the side of the precipitous Monash Valley. There are several interesting Turkish monuments on what used to be the Chessboard. Then drive round to The Nek. It is moving to look out from the Australian trenches to where the layered ranks of Turkish trenches and machine guns awaited the Light Horse.

Next drive up on to Chunuk Bair, the scene of Malone's last stand. You can make detours from here down to the Farm and on to Rhododendron Ridge, where there are remnants of a recently collapsed old tunnel system. You can drive or walk (depending on the state of the road) along the Sari Bair range to Hill Q (briefly held by Allanson's Gurkhas) and then up to Hill 971 – Koja Chemen Tepe – the highest point in the area. The views are stunning. With the whole tangle of valleys and ridges laid out below you, the insanity of Hamilton's plans for a night attack across this country will become all too clear.

Gallipoli Tour Day Three: Suvla

Start with a change of pace and a visit to an excellent little private museum full of the fascinating detritus of the battlefields in Biyuk Anafarta. Then move to the Turkish big guns from the 1870s, still located at the side of the road between the Anafarta villages. Although of archaic design, even in 1915, they were ideal for slow harassing fire on to the supply depots on the Suvla beaches.

Drive on to Scimitar Hill, the focus of incredibly bitter fighting, where the hills caught fire more than once incinerating the dead and wounded alike. Recently the ground to the north of the hill has been burnt off again and all the Turkish trench systems laid bare to see. An amazing sight.

Pass on to Green Hill and walk round Chocolate Hill. Here you will get a good view across the Salt Lake to Lala Baba. Then the programme really depends on time and the condition of the roads. W Hills, Hill 60 and the Lala Baba hills are well worth visiting. The A and B Beaches are idyllic and usually pleasantly deserted. Then round to visit Hill 10, the entrance to the Cut and the scene of the disastrous landing on C Beach inside Suvla Bay.

If transport can be arranged there is a wonderful walk from the Turkish Gendarmerie memorial all the way along Kiretch Tepe, down on to Karakol Dagh and out on to Suvla Point. This is quite challenging, but provides a breathtaking vantage point looking out over all the landmarks of the Suvla campaign. The sangars that criss-crossed the ridge and key posts like Jephson's Post can still be located. Everything at Suvla is bigger and takes more time than at Anzac as distances are measured in miles rather than hundreds of yards. It is, however, worth the extra effort and much of it is completely unspoilt.

Warning

This outline tour includes some rough country and you need to be reasonably fit to undertake it. Certainly do not attempt it alone in case of accident. Take plenty of water and a mobile phone and wear walking boots and trousers capable of resisting prickly thorns; shorts are a painful option! Also be aware of a slight risk from unsupervised farm dogs (a stout stick can make you feel better), but snakes are rarely seen and if you spot them they are usually trying their best to get away from you. Overall at Gallipoli a commonsense approach should see you all right. If in doubt, it is no disgrace to retrace your steps and drive round to the next point in the tour.

APPENDIX B
Glossary of Military Terms

Acronyms

AIF	Australian Imperial Force
AWOL	Absent Without Leave
BEF	British Expeditionary Force
CEO	Corps Expéditionnaire d'Orient
CIGS	Chief of Imperial General Staff
CO	Commanding Officer
CRA	Commander Royal Artillery
EMS	Eastern Mediterranean Squadron
HE	High Explosives
KOSB	King's Own Scottish Borderers
MEF	Mediterranean Expeditionary Force
NZ&AD	New Zealand and Australian Division
NZEF	New Zealand Expeditionary Force
PMLO	Principle Military Landing Officer
RAMC	Royal Army Medical Corps
RMLI	Royal Marine Light Infantry
RNAS	Royal Naval Air Service
RND	Royal Naval Division

Military units

Section	The sub-unit of an infantry platoon. About sixteen men usually commanded by a Corporal.

Platoon	The sub-unit of an infantry company. Four sections of about sixteen men. Commanded by a Lieutenant or Second Lieutenant.
Company	The sub-unit of a Battalion. At full strength about 250 men. Commanded by a Major.
Battalion	The building block of the army made up of four Companies. At full strength a Battalion could contain a thousand men, more often between 600–800, commanded by a Lieutenant Colonel.
Brigade	Made up of four Battalions. Approximately 3,000–4,300 men. Commanded by Brigadier General.
Division	Made up of four Brigades plus artillery units, engineers and support services, totalling between 12,000–20,000 men. Commanded by a Major General.
Corps	Between two and five Divisions with all the supporting arms and services. Commanded by a Lieutenant General.
Army	Two or more Corps. Commanded by General.
Artillery Battery	Basic unit of artillery. A Field Artillery Battery had six field guns and about 200 men. A Heavy Battery had four heavy guns and about 170 men. Together they made an Artillery Brigade.
Cavalry Squadron	The basic Cavalry unit of about 175 men.
Cavalry Regiment	Made up of three squadrons. Brigaded together as Cavalry Brigade.

Military terms

Ammonal	Type of high explosive
Chevaux de frise	Framework covered with long spikes
Cordite	Smokeless propellant in rifle cartridges
Defilade	Shielded or concealed from enemy fire
Dixie	Iron pot with a handle for cooking food
Dreadnought	Named after the first HMS Dreadnought launched in 1906. All big gun main armament.
Embrasure	Gap in the trench sandbags

Enfilade	Fire catching a position or unit from the flank
Hawser	Thick cable or rope used in mooring a boat
Kepis	Cap with a flat circular top worn by the French infantry
Lyddite	Type of high explosive
Melinite	Type of high explosive
Monitors	Shallow draft warships, weakly armoured and slow but with a big gun armament
Paravane 'kite'	Pair of towed winged (hydrofoiled) underwater objects with a cable between them to cut the mooring wires of mines
Parados	Raised side of a trench topped with sandbags that faced the enemy
Parapet	Rearward side of a trench
Picket boat	Small boat usually used as a guard boat
Picket/picquet	Small force of soldiers posted in advance of the main body to give warning of the approach of the enemy
Pinnace	Small boat used to carry messages or run errands by a larger ship
Poilus	French infantry
Pom-pom	Quick firing small calibre gun
Pre-dreadnought	Battleship with a mixed main armament of guns in contrast to the 'all big gun' dreadnoughts
Puttee	Cloth band wound round the leg from the boot to just below the knee to give support and protection to the lower leg
Salient	A salient is where the front line trenches project deep into enemy territory and are hence surrounded on three sides and vulnerable to enfilade fire
Sangar	Trench built up from ground level using stones and sandbags; usually built in rocky or swampy areas
Sap	Short trench dug out into No Man's Land
Sapper	A military engineer
Shrapnel	Artillery shell filled with lead pellets and exploded by a time fuse to create a 'shot gun' effect
Trench	The defensive ditches that protected the soldiers from direct fire

INDEX